AVID

READER

PRESS

LeBRON

JEFF BENEDICT

AVID READER PRESS

New York   London   Toronto   Sydney   New Delhi

Avid Reader Press
An Imprint of Simon & Schuster, Inc.
1230 Avenue of the Americas
New York, NY 10020

First Avid Reader Press hardcover edition April 2023

AVID READER PRESS and colophon are trademarks of Simon & Schuster, Inc.

For information about special discounts for bulk purchases, please contact Simon & Schuster Special Sales at 1-866-506-1949 or business@simonandschuster.com.

The Simon & Schuster Speakers Bureau can bring authors to your live event. For more information or to book an event contact the Simon & Schuster Speakers Bureau at 1-866-248-3049 or visit our website at www.simonspeakers.com.

Interior design by Carly Loman

Manufactured in the United States of America

10   9   8   7   6   5   4   3   2   1

Library of Congress Control Number: 2023931002

ISBN 978-1-9821-1089-5
ISBN 978-1-9821-1091-8 (ebook)

To Gary

*I grew up thinking you walked out on Mom and me. As a kid,
I was convinced you didn't care. About her. About me. As an adult,
I wondered why. I knew where to find you. But I never bothered. Then,
in my late forties, I got your number and called. When you answered,
you called me Son. Turned out, you had read and saved most
everything I'd ever written. Turned out, you were longing, too. You
traveled to my home. Met my family. Put your arms around me.
Told me you loved me. Told me you were proud. All those years . . .
I had it wrong. I learned that when a baby is born to two
unwed adolescents, a lot gets buried. I love you.
Thank you for being my father. This one's for you.*

CONTENTS

x CONTENTS

LeBRON

ONE

WHAT JUST HAPPENED?

A motorcade of shiny black SUVs exited Westchester County Airport and crossed into Connecticut, meandering along wooded back roads before turning onto a smoothly paved private drive lined on both sides with stone walls and large leafy oaks and maples. In the backseat of one of the vehicles, twenty-five-year-old LeBron James sat beside twenty-three-year-old Savannah Brinson, his soulmate since high school and the mother of their two little boys. In his eyes, she was the one thing more enchanting than the idyllic scenery visible through the windows as they eased to a stop in front of a house on an estate in Greenwich. Wearing black shades, a white T-shirt, and black cargo shorts, James stepped out and looked around. Golden light from the late-afternoon sun shone through the property's white picket fence, illuminating the lush green lawn, pink and purple impatiens, and chocolate-colored mulch. A stone path led to the sprawling New England Colonial. It was Thursday, July 8, 2010, and James had come to rehearse, have dinner, and relax. In a few hours, he was set to appear in a prime-time special on ESPN to reveal his decision whether to remain with the Cleveland Cavaliers or join one of the five teams that had been courting him for more than a year. The world's most celebrated basketball player couldn't foresee that by the end of the night he would be the most hated athlete in all of sports.

More than a half dozen people poured out of the other vehicles, including two of his best friends, twenty-nine-year-old Maverick Carter and twenty-eight-year-old Rich Paul. They were among the handful of people who knew James's plans. Carter and Paul, along with James's thirty-one-year-old chief of staff, Randy Mims, had been with James since his senior year of high school in Akron, Ohio, when LeBron had asked the three of them to come work for him, to be his inner circle. Smart, ambitious, and fiercely loyal to each other, they and James called themselves "the Four Horsemen." Mims hadn't joined them on this trip, but Carter and Paul followed James down the stone path toward the house, walking with a swagger. Especially Carter. James's business partner and an aspiring mogul, he was the one who had advised James to announce his decision in such an audacious way. James was the only athlete in America with the muscle to get ESPN's president, John Skipper, to green-light an hour for his own show. And Carter relished the idea of James using that muscle to do something more revolutionary than merely exercising his right as a free agent to choose one team over another. Rather, James was about to issue what amounted to a declaration of independence from the economic grip of team owners, from the filters that journalists at traditional media platforms put on him, and from the overall power dynamic that historically kept athletes—especially Black athletes—in their place.

Savvy and entrepreneurial, Paul was gearing up to become a sports agent, and he was uneasy over the way the decision was being announced. But he agreed with Maverick on one thing: LeBron was about to wreck the status quo.

Brimming with confidence, James took in the moment with his friends. He recognized how much leverage he possessed. In seven seasons in Cleveland, he had done things that no basketball player—not even Michael Jordan—had done. Ordained "the Chosen One" on the cover of *Sports Illustrated* during his junior year of high school and signed to a $90 million shoe contract by Nike before graduating, James had entered the NBA like a comet at age eighteen and promptly become the youngest and fastest player in league history to reach the collective milestones of 10,000 points, 2,500 rebounds, 2,500 assists, 700 steals, and 300 blocks. He was on pace to become the most prolific scorer-playmaker the game had ever seen. In 2004, at nineteen, he became the youngest NBA player to make the US Olympic basketball roster, and in 2008, at twenty-three, he won a gold medal. In the same year, he produced his first film through his newly formed production company, signed his first book contract, and went into business with Dr. Dre and Jimmy Iovine at Beats Electronics, which was later acquired by Apple. He also cultivated friendships with two of the richest men in the world, Warren Buffett and Bill Gates, both of whom were impressed with the cadre of sophisticated bankers and lawyers who were advising James and his inner circle. Of James, Buffett said, "If he were an IPO, I'd buy in."

By July 2010, James's estimated $50 million in annual earnings from his basketball salary and endorsement deals were just part of his burgeoning portfolio. His worth was on track to crest $1 billion within the coming decade. There had never been a billionaire playing professional team sports in America. James was determined to be the first.

At Nike, he had eclipsed Tiger Woods as the shoe company's most valuable brand ambassador. When Woods had crashed his SUV into a neighbor's tree and seen his reputation crumble in a sensational adultery scandal the previous fall, corporations dropped the golfer and increasingly gravitated toward James. American Express, McDonald's, Coca-Cola, and Walmart embraced the authenticity of James's devotion to family and his unrelenting commitment to his Akron roots.

Meantime, his global fame already transcended sports. Performing with Jay-Z, campaigning for Barack Obama, dining with Anna Wintour, doing a photo shoot with Annie Leibovitz and Gisele, and starting his own foundation, James ventured into politics, fashion, mass media, and philanthropy before his twenty-fifth birthday. In a recent one-year span, he was profiled on *60 Minutes* and appeared on the covers of *Vogue*, *Time*, *Esquire*, *Fortune*, and *GQ*. According to a leading celebrity index, James had surpassed Jay-Z in popularity. And Nike made James into a global icon through Hollywood-caliber television commercials that showcased his abilities as an actor and comedian. From China to cities across Europe, James became a household name.

About the only thing James hadn't done was win an NBA championship. But that, he had determined, was about to change. For more than a year he'd been clear that when his contract with the Cavaliers expired after the 2009–2010 season, he would look at his options and sign with the organization that was best equipped to field a team capable of winning rings. Everyone wanted in. Mayor Michael Bloomberg and the city of New York went as far as launching the "C'mon LeBron" campaign, putting up digital messages in Times Square and running ads on the mini-screens of taxicabs in hopes that James would join the Knicks. A Russian billionaire who owned the Brooklyn Nets tried to lure him by sharing his vision to help James become a billionaire. Even President Obama weighed in, making a pitch from the West Wing for his hometown Chicago Bulls. Billboards in Cleveland begged James to stay. Billboards in Miami pleaded with him to come.

Like any great entertainer, James wanted to be wanted. By everyone. At times he obsessed over the way people perceived him, especially when it came to his peers. The day before James traveled to Greenwich, free agent Kevin Durant used fewer than 140 characters on Twitter to announce his decision to sign a contract extenions with the Oklahoma City Thunder, saying, "I'm just not the guy that always wants to be in the limelight or have my business out there." Durant was James's closest rival in terms of talent. And Durant's low-key manner drew widespread praise from basketball writers, many of whom used his approach to take shots at James and his ESPN special. "An hour show? WTF?" a Fox Sports commentator wrote. Some players anonymously piled on. "With LeBron, it's all about him," one unnamed NBA player told a sportswriter. "He talks about wanting to be one of the greatest of all time, like Jordan, like Kobe. But Jordan and Kobe would never do this. He's trying to be bigger than the game."

James read what was written about him. The constant comparisons to Jordan and Kobe got old. But nothing stung more than being called selfish. In his mind, he was just approaching basketball the same way team owners did—as a business. Teams were willing to compete for his services. Why not meet with them and listen to their pitches? And why not try to orchestrate the best situation possible by talking to other players about joining forces to win championships together? That wasn't selfish. It was shrewd.

No one seemed to appreciate James's approach as much as Miami Heat team president Pat Riley. During the previous week leading up to the ESPN special, James met with more than a dozen executives from teams jockeying to entice him. Riley showed up with his championship rings, making it clear that he knew what it took to win them. He also wasn't threatened by James's taking it upon himself to recruit other great players to band with him for a championship run.

From a career standpoint, it was clear to James that Miami was the smart play. Still, the prospect of leaving Cleveland tore at him. Ohio was home. He had never lived anywhere else. He was comfortable there. And for reasons that few people other than his mother fully understood, James had a visceral connection to his hometown of Akron that made him feel indebted to the place that had made him. His head was telling him to go to Miami. His heart was tethered to Akron.

Determined not to disappoint his mother, he called her hours before flying to Greenwich and told her what he was thinking. He was the one, she told him, who had to live with the consequences of his decision. She encouraged him to do what was best for him.

Anxious to get the whole thing behind him, James felt a welcome sense of relief when he entered the Greenwich home of Mark Dowley. Wearing faded jeans and an untucked polo, Dowley didn't look the part of a senior partner at William Morris Endeavor (WME), the most influential talent agency in Hollywood. A marketing strategist, Dowley had arranged the details of the ESPN special. James didn't know Dowley particularly well. But Carter did, which was what mattered to James. He thanked Dowley for welcoming him and opening up his home.

Although Dowley's agency was based in Los Angeles, he resided in Greenwich, which factored heavily into his desire to stage the event there. It was to take place at the Greenwich Boys & Girls Club, and the proceeds from the ESPN show would be donated to Boys & Girls Clubs in the cities of the NBA teams that had been courting James.

Dowley introduced James to his awestruck twelve-year-old son and a few of his buddies. Some representatives from ESPN, Nike, and other corporate sponsors were on hand as well. James politely greeted people, then ducked into a private room and slipped into a pair of designer jeans and a purple gingham shirt, his phone relentlessly pinging with notifications. Just two days earlier, James had joined Twitter, tweeting for the first time: "Hello World, the Real King James is in the Building 'Finally.'" His impending decision was already trending on the up-and-coming social media platform. He was also getting inundated with text messages. One was from Kanye West: *Where u at?*

After making a spectacle of himself by upstaging Taylor Swift at the Grammy Awards, West had been off the grid in Hawaii, working on his fifth studio album, *My Beautiful Dark Twisted Fantasy*. Eager to witness James's decision in person, West had made his way to Greenwich and was trying to find Dowley's house. Without giving Dowley a heads-up, James sent West the address before sitting down with Carter and sportscaster Jim Gray to go over the program. Soon there was a knock at the front door. Stunned, Dowley's twelve-year-old blurted out: "Kanye's here!" The low-key rehearsal suddenly felt like a house party.

James had met Kanye through Jay-Z. They were friends. James was friends with a lot of rappers and hip-hop artists. They liked being in James's orbit. They gave him backstage passes to their shows. Invited him to their parties. Sat courtside at his games. Even saluted him in their lyrics. In many respects, they didn't just want to know LeBron, they wanted to be LeBron. As a basketball star, his fame surpassed all of them. Yet as dusk turned to dark, James was on the cusp of a whole new world of possibilities opening before him. Exiting the house with his entourage and filing into a van for a police escort to the Greenwich Boys & Girls Club, James couldn't help wondering: *How did a kid from Akron get here?*

Generators hummed and satellite trucks jammed the parking lot outside the Boys & Girls Club. Thousands of people wearing NBA jerseys and holding signs—COME TO THE NETS—lined the streets. Fans stood twenty deep, chanting, "Let's go Knicks" as a traffic cop with a bullhorn made a futile attempt to get them to step back. In a van trailing police officers on motorcycles, James rounded the corner as if on a float during a night parade. Flashes from cell phone cameras combined with streetlights, yellow headlights, blue and red police lights, and white spotlights outside the club to create a kaleidoscope of colors amid sirens.

Inside the van, James was nervous and thinking about leaving the Cavaliers. He quietly told Carter, "Let them know."

"We are coming to you live from Greenwich, Connecticut," a host in the ESPN studio in Bristol said as the network broadcast scenes from the chaos outside.

With Jay-Z's "Empire State of Mind" cranking on a boom box, kids screamed and pointed when LeBron *and* Kanye emerged from the vehicles. Teenage children of venture capitalists and Wall Street bankers reveled in the fact that for one night their town was the center of the basketball universe.

Grade-schooler Gigi Barter was overwhelmed when she arrived with her older brothers. "What's happening?" she shouted over the noise.

Her brothers had been taking her to the club for a few years. There had never been crowds outside. Giddy, her brothers explained that LeBron James was in town to announce he was joining the Knicks. It was going to be great.

Once inside, Gigi encountered a friendly face. The man who ran the club made sure she had a seat in the area cordoned off for club kids. He put her near the front, so she had a clear view of James.

A few minutes before 9:00 p.m., James stood outside the gymnasium with Savannah Brinson. Kanye stood nearby in dark sunglasses, a black blazer, and multicolored slippers. Dowley milled around inside, making sure everything was set. Rich Paul called the Cavaliers to inform the team that LeBron was leaving. To Paul this was like a divorce, and there was no easy way to break up with a spouse. Trying to soften the blow, he told the team's general manager that this was a business decision, not a personal one.

It didn't matter. Owner Dan Gilbert was furious. Four years earlier he had tried to lock James in with a five-year contract that would have avoided all this, but James had insisted on only signing a three-year deal. "When he said, 'I'm signing for three years,' we should have had the balls to say, 'Shove it,'" Gilbert told a journalist. "We should've said, 'Fuck you. Go. Let's see it.'"

While Paul dealt with the Cavs, James kept his focus on Brinson until an ESPN producer wearing an earpiece told him it was time.

"Wish me luck," James told Brinson, and gave her a hug and a kiss. Before turning to go, he displayed his teeth and asked her to check them for food particles.

Brinson loved how he always made her laugh. She gave him the A-OK and nudged him into the gym.

Jim Gray sat in a director's chair on a makeshift stage in the center of the gym. James sat opposite him in a matching chair. Under one basket, about sixty-five children were on folding chairs. Under the other basket and along the walls, a hundred or so adults in business attire sat in chairs. Police officers stood in the doorways. Despite being a seasoned pro, Gray looked unnerved. James appeared uncomfortable, too. Under the white lights, both men were sweating. A makeup artist touched up their foreheads. Without any cue, the audience remained as quiet as a congregation at a funeral.

From Bristol, ESPN's Stuart Scott told viewers that they were minutes away from James's decision. Gray's initial questions were stilted. Time dragged as James gave vague answers. Finally, nearly thirty minutes into the broadcast, Gray said, "The answer to the question everyone wants to know . . . LeBron, what's your decision?"

"Um, this fall . . . Man, this is very tough. Um, this fall I'm going to take my talents to South Beach and join the Miami Heat."

A hushed gasp could be heard in the gym. Gray seemed unsure what to say next. It was as if someone had paused live television. Outside, booing erupted.

The booing reverberated in sports bars from New York to Los Angeles. In Cleveland, there were tears of disbelief. James's nine words—*I'm going to take my talents to South Beach*—had rocked the NBA and its fans.

"How do you explain this to the people in Cleveland?" Gray asked.

"Ah, it's heartfelt for me," James tried to explain. "I never wanted to leave Cleveland. . . . And my heart will always be around that area."

Within minutes, fans in Cleveland took to the streets, setting fire to LeBron's jerseys and spewing profanity.

Unaware of what was transpiring back home, James stood up and stepped off the makeshift stage. He agreed to take a photo with the kids and motioned to them to come over. They swarmed him.

Older boys rushed past her, but Gigi Barter suddenly felt herself lifted into the air from behind. The man who ran the club handed her to James, who hoisted her onto his shoulders. With James's hands wrapped around hers, Gigi gripped his thumbs. Beaming, she couldn't believe she was on the shoulders of *LeBron James*. "I was the smallest person in the room," she later recalled. "I felt like the tallest person in the world. I literally felt like I could touch the sky."

Surrounded by children, James smiled for the camera.

After the kids were gone, James sat down for an interview with sports journalist Michael Wilbon, who was in an ESPN studio. "I've got to ask you," Wilbon said, "in Cleveland now there were places where they were burning your jersey. We've got some video of it right now."

James watched a monitor. Flames consumed jerseys with his name and number. In his earpiece, James heard Wilbon's voice: "If you can see that image . . . How do you feel about it?"

"One thing that I didn't want to do was make an emotional decision," he said. "I wanted to do what was best for LeBron James, and what LeBron

James is gonna do to make him happy. Put the shoe on the other foot. The Cavs would have got rid of me at one point. Would my family burn down the organization? Of course not."

On television and on social media, James was getting pilloried.

"He looks like a narcissistic fool," one prominent basketball writer said on ESPN.

Another basketball writer blasted the show as "shameless."

A prominent journalist called LeBron "an egotistical self-promoter."

One of David Letterman's producers weighed in on Twitter: "I'm keeping my 2 year old up to watch the LeBron James Special. I want her to see the exact moment our society hit rock bottom."

Even Jim Gray was getting mocked. "Foreplay from Jim Gray just as satisfying as I've always imagined it would be," comedian Seth Meyers tweeted. *Sports Illustrated*'s media critic referred to Gray's interview as "the kind of milking best done on a farm."

Back at Dowley's house, the CEO of Dowley's agency called from Los Angeles to congratulate him on the show's success. It was the most highly rated studio program in the history of ESPN. Thirteen million people were tuned in when James uttered the words *take my talents to South Beach*. Meantime, the Boys & Girls Clubs in six cities were recipients of record-setting donations to improve their facilities. But no one was talking about any of that. Instead, James was morphing into a heartless villain in real time. The *New York Times* had already posted a story online, declaring Miami "the new Evil Empire" and criticizing James for his "mercenary reach for championship rings."

"What we did was well intended," Dowley explained years later. "But no one remembers that we gave $5 million to the Boys & Girls Club. We did a terrible job with that. It just got subsumed."

By the time James boarded a private plane for a late-night flight to Miami, Cavaliers owner Dan Gilbert had worked himself into a rage. He published a letter in Comic Sans font on the team's website that began:

Dear Cleveland:

As you know, our former hero, who grew up in the very region that he deserted this evening, is no longer a Cleveland Cavalier.

This was announced with a several day, narcissistic, self-promotional build-up culminating with a national TV special of his "decision" unlike anything ever "witnessed" in the history of sports and probably the history of entertainment. . . .

You simply don't deserve this kind of cowardly betrayal.

He went on to call out James for his "shameful display of selfishness and betrayal" and his "heartless and callous action" that "sends the exact opposite lesson of what we would want our children to learn." With police officers stationed outside the Cavaliers' arena to deter vandals from tearing down the giant banner of James that hung from the building's exterior, Gilbert ended his rant with the closing sentiment "Sleep well, Cleveland."

No one felt worse about the situation in Cleveland than Maverick Carter. As the self-described leader and architect of the plan for a grandiose announcement, he had badly miscalculated the outcome. Sobered by the fallout, he wanted to disappear in a hole, where he couldn't see or hear anything.

James didn't have that luxury. After he was in the air, James said, "Fuck! What the hell just happened?"

No one said a word. Rich Paul had been on a lot of flights with James and Carter. Never had he been on one so awkwardly quiet.

"We fucked up," Carter said, reflecting on the situation years later. But in the moment, Carter was too dazed to weigh in.

Beleaguered, James turned inward. A big fan of Mafia figures from film and television, he had memorized lines from memorable scenes, like the time Tony Soprano felt vulnerable and tore into his consigliere for failing to protect him:

You got no fucking idea what it's like to be number one. Every decision you make affects every facet of every other fucking thing. It's too much to deal with almost. And in the end, you're completely alone with it all.

James loved *The Sopranos*, especially Tony. But James was nothing like the fictional crime boss. For starters, James wasn't confrontational. Rather than lash out at Carter, James held his tongue. Besides, he knew Carter felt wounded. There was no point in piling on. Plus, James valued relationships above all else. He and Carter had been best friends since James's freshman year of high school, when they were teammates. He viewed Carter more like a brother than a business associate. He wasn't about to do or say anything—privately or publicly—to distance himself from the decision to participate in the ESPN show. That would only embarrass Carter. Instead, James resolved to take the hit for Carter's miscalculation.

Dan Gilbert was a different story. He had deliberately attacked James's character and mocked his motives. Leaving Ohio was the most gut-wrenching decision James had made since joining the NBA. Akron was the only place he had ever lived. He'd fallen in love there. His children were born there. He and Savannah built their dream home there. They were so attached to their house that they planned to continue living there even after James signed his contract with the Heat. Strangely, reading Gilbert's letter numbed the pain of choosing the Heat over the Cavaliers and convinced James he'd made the right decision. *I don't think he ever cared about me*, James told himself.

It was around 3:00 a.m. when the plane touched down in Miami. Pat Riley was waiting for James on the tarmac. Exhausted and emotionally drained, James stepped off the plane and into Riley's embrace and rested his head on his shoulder. Then James and Brinson got into an SUV. The two of them held hands as they stared out the window into the Florida darkness. James was about to find out what it was like to be public enemy number one in every NBA city other than Miami.

Pulling away from the airstrip, Savannah put things in perspective with a simple reminder: You've been through worse than this. Much worse.

TWO

GLO AND BRON

It was way past bedtime in a housing project in Akron, Ohio. Inside one of the units, a shy little boy with a conspicuous name was hungry, awake, and alone. Fatherless, he lived with his mother. Just the two of them. But she was gone. Out for the night. She might be home by morning. Might not. Sometimes Mom disappeared for a few nights in a row.

Praying she'd return soon, the boy finally drifted off to sleep, only to be awakened by familiar sounds. Men yelling. A woman pleading. Gunfire. People scattering. Sirens. Doors slamming. More yelling. More sirens.

The boy didn't need an imagination to picture the danger around him. On plenty of occasions he'd seen things no child should see. Violence. Drug abuse. A menacing gang member. An intimidating cop. But it was the nighttime noises that unsettled him the most. He always knew when bad things were happening.

In these instances, there was no choice, he figured, but to lie there and wait for things to quiet down. Even then it was hard to fall back asleep. Some nights his anxiety made it impossible. Although he'd conditioned himself to block out what was going on around him, young LeBron James had one overriding concern—waking up and finding his mother alive and safe. Already without a father, he couldn't bear the thought of losing his mother.

During those dark childhood days, LeBron learned to fend for himself at an early age. "Like it or not," he said, "that's how my mom treated me." Yet LeBron never doubted his mother's love. He only questioned her whereabouts. "When you're there and you know your mother's not home," LeBron said, "you never know if those police sirens are for her. Or if those gunshots were intended towards her. So those are the nights, almost every night, that would stand [out]—hearing those sounds and hoping and wishing that it wasn't your parent on the other end."

LeBron eventually grew to love Akron. His character was forged there. His athletic gifts were discovered and shaped there. And his genius as an entertainer reflected his time in that place. But as a child, when he longed for security and companionship, he would often tell himself, *If I'm ever lucky enough to find a way out, I'm going to run as fast as I can.*

In 2009, LeBron James published a memoir about his high school years and the journey to winning a national championship as a senior. When the book came out, he was the NBA's reigning MVP. Yet he made his high school teammates the focus of his story. He even put them on the cover. In many respects, his approach to the book was the same as the way he played basketball, instinctively sharing the ball—sometimes, his critics insist, to a fault—and emphasizing team success over individual achievement. Whether intentional or not, by putting the spotlight on his friends and their respective backgrounds, LeBron downplayed key aspects of his own backstory. In that respect, the most tantalizing passage of his memoir may have been hidden on the dedication page:

To my mother, without whom I would not be where I am today

Readers routinely skip past dedication pages. And without context, LeBron's one-sentence tribute hardly seems revelatory. Nonetheless, it hints at hard and beautiful truths. On one hand, it holds clues to why LeBron is such a hands-on father and loyal husband. Similarly, it's a predicate to why he has devoted so much of his personal fortune to feed, clothe, and educate needy children, especially in Akron. Even the improbable durability of LeBron's tight inner circle stems from that statement. On the other hand, his pithy homage to his mother makes crystal clear that one of the richest, most successful athletes on the planet remembers his roots. Moreover, he looks back on them with appreciation and pride rather than resentment or shame.

Yet LeBron's origin story begs for illumination. Famous for his savant-like ability to recall game sequences in staggering detail or pull obscure statistics out of his head as if reading from a cheat sheet, he has a much more selective memory when discussing details about his childhood. This is not a self-serving exercise in deception. Rather, it says a lot about a son's inclination to shield his mother and her past from the unforgiving spotlight he lives under.

But this much is clear: when it comes to understanding LeBron James, all roads lead back to Gloria James and Akron, Ohio.

Dionne Warwick was America's number one female vocalist and her hit single "I Say a Little Prayer" had just surpassed 1 million copies sold when Freda M. James gave birth to Gloria Marie James on February 4, 1968. The lyrics—*The moment I wake up / Before I put on my makeup / I say a little prayer for you*—were intended to be a love song about a devoted woman praying for her man. In Freda's case, the song was more reflective of the way she looked at her baby girl. Freda's marriage was no fairy tale. Less than a year after Gloria's birth, Freda and her husband split up. Gross neglect and extreme cruelty were listed in court records as the grounds for divorce. Freda was in her early twenties. In addition to Gloria, she had two little boys. To make ends meet, Freda took a blue-collar job at the Western Reserve Psychiatric Habilitation Center and lived with her mother in a dilapidated Victorian at 439 Hickory Street, a dirt road bordered by railroad tracks on the edge of downtown Akron. The neighborhood was known as the Boondocks. Gloria grew up there with her mother and her grandmother.

Shortly after turning sixteen, Gloria got pregnant. During pregnancy she briefly stopped attending high school. On December 30, 1984, she gave birth at Akron City Hospital to a six-pound-ten-ounce baby boy she named LeBron Raymone James. The identity of the father remains one of the great mysteries of modern sports. Gloria preferred never to speak of LeBron's father, not even to LeBron. Once, when LeBron was a child, he asked his mother about his father's whereabouts. "She shut that shit down early," LeBron recalled. Rather than get into the father's identity, Gloria told her son not to worry about him. "It's me and you," she told him. LeBron stopped asking about his father.

Gloria had her reasons for not telling her son about his father. LeBron, meanwhile, was cut off from one of the primary roots in his family tree. His father's invisibility and the dearth of information explaining his identity and whereabouts led to bitterness. "I grew up resenting my father," LeBron said. "Everything was like, 'Fuck Pops.' You know, he left me. Why would he do that to my mom? She was a sophomore in high school when she had me."

When Gloria left the hospital with her newborn and brought him home to the Boondocks, the chances that her baby would become one of the most successful Black men in American history and one of the most recognizable people on earth were unimaginable. Gloria was a poor, teenage, single mother who was relying on her own thirty-nine-year-old single mother and her grandmother to help her adjust and learn how to care for a newborn. Almost immediately, the road ahead got even steeper. Shortly after LeBron's birth, Gloria's grandmother died. It was a blow to Freda, who assumed full responsibility over the household and became the sole stabilizing force for Gloria and LeBron. When Gloria returned to high school, Freda hoped her only daughter would graduate and that her only grandson would survive. Under the circumstances, these were lofty expectations.

Before LeBron's first birthday, Gloria started seeing Eddie Jackson, a twenty-year-old who had run track at her high school. Like a lot of young Black men in Akron in the eighties, Jackson struggled to find work. Instead, he found trouble. Before long, he needed a place to live and wanted to move in with Gloria. Freda had a reputation for taking in kids who had fallen on hard times, including some whose troubles were the result of poor choices. Jackson fit that description. Not one to judge, Freda allowed Jackson to live under her roof.

"To meet Gloria's mother, you would've met the most wonderful person in the world," Jackson once said. "If she trusted you, she loved you. If she didn't, she'd tell you to get the hell out of her face. And Gloria was the same way."

While forming a close relationship with Gloria, Jackson also took a liking to LeBron. Days before LeBron's third birthday, Gloria and Eddie got him a Little Tikes basketball hoop and a miniature rubber basketball. The plan was to surprise LeBron on Christmas morning. It would be a Kodak moment, a chance to see little "Bron Bron," as Gloria liked to call him, score for the first time. But early Christmas morning, Gloria and Eddie were the ones who got a surprise—Freda had suffered a heart attack sometime after midnight on Christmas Eve. Gloria and Eddie came home from a late-night party and found her on the floor. She was pronounced dead at St. Thomas Hospital. She was forty-two.

Gloria faced despair. In a three-year span she had gotten pregnant, withdrawn from school, given birth, lost her grandmother, returned to school while caring for a newborn, welcomed a live-in boyfriend, graduated, and, now, lost her mother. Life was suddenly going from precarious to frightening. How would she manage without her mother?

Determined that her child was going to have a merry Christmas, Gloria decided not to tell LeBron that his grandmother was gone until after he opened his presents. There was no ham in the oven, no stereo system with Nat King Cole singing about chestnuts roasting on an open fire and tiny tots with their eyes all aglow. The paint on the drafty living room windowsills was chipped. The curtains were faded and stained. But there was a small Christmas tree with red and silver garland. Later that morning, LeBron discovered a plastic basketball hoop with an orange rim and a red, white, and blue net towering above the other gifts. After opening everything else, he took the miniature orange ball with two hands, extended his arms above his head, rose up on his tippy toes, and managed to get the ball over the lip of the rim and through the net. LeBron smiled and a camera clicked. It was the last time Gloria would put up a Christmas tree during LeBron's childhood. "Christmas is not a happy time for me," Gloria said. "I pretty much had to step up and take care of things, and I was nowhere near prepared to deal with it all."

Freda M. James Howard was buried in Akron on LeBron's third birthday, December 30, 1987. "She is survived by daughter, Gloria James; sons, Terry and Curtis James; and grandson LeBron," her obituary read. With Freda's death, Gloria's safety net was gone. She had no childcare. She had no money. And she had no wherewithal to manage her mother's big, run-down house. The plumbing was failing. There were electrical problems. Her brothers lived there, too. But they weren't in a position to help, either. Nor was Jackson. He was unemployed and had his own personal struggles. Although he stayed in touch with Gloria, he moved elsewhere.

Meantime, Gloria couldn't even afford groceries and heat. Over the winter, a neighbor stopped in and found the house unfit for a toddler— dirty dishes spilling out of the kitchen sink, a hole forming in the living room floor, temperatures cold enough to make your breath visible. "It's not safe here," the neighbor told Gloria, imploring her to bring LeBron and move in with her. That day, Gloria stuffed what she could fit into a suitcase and bade farewell to her mother's home. With a miniature back-pack and a stuffed animal, LeBron followed his mother to the neighbor's place. It didn't have a spare bedroom. But there was a couch. For the next few months, Gloria and LeBron slept on it. Then they moved in with one of Gloria's cousins. Then with a guy Gloria knew. Then with one of Gloria's brothers. While the city proceeded to condemn and eventually bulldoze her mother's house on Hickory Street, Gloria and LeBron lived like no-mads. During this period, people who knew them referred to them as Glo and Bron, a mother and son just trying to survive. "I can remember numerous times when my son and I ran out of food and went hungry," Gloria said. "What kept us going was help from friends, family, and the community."

With his mother barely getting by on welfare and food stamps, LeBron struggled to form friendships with classmates or establish bonds with teachers. Without a permanent address, he frequently changed schools and developed into a quiet kid who seldom spoke up. "I was a scared, lonely young boy," LeBron said.

Despite the absence of a father and the inability of his mother to sup-port the two of them on her own, LeBron never grumbled or acted out. Sensitive to his mother's plight, he tried not to add to her stress level. "Being uprooted as a very young child is no way to live," LeBron said. "But complaining would do no good. It would only have put more pressure on my mom, who already felt guilty enough."

As LeBron put it years later, during his childhood he felt like so many African American boys who get lost in the hardness of life. "I didn't like looking for trouble," he said, "because I didn't like trouble. But I was on the edge of falling to an abyss from which I could never escape."

A chance encounter in the summer of 1993 altered the course of Le-Bron's life, revealing for the first time a potential pathway that would even-tually lead him out of the hopelessness that had enveloped him. While LeBron was playing with some other boys his age outside an apartment complex, a man named Bruce Kelker approached. Kelker was an acquain-tance of Gloria's. He was also a peewee football coach.

"You guys like football?" Kelker asked the group.

"That's my favorite sport," LeBron said.

At this point, LeBron had not played on a team. Nor had he received any basic instructions, such as how to properly throw or catch or tackle. He had, however, seen NFL games on television. Pro football had a magical quality with the colorful uniforms, big shoulder pads, shiny helmets, and mythical team names like Steelers and Cowboys and Giants and Lions. LeBron liked to draw and he would frequently sketch the logos of his favorite NFL teams on a pad that he kept in his backpack.

Kelker was looking for someone to play running back for his team, which meant he needed speed. He lined the boys up and had them run a footrace. LeBron left everyone in the dust.

"How much football have you played?" Kelker asked him.

"None," LeBron told him.

Determined to change that, Kelker wanted LeBron to start attending practices. But first he had to deal with Gloria. She was loud and clear that she didn't have money for the registration or the uniform. She didn't have a car, either. So there was no way to get him to practices. More important, she wasn't sure that such a physical game was right for her son—he was a quiet, reserved kid, not an aggressive one. "How do I even know football will be good for Bron Bron?" she asked.

Kelker was convinced that LeBron would be a great addition to his team. And he persuaded Gloria that football would be great for her son. He promised to take care of the registration and uniform costs. And he told her that she wouldn't have to worry about transportation. "I'll pick him up," he said.

Gloria could have said no. But it was evident that LeBron wanted to join the team. So she agreed. And it didn't take her long to recognize that she had made the right decision. The first time LeBron was handed the ball in a game, he raced eighty yards for a touchdown. Adults cheered. Teammates encircled him. Coaches smacked him on the shoulder pads and shouted words of encouragement.

LeBron wasn't used to the attention and praise, especially from male figures. But scoring felt exhilarating. That feeling and the sense of acceptance that it generated was repeated over and over that fall. LeBron scored seventeen touchdowns during his first season of peewee football. Defenders couldn't catch him, much less tackle him.

For Kelker and the rest of the coaching staff, it was easy to see that Le-

Bron was far and away the best player in his age group. They also couldn't ignore that his home life was fraught with risk. While on a waiting list for subsidized housing, Gloria and LeBron had moved five times in a three-month span. "I was tired of picking him up at different addresses," Kelker said. "Or showing up at one junked-up place and finding out they had already moved to another."

At least football provided some structure. But when the season ended, LeBron was totally adrift. That year, as a fourth grader, he missed nearly one hundred days of school. Things were so dysfunctional that LeBron's peewee coaches wanted to take him in. But most of them were younger single men who weren't well equipped to take on the responsibility of a nine-year-old. The one exception was Frank Walker, the coach everyone called "Big Frankie." Walker worked for the Akron Metropolitan Housing Authority. His wife, Pam, worked for an Ohio congressman. They owned a home and had three children.

Walker cared more about LeBron's personal welfare than his athletic prowess. And he knew that LeBron was hurting and needed a lifeline. It was apparent that he had seen and experienced hard things that had sapped some of the joy in his life and made him mature beyond his years.

The Walkers approached Gloria about having LeBron move in with them. It was a difficult subject to broach. Gloria knew she wasn't able to provide LeBron a stable home life. She didn't need any reminders that her situation was adversely affecting LeBron. "He didn't have a normal childhood," Gloria said. "I mean, hell, he done lived in some of the worst projects in town." Still, the notion of putting her son into the hands of another couple—especially another mother—was an agonizing one. She barely knew Pam Walker.

Without passing judgment on Gloria, the Walkers were offering to give LeBron security and family structure. He could share a room with Frankie Jr. There would be three square meals a day. He'd have a set bedtime. And school attendance would be an integral part of his daily routine. Frank made it clear that they had LeBron's best interests in mind.

Gloria knew she needed help. "I hated raising him that way—moving, moving, and moving," Gloria said. "I truly hated it." She added, "I wouldn't wish some of the stuff we went through on anyone. Not on my worst enemy."

Twenty-five years after her mother had gone through a divorce and taken on the full weight of raising her and her two brothers all on her own, Gloria was contemplating something potentially more traumatic. She could only pray that one day LeBron would come to understand that the lyrics from that old Dionne Warwick song that came out the year she was born summed up how she felt about him:

> *To live without you would only mean heartbreak for me.*
> *My darling, believe me,*
> *For me, there is no one but you.*

Gloria accepted the Walkers' offer.

THREE

IF YOU PASS THE BALL

Bewildered, LeBron listened as his mother informed him she needed to get her life to a better place. Until then, she told him, he'd be moving in with the Walkers. It wasn't clear where exactly she was going. The point was that they'd be apart.

The news was disorienting. It had always been them against the world. Glo and Bron. Suddenly it was just going to be Bron.

It was for the best, she tried to explain.

Best? To him it sounded unimaginable and frightening.

The situation wouldn't be permanent, she insisted, trying to soften the blow.

Would he see her?

She'd try to visit, she told him, as often as possible.

And she promised they'd be reunited once her life was more stable.

It was a lot to process for a nine-year-old.

LeBron didn't know what to expect when he arrived at the Walkers' three-bedroom Colonial on Hillwood Drive. He met the two daughters. And he put his things in Frankie Jr.'s room, where he'd be sleeping. LeBron was eighteen months older than Frankie Jr., and a superior athlete. Would Mrs. Walker resent him for that? What about the sisters? Would they accept him? LeBron had lots of questions, none of which he voiced.

There were also a lot of rules. LeBron was expected to wake up each morning at six o'clock to bathe and get ready for school. He had to be on time. And after school, homework came before anything else. The family ate dinner together each night. Afterward, there were chores—taking out the trash, doing the dishes, sweeping. And if he took a bath before bed, he could sleep in until six forty-five.

It was all foreign to LeBron. A schedule. A routine. Chores. He'd never emptied a garbage can or washed dishes or used a broom or a vacuum. Even the idea of being part of a family was new. The Walkers' eldest daughter didn't want anything to do with him. But LeBron soon discovered that she felt the same toward her younger brother. He and Frankie Jr. were instant buddies. And LeBron could tell that the youngest daughter looked up to him. It felt like having a little sister.

Even LeBron's school was new. The Walkers enrolled him in fifth grade at Portage Path Elementary, one of Akron's oldest schools, where more than 90 percent of the students were African American and most of them were on the free-lunch program. His teacher, Karen Grindall, took a personal interest in him. Years earlier she had taught Gloria and was familiar with some of the tumult in her past. Initially, Grindall worried that history might repeat itself with LeBron. However, he quickly established himself as one of her most disciplined students. He never missed school. He was always on time. And he never caused trouble. His favorite classes were music, art, and gym.

While he settled in at school, his reputation as a dominant youth football player grew. He even started to get his name in the paper. That fall, the *Akron Beacon Journal* reported: "The East B1 team ran only 11 offensive plays but scored on five of them to beat Patterson Park 34–8 last week in a Pee-Wee Football Association game. LeBron James scored three of the TDs, running for 50 and 18 yards for two of them and catching a 28-yard pass from Michael Smith for the other."

The recognition was a confidence booster. It especially helped to have Big Frankie Walker as his coach and Pam Walker looking after him at home. He no longer had to worry about storing his uniform and pads in the trunk of someone's car or wonder how he was going to get back and forth to practice. The cadence of a busy home life with two working parents who kept to a schedule suited him well. "I got the stability I craved," LeBron said. "I loved being part of the flow that is a family. . . . I saw how life was meant to be lived."

One day that fall, Big Frankie took LeBron and Frankie Jr. to shoot hoops in the backyard. Having seen how easily LeBron excelled in football, Walker introduced him to basketball, too, and showed him some fundamentals—how to dribble, how to shoot a jump shot, how to make a layup.

LeBron welcomed the experience of receiving instruction from a father figure. And he immediately embraced the adventure of trying to put a ball through a rim ten feet above the ground. The sensation of making a basket was akin to what he felt every time he reached the end zone with a football.

Walker noticed that although LeBron's dribbling ability was rudimentary and sloppy, he seemed predisposed to try to dribble with either hand, something most kids don't bother to learn. His long arms and leaping ability also impressed Walker. He had LeBron and his son play against each other.

LeBron had never played one-on-one. But he eagerly accepted the challenge.

Frankie Jr. loved basketball and had been playing with his father for a couple of years. He beat LeBron. But the fact that a nine-year-old who had never tried basketball was picking up the game so easily confirmed Walker's initial hunch—he needed to start taking LeBron to the gym.

The year that LeBron moved in with the Walkers, Walt Disney released *The Lion King*, and it quickly became the top-grossing animated film in history. The first time LeBron saw it, he couldn't believe it when Scar killed Mufasa. The treachery stunned him and brought tears to his eyes. LeBron loved the movie. But each time he watched it, that scene had the same effect on him.

There was a sentimental side to LeBron that he kept hidden away. One of the consequences of being driven from pillar to post for his entire childhood was that he suppressed his emotions and said as little as possible. He had trouble trusting adults. And he was reluctant to form friendships with kids, fearing his friends would disappear every time he and his mother picked up and moved on. The Walker home changed that. It was an emotionally safe place that opened LeBron's eyes to how much he had missed out on. He had watched *Family Matters* and *The Cosby Show* and often wondered what it would be like to be part of a middle-class African American family like the Winslows or an upper-class African American family like the Huxtables. The Walkers were the closest thing to those fictional families that LeBron had ever seen. Mr. and Mrs. Walker were loyal to each other and put the welfare of their children above all else. There were home-cooked meals and folded laundry, expectations and consequences for the children, birthday parties and holiday celebrations. Family was like a refuge.

For LeBron, living in the Walker home was also an opportunity to see a father in action and contemplate feelings he had long stifled. Out of respect for his mother's wishes, he never asked about his father. But fatherlessness inevitably causes a child to wonder, *Why didn't he want me?* While Big Frankie was taking LeBron under his wing, *The Fresh Prince of Bel-Air* ran an episode titled "Papa's Got a Brand New Excuse." In that episode, Will Smith's deadbeat father, Lou, finally shows up after fourteen years. Will loved living with his uncle Phil's family at the time, much the same way that LeBron loved living with Big Frankie's family. Yet as soon as Will's father showed up and indicated he wanted to take his son with him, Will packed his bag and was ready to go. Then on the day they were supposed to leave together, Will's father ditched him. Seeing the heartbreak on Will's face, Uncle Phil comforted him by telling him it was okay to be angry. Will tried to pretend he wasn't hurt. "Ain't like I'm gonna be sittin' up every night, askin' my mom, 'When's Daddy comin' home,'" he said. "Who needs him? He wasn't there to teach me how to shoot my first basket."

As LeBron watched the show, the story line hit home. It was as if Will Smith were speaking for him. For the first time, LeBron heard something that captured the pain he felt. Even the anger was authentic.

"You know what, Uncle Phil?" Smith boomed. "I'm gonna get a great job without him. I'm gonna marry me a beautiful honey and I'm gonna have me a whole bunch of kids. I'm gonna be a better father than he ever was . . . Because there ain't a damn thing he could ever teach me about how to love my kids!"

When Smith started crying, LeBron started crying.

"How come he don't want me, man?" Smith asked Uncle Phil, who put his arms around him.

The episode aired during a watershed year in LeBron's life. In various ways, Big Frankie became LeBron's Uncle Phil. Most days he picked up LeBron from school and drove him home from school. He taught him how to play basketball. And he steadily complimented him in ways that gave LeBron self-confidence. "This young man right here," Walker would proudly tell people, pointing to LeBron, "if he wants to be president of the United States, he can be the president of the United States." It was the kind of thing a proud father would say. But Walker meant it. "He doesn't get the recognition he deserves," LeBron would say of Walker many years later. "But he was the first one to give me a basketball and the first one to really show an interest."

Besides introducing LeBron to basketball, perhaps the most transformative impact Walker had on LeBron was putting him in an environment to meet other hardworking fathers who cared about the young boys in inner-city Akron. One of the men that LeBron met while living with the Walkers was Dru Joyce II. He would end up being the most influential coach LeBron encountered in his development as a basketball prodigy.

As a young man, Joyce had aspired to coach football for a living. But by the time Joyce graduated from Ohio University in 1978, his top priority was supporting his wife and raising a family. He set aside his dream of being a professional coach and took a job at Hunt-Wesson, a subsidiary of ConAgra, where he worked his way up to the position of senior sales rep. After he became a district manager, Joyce settled his family in Akron, where he and his wife, Carolyn, had two daughters. Then in January 1985—one month after LeBron was born—the Joyces had a son. They named him Dru Joyce III. He got his nickname "Little Dru" early on. When it became clear that his son preferred basketball over football, Joyce started coaching his son's youth basketball team in an Akron recreational league. That's when Joyce encountered young LeBron James.

Familiar with LeBron's budding reputation as an outstanding football player, Joyce watched with curiosity as he played point guard in a game against other boys his age. His ballhandling skills needed work, Joyce thought. But LeBron was at least four inches taller than everyone else. And he was using his size advantage to back defenders down the court, dribbling himself into position to score with relative ease. His skills were raw, but his instincts were advanced.

Before long, LeBron and Little Dru started playing ball together. LeBron liked him right away. Little Dru seldom spoke off the court. But on the court, he wasn't shy about telling LeBron what to do. Despite being the shortest guy on the floor, he acted like a coach. LeBron started calling him "the General." Little Dru had been playing basketball since he was four or five years old. But LeBron was so much bigger and stronger that he could beat Little Dru one-on-one. After every defeat, Little Dru would demand they go again. And again. And again. He had what LeBron referred to as "little man complex." Kids laughed at Little Dru and called him "Smurf," after the small blue cartoon creatures. It all contributed to the monumental chip on Little Dru's shoulder, inspiring him to work harder than all the other kids to prove himself. LeBron liked the way he would take on anybody, no matter the size disadvantage. For the first time, LeBron had a friend his own age who he didn't fear would disappear.

Fifth grade taught LeBron that he liked school. He went the entire school year without an absence. His perfect attendance record was a source of pride. It was particularly rewarding to see the look of approval in Pam Walker's eyes. She had been on him all year to keep his grades up and to aim high. With his athleticism, she repeatedly told him, he could earn a college scholarship. No one had ever mentioned college to LeBron before. The word *scholarship* wasn't even in his vocabulary. Mrs. Walker assured him he'd be able to get into any college he chose. He just needed to keep his grades up. His talent would take care of the rest.

LeBron had come to realize that his initial fears that Mrs. Walker might resent him for his athletic ability had been ill founded. There was no jealousy over the fact that LeBron was better than her son at sports. On the contrary, she treated LeBron like a fourth child. Over the course of the year, she had done everything from washing behind his ears to wiping away his tears to caring for him when he got the chicken pox.

Pam Walker wanted him to soar as if he were one of her own. That's why she felt conflicted when Gloria said she wanted LeBron to move back in with her at the end of the school year.

LeBron was also torn. The Walkers had become family to him. Their home felt like his home. He felt safe there. He felt wanted. "What we did for you," Big Frankie told him, "we did because we love you."

LeBron recognized how lucky he was to live with them. "Without that time spent at the Walkers," he said, "I don't honestly know what would have become of me." The pain and confusion he'd felt when his mom first sent him to the Walkers had also subsided. Eventually, well after LeBron was a parent himself, he looked at his mother's willingness to let him live with the Walkers as "a supreme sacrifice" that had put his interests above her own. "I know she hated to do it," LeBron said.

Although Gloria was eager to have LeBron back under her roof, the reunion was turbulent. At the start of sixth grade, Gloria lost the apartment she had planned to live in. LeBron had to temporarily move back in with the Walkers while Gloria figured out her next move. There was even talk of moving to New York.

LeBron was mature enough to recognize how hard it was for his mother to provide for them. Although she always managed to put food on the table, he didn't know how she pulled it off. There was a lot going on that was outside his control. He just knew that his mother's life wasn't easy and that he wanted to make her proud. "There were things I knew that I could see," LeBron later reflected. "There were things I couldn't see. But I never questioned. I didn't want to know."

With so much uncertainty, Pam Walker intervened. "There are times when I want to take him in my arms all over again," Pam said. But the situation was complicated. And recognizing the importance of trying to keep Gloria and LeBron together in Akron, Pam contacted a friend who managed a place called Spring Hill Apartments. The buildings were grim, and the neighborhood wasn't the most desirable. But Gloria qualified for low-income assistance. And with Walker's help, Gloria landed a two-bedroom unit. For the first time in his life, LeBron had his own bedroom. Spring Hill seemed like a place they could finally call home.

In sixth grade, LeBron still saw the Walkers. But he also started spending time at the Joyce home. It was like the Walkers' house: Both parents worked. There were three children. And the house had three bedrooms. But the Joyce home also had a rec room in the basement. It was a great place for boys to hang out, talk sports, and play video games like *NBA Live* and *Madden NFL*. Mrs. Joyce ran a tight ship. She worked for a nonprofit that focused on teaching middle school children to avoid sex and drugs. Her priorities permeated the Joyce household. The Joyces also went to church together as a family every Sunday.

Dru Joyce taught Sunday school with another parishioner, Lee Cotton, a FedEx driver who lived with his wife and kids in a part of town known as Goodyear Heights. Cotton had a son named Sian who was the same age as Little Dru and LeBron. Sian was even bigger than LeBron. He was so big that he exceeded the weight limit for his age group in peewee football.

Despite being taller than LeBron, Sian wasn't a good basketball player. But Joyce knew that Sian's father was an exceptional player and that it never hurt to have a big, bruising kid on the roster. He convinced Lee Cotton to help him coach a youth basketball team, and he recruited LeBron to join forces with Little Dru and Sian. The team was called the Shooting Stars.

LeBron was gung ho. But Gloria was skeptical. Although LeBron had said that he felt a stronger connection to Coach Dru than to any other man he'd ever met, Gloria insisted on attending a practice before deciding whether her son could play. Coach Dru said she'd be welcome. He had arranged for his team to practice at the Salvation Army on Maple Street. The court was quite a bit smaller than a regulation-size gym, there was almost no space between the court and the concrete walls that surrounded it, and the floor was covered in linoleum. None of that mattered to Gloria. She was only interested in the type of men who would be coaching her son.

Along with Lee Cotton, Coach Dru put the boys through some basic drills. There was a lot of energy and positive encouragement. It was easy to see how well the boys got along. Little Dru was a natural leader and intensely focused. Sian Cotton was an intimidating presence under the basket. And LeBron was the best all-around athlete. The three boys coexisted on the floor like brothers, and the other kids fed off their energy.

Gloria told LeBron he could join the team.

Dru Joyce knew LeBron was athletically gifted. In addition to being taller and faster than most of the other boys his age, he possessed uncanny leaping ability and quickness. There wasn't anyone in his age group who could guard him one-on-one. Even against older boys, scoring came easily to LeBron. Little Dru was a more disciplined and fundamentally sounder player. But LeBron could dominate even without mastering the fundamentals. It was a situation that irked Little Dru, prompting him to sometimes get on LeBron's case.

But Coach Dru didn't ride LeBron much. Inexperienced as a coach, Joyce was in it as a dutiful father who loved sports and cared enough about LeBron and the other boys to dedicate his weekends to teaching them life lessons, like the importance of teamwork. Had Joyce been a coaching guru with decades of experience scouting players, grading talent, and coaching in high-stakes tournaments, he might have envisioned that LeBron had it in him to someday become a professional ballplayer. He might have recognized the future economic value in James's intangible qualities—the equal dexterity in both hands that is common among piano players, the native self-confidence, the inexplicable reservoir of energy that seemingly enabled him to never get tired. But even if Joyce had been that coaching guru, it's unlikely that he would have dreamt, much less expected, that the ten-year-old on his rec league team, the kid hanging out in his basement, playing video games with his son, was a bona fide child prodigy.

One day, while riding home from practice with Coach Dru, LeBron listened to him suggest ways he could improve as a player. Without a father to talk to about his game, LeBron paid attention whenever his coach wanted to talk shop about basketball. On this occasion, Coach Dru encouraged him to integrate his teammates into the offense. "Bron," he said, "if you pass the ball, everyone is going to want to play with you."

LeBron seized on the last part of the sentence—*everyone is going to want to play with you.* Those nine words could not have had more impact if they'd been spoken by a celestial being. In his attempt to teach a fundamental truth about team sports—that when the star player is unselfish, teammates work harder and achieve more—Coach Dru had tapped into LeBron's hunger for friendship and acceptance. For a kid who had spent so much time alone, there was nothing LeBron wanted more than to be wanted.

LeBron never had to be encouraged to share the ball again. At a time when he was most impressionable, he shifted his focus from scoring at will to passing. He watched players like Magic Johnson and took pride in making no-look passes. Before long, he developed into the best ball distributor in Akron's youth basketball league. At times, LeBron was so determined to set up his teammates that Coach Dru had to tell him to take more shots. It was the beginning of a habit of being unselfish with the ball that would carry all the way to his days in the NBA, where he'd sometimes be criticized for passing instead of shooting in key moments. But as a youth player, his willingness to make the extra pass caught on with his teammates, turning Coach Dru's team into the gold standard of Akron's rec league.

"My Little League coaches always just taught us the right way to play the game of basketball," LeBron said years later. "The word 'ball hog' was something that we despised, and we never let creep into our ball club's view."

LeBron didn't know what to expect when his team qualified for the national Amateur Athletic Union (AAU) tournament in Cocoa Beach, Florida. He was eleven years old and had never been on a family vacation. The Shooting Stars felt like his family. The chance to go far away with them to play basketball sounded like a great adventure. One afternoon in the summer of 1996, LeBron filed into Coach Dru's minivan, along with Little Dru, Sian Cotton, and a handful of other players. Mrs. Joyce and her two daughters followed in a car packed with food and gear. Together, they embarked on a nearly nine-hundred-mile journey from Akron to a hotel not far from Cape Canaveral Air Force Station.

For LeBron and his friends, it was a great time to be stuck in a vehicle for hours with so much to talk about and so much to dream about. A seventeen-year-old high school kid from Lower Merion in Philadelphia named Kobe Bryant had just been picked by the Charlotte Hornets in the first round of the NBA Draft and been promptly traded to the Los Angeles Lakers. And a twenty-six-year-old up-and-coming rapper named Jay-Z had recently released his debut album, *Reasonable Doubt*. LeBron and Little Dru and Sian wanted to be pro athletes. And songs like "Dead Presidents II" and "Can't Knock the Hustle" got them primed to play.

The opening ceremonies were held at the Kennedy Space Center. When teams from all over the country paraded through the venue, LeBron felt like he was participating in the Olympics. But the games were only a small part of the overall experience. When LeBron saw the ocean for the first time, he was overwhelmed by its vastness. He'd never been on a beach before. Never felt sand beneath his feet. Never splashed around in salt water. It was hot and sunny. There were girls in bikinis. Compared to Akron, Cocoa Beach was an exotic place.

The Shooting Stars finished ninth in the field of sixty-four teams, many of which had spent much more time playing and practicing together. Coach Dru was proud. "You guys are going to do something special," he told his team afterward.

LeBron wasn't sure what his coach meant by that. But the trip to Florida had solidified in his mind that Little Dru and Sian Cotton were more than teammates—they were brothers. Together, they had gotten a taste of what it was like to venture outside Akron and play against some of the best basketball players in the country for their age group. Now that they'd proven to themselves that they could compete in the AAU national tournament, they wanted to get back there and see what it felt like to win it.

The next year, LeBron spent more and more time at Coach Dru's place. It became his home away from home. While there, he observed that Coach Dru had started reading books by great coaches that he admired, like UCLA's John Wooden. At the same time, LeBron knew that Lee Cotton was religiously taking his son to the local YMCA every weekend, doing drills, working on technique, and teaching him how to use his big body on the court.

With the help of his father, Sian caught up to LeBron and Little Dru in terms of his self-confidence as a player. That summer, the three of them played in sixty summer league games together as twelve-year-olds. All the hard work paid off. With the addition of a few sound role players, the Shooting Stars qualified for the twelve-and-under AAU national championship tournament in Salt Lake City.

The trip to Utah was a lot different from the one to Florida. The team did enough fundraising to afford to fly from Cleveland to Salt Lake City. LeBron had never been on an airplane. It should have been an exciting adventure, but he was in tears for most of the flight. "Since it was my first plane ride," he reflected years later in his memoir, "I might as well confess: I cried like there was no tomorrow, scared out of my wits, my ears an impacted mess because of the altitude."

LeBron may have been scared. But there was apparently more behind those tears than the fear of flying. "He loved his mother to death," Coach Dru said. "When she wasn't able to be there for him, it hurt him a lot. I remember his first plane ride. He cried the whole way. He wanted his mom. Those are heart-wrenching moments that I'll always remember about him growing up."

Though LeBron didn't like to talk about the situation, Little Dru and Sian were empathetic. Their parents were always around. And when it came to traveling and tournaments, Coach Dru and Lee Cotton were so reliable that it was easy to take their steady presence for granted. Not so for LeBron. There were voids in his life, and he was always cognizant of those who filled them.

But as unsettled as he'd felt on the plane, once they got to the gym, LeBron was fine. No matter what zip code he was in, he always felt at home once he stepped onto a court.

The AAU players in the twelve-and-under tournament were noticeably bigger and better than teams the Shooting Stars had played before. They faced one team with three kids who were six five. At six two, Sian was Coach Dru's tallest player. It didn't matter. Little Dru was a fearless point guard. Sian outmuscled taller guys. And no one could guard LeBron one-on-one. The role players did their part. The team won most of their games and finished tenth out of seventy-two teams. Coach Dru was pleased. They were getting better.

These experiences were life-altering, especially for LeBron. Air travel, he discovered, wasn't so bad. And the recurring thrill of playing in front of cheering crowds in national tournaments made it easier to imagine being a professional ballplayer. Basketball was a ticket to a life he'd otherwise never get to experience. Other boys in his Spring Hill apartment complex back in Akron didn't know what it was like to possess an airplane boarding pass or discover the miniature soap bars in a motel room or splash around in a heated pool in a faraway city. Basketball also provided him a family in the form of a team. So much of what LeBron wanted was fueled by what he'd gone without. "The great force of history comes from the fact that we carry it within us, are unconsciously controlled by it in many ways, and history is literally present in all that we do," the writer James Baldwin observed. "It is to history that we owe our frames of reference, our identities, and our aspirations." That applies to personal history, too.

Without a doubt, LeBron's past was informing the way he looked at his future. In school, when his teacher passed out a blank note card at the beginning of the year and instructed the students to write down three things they wanted to be when they grew up, LeBron wrote:

NBA Player
NBA Player
NBA Player

After collecting the cards, the teacher pointed out that LeBron had misunderstood the assignment—he was supposed to identify three things he wanted to be when he grew up, not one.

LeBron hadn't misunderstood. There was only one thing he wanted to be.

Coach Dru was convinced that for his team to win a national championship, he needed to add another player to put them over the top. After LeBron, the best thirteen-year-old player in the city was a kid named Willie McGee, who played on a team called the Akron Elite. After the Shooting Stars knocked off Akron Elite in the qualifying round for the AAU national tournament for thirteen-year-olds, Coach Dru decided to recruit McGee. He was living with his older brother, Illya McGee, who had attended the University of Akron on a basketball scholarship. Coach Dru tracked down Illya and asked if Willie could join his AAU team. Illya liked the idea. His little brother had been through a lot. The chance to play on a good team led by a positive male role model would be good for him.

Willie McGee was from Chicago, where he had watched both of his parents struggle with drug addictions. When his parents ended up in the criminal justice system, McGee went to live with his older sister, who was struggling to feed and care for her own two children, who were still in diapers. Fearing that her little brother would fall victim to the drugs and violence on the streets and recognizing that he needed a positive male influence in his life, she put Willie's clothes in a plastic garbage bag and sent him to Akron to live with his older brother. Illya made sure Willie had food and clothes, did well in school, and exhibited manners and respect. He also taught Willie how to play basketball. He was a really good basketball player, Illya assured Coach Dru, and an even better kid. Never any trouble. He was just quiet. Really quiet.

Coach Dru offered to drive Willie to his first practice with the team.

It was after school and LeBron was hanging out at Coach Dru's house until it was time to go to practice. Little Dru was doing his homework. Willie McGee was due to get dropped off any minute. LeBron and Little Dru wondered whether he'd fit in with their tight-knit group. Neither of them was in a talking mood when Willie entered the house. At six two, he was four inches taller than LeBron.

Little Dru didn't bother looking up from his schoolwork.

"What up?" LeBron mumbled.

The silence was awkward. Willie knew LeBron's reputation as a player. He knew nothing about his personality or Little Dru's. It wasn't until they were loading basketballs into Coach Dru's car that Little Dru finally introduced himself.

During the ride to practice, LeBron and Willie kept to themselves as Coach Dru scolded Little Dru for something that had happened at school. But as soon as they reached the gym and the music began playing and they started the layup line, the ice broke. LeBron and Little Dru and Sian Cotton had a love for basketball and a camaraderie that instantly appealed to Willie. Without saying a word, he matched their enthusiasm. He hustled. He dove for loose balls. He had a nice handle. He fought for rebounds. He defended. And he could score.

LeBron liked what he saw. After a few more practices, he invited Willie to spend the night at his apartment in the Spring Hill housing project. Sian slept over, too. Gloria cooked dinner for them. Then they settled in for an evening of video games. At one point, LeBron turned to Willie and said, "You pretty cool."

Willie didn't say anything. But he felt a connection to LeBron. Little Dru and Sian had solid families with hardworking fathers who dedicated all their discretionary time to raising their children. LeBron was more like him. They didn't have fathers. They lived on the edge.

Over time, LeBron made it easier for Willie to see that he could look at Coach Dru and Mr. Cotton as if they were family. They would take Willie and LeBron to church on Sunday. They pressed them to do their homework. They made Friday night sleepovers a regular thing. For LeBron, all the extracurricular stuff was the best part of being on a basketball team.

"One thing about Bron," Coach Dru said. "He never liked being by himself. When he found us, he found homes. He found father figures. He found one of the greatest things that happened to him—friendships."

As those friendships deepened, LeBron became more confident in expressing himself. One night during a sleepover, he looked at Willie and said, "You and I are good friends." Willie still didn't know how to react. He wasn't accustomed to anyone, much less another boy, talking to him that way. But it wasn't just LeBron who talked that way. Sian and Little Dru spoke their feelings as well. "They were more giving," Willie explained. "They were more accepting. It just got more comfortable."

Although Willie seldom said anything, he demonstrated loyalty to his new friends. When he saw a bigger player shove Little Dru in the handshake line after a game, Willie sprang to his defense, knocking the other player back. Coach Dru was a big proponent of sportsmanship. But he liked the way Willie came to the defense of a teammate. LeBron did, too. It told him that Willie was loyal. After that, he and Willie and Sian and Little Dru started calling themselves "the Fab Four."

In eighth grade, LeBron grew to six two. The added height enabled him to see over defenders more easily, altering the way he visualized the court and enabling him to become an even better passer when running the floor. LeBron also started routinely dunking the ball with two hands. The first time he dunked was in the gym at his middle school. He was in seventh grade and his friends were urging him to try it in a game. Although LeBron could get the ball over the rim with ease, he was reluctant to try dunking in games. Instead, he'd lay it in. Then one day during an AAU tournament in Cleveland, he elevated above the rim and jammed the ball through the cylinder. It was one thing to get a running start on a playground and create enough momentum to dunk a ball while not being challenged by defenders. But very few middle schoolers could get to the rim with the ball and throw it down in a game situation.

LeBron's newfound ability to dribble, drive, and dunk over defenders made the Shooting Stars nearly impossible to beat. The more experienced AAU teams started sending two and three defenders at LeBron whenever he got the ball. In those situations, he became adept at feeding his unguarded teammates for uncontested layups and open jump shots. For fourteen-year-olds, they played like a well-oiled machine.

In the AAU national tournament that year, the Shooting Stars went on a roll. At one point during a game in the quarterfinals, LeBron got the ball in the open court and raced toward the basket. With no one in front of him, he picked up his dribble just inside the foul line, took an extra step, went airborne, and threw down a two-handed jam that rocked the backboard.

He had established himself as the best player in the most competitive youth basketball tournament in the country. And the Shooting Stars reached the AAU national championship game for the fourteen-and-under division. The goal they'd set three years earlier was finally within reach. They were set to face the heavily favored Southern California All-Stars, a group of boys who had won the national championship for three consecutive years. They were stacked with elite athletes who could leap and dunk, including one who had already been profiled in *Sports Illustrated Kids*.

Coach Dru sensed that some of his players were feeling the pressure. The California All-Stars were an intimidating bunch. Cocky, too. During warm-ups, they strutted onto the court carrying Nike duffel bags and wearing Nike sneakers and matching red-and-white Nike uniforms. The Shooting Stars didn't even have a sponsor. LeBron and his teammates had scraped and scrimped—holding car washes, hosting barbecues, and going door-to-door in Akron for donations—just to pay for their uniforms. Next to the All-Stars, they looked like paupers. Right before the game, Dru brought his team together in the locker room and assured them that he shared their dream to win it all. But he wanted them to know that they had already given him everything a coach could possibly want from his team. "I just want you guys to play and play well," he told them. "You don't have to win."

His speech was intended to put them at ease. But when LeBron and his teammates took the floor for the opening tap at the Disney sports complex in Orlando on July 8, 1999, their hearts were racing. "Y'all from Akron?" one of the All-Stars said condescendingly. His teammates snickered. Another one chimed in: "Y'all country boys?"

LeBron felt scorned. So did the others. Akron had indeed been an obscure place on the AAU basketball map. But the Shooting Stars had built a reputation for playing a team-oriented, hard-nosed brand of basketball that landed them in the late rounds of the tournament each year. And LeBron had become a familiar name to coaches and players throughout the AAU circuit. It pissed him off that these guys from Southern California were looking down on him and his teammates like a bunch of second-rate players from the sticks.

Early on, the Shooting Stars fell far behind, trailing, 45–30, at the end of the first half. But they rallied in the second half. LeBron led the way, slashing his way to the basket, throwing no-look passes that were converted into layups, and blocking shots on defense. With a minute to play, he dribbled up the left side of the court using his left hand, crossed over to his right hand to avoid a defender, and then twisted his way through two more defenders to make a layup off the glass that prompted the announcer to shout, "Oh! What a move by James!" The acrobatic shot cut the All-Stars' lead to three. Then, with four seconds remaining and his team trailing by two, Coach Dru called time-out. The objective was to successfully inbounds the ball and advance it the length of the floor in time to get a shot off. The plan was simple—get the ball to LeBron.

LeBron had long dreamt of hitting a game-winning shot at the buzzer. He couldn't count how many times he had acted out the scenario in the gym, shooting over imaginary defenders as time ran out. In his mind, he could see what he was about to do. Moments later, LeBron had his head turned and was surveying the court, when Sian lofted the inbounds pass over LeBron's head. Looking back just in time, LeBron spotted the ball and caught it in stride. Using two dribbles, he raced along the side court, past two defenders. Crossing half-court, he took one more dribble and went airborne as a third defender ran toward him and leaped with an outstretched arm. His momentum carrying him toward the basket, LeBron launched an NBA-range three-point attempt from thirty-five feet away. The crowd was silent as the ball traveled on a perfect trajectory, landed in the cylinder, then rimmed out as the horn sounded. Relieved, the All-Stars leaped for joy. LeBron stood frozen where he had landed and buried his head in his hands, his teammates staring at him. They lost, 68–66.

The trip back to Akron was long and quiet. Coach Dru figured he'd never coach the boys again—later that year they'd all be heading off to high school. It felt like the end of a great ride. But the boys had other plans. Earlier that year they had started talking seriously about attending the same high school so they could continue playing together. Their homes were spread out all over town. But Akron had multiple high schools and the school system afforded them the option to select the same school. The loss to the Southern California All-Stars was a bitter experience. But it solidified their commitment to play ball together in high school.

They had unfinished business.

FOUR

WE ALL WE GOT

Little Dru kept a pull-up bar mounted in his bedroom. LeBron would watch him as he hung from it in hopes of stretching his body. Little Dru would have done just about anything to get taller, anything to become a better basketball player.

Knowing how diligently his son worked to improve his game, Coach Dru was always looking for ways to help him. When he caught wind of basketball clinics being held at the Jewish Community Center in Akron on Sunday nights, he brought Little Dru. The clinics were being run by thirty-eight-year-old Keith Dambrot, a stockbroker who had previously been the head basketball coach at Central Michigan University. Coach Dru knew little about him. But anyone who had coached Division I basketball in his early thirties had to be pretty impressive, he figured.

Short and fiery, Dambrot took an instant liking to Little Dru, who was in seventh grade when he first attended and was barely four foot ten. When Dambrot looked at him he saw himself—a gym rat who compensated for his lack of size by honing his long-range jump shot and his ball-handling skills. Dambrot took Little Dru under his wing, complimenting his work ethic and his competitive drive.

Little Dru liked Dambrot right away and started attending regularly. Every other coach would harp on the idea that he had to get bigger if he expected to play in high school. Dambrot never said a word about Little Dru's size. He just focused on the mechanics of dribbling and passing and the importance of things like footwork and shooting technique. He was all about the fundamentals. Little Dru thrived, distinguishing himself as the most fundamentally sound player at Dambrot's clinics.

LeBron soon started going with Little Dru on Sunday nights. The first thing he noticed was that they were the only Black kids at the Jewish Community Center. LeBron hadn't had much exposure to white people. And as a seventh grader, his views on race were just starting to form. When he observed that Coach Dambrot constantly used Little Dru every time he wanted to illustrate to the other kids the correct way to perform a drill, LeBron wondered if it was racist to always single out one of the only two Black kids. But he soon dismissed the idea, concluding that Dambrot favored Little Dru. And Little Dru liked demonstrating proper technique. It was obvious that Little Dru and Dambrot got along well. There was a certain chemistry between them. And LeBron adapted quickly to the new environment. Before long, Sian Cotton and Willie McGee started coming to the clinics. The four of them easily stood out as the best players in the gym.

In July 1998, about a year after Coach Dru first started taking his son to work with Keith Dambrot at the Jewish Community Center, Dambrot was hired as the new head coach at St. Vincent–St. Mary, a private Catholic high school in Akron. The news dredged up reports of Dambrot's controversial departure from Central Michigan University five years earlier. The *Akron Beacon Journal* reported that Dambrot had been fired for using the N-word in 1993. That year, after a frustrating loss to Miami University of Ohio, Dambrot allegedly said to his players in the locker room: "I wish we had more niggers on this team." Days later, his comment was reported in the student newspaper, touching off protests on campus. At the time, Dambrot did not deny using the racial slur. Instead, he told the press: "It was not used in any racially offensive manner. Our team understood the connotation of the word as I used it and were not offended."

After the school fired him, Dambrot filed a federal lawsuit against the university, challenging his termination as a violation of his rights to free speech and academic freedom under the First Amendment. Insisting they weren't offended by his use of the N-word, nine Black players on the Central Michigan team joined the lawsuit in support of Dambrot. "All the people who said he should be fired, they weren't there when he said it," one of the players said at the time. "They don't understand the situation. It was a bad choice of words, but you had to be there to understand it." Dambrot's suit was ultimately dismissed by a judge and for five years he was unable to find a coaching job. Then St. Vincent–St. Mary decided to give him a chance.

"Obviously, I made mistakes and I apologized for them," Dambrot told the *Akron Beacon Journal*. "I paid a pretty good price for it, and I accept that." Dambrot thanked St. Vincent–St. Mary for giving him a second chance. The high school's athletic director, Jim Meyer, defended the school's decision. "We checked and we liked what we heard about him," Meyer said. "He works well with young athletes, and that was important to us." The decision to hire Dambrot to coach high school ball was framed as "an opportunity for redemption."

Coach Dru got pushback for letting Little Dru go to Dambrot's clinics. An associate told him he should stay away from that guy. But Coach Dru wasn't familiar with the specifics in Dambrot's past, and he wasn't going to shun him based on media reports. All he had to go on was what he had witnessed firsthand, which was that Dambrot was an excellent coach who had consistently treated his son and the other boys with respect. Little Dru thrived under Dambrot's instruction and signed up for a summer basketball camp with him. So did LeBron and the others.

Initially, LeBron, Little Dru, Sian, and Willie weren't directly impacted by the swirl around Dambrot and the fact that he was heading to St. Vincent–St. Mary. They were about to enter eighth grade at the middle school. And after that the four of them would be heading off to Buchtel High, a public high school in Akron with an exceptional basketball team. LeBron already had it all mapped out in his mind. "I knew the athletic reputation of the school; every Black kid in Akron did," LeBron said. "I was already having fantasies about how it would be—the four of us marching in as Big Men on Campus who would lead Buchtel to a state and national championship."

It was no secret within the Akron youth basketball circuit that the four best players on Dru's AAU team were a tight bunch with hopes of playing together in high school. Eager to ensure that they ended up at Buchtel, the school's basketball coach added Dru Joyce to his staff as an assistant coach, a shrewd move on Buchtel's part. He began coaching there during Little Dru's eighth-grade year, while Little Dru was still in middle school. Buchtel assumed that Coach Dru would deliver his son, who would in turn bring along LeBron and the others.

But during eighth grade, Little Dru cooled to the idea of going to Buchtel. The varsity team there was loaded and he didn't think the coaching staff would take him seriously. Little Dru knew he'd end up playing on the junior varsity team. In the back of his mind, he also had the feeling that LeBron was the only player from the Shooting Stars that Buchtel really wanted. He let LeBron know that he was having second thoughts about going there. "Man, I don't think this is gonna work," he said. "I don't think they're gonna give me a chance."

LeBron didn't think much of his friend's concerns. To him it was simple: if you were an inner-city kid, you went to Buchtel. It was an all-Black school. Everyone expected them to go there. Plus, Coach Dru was on the staff. Why would they go anywhere else?

But Little Dru was serious about spurning Buchtel. He'd gone there with his dad for open gym. The guys on the varsity team had been pretty dismissive of him, mainly due to his size. Discouraged, Little Dru had a heart-to-heart with his father.

"Dad, they're not gonna give me a chance here," Little Dru told him.

Coach Dru tried to reassure him.

"Dad, I'm not going to Buchtel," he finally said.

"What do you mean?" Coach Dru asked. "I'm on the coaching staff. Everything's in place."

"I wanna go to St. V," Little Dru told him.

Coach Dru paused.

"I know Coach Dambrot will give me a chance," Little Dru continued.

At first, Coach Dru was angry. Not at his son. Not at Dambrot. At the situation. He'd been offered the assistant coaching position at Buchtel with the expectation that he'd deliver LeBron and his other top AAU players. Now he was going to have to tell the head coach that he couldn't even deliver his own son? It was humiliating.

Yet Coach Dru recognized that his son had developed a bond with Coach Dambrot. After calming down, he decided he wouldn't stand in his son's way. Instead, he told the head coach at Buchtel he was going to resign.

LeBron, Sian, and Willie looked at Little Dru like he was crazy when he told them he'd decided he was going to St. Vincent–St. Mary. The school was known for academics, not basketball. And as a private Catholic school with tuition that exceeded $5,000 per year, the students were almost exclusively white kids from the suburbs. LeBron wanted nothing to do with a school like that. "I was on some 'I'm not fucking with white people' [kick], 'cause I was so institutionalized growing up in the hood," LeBron said years later. "It's like . . . they don't want us to succeed."

Convinced that he and his friends should stick with the original plan to go to Buchtel, LeBron tried to talk Little Dru into changing his mind. What about their pact to win a national championship? To stick together?

Little Dru held his ground. He didn't try to sway his friends. But he remained adamant about going to St. V. Coach Dambrot had assured him that he was willing to put freshmen on the varsity squad. And if a freshman outworked a senior, Coach Dambrot told him, he wasn't afraid to play the freshman. Little Dru felt his best chance of playing varsity basketball was with Dambrot.

For a few weeks, LeBron thought the Fab Four were actually going to split up. Gradually, though, Willie and Sian started coming around to Little Dru's way of thinking. First Willie met with Dambrot, who told him he'd love to have him on his team and that he'd have a chance to compete for a varsity spot as a freshman. Then Sian started getting the vibe that the Buchtel coaches were really only interested in LeBron. Sian wanted to play for a coach who wanted him. And he wanted to keep the Fab Four together. He decided he was willing to follow Little Dru and Willie to St. V.

LeBron couldn't help thinking that the coaches at Buchtel had made a mistake by overlooking Little Dru. He was the ringleader of the Fab Four. By focusing on the fact that he was tiny by basketball standards, the Buchtel coaches failed to see the determination in his heart and the size of the chip on his shoulder. Those were the qualities that made Little Dru such an attractive teammate. LeBron was also getting the sense that the Buchtel coaches had underestimated him as well. Sure, they liked him as a basketball player. But they didn't really understand him and the bond he felt with his friends. He was getting the impression that the Buchtel coaches saw him as a kid from the projects who didn't have it in him to go to a nearly all-white Catholic school with high academic standards and a dress code. It bothered him to be underestimated.

LeBron was considering venturing way outside his comfort zone to attend a school where he'd be very much an outsider. He fully suspected that the white students and faculty at St. V would look down on him and knew that the African American community might turn on him for not going to Buchtel. It would have been a lot easier to just conform. But his first allegiance was to his friends. They had given each other their word. Ultimately, this decision was about more than basketball. It came down to staying true to each other. "We all we got," Sian liked to say. LeBron agreed. But he realized that choosing to go to St. V as a group was fraught with race and class implications. This would be viewed as something much bigger than simply choosing one school over another. For him it was a defining moment, one that would dramatically alter the course of his basketball life.

In Keith Dambrot's first year at St. Vincent–St. Mary, he coached his team to a 16-9 record, and they qualified for the state tournament. His best player was a six-four forward, Maverick Carter. A junior, Carter was the leading scorer and a superb all-around athlete with natural leadership traits. Together, Dambrot and Carter were quickly changing the perception of the St. V basketball program.

LeBron was four years younger than Maverick, but he'd known Maverick since they'd been little kids. They'd met at Maverick's eighth birthday party. At the time, LeBron lived in a housing project that was next to Maverick's neighborhood. Although they didn't live next to each other for very long, they continued to cross paths in Akron, and a friendship evolved. They were the two boys with unusual names. Maverick had been named after the late-fifties television show *Maverick*, starring James Garner as the poker player Bret Maverick, who gambled his way in and out of trouble in the Old West. Carter's grandmother loved that show. She also loved gambling. After hours, she'd open her basement so people in the neighborhood could play poker and shoot craps.

Like LeBron, Maverick had been raised primarily by his mother, who was employed by the county for nearly thirty years as a social worker. Maverick's father had done prison time for drug possession with intent to distribute.

Hoping to play in the NBA, Maverick was determined to go to college on a basketball scholarship. He welcomed the arrival of Coach Dambrot to St. V and immediately bought in to his intense coaching style. Maverick figured it would only further his own aspirations.

During the summer of 1999, Coach Dambrot held a basketball camp at the Jewish Community Center. He invited Maverick and some of his other varsity players to work at the camp. LeBron, Little Dru, Sian, and Willie attended. It was the same summer that they had lost by two points to the Southern California All-Stars in the AAU national championship game in Orlando. And they were in the midst of working through their decision to stick together and go to St. V.

Due to the four-year age gap, Maverick and LeBron hadn't played much ball together. But during the camp, Maverick could see that LeBron was different from all the other boys, slashing to the basket and making precision passes to open teammates. He was more cerebral in his play than the guys Maverick was competing against in high school. It was tempting to think about what it would be like to see LeBron in a St. V uniform.

Dambrot couldn't help wondering the same thing. Over the years, as a college coach, he had scouted his share of teen basketball players. In LeBron he saw an "it" factor—that hard-to-describe quality that very few players possessed, that rare talent combined with an inner drive that can't be taught or coached. That summer, LeBron and his buddies played against some of Dambrot's varsity players in a pickup game. Dambrot's assistant coach, a hard-nosed guy in his thirties named Steve Culp, joined the game and went one-on-one with LeBron. At one point, Culp intentionally toyed with LeBron, dribbling in a way that dared him to try to steal the ball. When LeBron lunged, Culp quickly changed his dribble from his right hand to his left and cut toward the basket, causing LeBron to lose his balance and land on his butt. As Culp scored easily, everyone laughed. The next time Culp brought the ball up the court, he expected LeBron to back off. Instead, LeBron was up in Culp's face, pressing and challenging him to try that move again. And on offense, LeBron was demanding the ball so he could take it at Culp. Again. And again. After the game, Culp told Dambrot, "This kid is going to be unreal."

Dambrot agreed. Unlike the other kids, LeBron wasn't just playing to win. He was playing to be recognized. He wanted to be somebody. *How great would it be to coach a kid like that?* Dambrot thought. But he wasn't about to try to recruit LeBron. Like everyone else in town, he figured LeBron was a lock to go to Buchtel.

LeBron wasn't talking to Dambrot about the prospect of playing for him. But Maverick's presence at St. V helped solidify his thinking. LeBron looked up to Maverick more than to any other teenager in Akron. He had the things that LeBron wanted—his own car, a pretty girlfriend, a tattoo. Maverick was so cool that when he walked he kind of strutted. Plus, Maverick was an inner-city kid who was thriving at a predominantly white school. His experience gave LeBron confidence. He already knew he was good enough to start for the varsity team. And the chance to be on the floor alongside Maverick during his senior year was appealing. "Maverick," he would say years later, "was the main reason I came to St. Vincent–St. Mary's."

Gloria couldn't afford the tuition for LeBron to attend St. V. But Dambrot knew that, and the school was equipped to provide scholarships for needy students. About a quarter of the school's 550 students received financial aid. Tuition wouldn't be an impediment to LeBron and his friends.

As soon as word began to spread through the youth basketball circuit in Akron that all four of the stars from Coach Dru's AAU team were heading to St. V, the backlash began. Someone called Sian Cotton's home and left a message that implied Dambrot was a racist based on the things he'd allegedly said to his players at Central Michigan years earlier. Lee Cotton had played basketball against Dambrot in high school. While he found the comments attributed to Dambrot troubling, they were inconsistent with the man that Cotton remembered. Rather than rely on innuendo, he spoke directly to Dambrot about the incident that had gotten him fired. Contrite, Dambrot admitted he'd been foolish. But he insisted his words had not been intended to be demeaning. He encouraged Cotton to look at the testimony from his lawsuit against Central Michigan.

Lee's wife, Debra, tracked down the court documents. A key passage from the judge's decision read:

In January of 1993, Dambrot used the word "nigger" during a locker room session with his players and coaching staff either during the half-time or at the end of a basketball game in which the team lost to Miami University of Ohio. According to Dambrot's testimony, Dambrot told the players they hadn't been playing hard enough and then said, "Do you mind if I use the N word?" After one or some of the players apparently indicated it was okay, Dambrot said, "You know we need to have more niggers on our team. . . . Coach McDowell is a nigger. . . . Sand[er] Scott, who's an academic All-American, a Caucasian, I said Sand[er] Scott is a nigger. He's hardnose [sic], he's tough, et cetera." He testified he intended to use the term in a "positive and reinforcing" manner. The players often referred to each other using the N-word during games and around campus and in the locker room. Dambrot stated he used the word in the same manner in which the players used the term amongst themselves, "to connote a person who is fearless, mentally strong and tough."

The Cottons also received a call from one of Dambrot's Black players, who confirmed that Dambrot had first asked them if it was okay for him to use the N-word.

Lee Cotton accepted Dambrot's explanation and felt comfortable with letting his son play for Dambrot. Coach Dru was also at peace with the situation. But he talked to Dambrot and suggested that he add him and Cotton to his coaching staff. The intention wasn't intended to diversify Dambrot's staff—he already had an African American man working as an assistant coach, and another assistant coach who was a woman. Dru understood what his son and his friends would be up against. He thought it would be a good idea to have him and Lee Cotton around to support the boys during a critical transition period.

Dambrot agreed and welcomed them aboard. After all, they'd been coaching the Shooting Stars for four years and knew LeBron, Little Dru, Sian, and Willie much better than he did.

Right away, Coach Dru got flak. He was on the street in Akron one day when a car pulled up. Dru Joyce knew the driver, who worked for the Akron public schools. "Hey, Dru," the man said, "I understand you're pimping for St. V now."

Cotton took even more verbal abuse. "St. V isn't going to take care of you," one guy told him. "White people aren't going to take care of you."

But what bothered both Joyce and Cotton most was what people from their own community were saying to their sons. "You're all fucking traitors," one man told Sian. "And your coach is a pedophile." (There was never any substance to that charge.)

It didn't matter. Four African American boys from the inner city were headed to a Catholic school to play for a Jewish coach.

FIVE

THE FRESHMAN

LeBron was going to St. V to play basketball. But football was his first love. And football was a much bigger deal than basketball at St. V. In the previous decade the school had won three state championships in football. The current team had two former NFL players on the coaching staff. Sian, who had aspirations of going to college on a football scholarship, had gone out for the freshman team. Willie was playing, too. Eager to join his friends, LeBron talked to his mother.

Gloria didn't want to hear it. Football is violent. All it took was one knucklehead crashing helmet-first into LeBron's knee and his basketball dreams would be in jeopardy. Forget about it, Gloria told LeBron. Focus on basketball and academics.

By this time, LeBron's dream had become Gloria's dream. She'd begun to see basketball as a legitimate pathway that could lead her son out of poverty and into a life-changing career. For the overwhelming majority of high school athletes, a career in professional sports is a pipe dream. But when LeBron was in eighth grade, Gloria realized that her son wasn't like most student-athletes. This conclusion was more than mere motherly pride. The men who coached LeBron were saying things about him that they weren't saying about their own sons.

At the same time, the idea that LeBron had the potential to one day play in the NBA was being enthusiastically reinforced by Gloria's long-time friend Eddie Jackson. Ever since LeBron was little, Jackson had taken an interest in him. There had been a significant stretch of LeBron's life, however, when Jackson wasn't around. When LeBron was in grammar school, Jackson was arrested and charged with selling a half ounce of cocaine to an undercover officer in a school zone. He ended up spending time in prison. "I had made a bad choice," Jackson told the *Plain Dealer* after his release. "I made a promise to God. Not to man. Not to my kids, my friends, my sister, brother, mother, anybody. I made it to God that if he grants me my freedom, I will never, ever do it again, or forsake Him in that manner. That is as real as it gets."

When LeBron was in eighth grade, Jackson started dabbling in real estate in and around Akron. He also reconnected with Gloria and the two of them started attending LeBron's AAU games together.

Jackson had played high school sports in Akron and he understood the racial dynamics around LeBron's decision to attend St. V. Both Jackson and Gloria were initially uncomfortable when they heard some of the things that Dambrot had reportedly said to his college players in the past. But Jackson made the effort to speak with Dambrot one-on-one, and he came away convinced that Dambrot wasn't a racist. Moreover, Jackson believed that Dambrot's intense, no-nonsense approach to coaching was ideal to prepare LeBron for the next level. "You had a Division I college mentality coaching these kids," Jackson said. "When he looked at the kids, they would straighten the hell up."

LeBron trusted Jackson. He liked looking up and seeing Jackson and Gloria in the stands at his AAU games. It also mattered to him that Jackson felt he had made the right choice by electing to play for Dambrot, and that his mother approved of Dambrot, too.

Yet LeBron's desire to play football remained. Weeks before school started, LeBron walked to the campus on the first day of football practice. On one field, Sian and Willie did calisthenics with the freshman team. On another field, Maverick Carter hauled in passes with the varsity. Maverick was the best receiver on the team. Watching him, LeBron wished he could showcase his own pass-catching abilities. Instead, in between whistles and cursing from coaches, he paced the sideline like a spectator. He returned the next day and the day after that, spending his afternoons hanging around the field while the team went through two-a-day practice sessions.

Gloria knew what he was up to. She agreed to listen as he made a last-ditch effort to change her mind.

His friends were out there, he said. He wanted to be with them. And the coaches were skilled. They were pros. Mark Murphy had played safety for the Green Bay Packers. And Jay Brophy had played for the Miami Dolphins.

Brophy's name got Gloria's attention. She knew him. Brophy was a bit older than she was. But he had grown up in the area and had attended Buchtel High. Gloria agreed to talk to him.

A brawny former linebacker with big shoulders and powerful arms, Brophy stood six three. He listened intently as Gloria explained that Le-Bron had a bright future as a basketball player and that she wasn't keen on his playing football. But, she said, LeBron had prevailed on her and she was going to let him play.

"Jay, just don't let my baby get hurt," she said.

Brophy grinned. "Gloria, if you look at your baby, he's not such a baby anymore," he said.

She nodded and smiled.

"We'll take care of him," Brophy told her.

The next day, LeBron ran out of the locker room in cleats and pads. Standing six four and weighing 180 pounds, he made an instant impression. The freshman coach told him to play receiver. He started making one-handed catches and evading would-be tacklers with his extraordinary speed and quickness. But he quickly became frustrated with the way practices were going and volunteered to play quarterback. The first time he stepped into the huddle, he looked at his teammates and said, "I'm QB now."

Starting high school was intimidating enough. But the added element of entering such a different world at age fourteen made LeBron even more uneasy. St. V had a mandatory dress code: slacks with a belt, shirts with collars, and dress shoes. LeBron didn't even own clothes like that. There were also grooming standards. Tattoos, earrings, braids, and facial hair were forbidden. But his biggest source of angst was being around so many white people. Led to believe that white people didn't want anything to do with Black people, LeBron adopted the same attitude toward them. Yet he would be surrounded by white teachers and white students. At a loss as to how to get along with them or what to say to them, he was determined to close ranks and just stay close to Little Dru, Sian, and Willie. *We're here to play ball*, he told himself. *That's it.*

Maverick Carter's perspective on race was evolving, and he suggested a different approach. During his time at St. V, Maverick had made friends with lots of white kids and had become quite popular throughout the school. Sports, in Maverick's view, were a natural environment for breaking down barriers and building unity. Optimistic by nature, Maverick had no doubt that once LeBron started playing sports he'd be embraced by the St. V community and that he'd grow to love the school. Still, Maverick wasn't naive enough to think that everyone was thrilled about the newcomers. Right or wrong, the prevailing narrative was that LeBron was the ringleader of four African American freshmen who had been recruited to the school principally to play basketball.

LeBron relied on Maverick for tips on which teachers would be friendly and which ones might look for a reason to come down hard on him. He also trusted Maverick to give him a heads-up on the students who would welcome him and the ones who would treat him like an outsider. The biggest shock LeBron experienced at the beginning of ninth grade was the weight of having so many strangers' eyes on him when he walked the school's carpeted hallways in a collared shirt with a backpack slung over his shoulder. His minority status had never felt so pronounced.

The best piece of advice LeBron received in this period was from Coach Dru: *Treat people at St. V the way you want to be treated.* The man who had nurtured LeBron's unselfish playing style by telling him everyone would want to play with him if he passed the ball more often once again offered up a simple lesson with profound ramifications. Drawing on his religious convictions, Coach Dru took the Golden Rule, which Jesus Christ introduced in the Sermon on the Mount—*Do unto others as you would have them do unto you*—and instructed LeBron to behave that way toward his classmates and teachers in high school.

Patrick Vassel had grown up in Akron and gone to Catholic schools for grades one through eight. When it came time to choose a high school, he did what most Catholic kids in the area did—visited the city's three coed Catholic high schools: Walsh Jesuit, Archbishop Hoban, and St. Vincent–St. Mary. His mother and his older sister had attended St. V, so Vassel applied there and was awarded a couple of scholarships to help offset the annual tuition. Then Vassel did the math to see how much his parents would have to contribute to make up the difference. Although there were affluent kids at St. V, Vassel was among the 25 percent or so who received tuition assistance.

An honors student, Vassel was into the arts, especially theater. But his favorite sport was basketball, and he had his sights set on making the freshman team at St. V. He'd played in Akron's Catholic Youth Organization league and attended Keith Dambrot's annual summer basketball camp at the Jewish Community Center. Through the camp, he had met LeBron, Little Dru, Sian, and Willie. Even though Vassel and LeBron were the same age, they were on a very different level in terms of basketball skill. Sometimes Dambrot would assign LeBron to work with Vassel and other kids in his group on drills. When he learned that LeBron and his three friends would be attending St. V, Vassel was thrilled.

In the first week of school, LeBron recognized Vassel from the camp and said hello. They ended up in the same religion class, and they had a study hall together. Vassel had already formed a positive opinion of LeBron, but most of the 115 students in the freshman class didn't know him or his three friends. When LeBron would congregate in the hallway with Sian and Willie and Little Dru, some of Vassel's friends were critical. "They're just talking and laughing," Vassel told his friends. "They're not doing anything wrong."

Privately, Vassel admired LeBron and the fact that he seemed so self-assured and confident. It seemed to Vassel that LeBron already had a sense of purpose. Vassel, on the other hand, was trying to figure things out. He fretted over the fact that he had no idea where he was going or what he was going to do with his life. A part of him wished he could be more like LeBron in that respect.

When tryouts were announced for the freshman basketball team, Vassel showed up. It didn't bother him that LeBron, Little Dru, Sian, and Willie weren't required to try out. Dambrot had decided to put them on the varsity squad. That meant there were four open spots on the freshman squad. Vassel made the team.

When the start of basketball season arrived toward the end of the fall, LeBron was still finding his footing at St. V. But Gloria's decision to let him play football had accelerated the adjustment process. It also enabled him to spend more time around Maverick and some of the other upperclassmen.

Early in the football season, Coach Brophy and Coach Murphy stepped away from the varsity football practice one afternoon to watch the freshmen. They couldn't help marveling at how much more advanced LeBron was compared to the other ninth graders. Watching him haul in passes, Brophy and Murphy felt he should be moved up to varsity. "All you had to do was look at him play and the strides he'd make while catching balls," Brophy said. "You could see with LeBron just how he could run patterns."

Brophy and Murphy met with varsity head coach Jim Meyer and pled their case to elevate LeBron to varsity. Meyer was against putting freshmen on the varsity team. Conventional wisdom indicated that ninth graders simply weren't developed enough physically. There was a risk of injury by putting a freshman on the field with seniors. But LeBron was already taller than practically everyone on the varsity team. And as a receiver, he was also more talented. "There's no sense in leaving him down there," Brophy said. Meyer gave in.

But Maverick was the top receiver and there was a crop of juniors and seniors behind him, including the head coach's son. It was LeBron's first taste of the politics of high school sports. Relegated to the sideline, LeBron never played. As the season dragged on, Maverick encouraged his friend to keep his head up and to continue working hard in practice. LeBron never complained.

Then, on November 13, 1999, St. V faced Wickliffe in the state playoffs. Maverick started. But he felt ill and eventually exited the game. Meantime, the St. V offense couldn't get anything going. After three quarters, St. V trailed, 15–0. Finally, with LeBron on the bench, the team's quarterback couldn't stay quiet any longer. He'd watched LeBron in practice and knew what he could do. "Put him in," the quarterback told the coach.

Meyer hesitated. LeBron hadn't seen game action all year. He wasn't familiar with all the plays.

"I don't care if he only knows one play," the quarterback pleaded.

Brophy agreed.

With time running out on the season, Meyer finally called the freshman's number.

Adrenaline pumping, LeBron snapped his chin strap and trotted onto the field. He caught the first pass thrown his way, outleaping the defender and prompting Brophy to yell, "The kid can't cover him!" The quarterback kept going to LeBron. Again. And again. In the fourth quarter, LeBron caught nine passes for more than one hundred yards and scored two touchdowns. The players on the St. V sideline were hollering. The fans were screaming. LeBron's heroics had completely swung the momentum. But St. V ran out of time and lost the game, 15–14.

Dejected, the team filed into the locker room. This was a game they should have won. Instead, the season was over. LeBron said nothing. His teammates weren't so quiet. They all felt LeBron should have been playing the entire season.

Unlike the football coach, Keith Dambrot had no hesitation in starting LeBron as a freshman on the varsity basketball team and didn't need anyone to persuade him. Dambrot's only doubts were directed at himself. Convinced that LeBron was a generational player, he was intimidated by the prospect of coaching him. It was one thing to have him at his clinics and camps. It was another thing to have him on his roster when every other school in the city would be gunning for them. There was another aspect to LeBron's situation that weighed heavily on Dambrot—he understood the circumstances that LeBron had grown up in. Basketball wasn't just a game to LeBron—it represented a chance to make something great out of his life. A lot was riding on LeBron's next four years. And Dambrot couldn't stop thinking about the fact that he had never coached a player with so much potential. What if he didn't coach him properly? What if he didn't do everything possible to help LeBron maximize his talent?

When LeBron showed up for the first day of basketball practice, his attitude was a lot different than it had been on his first day of football practice. He knew how good he was at basketball. He knew he was going to start even though he was a freshman. And he knew Dambrot. Varsity basketball, LeBron figured, was going to be a cinch.

Then Dambrot put his players through the first set of drills.

"That was *fucking* terrible!" Dambrot barked at LeBron.

LeBron was stunned. He had never heard Dambrot talk that way. And Coach Dru had never yelled at LeBron like that. No one had.

Dambrot was just getting started.

"What the fuck is that?" Dambrot boomed at LeBron the next time he did something that wasn't up to the coach's standards.

LeBron had never considered lashing out at a coach. But the urge was building. *I'm about to do something to this dude*, he told himself.

"You're fucking up," Dambrot yelled at him for something else.

LeBron was the target of more high-volume F-bombs than anyone on the floor. Meantime, Dambrot called Sian a coward and was so hard on Little Dru that Little Dru wanted to fight him. Even Willie, who never showed emotion, was giving Dambrot the death stare.

Practice felt like two hours of boot camp. Afterward, there was nearly a mutiny in the locker room. LeBron wondered what the hell had happened to the mild-mannered guy from the Jewish Community Center. He concluded that Coach Dambrot was an insane asshole. The other freshmen agreed. It felt like they'd made a huge mistake. They should have gone to Buchtel.

Prior to LeBron's arrival, Maverick had relished being the best player and the team captain. He liked the attention, especially from Dambrot. He didn't mind that Dambrot was knocking LeBron and the other freshmen down a few pegs. They were a cocky bunch. But Maverick also recognized that LeBron had more talent than he did and that it was only a matter of time before the freshman would outshine the captain. Instead of becoming jealous, Maverick felt it was his duty as a senior to lead by taking LeBron under his wing.

Maverick played a pivotal role in bringing LeBron and his friends around. He recognized that LeBron was used to Coach Dru's manner of coaching, without screaming and shouting profanity at his players. But Maverick also appreciated that Coach Dru didn't have the coaching experience that Dambrot did. There was a method to Dambrot's madness. If these guys wanted to play varsity as freshmen, they needed to toughen up and take it. And if they wanted to compete for a state championship, they needed to work harder and complain less.

In LeBron's eyes, Maverick had credibility. He was a natural leader who had already received a full-ride basketball scholarship offer to attend Western Michigan University. Boys at school wanted to be like him. Girls wanted to date him. More than anything, LeBron wanted to play alongside him, even if that meant enduring Dambrot's tirades.

Maverick's maturity enabled Dambrot to push LeBron even harder. "I was on his ass nonstop," Dambrot later explained. "He probably didn't like it. But I never felt like he didn't want it. I always felt like he knew what I was trying to do."

* * *

St. V opened the basketball season on the road against Cuyahoga Falls in early December. LeBron was the only freshman in the starting lineup. Maverick was the only senior. They each scored fifteen points, leading the team to a blowout victory, 76–40. The other three freshmen came off the bench and played valuable minutes, especially Little Dru. It was a preview of things to come. Over the next month, St. V kept on winning. LeBron and Maverick kept on scoring. And the freshmen got better with each game.

By the time the team got to 10-0, LeBron was averaging more points per game than Maverick and the local writers who covered the team were increasingly referring to LeBron as "leading" the team to victories. Maverick was playing exceptionally well. But LeBron did things on the court that electrified the crowd. No-look passes. Dunks. Shot blocks. Maverick was the captain. But LeBron had quickly become the star attraction.

Coach Dambrot was sensitive to how this might affect Maverick. After all, he had worked hard for four years to become the best player and the leader of the team. As a senior, this should have been his time to shine, but he was being eclipsed by a freshman. Dambrot recognized that LeBron was the most talented player on the floor, night in and night out. But even LeBron looked to Maverick for leadership. To prop up his team captain, Dambrot pulled Maverick aside for a pep talk. After reminding him that the goal was to win a championship, he gave him some simple wisdom: "A high tide raises all ships."

Maverick didn't say much, leaving Dambrot to wonder whether his message had gotten through.

When LeBron wasn't in class or at the gym, he was usually at the library. Mainly he went there to see Barbara Wood, the school's librarian. Wood had a long history with St. V. She graduated from the school in 1965 and six of her children graduated from there as well. Mrs. Wood had worked in the school bookstore, taken over the booster club, organized the pep rallies, started senior nights, and was like a den mother to a lot of the student-athletes who visited the library. But she took a particular interest in LeBron. To her, he was unusually mature and refreshingly humble for a kid with so much talent. They talked often and she never let him get away with improper grammar. "There is no such thing as fiddy cent," she'd tell him with a smile. "It's *fifty cents* . . . with an *s.*"

LeBron adored Wood. He'd go to the library just so he could sit at her desk and chat. Sometimes they'd go on the computer together and enter his name in the new online search engine called Google to see how many articles they could find that mentioned his name. As the school year progressed, especially toward the end of basketball season, LeBron's mentions on Google gradually increased.

LeBron also took a liking to Wood's daughter Mia. Aware that more than a few girls at St. V had their eye on him, LeBron found common ground with Mia. They were the same age and she was arguably the best female athlete in the freshman class, starring on both the soccer team and the basketball team. Best of all, her interest in LeBron wasn't rooted in his budding popularity. She liked the fact that he treated her with respect.

The whole experience helped reinforce what Maverick had been telling LeBron from the beginning—that sports are the most unifying thing.

With a 19-0 record, St. V cracked the *USA Today* national poll for the first time in school history in late February 2000 with a ranking of number twenty-three. Days later, over five thousand fans packed James A. Rhodes Arena to watch the regular season finale between St. V and archrival Archbishop Hoban. At the beginning of the game, LeBron brought the crowd to its feet and left his opponents in awe when he appeared to be suspended in the air while flying toward the basket for a fast-break dunk. He led the way with twenty-seven points and his team dominated, winning, 90–58, and becoming the first team in school history to go undefeated. Afterward, Dambrot told reporters: "He's one of the best freshmen you'll ever see."

LeBron knew the reporters would flock around him. Determined to deflect the attention toward Maverick, he downplayed his performance and pointed out that his friend was the real leader of the team.

"This is a great feeling because no one really knew what to expect from us," Maverick told the press. "We have guys who came together and just worked hard all year long and this is our reward."

A reporter asked Maverick about LeBron's twenty-seven-point performance.

"I don't care if I score two points in a game or twenty-seven," he said. "I want to win. I want the team to win."

Dambrot's message from earlier in the season had clearly gotten through. Maverick was all in. Winning had snuffed out any chance that jealousy would drive a wedge between him and LeBron.

It was the eve of the state championship game and St. V was 26-0. That awful first day of basketball practice felt like ancient history. LeBron beamed when Coach Dambrot pulled him aside and told him privately that he was the best player in the state of Ohio. He no longer resented Dambrot's yelling and swearing—he welcomed it. His coaching style had made him a smarter, tougher player. Dambrot, he recognized, was the most skilled coach he'd ever been around. And he'd done a masterful job blending four freshmen into a team led by Maverick.

When the *Plain Dealer* named Maverick Carter the Ohio State basketball player of the year, LeBron was the first to congratulate him. It was like seeing his older brother receive a well-deserved honor. The only thing that remained to cap off a perfect season was to win one more game.

Thirteen thousand fans turned out for the state championship game on the Ohio State campus between St. V and Jamestown Greeneview. LeBron scored the first eight points, including a dunk and a long-range three. He ended up making ten of twelve shots and leading the team with twenty-five points and nine rebounds. But Little Dru came off the bench and stole the show. The five-foot-three, ninety-five-pound freshman made seven consecutive three-point shots. With the crowd going wild as Little Dru's seventh three-pointer went through the net, LeBron gave him a bear hug, lifted him off the floor, and carried him to the bench during a time-out. Dating back to when they were eleven years old, the two of them, along with Sian and Willie, had played together in more than three hundred basketball games. Almost a year earlier they had made a difficult and unpopular decision to come to St. V. On the cusp of winning the state championship, it felt like they had been vindicated.

Moments later, LeBron stood by Maverick as the game clock wound down. Maverick had scored just six points. But he had played almost every minute of the game and his leadership had set the tone. Beaming, LeBron embraced him. "No matter how many points you score," LeBron told him, "or what you do, I will always love you."

"I love you, too," Maverick said.

They were 27-0. They were state champions. And they were best friends. They felt on top of the world.

SIX

THE MOST CROOKED STREET IN AMERICA

In April 2000, Chris Dennis arrived at the NCAA Final Four in Indianapolis with a VHS tape that he guarded as if it were a rare gem. A native of Oakland, California, Dennis had been living in Akron in 1998, when he attended his younger brother's youth basketball game. But Dennis ended up focusing his attention on another kid who was bigger and much more advanced than his little brother. He inquired and learned the kid's name was LeBron James. At the time, Dennis maintained close ties with Calvin Andrews, the cofounder of the Oakland Soldiers, one of the top AAU basketball teams in the country. After seeing LeBron play, Dennis telephoned Andrews back in Oakland. "I saw a kid that will be better than Jason Kidd," he told him.

Andrews was in no mood for hyperbole. No thirteen-year-old, he felt, was worthy of being compared to one of the most talented point guards in the NBA.

Undeterred, Dennis went to see LeBron play as often as possible. He also befriended Gloria and Eddie Jackson. And he closely tracked LeBron's progress through his freshman season at St. V. During the Ohio State high school basketball tournament, Dennis filmed one of LeBron's games. He took the tape to Indianapolis with one goal in mind—to show it to the most influential man in the basketball sneaker universe.

Sixty-year-old John Paul Vincent Vaccaro preferred to be called Sonny. Just about everyone in the basketball industry thought of Vaccaro as the godfather of the sneaker business. Back in the sixties, Vaccaro had founded a national all-star game for high school basketball players. Over the next twenty years, he ingratiated himself with top college coaches and elite high school players throughout the country. Eventually, he went to work for Nike, and in 1984 Vaccaro signed twenty-one-year-old Michael Jordan to the richest athlete-endorsement deal in history. At the time, Converse and Adidas dominated the sneaker business. Nike's decision to pay the unproven Jordan $250,000 in his rookie year was considered reckless within the industry. But in Jordan's first year in the NBA, Nike sold over $126 million worth of his signature Air Jordan sneakers. Suddenly, Nike soared past its competitors and Vaccaro emerged as a visionary.

The same year that Vaccaro signed Jordan he also convinced Nike to start sponsoring an annual basketball camp for elite high school players. Vaccaro created the concept and the name, ABCD Basketball Camp. The initials stood for Academic Betterment and Career Development. In a shrewd business move, Vaccaro held on to the rights to the name, while Nike financed the camp. At the time, there were plenty of elite camps, but all of them charged an entrance fee. Vaccaro did away with the fee. Instead, he invited top college coaches to the camps and outfitted them in Nike gear. Additionally, every elite high school player who attended the camp went home with one thousand dollars' worth of Nike shoes and apparel. It didn't take long for Vaccaro's summer camps to become the premier showcase for high school basketball players throughout the country and for Nike to become a powerful fixture in the college basketball scene, signing sneaker deals with coaches and reeling in colleges and universities with apparel contracts. All the while, Vaccaro had the inside track to landing endorsement deals with future NBA stars coming out of the college ranks.

Through his history with Jordan and his control of the camps, Vaccaro became the sneaker industry's kingmaker. Eventually, he left Nike and took his ABCD Basketball Camp to Adidas, where he signed a string of high school athletes to endorsement deals, including Kobe Bryant and Tracy McGrady. At Adidas, Vaccaro relied on a network of AAU coaches and scouts, who helped spot and recruit elite high school players to the Adidas family. Two of Vaccaro's longtime associates on the AAU circuit were Calvin Andrews and Mark Olivier from Oakland.

At the Final Four in Indianapolis, Chris Dennis joined Andrews and Olivier in the Adidas suite. At one point, Dennis put his LeBron video in a VCR and pushed play. Andrews and Olivier liked what they saw. "Damn!" one of them said.

When Vaccaro entered the suite, he saw the guys crowded around a television set and asked what they were watching.

"His name's LeBron James," Olivier said.

Vaccaro flashed a blank expression.

"He's a freshman from Akron, Ohio," Olivier said. "Chris thinks he's gonna be better than Jason Kidd."

Vaccaro rolled his eyes and stepped toward the television as the men moved aside. Squinting, Vaccaro spent a minute watching the video of LeBron that Dennis had shot from a distance. "He looks like a peanut," Vaccaro said.

Dennis assured Vaccaro that LeBron was the real deal and suggested he should invite LeBron to the Adidas ABCD Camp.

"C'mon, Chris," Vaccaro said, stepping back from the television. "I can't invite 'im to camp."

"Why not?"

"For Chrissake," Vaccaro snapped. "He's a *ninth* grader!"

Realizing it might take time to convince Vaccaro, Dennis turned his efforts toward Andrews and Olivier, lobbying them to put LeBron on their power-house AAU team in Oakland. They had an under-seventeen team and an under-sixteen team, both of which were stacked with kids who were deemed legitimate NBA prospects. Although LeBron was only fifteen, Dennis believed that he could dominate on either team. And Dennis had already talked to Coach Dambrot, who agreed that LeBron was more than capable of holding his own against any high school talent in the country. Moreover, Dambrot thought it would be good for LeBron's development to join the Soldiers.

Intrigued by the prospect of adding LeBron to his team, Andrews agreed to offer him a roster spot for the Elite 8 tournament later that summer. But he said that the Soldiers didn't have a budget to fly LeBron back and forth or cover his lodging.

Olivier stepped up and said he'd happily host LeBron at his house. Meanwhile, Dennis and Dambrot agreed to figure out the airfare.

There was one other issue: Andrews knew that the kids on his team probably wouldn't take too kindly to an outsider taking a roster spot.

Everyone agreed that it would be up to LeBron to win them over. But they weren't going to tell him that.

*   *   *

LeBron liked the idea of going to the Bay Area to play in a tournament. But he didn't want to go alone. Although there wasn't a roster spot for Little Dru, LeBron wanted him to come along. In late July 2000, the two of them landed at San Francisco International Airport. Outside the terminal, they met Olivier and climbed into the backseat of his car. A long way from home, neither of them said a word as they exited the airport and sped down the highway.

Struggling to strike up a conversation, Olivier finally looked at the two of them in his rearview mirror and said, "Have you guys ever heard of the most crooked street in America?"

Neither of them knew what Olivier was talking about.

"Y'all want to go?" Olivier asked.

LeBron shrugged. Soon, he was looking out the window at stately homes in San Francisco's Russian Hill neighborhood. He took it all in as Olivier played tour guide.

"This is Lombard Street," Olivier said.

LeBron had never seen anything like the winding curves and switchbacks, not to mention the stately Victorian mansions that bookended the city's most famous street.

After showing them around, Olivier took them to his modest home and introduced them to his two kids and his pregnant wife, who took the boys to Berkeley to get pizza. Starting to feel at home, that night the boys slept on couches in Olivier's living room.

The Olivier family were very welcoming. The players on Olivier's AAU team were not. The Soldiers' seventeen-and-under team was led by Chuck Hayes, who was destined for a career in the NBA. The sixteen-and-under team was led by Leon Powe, a sixteen-year-old sophomore at Oakland Tech High School who was considered the number one player in the nation in the Class of 2003.

The national writers who ranked high school players hadn't heard of LeBron. Akron was a backwater region in the high school basketball scene. On top of that, St. V wasn't a premier prep school. Therefore, LeBron wasn't ranked among the top sophomores in the class of 2003. Nonetheless, the Soldiers' coaches put him on the seventeen-and-under team with Hayes. It offended Hayes that a fifteen-year-old who wasn't even from the Bay Area was suddenly on his team. Powe was even more put out—a guy who was younger than he was had leapfrogged him to play on the older squad.

In the first game, however, LeBron turned heads. Despite having no familiarity with the guys or the plays they ran, he quickly grasped what they were doing and managed to blend right in—making steals, feeding the ball to his teammates, and scoring at will with a variety of jump shots, layups, and dunks.

While Hayes was impressed, Powe was concerned. At one point, he told Olivier he needed to talk to him in private.

"What's up, big fella?" Olivier asked.

"This dude isn't in my class, is he?" Powe said.

"Big fella, I'm afraid so."

"There goes my number one spot," Powe replied.

The trip to the Bay Area was essentially a test run to see if LeBron would be a good fit in the Soldiers' system. His performance convinced the coaches that they had to have him. LeBron's unselfish play also won over the players. Even Powe couldn't deny that LeBron was an ideal teammate.

LeBron liked Powe right away, too. They shared a common work ethic, as well as some similar life experiences that helped them bond more quickly. The eldest of seven children, Powe was raised by a single mother. His house had burned down when he was seven years old, forcing him and his family to the streets. Homeless, the family moved twenty times over the next six years, shuffling from shelters to motels and eventually living in an abandoned car. When Powe was ten, his mother got caught stealing groceries and was sentenced to ninety days in jail. Powe and his siblings ended up in foster care.

For Powe, basketball was a lifeline. When he stepped onto the court, he played as if his mother's welfare rested on his shoulders. LeBron related to that and believed that he and Powe would get along just fine.

Olivier and Andrews were thrilled, as was Chris Dennis. By the time they put LeBron on a flight back to Akron, his place on the Soldiers AAU team was solidified. The plan was for LeBron to return at the conclusion of his sophomore season at St. V and play in a series of national tournaments on the West Coast.

In the meantime, Dennis briefed Vaccaro and made a push for him to visit St. V to watch LeBron play.

"I'm not going to fuckin' Akron," Vaccaro told him.

Instead, Vaccaro authorized a shoe contract for the St. V team. For LeBron's sophomore year, the team would wear Adidas shoes.

For Vaccaro it was an easy call—if the kid from Akron was good enough to dominate on the Soldiers, then it made sense to put him and his high school teammates in Adidas sneakers sooner rather than later. In the grand scheme of things, it cost Adidas next to nothing to supply a high school with sneakers. In return, Vaccaro was establishing an inside track to LeBron.

One night during the summer of 2000, Sian Cotton slept at LeBron's apartment. In the morning the two of them were eating cold cereal, when LeBron noticed Sian was staring at him with a quizzical expression.

"You grew two inches last night!" Sian said.

LeBron liked Sian's sense of humor.

But Sian wasn't fooling around. He genuinely thought LeBron had grown taller overnight. In fact, LeBron had undergone a growth spurt that summer. By the start of his sophomore year, he was six six and weighed two hundred pounds. His size made him an even more attractive target as a receiver on the varsity football team. Despite breaking his left index finger early in the season, LeBron refused to sit out and ended up leading the football team with forty-two receptions for eight hundred and twenty yards and seven touchdowns.

In addition to being named to the All-Ohio team as a wide receiver, LeBron was garnering a lot of interest from college football recruiters. One day, in between classes, his football coach introduced him to Urban Meyer, a young wide receiver coach at Notre Dame, who had come to St. V on a recruiting trip.

LeBron shook his hand and introduced himself.

Meyer marveled at his height and the size of his hand.

"Why don't you come up to Notre Dame?" Meyer said. "Because we'd love to talk with you."

"I appreciate that," LeBron said.

After LeBron hustled off to his next class, his football coach warned

Meyer not to get his hopes up. "That's the next Michael Jordan," the coach told Meyer, who was oblivious to the fact that he had just met a basketball prodigy.

LeBron wasn't serious about visiting Notre Dame. Nor was he genuinely interested in entertaining any offers from college football recruiters. As much as he enjoyed football and the adulation that he got from it, he kept his focus on basketball, where he'd been doing some recruiting of his own.

Prior to the start of his sophomore year, he had heard that a kid named Romeo Travis, one of the better basketball players at a public school in Akron, was looking to transfer. LeBron knew Romeo. They were the same age, and Romeo had lived in a housing project that LeBron had lived in. Romeo had a tough exterior and a reputation for being angry all the time. A lot of that anger stemmed from the way he was raised and the experiences of his youth. His father was absent in his life and his mother was on welfare. Romeo had always been forced to fend for himself.

Although Romeo didn't trust people and was hard to get to know, LeBron approached him about transferring to St. V. A private Catholic school with a predominantly white student body and a bunch of restrictive rules. Romeo preferred one of the city's other public schools. But he knew that LeBron was the best player in the city. And the fact that LeBron wanted him to join his team carried a lot of weight. He agreed to transfer to St. V.

The harder sell for LeBron was convincing his teammates to welcome Romeo. Little Dru, Sian, and Willie didn't like him. They had clashed with him plenty of times in youth basketball games. Their collective attitude toward him was that he was an asshole. But LeBron pointed out that Romeo was a beast—at six six, he was an exceptional athlete who played the game like an enforcer. With Maverick no longer on the team, they needed a guy who could be a presence on the floor. It wasn't hard to imagine how intimidating St. V would be with Romeo and Sian playing together under the basket.

Reluctantly, the Fab Four went along with the idea of having an outsider join the team.

Bent on winning another state championship, Coach Dambrot welcomed the addition of Romeo. But he cut him no slack. Dambrot practically ran him into the ground during the first week of practice.

Romeo wasn't used to the conditioning drills that were expected at St. V. He also wasn't ready for Dambrot's in-your-face coaching style. He learned quickly that despite his size and athleticism, he'd begin the season on the bench—Dambrot expected him to work his way into the starting lineup. Nothing would be given to him.

Little Dru, on the other hand, was named the starting point guard. And the friction between him and Romeo was immediate. The two of them repeatedly went after each other in practice, arguing and calling each other names. Little Dru thought Romeo was lazy. Romeo viewed Little Dru as an "arrogant dickhead." One time, after the two exchanged words, Romeo punched Little Dru in the face. Sian couldn't stand Romeo and was always quick to come to Little Dru's defense. Even Willie had no tolerance for Romeo's attitude. The guys nicknamed him the Brawl Street Bully.

About the only guy on the team who didn't fight with Romeo was LeBron.

Convincing Romeo to come to St. V was LeBron's first foray into team building. Initially, the situation not only caused fissures within the team, but Romeo's presence also reignited the bitterness that Akron's Black community felt toward the St. V basketball program. The players weren't the only ones taking heat. Coach Dambrot faced more criticism for stealing away another "ringer" from the public school system. And there was also some resentment within the St. V community as yet another roster spot on the varsity basketball team was taken away from boys whose families had long ties to the school.

It didn't help that Romeo sometimes went out of his way to voice how much he disliked St. V. "Too many whites at this school," he once yelled loud enough for some white students to hear. And he didn't hesitate to say things like "Who the fuck are you talking to?" if someone dared to ask him something he didn't feel like answering. Although he was plenty smart enough to keep up with the school's academic standards, he bristled against the dress code and often missed school. It wasn't until he faced the threat of academic probation and suspension from the basketball team that Romeo finally picked up his attendance and his grades.

Despite all of this, LeBron thought he had Romeo figured out. He pegged him as a lonely kid, one who didn't know how to make friends easily. But he was a hell of a ballplayer who could help them win. It was only a matter of time, LeBron figured, before playing together and racking up some victories would chill the animosity.

St. V opened the 2000–2001 season by blowing out two powerhouse teams from Virginia and Wisconsin. The growth and maturity of LeBron, Sian, and Little Dru was notable. And with Romeo coming off the bench, the team looked even stronger than the previous year's squad. About a month into the season, St. V was 9-0 and ranked number three in the nation. Riding a thirty-six-game winning streak that stretched all the way back to the start of their freshman season the year before, LeBron and his teammates faced Oak Hill Academy, the number-one-ranked boys basketball team in America, on January 13, 2001. The fact that Coach Dambrot managed to schedule a game with the vaunted prep school was a testament to how far his team had come in such a short period of time.

Oak Hill was in Mouth of Wilson, Virginia, and it had fewer than two hundred students in grades nine through twelve. But it had become a virtual basketball factory, churning out blue-chip recruits for elite college programs year after year. The two starting guards, both seniors, were heading to Kentucky and Syracuse. A third player, DeSagana Diop from Senegal, stood seven feet tall and weighed three hundred pounds. Several NBA scouts were on hand among the college recruiters to check out Diop.

Despite being much younger and significantly overmatched physically, St. V outworked Oak Hill from the opening tip, getting ahead early and holding the lead for most of the game. Romeo and Sian battled Diop under the basket. Little Dru hit a bunch of three-pointers. But LeBron carried the team, scoring a game-high thirty-three points and dominating Oak Hill's two college-bound guards. He was so unstoppable that at one point the nearly six thousand fans in attendance gave him a standing ovation.

But Oak Hill eventually took the lead in the fourth quarter. Battling dehydration, LeBron's legs were cramping so badly it hurt to stand. With seconds left and St. V trailing by one point, LeBron got the ball and put up a running jump shot that went in, rolled around the rim, and popped out as the buzzer sounded. St. V lost, 79–78.

Exhausted, LeBron began to cry. The other guys did, too. Even Romeo let go of his emotions, bawling as one of the assistant coaches wrapped his arms around him.

Dambrot hated losing. But he loved what he was seeing.

"It's supposed to hurt," he told his players in an emotional speech after the game. "Losing always hurts."

LeBron blamed himself. With two minutes left in the game and St. V clinging to a one-point lead, LeBron had missed a couple of key free throws. He was beating himself up for not converting them.

Dambrot set LeBron straight, telling him that those missed free throws weren't the reason they lost the game. The fact was that LeBron had just played the best game of his life and he'd done it against the best team in the nation. Dambrot could not have been prouder.

A few days after St. V lost to Oak Hill, Dajuan Wagner of Camden High in New Jersey scored one hundred points in a game that his team won, 157–67. Camden was one of the top five ranked teams in the country and Wagner was generally considered the best high school basketball player in America. A senior, he had already signed a commitment letter to attend the University of Memphis and play for Coach John Calipari. In the game where he scored one hundred points, Wagner shot the ball more than sixty times. After the game, *Sports Illustrated* called him the "player of the century." But a month earlier, Wagner and two other young men had beaten up a student in the hallway at school. The victim required medical treatment, including stitches above his eye. Wagner, who was found guilty of simple assault and threatening a student, was sentenced to probation and had been dubbed "the next Allen Iverson," the hyper-talented point guard who had a reputation for being the NBA's bad boy.

While Wagner garnered national attention for his one-hundred-point game and his off-the-court persona, Coach Dambrot reminded the local media covering St. V that LeBron was built differently. "LeBron's LeBron," he told the press. "He's very unselfish. He can get 35 points, but he refuses to do that."

To LeBron, the notion of taking sixty shots in a game was anathema. He would have rather notched one hundred assists than scored one hundred points. This team-first mentality was largely an extension of his personality—he was unselfish and liked to please people, especially his friends. So sharing the ball and sharing credit for success came naturally to him. But his play was also a by-product of a steady stream of youth coaches who emphasized teamwork over individual achievement. Coach Dambrot saw that LeBron possessed an unusually high basketball IQ. It surprised Dambrot that the most talented player he'd ever seen was so receptive to being coached, not to mention pushed. The primary reason that Dambrot got away with treating St. V like a college team was that LeBron had bought in to his approach and would often refrain from scoring, particularly early on in games, in order to demonstrate by example the importance of being unselfish with the ball.

Off the court, LeBron's behavior was driven by his desire to please his mother. In hard moments, he'd tell her that one day she wouldn't have to worry—he'd buy her a fine home and a nice car and anything else that would ease her life. When she gave him permission to get a tattoo, he chose to have "Gloria" imprinted on his arm. It was a great reminder to focus on his priorities. By the time he was a sophomore, he'd already decided he was never going to touch drugs. He'd already decided he'd never steal, despite plenty of opportunities to do so. And although he was more physically imposing than his peers, he preferred the role of peacemaker. Aware that lots of people had an eye on him because of his athletic abilities, he was determined to never do anything that would land him in the news for the wrong reasons. "I didn't go looking for trouble because I didn't like trouble," he once said about his adolescent years.

The Oak Hill game was LeBron's coming-out moment. It was his best performance yet, and it had been witnessed by NBA scouts and college coaches. They had come to watch players from Oak Hill, but LeBron got their attention. In the weeks that followed, Coach Dambrot was inundated with inquiries about LeBron. Despite being forbidden by NCAA rules from talking to LeBron until his junior year, more than one hundred coaches wrote letters and expressed interest in recruiting him to play college basketball. Suddenly, LeBron was on the radar of every top program in America.

The game against Oak Hill was also a validation for St. V. Relying heavily on a group of sophomores, Dambrot's squad had proven they could compete with any team in the country. They went undefeated the rest of the way and finished the regular season 19-1. During that period, St. V also took on the outward appearance of an elite program, largely due to the interest that LeBron was generating from Adidas, which supplied them with more gear—sweat suits, gym bags, practice shirts.

For Chris Dennis, this was a coup. He was consistently trying to curry favor with LeBron and Gloria. The fact that he had been the conduit to outfitting LeBron's team with sneakers and gear was a feather in Dennis's cap.

Dambrot could only shake his head. During his days as a college coach he had always struggled to land a shoe contract. Suddenly, thanks to LeBron, St. V was dressed like a college team.

During LeBron's sophomore year, he averaged 25 points, 7 rebounds, 6 assists, and 4 steals per game. At the beginning of March 2001, he became the first sophomore to be named to the *USA Today* All-USA First Team. The distinction clearly established him as the best sophomore in the country.

With the state tournament still to come, Coach Dambrot made sure not to let the recognition go to LeBron's head. "Best sophomore in the country, my ass," Dambrot told him. "You don't even play defense."

Led by LeBron, St. V tore through the playoffs. Then more than seventeen thousand spectators turned out for the championship game, setting an attendance record for a high school basketball game in Ohio. In a complete team effort, St. V rolled to its second-straight championship. Even Romeo had bought in to the team's unselfish attitude, becoming one of the team's leading scorers and rebounders, despite never starting a game. He kept complaining, but the reality was that he loved the satisfaction of winning a state championship. And now that he'd experienced what it was like to reach the top, he wanted to do it again. They all did. After all, they had a great coach, and they had the best player in the state. As a sophomore, LeBron became the youngest player to ever be named Ohio's Mr. Basketball.

But LeBron had no time to savor the state championship and all of the individual accolades. As soon as his high school basketball season ended, he was on a flight to Los Angeles for his first national AAU tournament with the Oakland Soldiers.

In a layup line before a game, LeBron held an ice cream cone in one hand while dribbling with the other hand. Teammate Leon Powe couldn't help laughing. LeBron made AAU basketball fun. Not only could he jump out of the gym, but he was always grinning and doing silly things that lightened the mood and made his teammates laugh.

LeBron was so busy clowning around that his coaches for the Soldiers felt he wasn't always as intense as they preferred. Sometimes it took something external to get him to go all out. Early in the Pump N Run tournament in Los Angeles, an opponent went out of his way to send a message of intimidation by hammering LeBron while he was in the act of shooting. LeBron's coaches didn't mind because it was as if the hard foul flipped a switch. LeBron's demeanor changed and he started dominating to the point that his coaches almost felt sorry for the competition. The Soldiers won the tournament, and Leon Powe decided he was perfectly content being LeBron's wingman.

LeBron's performance in LA persuaded everyone—his Soldiers coaches, Chris Dennis, Coach Dambrot, and Coach Dru—that they had to get LeBron in front of Sonny Vaccaro. By this point, they were all of the mind that LeBron was talented enough to go straight from high school to the NBA. But it was critical to further raise LeBron's profile. The key was to get him into the Adidas ABCD Camp that would be held in New Jersey later that summer. All of the top players in the country would be there. Since LeBron was so young, it was important to get Vaccaro's endorsement. If Vaccaro got behind LeBron, his world would change.

Since Vaccaro was unwilling to fly to Akron, the group worked together to stage a private audition for LeBron on the West Coast. It was a big production. Everyone pitched in.

Olivier and Andrews agreed to secure a venue and some top-notch AAU players to participate in a couple of exhibition games.

Dambrot and Dru handled the logistics in Akron, making sure LeBron didn't miss classes and agreeing to accompany him on the trip.

Chris Dennis worked with the marketing rep at Adidas to get custom shoes designed for LeBron to wear at the audition.

And Adidas put up the money—covering the flights, hotels, and meals for LeBron, Gloria, and Eddie Jackson.

All LeBron had to do was pack a bag and get in the right frame of mind for another weekend trip to the West Coast. And for that, there was nothing better than one of his favorite songs—Tupac's "California Love."

Now let me welcome everybody to the Wild Wild West
A state that's untouchable like Eliot Ness
The track hits your eardrum like a slug to your chest
Pack a vest for your Jimmy in the city of sex.

At his home in Southern California, Sonny Vaccaro splashed a little co-
logne on his chest and packed an overnight bag while Bobby Darin music
played on his home sound system.

Now on the sidewalk, huh, huh, whoo sunny morning, un huh
Lies a body just oozin' life, eek
And someone's sneakin' 'round the corner
Could that someone be Mack the Knife?

Vaccaro wasn't totally convinced that LeBron was as good as Chris
Dennis and the boys made him out to be. But if he was that good, Vaccaro
knew the psychology of recruiting kids better than anyone. The most important thing wasn't to win over the player—it was to win over the mother.
And Vaccaro had the ultimate secret weapon in that department: his wife,
Pam. She didn't care about recruiting or sneaker contracts or money. She
cared about relationships and people, which is what made her such an
ideal partner to Sonny.

On a Friday evening in May 2001, Sonny and Pam boarded a flight in
Burbank and headed for Oakland.

Later that evening, LeBron and Gloria were in their room at the Oakland Downtown Marriott when they got a visit from Chris Dennis, Calvin
Andrews, and Chris Rivers. Rivers worked for Adidas, and he was carrying a shoebox under his arm. After exchanging pleasantries, he removed
the lid and pulled out a custom-designed green and gold sneaker.

LeBron's eyes widened.

Rivers tossed the shoe to him.

LeBron caught it, immediately noticing that his initials—*LBJ*—and his
number—*23*—were embossed on the heel.

"Oh my God," he said, cradling the shoe like a piece of fine china.

It was the first time that Adidas had ever created a personalized shoe
for a high school player. Not even Kevin Garnett, Kobe Bryant, or Tracy

McGrady—the three biggest stars to go straight from high school to the NBA—had had custom sneakers in high school.

Gloria nodded her approval.

LeBron couldn't stop smiling. "I want to play in these tomorrow," he said.

"I'll give you the other shoe if we all agree you're with the Adidas family," Rivers said.

"I'm with the family," LeBron said. "I'm with the family."

Rivers tossed him the other shoe.

The plan was to meet for breakfast at the hotel. LeBron waited with Gloria in the lobby, wondering what it would be like to meet the legend credited with signing Michael Jordan and Kobe Bryant to their shoe deals. Before long, he spotted a man in a black turtleneck walking toward him, an attractive woman at his side.

Vaccaro introduced himself and extended his hand.

LeBron smiled and shook it.

Pam hugged Gloria. Then Sonny embraced her.

Gloria didn't trust many people. But when Sonny and Pam put their arms around her, she sensed that her son's dream was going to be realized. It was like a hand had reached into the ditch she was stuck in and was offering to pull her and her son out.

The four of them sat down in a booth. While LeBron ate a big breakfast and Sonny sipped coffee, Gloria and Pam did most of the talking. The main topic of discussion was the pressures facing LeBron. Everyone, Gloria explained, expected him to act like he's thirty.

Sonny wasn't surprised.

"But he's still a kid," Gloria said.

"He can only be fifteen when he's fifteen," Pam said.

LeBron was instantly comfortable in Sonny's presence. In a couple of hours, he would perform in two exhibition games while Sonny looked on. Rather than be intimidated, LeBron felt at ease. At one point, he referred to Vaccaro as "Uncle Sonny."

Vaccaro smiled. *I like this kid*, he thought.

Standing to leave, Pam and Gloria hugged again.

* * *

Wearing Adidas shorts and an Adidas jersey, LeBron laced up his custom sneakers. He and nine other players were warming up in the gym as the Adidas representatives and his AAU and high school coaches looked on. There was a lot of chatter in the gym until Vaccaro walked in. Then it got so quiet that the sound of Vaccaro's hard-soled shoes echoed on the hardwood as he made his way to the bottom row of the pullout bleachers. Pam waved and smiled at Gloria, seated a couple of rows behind them.

Dambrot was more nervous than LeBron. He realized how rare it was for a teenager to get an audition in front of Vaccaro. Even Kobe Bryant hadn't gotten to play an exhibition game in front of the sneaker executive when Kobe was in high school. In order to maximize the opportunity, LeBron was going to have to do something he wasn't used to—play selfishly. For once, Dambrot wanted LeBron to show off his scoring ability.

LeBron started the first game the way he usually did—involving his teammates and trying to showcase his passing abilities. Everyone seemed to have the jitters. As soon as the first game ended, Dambrot motioned with his hand for LeBron to step away from the court.

LeBron followed him into a hallway.

"LeBron, look, I'm not gonna tell you what to do," he said. "But that's a pretty powerful guy watching and you're out there fuckin' around. You need to *play*."

"Coach, my shorts are bothering me," he said, tugging at the drawstring, which had a knot in it that was preventing him from tightening the waistband. As a result, his shorts kept slipping below his waist.

Dambrot didn't want to hear it. "You better stop playing with your shorts and start playing harder," he said. "There's going to be a lot of money determined by what he thinks of you."

Cinching the knot, LeBron jogged back into the gym. As soon as the second game started, he nailed a jump shot. Then, anticipating where an opposing player was going to pass the ball, LeBron sprang into the passing lane, stole the ball, took a couple of dribbles, and soared to the basket, throwing down a thunderous dunk that shook the backboard. Then, on another possession, he dribbled the length of the court before zipping a no-look pass to a teammate for an easy basket. He followed that up with another dunk.

For a moment, Vaccaro thought LeBron was going to hit his head on the rim. About ten minutes into the second game, Vaccaro stood and started walking out.

"Sonny?" Pam said.

Without looking back, Vaccaro kept going, exiting the gym.

The game momentarily halted. No one knew what was happening.

Pam looked at Gloria, waved goodbye, and also left the gym.

A few minutes later, Vaccaro hailed a cab.

"Where you headed?" the driver said.

"The airport," Vaccaro barked.

Pam knew something was out of the ordinary. Sitting beside him in the backseat, she watched him look out the window. "Sonny?" she said.

Since the Michael Jordan era, only three players had gone directly from high school to the NBA and become superstars—Kevin Garnett, Kobe Bryant, and Tracy McGrady. Vaccaro was convinced that LeBron was more talented than all three of them.

"I can't explain it to you," he said. "Pam, he's unbelievably gifted. He's just doing things that can't be taught."

Vaccaro knew that there was going to be a race among the shoe companies to land him. An obscene amount of money would be spent. And Nike would be Vaccaro's main competition. But by the time Nike started seriously pursuing LeBron, Vaccaro planned to be in the pole position.

That night, Vaccaro called his colleagues. LeBron, he told them, was the greatest high school player he'd ever seen. He was so talented, in fact, that Vaccaro felt he was capable of playing in the NBA after his junior year of high school. Without question, he said, LeBron should play at the Adidas ABCD Camp in July. It was time for everyone to see just how good this kid could be.

There was one more thing. Vaccaro wanted to make St. V a full-fledged Adidas school. In addition to sneakers and gear, he wanted LeBron's high school team to wear uniforms that were custom-made by Adidas. For LeBron's junior year, St. V should be the best-dressed high school team in America.

Chris Dennis was over the moon.

Satisfied, Vaccaro hung up, put on his favorite Bobby Darin record, and poured himself a drink.

SEVEN

THE LAD

During his freshman year at Western Michigan, Maverick Carter came to grips with the fact that he was never going to play in the NBA. That year, he started in seven of his team's twenty-eight games. Not bad for a freshman. But when Western Michigan played Indiana, Texas Tech, and Michigan, Maverick went up against guys who had NBA bodies—big, strong, and athletic. No matter how hard he worked, he knew he was never going to be as big or as good as those guys. Taking a pragmatic approach to his future, he withdrew from school after the spring semester and moved back to Akron, where he planned to enroll at the University of Akron and focus on his studies.

For Maverick, the other draw in returning to Akron was LeBron. While he had no illusions about his own future in pro basketball, he was certain that LeBron was headed for the big time. He was already better than anyone at Indiana or Michigan that Maverick had played against. And with shoe companies and recruiters already pursuing his friend, Maverick wanted to be around to help him navigate his remaining two years of high school. One of the first things he did when he got home was talk to LeBron about coaching his AAU team, the Northeast Ohio Shooting Stars. LeBron loved the idea. So did the guys. They all looked up to Maverick, both as a teacher and as an example off the court.

For LeBron, the good news of Maverick's return coincided with some unexpected bad news—Coach Dambrot was stepping down as the head coach at St. V to take a job as an assistant coach at the University of Akron. LeBron found out from a reporter. Little Dru and Sian heard it from a reporter, too. To them, it felt like a sucker punch. They had taken a tremendous amount of flak for going to St. V to play for him. They fully bought in to his brand of coaching. In two seasons together they'd gone 53-1 and won two state championships. They were poised to be the number one team in the country as juniors. And this guy was bailing on them?

For Little Dru, Dambrot's departure was particularly painful. Dambrot had told him that he was going to be there for four years. On that basis, Little Dru had persuaded LeBron and Sian and Willie to go to St. V. As far as Little Dru was concerned, Dambrot had lied to him and lied to his friends.

Sian agreed. "He used us," he said. "He used us to get back to college."

For Romeo, Dambrot was the one coach he had finally started to trust to help him reach his full potential. His departure represented just another adult who had gone back on his word and disappeared.

LeBron felt scorned and deceived. He'd put his faith in Dambrot. All of the boys had. They were loyal to him. The realization that loyalty could be so easily cast aside made LeBron so angry that he never wanted to see or talk to Dambrot again. When Dambrot finally reached out to him, LeBron showed his resentment by referring to him as "Mr. Dambrot."

The jab stung Dambrot. The greatest honor of his basketball career was hearing the best player he ever coached refer to him as "Coach." But those days were over.

LeBron and his friends felt so spurned that they were ready to transfer to a different school. Little Dru suggested Buchtel. Nobody objected.

Coach Dru was just as blindsided when Dambrot called him at home and told him that he was leaving. In disbelief, Dru listened as Dambrot said it was one of the hardest decisions he'd ever made. The kids, he acknowledged, had resurrected his career. But he explained that his goal and his dream had long been to return to college coaching. And with all the agents and shoe companies circling around LeBron, he feared that there might be a scandal coming. There was just too much money riding on LeBron. And since Dambrot had already been through one major scandal, he couldn't risk being associated with a second one. "I've got to get out of this thing," he told Dru.

Dru couldn't help wondering the obvious—who would fill Dambrot's shoes?

"I want you to take over," Dambrot said.

Dru wasn't interested. There was way too many expectations on the upcoming season—for LeBron, for the rest of the boys, and for the school. The pressure would be enormous. "No," he told Dambrot. "I don't want to mess this thing up."

But Dambrot felt strongly that Dru was the ideal person to step in.

"These are your kids," Dambrot told him. "You brought them to me. They'll play hard for you."

Dru appreciated Dambrot's words. But he couldn't ignore the sense of foreboding he felt about the magnitude of taking over a nationally ranked team with the country's best player. Moreover, he couldn't imagine that St. V would offer him the job even if he was interested.

Dambrot told him not to worry about the school. "I'll support you in front of the board," he said.

That night, Dru talked to his wife about the situation, and he told her that despite Dambrot's support, he was still going to turn down the opportunity.

"Dru, how can you say no?" she said. "This is God honoring all those years that you have been with those boys. All those times you drove up and down the highway."

He could hardly argue against her point—no one had invested more time or made more sacrifices for those boys, dating back to grammar school. And he'd never received a dime for what amounted to thousands of hours spent taking the Shooting Stars all over the country for tournaments. Nor had he been compensated for his two years as an assistant coach under Dambrot. He'd done it all as a volunteer.

His wife reemphasized her view: *This is your time!*

With her backing, Dru decided to go for the job. And with Dambrot's endorsement before the St. V board of trustees, the school offered him the position of head coach.

When LeBron found out that Coach Dru was taking over at St. V, he changed his tune about transferring to another school. All of the boys did. They'd matured a lot in their two years at St. V and they recognized that they were about to be part of something bigger than basketball. "Once Coach Dru had been selected the first African American head coach in the history of St. V, there was no way any of us were going anywhere," LeBron explained.

LeBron's summer schedule was jam-packed with tournaments throughout the country. One of his first commitments was an AAU tournament in Chicago. LeBron's team went to the finals, but ultimately lost. During the tournament, a man approached Maverick and introduced himself as Greg Ryan and said he worked with Michael Jordan's trainer at a place in the city called Hoops. It was Michael Jordan's private gym, and a lot of pros trained there in the off-season. Ryan offered to give Maverick and LeBron a tour of the place.

LeBron was eager to take Ryan up on his offer. In between games, he went with Maverick to check out Hoops. The minute they stepped inside, it felt like they'd entered basketball heaven. There were two courts and a small weight room with the most technically advanced equipment available. This was the place where Michael Jordan trained.

Ryan introduced them to Tim Grover, Jordan's trainer. Although Jordan was retired, he still worked out with Grover.

LeBron hadn't spent much time lifting weights.

Grover took the opportunity to explain why lifting was so important. He also talked to LeBron about technique.

LeBron was in awe. Jordan was his idol. His posters hung from LeBron's bedroom walls. He wore Jordan's number at St. V. It was hard to believe that he was talking to Jordan's trainer about how to strengthen his body.

At the end of the visit, Ryan invited LeBron and Maverick to come back. Later in the summer, a bunch of NBA players would be around, working out and playing pickup games. It would be a good opportunity for LeBron to be in the gym for a week or so. Ryan told LeBron and Maverick that they were welcome to stay with him while they were in town.

Maverick couldn't believe the offer. Neither could LeBron. After the AAU tournament, they told their mothers about Greg and his invitation. And they lobbied for permission to go back to Chicago and stay with him for a few days. It wasn't going to cost them anything other than the price of gas to get back and forth. And LeBron would be training with some pros. Ultimately, Gloria and Maverick's mother agreed to the idea. A date was set for later in August.

But first LeBron had to travel to Colorado for the USA Basketball Men's Youth Development Festival. Twenty-four of the best high school players in the country had been invited to participate. When LeBron arrived, he met his roommate, Carmelo Anthony, a six-seven forward from Baltimore who went by the nickname "Melo." He'd been attending a Catholic high school in the Baltimore suburbs, but he was heading to Oak Hill for his senior year, and then on to Syracuse University on a basketball scholarship.

LeBron and Carmelo instantly hit it off. On the court, they were the two most dominant players. They both averaged a tournament-high twenty-four points per game, and they both shot 66 percent from the field. LeBron's team won the gold and Carmelo's team won the silver. But it was the time they spent alone, talking, that enabled them to get to know each other and form a bond. It turned out that Carmelo felt the same way about his mother—he referred to her as "the best mother . . . hands down"—as LeBron felt about Gloria.

LeBron learned that Anthony had been two years old when his father died from cancer. The only thing his father left him was a gold chain with a Jesus emblem that Anthony wore everywhere—until his best friend stole it. As a boy, Anthony had lived in Brooklyn, and some of his fondest childhood memories were taking long train rides with his mother from their apartment in Red Hook to Manhattan to visit the American Museum of Natural History to look at natural-science exhibits or the Metropolitan Museum of Art to look at paintings. That was before his mother moved the family to Baltimore, before he knew that he was destined to be a professional basketball player. By his junior year of high school he was the player of the year in the city of Baltimore and generally considered the second-best high school player in the country. That summer, though, he'd begun to learn that basketball wasn't just a game—it was a business. When he met LeBron, Anthony had no desire to go to Oak Hill Academy. He wanted to finish his high school career in Baltimore. But the coaching staff at Syracuse was emphatic that it was too dangerous for their blue-chip recruit to remain in Baltimore—the city had 256 murders that year—and adamant that he finish up at the Virginia prep school.

In LeBron, Anthony felt he'd found a brother. Although LeBron had beaten him in the championship and everyone was referring to him as the next Jordan, Anthony wasn't jealous. Years later, he reflected on that first encounter with LeBron. "He was excited to see me play, just as I was excited to learn about him and see what his skill set was like," Anthony said. "We had a great time playing together; I felt like I had known LeBron my whole life."

LeBron felt similarly toward Anthony. When he got back to Akron, he told all his friends that he'd met this kid named Melo who was the best basketball player he'd seen at the festival. Privately, he hoped that someday he and Anthony might be teammates.

The one player in the country who was ranked ahead of Anthony by most of the recruiting services was Lenny Cooke, an eighteen-year-old from New York City. A playground legend, Cooke was projected to go straight from high school to the NBA as a top lottery pick. The most important date on LeBron's summer 2001 calendar was Sonny Vaccaro's Adidas ABCD Camp in New Jersey. And Lenny Cooke would be there. Coaches from every major college basketball program would be on hand, along with plenty of NBA scouts. *Sports Illustrated* and a slew of national publications that cover basketball would also be present. Everyone in attendance would be anticipating a showdown between Cooke—the reigning MVP of the ABCD Camp from the previous year—and the newcomer from Akron being heralded by the camp's founder as the best he'd ever seen.

"At this point in his life, [LeBron] is the most mature on the court, and the most gifted on the court," Vaccaro told the press in the run-up to the tournament. "He has a chance, when it's all over, to be one of the greatest players to ever play the game."

LeBron didn't know what Vaccaro was saying about him. Nor did he know much about Cooke, other than the fact that he was apparently a big deal and he'd been the MVP the previous year. Right before leaving for New Jersey, LeBron started keeping a journal. In his first entry, he described his attitude heading into the ABCD Camp:

> I'm going in trying to be MVP of the whole thing. I don't really feel like I have to prove myself, but if people have any doubts about me, they just gotta come watch me play.

On the night before the start of the camp at Fairleigh Dickinson University in Teaneck, New Jersey, Kobe Bryant addressed the 220 high school players in attendance at one of the gymnasiums. "The main thing I want to tell you guys," Bryant said, "is don't put all of your eggs in one basket." Bryant encouraged the kids to go to college. It was important, he told them, to have something to fall back on.

LeBron listened intently. And he kept quiet when Kobe invited those in the audience to ask questions. But Lenny Cooke immediately made his presence known by publicly challenging Kobe. "When are you gonna play me one-on-one?" he said to Kobe.

Cooke's bravado got everyone's attention.

Kobe chuckled. "When you get to the league, I'll beat you in various ways," he told Cooke.

Cooke was big and loud and cocky. He was vocal about the fact that he had no interest in college. He even had a camera crew trailing him for a documentary film being produced about his journey to NBA stardom.

But no matter how hard Cooke tried to seize the limelight, the national media covering the tournament gravitated toward LeBron and the intriguing question of whether he might try to enter the NBA Draft after his junior year of high school. Vaccaro had been telling basketball writers that LeBron was *that* good. One of the journalists that Vaccaro had talked to was *New York Times* columnist Ira Berkow, one of the most influential sportswriters in America.

At the outset of the tournament, Berkow talked to Gloria about her aspirations for her son.

"What I want for LeBron is happiness," Gloria told him. "He loves basketball. But I would like to see him graduate with his class from high school, at least. But we'll make a decision when the time comes. He's a level-headed boy. He's never given me a lick of problems. He's mannerable and respectful."

Berkow talked to LeBron, too, and asked him about his plans.

"College is important," LeBron told him. "You can't play basketball all your life. You should prepare for something else too."

This was the first time that LeBron and Gloria had interacted with someone from the national media, especially someone of Berkow's stature. He had just won a Pulitzer for his landmark story "The Minority Quarterback," which was part of a *New York Times* series called "How Race Is Lived in America." Keenly aware of the temptations and land mines that awaited LeBron, Berkow pointed out to him that one month earlier, the Washington Wizards had made history by making Kwame Brown the first high school player to be selected number one overall in the NBA Draft. And Brown had just signed a three-year, $12 million contract.

"That's a lot of money," LeBron told Berkow. "But we've struggled this long. A couple more years won't make that much difference."

The reference to *we* in LeBron's answer stood out like a beacon at a tournament where so many of the players were conditioned to view everything through the prism of *me*. After talking to LeBron and Gloria, Berkow wrote a column titled "Hitting the Lottery as a Junior?" In it, he wrote that one individual stood out among the 220 best high school players in the world who had convened at the Adidas ABCD Camp:

> He is a 16-year-old from St. Vincent–St. Mary High School in Akron, Ohio, who will be a junior in the fall. Many of the gathered connoisseurs believed that the lad, LeBron James, a 6-foot-7, 210-pound point guard, shooting guard and small forward—sometimes he plays as if he is all three in one, a kind of hoops Swiss Army knife—would have been taken in the first round of the most recent N.B.A. draft, possibly a lottery pick.

The column marked the first time that LeBron had been featured in a widely read national publication, and Gloria could not have asked for a more resounding and classy introduction of her son to the sports world. Describing him as a kid with "hair tufted out and his pants baggy," Berkow also quoted basketball heavyweights, including one who said LeBron already had a better feel for the game than NBA superstars Vince Carter and Tracy McGrady.

Hours after Berkow's column was published, LeBron's team was scheduled to play Lenny Cooke's team in the marquee game of the tournament. Armed with clipboards and pencils, hundreds of coaches and scouts, including Louisville head coach Rick Pitino and Milwaukee Bucks general manager Ernie Grunfeld, took their places in the seats nearest the court. Journalists sat courtside with notepads. The top high school players on neighboring courts stopped to watch the action. And Vaccaro roamed the perimeter of the gym as if he were an oracle whose congregation was about to witness what he'd been predicting.

During pregame warm-ups, a loud contingency of Cooke's friends from New York made their presence known. All tournament long, people had been telling LeBron that he'd never be able to stop Cooke. In the layup line, LeBron turned to his teammate Leon Powe and quietly said, "We're just going to see. Wait 'til the game starts."

Cooke's team came away with the opening tip and the ball went right to Cooke.

LeBron crouched down in a defensive stance.

After juking and jab-stepping, Cooke never looked at his teammates as he dribbled the ball twenty-nine times before pulling up and nailing a jumper over LeBron. His supporters erupted.

On the next possession, Cooke took the ball again. LeBron guarded him again. And again, without ever looking at his teammates, Cooke dribbled the ball sixteen times before knocking down another jumper. Running back down the court after his second basket, Cooke shouted to the crowd, pumping up his friends, who were ridiculing LeBron.

On the other end, LeBron rose at the top of the key and launched a three-point bomb that was all net. Then he called for the ball again and knocked down another three from the corner, and that one, too, was all net. The second one generated a collective "WOW" from the crowd. Next, he dunked off a fast break. Then he grabbed an offensive rebound that he reverse-dunked, jamming the ball through the rim with two hands. In a quick flurry, he put up ten points. And on defense, he put the clamps on Cooke, exposing a glaring weakness in the top-rated player's game— his inability to create offensive shots for himself or his teammates when closely guarded by a player of equal size and strength. Meanwhile, on the other end of the floor, LeBron's offensive dominance revealed an even more fatal flaw in Cooke—he simply could not guard a player with superior quickness and ballhandling abilities.

Playing alongside LeBron, Powe poured in more than twenty points and shut down the second-best scorer on Cooke's team. But he was in awe as LeBron relentlessly took it to Cooke, attacking the rim, scoring at will, and feeding his teammates with no-look passes that left college coaches and NBA scouts gawking. LeBron led all scorers with twenty-four points, while holding Cooke to nine points for the entire game.

With six seconds to go and LeBron's team trailing, 83–82, everyone in the gym knew the ball was going to him on the inbounds pass. Cooke was exhausted. And after being burned by LeBron the entire game, he wanted no part in guarding him one-on-one. But Cooke's teammates didn't want to guard LeBron, either, leaving Cooke to do it.

Blowing past Cooke, LeBron dribbled the length of the floor. Then, with Cooke on his heels, LeBron elevated from well beyond the three-point line, bringing his knees up and kicking his feet back. Hanging in the air as Cooke ran past him, LeBron floated a thirty-foot shot that zipped through the air and whipped through the net without touching the rim as time expired, sending the gym into a frenzy. LeBron's team had won, 85–83.

Cooke's jaw dropped. "How'd he make that?"

It was a majestic shot. Watching from courtside, Vaccaro stood frozen, marveling at what he'd just witnessed. "It was as if God touched it," he would later say.

The college recruiters and pro scouts all saw the same thing—LeBron James was at his best when all eyes were on him. At the ripe age of sixteen, he seemed built for pressure. There was no question in anyone's mind that he was the best high school player in America. LeBron hadn't just beaten Lenny Cooke, he had destroyed him.

After the game, LeBron saw Cooke standing with a bunch of his friends. As LeBron walked toward them, Cooke saw him coming and stepped away from his guys. LeBron congratulated him on a good game. Then LeBron shook his hand. He wanted Cooke to know that he respected him and his game.

Cooke nodded.

Then LeBron walked off.

Cooke went back to his friends. "That kid over there," Cooke said, "he is serious!"

"LeBron James?" one of his friends asked.

"LeBron James," Cooke said. "That nigga legit."

In one weekend in Jersey, LeBron James arrived as the best high school basketball player in America, and Lenny Cooke fell apart. He never made it to the NBA.

EIGHT

A DIFFERENT FLOOR

Coach Dru couldn't help feeling overwhelmed by what he sensed was coming. First LeBron got recruited to play on the top AAU team on the West Coast. Then Sonny Vaccaro took a personal interest in him and St. V received all kinds of free shoes and gear. Suddenly, Michael Jordan's people were inviting LeBron to work out. Then LeBron got profiled in the *New York Times*, dethroned the top high school player in the country, and won the MVP award at the most prestigious summer camp in the country. It boggled Dru's mind that a sixteen-year-old kid who had yet to grow facial hair and get his driver's license could whip out his flip phone and get Vaccaro on the line or call someone to schedule a time to train at Michael Jordan's private gym. Dru wasn't used to running in these circles. But he knew enough to realize that LeBron was already an extremely valuable commodity and more and more people would be angling to get access to him.

When Dambrot was the coach, he used to routinely warn LeBron not to take any money from anyone while he was still in high school. Dambrot warned LeBron to especially avoid street agents who wanted to get their hooks into him.

Dru felt responsible to pick up where Dambrot had left off. Protective of the budding superstar he had started coaching in a drab gym at the Salvation Army in Akron, Coach Dru reiterated to LeBron the importance of steering clear of anyone offering him money.

LeBron appreciated the advice. But he assured Dru he had nothing to worry about. He had never taken a dime from anyone, and he wasn't about to change his approach.

LeBron's coaches weren't the only ones with concerns about the buzz being generated around him and the money that was bound to follow.

Eddie Jackson also had strong opinions. But Jackson looked at the situation from a different perspective. By this time, he knew LeBron saw him as a father figure and had even started referring to him as his dad. It was the ultimate compliment, and Jackson wore it like a badge of honor. But it was a heavy badge for Jackson, who had no experience with the kinds of opportunities in front of LeBron. Nor had Jackson ever dealt with Fortune 500 companies, the media, or the burden of celebrity.

Nonetheless, Gloria was leaning on Jackson for support. And Jackson wanted to play an active role—the kind of role a father would play—such as paying for LeBron to travel to camps and tournaments. He also wanted to be involved in the impending discussions with Adidas and Nike. But Jackson was strapped for cash. And in order to play the part he envisioned for himself, he needed money for things like traveling expenses. With that in mind, days before LeBron participated in the Adidas ABCD Camp, Jackson went to see an old friend.

Joseph Berish had once been a dancer with Chippendales, the dance troupe known for male striptease performances. He had met Jackson in the early nineties at the YMCA in Akron, where they had played basketball together. Shortly after they became friends, Jackson introduced Berish to Gloria and LeBron, around the time that LeBron was starting middle school. In the ensuing years, Berish had visited Gloria's apartment multiple times and considered her a friend.

When Jackson talked to Berish in early July 2001, he asked if Berish or anyone he knew could provide him and Gloria with financial assistance while they helped further LeBron's basketball career. Eager to help, Berish introduced Jackson to Joseph Marsh, a close friend who had worked as a promoter for the Chippendales dancers. Marsh, who lived in the Akron area and had founded an Ohio-based entertainment company called Magic Arts & Entertainment, was also magician David Copperfield's longtime producer. Jackson was impressed.

Marsh wasn't familiar with LeBron. But Berish and Jackson filled him in. Then Jackson made his case for a $100,000 loan.

It didn't take Marsh long to recognize that LeBron's NBA prospects were legitimate. So he agreed to lend Jackson the money. But rather than giving it to him in one lump sum, Marsh proposed an initial advance to Jackson in the amount of $25,000, followed by a second installment of the same amount later in the fall. Then the remaining $50,000 would be paid to Jackson in monthly increments of $2,500, with the final installment due in June 2003, just as LeBron would be graduating from high school. Marsh also proposed a 10 percent interest rate on the loan.

For his part, Jackson promised to include Marsh in LeBron's future endorsement deals. And Jackson agreed that Marsh could produce a documentary film on LeBron.

Jackson signed a promissory note, and at the end of July he received $25,000. At the same time, Jackson got into a dispute with someone at a bar in Akron. He ended up being charged with disorderly conduct and pleaded no contest. But he wasn't about to let the setback get him down.

Jackson and Marsh were in business together.

Lynn Merritt was senior director of Nike Basketball, a position that put him in charge of the company's endorsement deals with basketball players throughout the world. Nike had roughly seventy-five professional basketball players under contract to endorse its products. As the top executive at Nike's biggest division, Merritt was expected, among other things, to always be on the lookout for future talent. And from Merritt's vantage point, there was no one on the horizon who stood out more than LeBron. Michael Jordan was the best salesman in Nike's history. LeBron James, it seemed to Merritt, could become the best salesman of the next generation.

Merritt had started tracking LeBron shortly after Sonny Vaccaro entered the picture. Merritt knew that Vaccaro and Adidas would be formidable competitors in Nike's quest to land LeBron. But Merritt was methodical. He did his homework. He visited Akron. He was never pushy. And he got to know the people in LeBron's orbit, taking a genuine interest in them. Merritt showed a particular interest in Maverick Carter.

Maverick met Merritt around the same time that he came to the realization that he wasn't going to be an NBA player. To Maverick, Nike had always represented the holy grail of footwear in terms of status and design. As a kid, he had dreamed of owning Air Jordans. As a teenager, he felt empowered when he stepped onto the court in a pair of Nikes. But he'd never thought about the people who work at Nike until he encountered Merritt. Immediately, Maverick's curiosity took over. He peppered Merritt with questions about the company: "How does Nike decide who they want to endorse their shoes? . . . How are the commercials made? . . . Who designs the shoes? . . . How are they designed?"

Merritt was impressed with Maverick's questions. They demonstrated a genuine desire to learn. And he couldn't help noticing that Maverick was an exceptional listener. He absorbed information like a sponge. After a couple of interactions, Merritt offered Maverick an internship.

Maverick was shocked. The thought of interning for someone of Merritt's stature was intimidating. But the opportunity to associate with Nike was like a dream come true, a fringe benefit of being friends with LeBron. Rather than let self-doubt creep in, Maverick jumped at the chance.

In the fall of 2001, Maverick would start his internship at Nike. And Lynn Merritt would be his mentor.

Over the summer, word leaked out that Michael Jordan, at age thirty-eight, might come out of retirement for the second time. With rumors swirling, LeBron and Maverick headed back to Chicago to spend a week with Greg Ryan, working out at Hoops. When they arrived, they encountered more than a dozen top NBA players—Anfernee "Penny" Hardaway, Ron Artest, Paul Pierce, Jerry Stackhouse, Antoine Walker, Tim Hardaway, Michael Finley, Juwan Howard, Charles Oakley, and others. It was a collection of some of the biggest and toughest enforcers in the league, along with some of the most talented offensive players in the game. Each day they'd arrive, spend an hour lifting with a team of trainers, and then they'd play pickup games.

Jordan wasn't around. But his personal trainer, Tim Grover, ran the place. And for LeBron, it was an opportunity to be in Jordan's inner sanctum, watching some of the greatest players in the world train. It was immediately apparent there were no boys in this world. These dudes were *men*. Drenched in sweat and their bodies chiseled with muscle, they weren't playing—they were running and banging and talking trash in their own unique vernacular.

The NBA players didn't pay much attention to LeBron. But partway through the week, Grover arranged for LeBron to get in one of the pickup games. LeBron laced up his sneakers. Like an interloper, he stepped onto the floor and immediately realized it was different from any floor he'd been on. The dimensions were the same. But the players were so much bigger that the driving lanes to the basket were harder to see. Everyone's arms were so much longer that the passing lanes were much narrower. It was as if the court had shrunk.

LeBron ended up guarding Jerry Stackhouse, who made a point of taking him to the hole, demonstrating that LeBron wasn't ready to defend at this level. And Antoine Walker talked shit the whole time, giving LeBron a taste of what he was in for in the NBA.

But LeBron maintained his poise. Although he had trouble guarding guys on defense, he was able to get up and down with them on offense, making several impressive passes and knocking down a couple of shots. It was a tremendous confidence boost to receive a pass from an NBA great and turn it into a bucket.

For Maverick, it was impossible not to swell with pride as he watched LeBron visit the world he'd soon occupy as a full-time resident. He was running with millionaires who drove luxury cars, were married to beautiful women, and were raising families. They were pros. And seeing LeBron play with them made it easier to visualize LeBron's future.

At the end of each day, after all the players left, LeBron and Maverick stayed behind to help Ryan and Grover clean up. One afternoon toward the end of the week, they were walking out the door when they spotted a red Ferrari coming down the street. As it came to a stop, they noticed who was driving—Michael Jordan.

"Ho-lee shit," Maverick said.

LeBron froze, staring at Jordan as he stepped out of the car and walked toward them. LeBron had never seen his idol up close. It looked as though he were levitating.

Jordan had a lot on his mind at that time. After being away from the game for three years, he was gearing up to come back. He realized that at his age, he probably wouldn't be able to play at the same level people had become accustomed to when he had walked away from the game. One of the lessons he'd learned during his career was that it was impossible to live up to other people's expectations; all he could do was set his own expectations and try to meet them. Another thing he'd learned was the power of silence. He still hadn't told anyone about his comeback plans. He was keeping all that close to the vest.

Approaching the gym, Jordan looked at LeBron, said hello, and invited him and Maverick back inside.

They followed Jordan to the weight room. Grover and Ryan joined them. No one else was around.

Jordan smiled at LeBron, the kid who people were saying would be his heir.

LeBron met his gaze.

Surrounded by weight machines, Jordan kept it light, talking in general terms about the NBA and what it meant to be a professional.

LeBron listened and nodded. The experience was too surreal to process.

The conversation lasted about fifteen minutes. And Jordan dispensed no advice. But he gave LeBron something more valuable than words: his cell phone number.

Maverick was stunned.

LeBron didn't know what to say. Jordan's shoes were on his feet. And now Jordan's number was in his pocket. At sixteen, LeBron had joined a very select club of people in the world who had direct access to Jordan.

It was late when LeBron and Maverick left Chicago for the five-plus-hour drive back to Akron. In the morning, LeBron had to be at St. V for the first day of school. There wouldn't be much time for sleep. But with Maverick at the wheel and LeBron playing DJ from the passenger seat, music pulsed from the stereo as they sped down I-90 past South Bend and crossed into Ohio. In between songs, they couldn't get over the fact that they had met Jordan.

"It was like listening to God speak," Maverick said.

LeBron was flying high. Over the past few months it was as if he had lived a lifetime. He didn't want the summer to end. He just wanted to keep on soaring.

In his journal, he quickly summarized his experience in Chicago:

I didn't get to play with Mike, but I did get some run with a lot of the other NBA guys, and I talked to Jordan a little bit. He didn't really give me any advice, he just told me to keep my head on straight. We all went out to dinner at his restaurant—the steak and mashed potatoes were tight.

* * *

The aroma from Pam's Italian-style chicken pasta wafted through the Vaccaros' Calabasas home. It was Saturday, August 25, 2001, and Sonny was in the living room, thumbing through his vast record collection in search of just the right artist for the occasion. Gloria and Eddie Jackson had flown out from Akron and were coming for lunch. The trip was Eddie's idea, and Sonny was determined to treat LeBron's family the way Sonny treated his own family—by opening his home, stuffing them with home-cooked Italian food, and surrounding them with good music. Sonny settled on Ray Charles to set the mood.

When Gloria and Eddie arrived, Sonny gave them a tour of the place. He showed off his original Elvis Presley jukebox, the outdoor Jacuzzi, the swimming pool, and the lush red tomatoes in his vegetable garden. There was even a backyard swing that Sonny invited them to try out. Everything looked idyllic as jazzy songs like "Them That Got" piped through a state-of-the-art sound system that filled the backyard:

> I see folk with long cars and fine clothes
> That's why they're called the smarter set
> Because they manage to get
> When only them that's got supposed to get
> And I ain't got nothin' yet.

Gloria commented that she'd never seen such a fine home.

Nor had Jackson ever visited a house that had an in-ground pool and a Jacuzzi.

They spent the entire afternoon with the Vaccaros. After lunch, Sonny and Eddie talked in the backyard. Gloria helped Pam with the dishes. Among other things, they discussed LeBron's desire to continue playing high school football. Gloria had already told him no. She'd allowed it when he was a freshman and sophomore, but given the trajectory of his basketball career, she felt it was time to put her foot down.

LeBron had accepted his mother's decision. But the night before Gloria and Eddie showed up at the Vaccaros' home, LeBron had attended the first football game of the season for St. V. He had watched as Sian, Willie, and Romeo helped lead the team to victory. He hated being a spectator.

Gloria knew how LeBron felt. She wondered what Pam thought.

"Don't let him play football," Pam told her.

Gloria went on about how much she loved LeBron and hated to disappoint him. She just wanted to do what was best for him, she insisted. Sometimes, she admitted, it was hard to know what to do.

Pam told her that if she decided to let him play, she needed to be sure to take out an insurance policy on him.

After spending a day with the Vaccaros, Eddie and Gloria flew to Oregon to meet Nike chairman Phil Knight and spend time with Lynn Merritt. While at the company's Beaverton headquarters, they also toured the Nike campus. It was a lot to absorb. But the more time they spent around Merritt, the more impressed they were with his professionalism and his vision for LeBron with Nike. They came away convinced that LeBron was in a great position.

When Eddie and Gloria got back to Akron, LeBron talked to his mother about football. While Gloria had been out west, the R&B singer Aaliyah had died in a plane crash shortly after taking off from an island in the Bahamas. She was twenty-two. LeBron told his mother that hearing about the pop star's death had affected his thinking. *Life is short* may be a cliché, but it was true.

"Tomorrow is not promised to anyone," Gloria told him.

LeBron agreed, which was precisely why he didn't want to miss the opportunity to do something that brought him tremendous joy and gave him a more rounded high school experience—play football with his friends.

Gloria turned to Eddie. It was time to get that insurance policy.

Eddie found a broker in North Carolina who had insured top NBA prospects with basketball scholarships at Duke University. The broker had never heard of insuring a high school junior. But he worked with Eddie to issue a multimillion-dollar policy for LeBron.

Jay Brophy was thrilled when LeBron told him he was joining the team in time to play in the second game of the season. Brophy even got a call from Gloria, who told him: "Jay, take care of my baby." To minimize the risk of injury to LeBron, Brophy made sure that the rest of the team knew not to hit him during practice. Brophy also made it clear to LeBron that he didn't want him running pass patterns across the middle of the field, where violent collisions were more common.

LeBron liked playing for Brophy and was happy when he'd been named the new head football coach over the summer. At the start of the 2001 season, Brophy had decided to go with two quarterbacks and play them on a rotating basis. One of them was Willie McGee. Once LeBron rejoined the team, Brophy told both quarterbacks there was a new play in the playbook: when in doubt, throw the fade to LeBron.

Willie knew that play well. He and LeBron had been playing football together since the Pop Warner days. And throughout the 2001 season, they hooked up on a lot of pass plays. The other quarterback had good chemistry with LeBron, too.

Early in the season, the team traveled an hour away to play a school located in rural Ohio, near Amish country. That night, LeBron put on a show, making six receptions for nearly 150 yards. One play in particular ignited the crowd. The St. V quarterback threw an errant pass that was headed out-of-bounds. Coach Brophy raised his arms to catch the ball when suddenly LeBron leaped into the air and snagged it with one hand before landing with both feet inbounds. It was the kind of circus catch that Brophy was used to seeing NFL great Randy Moss make.

After the game, Amish people surrounded the St. V bus. There were so many of them that the bus driver couldn't drive off. After realizing why all of these folks were making it impossible for his team to leave, Coach Brophy went to the back of the bus. "L.J.," he said, "do you mind signing some autographs so we can get out of here?"

LeBron had never been around Amish people. Neither had Romeo or Sian or Willie. With his teammates staring at him, LeBron stood up and got off the bus.

The strangers immediately swarmed him.

Towering over the crowd, LeBron signed everything that people put in front of him—game programs, clothing, scraps of paper, bare hands.

Looking on, Romeo was struck by what he was witnessing—people who had a reputation for being so insular had accepted LeBron, and by extension, they had accepted everyone on the St. V team. "They showed us love," Romeo said, reflecting on that moment years later. "That showed that [LeBron] was then a transcendent athlete, that he was crossing barriers that normally they don't let you cross no matter who you are."

Beaming, LeBron got back on the bus for one of those rides home with his sweat-drenched teammates that he wished would never end.

Despite being double-teamed week after week, LeBron hauled in thirteen touchdowns and had more than 1,200 receiving yards during the nine regular season games he played in. For the second year in a row, he earned All-Ohio honors in football, and college recruiters were clamoring to get an audience with him. Coach Brophy had gotten calls from Ohio State, Alabama, Miami, Florida State, Notre Dame, USC, South Carolina, and a slew of other schools. Brophy had always assumed that LeBron wasn't going to play college football. But the interest level in LeBron as a football player was unlike anything Brophy had ever seen. He figured he should at least confirm his understanding that LeBron wasn't interested in a football scholarship. That way, Brophy could put these recruiters out of their misery.

One afternoon he tracked LeBron down in the library, where he was visiting with Mrs. Wood.

Brophy asked LeBron if he had any interest in playing college football. He'd been getting a lot of calls from recruiters.

"Coach, I'm ninety-nine percent sure I'm probably going to the NBA. But I wouldn't rule it out."

Wouldn't rule it out? Brophy was surprised to hear that.

Moments later, LeBron dropped the serious expression and started laughing. "No, Coach," he said. "I'm kidding. I'm gonna play basketball."

Brophy smiled. When football season ended, he was going to miss LeBron, whom he looked at as an old soul. No one else on the team was capable of carrying on an in-depth conversation with him about NFL players from the seventies and eighties. If St. V had offered a class in NFL history, LeBron would have earned an A-plus. One time he was going on and on about Chicago Bears Hall of Fame running back Walter Payton. Finally, Brophy asked him how he knew so much about a guy who had retired when LeBron was three years old.

"Coach, I've got ESPN Classics," he said, smiling.

Basketball season had yet to begin and Coach Dru was already swamped with the administrative aspects of his new job. For starters, the demand for tickets to see LeBron and his teammates had gotten so out of hand that the school had decided to shift its ten home games for the 2001–2002 season to the University of Akron's James A. Rhodes Arena, which held 5,200 spectators. St. V was even offering season-ticket packages for $120. More than 1,700 had been sold. Meanwhile, tickets to some of the St. V road games were being sold by Ticketmaster.

At the same time, Coach Dru had inherited a schedule that Coach Dambrot had put together with an eye toward solidifying St. V as a national powerhouse. Slated to compete against elite teams from Pennsylvania, Missouri, New York, and Virginia, as well as participate in a series of national tournaments, Dru and his players were destined to rack up thousands of frequent-flier miles. There were hotels to book, buses to reserve, and class schedules to arrange to ensure that the boys were able to minimize school absences.

But the biggest source of anxiety heading into Dru's first season as head coach was expectations. The team had gone 53-1 in two seasons under Dambrot. And now that LeBron was widely regarded as the best high school player in the country, Dru had no margin of error. If his team didn't win a national championship, he'd never live it down. Making matters worse, two of the first three games on the St. V schedule were against teams that were ranked in the top ten of the *USA Today* preseason national poll. Yet Dru had no idea whether LeBron, Sian, Romeo, and Willie would be available to play when the season started. Due to the success of the football team—St. V had qualified for the state playoffs—the four of them weren't allowed to practice with the basketball team, much less play in games, until football season was over.

LeBron knew that Coach Dru wasn't thrilled with his playing football. Then, after leading his football team to victory in the first round of the state playoffs, LeBron delivered some news that only added to Dru's worries. LeBron wrote about the situation in his journal:

I broke my left index finger in the first playoff game—it was my first break. A lot of people kind of panicked. But not me. I kind of kept it secret. Didn't let it get out to the public until like a week before basketball started. I just had a little cast on it to keep from jamming it again, but it's fine now. It's not really a problem for basketball, 'cause it's my left hand, my non-shooting hand, and Coach Dru knew I had a little time to let it heal, anyway.

From his apartment on the top floor at Spring Hill, LeBron could look out the window and see the St. V football stadium. He loved playing there. He loved football. It was a game that came naturally to him. But basketball represented so much more to him than a game. The last thing he saw before going to sleep each night and the first thing he saw when he woke up each morning were images of Michael Jordan looking down on him from the walls of his bedroom. To LeBron, Jordan was the ultimate athlete. During football season, LeBron heard the news on ESPN: "Speculation has ended. Rumors confirmed. The greatest player of all time is back. And he's wearing a Wizards uniform." The fact that LeBron had been with Jordan a month earlier when Jordan was planning his return gave LeBron a unique historical connection to Jordan, fueling LeBron's desire to become like him and one day have his own image on the bedroom walls of children. Football was his fun. Basketball was his life.

With the Ohio State football semifinals days away, LeBron joined Sian, Romeo, Willie, and the rest of his teammates on the practice field. Dressed in sweat suits, cleats, and helmets, they did a walk-through, going over the plays.

As LeBron went through the motions with the football team out on the field, the St. V basketball team was in the gym. With the first game of the season less than one week away, Coach Dru had organized an informal scrimmage game. But with four of the team's best players unavailable, the mood in the gym was flat.

Then, with Romeo trailing, LeBron burst through the gym doors, ripped off his sweatpants, removed his sweatshirt, and stepped onto the court, motioning for one of the guys who was guarding Little Dru to step off. As soon as football practice had let out, LeBron had ditched his cleats and helmet and run to the gym.

Trash-talking, Little Dru baited LeBron, asking if he could hold his own.

LeBron sprang, stole the ball, sped downcourt, elevated, cocked his arm back, and rammed home a rim-rattling dunk. Everyone started hooting and hollering. In an instant, the gym was infused with energy.

"Yeah, I can hold my own, motherfucker," LeBron said to Little Dru, getting in his face.

Little Dru took the ball and went right back at LeBron.

Romeo got in the game and started banging people down low.

Guys battled for rebounds, scrapped for loose balls, and set hard screens on each other. It was precisely the kind of energy that Coach Dru and his staff had been craving from his team.

Eventually, everyone stopped for a breather and one of the players approached LeBron about a previous sequence where a play had broken down.

LeBron knew precisely which play was in question.

"Why didn't that play work?" his teammate asked.

"Well, you started too early," LeBron said, going into teaching mode.

With the coaches looking on, the players gathered around LeBron as he walked everyone through what had transpired moments earlier. Then he explained to his teammate what he had done wrong. "You were in a low post," LeBron told him. "And you should have been in a high post."

The player nodded, and the guys fist-bumped.

Coach Dru couldn't wait for football season to end.

During the fall, Eddie Jackson received his second $25,000 installment from Joseph Marsh. Marsh was already looking ahead to the documentary about LeBron. And since Marsh had put up the money, he expected to control the rights to the film. He also wanted to keep 50 percent of the proceeds. It was all new to Jackson. But since Marsh was the one with the capital, he was calling the shots.

At Marsh's urging, Jackson agreed to meet with Lionel Martin, a New York–based filmmaker who had directed dozens of music videos for 2Pac, Snoop Dogg, Whitney Houston, and a host of other recording artists. Marsh felt Martin could be a good fit to direct a film on LeBron.

While Jackson and Martin were making plans, LeBron had his hands full trying to keep up with the day-to-day tasks that came with being sixteen, such as turning in class assignments, keeping up his grades, and learning to drive. Report cards had just come out, and his grades were solid, especially in Earth Sciences—his favorite class. And right as football season was winding down, he passed his driver's test and obtained his license.

As a reward, Jackson used money he had borrowed from Marsh to purchase a used Ford Explorer for LeBron. On Thanksgiving night, LeBron drove to the movie theater, where he planned to see *Black Knight* starring Martin Lawrence. Making his way to his seat, he heard someone say in a hushed tone: "There's LeBron James."

The independence that came with having his own car and being able to drive himself places was a new experience, as was being recognized and whispered about in a public place. They felt good, especially the recognition. They also made him itch even more to get on with basketball season.

Two days later, on November 24, 2001, St. V lost to Licking Valley in the state football playoffs. Afterward, LeBron turned in his helmet and hung up his cleats. He would never play organized football again.

In its 2001–2002 basketball preview, the *Akron Beacon Journal* wrote:

> You almost expect to wake up one morning and see LeBron James' leaping likeness staring back at you from the wall of a downtown office building. Today, Akron.
> Tomorrow, Times Square.

Expectations were sky-high. But so was the level of resentment that was mounting against LeBron and his teammates. St. V had become the team that everyone else loved to hate. They had the best player in the country. They were the best-dressed team with their Adidas sneakers, Adidas uniforms, and personalized Adidas headbands. They were media darlings. And they'd won two straight state championships and were projected to go undefeated and win a third. In sports, the team at the top always wears a target.

LeBron's attitude was: *If people want to turn us into arrogant victors, let them. If people want to think we're too cocky, let them.*

In the locker room before games, the St. V players got amped up by blasting Jay-Z's new album *The Blueprint*. Songs like "Takeover" reflected the way St. V players felt toward the competition.

> *We bring knife to fistfight, kill your drama*
> *Uh, we kill you motherfuckin' ants with a sledgehammer.*

The St. V players relished the moment when they'd enter the gym and meet the gaze of the opposing team. Instantly, it would become clear whether the opponents were starstruck or itching for a fight. Those who were in awe were afraid to make eye contact. Those who were looking to send a message would stare and glare. "None of those poses mattered," LeBron explained. "Because we knew what was going to happen right at tip-off."

In the season opener, St. V trounced a high school from the Cleveland suburbs by forty-one points. Then St. V played back-to-back games against teams in the *USA Today* Top Ten. First up was Germantown Academy, a private school outside Philadelphia with a six-six senior headed to the University of Florida, a six-seven senior headed to Duke, and a six-eleven senior headed to Vanderbilt. Despite the significant height disadvantage, LeBron poured in thirty-eight points and pulled down sixteen rebounds, while Romeo and Sian, who had bulked up to 285 pounds, outmuscled everyone underneath the basket. St. V won, 70–64.

Seventh-ranked Vashon High from St. Louis was no match, either. LeBron scored twenty-six and St. V smothered them with defense, winning, 49–41.

After knocking off Germantown and Vashon, LeBron noted that St. V was being described in the media as one of the top teams in the country. He didn't disagree. But he saw one big difference between his team and the other elite programs. "We ain't got four All-Americans," he wrote in his journal. "We only got one, and it's me." But he loved his teammates and the way they played.

But Coach Dru didn't like what he was seeing. With each victory, his players were getting more arrogant and more disrespectful. In games, they sometimes ignored his instructions. In practice, they argued with him and bickered with each other. At times it felt like pulling teeth to get the guys to focus and put in the maximum effort. On one occasion, Dru got so fed up with the way practice was going that he ordered the players to run. But they refused. Exacerbated, Dru canceled practice. And more than once he had to reprimand guys for violating his rule against cussing. After Romeo used a series of obscenities in practice, Dru made him do one hundred push-ups.

Even the players' choice of warm-up music had become an issue. Already turned off by the petty infighting and lack of discipline, Coach

Cotton let it be known that he didn't approve of all the F-bombs and references to "bitches" and "hos." If it weren't for his allegiance to Sian, he would have quit the team.

Part of the dissension in the ranks was a reaction to Dru's coaching style. Although they wouldn't admit it, LeBron and his teammates missed Dambrot. They were still pissed at him for leaving, yet they longed for his confrontational, in-your-face approach to coaching. They missed his yelling and even his obscenity-laced outbursts. The bottom line was that Dambrot had made them feel as though they were playing for a college coach who knew how to win. With Dru, it felt as though they were playing for a father figure. That had been fine when they were kids. But they were older now and had experienced winning. They felt invincible. So Dru's repeated warnings that they were ripe for being picked off by an inferior team fell on deaf ears.

St. V was 7-0 when they faced Amityville Memorial High of Long Island in the championship game of a holiday tournament in Delaware. The game fell on LeBron's seventeenth birthday, and Amityville, the reigning state champions from New York, was looking to spoil the party. With St. V trailing by three and with five seconds to play, LeBron nailed a three-pointer and got fouled. After LeBron made the free throw to put his team up by one, Coach Dru called time-out.

In the huddle, he told his guys he wanted them to put pressure on the inbounds pass. But the team had other ideas and made it clear they were going to defend the play differently.

On the inbounds pass, Amityville's speedy point guard got free. LeBron fouled him. The point guard made both free throws. And St. V lost by one point.

Frustrated, Coach Dru could only hope that the loss would take some air out of his players' egos.

It was wishful thinking.

NINE

GET IN THE CAR

Adidas had the edge in the LeBron sweepstakes. But Nike was playing the long game. And Michael Jordan was Nike's ace in the hole. On January 31, 2002, Jordan and the Washington Wizards were in Cleveland to play the Cavaliers. Eddie Jackson had telephoned Cavaliers head coach John Lucas to ask him to set aside tickets for LeBron and a few of his friends. Arrangements had also been made for LeBron to meet with Jordan after the game.

That afternoon, LeBron had basketball practice. He noticed an unfamiliar face in the gym. Afterward, in the locker room, a member of the St. V athletic department approached and introduced twenty-eight-year-old Grant Wahl, a writer from *Sports Illustrated*.

Assigned to cover soccer and college basketball for the magazine, Wahl had first heard about LeBron shortly after the Adidas ABCD Camp the previous summer. One of Wahl's colleagues at the magazine had mentioned LeBron's performance against Lenny Cooke in a column. Intrigued, Wahl did some poking around. Numerous NBA scouts told him that even as a high school junior, LeBron was good enough to be the number one pick in the draft. The more Wahl heard, the more eager he became to profile the kid from Akron whom basketball insiders were describing as the heir apparent to Jordan. As soon as he got approval from his editor to approach LeBron about the prospect of being profiled, Wahl hopped on a plane and flew to Ohio. It was all very last-minute and everything hinged on whether Wahl could convince LeBron to give him access.

Now, flanked by his friends in the locker room, LeBron stared skeptically at Wahl, a total stranger who had arrived out of the blue, and thought, *Who's this guy? What's he want?*

Feeling like he didn't belong, Wahl knew that a busy locker room wasn't an ideal environment to get acquainted. Sensing LeBron's reluctance, Wahl asked if they could talk for a minute in private.

LeBron went with him to a quiet corner.

First, Wahl apologized for showing up without any advance warning. Then he outlined his objective—to write a piece that would enable *Sports Illustrated* readers to know more about LeBron and what his life was like. "I think this is gonna be a really cool story," Wahl told him.

LeBron listened as Wahl explained that in order for him to do justice to the story, the two of them had to spend some time together. And Wahl had a creative idea for how to make that happen.

"I hear you're going up to Cleveland for the game tonight," Wahl said. "I got a rental car. I'd love to take you up there."

LeBron hesitated. He hadn't expected Wahl to offer to drive him and his friends to Cleveland. It was an unusual request. And LeBron wasn't sure that he wanted Wahl tagging along. He didn't even know this guy.

"I'd really appreciate the opportunity," Wahl said.

Opportunity? Standing in the bowels of his high school, LeBron considered whether to take a ride with a total stranger. Barely seventeen years old, he couldn't foresee the life-altering implications of Wahl's proposition. Without consulting his mother or his coach or any other adult, LeBron took less than a minute to size up Wahl. The opportunity to appear in the most influential sports magazine in America outweighed his reservations. He decided he'd get in the car.

Later that evening, LeBron left his apartment wearing an Adidas stocking cap and a black coat and carrying a binder full of CDs. He got into the front passenger seat of Wahl's rental car, while Maverick and Frankie Walker Jr. piled into the backseat. It had been seven years since LeBron had bunked in Frankie's bedroom, but they had remained close and whenever LeBron was doing something fun, he tried to include his old friend. If Wahl wanted a glimpse of his life, LeBron figured, he might as well get to know his friends and the music that formed the soundtrack of their day-to-day experiences. LeBron removed Jay-Z's *The Blueprint* from the binder, popped it in the car's sound system, and turned up the volume.

As soon as Wahl started driving, the implications of having a teenage passenger who was soon to be worth tens of millions of dollars hit him.

The music was thumping, and Wahl was navigating down roads he'd never been on. Anxious, he told himself, *Make sure this guy gets back in one piece.*

On the way out of town, they stopped for fast food. While waiting in the drive-thru line, Wahl looked at LeBron. There's a chance, he told him, that this could be a cover story.

LeBron's eyes widened.

Yet, Wahl had a problem—he had no idea how he was going to get into the game. He had neither a press credential nor a ticket.

Once they reached Gund Arena, Maverick led the group to a designated area, where he and LeBron and Frankie presented their photo IDs in exchange for floor seats. Then Maverick and LeBron, looking at Wahl, told security personnel words to the effect of *He's with us.*

After some back and forth Wahl was in.

Trailing LeBron, Wahl watched as LeBron made his way to his floor seat, signing autographs and posing for pictures.

The game ended in dramatic fashion with Jordan knocking down the game-winning shot at the buzzer. Moments later, a sharp-dressed, mysterious-looking man greeted LeBron and Maverick by name and invited them to follow him into the tunnel that led to the Wizards locker room.

LeBron and Maverick carried on with the man as if he were an old family friend. When the man stepped away, Wahl asked, "Who was that guy?"

"Uncle Wes," LeBron said.

Wahl had never previously encountered William Wesley, considered by many to be the most influential behind-the-scenes power broker in the NBA. Closely aligned with Jordan and Nike, Wesley had been described by a *Chicago Sun-Times* writer this way: "I thought he worked for the Secret Service or the FBI or the CIA. Then I thought he was a pimp, providing players with chicks, or a loan shark or a bodyguard or a vice commissioner to the league."

But to LeBron, Wesley was just Uncle Wes, a new presence in LeBron's expanding orbit. Wesley had befriended Eddie Jackson. He had inconspicuously attended a few of LeBron's games at St. V. And he'd even introduced LeBron to Jay-Z the previous summer. However, LeBron didn't divulge any of that to Wahl.

Eventually, Wesley reappeared with Jordan, who strode toward LeBron in a perfectly tailored blue suit.

LeBron smiled and shook his hand.

Jordan noticed that Gloria wasn't around. "Where's Mama?" he asked.

"She's in New Orleans," LeBron said.

Wahl marveled at what he was seeing. It reminded him of the famous photograph of sixteen-year-old Bill Clinton meeting his idol, President Kennedy, in the White House Rose Garden in 1963.

After talking hoops with LeBron for a few minutes, Jordan had to jet.

"One dribble, stop and pull up," Jordan said. "That's what I want to see."

LeBron nodded.

And Jordan was gone.

"That's my guy," LeBron said.

Wahl could see the story unfolding before his eyes.

On the drive back to Akron, LeBron peppered Wahl with questions: "What's it like being a writer? . . . Do you have family?"

Wahl was impressed with LeBron. He was neither pretentious nor a diva. And he treated his friends like brothers.

By the time they got back to Akron, it was close to eleven o'clock on a school night. But LeBron said he was hungry and suggested they all go to Applebee's.

Wahl was game.

LeBron had already come to appreciate that there was a lot more to being a professional basketball player than simply playing and practicing—it was a full-time commitment that encompassed a lot of additional responsibilities that many athletes found burdensome, such as dealing with the media. From the moment he entered high school, LeBron had become used to being around sportswriters from the *Akron Beacon Journal* and the *Plain Dealer*. They covered all his football and basketball games, and their stories played an important role in raising his profile throughout Ohio. LeBron liked those guys, and he had learned how to talk to them. But now that he was cooperating with *Sports Illustrated*, he was about to learn an even more valuable lesson—that a picture could be much more potent than words when it came to shaping his image.

Just before eight o'clock in the morning, LeBron pulled into the parking lot at St. V. It was Super Bowl Sunday and the high school was deserted. LeBron was looking forward to watching the heavily favored St.

Louis Rams play the New England Patriots later. The underdog Patriots had a little-known quarterback named Tom Brady, who would be playing in his first Super Bowl. But before all of that, LeBron had to focus on his first photo shoot with a national magazine. He went inside the darkened building, where twenty-five-year-old Michael LeBrecht, a fledgling photographer who normally worked as an equipment assistant, broke out his camera.

LeBrecht had never done a cover shoot for the magazine. But he had met LeBron at the Adidas ABCD Camp the previous summer. LeBrecht's best quality was his ability to relate to young people and put them at ease—he particularly impressed Gloria with the way he treated her and her son. He also had a great eye for portrait shots.

LeBron posed for LeBrecht with a variety of backdrops—at a desk, at his locker, and in the gym, dribbling and dunking. LeBrecht's assistant even sprayed mist on LeBron's face to create the impression that he was sweating. The process took hours.

Coach Dru was around for part of the shoot. He'd never seen something quite so elaborate. *This is crazy*, he thought.

But the goal was to come away with one image—a money shot for the cover—that would introduce the world to LeBron James. Ultimately, LeBrecht had LeBron pick up a basketball that had been spray-painted gold for effect.

Dressed in his St. V jersey and sporting a green headband, LeBron held the ball in his right hand, bringing his arm back behind his head, like he was preparing to dunk a golden globe. He extended his left arm forward, spreading his fingers wide, as if he were halting traffic. And he widened his eyes and opened his mouth, as if to declare, *Look out! Here I come.* Playful and charismatic, LeBron needed no direction.

Using just two small lights to illuminate LeBron against a black backdrop, LeBrecht had his cover shot—*click!*

When LeBron first saw the basketball schedule at the beginning of the school year, he was pleasantly surprised to see that his team was playing Oak Hill for the second year in a row. It meant that he'd get to face his new friend, Carmelo Anthony. He circled that game as the one he looked forward to the most.

Oak Hill had a record of 24-1 and was ranked number four in the country.

St. V was 15-1 and ranked number five.

The two teams were staying at the same hotel in Langhorne, Pennsylvania. On the night before the game, LeBron met up with Carmelo in the lobby. They picked up the conversation right where it had left off the previous summer when they had roomed together in Colorado. By this point, Carmelo was looking for a friend who could be like a brother. LeBron, meanwhile, felt the friendship they were forming could last a long time. It was getting late and they'd been alone for more than two hours when the coach for Oak Hill approached.

"I know y'all are friends," he said. "But you have a game to play tomorrow."

The next day, the atmosphere at the PrimeTime Shootout at Sovereign Bank Arena in Trenton, New Jersey, had the feel of something much bigger than a high school basketball game. More than eleven thousand spectators and a throng of basketball writers showed up to watch the two best high school players in the country go head-to-head.

The previous summer, when LeBron and Carmelo had been at the Adidas ABCD Camp, LeBron had gotten some personal advice from NBA all-star Tracy McGrady, who had told him: "When you get on the court, you have no friends. No matter who you're playing, you gotta kill 'em." LeBron had taken that approach against Lenny Cooke. He had also brought that mindset to every game St. V had played thus far in his junior year. But Carmelo was LeBron's friend and LeBron couldn't look at him any other way. As soon as the game between St. V and Oak Hill got underway, the two players with the highest basketball IQ put on a master class that left everyone else spellbound. Dueling as if they were alone on a private stage, LeBron scored thirty-six points and Carmelo scored thirty-four. LeBron was named MVP of the game, and Carmelo led his team to victory, 72–66. It came to be regarded as one of the best high school basketball games ever played.

St. V fell to 15-2. But LeBron and his teammates rationalized the situation: on a night when everyone on the team except LeBron had shot poorly, they had lost by only six points to a team that had six players heading to Division I colleges on basketball scholarships.

* * *

It was rare for *Sports Illustrated* to put a high school athlete on the cover. In the magazine's forty-two-year history, it had happened only seven times. From an editorial standpoint, there were commonsense reasons to avoid featuring teens on the front of a magazine read by millions of adults. Chief among them was the realization that putting a minor on one of the most widely read magazines in the world created overwhelming expectations that were virtually impossible to meet. The first time the magazine had tried the experiment was in 1966 when it had featured Rick Mount, a high school senior from Lebanon, Indiana, standing on a farm with red barns and white rail fences. The tagline had read: "Brightest Star in High School Basketball." Mount had ended up playing for Purdue and having a short, undistinguished pro career. The last time the magazine had featured a high schooler had been in 1989. Jon Peters, an eighteen-year-old pitcher from Brenham, Texas, with a high school record of 51-0, appeared under the cover line "Superkid." Peters never made it to the big leagues. After accepting a scholarship to play for Texas A&M, he had undergone four arm surgeries that ended his baseball career before he turned twenty-one.

It had been over twenty years since the magazine had last featured a high school player on the cover. And it had never featured a high school junior. Except for fourteen-year-old gymnast Kristie Phillips, whom the magazine had dubbed "the New Mary Lou"—Phillips subsequently failed to qualify for the US team and ended up attending Louisiana State University on a cheerleading scholarship—LeBron would be the youngest prospect to occupy the cover.

For the editors, it was a big decision. But the magazine's outgoing managing editor, Bill Colson, liked the idea. It was risky and edgy. And LeBron's charisma was bound to create a splash. Colson came up with the cover line "The Chosen One: High school junior LeBron James would be an NBA lottery pick right now."

On one hand, Grant Wahl was thrilled. But he couldn't ignore his reservations. *Man*, Wahl thought. *I hope we don't ruin this kid's life.*

LeBron was in school on February 13 when his face began appearing on newsstands from New York City to Los Angeles and in mailboxes from Key West to Spokane. Other media outlets, from ESPN to sports talk radio stations throughout the country, were buzzing about the cover. The *Today* show and *Teen People* magazine were calling. And in Ohio, Grant Wahl did a blitz of interviews on local radio shows. Sitting in a room at the school, LeBron opened the magazine, looked inside, and read:

> Ohio high school junior LeBron James is so good that he's already being mentioned as the heir to Air Jordan.

It was heavy praise. And with the *Sports Illustrated* publicity machine going full tilt, LeBron was the talk of the sports world.

The impact at St. V was immediate. When LeBron walked the hallways, his peers looked at him with newfound awe. The athletic department was deluged with calls from reporters around the country who wanted to interview him. Fans showed up at the school, barging into basketball practice to get a glimpse of LeBron. The magazine may have dubbed him "the Chosen One," but at St. V he was "the King." LeBron had even started referring to himself as King James.

"Maybe naively, I didn't really understand what it truly meant to be on the cover of *Sports Illustrated*," LeBron reflected on the experience years later. "I was arrogant, dubbing myself King James. My head did swell. In hindsight I should have kept quiet, but I also was what I was—a teenager. And every reporter in the world seemed to be rushing toward me at once."

All of the adulation wreaked havoc on LeBron and his teammates. Four days after the magazine came out, St. V faced George Junior Republic, a residential reform school for disadvantaged youth in Pennsylvania. The game was held at Youngstown State University. A standing-room-only crowd exceeding 6,700 fans packed the arena. The opposing coach gave his players two simple instructions: foul LeBron in transition and do *not* let him get to the rim.

His players wasted no time carrying out the game plan. When LeBron drove to the basket, he was purposely hit so hard that he was knocked to the floor. Then LeBron got knocked down a second time. The second foul was so egregious that LeBron could have easily been injured. Furious, Gloria stormed onto the court and had to be restrained.

After that, LeBron stopped driving and started settling for jump shots. St. V lost in overtime to an inferior team, 58–57. Coming on the heels of the loss to Oak Hill, it marked the first time that LeBron and his teammates had lost two straight games in high school. The mood in the locker room afterward was so bad that Coach Dru told the throng of reporters that none of his players were available for comment. But when LeBron emerged, he was inundated by a crowd of roughly one hundred people who had copies of *Sports Illustrated* and wanted his autograph. A man outside the arena had been selling them prior to the game at five dollars a pop.

The next day, a small mob of autograph seekers stormed into the gym at St. V, interrupting practice. It was becoming obvious that the school had to do something to protect LeBron and his teammates. For the next road game, a police escort led the team bus to the arena. When LeBron and his teammates stepped off the bus, fans were lined up twelve-deep to greet them. Some of them had been waiting for hours. "We love you, LeBron!" they shouted. Many of the onlookers were girls, screaming and vying for LeBron's attention.

LeBron's teammates got swept up in the euphoria.

"It was almost like playing in the NBA," Sian Cotton explained. "Girls at our hotels. People trying to get up to our rooms."

Celebrities started showing up at St. V games, too. When the Lakers were in Cleveland to play the Cavaliers a couple of weeks after the *Sports Illustrated* piece ran, Shaquille O'Neal showed up to watch LeBron play. His entrance caused so much commotion that the game had to be stopped. Sian Cotton, who idolized Shaq, was starstruck. Fans moved like a pile of ants toward him in hopes of shaking his hand. A couple of days later, ESPN dispatched a production crew to St. V, turning the locker room into a makeshift set for on-camera interviews that the network intended to film with LeBron, his teammates, and Coach Dru for a special segment that would air on *SportsCenter* at the end of February.

Meanwhile, the resentment toward the team only escalated. In a sold-out game against crosstown rival Archbishop Hoban at Rhodes Arena, all of the opposing players came out for pregame warm-ups wearing T-shirts that had THE CHOSEN ONE printed on them. Fired up by the gimmick, LeBron and his teammates punished Hoban early, building a big lead. Then the Hoban coach sent in a bench player who was built like a linebacker. He quickly manhandled LeBron, hammering him with a couple of rough fouls. Eddie Jackson, who was sitting courtside next to the St. V bench, didn't like it. He got up and went toward the Hoban bench, where he started venting. When security intervened, Eddie got more heated. The police ended up escorting him out of the building. St. V won by thirty-nine.

Although his team was winning, Coach Dru was overwhelmed. When he had signed on to coach the team, he had never planned on sitting for interviews with *Sports Illustrated* and ESPN. He had never anticipated that his players would be treated like celebrities—spritzed for photo shoots, talked about on network television as if they were household names, and trailed by autograph seekers, cameramen, and girls. Nor was he prepared for a level of scrutiny and resentment that went far beyond anything Coach Dambrot had experienced in the previous two years. Dru had read a lot of books on coaching, but there was no manual for how to deal with the circus-like atmosphere that engulfed his program.

On top of all the media coverage, Dru saw things slipping in practice. Although the team bounced back from the back-to-back losses and started beating teams by wide margins, St. V had lost its sense of urgency. In practice, they were quick to question Dru's instructions, as if they knew better than he did. And away from the court, the guys were partying.

Although he was caught up in the moment, LeBron also realized what was going on. "The *Sports Illustrated* cover had made us all into rock stars," he reflected years later, "only reinforcing our sense of our own invincibility."

An incident toward the end of the season crystallized how challenging things had become for Coach Dru. After Romeo used the F-word multiple times in practice, Coach Dru ordered him to do push-ups.

Romeo had a favorite retort: "Fuck you."

At wit's end, Dru kicked him out of practice.

After his freshman year, Patrick Vassel had known his basketball days at St. V were over. The team was simply too talented and the competition too stiff. Instead, Vassel set his sights on his honors classes, the school's theater club, and his budding interest in student government. But Vassel continued to see LeBron regularly at school. Their hallway lockers were next to each other.

Vassel was tightly wound and worried incessantly about his grades, the burden of choosing a college, and what he was going to do with the rest of his life. It was a lot to think about. When he looked at LeBron, he saw self-assurance and self-confidence, a guy who had focus and direction and knew exactly where he was going in life. One day, the two of them were at their lockers when LeBron dropped a piece of paper. Vassel looked down and immediately recognized it as a pre-ACT report. It was an important document for students preparing to take college-entrance exams.

Vassel picked up the paper and handed it to him.

Without looking at it, LeBron stuck it in his locker and closed the door.

Vassel envied his attitude toward it.

"Here I was with my AP classes and my Midwest white anxiety about everything in the world, trying to make sure my locker was locked," Vassel explained. "He was just so the opposite of me. His relationship to the ACT report was: 'This is not an important piece of paper. I'm not worried about it.' And I couldn't fathom that. He had an awareness when something really mattered and when something really didn't matter."

But LeBron's life was hardly free of stress. He simply became adept at cordoning off the more complex aspects of his life. At times, it seemed, everything he touched was a double-edged sword. For instance, he loved seeing himself on the cover of *Sports Illustrated*. He was so proud that he stockpiled stacks of the magazine in his bedroom. But being compared to Michael Jordan? That felt more like a curse than a compliment. The worst part was that there was no one else who could relate to what he was going through—no one else was being portrayed as the second coming of the greatest basketball player of all time.

The pressure he felt was immense. He even tried marijuana more than once with his friends, but he didn't like the way it made him feel, especially on the court. So he abandoned that pretty quickly. As much as he loved basketball, the burden of feeling like he was always onstage—even when he was doing something as routine as going into a study hall—took a toll.

One of the things that helped him escape was watching other people perform, especially in movies and television shows. In his junior year of high school, he even took an interest in the plays and musicals at St. V. With the state basketball tournament fast approaching, LeBron went to see the school's production of *Annie*.

Vassel was involved in the production and was thrilled to see LeBron in the audience.

For LeBron, it was his first time seeing a live performance of the musical about the orphan girl taken in by the billionaire Oliver Warbucks. It was a nice escape from the whirlwind that had become his life.

When LeBron cheered, Vassel felt a sense of pride and purpose.

More than twenty thousand fans packed a sold-out Gund Arena in Cleveland for the semifinal round of the state tournament. It was the largest crowd ever for a high school game in Ohio. The only time the Cavaliers had sold out that year was when Jordan and the Wizards had been in town. LeBron was as big a draw as Jordan. He had received *Parade*'s Player of the Year trophy, making him the first junior to be recognized as the nation's top player. He was also set to receive the Ohio Mr. Basketball Award from the Associated Press for the second straight year. But it was the afterglow of his cover treatment in *Sports Illustrated* that caused fans to treat him and his teammates more like a rap group than a high school basketball team. Fans had camped out on the street before tickets went on sale, and scalpers were getting as much as $200 a ticket on the street just before tip-off.

St. V won by forty. And in the rounds that followed, the crowds kept turning out and St. V kept winning. Everyone expected them to win a third straight state title.

Coach Dru warned his team about being overconfident.

But LeBron and his teammates dismissed his concerns. St. V had gone unbeaten since dropping those two games back in mid-February. They were blowing teams out. And in the championship game they were set to face Roger Bacon, a Catholic school that St. V had already beaten earlier in the season. LeBron's attitude was: *We're St. Vincent–St. Mary. Nobody can mess with us. They're a predominantly white team with a few Black kids. How can they beat us?*

The night before the game, the players and the cheerleaders carried on in the hotel until way past midnight. Coach Dru erupted, bawling everyone out, ordering the cheerleaders back to their rooms, and questioning the commitment of his players. But even after he went back to bed, the players continued carrying on until dawn, some of them sneaking girls into their rooms.

The game didn't go as expected. Unintimidated, Roger Bacon led by one at the half. They were up five heading into the final quarter. Late in the fourth quarter, Romeo fouled out. Then with Roger Bacon clinging to a three-point lead with seventeen seconds left, St. V missed a three-point attempt and then fouled the rebounder. In frustration, Little Dru hurled the basketball at the rim, drawing a technical foul.

"What are you doing?" LeBron yelled, shaking him. "There's still time left."

The technical foul awarded Roger Bacon two shots and the ball, putting the game out of reach. Humiliated, Dru's eyes welled up. Sian wrapped his massive arms around him. Willie started crying. Romeo had tears in his eyes and was so furious he was looking to fight someone.

LeBron was about the only one who didn't cry. He and his teammates had no one to blame but themselves. They were the superior team. But they had developed swollen egos. At times they had acted like jerks. And they had ignored the coach and his warnings one too many times.

LeBron approached the Roger Bacon players and shook each player's hand.

It had been a long, exhausting season. And the way it ended left a bitter taste in his mouth.

TEN

HUSTLE

LeBron and Maverick were spending more and more time together. They talked daily. And when LeBron needed to get away, he'd call Maverick, who would leave campus at the University of Akron at the drop of a hat and go pick up his friend and take him for a ride. In the aftermath of the *Sports Illustrated* cover story, they discussed the onslaught of people angling for access to LeBron. By the spring of 2002, LeBron and Maverick started using the term *inner circle* and agreed on the need for LeBron to form one. In Maverick's view, LeBron was like gold—the more it's touched, the more it loses its shine. Maverick wanted to restrict the number of people who had access to his friend.

LeBron agreed that it was time to shrink the circle around him, limiting it to close friends and family. *If you haven't been in the circle since day one*, he felt, *you're never going to be in it.* And he trusted Maverick as the ideal gatekeeper to the circle.

At the end of March 2002, the two of them decided to go to the Final Four in Atlanta. The high school season had been a grueling one and they were looking forward to the getaway. Instead of flying out of Cleveland, they were standing in the Akron-Canton Airport, awaiting a regional flight, when LeBron spotted a short, wiry, young Black man wearing a throwback Houston Oilers football jersey with the number 1 and the name MOON across the back. The numbers and letters were white with classic red trim.

LeBron and Maverick walked toward the man.

Where'd you get that? LeBron asked.

The man said he sold them.

Impressed, LeBron mentioned he collected them.

A few minutes later it was time to board.

After landing in Atlanta, LeBron and Maverick ran into the same man in baggage claim.

If you guys are gonna be down here, he told them, you should go to Distant Replays.

LeBron had never heard of Distant Replays.

The man told him it was a store that carried vintage sports jerseys. The store was the man's supplier. He handed LeBron a business card with the store's address. On the back side he had written his cell number and his name: Rich Paul.

Drop my name, Paul told him. They'll give you a discount.

Maverick had started looking at every outsider who approached LeBron's orbit with skepticism—*Some dude in a Warren Moon jersey is handing out his card in baggage claim?*

LeBron wanted to check out Distant Replays, so that weekend he and Maverick found the store. After picking out a vintage Los Angeles Lakers jersey, LeBron went to the checkout counter and told the clerk that Rich Paul was a friend.

The clerk got the owner, who looked skeptically at LeBron and Maverick. Convinced they were bullshitting him, the owner telephoned Paul. "Hey, there's some kids in here," he told him. "They're dropping your name."

Paul confirmed that he knew them and had referred them to the store.

Satisfied, the owner hung up and gave LeBron the Rich Paul discount.

Maverick made a mental note—Paul had some sway.

When LeBron got back to Akron a few days later, he telephoned Paul to tell him how much he liked the Magic Johnson jersey and to thank him for the tip.

Paul was glad it had worked out.

LeBron invited him to come to Akron to hang out.

Paul figured he'd bring some jerseys.

In the aftermath of losing the state championship game, Coach Dru did a lot of soul-searching. He knew what people were saying about him— that he wasn't up to the task of coaching a nationally ranked team that included the best player in the country. One local columnist wrote: "The biggest difference between this year's St. V team and the past two is the leader—Dru Joyce."

Never mind that St. V had gone 23-4, beaten some of the best teams in the country, made it to the state championship game, and finished the season ranked among the top twenty by *USA Today*. The notion that Dru had done a subpar coaching job overlooked the enormity of what he had taken on. The schedule he had inherited had much stiffer competition than those of the previous two years. The unprecedented national media exposure generated by LeBron created distractions that Dambrot had never had to contend with. And Dru's players were no longer the same malleable kids that Dambrot had coached—they had evolved into young men with swollen egos and a sense of invincibility. *It's never going to go back to the way it was when this group were freshmen*, Dru told himself with nostalgia for a simpler time.

When Dru looked back on the season, he couldn't help blaming himself for having gotten too caught up in the wins and losses, rather than focusing on the development of the boys. *My job*, he told himself, *is to help them become men*. He felt he had come up short in that department.

Little Dru knew that he and his teammates hadn't been easy to coach as juniors. He knew what people were saying about his father. He'd also read what some of the reporters were saying about him.

"Dad, don't worry about it," he told him. "We're going to show them next season."

Coach Dru's wife agreed with her son. "Let's just show people who you guys really are," she told them.

Emboldened by his family's support, Dru decided to lean in to the task in front of him, vowing that the boys he'd been mentoring since grade school would have a life-affirming experience as seniors. Rather than trying to engineer a softer schedule that promised an easier path to a championship, Dru went the other way. He set out to assemble the most challenging schedule in team history, one that would give the core group of players he'd been with for so long the chance to achieve the thing they'd been chasing since they started playing AAU ball as kids—a national championship.

He got to work lining up games for the 2002–2003 season against a slew of national powerhouses, including a handful of the nation's top twenty-five teams: Oak Hill Academy in Virginia; Percy L. Julian in Chicago; Mater Dei in Santa Ana, California; Redford High in Detroit; and Richard J. Reynolds High in Salem, North Carolina.

No one was going to be able to say that Coach Dru and St. V had taken the easy road.

At LeBron's invitation, Rich Paul started making trips to Akron. From the outset, LeBron's friends didn't like him. To them, Paul was an outsider, a guy who would use LeBron to help him push throwback jerseys in Akron.

But LeBron saw something different in Paul—a self-made man. Although he was only twenty-one and had dropped out of college, Paul was running a lucrative business out of the trunk of his car. He was buying vintage jerseys at $160 each from his wholesale supplier in Atlanta, and then selling them in Cleveland for $300 each. In an ordinary week he sold between $10,000 and $15,000 worth of shirts, putting him on pace to clear a half million dollars that year. Business was so good that he was looking to open a store in one of the Cleveland malls. It didn't matter to him that he didn't have a business degree. When he was sixteen he owned two cars. And he had purchased his first home when he was nineteen. Opening his own store at twenty-one was no big deal.

LeBron had never met anyone quite like Paul. The more he learned about him, the more he wanted him around. And LeBron had always been of the mindset that you can't have too many friends. He had his "inner circle," people he looked to for guidance—Eddie, Coach Dru, Maverick. He had his "best friends"—Little Dru, Sian, and Willie. But LeBron also had long made a habit of collecting new friends the way a world traveler collects stamps in his passport—Leon Powe, his AAU teammate in Oakland; Barb Wood, the St. V librarian; Carmelo Anthony, his summer camp roommate in Colorado. LeBron also had a knack for getting along with outsiders. No one else could have persuaded Romeo Travis to come to St. V, or convinced the team to let him in.

Unclear just where Paul might ultimately fit along the spectrum, LeBron was undeterred by the way his friends viewed him. When he had something on his calendar, he'd let Paul know. And although LeBron typically called on short notice, Paul always responded the same way: "I'll be right there."

When LeBron invited Paul to attend his AAU tournament in Chicago in June 2002, Paul dropped everything and went. But things didn't go as either of them had anticipated. In a game when LeBron's team was way ahead, LeBron went up for a dunk. While airborne, he was undercut by an opposing player. His feet knocked out from under him, LeBron landed hard on his wrist, snapping it.

The referee immediately ejected the opposing player for committing a flagrant foul.

Writhing in pain on the floor, LeBron cried, "Why me? Why me?"

Gloria had had it. The nasty reality was that all the hype around Le-Bron had turned him into a target. And all the talk about his hanging out with Jordan and being courted by sneaker companies had only aggravated the situation, generating more envy and resentment. But Gloria was look-ing at the bottom line—rivals were messing with her son's future and that shit had to stop.

LeBron was taken by ambulance to an area hospital. Michael Jordan's personal orthopedist treated him. And after his left wrist was reset and his arm placed in a cast, LeBron was told he'd be out of action for about eight weeks.

Over the remainder of the summer, while LeBron was sidelined and un-able to participate in AAU games or tournaments, he spent a lot more time with Paul. That LeBron's injury afforded him time to get to know Paul on a more personal level was a silver lining.

For Rich Paul, the scene in Chicago was a window into the cutthroat nature of the world that LeBron had entered. But it was tame compared to the place that Paul had come from.

Born in Cleveland in 1981, Paul was raised in an apartment in the city's gritty Glenville section. But he really grew up in his dad's bodega, called R & J Confectionery, which was located beneath the apartment. Rich Paul Sr. sold the things that people craved—beer, cigarettes, lottery tickets, and snacks. He even carried fresh donuts. The bodega was the hub of the neighborhood, and it attracted all types—drug dealers and addicts, prostitutes and johns, dice players and numbers guys. Even some thieves and killers. There was a reason that Rich Paul Sr. always carried a gun. But none of the characters that comprised his customer base messed with his kid. Rather, they helped raise him. They even looked out for him. To them, he was "Lil Rich," the kid who worked for his dad, the kid behind the counter who liked thumbing through the luxury lifestyle magazine *Robb Report*, the kid who memorized which cigarettes everyone smoked and which tickets they liked to play.

Rich Paul Sr. not only showed his son how to work and get along with all types of people; he also taught Lil Rich how to shoot dice and play cards when he was eight years old. They were tools, his father told him, to generate money in the future if he ever got in a pinch. Lil Rich got good at dice at a young age. He started winning a hundred here and a hundred there. He got used to having cash in his pocket. Then one day when he was thirteen, he got robbed at gunpoint during a dice game. In that moment, he kept his cool, remembering what he'd been taught—*Keep your eyes on the guy with the gun.* A killer, he had learned, can look you in the eye and pull the trigger. But if the gunman had trouble looking you in the eye, he probably didn't have it in him to pull the trigger. The guy who entered the dice game with a gun wouldn't look Rich in the eye. So Rich dropped the money and backed away.

LeBron loved listening to Rich. He also was pleasantly surprised to find that they had gone to similar high schools. Rich Paul Sr. did what he had to do to support his family. But he wanted his son to have a better life. He wanted him to get a formal education. So he paid the steep tuition and sent Rich across town to Benedictine High, a Catholic school with a predominantly white student body, high academic standards, and a strict dress code. Rich didn't like it. He felt out of place. And he purposely tried to flunk out during his freshman year. One afternoon his father picked him up after school and asked him on the drive home if he knew how Marvin Gaye had died.

"Overdose," Rich said.

"No," Paul Sr. told him. "His father killed him, and that's what'll happen to you if you disrespect me the way you've been doing."

It was the first time Rich had ever heard his father talk to him that way.

"Get your shit together and turn these grades around," his father said. "Or I'm going to take you out of this world."

Rich graduated with a 3.7 GPA. Not long afterward, in 2000, his father died of cancer. Rich had looked on his father as a hero and his loss left a great void, one his mother wasn't able to fill. Rich wasn't nearly as close to her, but that wasn't by his choice. She had gotten addicted to drugs when he was young, and she remained a user for most of his upbringing. At times, her addiction and her attempts to feed it left Rich and the rest of his family without money for food. Rich worried about his mother. It got to the point where he wouldn't watch television shows or movies that dealt with sexual assault because that theme conjured up fears of what might happen to his mother when she was out on the streets.

LeBron couldn't get over how much they had in common. "Inner city, dad passing away, obviously mom wasn't there all the time—I related to that *right away*," he recounted.

LeBron also admired Rich's work ethic. Rich described himself as a hustler. In some circles, that term has a negative connotation. But LeBron knew Rich's brand of hustler—someone who had learned early on how to outwork everyone else and become self-sufficient. Paul had inherited those traits from his father. LeBron also seemed to have been born with the hustle gene. He'd been a dreamer ever since he'd been left alone at night as a little boy. He'd been a hard worker since the first time Big Frankie had put a basketball in his hand. He'd been generous since Coach Dru had encouraged him to share the ball. And he wasn't afraid to take risks—going to a predominantly white school, playing for a coach with a controversial past, opening up to a writer at *Sports Illustrated*.

Over the summer of 2002, LeBron had discovered someone who had given him the feeling that he wasn't alone. Years later, LeBron reflected on that period this way:

> *The conversations that we were having were so much bigger than just basketball. It was just life. Everything from fashion to the hustler's mentality to family to growing up the way we grew up to music to. . . . It wasn't just "Hey, man, it was great to see what you did today in the game." That shit gets boring and old. The guy was teaching me shit that I thought I knew—but he had more years on me.*

It got LeBron thinking that perhaps he should make room in his inner circle for one more person: Rich Paul.

Burke Magnus oversaw men's college basketball programming for ESPN. The thirty-six-year-old executive scheduled all the men's games that aired on the network, and he managed the rights associated with those broadcasts. In 2002, ESPN did not broadcast high school basketball games. There had been plenty of proposals over the years to televise high school sports, but they'd all been shot down, mainly due to the notion that making money by airing high school games seemed exploitative.

Magnus thought that the time had come to look at the situation differently. The tipping point for him was when LeBron landed on the cover of *Sports Illustrated*. That event, Magnus felt, was all the validation ESPN needed to justify a bold experiment—airing a regular-season high school basketball game in prime time. *We are in the live sports business*, he reasoned. *LeBron is on the tip of everybody's tongue. He's the guy. We should do one of his games live.*

Not everyone at ESPN agreed. When Magnus's idea first got raised in a programming meeting, there was pushback. "I'm not sure why we'd do this," one colleague said. "We're rushing this kid into the spotlight."

Rushing him into the spotlight? Magnus was incredulous. "I'm like, 'Really?'" Magnus recalled thinking at the time. "'The guy's been on the cover of *Sports Illustrated*. Did you guys not notice that?'"

Nonetheless, the financial aspect of the equation had some folks at ESPN asking: "Should we be doing this?"

With all the consternation, some of Magnus's colleagues couldn't help wondering at the time whether LeBron was worth all the fuss. More than one of them wondered: *Is this guy really that good?*

Undeterred, Magnus forged ahead. He couldn't vouch for LeBron's bona fides as an NBA prospect. Magnus had never seen him play live. And besides, Magnus was no x's and o's guy. But he saw something that impressed him—instead of going to one of the elite prep schools, such as Oak Hill Academy, that functioned like factories churning out blue-chip high school players, LeBron had chosen to stay in his hometown and play with a bunch of his childhood friends at a little-known, local Catholic school. *He isn't a mercenary for the sake of his own career*, Magnus thought. *He's playing at his hometown school with his buddies.*

As a guy who had attended a Catholic high school in Jersey, Magnus found LeBron appealing. And with the backing of his bosses, he got the green light to televise one of LeBron's games in the 2002–2003 season. After looking over the St. V schedule, it was easy to circle the one with the most appeal—St. V versus Oak Hill.

Picking the game was easy. Figuring out how to air it was another thing altogether. No one at ESPN knew where to start. *Who do we go to*, Magnus wondered, *to get the rights to broadcast a high school game?*

Eddie Jackson had a bone to pick with Grant Wahl. He didn't like the way that Wahl had characterized him in his cover story about LeBron. In a phone call, Jackson vented to Wahl about two passages. The first one stemmed from something LeBron had said about his childhood during his interview with Wahl. "I saw drugs, guns, killings; it was crazy," LeBron told him. "But my mom kept food in my mouth and clothes on my back." That quote made it into the magazine in a section of the story that described the challenges of LeBron's "unsettled home life." Against that backdrop, Wahl wrote:

> Nor did it help that Jackson, who has been in a relationship with Gloria since LeBron was two, spent three years in jail after pleading guilty to a 1991 charge of aggravated cocaine trafficking.

Jackson didn't see why something in his past belonged in a story about LeBron. *Why dredge up something from over ten years ago?*

The other passage that upset Jackson followed a paragraph that mentioned the meeting that he and Gloria had had with Nike chairman Phil Knight. It read, in part:

> Jackson knows LeBron's in the driver's seat, yet he also knows first-hand that the distance from jail to the office of a multinational's chairman is shorter than you'd think. Not long before his meeting with Knight, Jackson pleaded no contest to a disorderly conduct charge and received a suspended 30-day sentence for his role in an altercation last July at an Akron bar.

Gloria didn't like the references to Jackson, either. The story, she thought, was supposed to focus on LeBron. So why mention that Eddie had gotten into a dispute in a local bar? That created the impression of guilt by association. Besides, who didn't have a friend or family member with a record or a drinking problem?

LeBron knew how Gloria and Eddie felt, which influenced the way he felt. He liked the cover and what it did for him—he got *Chosen 1* tattooed across the top of his back—but he didn't like the words on the inside of the magazine that humiliated the man he considered his surrogate father.

One thing was clear—now that the spotlight was on LeBron, everyone close to him would feel the heat. Midway through the summer that became even more clear when federal authorities accused Jackson of mortgage fraud. He was charged with engaging in corrupt activity, tampering with records, forgery, and money laundering. Jackson was not a public figure, and his case surely would have been ignored by the local media but for his connection to LeBron. It didn't take long for the national media to also focus on Jackson's latest legal troubles.

Fearing he'd soon be heading off to prison, Jackson told LeBron that he could use his soon-to-be vacant house at 573 Moreley Avenue in Akron. LeBron knew the place well—the modest, single-family brick home was less than a block away from Buchtel High.

Jackson was in trouble and there was little he could do to reverse his fate. But when his best friend, Randy Mims, came to him and said he needed a temporary place to stay, Jackson didn't hesitate. He told Mims he was welcome to move into his house on Moreley Avenue. But, Jackson told his friend, there was one catch—LeBron would occasionally be staying there, and when he did, he'd been promised the master bedroom. Mims would have to take the guest room.

LeBron was thrilled when he learned that he and Mims would both have the use of Jackson's house. LeBron had known Mims since LeBron was four or five. Mims was ten years older than LeBron but like an extended member of the family. Big and burly, Mims was humble and reliable. He worked for Cingular Wireless. And soon after Mims moved into Jackson's house, LeBron noted that Mims was always in a shirt and tie, and that he never took days off. He looked and acted very businesslike.

Maverick liked Mims, too. Maverick had grown up down the street from Mims's grandmother. Maverick didn't know many people who were as reliable and trustworthy as Mims.

The more LeBron watched Mims, the more he got to thinking. "Man, if I ever get in the NBA," he told him one day, "I want you to work for me."

Mims was flattered. But he couldn't imagine what a job working for LeBron might look like. After all, he worked for a wireless carrier.

LeBron didn't care about that. He was looking for people he could trust. They could figure out the job later.

Maverick agreed.

In the summer of 2002, Kobe Bryant decided to leave Adidas. With his departure, twenty-three-year-old all-star Tracy McGrady slipped into the top spot as the signature athlete at the shoe company. For Vaccaro, the pressure to land LeBron was mounting. He was counting on one of his former apprentices to help him.

David Bond had learned the sneaker business under Vaccaro at Nike, where he ultimately worked his way up and became head of the basketball business unit there. While at Nike, Bond had kept close tabs on who the top performers were at all the major basketball camps, and he stayed in close contact with the top AAU coaches, all of whom were conduits to elite players. It was all part of the *Who's next?* mentality ingrained in the Nike culture.

But not long after Vaccaro left Nike, Bond followed. Thanks to a non-compete clause in his contract, he spent a year away from the business. It was during the year he was away that LeBron burst onto the national scene. Then, in the fall of 2002, Bond joined Adidas in an executive role. On his first day with the new company, he discovered piles of what appeared to be Tracy McGrady's signature shoe—the T-Mac 2. But all the shoes were green and gold, which made no sense to him—McGrady played for the Orlando Magic, whose team colors were blue and white. *What are these?* Bond wondered, examining the shoes.

A colleague explained that those shoes were for LeBron James and his high school team.

"Really?" Bond said. "We're doing signature shoes for a high school kid?"

Vaccaro was glad to have Bond aboard. But he realized that Bond needed to be brought up to speed. At Nike, the criteria that was used to assess the viability of basketball players for shoe contracts rested heavily on outward appearance and likability. Jordan was the prototype—six six, super athletic, and possessed with so much flair that even his layups and finger rolls looked majestic. Plus, he had a smile straight out of central casting and was handsome enough that if he hadn't been a basketball player he could have been a model. Equally important, by avoiding politics and staying mum on social issues, he hadn't alienated half of America.

Bond wondered if LeBron had those qualities.

"Forget all that," Vaccaro told Bond. "LeBron's gonna be so good, so dominant, that it won't matter. He'll be on the cover of *Sports Illustrated* a hundred times. He will be the first story on *SportsCenter* four nights a week."

Bond didn't want to get into an argument with the guy who he considered the Nostradamus of basketball. He was just questioning whether Vaccaro, who had signed Jordan to his first Nike deal, thought that LeBron had the kind of charisma that Michael had. "Because he's gonna cost more than Michael," Bond said.

"Hey, David, you gotta trust me. We gotta go all in. If we sign LeBron, it will change the course of the industry."

"I'm on your side," Bond said. "I get it."

Vaccaro felt that in order for Bond to truly get it he needed to meet LeBron. He told Bond that they were going to Akron. Since Bond was going to be overseeing the development of the signature shoe that LeBron would wear once he turned pro, Bond should get acquainted with the talent.

It was September and LeBron had just begun his senior year when Vaccaro and Bond rolled into town in a rental car they'd picked up at the airport. Vaccaro stopped at a joint in Akron and ordered twelve large pizzas to go. Bond couldn't understand why Vaccaro was buying so many. *How much can this kid eat?*

When they reached the Spring Hill housing project and stepped out of the car, people were milling around, streaming in and out of the building. Bond observed that he and Vaccaro were the only white people in sight. And they were drawing a lot of strange looks as they each hefted a pile of pizza boxes and made their way across the parking lot toward LeBron's building. Bond felt out of his element as he trailed Vaccaro up flights of stairs, past mothers and kids. The thirty-five-year-old father of three lived in a modern home in the suburbs of Portland. He'd never been inside a housing project. He'd never been inside the home of a Black teenager.

The door to LeBron's apartment was open and it looked like half the neighborhood was packed inside.

Acting as if he were intimately familiar with the place, Vaccaro entered like Santa Claus delivering gifts.

Gloria threw her arms around him, grabbed a pizza, and invited her neighbors to eat up.

As soon as Vaccaro set the remaining boxes down, people started grabbing slices. Bond instantly realized why Vaccaro had bought so much food—they were feeding the building.

Wearing gym shorts and a backward baseball cap, LeBron sat on the couch in front of a fifty-inch television. With *SportsCenter* on the screen, he autographed copies of *Sports Illustrated* for neighbors and friends. Mountains of shoeboxes from Reebok, Nike, and Adidas lined the walls of the cramped room.

"Uncle Sonny," LeBron said, looking up, pen in hand, grinning.

"Hey, LeBron," Vaccaro said.

LeBron stood and hugged Vaccaro.

"This is David," Vaccaro said over the noise. "He's new."

LeBron looked at Bond, nodding.

"He's the guy that's gonna make the product," Vaccaro continued. "He just wants to get to know you."

LeBron extended his hand and said hello.

Nervous, Bond was overwhelmed by LeBron's size. He'd been around plenty of tall, wispy high school players at Nike tournaments. But he'd never seen one built like LeBron. *My God*, he thought. *This guy is like Paul Bunyan.*

While Vaccaro chatted with Maverick and some of LeBron's friends, Bond made small talk with LeBron, asking him what he was looking for in a signature shoe.

Eventually, Gloria cleared everyone out and Bond got down to business, erecting a small tripod on the table and attaching a video camera. Looking through the viewfinder, he focused in on LeBron's face.

Relaxed and chewing on a slice of pizza, LeBron stared at the lens.

The objective, Bond explained, was to do an informational interview that would help the development team back at Adidas. He had a series of get-to-know-LeBron questions. He began with a cheesy one that was designed to be an icebreaker: "What position do you see yourself playing in the NBA?"

LeBron named the five starters on the Atlanta Hawks and said, "On that team, I'd be a three." Then he named the starting five for the Boston Celtics. "There I think I'm a two or a three."

He went through the starting five for the Chicago Bulls, then the Cleveland Cavaliers, then the Dallas Mavericks.

Looking on, Vaccaro nodded slightly.

Bond was floored.

Over the next few minutes, LeBron worked his way through the lineups of all twenty-nine teams, suggesting where he'd best fit into each one. After listing the starting five on one of the worst teams in the league, he joked, "Oh, on this team I can play any position."

While people chuckled, Bond marveled. *This guy,* he said to himself, *has memorized the entire NBA. In alphabetical order!*

At the end of the interview, LeBron gave Bond a handshake-hug, double-tapping him on the back.

Bond tried reaching around LeBron to tap his back. *My goodness, he's got a big back,* he thought.

In the car, Bond looked at Vaccaro and said: "You're right. He's special."

Back at Adidas headquarters, Bond and his team watched the interview with LeBron. One of the staffers collected the starting lineups for all twenty-nine teams and cross-checked it against the 145 players LeBron had rattled off.

"My God," one of the team members said. "He's like Rain Man."

"He has a mind that's very unusual," Bond said. "He retains information in a different way."

He was starting to get what Vaccaro was saying: *We have to spend whatever it takes to win the day. We have to get LeBron to Adidas.*

ELEVEN

PRIME TIME

Gloria James had a reputation for cutting to the heart of the matter, especially when it involved her son. In 2002, she started noticing the way girls were looking at LeBron—like a ticket to riches. And not just girls. Women in their twenties, too. There were even some thirty-year-olds who wanted to date him. "There are a lot of females," Gloria told a reporter at the start of LeBron's senior year, "who would love to hem him up with a baby."

LeBron wasn't worried.

But Gloria reminded him that there were people out there who would try to take advantage of him. He was already famous. Soon he'd be rich, too. The combination of fame and wealth was a dangerous magnet, particularly to street-smart girls who knew how to open doors with a smile. At LeBron's age, Gloria felt, it could ruin his life if he got someone pregnant.

LeBron didn't view all the attention from girls as a risk. On the contrary, he liked it. As far back as eighth grade he had fantasized about what it would be like to win a state championship in high school. The best part, he had felt at the time, would be the opportunity to meet the prettiest girls at Buchtel High, which he'd thought he'd be attending. But he had ended up at St. V, where his experiences far exceeded his wildest dreams. By the time he appeared on the cover of *Sports Illustrated*, LeBron was being approached by the prettiest girls everywhere he went, from rural towns throughout Ohio to the suburbs of Cleveland to cities as far away as Chicago, Los Angeles, and Las Vegas. Even LeBron's teammates were basking in the glow of his fame, reveling in their newfound popularity among the girls.

But with just one more year of high school remaining before her son entered the NBA Draft, Gloria looked at the months ahead as fraught with peril. "Just protect yourself," she told LeBron. "Be smart."

Although LeBron got gratification from the way women looked at him when he traveled to other towns or entered faraway basketball arenas, the girl he had eyes for lived nearby in Akron. At the start of his senior year he had spotted her at a football game. She was a cheerleader and a softball player at Buchtel High and far and away the most beautiful girl in the school. The irony wasn't lost on LeBron—had he gone to Buchtel as originally planned, she'd be cheering for him and his original dream would have been fulfilled according to plan. But he hoped it wasn't too late to land a date with the prettiest girl at Buchtel.

LeBron had a friend who knew the cheerleader's name: Savannah Brinson. She was a sixteen-year-old junior.

Eager to meet her, LeBron asked his friend to get Brinson's phone number.

But Brinson rebuffed him. "Nope," she told LeBron's friend. "I'll take *his* number."

Brinson's response made LeBron want to meet her even more. He passed along his number.

But weeks went by, and Brinson didn't call.

Her silence told LeBron a few things. She didn't seem to be enamored with him. It wasn't even clear that she knew much about him or that he was headed to the NBA. In other words, Savannah Brinson wasn't acting like the kind of girl who Gloria was worried about.

LeBron remained hopeful.

After some research, Burke Magnus and ESPN learned that no television outlet could broadcast one of LeBron's games without permission from St. V. The school owned the television rights. LeBron was such a big draw that St. V had already entered a profit-sharing arrangement with Time Warner Cable to offer ten games on pay-per-view at $8.50 per game to subscribers in northeast Ohio. Magnus, however, was interested only in St. V's game against Oak Hill, a contest that the two schools had agreed to play at a neutral site in Cleveland on December 12.

Working through a promoter who understood the ins and outs of the high school sports world, ESPN and St. V came to terms on an arrangement that would enable the network to showcase the game against Oak Hill in prime time. The school did not charge a rights fee to ESPN, but the promoter who helped broker the arrangement received $15,000.

ESPN assigned the network's top talent to call the game—Dick Vitale and Bill Walton. Magnus also put together a half-hour show devoted to LeBron, which would immediately follow the broadcast. Meanwhile, he planned to promote the game across all of ESPN's platforms, including frequent mentions on *SportsCenter.*

With so much riding on the broadcast, *ESPN The Magazine* was enlisted to cross-promote the game. The magazine had planned to put LeBron on the cover of the December issue, which would hit newsstands just in time to coincide with the Oak Hill game. The assignment to write the story fell to Tom Friend, who went to Akron during the preseason to spend time around LeBron and the team. At the same time, the *New York Times* dispatched its basketball writer, Mike Wise, to Akron to profile LeBron. It was a foregone conclusion that LeBron was going to be the number one pick in the next NBA Draft. And with ESPN taking the extraordinary step of showcasing one of LeBron's high school games, the *Times* wanted to get ahead of the ESPN broadcast.

LeBron loved the fact that one of his games was going to be on ESPN. It would mark his first chance to perform in front of a national audience. It was surreal seeing the game teased on *SportsCenter.* But he was leery about talking to Tom Friend and Mike Wise, both of whom requested interviews. LeBron talked to Maverick, who shared his reservations.

Reluctantly, LeBron agreed to talk to both writers, but he was careful not to say anything revelatory. Maverick said more to Mike Wise than LeBron did. And LeBron ended up shutting down completely after Tom Friend asked a question along the lines of "What do you know about your dad?" LeBron wasn't about to talk to a stranger with a pen and a notepad about something that was too sensitive to talk about with his own mother. "I keep that far, far away," LeBron told Friend.

Gloria and Eddie also talked to both writers. When the identity of LeBron's father came up, Gloria told Wise: "Eddie is his dad. Always has been. He's been a great father and a great friend to me. LeBron loves him and trusts him." Wise accepted that.

Tom Friend was more of a bulldog. He investigated the background of an alleged sexual partner of Gloria's and dug into Akron court records in search of Gloria's history with law enforcement. Eventually, he got Gloria on the phone and confronted her with his findings. Friend also looked into Eddie's criminal history and questioned his motives with respect to LeBron.

LeBron didn't like the direction the story seemed to be taking. Basketball season hadn't even begun, and it felt like his family was on trial.

School officials were going all out for LeBron's final year at St. V. Brand-new gold carpet with thick padding and the words FIGHTING IRISH embossed on the surface was installed in the locker room. The room was also outfitted with new lockers that had been painted dark green with a glossy finish. The team played its home games at the University of Akron, but the players would dress for practice each day in class and comfort.

Although LeBron never liked being alone, he was by himself when he ducked into the locker room one afternoon to see how it had come out. He was greeted by the scent of new carpet and fresh paint. And he discovered a man painting the school mascot—a leprechaun—on the wall. Without saying a word, LeBron admired how the image really popped.

After a few moments, Joe Phillips, a little-known local artist who had attended St. V, sensed he wasn't alone. Looking over his shoulder, he was stunned to see LeBron, who complimented his work and mentioned how much he liked to draw. Gratified, Phillips found it surreal to be talking about art with the most famous person in Akron.

For LeBron, the overhaul of the locker room was a metaphor for what the team needed—a fresh approach. He was ashamed about the previous season and the way it had played out, especially how it ended. St. V never should have lost the state championship. He'd been talking to his teammates, and they were all on the same page in terms of what they needed to do to achieve the dream of winning a national championship—buckle down and do things Coach Dru's way.

Coach Dru wasted no time testing the resolve of his seniors. With the season opener days away, he called them into his office. With the door closed, he asked them point-blank about the rumor he'd heard—that they'd been going to a hotel in Akron and bringing in girls and drinking alcohol and smoking pot.

LeBron, Willie, Little Dru, and Sian admitted to smoking pot. Romeo admitted to drinking.

"Can you imagine the headlines tomorrow: 'St. V Starting Five Arrested in a Hotel. Possession of Marijuana'?" Dru asked.

The guys hung their heads. They knew Dru was right.

"You guys have to be smarter than that," he said.

The players agreed.

Coach Dru wasn't done. He was tired of all the cursing and the pre-game rap music, too. So he was implementing a new rule—no more pre-game music in the locker room. Those days were over.

But the hardest news that Coach Dru gave his players was his decision on the starting five for the 2002–2003 season:

Dru Joyce
LeBron James
Sian Cotton
Romeo Travis
Corey Jones

Corey Jones was the only junior in the lineup. He was also a newcomer who liked to describe himself as a six-one white kid with a decent jump shot. His jump shot was more than decent, he was one of the best pure shooters among high school players in Ohio, especially from three-point range. But Jones hadn't grown up around LeBron and his friends. Nor did Jones have a deep connection to St. V. He'd never even seen a St. V game until he transferred to the school a year earlier as a sophomore and joined the team. LeBron and the guys had welcomed Jones because the kid could play. But taking Willie's spot in the starting lineup was a big deal.

LeBron was concerned with how Willie would take the news. The previous year, Willie had struggled on the court. And the pressures of playing on the St. V team had gotten to him. After one game, LeBron found him on the team bus crying. Willie tried to pull himself together before all the guys saw him that way. But LeBron sensed his friend was hurting. "Are you all right?" he asked.

Willie didn't say much. But LeBron figured out what was going on. Sian was getting recruiting letters from football teams. Little Dru and Romeo were getting letters from basketball recruiters. And everyone knew where LeBron was going. Willie was the only one who wasn't getting recruited. That realization only added to the pressure that came with playing on the most scrutinized high school basketball team in America.

The one thing that helped Willie was his decision to run for student body president. He was a long shot to win, but he wanted to show people that there was more to him than just being an athlete. His teammates rallied around him and Willie ended up winning, making him the first African American at St. V to be elected president of a class since the seventies.

Willie didn't say much when he learned that he wouldn't be starting his senior year. But LeBron and his teammates couldn't help worrying about him.

A players-only meeting was called, and Willie led things off. He reminded LeBron, Sian, and Little Dru that they'd been friends since they were kids. And this was going to be the last time they would ever play together. This was the last chance they'd have to reach what they'd been chasing since they had started playing AAU ball together—a national championship.

"This is our last year together," Willie said. "If anybody says anything about Coach Dru, I'm going at them. I won't have it."

His team-first attitude galvanized everyone.

"When Willie didn't start," Romeo said, "he could have cried and bitched about it. But he didn't. When I seen that, I realized it was something bigger than individuals. It was something bigger than all of us."

Romeo was so impressed that he addressed the team. "Today is one of the biggest, most pivotal times of our lives," he said. "One link breaks, everything falls apart. You can't ride a bike with no chain. You know what I mean? Think of it as a 'we.' A unit!"

LeBron had never heard Romeo talk that way. None of the guys had. It was a testament to Willie's influence. Looking around the room, LeBron saw that everyone was moved.

For the first time, Sian felt love for Romeo. They all did.

"Let's just go ahead and take care of business and win a national championship," LeBron told them.

After the players-only meeting, LeBron, Little Dru, Sian, and Willie got together and decided to change the Fab Four to the Fab Five. Romeo was in the club.

A few days later, St. V faced George Junior Republic, the team that had upset them the previous year by manhandling LeBron with intentional fouls. Coach Dru told his team that the opposing coach intended to use the same dirty tactics again.

St. V started the game in a full-court press and never let up. Even when

St. V started running away with the game, they kept pressing and pressing and pressing. Right down to the final seconds. The final score was 101–40. This time it was the other coach's turn to complain about tactics.

But Coach Dru didn't care. His team was 1-0. The season of vindication had begun.

On December 11, 2002, LeBron appeared on the front page of *USA Today* and on the cover of *ESPN The Magazine*. On the same day, Eddie Jackson appeared in a courtroom in Cleveland, where he admitted to mortgage fraud and to using a stolen check worth $164,000 to open a personal management account with Salomon Smith Barney Inc. "It seems that whenever Eddie goes back to drinking," his defense attorney told the court, "he makes bad decisions."

The judge sentenced Jackson to serve three years in a federal prison starting in January. In the meantime, Jackson was ordered to remain on house arrest in Akron.

While Jackson was in court, LeBron was in school. In his English class he was studying *Macbeth*. The story of the power-hungry Scottish thane who seized the throne by murdering his king was new to LeBron. Like many teens, he found Shakespeare's words difficult to interpret. Even when Macbeth disemboweled and beheaded a slave, the graphic violence was easy to gloss over:

Till he unseam'd him from the nave to the chaps,
And fix'd his head upon our battlements.

LeBron's teacher Shawn-Paul Allison helped bring *Macbeth* to life, especially the cautionary bits about ambition and power and treachery. But as a Black teenager from Akron, LeBron felt nothing spoke to him like the lyrics of rap artists. When LeBron was nine years old, rapper Christopher Wallace released the groundbreaking album *Ready to Die*. Three years later, Wallace, who went by the name the Notorious B.I.G., was gunned down in a drive-by shooting in Los Angeles at the age of twenty-four. Shortly after that, LeBron began to pay closer attention to the words in Wallace's song "Things Done Changed."

If I wasn't in the rap game
I'd probably have a ki, knee-deep in the crack game
Because the streets is a short stop
Either you're slingin' crack rock or you got a wicked jump shot
Shit, it's hard being young from the slums
Eatin' five-cent gums, not knowing where your meal's coming from.

In a few rhymes, Wallace spoke to LeBron in ways that were more relatable than anything Shakespeare wrote. To LeBron, Biggie was a poet. On hard days, like when he learned that Eddie Jackson was going to prison, LeBron could be alone in his bedroom, blasting Biggie Smalls and knowing exactly what he meant—that if he hadn't been a rapper, his choices would have been drug dealing or basketball. LeBron didn't need a teacher to put that into perspective for him. He knew that basketball had been a refuge from the streets.

Knowing that in a matter of months he'd be a professional basketball player, LeBron struggled to stay focused in school. He took the ACT just because. Although his 3.2 GPA wouldn't matter to NBA teams, he nonetheless tried to keep his grades up. Out of guilt, he squeezed in homework when the team traveled. He even took his English teacher up on the offer to earn extra credit by sketching a picture of Macbeth.

Ever since Gloria had given him his first sketch pad when he was a little boy, LeBron had liked to draw. Initially, his pencils and pad were tools to help him escape. This time wasn't much different. Drawing a king who became paranoid and trusted no one felt less like a school assignment and more like stress relief.

When LeBron turned in his work, his English teacher was so impressed with the sketch that she affixed it to her classroom wall. It would remain there until years later when LeBron was widely known as King James and was more familiar to youth throughout the world than Macbeth, at which point his teacher took the sketch down and placed it in a bank vault.

The day after Eddie Jackson was sentenced to prison, LeBron and his teammates traveled to Cleveland to face Oak Hill Academy. Outside the arena, fans in winter coats boisterously streamed through turnstiles as event staff collected their tickets. Inside, a member of the ESPN broadcast team set the scene for viewers who were tuning in across the country: "A high school game in Cleveland has attracted a crowd of ten thousand here tonight. But it's not just any high school game. It's phenom LeBron James against the number-one-ranked team in the country—Oak Hill. LeBron mania goes national tonight."

Standing in a layup line with his teammates during warm-ups, LeBron looked over his shoulder and saw Dick Vitale and Bill Walton near center court, holding microphones and looking into a camera. He knew they were talking about him. And he realized the significance of the moment. When one of his teammates wasn't sufficiently focused on the warm-up routine, LeBron whispered in his ear, "Pay attention," and nodded toward Vitale.

When LeBron noticed that Vitale had finished his pregame bit for the television audience, he walked toward him, hugged him, and thanked him for coming.

Vitale felt LeBron's overwhelming physical presence—the thick, broad shoulders, the powerful chest, and the rock-hard biceps. But his maturity left a more lasting impression. *The teenager thanked* me *for coming,* he thought.

It was clear to Vitale that LeBron was a man among boys. He wasn't just a superior player. He seemed to appreciate the power of television and the significance of performing in front of a national audience. And he appreciated the influential role that people like Vitale played in the game.

The contest against Oak Hill wasn't close. After losing to them on two previous occasions, LeBron and his teammates put on a clinic. Early on, LeBron dazzled the crowd with a no-look pass on a fast break.

"Are you serious?" Vitale said on the air. "Are you ser-i-ous! How many college guys or NBA guys can make that pass in transition?"

With the cameras trained on him from all angles, LeBron exuded sheer joy. There was no scowling. No trash-talking. No posturing. He was at home under the spotlight, doing what came naturally to him—playing above the rim in front of a crowd. In his first prime-time appearance, he finished with 31 points, 13 rebounds, and 6 assists. St. V had pummeled the number one team in the country, 65–45.

"He's the truth, the whole truth, and nothing but the truth," Vitale said on the air.

Looking on, Burke Magnus was enthralled. He didn't consider himself a basketball expert. He certainly wasn't an *x*'s and *o*'s guy. But he had an uncanny ability to look beyond the horizon. And after seeing LeBron in person, he had no doubt that he was looking at a future television star. LeBron wasn't just a great player—he was a great performer. He had charisma. He was the rare talent who people from every demographic would pay to see. And the ratings confirmed it. The St. V–Oak Hill game was the most-watched event on ESPN2 in two years, and it was the third most highly rated basketball game in the network's history.

Yet in the aftermath of the game, ESPN faced renewed criticism for broadcasting a high school game. CBS's longtime college basketball announcer Billy Packer said that Vitale and Walton should have declined to call the game. TNT's Charles Barkley said, "They're not giving the kid any money. . . . I just don't think it's right that we should start exploiting high school kids." And *Baltimore Sun* sports columnist Laura Vecsey opined, "What plausible reason could there be for watching a 17-year-old senior play a game of high school basketball—on national television—last night?"

ESPN's decision to broadcast LeBron's game was even being debated on ESPN's airways. With his wife sitting beside him at his home in Connecticut, Magnus watched talking heads complain that the network was exploiting the youth of America.

"They're talking about *you*," his wife said.

She was being facetious. But Magnus knew that there was truth to the comment. Nonetheless, he was already scrambling to secure the rights to another one of LeBron's games—the upcoming contest against fourth-ranked Mater Dei, which was scheduled for early January in Los Angeles.

In the short term, LeBron's game against Oak Hill had sparked the momentum for ESPN to put him on television as much as possible. In the long term, the LeBron experiment led to ESPN's launching ESPNU, a new channel that would end up featuring a lot more high school games as the years went on, and the debate about exploiting kids faded away.

Everyone at St. V was buzzing about the basketball team's appearance on ESPN. In the library, LeBron and a group of his classmates crowded around a television that librarian Barb Wood had connected to a VCR. At one point, LeBron got out of his seat and fast-forwarded the tape to his favorite play of the game. "Watch," he said as he pushed play and appeared on-screen, making a no-look pass to a teammate for a layup.

The experience of seeing himself on television was intoxicating.

But privately, LeBron was hurt by ESPN's cover story about him, which had been published to coincide with the game. It was bad enough to be referred to as a "narcissist" in the opening paragraph. But what really upset LeBron was the way the magazine characterized his family. Gloria was described as "a testy, diminutive woman" who "got pregnant at 16." The article advanced the theory that LeBron's biological father was a casual sex partner of Gloria's, a man who had been convicted of arson and theft and was "well-known within the state and county penal systems."

The unproven implication that LeBron's father was a casual sex partner of Gloria's was hard to read and was particularly degrading to Gloria. No one would want to see his mother talked about so crudely, especially in a national magazine dedicated to sports and entertainment.

The story continued:

Glo's always been late to bed, late to rise—"I ain't into mornings"—and she's seen her share of trouble as well, having spent a total of seven days in county jail. According to Akron court records, she's been cited over the years for playing music too loudly, criminal trespassing, contempt of court and disorderly conduct. It's something she plays down—"there wasn't any drugs involved"—but it was never trivial to her son. Out of shame, he stopped going to elementary school.... "In fourth grade, I missed 82 days of school," LeBron says. "Out of 160."

Nothing stung more than seeing something he had said to a reporter being used to imply that he was ashamed of his mother. LeBron wished he'd never talked to *ESPN The Magazine*.

Gloria and Eddie were fuming, too. The story repeatedly referred to Eddie as an "ex-con" from Gloria's past who resurfaced right as LeBron was emerging as a basketball talent in eighth grade, just in time to capitalize on his success. The narrative pitted Gloria and Eddie against the Walker family and others in the community, suggesting that LeBron's life had become more chaotic when Eddie reentered the picture. The story went on to claim that LeBron had asked Eddie to be his financial advisor and that LeBron's life had become a "circus."

It didn't make sense to LeBron that ESPN was hyping him up on television while tearing down him and his family in print. He would never look at journalists the same again.

Savannah Brinson wasn't playing hard to get. She had simply forgotten that a guy at St. V had given her his phone number. A few weeks into basketball season, she found the number and figured she'd call him.

Thrilled when he heard her voice, LeBron played it cool and invited her to one of his games.

Brinson had never seen LeBron play basketball. Oblivious to his talents as an athlete and his status in the basketball world, she accepted his invitation. When she entered the arena, it took her only a few minutes to realize that thousands of people were on hand to watch the guy whose number was in her pocket. *Wow*, she thought. *This guy is pretty popular.* The situation was overwhelming and exhilarating at the same time.

Afterward, LeBron invited Brinson to go with him and his friends to Applebee's. The guys immediately made her feel welcome. And at the end of the night, LeBron asked her out on a date. He wanted to get to know her.

Born August 27, 1986, Savannah Brinson was the youngest daughter of Jennifer and JK Brinson. Her mother was a nurse. Her father had been a custodian at Bridgestone and spent nineteen years at BFGoodrich before taking a job with Akron Paint & Varnish Engineered Coatings. Together, her parents were working-class people who had developed a reputation in town for taking in folks who were down on their luck or going through hard times. They approved of Savannah's going out with LeBron.

When LeBron picked up Savannah to take her to the Outback Steakhouse, she was wearing a black and pink two-piece outfit. LeBron couldn't get over how good she looked. He was too excited to remember what they talked about over dinner that night. But the image of what she wore was seared into his memory.

Determined to impress Savannah's father, LeBron made sure to get her home on time.

Savannah's parents liked what they saw.

LeBron just wanted them to see that he respected their rules.

After dropping Savannah off, LeBron discovered that she had left behind her take-home container in his vehicle.

Moments later, Savannah was surprised to see him back at her door.

He smiled and handed her her leftovers.

It was a small gesture. But it impressed her much more than anything she'd seen him do on the basketball court. A boy who is sensitive enough to think of the little things in a dating relationship was a rare find. She couldn't wait to see him again.

Exhilarated, LeBron drove off. With everything happening so fast, it was hard not to speed.

TWELVE

TRADING PLACES

Snow was falling and a single piece of paper with the words SOLD OUT was taped to the box office window outside the Palestra in Philadelphia. It was Christmastime and LeBron was nearby in his hotel room, trying to muddle his way through a homework assignment. But there were distractions. The ESPN story had really upset his mother and Eddie, while causing a lot of fallout in Akron. People like the Walker family, who had talked to the magazine, regretted their decision. For LeBron, it was getting harder and harder to trust anyone in print media. The television guys—the Dick Vitale types—were different. They were more like entertainers. And Bill Walton and Jay Bilas had played the game, and now they were getting paid to analyze the game on the air. He liked those guys. But it seemed like some of the writers were playing a different game: Gotcha!

One of the exceptions was David Lee Morgan at the *Akron Beacon Journal*. His coverage of LeBron and the team didn't feel slanted. And Morgan's writing reflected the fact that LeBron was still a teenager who happened to have a gift that gave people something to look forward to every time he stepped on the court.

Wishing there were more writers around like Morgan, LeBron took out a holiday card and wrote:

Dear Mr. Morgan,

Thanks for all your support.

LeBron

Then he put the card in a mail drop in Philadelphia. *It can't hurt to have a writer like him in my corner*, LeBron thought.

A short while later, LeBron and his teammates took on Strawberry Mansion High School in front of nine thousand fans. Even 76ers all-star guard Allen Iverson dropped by to catch a glimpse of LeBron. The raucous Philadelphia crowd supported their hometown team and tried to rattle LeBron early. But he fed off the energy, swatting away opponents' shots, making passes that caused people to shake their heads, and throwing down a dunk that brought everyone out of their seats. St. V ran away with the game and led, 74–34, with five minutes remaining. Still, no one left early. In the city where Wilt Chamberlain had set a high school scoring record, the basketball aficionados gave LeBron an ovation fit for a king.

Gloria was determined to do something big for LeBron's eighteenth birthday. And she wanted it to be a surprise. She'd been talking to Celtics star Antoine Walker, who had acted as a sounding board for her and LeBron. Walker was one of a handful of NBA players who had purchased luxury vehicles from a boutique auto dealership in Los Angeles whose clients included Denzel Washington, Jennifer Lopez, Ice Cube, Queen Latifah, and Justin Timberlake. Working directly with the owner of the dealership, Gloria ordered a pewter-colored Hummer H2 and had it outfitted with television screens, a PlayStation 2, a DVD player, speakers, leather seats, and custom *King James* logos. The dealership arranged to ship the vehicle to Akron from LA on a truck. Gloria had the Hummer registered in her name.

The base price of the Hummer was $50,000. With all the extra bells and whistles, the delivery fee, and the taxes and insurance, the total price tag was closer to $80,000. To finance the purchase, Gloria approached U.S. Bank in Columbus, Ohio. She had no income and no collateral. But every credible news source in the country from the *New York Times* and the *Wall Street Journal* to *Sports Illustrated* and ESPN had quoted NBA sources saying that LeBron James would be the number one pick in the upcoming NBA Draft. Under the NBA's collective-bargaining agreement, the top pick in the draft automatically received a three-year contract worth $13 million. The only wild card was how much LeBron would get for his shoe contract, but there was no doubt that it would exceed his NBA salary.

The bottom line for the bank was that in a matter of months, LeBron and his mother would have no problem paying off the car loan. Gloria's loan application was approved, and she signed a promissory note.

LeBron was stunned when the tricked-out, military-grade vehicle arrived shortly before his birthday. There were a few fancy cars in the St. V student parking lot, but no one drove anything as audacious as a Hummer. Driving his friends around town was going to be an adventure. Seeing Savannah in the passenger seat was going to be even better.

Frederick R. Nance was arguably the most revered lawyer in Cleveland. He was also one of the city's most sophisticated litigators and dealmakers. A senior partner at the international law firm Squire Patton Boggs, he had been inspired to become a lawyer during the sixties, when he had seen vehicles with machine guns rolling through the streets of Cleveland while people rioted. Convinced there had to be a better way to bring about change, Nance pursued a law degree at the University of Michigan. Then he came home, worked his way up at one of the most storied firms in town, and ended up at the forefront of development initiatives that helped revitalize Cleveland's economy. By the time Cleveland Browns owner Art Modell dealt a devastating blow to the city by moving his franchise to Baltimore in 1995, Nance was a natural choice to help the city retain the Browns' name and colors. In a bruising legal battle, Nance negotiated a complex deal between the city of Cleveland, the city of Baltimore, Art Modell, and the NFL. In the end, Cleveland got a new football team and a brand-new stadium, which opened in 1999.

The NFL was so impressed with Nance that when Commissioner Paul Tagliabue announced his retirement, numerous team owners put forward Nance's name as a candidate to become the next commissioner. Had that happened, Nance would have become the first African American to hold the position. But Nance lost out to Roger Goodell.

In late December 2002, Nance received an unusual request—to meet a kid in high school who needed a lawyer. The kid was LeBron. The request to meet him came from Gloria. A longtime friend of Eddie Jackson had recommended to the family that they consider retaining Nance.

Nance wasn't familiar with LeBron. And he didn't typically take on teenage clients. Moreover, it quickly became clear that LeBron wasn't in any kind of trouble and that there was no specific legal matter to address. Gloria explained that LeBron was about to turn eighteen and that he was putting together a team to help him prepare for signing a shoe contract and entering the NBA Draft. Her son was going to need a good lawyer, someone experienced with handling complex business deals. And Gloria and Eddie had been told that Fred Nance was the go-to guy in Cleveland.

Intrigued, Nance traveled to Ohio State University in Columbus on December 28, where he sat with Gloria and watched LeBron play for the first time. With eighteen thousand fans cheering him on, LeBron scored twenty-seven points and led St. V to an overtime victory.

After the game, Nance agreed to represent LeBron.

A thirty-foot-long white Cadillac Escalade with frosted windows awaited LeBron and his teammates when they emerged from Los Angeles International Airport in the midafternoon on January 2, 2003. A chauffeur in a suit opened the doors. Wearing a Reebok jacket, an Adidas backpack, and Nike sneakers, LeBron climbed in and looked: two wet bars, an eight-speaker stereo system, a satellite television, and plush leather seats. There was even a sunroof. Giddy and loud, Gloria and the team filed in behind him.

When Eddie Murphy climbed into a limo for the first time in *Trading Places*, he was playing Billy Ray Valentine, a fictional poor man from the streets who swaps places with a rich stockbroker. For LeBron, this was no movie. It was real life. Although he and his mother still lived in a cramped apartment in a government housing project, LeBron no longer had to dream about the future. Courtesy of the promoter who had convinced St. V to play in the Dream Classic tournament, LeBron had a vehicle to deliver him from one life to another. And it was big enough to accommodate his mother and all his friends.

After a stop for dinner at P.F. Chang's in Santa Monica, LeBron popped his head through the sunroof. Aiming a handheld video camera toward the ocean, he looked through the viewfinder at the sunset. As a scared, lonely young boy, he couldn't have imagined that there were places in the world that looked this way. Handing the camera to one of his teammates, LeBron tore off his shirt. With the Pacific air warming his chest, he rapped while Jay-Z music pulsed so loudly that it shook the windows. His team-mates cheered him on.

Gloria swelled with joy. That was her boy.

With the college football national championship on the line, the Ohio State–Miami game was on the television, the volume muted. But Sonny Vaccaro wasn't paying attention to it. It was the night before the Dream Classic tournament, and Sonny Vaccaro was pacing in a hotel suite next to the UCLA campus, waiting for LeBron and Gloria to knock on the door. For two years, Adidas had been in the pole position in the race to land LeBron. But thanks in large part to the influence of Michael Jordan and the networking of Lynn Merritt, Nike had caught up. Reebok was in the hunt, too. But Vaccaro was only concerned with Nike. Hell, Merritt had been mentoring Maverick Carter for almost two years, and some of the Nike staff working under Merritt had been a steady presence in Akron since the beginning of LeBron's senior year. "Nike reps have been living in Akron so long," Vaccaro quipped to a colleague, "they will have to pay Ohio taxes."

Adidas was still working every angle. The suite adjacent to Vaccaro's was stocked with shiny new Adidas sweat suits, sneakers, and towels with the words *St. Vincent–St. Mary* embossed on them. There were custom T-shirts with each player's name on the back. And brand-new white uni-forms, custom-made for the game against Mater Dei, hung on a rack, each player's name sewn on the back. When St. V stepped onto the court, LeBron and his teammates would be dressed as well as the Los Angeles Lakers.

In the end, though, flashy uniforms and cool merch weren't going to win the day for Adidas. If Vaccaro wanted to overcome the allure of Air Jordan, he knew there was only one thing left to do—go for broke. It was well understood by industry insiders that Nike was prepared to spend upward of $25 million to sign LeBron. That figure would represent the richest price ever offered by a shoe company to secure a basketball player's services—even Michael Jordan hadn't received anything remotely compa-rable to that kind of money for his Nike deal—prompting the *Wall Street Journal* to weigh in that "somebody is going to lose their shirt on this kid."

But Vaccaro disagreed and was prepared to push the envelope a lot further. He'd been talking with his associate David Bond and other senior executives at Adidas about what it was going to take to win the day.

Shortly after Ohio State upset Miami, he heard the knock on the door.

LeBron had had a busy day—a shootaround with the team, a press conference, a luncheon in Beverly Hills. And he'd just spent three hours watching the football game. It was late. But the night felt young as he trailed his mother into Sonny's suite, wearing baggy jeans and a T-shirt.

Gloria couldn't help being a bit nervous. This was a business meeting, and normally she'd lean on Eddie Jackson for support. But Eddie was homebound in Ohio.

Sonny and Pam led them past David Bond into a private room and closed the door. LeBron sat on the bed, his back resting against the headboard. Gloria sat next to him.

After some back-and-forth about the formal offers that would soon be coming from Adidas, Nike, and Reebok, Sonny cut to the chase.

"LeBron, where do you think things are going?"

"Maybe like five million dollars a year?"

"That's what you think?" Sonny asked.

LeBron nodded.

Sonny smiled. "LeBron, you're gonna break the bank."

LeBron's eyes widened.

"You're going to get way more than that," Sonny continued.

Gloria looked at LeBron.

"You're worth a hundred million dollars," Sonny said.

A hundred million? LeBron and Gloria were speechless.

"That's where things should go with you," Sonny told him.

LeBron and Gloria simultaneously sprang from the bed and threw their arms around Sonny and Pam.

Listening from behind the door, David Bond heard celebrating. *Ho-lee shit!* he thought. *Sonny went there.*

Moments later, the door opened and Gloria emerged, her hands shaking.

"Good time for a drink," she said.

Bond agreed and led her to the minibar.

*   *   *

Shirtless, LeBron sat on a chair in the UCLA locker room, dressing for the game. A few feet away, Maverick Carter held a stick with a cutout of LeBron's smiling face. Playfully hiding his face behind LeBron's, Maverick was feeling good—LeBron was on top of the world, St. V was 7-0 and ranked ninth in the country, and they were in LA to take on fourth-ranked Mater Dei.

But LeBron was tense. He felt an extra incentive to beat these guys. The core players on the Mater Dei roster were the same guys who had beaten LeBron, Sian, Little Dru, and Willie in the AAU national championship game in eighth grade. These were the guys who had looked down on them for being from Akron.

LeBron wanted to settle a score. But St. V was going to have to do it without Sian, who was one of just seventy-eight high school football players in the country invited to play in the high school All American Bowl that weekend. A football scholarship was Sian's ticket to college. So he couldn't miss the bowl game, which meant the team was going to have to play without him.

"Guys," Coach Dru told the team, "there won't be any magic out there tonight."

Magic? LeBron grinned. He had something up his sleeve.

Bill Walton called the game with Dan Shulman and Jay Bilas for ESPN2. The action had hardly begun when Romeo blocked a shot by Mater Dei's best player. The ball ended up in LeBron's hands at Mater Dei's foul line. As he turned and began to race downcourt, LeBron spotted Romeo out of the corner of his eye, trailing him. Dribbling past midcourt, LeBron had only one defender to beat. Streaking into the lane and accelerating toward the rim as the defender slid in front of him, LeBron bounced the ball back between his legs. As LeBron's momentum carried him past the backboard and out-of-bounds, Romeo caught the ball in stride just inside the foul line. Without taking a dribble, Romeo elevated and threw down a two-handed dunk. The crowd erupted. "This is a town that has seen phenomenal passing, from Walt Hazzard to Greg Lee to Magic Johnson," said Walton, "and now LeBron James, laying the dime down."

Sitting courtside beside Lynn Merritt, Nike CEO Phil Knight marveled. A coach can teach a player how to pass, but you can't teach a player to see. By delivering a perfect bounce pass to a trailing teammate without ever looking over his shoulder, LeBron appeared to have eyes in the back of his head. It was a rare display of basketball artistry that Los Angeles fans had gotten used to seeing from Magic during the Lakers' Showtime years.

From his courtside seat, Sonny Vaccaro looked at Knight looking at LeBron like an action figure from another planet with a transcendent capacity to turn his teammates into stars.

St. V won again, marking the third time in three weeks that they had knocked off a top ten team.

After the game, Vaccaro approached Knight and whispered in his ear, "Be ready for a fight."

Knight smiled.

Vaccaro didn't.

THIRTEEN

HIGHER EDUCATION

Rich Paul was a young guy. But he had a mature outlook. "You're born into the world under circumstances you can't control, that maybe you wouldn't choose," Paul once said. "But whatever those are and how they are faced will determine how you then move through the world as an adult."

Maverick Carter couldn't help being impressed with LeBron's new friend. Despite having dropped out of college, Paul seemed smarter than most adults that Maverick had encountered. And within a year of meeting Rich, Maverick was on the verge of dropping out of college himself in order to work full-time helping LeBron advance his NBA career. During this period, Maverick had started to feel a kinship with Rich. They bonded over similar life experiences and a shared outlook toward the future. Brimming with ambition, they were both determined to break down the walls that had limited how far their fathers could go in life. And they were both relentlessly determined to do whatever it took to protect LeBron and advance his interests.

One of the first times that Maverick and Rich joined forces to support LeBron occurred in the aftermath of LeBron's successful trip to Los Angeles. The day after LeBron and Gloria got back to Akron, they said good-bye to Eddie Jackson, who headed off to a prison in Pennsylvania, ninety miles east of Pittsburgh. For the next three years, Eddie would be known as inmate no. 38980-060.

Eddie promised to write.

Gloria was beside herself. As her son was ascending, her confidant was going away.

LeBron struggled to come to grips with what was happening. There was no instruction manual for coping with the trauma of watching a parent go to jail.

Both Maverick and Rich knew that LeBron viewed Eddie as a father. And although they couldn't snap their fingers and make the loss and confusion go away, they could both relate to the experience of watching loved ones go into the teeth of the criminal justice system. Maverick's father had done time, so Maverick knew firsthand the range of emotions that come with having a parent behind bars. And Rich had grown up in a neighborhood where cops had routinely manhandled young Black men. One day, two officers had entered Rich Paul Sr.'s store and grabbed Rich's brother. After words were exchanged, one of the officers struck Rich's brother in the face with his gun. Rich Paul Sr. sprang from behind the counter with a pistol in each hand and confronted the cops, telling them, "This ain't gonna be no Rodney King." The police ended up backing down.

Now that it was LeBron's turn to have a loved one in the crosshairs of the justice system, Maverick and Rich communicated a unified message to LeBron: *We're with you.*

On the same day that Eddie Jackson entered prison, *USA Today* released its new rankings. Fresh off the victory over Mater Dei, St. V had vaulted to the number one spot. The news that St. V was the top team in the country rippled through the school, touching off a celebration. After the principal made an announcement over the public-address system, the school day ended with a makeshift pep rally. Students painted their faces green and yellow. The marching band, led by the trombone players, blasted the school's fight song. And the basketball players were feted like conquerors who had vanquished every foe and put St. V on the basketball map.

For Sian, Little Dru, Willie, Romeo, and the rest of the players, it was one of the best days of their lives.

LeBron reveled in the moment of unprecedented school unity. But privately, he was hurting. When the cheering stopped, he went to see Coach Dru.

Fully aware of what was on LeBron's mind, Dru searched for a way to buoy him. "You should dedicate the rest of the season to your father," he told LeBron.

LeBron hadn't thought of that.

"That would send a message," Dru continued, "to people who have ill will toward your father."

That night, St. V played Cleveland's Villa Angela–St. Joseph. With Coach Dru's words on his mind, LeBron scored forty points and dunked the ball seven times, including one dunk that was probably the most impressive one of his high school career. Late in the third quarter, LeBron brought the ball between his legs while elevating, then slammed it through the rim with two hands, prompting a rapturous standing ovation from the crowd. Afterward, David Lee Morgan wrote in the *Akron Beacon Journal*, "The show LeBron James put on was . . . uh . . . um . . . err . . . indescribable."

Basketball had long been LeBron's magic carpet, transporting him away from everything going on around him to a state of bliss. The best part of the ride was seeing the fixed stare in his audience. Nothing compared to the adrenaline rush generated by the sound of applause. Validation never got old.

But the joy from LeBron's forty-point masterpiece was short-lived. Days later, the Ohio High School Athletic Association (OHSAA) contacted St. V and inquired about LeBron's Hummer. Aware that Gloria James lived in a government housing project, OHSAA commissioner Clair Muscaro requested documentation from the school on who had purchased the vehicle and the source of the financing. Under the association's bylaws, a student-athlete would forfeit amateur status by "capitalizing on athletic fame by receiving money or gifts of monetary value." Muscaro insisted that he owed it to the other schools to look into the matter. "If he has violated any of the rules," Muscaro told the Associated Press, "he would have to give up his amateur eligibility from the time the car was delivered."

By that afternoon, ESPN's *SportsCenter* reported that LeBron's Hummer was the subject of an inquiry. The story quickly spread beyond the sports pages. With US troops in Afghanistan and the Bush administration ramping up to invade Iraq to depose Saddam Hussein, the *New York Times* ran the following headline on January 14, 2003: "LeBron James's S.U.V. Prompts an Investigation." That same day, CNN's *Wolf Blitzer Reports* covered LeBron's Hummer situation as if it were a matter of national interest.

Gloria was irate. From where she stood, everyone had been capitalizing on her son—tournament promoters, ESPN, *Sports Illustrated*, cable television providers, the media, and even St. V. Yet someone was threatening to take away her son's eligibility because she had done something special for him? *Now that's rich*, she thought.

Angry and embarrassed, Gloria called attorney Fred Nance, who agreed to handle the matter.

LeBron was angry, too. The *New York Times* had pointed out that Gloria lived in public housing. "Asked how she could secure such a loan," the *Times* reported, "a person with knowledge of the family's situation who spoke on condition of anonymity said, 'LeBron James is collateral enough.'" It felt to LeBron like the press was going out of its way to embarrass his mother. But LeBron dealt with insults and adversity differently than his mother did. While Gloria would speak her mind, LeBron kept his emotions bottled up until he got on the hardwood.

At St. V's next home game at the University of Akron, LeBron showed up with a remote-controlled Hummer. During pregame warm-ups, he brought the toy onto the court and maneuvered it around the floor at high speeds. His teammates laughed while reporters took in the scene. It was a playful way of giving the middle finger to OHSAA and anyone else asking questions about his mother.

Then LeBron went out and dropped fifty points on the opposing team, whose fans were wearing T-shirts with the words I WISH MY MOMMY BOUGHT ME A HUMMER. LeBron set a record that night, nailing eleven three-point shots. When Coach Dru lifted him from the game with a minute to play and St. V up by more than thirty points, the hometown crowd gave LeBron a long, rousing ovation. Meanwhile, Gloria, wearing a jersey that said LEBRON'S MOM, walked toward the visitor's section of the stands and used a picture of LeBron's face to fan herself. St. V improved to 11-0.

Akron Beacon Journal reporter David Lee Morgan tried to look at the situation from the perspective of LeBron and Gloria. After the game, Morgan interviewed Coach Dru, who told him, "I really think this is a class issue. Because LeBron is of a certain station in life, he's not supposed to have that. . . . Here we are about to go to war, about to send a lot of young men to where they lose their lives, and we're focusing on his birthday gift."

Fred Nance reviewed the OHSAA bylaws governing gifts and concluded that Muscaro's investigation was much ado about nothing. There was no prohibition against a parent giving a child a gift. The fact that the gift was beyond Gloria's financial means was irrelevant. The only question was whether Gloria had indeed purchased the vehicle. And the vice president of U.S. Bank in Columbus provided the answer by faxing a letter to OHSAA verifying that it had loaned the funds to Gloria that were used to purchase the vehicle.

After OHSAA received documentation from the bank, Muscaro still declined to clear LeBron. "All I can say is that the investigation is still ongoing," he told the press.

Nance told Gloria and LeBron not to worry—they'd done nothing wrong. When the grandstanding was over, the matter would be resolved in their favor.

For LeBron and Gloria, it was a new experience to have a powerful lawyer in their corner. But LeBron was also unaccustomed to needing a lawyer. He'd never been in trouble. He'd never even been investigated. Although he recognized in hindsight that it would have been wiser for his mother to wait a few more months before giving him a Hummer, he also realized that in a few more months he'd have so much money that his mother would have been deprived of the opportunity to surprise him with a luxury vehicle. It aggravated him that his mother's attempt to express her love for him had been used to call his eligibility into question. But it was particularly galling to see journalists exaggerate the situation.

"As the national media jumped on top of one another like excited spectators at a car crash," LeBron wrote a few years after the fact, "the equally ravenous Ohio High School Athletic Association scrutinized the loan my mom had gotten with the kind of intensity the IRS reserved for a mobster's tax return."

But it wasn't just the national media who were going after Gloria. Even some writers at the hometown paper were getting in on the act. In a piece titled "James' Problems Began with Misguided Mother," an *Akron Beacon Journal* columnist wrote:

> Like a good son, LeBron James sees his mom through loving eyes, speaking of her only in glowing terms. What he didn't see were the dollar signs in her eyes. As a person who has never had money, the prospect of having millions and millions of dollars clouded Gloria James' judgment.

LeBron never felt threatened by the Hummer investigation. He knew he'd done nothing wrong. But the experience and the way the media covered it went a long way to convincing LeBron and Gloria that journalists just want a piece of you, something for nothing.

Although Eddie Jackson was in prison, he still had a lot of friends on the outside, many of whom he tried to remain in contact with through letters and occasional phone calls. One of Jackson's friends was Joseph Hathorn, who worked at Next Urban Gear, a retail store in Cleveland that sold vintage jerseys. Hathorn was also a trustee of Project: LEARN, a nonprofit focused on improving adult literacy. During the Hummer investigation, Hathorn reached out to LeBron and said he'd heard that LeBron had made the honor roll. He congratulated LeBron and invited him and his friends to visit the store.

Days later, LeBron drove a bunch of his friends to Cleveland in the Hummer. When they entered the store, Hathorn mentioned that lots of professional athletes and celebrities had shopped there. He pointed to all of the autographed pictures on the wall.

At Hathorn's suggestion, LeBron signed a picture of himself to be added to the wall.

While LeBron milled around the store, Hathorn grabbed a couple of jerseys and removed the price tags.

LeBron was about to leave when Hathorn handed him a bag. "There's something in there for you," he said.

LeBron looked inside and discovered two vintage jerseys—those of Gale Sayers and Wes Unseld. He looked up at Hathorn. "You don't have to do that," LeBron told him.

Hathorn said he was proud of LeBron for making the honor roll. The shirts were his gift.

"Thank you," LeBron said. "I'm glad somebody recognizes that I'm a good student."

LeBron was too polite to tell Hathorn that he already owned a vintage Wes Unseld jersey.

On January 27, 2003, OHSAA commissioner Clair Muscaro finally cleared LeBron of having violated any rules when he received a Hummer from his mother for his birthday. Three days later, Muscaro read a story in the *Plain*

Dealer that mentioned LeBron's recent visit to Next Urban Gear. A store employee had indicated that LeBron had received two vintage jerseys in exchange for autographing a photo of himself for the store's wall.

Muscaro couldn't help himself. He called the store and spoke to the employee who had been quoted in the story. The employee said that he wasn't the one who had given the jerseys to LeBron. But he confirmed that the two jerseys were valued at $845. He added that he couldn't say for sure what had transpired between LeBron and the employee who had given him the shirts. Muscaro also spoke to the store's co-owner, who warned him that aspects of the newspaper story about LeBron's visit to the store might have inaccuracies. The co-owner offered to talk to his employees and get to the bottom of what had taken place, but he would need the remainder of the day to get to everyone.

Muscaro telephoned St. V and asked to speak with LeBron.

LeBron was in class when Muscaro called. When he got word that Muscaro wanted to speak with him about vintage jerseys and a story in the paper, LeBron couldn't believe it. Hoping to avoid another controversy, he left school, drove home, retrieved the two throwback jerseys, and headed to Cleveland to return them.

Gloria, meanwhile, advised the school that LeBron would not be talking to Muscaro. Fred Nance would be handling the matter, and any outreach by OHSAA should go through him.

St. V passed that information along to Muscaro when he made a second attempt to reach LeBron at the school.

Although Muscaro had just dealt with Nance on the Hummer investigation, he made no attempt to go through Nance to get LeBron's side of the story. Instead, Muscaro called Nance's office shortly after three o'clock that afternoon and notified him that he'd made his decision. Minutes later, Muscaro issued a formal statement announcing that LeBron James was banned for the remainder of the season. "In talking with the store's personnel, I was able to confirm that on January 25, the merchant gave the clothing directly to LeBron at no cost," Muscaro said. "Accordingly, this is a direct violation of the OHSAA bylaws on amateurism because LeBron did capitalize on athletic fame by receiving these gifts."

It was the first time in fourteen years that OHSAA had invoked the gifts prohibition rule to declare a student-athlete ineligible.

LeBron had just left the store and was driving back to Akron when he got a call on his cell phone from Nance. Speechless, LeBron listened as Nance broke the news.

LeBron struggled to process what he was hearing—his high school career was over.

It was clear to Nance that Muscaro had jumped the gun. After spending nearly three weeks on a Hummer investigation that should have been concluded within days, Muscaro was throwing the book at LeBron just twenty-four hours after reading a short newspaper story about two vintage jerseys. But before Nance could formulate a plan on how to proceed, he needed time to do what Muscaro had failed to do—gather all the facts.

St. V was scheduled to practice that afternoon at five thirty. By then, Muscaro's decision to banish LeBron had already ricocheted across the country. It was being discussed on sports radio talk shows from New York to Los Angeles. And it was the lead story on ESPN's *SportsCenter*. When LeBron pulled into the school parking lot, he saw television satellite trucks lined up across the street and a crowd of reporters and random people gathered outside the gym. A man in a trench coat with a box over his head with eyeholes cut out was holding a handmade sign that said OHSAA SUCKS.

Wiping tears from his eyes, LeBron stepped out of his Hummer and into the tumult. A small mob of photographers and cameramen rushed toward him. Outmaneuvering them, LeBron darted into the school through a back entrance.

The team was in the locker room.

LeBron entered as Coach Dru was telling his players what was going on. In addition to declaring LeBron ineligible for the remainder of the season, OHSAA also had declared that St. V's most recent victory over Buchtel would be treated as a forfeit because it had occurred the day after LeBron was given the jerseys. As a result, the state had changed St. V's record from 14-0 to 13-1.

The boys were bewildered. *No team could beat them, but some dude could just take away their undefeated season?*

LeBron buried his face in his hands.

Feeling like they were being hit from all sides, Dru told his guys that the focus now had to be on the team. They were going to have to come together and learn to play without LeBron. He also gave them some advice on how to handle the crush of reporters that would be waiting for them at the conclusion of practice. "Nobody talks to anyone," he said.

That night, LeBron was reeling. He viewed Muscaro as a one-man posse that had wreaked havoc on his triumphant senior season and snuffed out his dream to win a national championship with his childhood friends. But LeBron also looked in the mirror and couldn't help feeling guilty for letting down his teammates. Angry at himself, he wished he'd never taken those damn jerseys. He told himself that he should have known better.

The abrupt end to LeBron's basketball season was an unimaginable result that neither Maverick nor Rich knew how to reverse. Eddie might have had words of wisdom, but he was behind bars. And Gloria was beside herself. The worst part was that school officials seemed content to go along with OHSAA's decision. In one day, it seemed, all hell had broken loose.

Fred Nance had a different perspective, one that came from years of dealing with big conflicts and big egos. He remembered what it was like the morning after the Cleveland Browns had loaded up eighteen-wheelers in the middle of the night and left town for Baltimore, leaving behind shuttered offices, a vacant stadium, and a devastated fan base. In that case, one man—Browns owner Art Modell—had in fact wreaked havoc on the city's psyche and its economy. In the big scheme of things, LeBron's case was not nearly as consequential. Yet Nance recognized that LeBron was going through something extraordinary, especially for a high school student. And the national media was covering the situation like a sporting event.

Looking at LeBron's banishment from a legal perspective, Nance felt that his client had certainly been harmed—there had been a rush to judgment, which led to an excessive punishment. In Nance's world, the legal term for Muscaro's decision was *arbitrary and capricious*. The remedy was not overly complicated. But the first step was for LeBron to do something that doesn't come easily to anyone who feels they've been wronged—demonstrate contrition.

Before going to bed that night, LeBron sent a letter to Muscaro:

I want to start by apologizing for this and any other recent controversy involving me. As you might imagine, there are as many minuses as there are pluses associated with having become something of a celebrity, and I have been forced to make some very important adjustments in my personal lifestyle because of it.

In the letter, LeBron took responsibility for his actions, acknowledging that he had visited the store and had accepted two jerseys. But he indicated that he had been unaware of their value, and he explained that he had returned them as soon as he realized that he might have violated a rule. He closed his letter by speaking from the heart:

> Commissioner Muscaro, I have worked long and hard at realizing two dreams. Being a good student and an exceptional athlete. Basketball is my life. My senior year is very, very important to me and I want to complete it with honor and distinction.

Nance was impressed. He knew plenty of adults who wouldn't have been willing to muster the humility to write a letter like that.

LeBron hoped it would make a difference.

It didn't. OHSAA seized on the sentence in the letter where LeBron acknowledged receiving the jerseys as an admission that he had profited from his athletic achievements. In other words, OHSAA treated the letter like an admission of guilt. Muscaro wasn't budging.

LeBron concluded that the letter had done no good.

But Nance was focused on how a judge would view LeBron's letter, and, more important, Muscaro's reaction to it. The combination of such a harsh punishment and a cavalier response to a teenager's written apology had set the table for a legal challenge.

Nance prepared a motion for a temporary restraining order and a preliminary injunction to block OHSAA from revoking LeBron's eligibility.

St. V librarian Barb Wood was not the kind of person to seek out media attention. And she steered clear of controversy. But when she learned that OHSAA had banned LeBron, she couldn't keep quiet any longer. "People couldn't wait for him to fail," she told David Lee Morgan at the *Akron Beacon Journal.* "They couldn't wait to knock him down. It's just so sad because I see him come to school every day and I see how hard he works in class every day. When I found out, it just made me sick to my stomach."

Patrick Vassel felt the same way. He'd been watching LeBron since middle school when they'd been in Coach Dambrot's summer basketball camp together. Each year it had become harder and harder for Vassel to comprehend the enormity of everything going on around his high school locker mate. In Vassel's mind, LeBron had lifted St. V to new heights, giving the school an identity. His individual success had created opportunities for plenty of other people at the school to shine. Vassel was among them. As a leading member of the student government, Vassel was frequently called upon to interact with members of the national media who came to the school to write stories about LeBron. When a *New York Times* feature writer visited Akron earlier in the school year, Vassel had been his escort. He even ended up getting interviewed and quoted in the *Times*, an experience that he found surreal.

For Vassel, the opportunity to meet journalists from some of the most esteemed publications in the country was more educational than what he could learn from a textbook. On February 2, Vassel went to Rhodes Arena to cheer on the basketball team. The gym was packed, and LeBron was in street clothes. And lots of reporters were on hand to document the outcome of St. V's first game without its star player. Shortly after the game got underway, Vassel got a tap on the shoulder from a school administrator.

"Do you want to come sit with Deion Sanders at halftime?" she asked.

Vassel was speechless. In the nineties, Sanders had played professional baseball and professional football at the same time, earning the nicknames "Prime Time" and "Neon Deion." Vassel had loved watching him play.

The administrator explained that Sanders was on assignment from CBS News. He was in town to interview LeBron for a segment on *The Early Show*. The school was looking for a student who could spend some time with Sanders during the game.

"Sure," Vassel said.

LeBron wasn't built to be a spectator. Wearing a cream-colored suit over a black shirt, he sat on the bench with the second string, cheering on his teammates in a hard-fought contest against the Canton McKinley Bulldogs. For much of the game, it looked as though St. V might lose. But they ended up winning by one point.

Afterward, LeBron went off with Deion and a camera crew from CBS. As a boy, LeBron had loved watching Sanders. He was one of his favorite players. Now he was being interviewed by him.

Sanders wasn't like the writers LeBron had talked to. In 1989, when Sanders was twenty-two, he hit a home run in a Yankee uniform and scored a touchdown in a Falcons uniform *in the same week*. As a former athlete who had spent his career in the limelight, Sanders was coming from a totally different place than other journalists did. Rather than asking probing questions, he related to what LeBron was experiencing and afforded him an opportunity to say what he wanted to say.

Comfortable, LeBron told Sanders, "If I had known I was violating anything, I would have never done it. I would have never jeopardized my eligibility. I would have never jeopardized my team. It was just me and a bunch of my friends went in there and the guy said, 'You know, I'll give you a couple of jerseys for your reward for being on the honor roll.'"

Sanders could relate.

LeBron's sit-down with Sanders aired on CBS the same day that a new headline appeared on ESPN.com: "Please Don't Cry for LeBron James." *ESPN The Magazine's* Tom Friend was back, this time with an opinion piece that pulled no punches. Insisting that LeBron wasn't a victim, Friend wrote, "Don't tell me he hasn't had his hand out. It's been out." And he insisted that the court in Ohio should question LeBron about his finances. "There's more here than meets the eye," he wrote. "More than we even know about."

LeBron and Gloria had felt wounded after Friend's cover story a month earlier. The opinion piece came across like an attempt to pour salt in the wound. "Just because he doesn't have a strong parent telling him to say no," Friend wrote, "that doesn't mean he's crooked. It just means he is what he is."

Lines like that helped deepen LeBron's distrust of print journalists and landed *ESPN The Magazine* on his blacklist.

* * *

James R. Williams was the first African American to serve as the Summit County Court of Common Pleas judge. Earlier in his career, he had been appointed by President Jimmy Carter to be the US Attorney for the Northern District of Ohio. He had a distinguished record as a civil rights leader. It fell to him to consider LeBron's request to have his eligibility restored.

Reporters packed the courtroom when Fred Nance argued his points:

Muscaro failed to notify LeBron that an investigation was underway.

Muscaro failed to provide LeBron with notice of the accusations against him.

Muscaro failed to provide LeBron with a hearing.

Muscaro failed to talk to Joseph Hathorn, who had given LeBron the shirts, choosing instead to rely on the word of a store clerk who wasn't involved in the transaction.

Nance then introduced sworn statements from employees at the clothing store in Cleveland, including one from Joseph Hathorn, whose testimony of what had transpired was more complete than the conjecture put forward by OHSAA.

In sum, Nance argued, LeBron had received a gift from a family friend who wanted to recognize LeBron for his academic achievement. "The circumstances of the public pressure Muscaro must have felt from finding no violations regarding the Hummer purchase must have impacted the undeniable rush to judgment in this instance," Nance said. "The two events, separated by a mere four days, obviously impacted Muscaro's judgment."

A lawyer for OHSAA argued that Muscaro's decision was dictated by the rules. Moreover, he argued that Muscaro's decision had not subjected LeBron to "irreparable harm," which was the standard for granting LeBron's request for a restraining order. "His prospects with the NBA are well known and will not be adversely affected by the loss of his amateur status," the OHSAA lawyer argued.

Twenty-four hours later, Judge Williams issued his ruling: "LeBron James' eligibility is restored as of this day, February 5, 2003, and he can begin practicing with the team."

Nance was like a velvet hammer coming down on a mosquito. For LeBron, the experience was a master class in dealing with adversity. It was also a preview of how his athletic superiority and the extraordinary wealth that came with it would afford him access to the levers of power, and how those levers could be pulled to make the wheels of justice move faster to deliver a more favorable outcome. Looking ahead to his upcoming shoe contract negotiations and his NBA career, LeBron felt grateful to Eddie Jackson for his role in bringing Nance into the family. LeBron considered Nance a keeper.

Maverick also admired Nance. He appreciated that Nance had helped navigate LeBron back into action just in time for St. V's highly anticipated tournament game against Westchester High, a team from Los Angeles that was ranked seventh in the country. Westchester was led by Trevor Ariza, a star recruit who was headed to UCLA on a basketball scholarship. Maverick recognized that Westchester was the only team left on the schedule with a legitimate shot at beating St. V.

LeBron was already raring to go. But before the game, Maverick told LeBron that Trevor Ariza's mother had been talking trash about LeBron. According to Maverick, during LeBron's suspension, Mrs. Ariza had told a Los Angeles newspaper, "This guy LeBron's suspended. Good. Now my son can finally showcase. He's the number one player in the country. He's been better than LeBron all along." It was unclear where Maverick had gotten his information. But that didn't matter. His relaying it to LeBron had the intended impact.

Camera shutters clicked when LeBron skipped onto the court during warm-ups at sold-out Sovereign Bank Arena in Trenton, New Jersey. Busloads of fans from Akron—retired autoworkers, mechanics, custodians, and blue-collar workers who had dug deep to come up with the $70 round-trip fare—roared, and more than one hundred credentialed journalists jockeyed for proximity to LeBron as he made his return. While scalpers were getting $2,500 per ticket out on the street, LeBron got in the mood while channeling the words to Eminem's new hit "Lose Yourself":

This world is mine for the taking
Make me king as we move toward a new world order
A normal life is borin', but superstardom's close to postmortem
It only grows harder, homie grows hotter.

"Tonight's the night," LeBron told his teammates.

He stepped onto the court and a fan yelled, "Show me something, Le-Bron."

In a first-quarter flurry, LeBron nailed jumpers, made layups, dunked three times in a one-minute span, and hit a three from thirty-seven feet. By halftime he had thirty-one points.

Coach Dru decided to just sit back and let him go.

In the most explosive offensive display of his high school career, Le-Bron went off for fifty-two points, single-handedly outscoring Westchester, which had forty-three points when LeBron finally checked out of the game with two and a half minutes remaining. Exhausted, he made his way to the bench as the crowd serenaded him with cheers.

Big Frankie Walker was among those who had made the trip from Akron. Overcome with pride, he shouted at the boy who had lived with him in fifth grade, "That's how you play basketball!"

Afterward, journalists converged on LeBron.

"So tell us, LeBron, did you and your teammates feel any pressure tonight?" a reporter asked.

"No pressure at all. A lot of people were asking if we were good enough to be the number one team in the country, and I think we proved tonight that we were," LeBron said.

"I was talking about controversies," the reporter said. "Have you felt pressure over all of the coverage?"

"Nope."

"You've complained about the media," another writer said. "Do you think it's right to complain? After all, the media made you famous."

"I never complained about the media. Never. I worked hard. Put in all the hours. Anyway, y'all didn't make me famous. I made myself famous."

St. V cruised through the remainder of its schedule. The state championship game against Kettering Archbishop Alter was more like a coronation than a contest. LeBron turned in another dominant performance, leading all scorers. When the final second ticked off the clock, Little Dru heaved the ball into the air and Coach Dru burst into tears. The players mobbed each other. They were the undisputed number one team in the USA Today rankings. They were national champions.

Looking around at Little Dru and Willie and Sian and Romeo, Le-Bron's mind filled with memories—growing up fatherless, the fears that his mother would never come home and he'd end up completely alone, the Walkers, Coach Dru, the brotherhood with the Fab Five. He couldn't help thinking how critical it had been for them to stick together when the Black community of Akron had accused them of being traitors for choosing a predominantly white private school over a predominantly Black public school.

After cutting down the net, LeBron was named MVP of the championship game.

"I'm glad I was named the MVP," LeBron said in accepting the award. "But there is a guy who played a lot better game than I did, so I'm giving this to Corey because he deserves it."

Jones had been second in scoring and played a flawless game. Overwhelmed, he walked toward LeBron.

In the final act of his high school career, the leading man passed the trophy to a role player.

The Fab Five threw their arms around the short white kid with a wicked jump shot.

The next day, the headline in the *Akron Beacon Journal* read "LeGone with the Win."

FOURTEEN

IN THE ROOM

It was a Monday morning in late March. Normally, LeBron would have been in homeroom at St. V, dressed in school clothes, with a backpack containing books strapped over his shoulders. Instead, he was in a locker room at a rec center in the suburbs of Cleveland, putting on his work clothes. Moments later he stepped onto the court for a practice session one day prior to the McDonald's All-American high school basketball game.

Scouts from all twenty-nine NBA teams were on hand for the workout. Since none of the other all-Americans had yet entered the gym, all eyes were on LeBron in his red McDonald's jersey. His six-eight, 240-pound frame was thick with muscle through the shoulders, chest, and thighs. His chiseled figure didn't appear to have an ounce of body fat. It was hard not to gawk at his supernatural athleticism. With an ethereal forty-four-inch vertical leap, the top of LeBron's head was above the rim when he dunked. At eighteen, he could already jump higher than every player in the NBA.

When the other high school all-Americans began trickling onto the court, the contrast between LeBron and them was stark. They were all pro prospects, tall and skilled. But LeBron was far more physically imposing, a man among boys. The scouts were also attuned to the more subtle distinctions, noting that LeBron had a habit of being the first person on the court for practice and the last one to leave. The rare combination of superior skill and indomitable drive was a priceless commodity in the commerce of professional sports.

Perhaps the most difficult thing for a scout to ascertain was what was going on inside a prospective player's head. At a time when some of the McDonald's all-Americans were still figuring out which college to play for in the fall, LeBron had much weightier matters on his mind. For a long time, he'd viewed it as his responsibility to provide a comfortable home, a car, and lifetime financial security for his mother. The time had come for him to formally notify the NBA in writing that he was entering the draft, where he was a lock to be the number one overall pick. He also had to choose between the three shoe companies vying for his services, a decision that would affect his net worth much more than which NBA franchise he ended up joining. But before dealing with the NBA or the corporations that were already lining up to offer him lucrative endorsement deals, LeBron had to choose a sports agent to help him navigate his next moves. It was a lot to contemplate for a high school senior.

Yet, the following day, none of those distractions were evident when LeBron played in the all-star game. In front of a record-setting crowd of nearly twenty thousand spectators, including Jay-Z—the man whose music was the soundtrack to LeBron's life now sat courtside to watch him play—LeBron displayed laser-like focus, showcasing his skills and earning MVP honors. In a postgame ceremony broadcast on ESPN, legendary UCLA basketball coach John Wooden congratulated LeBron and awarded him the trophy. Asked to comment on his performance, LeBron said, "First of all, I'd like to give a shout-out to my father."

Eddie Jackson had been incarcerated for three months at this point. But he remained on LeBron's mind. They stayed in touch through phone calls. And Eddie wrote letters to LeBron and Gloria as well.

Eager for updates, Eddie felt marginalized at a time when LeBron was facing some of the biggest decisions of his life. Attempting to remain involved, Eddie continued to call the representatives from Nike, Reebok, and Adidas. He also continued to weigh in on whom he thought LeBron should choose to be his agent.

Most NBA insiders figured that LeBron would sign with someone like Arn Tellem, who was generally regarded as one of the most powerful agents in the league. Tellem controlled more than 15 percent of the league's players, including many of the game's biggest stars. He was also close to Sonny Vaccaro, who thought he'd be a good fit for LeBron. Another leading candidate was Leon Rose, who was tight with NBA power broker William Wesley. Although LeBron respected both Vaccaro and Wesley, neither of them tried to influence his thinking on agents.

Ultimately, LeBron went in a different direction. In the spring, he quietly settled on forty-two-year-old Aaron Goodwin as his agent. On the surface, LeBron's choice was unconventional. Goodwin represented a relatively small roster of clients and he'd never represented a number one overall pick in the draft. His experience negotiating top-of-the-market endorsement deals was limited. Compared to some of the more established agents, Goodwin was still an up-and-comer. Nonetheless, Goodwin had always been two steps ahead of the competition in the chase to land LeBron. Back in 2001, he had watched LeBron play in an AAU game in Oakland. Around that time, he met Eddie Jackson and the two of them began talking about the prospect of Goodwin's representing LeBron. It was a conversation that lasted eighteen months.

"I recruited LeBron James for more than a year without people realizing I was there," Goodwin said in a rare interview in 2003. "There were people looking for me. Reporters were looking for me, but they didn't have a clue what I looked like. That's the way I like it. I like what I've established."

By the start of LeBron's senior year, Goodwin was practically residing in Akron, where he had also cultivated a relationship with Gloria and gained her trust. Once he was embedded with Eddie and Gloria, Goodwin also arranged for several of his NBA clients to befriend LeBron. Ultimately, Fred Nance vetted Goodwin and was impressed with his ability to represent LeBron.

"I thank Gloria and Eddie all the time for giving me this once-in-a-lifetime opportunity," Goodwin said after he officially joined LeBron's team.

Goodwin stepped into an unprecedented situation—LeBron was positioned to become one of the richest athletes in the world even before playing his first NBA game. Agents take a commission on every endorsement deal they close. With the negotiations with Nike, Reebok, and Adidas headed for uncharted territory, Goodwin turned to attorney Fred Schreyer to help him navigate the offers. It was a shrewd move on Goodwin's part.

Schreyer was the general counsel and chief financial officer for the Professional Bowlers Association. But prior to joining the PBA, Schreyer had been a senior executive at Nike, where he had handled the company's biggest shoe contracts with athletes. No one was more versed in dealing with Nike than Schreyer. And Schreyer would be invaluable in scrutinizing the competing offers from Adidas and Reebok.

While Goodwin ramped up for a round of pitch meetings with the shoe companies, he also stepped into a sticky situation that threatened to entangle LeBron. When Eddie Jackson had gone to prison, he had left behind a lot of unfinished business with Joseph Marsh and Magic Arts & Entertainment. It had been nearly two years since Eddie had approached Marsh about a loan for the stated purpose of covering travel expenses for Eddie and Gloria to meet with shoe company executives on LeBron's behalf. In the interval, LeBron's fame had skyrocketed. As a result, the value of the rights to a film based on LeBron's life had significantly increased. And the opportunity to produce the film was worth far more to Marsh than the interest he stood to collect on the $100,000 he had lent to Jackson.

Once Eddie had gone to prison, Marsh had started dealing more exclusively with Gloria. Eager to get the documentary into production, Marsh put together a business and marketing plan for the film, which was tentatively titled *King James: The LeBron James Story*. Marsh's initial recommendations for a director had not worked out. After consulting with Gloria, Marsh then sent the plan to filmmaker Spike Lee, informing him that Magic Arts & Entertainment represented LeBron in an upcoming documentary. "Gloria James, LeBron's mother, has expressed an interest in having you as an integral part of this documentary, perhaps as the director or as a producer," Marsh wrote to Lee in April 2003.

A month later, Marsh updated Gloria in a letter:

> Per your request, we approached Spike Lee with regards to directing our upcoming documentary on your son LeBron. Unfortunately, we are being told that Spike Lee is not available at this time to direct the project. You had mentioned before that you have spoken directly to Spike. . . . Would you like to attempt putting a call in to him in hopes of persuading him to be involved?
>
> If Spike Lee is unavailable, is there a short list of other people that you and LeBron would like for us to solicit as the director? If not, we have a few people that we feel are very talented and are available immediately to begin working on the project.

While trying to attach a director to the project before the summer, Marsh made two payments to Gloria, one in April and one in May. Those payments totaled $5,000, completing Marsh's original loan obligation to Eddie Jackson and further solidifying his view that he had been granted the exclusive rights to produce a film on LeBron.

Goodwin sensed conflict ahead. But he kept his focus on the issue at hand—securing LeBron's first endorsement deal.

LeBron knew that Eddie had dealings with Marsh. LeBron was also aware that his mother was in communication with Marsh. But LeBron already had enough on his plate. He was more interested in spending his limited discretionary time with Savannah Brinson than making a documentary.

LeBron and Savannah had only been dating for about six months, but that had been long enough for LeBron to recognize one of her most attractive qualities—she was unusually levelheaded, particularly for her age. LeBron had seen his share of drama queens. Savannah was the antithesis of that. For him, their time together was like a refuge. Around her, he could drop his guard, be a teenager. She was someone he could confide in.

For Savannah, there were aspects of dating LeBron that were surreal, not the least of which was the steady presence of photographers, cameramen, and autograph seekers. Going on dates in an $80,000 luxury vehicle was a trip. So was the experience of seeing her boyfriend on magazine covers and television screens. And LeBron was the only boy she'd ever met who had his own high-powered attorney in Cleveland.

Yet none of those things were what attracted Savannah to LeBron. She was drawn to his self-confidence and sense of direction. It was reassuring to be with a teenage boy who was so goal-oriented. His life was already mapped out. And while there were a lot of other girls vying for LeBron's attention, his heart was set on the one who had originally rebuffed him by declining to give him her number. LeBron was never going to let her live that down.

But LeBron had plenty of reasons to keep their relationship under wraps. He lived under a microscope. Anyone close to him was vulnerable to media exposure, and the last thing he wanted was to subject Savannah to the kind of harsh scrutiny that his mother had already undergone. It was best that the media not even know that he had a girlfriend. For her sake, Savannah should remain anonymous.

For two teenagers, the entire situation was daunting. LeBron was about to venture into the fast lane. Savannah still had another year of high school in Akron. How was this all going to go? What would happen to them? Would they last?

LeBron had a simple mantra: *Don't worry.*

At the end of April, LeBron stood at a podium in the St. V gymnasium and declared that he was forgoing college and entering the NBA Draft. Looking out at his friends, fellow students, and more than fifty journalists from around the country, he paused, remembering that time in middle school when he had written "NBA" three times on a three-by-five card after his teacher assigned him to list three careers that interested him. "It's been a longtime goal," LeBron told the audience. "And I'm happy it's finally coming true."

Days later, LeBron stepped into the boardroom at Reebok's headquarters outside Boston. Accompanied by his agent and his lawyer, LeBron sat next to his mother at the longest table he'd ever seen. Maverick took a seat at the table, too.

Reebok CEO Paul Fireman welcomed everyone and made it clear to LeBron from the outset that his company was prepared to treat him as the most important athlete in Reebok's history. It was a not-so-subtle way of distinguishing Reebok from Nike, where LeBron would be in a crowded field of superstar athletes.

Todd Krinsky, an executive over Reebok's clothing and shoe division, outlined the company's new initiative to blend music and sports in hopes of appealing to hipper, younger consumers. Reebok had just signed Jay-Z to an endorsement deal that included his own signature sneaker, the S. Carter. Reebok was also working on a deal with Pharrell Williams. And Reebok put LeBron in the same category as these entertainers. LeBron was a next-generation athlete with tremendous crossover appeal.

After the presentation, Reebok put its offer on the table: $100 million over ten years.

The room fell silent.

LeBron was astounded. Sonny Vaccaro had told him he was worth a hundred million. But that number had always felt more magical than literal.

Gloria's eyes welled up.

Aaron Goodwin tried to maintain his composure. He hadn't been expecting a nine-figure offer from Reebok.

Neither had Fred Schreyer, who remembered when Tiger Woods had turned pro, in 1996, and Nike signed him to a five-year endorsement deal worth $40 million. It was the most lucrative shoe deal ever offered to an amateur athlete. Reebok's offer to LeBron blew the Tiger deal away.

Looking to close, Paul Fireman pulled out a pen and reached for a check.

LeBron had no idea what Fireman was doing at the other end of the table.

Fireman signed the lower right-hand corner and slid the check across the table.

Goodwin picked it up and noted the amount: $10 million, made payable to LeBron James.

Goodwin showed it to LeBron and Gloria.

Gloria cried.

LeBron stared at all those zeros.

Fireman's proposition to LeBron was simple—sign with Reebok now and he'd walk out the door with a $10 million advance.

Sweating, Maverick stood and undid the top buttons on his shirt. *Holy shit*, he thought. *This shit is real.*

Goodwin and Schreyer needed a moment to confer with their client.

Fireman gave them the room. He and Krinsky stepped out, and the door clicked shut behind them.

Gloria was vocal. She didn't see what there was to confer about. Reebok's offer surpassed everyone's expectations. LeBron could walk out the door an instant millionaire ten times over.

LeBron was at a loss for words. He'd just flown in from Akron. He lived in the projects. Their subsidized rent was around $22 a month. His mother was unemployed and had to pay for groceries with food stamps. The check in his hand offered an escape from all of that. It was an instant ticket to a new life. All he had to do was say yes.

Gloria was ready to walk out with the check.

Goodwin wanted everyone to take a beat. Reebok's offer was off the charts. And Fireman had made a bold move by putting $10 million on the table. But this was a preemptive bid, one that was intended to preclude LeBron from talking to Adidas and Nike. Goodwin reminded LeBron that the game plan was to meet with all three companies before deciding.

Schreyer agreed. Although it was nerve-racking to turn down $100 million, he felt that the prudent move was to wait and see what Adidas and Nike had to offer.

Holding the check, LeBron felt torn.

Fireman and Krinsky reentered the room and took their seats.

Stoic, LeBron pushed the check back to Fireman.

Fireman and his team were disappointed. But they couldn't help being impressed. Todd Krinsky looked on in amazement as LeBron left Reebok's headquarters that evening. *He's a man already*, Krinsky thought. *He knows what's about to come to him.*

On his way to homeroom the following morning, LeBron thought: *Holy shit! I can't believe I left that on the table.*

He didn't dwell on the thought very long. It was a Friday and LeBron's classmates were gearing up for senior prom that weekend. But LeBron had other plans. As soon as school let out, he hustled off to an airfield, where a private jet awaited. The plane had been chartered by Sonny Vaccaro to whisk LeBron to Los Angeles for the pitch meeting with Adidas. There were enough seats on the luxury aircraft for LeBron's friends and advisors. Everyone climbed aboard.

Sonny had long admired the way LeBron always tried to include his high school teammates in everything he did. At LeBron's request, Sonny had secured courtside seats for them to take in that night's playoff game between the Spurs and the Lakers. A limousine picked up LeBron and his friends at LAX and delivered them to the Staples Center. Wearing a fake diamond in each ear, a backward Lakers cap, and an unzipped letterman jacket over a white T-shirt, LeBron entered the arena as if he were stepping into a future home. Hollywood moguls, pop stars, actors, and athletes occupied the seats closest to the court. The Laker Girls danced. Music pulsed. And Kobe Bryant and Shaquille O'Neal were trying to lead the Lakers to a fourth consecutive NBA championship. But the Spurs, led by David Robinson and Tim Duncan, stood in the way. The atmosphere was alluring.

Partway through the second quarter, Shaq was whistled for his second foul. Dressed in black and wearing Ray-Bans, Jack Nicholson rose from his courtside seat and tore into the referees. With his new movie, *Anger Management*, atop the box office charts, Nicholson shouted and pointed his finger as if he were in character, revving up the crowd. When the referees told him to sit down, Nicholson got louder. "This is the NBA!" he barked. "You can't tell me to sit down."

Egged on by Nicholson's defiance, fans rose to their feet, cheering him and booing the referees. The tension in the building prompted the officials to consult with security about having the Oscar winner removed from the arena for stepping onto the court. But security advised against it, saying the move might start a riot. Instead, the officials warned Nicholson that he better not set foot on the court again.

"They can't run me out of here," Nicholson sneered. "They're not going to get me out of here. I can stand here if I want to. I pay good money for my ticket."

LeBron took it all in as Nicholson's outburst ignited the crowd and Kobe led the Lakers on a run. It was the kind of moment that LeBron longed to star in—the best player in the NBA, competing in front of world-famous entertainers on a grand stage, the crowd going wild. It was a reminder of what LeBron had already figured out—that at its core, a professional sport was much more than a game; it was show business.

Suddenly, a producer from TNT approached LeBron. Courtside reporter Craig Sager wanted to interview him.

LeBron obliged. Stepping into the glow of the white light and facing the camera, LeBron felt the eyes of Lakers fans settling on him.

"With me, perhaps the most highly acclaimed player to ever participate in high school basketball," Sager said. "LeBron James, first of all congratulations on an outstanding career and a national championship. How difficult was it to handle all the attention and publicity?"

"I think for any normal person it would be pretty hard," LeBron said. "You know, from growing up and having so much adversity in my life, I think it was pretty easy. And with a couple of my teammates and coaches, it made it a lot easier."

"You'll be in the draft. But you don't know who you'll be playing for. Who would you like to play for?"

"Man, this is my long-term goal. I'll play for anybody."

Back in Akron, St. V students and teachers who were watching the game couldn't get over the fact that LeBron was on live television *in Los Angeles.* That afternoon, he'd been at school. In a post-9/11 world, it wasn't possible to get from Akron to Los Angeles that fast on commercial flights.

But LeBron was already accustomed to the kind of high-speed travel normally reserved for corporate titans. He'd also become pretty deft at doing live interviews.

"Why are you here tonight?" Sager asked LeBron.

It was a loaded question, one that required LeBron to parse his words.

"I'm here to watch Kobe and Shaq," he said. "Shaq came to my game two years ago and I'm here to watch them try to get a victory."

Everything LeBron said was true. Yet he had cleverly avoided any mention of Adidas as the impetus for his trip to LA and his presence at the game.

Staring at his television, Sonny Vaccaro nodded. *Smart kid*, he thought.

As LeBron returned to his seat, Kobe drove the lane and put up an acrobatic shot. But TNT announcers Mike Fratello and Marv Albert were focused on LeBron.

"That young man, Marv, that Craig just talked to," Fratello said, "really has handled himself extremely well under the pressures this year that he was put under."

LeBron awoke to bright sunshine, warm air, and a view of the water. Sonny had put him and Gloria up in a beachfront hotel in Santa Monica. LeBron recognized that Sonny always went out of his way to treat Gloria like a VIP. LeBron was also aware that Sonny had publicly defended Gloria when journalists had portrayed her as money hungry.

Most of the stories that had been critical of Gloria were written by journalists who had no firsthand experience with poverty. These sportswriters were predominantly white men with no reference point for what it was like to raise a child on your own as a sixteen-year-old Black girl. Sonny didn't know what that was like, either. But he'd gotten to know Gloria well enough to see a side of her that the media overlooked. "She could've taken hundreds of thousands from various people," Sonny told the *Akron Beacon Journal* in the spring of 2003. "There's nobody from the agents to the financial managers to would-be investors that would not have fronted them whatever they wanted or needed. Gloria didn't ask for or take anything."

The best chance that Adidas had in landing LeBron rested in the relationship Sonny had established with him and Gloria.

Around noon, LeBron and Gloria got into a limo that delivered them to an opulent mansion in Malibu. It belonged to a mover and shaker in the music industry. Sonny had rented the place for the weekend. And he had it staged for the occasion. Bobby Darin's "Beyond the Sea" played in the background when Sonny opened the door and greeted LeBron and Gloria.

"C'mon," Sonny said. "Check out the view of the ocean."

LeBron and Gloria walked across the marble floors, past a spread of catered food and an endless array of beverages on ice, toward a spacious room with floor-to-ceiling windows that overlooked a swimming pool and provided a panoramic view of the Pacific. It was like seeing the future.

The vibe of the Adidas pitch felt much more relaxed than the Reebok meeting had. Flanked by Gloria and Goodwin, LeBron sat on a couch that faced the water. The Adidas team sat opposite him. A long glass coffee table was between the two sides.

Vaccaro turned it over to his associate David Bond, who presented the branding plan, the marketing plan, and the product plan. Eventually, the conversation shifted to money. An attorney for Adidas entered the room with a file in his hand. He removed a contract for Goodwin to review. It contained a lot more legalese than the Reebok offer had.

Adidas appeared to be offering LeBron $100 million over seven years. But a closer inspection of the fine print revealed that a lot of the money was tied up in royalties and contingent on LeBron's hitting various benchmarks, such as playing in a certain number of games and scoring a certain number of points. The amount of guaranteed money was closer to $70 million, which was a far cry from what Sonny had led LeBron and Gloria to believe was coming.

Goodwin looked at Sonny and pointed to the contingencies provision in the offer. "This isn't what we talked about," Goodwin told him.

Sonny's jaw dropped as he looked at the language. He stood and motioned for the Adidas lawyer and Bond to follow him.

"What the fuck are you doing?" Sonny said to the attorney.

In a heated exchange, Sonny and Bond learned that a last-minute decision had been made at corporate headquarters in Germany to lower Adidas' risk by putting performance-based provisions in the contract.

Bond couldn't believe what he was hearing. They had agreed ahead of time to offer LeBron $100 million guaranteed.

But the CEO of Adidas was not as certain as Sonny and Bond that committing $100 million to an eighteen-year-old who had yet to play against NBA competition was a wise move, so the offer was changed.

It was a fateful decision that would alter the company's history.

Furious, Sonny knew what this meant—Adidas was out of the running. Reebok's offer was fully guaranteed, no strings attached. Adidas had no chance with a contingency-based offer.

Embarrassed, Sonny had a sidebar with Goodwin.

Left alone on the couch, LeBron and Gloria stepped outside to look at the water. It felt as though the ground had shifted beneath them; the mood had gone from optimistic to awkward.

After a few minutes, the two sides reconvened, and Sonny told everyone: "We're done here."

Then Sonny and Pam talked privately with LeBron and Gloria. With a forlorn expression on his face, Sonny apologized for the Adidas offer. "That wasn't what was supposed to happen," he said.

LeBron nodded.

To Sonny, it felt as though he had spent three years helping LeBron prepare for liftoff. All that time, Sonny thought he'd be along for what promised to be the kind of ride that would transform the shoe industry. But now that it was time for ignition, Sonny realized he wouldn't be joining the kid he'd gotten more attached to than any athlete he'd ever recruited. It felt like saying goodbye to a family member who wasn't coming back.

Gloria felt it, too. So did Pam.

Sonny looked at LeBron. "Go to your next meeting," he said. "But don't tell them what our number was. Negotiate the highest number you can. Do what's best for you."

LeBron hugged him.

"We know what you've done for us, Sonny," Gloria said. "We'll never forget this."

Pam put her arms around Gloria. "I love you," she said.

On the drive home that day, Sonny could hardly bring himself to say *Adidas*.

"They lied to me," he said.

Pam nodded.

"You know what I'm going to do," he said.

"You're going to quit, aren't you?" she asked.

"Yeah. I'm done."

A week later, Nike sent a private jet to bring LeBron, Gloria, and Maverick to Beaverton, Oregon. Nike's corporate headquarters lacked the glamour of an oceanside mansion. But for LeBron, being on the Nike campus was like entering a fantasyland. There were buildings that featured larger-than-life images of the immortals—Michael Jordan, Tiger Woods, Bo Jackson. LeBron entered the Mia Hamm building and walked down a long hallway lined on both sides with glass cases containing Air Jordans and other iconic sneakers worn by NBA stars. At the end of the hall was one empty case that was illuminated by a light, making it easy for LeBron to envision his shoes in the hallowed passageway.

LeBron entered Phil Knight's conference room and saw that it was decked out with a variety of merchandise: workout clothes, swimwear, bathrobes, towels, socks, underwear, basketballs, gym bags, and sunglasses—all branded with LeBron's name. Nike had also stocked the room with LeBron's favorite breakfast cereal, Fruity Pebbles.

Lynn Merritt had thought of everything. And he was one step ahead of Reebok and Adidas on the sneaker front, too. Instead of showing LeBron sketches of what his shoes could look like, Merritt had sample shoes for LeBron to try on. Nike's signature LeBron shoe was called Zoom Generation I, and it was patterned after his Hummer—the Nike stripe looked like the trim on the Hummer's wheel well and the eyelets for the laces resembled the vehicle's door handles.

Gloria loved the design.

LeBron slipped the shoes on. They fit as if they'd been tailored to his feet. He could see himself wearing them in the NBA.

Goodwin had never seen such a compelling sales pitch.

When it came time to talk money, Nike had expected LeBron and Gloria to step out. It wasn't customary for an athlete to be present while the suits talked terms with the agent.

But LeBron insisted on being in the room. And he wanted his mother in the room, too. And Maverick.

When Nike CEO Phil Knight realized that LeBron wanted to be involved in every step of the process, he obliged, inviting LeBron into a private room with the lawyers.

It ended up being an underwhelming experience. Nike's offer was around $70 million, including $5 million as a signing bonus. But Knight didn't sign a check on the spot. If LeBron accepted Nike's offer, he'd be going home empty-handed. The bonus would come . . . well, later.

Goodwin let it be known that Nike's offer wasn't going to cut it.

That night, LeBron and his team had dinner at Lynn Merritt's home. Afterward, while LeBron played video games with Merritt's teenage son, Goodwin and Schreyer negotiated with Merritt. It was clear that the two sides were far apart.

The mood on the flight back from Beaverton was pensive.

Maverick Carter had interned at Nike for two years. He'd learned a lot from Lynn Merritt. But Maverick had no degree in business, no background in law or finance. Nor was he experienced in the art of dealmaking. Yet Maverick had been in the room for the negotiations with Reebok, Adidas, and Nike. LeBron had insisted that his friend be given a seat at the table. It was an extraordinary opportunity, affording Maverick a glimpse of how CEOs Paul Fireman and Phil Knight operated. Maverick also got a deeper appreciation of just how much pressure LeBron was under. When Fireman put that $10 million check on the table, Maverick had been overwhelmed. "I can't say I would have turned it down," he later admitted to LeBron. In that moment, Maverick's view was: *Let's take this check and get the hell out of here.*

The experience of watching LeBron navigate his way through such a pivotal moment in his life inspired Maverick to do more to help his best friend succeed. The opportunity also stoked within Maverick a desire to one day be a power player in his own right. Until then, he was content to sit at the table and learn.

LeBron recognized that Maverick was inexperienced. But Maverick was trustworthy and loyal. LeBron had a lawyer and an agent to give him legal and financial advice. But he relied on Maverick as his confidant, and shared things with him that he didn't discuss with his lawyer or his agent. When they got back from Oregon, they talked about Nike and Reebok and the future.

LeBron realized he was facing a monumental decision.

Maverick felt the weight of it, too.

LeBron's heart was with Nike. But in his head, he couldn't dismiss Reebok. It would have been an easy choice if Nike had simply put up more money. Alas, Nike had not done that.

In the meantime, Goodwin reengaged with Reebok. And two days after LeBron got back from Oregon, Reebok dispatched a team of executives and lawyers to Akron to seal the deal. Holed up in a hotel room, the Reebok group went to work on a new term sheet that would raise the final number to $115 million over seven years.

In a nearby room in the same hotel, LeBron met with Goodwin and Schreyer. At LeBron's request, Goodwin made a final run at Nike. Goodwin gave Nike until the end of the day on May 21. That evening, Nike faxed a new offer—$90 million over seven years. At signing, LeBron would receive $10 million.

Nike had come up significantly. But so had Reebok. The bottom line was that LeBron stood to receive roughly $25 million more by signing with Reebok.

Late that night, LeBron was with Maverick in a restaurant behind the hotel, mulling over his situation. At eighteen, he had an opportunity to realize a dream. He'd long envisioned himself soaring in the same rare air that his idol had occupied. When LeBron was growing up, Michael Jordan was a real-life superhero. Nike had had a big hand in that, designing Jordan's iconic logo and creating the epic commercials that made him the brightest star in sports.

LeBron yearned to shine as brightly as Jordan. But in order to get where he wanted to go, the boy who had spent his whole life in poverty would have to leave $25 million on the table. Picking at french fries, LeBron made up his mind. It was a defining moment.

Just after midnight, Goodwin and Schreyer entered the restaurant and slid into LeBron's booth. They needed his decision.

"I want to go with Nike," LeBron told them.

FIFTEEN

CRAZY RIGHT NOW

No Cleveland sports team had won a title since 1964, when the Cleveland Browns won the NFL Championship, two seasons before the first Super Bowl was played. Since then, the city had endured a thirty-nine-year drought that included some of the most devastating defeats in modern sports history. In 1987, the Browns were on the verge of winning the AFC Championship and going to the Super Bowl when Broncos quarterback John Elway drove his team ninety-eight yards in fifteen plays to tie the game with seconds to go in regulation, in what became infamously known in Cleveland as "the Drive." The Browns lost the game in overtime, and Cleveland was crestfallen. A year later, in a play known in football annals as "the Fumble," the Browns were about to score the game-winning touchdown in the AFC Championship game when the team's top running back had the ball stripped from him on the goal line with a minute left to play. Once again, the Browns lost an opportunity to go to the Super Bowl. Then, in 1989, the Cleveland Cavaliers were one second away from closing out the Bulls in a five-game playoff series when Michael Jordan hit "the Shot," an iconic buzzer-beater that gave his team a one-point victory. And in 1997 "the Blown Save" by relief pitcher José Mesa cost the Cleveland Indians the World Series.

Growing up forty miles south of Cleveland, LeBron was well versed in the city's tortured sports history. He also knew that Clevelanders had their hearts set on seeing him reverse the city's bad fortunes and leading the Cavaliers to basketball glory. Those dreams hinged on the NBA lottery, which was set up to give the teams with the poorest record the best chance of securing the top pick in the NBA Draft. The Cavaliers had finished the previous season 17-65, tied with the Denver Nuggets for the worst record in the league. Among the thirteen teams that had missed the playoffs and therefore qualified for the lottery, the Cavaliers and the Nuggets each had a 22.5 percent chance of winning the right to select LeBron.

"Cavs fans have hope," one sports columnist wrote on the eve of the lottery. "If this cursed franchise can finally muster enough luck to win the NBA lottery—a 22.5 percent shot in the dark—maybe anything is possible. Such as a trip to the NBA Finals in your lifetime."

Just hours after signing with Nike, LeBron hosted a party for his high school teammates and coaches at an Akron hotel, where they planned to watch the lottery proceedings together. It was a last hurrah before they graduated and entered the next phase of their lives. Sian had accepted a football scholarship from Ohio State University. Willie was headed to Fairmont State University in West Virginia on a football scholarship. Romeo and Little Dru were heading to the University of Akron, where they'd be playing basketball and reuniting with Coach Keith Dambrot. And Coach Dru, who had been named coach of the year by *USA Today*, had cemented his future at St. V. All that remained was to find out where LeBron was heading.

They all crowded around a television as ABC sportscaster Mike Tirico opened the live broadcast from the NBA studios in Secaucus, New Jersey. "Earlier today, LeBron James signed a ninety . . . *million* . . . dollar endorsement contract for sneakers," Tirico said. "Needless to say, they're counting on him for a lot, all the way around."

Gloria was in the hotel room, too, standing beside St. V librarian Barb Wood, who had always known that LeBron was going to do big things. But what Wood was seeing was hard to fathom.

With representatives from the lottery teams in the studio, a league official stood at a podium and methodically opened a stack of thirteen sealed envelopes. When he got to the last one, loud cheers filled the hotel ballroom in Akron as the NBA official declared, "The first pick in the 2003 NBA Draft goes to the Cleveland Cavaliers."

Applause also filled the NBA studio as Mike Tirico approached the jubilant Cavaliers team owner, Gordon Gund.

"Mr. Gund, congratulations," Tirico said. "With LeBron James being from Akron, Ohio, I'm sure there has to be a lot of excitement in the organization."

"You know," Gund said with a straight face, "we don't know who we're gonna pick yet."

Everyone in the studio cracked up.

Gund laughed, too. "I'm very excited for the fans in Cleveland," he continued. "This is a great day for them and for all of that market—for Akron, Cleveland, all of northeastern Ohio. A big day in Cleveland sports."

The next morning, the phone lines at the Cavaliers' front office were jammed. The team with the lowest attendance in the NBA had a run on tickets. Over the next three weeks, the Cavaliers sold thousands of season-ticket packages. Even before the kid from Akron was officially a Cavalier, Cleveland fans were banking on him to be the city's savior.

The weight of the expectations seemed to roll off LeBron's back. In his youth, he'd had visions of what it would be like to be a superhero who watched over a city and took down bad guys. His favorite action figure was Batman. Eager to play a Bruce Wayne–like role, LeBron arrived in New York for the NBA Draft. For an appointment set up by the league, LeBron and some of the projected first-round draft picks—Carmelo Anthony, Dwyane Wade, Chris Bosh, and others—visited the New York Stock Exchange and met with Chairman Richard Grasso. Traders shouted, "LeBron!" and clamored for his autograph as he walked with Grasso across the trading floor.

"What round do you think you'll get drafted in, first or second?" Grasso asked with a smile.

"Probably the second," LeBron quipped.

Moments later, from the balcony above the trading floor, LeBron reached for the opening bell. The ink on his high school diploma was barely dry and his net worth was already on par with that of the CEO of the New York Stock Exchange. With the bell ringing and cheers filling the stock exchange, LeBron looked down and smiled at the boisterous traders.

LeBron couldn't deny that New York would be a great place to play. It was a basketball mecca. And Eddie Jackson had always wanted LeBron to play for the Knicks, a storied franchise that played in the World's Most Famous Arena. But when LeBron entered Madison Square Garden on June 26, 2003, he was going there as Cleveland's white knight, ready to claim his newly minted Cavaliers uniform and do battle with the Knicks and everyone else in the league. His goal was to turn northern Ohio into the center of the basketball universe.

Dressed in a white suit, a white shirt, and a white silk tie, LeBron sat beside his mother at one of the head tables, chewing his nails and waiting for the first pick to be announced. When Commissioner David Stern called his name, LeBron stood, kissed Gloria, and walked across the stage to raucous cheers. After shaking Stern's hand, LeBron faced ESPN's Michele Tafoya.

"You will most certainly be the most scrutinized rookie in the history of the NBA," she said.

New York fans in the audience started chanting, "O-VER-RA-TED! O-VER-RA-TED!"

Unfazed, LeBron smiled, held up his Cavaliers jersey with one hand, looked at the television camera, and pointed. "All right, Cavs fans back at home," he said, tapping his heart with his fist.

Cleveland had its first bona fide sports superstar since Jim Brown retired from the NFL in 1966 to pursue an acting career.

A week after the NBA Draft, LeBron was invited back to New York City by Jay-Z to spend a week with him and attend the most competitive streetball tournament in the country—the Entertainers Basketball Classic, held each summer at the storied Rucker Park in Harlem. Jay-Z, who was born Shawn Carter, owned a team in the tournament called Team S. Carter. It was expected to compete for the championship, which was known on the street as "the Chip." LeBron, who had been in steady contact with Jay-Z since the two of them had spent time together around the McDonald's All-American Game back in the spring, readily accepted Jay-Z's invitation. And he brought Maverick along.

Jay-Z had long felt that rap artists and basketball players were joined at the hip. But the connection Jay-Z felt with LeBron was different. And it ran much deeper than two celebrities who liked being around each other. Like LeBron, Jay-Z had grown up in a public housing project called Marcy Houses, which occupied six blocks in the Bedford-Stuyvesant section of Brooklyn. Like LeBron, Jay-Z had no relationship with his father, who had abandoned him and his mother when Jay-Z was a boy. And like LeBron, Jay-Z was close to his mother, who also happened to be named Gloria. He'd become her protector and her provider.

LeBron had found a kindred spirit in Jay-Z. But Jay-Z was fifteen years older than him. So LeBron was getting to know Jay-Z at a time when the thirty-three-year-old artist was reflecting back on his life as a younger man. While LeBron was hanging out with him, Jay-Z was writing a new song called "December 4th"—titled after Jay-Z's birthday—that referenced the "demons" inside him from being "a kid torn apart once his pop disappeared." The raw, autobiographical lyrics revealed Jay-Z's state of mind as a teenager:

> Hard enough to match the pain of my pop not seein' me
> So with that disdain in my membrane
> Got on my pimp game
> Fuck the world, my defense came.

LeBron discovered that as a young boy, Jay-Z had loved to read and write down rhymes. He had imitated Michael Jackson and been so good with words that other kids in the projects had nicknamed him Jazzy. But after his father walked out, Jay-Z turned to drug dealing before finding his path and making his first record at age twenty-six. Music, he told LeBron, had saved him. But Jay-Z had learned a hard lesson. "You enter the room, your résumé enters with you," he acknowledged to a writer. "So [even now] every time I enter a room, it's still that thing of: 'That's Jay-Z. He used to be the drug dealer from Marcy Projects.'" He'd learned to block that out. But still.

LeBron never looked at Jay-Z that way. He revered Jay-Z's artistry and respected his candor.

One of the things that impressed Jay-Z about LeBron was that he exhibited no outward signs of disdain or lasting pain from growing up without a father. And despite the hardships that LeBron and his mother had experienced, LeBron had never adopted a fuck-the-world mentality as a defense mechanism in his youth. Rather, LeBron had found his path in fifth grade when a father figure had put a basketball in his hands. And LeBron had never detoured from the path. At eighteen, LeBron's résumé contained just one thing: *basketball player extraordinaire*.

LeBron's and Jay-Z's lives intersected at a time when the artist was also at a crossroads in his career. Long established as the most successful rapper in the world, Jay-Z had cofounded his own record label—Roc-A-Fella Records—which enabled him to capture a significantly larger share of profits and royalties from his music than other recording artists did. He was also working with up-and-coming artists like Kanye West, whose debut studio album was in the works. At the same time, Jay-Z was branching out, launching a clothing line called Rocawear and looking to expand his business interests outside the music industry. He was also in a relationship with twenty-one-year-old pop star Beyoncé, making them one of the most visible couples on the planet. On many levels, Jay-Z had a more complicated life than LeBron did.

Yet Jay-Z could see that LeBron's life was destined to become much more complicated. LeBron had experienced fame much sooner than Jay-Z had. And Jay-Z welcomed the opportunity to take LeBron under his wing.

Similarly, LeBron embraced the opportunity to see Jay-Z's world as a protégé. A couple days after arriving in town, LeBron sat beside Jay-Z on the Team S. Carter bus as it wound its way from Brooklyn to the Bronx. Rain had forced tournament organizers to shift the games to the iconic Gaucho Gym for the day. Looking through the tinted windows, LeBron could see the throngs of people waiting outside as the vehicle came to a stop. After the players exited, the crowd surged forward as LeBron stepped off the bus.

As if taking a prizefighter to the ring, Jay-Z led LeBron into a shrinking funnel of fans, video cameras, and security guards. The chaotic scene was the first time that the two stars had stepped out together in public. Inside the gym, LeBron sat beside Jay-Z on the bench, cheering on Team S. Carter while fans marveled at the sight of the number one draft pick in the NBA teamed up with the iconic hip-hop mogul.

While LeBron was in town, Jay-Z took him to the grand opening of his 40/40 Club, a luxury sports bar in Manhattan. A well-heeled crowd packed the main floor, which featured giant plasma TVs above the bar and an impressive collection of rare sports memorabilia encased in glass. LeBron stayed upstairs in the VIP lounge, where a handful of celebrities played pool and a few NBA stars sat on plush leather furniture playing cards, while a curvaceous hostess in a short skirt served cognac and cigars. LeBron was with Jay-Z, who was having a private conversation with Timothy Zachery Mosley, the influential record producer known throughout the rap industry as Timbaland. It was well after midnight, and Jay-Z was lamenting how the hip-hop industry had changed since the untimely deaths of the Notorious B.I.G. and Tupac Shakur, both of whom had been murdered in drive-by shootings in the nineties.

"It's not like it was with Big and Pac," Jay-Z said.

Cigar smoke wafted through the air as LeBron checked his phone. Even in a VIP setting, he was in his own rare space, privy to a private conversation between two kings of the hip-hop industry.

There was plenty to celebrate—days earlier, Beyoncé had premiered songs from her first solo album, *Dangerously in Love*, including the smash hit single, "Crazy in Love." The music video that accompanied the song opens with Jay-Z rapping, "Yes! Whoo, ow! So crazy right now," as a sultry-looking Beyoncé, in red heels, tight jean shorts, and a white halter top, struts down the middle of a city street and seductively says, "You ready?" She then sings, "Uh-oh, uh-oh, uh-oh" while the video slows down and the camera zooms in on her as she gets down and starts to gyrate on a loading dock. The lyrics had been cowritten by Jay-Z and Beyoncé and brashly showcased the status of their romance.

While Jay-Z was thrilled about the direction of his relationship with Beyoncé and her skyrocketing career, he was ready to make changes in the direction of his own career. He had already reached the top of the mountain in hip-hop. In fact, he was the mountain. But he knew there were other mountains out there, and he was itching to climb them.

"Hip-hop's corny now," he said to Timbaland, confiding that his forthcoming album would be his final record.

LeBron would never reveal what he had heard. Discretion, he already figured out, was the key to navigating the corridors of power and fame.

By the time LeBron left New York and headed back to Akron, Jay-Z had made it clear that he was family now.

As soon as LeBron's first check arrived from Nike, he told his mother that whatever she needed, he would give it to her. For starters, he told her, he was buying her a new house. And not just any house. "A house with some grass," he told her with a smile.

For the first time in her life, Gloria James didn't have to worry about money.

LeBron also had plans in mind for Maverick Carter, Rich Paul, and Randy Mims. LeBron met separately with each of them to discuss the future.

LeBron talked to Maverick first, and he focused the conversation on Nike.

"I want you to go work there," LeBron told him.

Maverick wasn't expecting that.

But the move made sense to LeBron on various levels. First, LeBron wanted one of his guys—someone he trusted—to be his eyes and ears within Nike. And Maverick was the obvious choice, as he'd already spent time at Nike, where he'd learned the ropes and built a solid relationship with Lynn Merritt. Second, LeBron saw big things in Maverick's future. And he wanted to help his friend gain valuable work experience.

"I've already worked it out for them to hire you," LeBron told Maverick.

Maverick felt incredibly lucky to have a friend who possessed the clout to "work it out" with Nike. To Maverick, the Nike campus was like a playground. The prospect of working there full-time was a dream come true. It was also scary. Interning was one thing. But moving to Beaverton and becoming a Nike employee was something different altogether. He'd be expected to work alongside some of the most talented and experienced marketers and designers in the industry. What if he didn't measure up?

LeBron wasn't worried.

Emboldened by LeBron's backing, Maverick remembered something his grandmother used to say: "If you got a hunch, bet a bunch." Maverick had more than a hunch that joining Nike was the safest bet he'd ever make. He withdrew from college, packed his bags, and headed to Oregon.

LeBron's conversation with Randy Mims was more of a continuation of the one LeBron had begun with him a year earlier when he had told Mims that he wanted to hire him one day. Well, LeBron told him, that day was here. He invited Mims to be his full-time personal assistant. He wanted Mims to go everywhere with him, whether it was to New York to film a commercial, to Oregon to meet with folks at Nike, or on the road during the NBA season.

Honored to function as the gatekeeper to LeBron and the one responsible for getting him everywhere he needed to be, Mims walked away from his job and went on LeBron's payroll.

LeBron told Rich Paul that he wanted him on his payroll, too. But LeBron told Rich that he hadn't yet come up with a specific role for him. They'd figure it out together, LeBron told him. In the meantime, he offered Rich an annual salary of $50,000 and handed him a check covering his first two weeks' pay.

Rich knew full well that LeBron was now a multimillionaire. As such, he could easily afford to pay Rich a lot more than $50,000 a year. Hell, LeBron had so much money that he could give his friends whatever they wanted. Instead, he had urged Maverick to uproot and take an entry-level position at Nike, where he'd be working long hours and earning a modest wage. Similarly, LeBron was expecting Randy to essentially work twenty-four seven on a modest salary. And now he was asking Rich, who was running his own business, to work for less than he earned selling throwback jerseys.

. But rather than resent LeBron, Rich gravitated toward him. A sense of entitlement, in Rich's mind, was a dangerous thing. It bred laziness and took away the incentive to work hard. Rather than offer his friends special treatment, LeBron was providing special opportunities. If LeBron had gone about it any other way, Rich would have turned him down. Although his vintage jersey business was thriving, he committed to LeBron.

Maverick was twenty-two. Rich was twenty-one. Randy was twenty-four. Unified in their belief that LeBron had offered each of them a once-in-a-lifetime opportunity, they felt a deepened sense of loyalty to their eighteen-year-old friend. Together, they started calling themselves the Four Horsemen.

LeBron signed a $13 million, three-year contract with the Cavaliers. The contract contained an option for a fourth year that would bring LeBron's earnings to $19 million. He signed the paperwork just in time to play with the Cavaliers in the Reebok Pro Summer League in Boston in mid-July. The games were part of the NBA's developmental initiative for rookies and free agents. While standing in a layup line during warm-ups prior to a game against the Celtics, LeBron spotted Reebok executive Todd Krinsky sitting courtside.

LeBron knew that the negotiations between his agent and Reebok hadn't ended well. There had been sharp words when Aaron Goodwin went to Reebok's hotel room in Akron to deliver the news that despite Reebok's higher offer, LeBron had decided to go with Nike.

Krinsky was still smarting when he saw LeBron warming up in a pair of Nikes.

LeBron stepped out of line and walked over to him.

"Listen, man, I just want to tell you that you guys gave a great pitch," LeBron said.

Krinsky was disarmed.

"It's nothing personal," LeBron continued. "In the end, I just went with my heart and went with what I thought was right for me."

Krinsky was struck by LeBron's candor and sincerity. *Shit, he didn't need to do that,* he thought as he watched LeBron return to the layup line. *This kid is* eighteen.

Lynn Merritt was also dazzled by LeBron's precociousness. No one at Nike had been more bullish about signing LeBron than Merritt. In 2003, Nike had committed $274 million in endorsement contracts to seventy-five basketball players. From Nike's perspective, its commitment to Le-Bron was far more substantial than the money Reebok had offered. By awarding a $90 million contract to LeBron, Nike had set him apart from everyone else in the Nike family. For Merritt, the disproportionate invest-ment in LeBron was a sound decision. In high school, LeBron had sold out arenas all over the country and generated higher television ratings than most college games and even many pro games. From Merritt's per-spective, LeBron had demonstrated that his style of play and his person-ality appealed to a mass audience. Not even Michael Jordan had entered the NBA with as much fanfare as LeBron had. "With Michael, you really didn't see it until his second year, but with LeBron we're starting right away," Merritt told the *New York Times.* "He's coming in with so much cachet and visibility."

It was no coincidence that Nike had offered LeBron the richest sneaker deal in history just one month after Jordan announced his retirement, stepping away from professional basketball for the final time. Jordan had put Nike on the map, and over a two-decade span he had been the big-gest rainmaker in the athletic-footwear industry. Throughout the world, the Air Jordan brand was unparalleled. But Nike's business plan centered around two words—*over* and *next.* The Jordan era was over. The LeBron era was next.

It was also no coincidence that Nike had signed an endorsement deal with Kobe Bryant one month after coming to terms with LeBron. From Nike's perspective, Kobe was the bridge between the Jordan era and the LeBron era. When Jordan retired, Kobe assumed the title of best player in the NBA. At twenty-four, he had already won three NBA championships, and his playing style was closely patterned after Jordan's. No one would argue that LeBron was a better player than Kobe in 2003. But LeBron was clearly more advanced than Kobe had been when Kobe had entered the league. And most NBA insiders felt it was only a matter of time before LeBron surpassed Kobe as the game's best player. Nike already considered LeBron a superior salesman to Kobe, which the company demonstrated in its decision to offer Kobe a four-year, $40 million endorsement deal. Nike had paid LeBron more than twice as much money, and they had committed to being in business with LeBron for almost twice as long.

"Bryant's track record as a sneaker pitchman is spotty," the *Wall Street Journal* opined. "His last signature shoe with Adidas, a futuristic-looking sneaker reminiscent of an igloo, bombed in stores, and part of the shoe's poor performance was attributed to Mr. Bryant's lack of street credibility in the eyes of urban teens who are the biggest buyers of athletic shoes."

LeBron, on the other hand, was the epitome of an urban teen. And he embraced his urban roots, often going out of his way in press conferences and interviews to talk about his neighborhood, his mother, and the struggles they had endured in Akron. Plus, LeBron's budding relationship with Jay-Z had further elevated his presence as a rare athlete whose star was also rising in the music world. In mid-July, Jay-Z's "Roc the Mic" tour passed through Cleveland. LeBron spent some time with Jay-Z on his tour bus. While they hung out together on a couch—Jay-Z in a green T-shirt and a green baseball cap; LeBron in a vintage Alex English jersey over a white T-shirt with a piece of gold Jesus jewelry dangling from his neck— they got a visit from Sway, a hip-hop correspondent for MTV.

"Look who we got in here," Sway said. "These are the type of cats that hang around Jay. You know, just randomly fall up on the bus. Hottest guy in the country right now. LeBron James."

"Yes, sir," Jay-Z said.

"What brings you to the concert?" Sway asked.

"C'mon, man," LeBron said. "You know what brings me to the concert. It's this man sittin' right here next to me."

Jay-Z laughed and nodded at LeBron. "That's an extended family member right there," he said.

"Who you lookin' forward to pairing up against?" Sway asked. "Kobe Bryant? Tracy McGrady?"

"I'm prepared to play against the NBA," LeBron told him. "The Cavs versus whoever we got that night. We tryin' to make the playoffs. Individual things don't mean nothin'. It's all about the team."

"That's why I love him," Jay-Z said.

"Shaq, Kobe, Chris Webber, a few NBA players took a stab at making rap records," Sway said. "And I see you hangin' with Jay."

LeBron grinned.

"C'mon, man, this is MTV," Sway said. "If that's what's about to take place, is there a chance you might be makin' an album?"

LeBron looked at him like he was crazy. "No, man. There's *no chance*. No chance at all."

"Ever?" Sway asked.

"I'm God-gifted in one thing, and that's basketball," LeBron said. Then he pointed at Jay-Z. "I'm gonna let my man handle the other side."

Jay-Z smiled. "That's real family right there," he said. "That's my boy right there."

LeBron had yet to play an NBA game. Yet his stature in the hip-hop community was soaring. It was a situation that gave Nike's Lynn Merritt great peace of mind. Nike had run focus groups and conducted consumer surveys, both of which indicated that LeBron's appeal among consumers transcended age, ethnicity, and demographics.

From Nike's perspective, Michael Jordan had been a phenomenon it would be tough to duplicate. But Kobe and LeBron were the next generation's two brightest stars.

The NBA took a similar view of Jordan's exit from the stage—Kobe and LeBron were the league's faces of the future.

The demands on LeBron—from Nike and the NBA—were about to intensify.

SIXTEEN

PRESSURE

On July 18, 2003, authorities in Colorado charged Kobe Bryant with sexually assaulting a nineteen-year-old woman who worked at a resort hotel in the Rocky Mountains where Bryant had been staying. Bryant's accuser had been treated at a local hospital and provided graphic testimony to the police. The district attorney who brought the charges against Bryant described the legal definition of felony sexual assault in Colorado as "sexual intrusion or sexual penetration" and "submission of the victim through the actual application of physical force or physical violence." If convicted, Kobe was facing four years to life in prison.

Hours after being charged, Kobe held a news conference in Los Angeles. "I'm innocent," he said. "I didn't force her to do anything against her will. I'm innocent." Kobe's wife, who had recently given birth to their first child, added, "I know that my husband has made a mistake—the mistake of adultery. He and I will have to deal with that within our marriage, and we will do so. He is not a criminal."

News of the charges sent shock waves through the NBA. Headlines connecting the game's top player with rape allegations flooded the internet and appeared in newspapers across the world. *Sports Illustrated* even put Kobe's mug shot on the cover with the word ACCUSED under his face. But this was much bigger than a sports story.

Commissioner David Stern issued a statement: "As with all allegations of a criminal nature, the NBA's policy is to await the outcome of a judicial proceeding before taking any action." The court of public opinion was not so patient. And Kobe's endorsement partners didn't waste any time scrapping ad campaigns. The Coca-Cola Company, for example, stopped airing its commercials with Kobe. And a few weeks later, Coca-Cola signed LeBron to a six-year endorsement deal worth $12 million.

The NBA's image took a hit, too.

"Beyond immeasurable damage to Mr. Bryant's once-flawless endorsement reputation," the New York Times reported, "the charges deepened the image problems of the NBA. For the past two summers, some of the league's marquee players, including Allen Iverson of the Philadelphia 76ers, have been in trouble with the law."

With Kobe's reputation in tatters, LeBron flew to the West Coast to film his first Nike commercial. The Cavaliers were scheduled to open the regular season later in the fall at Arco Arena in Sacramento against the Kings. For the commercial, Nike staged a game between the Cavaliers and Kings at Arco Arena, using players from both teams, along with hundreds of extras, who were brought in to be fans. The Kings announcers were used in the ad as well.

Nike titled the commercial "Pressure," and it opened with LeBron handling the ball for the first time in his NBA debut. Being guarded by Kings point guard Mike Bibby, LeBron stops and surveys the court. "Is he gonna be able to handle it?" one announcer says to the other as LeBron freezes and the camera zooms in on his face. For the next fifty-two seconds—an eternity in television commercials—LeBron stands frozen while the arena goes silent. "You talk about not being able to handle the pressure," one of the announcers whispers. "You're a joke!" a fan yells from the stands. "C'mon, young fella," Hall of Fame player George "Iceman" Gervin says to himself from a courtside seat. Finally, LeBron laughs. Fade to black, and the Nike swoosh appears on-screen.

The commercial and the question it posed—was he going to be able to handle the pressure?—attempted to make light of the load LeBron was carrying. But even before Kobe's legal troubles, the NBA had already been looking to LeBron to do more than any rookie in league history. Over the summer, LeBron's jersey had become the league's top-selling product among all NBA-licensed merchandise. Team-wide, only the Los Angeles Lakers merchandise was outselling the Cavaliers merchandise in NBA stores. On the television side, the NBA planned to feature the Cavaliers in thirteen nationally televised games during the 2003–2004 season. In the previous season, the Cavaliers had not appeared in one nationally televised game. Broadcaster Charles Barkley spoke out against the league for the way it was handling LeBron. "I think the NBA has done him a disservice showcasing him so much this early, putting him on TV all the time," Barkley said. "I think he's got a real chance of being a stud in three or four years. But right now, he's got a long way to go."

At the end of the summer, LeBron went to New York to film a television spot with TNT, the league's longtime broadcasting partner. The NBA chose filmmaker Spike Lee to shoot the commercial, which features LeBron dangling from a crib while kids sing "Rock-a-Bye Baby." For LeBron, it was an opportunity to spend time with the filmmaker he most admired. In addition to making movies such as *He Got Game*, *Do the Right Thing*, and *Mo' Better Blues*, Lee had created and starred in landmark Nike commercials with Michael Jordan. For his 1986 film, *She's Gotta Have It*, Lee had created a fictional character named Mars Blackmon, a Brooklyn-born New York Knicks fan who likes Air Jordan sneakers. Not long after the film's release, Lee played Mars Blackmon in a series of Nike commercials with Jordan. In addition to popularizing the phrase "It's gotta be da shoes," the Spike Lee–Michael Jordan commercials were so popular that they were credited with revolutionizing the sneaker industry and elevating Air Jordans into a worldwide fashion brand.

Lee impressed upon LeBron the significance of the moment he was in. Lee had watched with great sadness as Kobe Bryant's sexual-assault case dominated the headlines. From Lee's perspective, LeBron was joining the NBA at a critical time for African American athletes. Partly due to Kobe's case, the image of Black athletes was suffering.

LeBron listened as Lee emphasized how important it was for him to perform well on the court. But it was just as important, Lee said, for him to perform off the court.

LeBron recognized that Lee was speaking as a friend. And Lee's words resonated with him. LeBron had been startled when he had visited Nike's headquarters and seen the notorious commercial from 1993 in which Charles Barkley iconically declares, "I am not a role model. . . . Parents should be role models. Just because I dunk a basketball doesn't mean I should raise your kids." LeBron disagreed. "That's ridiculous," LeBron said later. "I have no problem being a role model. I love it. I have kids looking up to me and hopefully I inspire these kids to do good things."

Lee found LeBron's outlook refreshing. Still, Lee had been around the world of celebrity for a long time. He'd seen a lot in his day. Yet he sensed he was looking at a young man who was going to likely see and experience so much more than he had—potentially more than any other Black athlete in his generation had. There was so much promise. There was so much danger.

The pitfalls of male celebrity—drugs, falling in with the wrong crowd, and especially womanizing—were temptations that LeBron recognized and guarded against. Although he had tried marijuana in high school, he hadn't liked it, and he'd never been interested in touching harder drugs or anything else that would interfere with his quest for peak athletic performance. In terms of choosing his friends, LeBron surrounded himself with Mav, Rich, and Randy, three guys who respected and admired his determination to keep his nose clean and protect his good name. And when it came to the ladies, LeBron was often in proximity to plenty of glamorous ones. But although he noticed beautiful women as much as the next guy, he kept his mind's eye trained on Savannah. Although he wasn't with Savannah as much as he would have liked, due to his demanding basketball and business schedule, his heart belonged to his seventeen-year-old high school soulmate.

LeBron didn't say any of that to Lee. But LeBron frequently told himself, *Kids look up to me.*

Nonetheless, in the aftermath of Kobe's arrest, Lee also made sure to get his point across to LeBron's agent, Aaron Goodwin.

"This can't be messed up," Lee told Goodwin.

In prison, Eddie Jackson felt increasingly isolated and discouraged. LeBron's career was taking off. Gloria's financial situation had forever changed. Aaron Goodwin was closing deals left and right. Everyone, it seemed, was thriving. Everyone except Jackson. The reps from the shoe companies no longer stayed in touch with him. People trying to get to LeBron no longer bothered with him. He hadn't even heard from Gloria in over three months. The only person who seemed to be chasing Jackson now was Joseph Marsh, who had become impatient.

Marsh felt that he had held up his end of the bargain, lending Jackson and Gloria $100,000. Yet the documentary was going nowhere. And since LeBron had turned pro, Marsh was having trouble getting ahold of Gloria. To Marsh, the writing was on the wall. He wrote to Jackson and made it clear that it was time for him to pay up.

In late July, Jackson wrote Marsh a letter, apologizing for the situation and saying he hadn't talked to Gloria in months. He added:

> However, I did write her and told her to call you and get things handled. I just called A.G., the agent, to see how soon he can get down here to visit me so I can talk to him. So let me go to work on all of that.
>
> Man, I'm sorry that things have not been handled by now. Hopefully it will be, because I really appreciate everything that you have done for me and my family.

Jackson eventually connected with Goodwin. And Goodwin made contact with Marsh. But the back-and-forth between Goodwin and Marsh quickly hit an impasse. And in September, Marsh served Jackson with a demand for full payment of the loan and interest—$115,000 and change.

Days later, Jackson wrote another letter to Marsh:

> As I stated over the phone we are trying to handle this matter. I thought it was handled. I spoke with Aaron. He said he just wanted you to sign a contract stating that you will not go to the media, even after you are paid.
>
> Sorry for you having to go through this, because I really appreciated everything that you have done.

In October, Marsh sued Jackson and Gloria for breach of contract and unjust enrichment. Shortly thereafter, Marsh also sued LeBron, alleging that he had breached an oral contract by refusing to cooperate in the production of a documentary or participate in any other business relationship with Marsh. Marsh demanded $10 million in damages regarding the documentary and $5 million in damages regarding the other business relationships.

On the eve of training camp, LeBron was suddenly a defendant. The litigation was a distraction that LeBron handed off to Fred Nance, who filed an answer to the complaint. In it, LeBron denied that Eddie Jackson had acted with his authority. He also denied that Gloria had been his agent or acted with his authority.

* * *

During the sixties and seventies, Paul Silas had an illustrious NBA career, establishing himself as one of the league's elite defenders and winning three championships. After his playing days ended, Silas had spent more than fifteen years as an NBA coach. In 2003, the Cavaliers hired Silas to be the team's new head coach. One of his primary roles was to mentor LeBron.

Not much surprised Silas. But he'd never seen a rookie who had come into the league with so much hype and expectation. Nor had he ever encountered a rookie with so much money. When LeBron first showed up for team workouts, Silas observed veteran players talking about him. "What has he done to warrant all this hype?" they said.

Silas told LeBron that everyone would be gunning for him. And by *everyone*, Silas was including some of LeBron's teammates. Even before the draft, Silas was picking up on the vibes of resentment within the team. "We have better players than him at his position already on our team," Cavaliers forward Carlos Boozer said at the time.

But the player Silas figured would be most threatened by LeBron was Ricky Davis. He led the team in scoring and was considered the best player on the roster. And he viewed himself as the team's leader. In the preseason, Davis talked to *Sports Illustrated* writer Jack McCallum, who was working on a feature story for the magazine's NBA preview issue. "LeBron is going to help me," Davis told McCallum. "With a great athlete like myself and a great athlete like him, we can pull it all together."

Davis was used to being the most important player on the Cavaliers roster. But when the NBA preview issue came out, LeBron was on the cover under the headline "The Importance of Being LeBron." It was a not-so-subtle message to Davis and everyone else that LeBron wasn't just the most important player on the Cavaliers. He was the most important player in the NBA.

Silas spent a lot of one-on-one time with LeBron during training camp, preparing him for the ways that opponents were going to come at him. "You can't be a punk," Silas told LeBron. "When they come at you, you've got to go right back at them."

LeBron knew he was a marked man. But he told himself, *This is the life I have chosen.*

*   *   *

Normally, the Sacramento Kings issued a couple dozen media credentials for a regular-season game. But for the season opener against the Cavaliers on October 29, 2003, the Kings issued 340 credentials. The media interest in LeBron's first game exceeded the normal interest in an NBA playoff game.

Earlier in the day, LeBron called his St. V teammates back home. A bunch of them had gathered in Akron to watch the game together. Although he was in the league now, LeBron stayed in close contact with his best friends. He was closer to them than anyone on the Cavaliers. He told them he was ready to go.

The sold-out crowd in Arco Arena booed when LeBron was introduced.

LeBron tried to block out the noise. *Stay composed*, he told himself. *Focus on the court. I need to work hard every minute.*

Right before tip-off, Nike aired the LeBron commercial. A little over a minute into the game, LeBron brought the ball up the floor for the first time. But unlike in the commercial, LeBron didn't freeze. He accelerated. "On the run, this is the best part of his game," the announcer said as LeBron drove into a pack of Kings and lobbed a no-look alley-oop pass from the top of the circle to a streaking Ricky Davis, who elevated, caught the pass, and dunked it, electrifying the crowd. "And there's his first assist, and it's a beauty!" the announcer said.

A little over a minute later, LeBron scored his first two points as a pro, knocking down a fifteen-foot jump shot. Moments later, he hit another jumper.

"That's our boy," his teammates back in Akron said with pride.

On Cleveland's next possession, LeBron came off a screen and ended up being guarded by the Kings' six-foot-eleven center, Brad Miller. Confident he could beat Miller one-on-one, LeBron dribbled toward the baseline, into the corner near the Cavaliers' bench. With Miller coming toward him, LeBron elevated, fading away from Miller and the basket. With his momentum propelling him backward, toward the sideline, LeBron kicked out his right leg and at the last possible moment shot the ball just over the tip of Miller's outstretched hand. "Oh, way off balance, over a seven-footer," the announcer said as the ball arced upward.

To the untrained eye, LeBron's shot looked ill-advised, like a rookie mistake, some kind of circus shot that kids might try on a playground. But LeBron hadn't learned how to play basketball on playgrounds. Although he'd grown up in an urban environment, he'd spent very little time playing pickup games on blacktop. Instead, he'd spent thousands of hours in gymnasiums, training on hardwood floors. What most people didn't realize was the critical behind-the-scenes role played by the coaches in LeBron's life. In addition to being dedicated to family, faith, and his profession, Coach Dru and Frankie Walker and Lee Cotton and Keith Dambrot were basketball purists. They preached passing over scoring, teamwork over individualism. But in the end, they all recognized that LeBron was a prodigy who could do things with a ball that couldn't be taught. He had instincts and physical gifts that were beyond anything they'd seen. The most important thing that Dru and LeBron's other coaches had done was keep LeBron and his friends off the streets and in the gym, giving LeBron a place to practice and practice and practice. His brilliance was in making the extremely difficult look easy.

As LeBron landed out-of-bounds and stumbled over the legs of his Cavaliers' teammates seated on the bench, his perfectly arced shot dropped through the net. "And he knocked it down!" the announcer said in amazement.

Back in Akron, LeBron's teammates were proud, but not surprised.

"He used to hit that shot on Willie all the time in practice," one of them said.

The rest of them started laughing. They all remembered how LeBron would practice that fadeaway jumper over Willie McGee time and time again. What LeBron was doing to the Kings was no circus act. It was the result of relentless work.

Feeling unstoppable, LeBron intercepted an errant pass under the Kings' basket, drove the length of the floor in traffic, and bounced a no-look pass to teammate Carlos Boozer for a dunk. On the Kings' next possession, LeBron intercepted a pass at midcourt, sped toward the Cavaliers' basket, and took flight from the foul line. His head even with the rim, he hammered down a one-handed jam. On the Kings' next possession, LeBron stole the ball *again* and raced downcourt all alone. But instead of dunking it, he stopped, waited for teammate Ricky Davis, and pitched it to him for a flashy reverse dunk.

Coach Silas liked what he was seeing. The Cavaliers ended up losing the game. But LeBron led all scorers with twenty-five points and had a game-high nine assists to go along with six rebounds and four steals.

ESPN's Jim Gray interviewed LeBron as he walked off the court.

"Did you surpass your own expectations on an individual level?" Gray asked.

"I try not to think about that, with a loss. I thought we really had an opportunity to get this win tonight and it just didn't go our way."

Dressed in a stylish black suit, Gloria waited outside the Cavaliers' locker room. When the players emerged and headed to the team bus, she intercepted LeBron and threw her arms around him.

LeBron held her tight. Then he boarded the bus for the ride to the airport.

The team landed in Phoenix at two thirty in the morning.

LeBron's life in the NBA had officially begun.

The television ratings for LeBron's first NBA game were off the charts. In northern Ohio, viewership was up 433 percent from the Cavaliers' first game the previous season. Nationally, it drew more eyeballs than any game ESPN had broadcast the previous year except for one. Not bad for a game that aired at 10:30 p.m. on the East Coast.

In the locker room prior to the game against the Suns at America West Arena, LeBron noticed that the analysts in the TNT studio were talking about his performance against the Kings. LeBron turned up the volume and smiled as TNT showed the highlight of him stealing the ball and dishing it to Ricky Davis for a dunk. "You see that?" LeBron said, pointing to a few of the reporters in the locker room. "That's unselfish."

The reporters filed into a room with Coach Silas.

LeBron ducked his head in and suggested that Silas wrap it up.

"Chill," Silas told LeBron.

Then Silas looked at the reporters. "He wants his office back. That's all right with me. No problem, Mr. King James."

That night, LeBron scored twenty-one points against the Suns. And he pulled down twelve rebounds and eight assists. His team lost again.

*   *   *

In the Cavaliers' third game, Ricky Davis berated LeBron for not passing him the ball. After that moment, Silas noticed that LeBron started holding back on offense. It appeared that LeBron was stifling himself in an effort not to overshadow Davis. The last thing Silas and the Cavaliers organization wanted to see was LeBron hold back.

On December 15, 2003, the Cavaliers traded Ricky Davis and two other players to the Boston Celtics. It was the beginning of an overhaul of the entire Cavaliers' roster to build a team around LeBron.

The Davis trade coincided with Nike's official release of LeBron's signature sneaker, now called Air Zoom Generation. To help launch LeBron's signature shoe, Nike also unveiled its second LeBron commercial, which was called "Book of Dimes." The commercial was set in a gymnasium that had been converted to a church with comedian Bernie Mac playing the preacher. The congregation consisted of a slew of NBA Hall of Famers—Jerry West, Moses Malone, Julius Erving, and George Gervin. The biggest stars in the WNBA comprised the choir—Sue Bird, Tamika Catchings, Sheryl Swoopes, Chamique Holdsclaw, and Dawn Staley.

Reading from the "King James Playbook," preacher Bernie Mac praises LeBron.

"Basketball's Chosen One asked the soul of the game for court vision, and it was granted to him," Mac says. "Can I get a layup?"

"Layup!" the congregation says.

Moments later, Mac shouts that he feels the soul of the game coming over him as the gym doors burst open and LeBron dribbles into the church, firing no-look passes to members of the congregation. Anyone who catches one of his passes is blessed with celestial scoring abilities. People are flying through the air, dunking, and the ad ends with the choir singing: "Pass! Pass! Pass! Pass! Pass!"

This ad was more LeBron's idea than Nike's. LeBron had talked with Lynn Merritt a lot about wanting to make commercials that were authentic to his personality. He loved passing. But he also loved humor. And LeBron liked the idea of including players that he had admired growing up—Dr. J, Iceman—and the top female players in the game. But he especially liked having one of his favorite comedians playing the preacher.

The commercial debuted during NFL games in December, guaranteeing maximum exposure. The reception was like music to the NBA's ears. "Turns out Nike's gone clean-cut," *Slate* magazine said. "They've got Le-

Bron smiling, which is decidedly un-gangsta. And perhaps most interesting, this whole spot is about LeBron's devotion to team, not about the jaw-dropping playground moves that often get used to sell sneakers."

LeBron's shoes listed for $110 per pair. They went on sale across the country in mid-December and were sold out everywhere before Christmas. At the same time, LeBron's jersey sales eclipsed six hundred thousand through the first few months of his rookie season, grossing an estimated $69 million. And the television ratings for NBA games were up 15 percent on ESPN and more than 20 percent on TNT.

Shortly after LeBron turned nineteen, in the middle of his rookie season, Savannah Brinson learned that she was pregnant. The situation instantly frightened her. *What am I going to tell my parents?* she fretted. She also feared the implications for LeBron. *What's going to happen to LeBron's career?*

Bawling, Savannah informed LeBron that she was carrying his child.

It was a sobering moment for both of them. Neither of them had planned on this. LeBron had the weight of Nike and the league on his shoulders. Savannah was a scared seventeen-year-old high school senior. But they were both fully committed to keeping the child.

The situation was complicated, but LeBron felt it was manageable.

"It's not going to slow me down," he told Savannah. "And it's not going to slow you down."

Savannah couldn't help feeling overwhelmed.

"We're going to keep doing what we have to do," LeBron told her.

Over the next couple of months, LeBron led the Cavaliers to a strong finish. The Cavaliers finished the season 35-47, missing the playoffs by just one game. He led the team in minutes played, scoring, assists, and steals. And he became the youngest player in NBA history to be named Rookie of the Year.

As soon as the season ended, LeBron headed to Akron and took Savannah to her senior prom. He complimented her on how beautiful she looked wearing an outfit that she had designed herself—a halter top with a mermaid bottom and rhinestones.

She was five months along. They were about to become parents.

SEVENTEEN

NO HARD FEELINGS

Just a few months before the 2004 Summer Olympics in Athens, LeBron got an unexpected invitation to join the US men's basketball team. The Olympic team was in disarray. Nine of the twelve NBA veterans from the USA squad that had won the FIBA Americas Olympic Qualifying Tournament a year earlier had decided not to go to Greece. And most of the NBA stars who had been recruited to fill vacant roster spots had also declined for a variety of reasons: Kobe Bryant was consumed with his upcoming trial. Others preferred to stay home and rest their bodies during the NBA offseason. And several prominent NBA players had security concerns about playing in the first Olympic games since 9/11. US forces had recently captured Saddam Hussein. But 9/11 mastermind Osama bin Laden was still in hiding. And in the aftermath of President George W. Bush's invasion of Iraq, anti-American sentiment was on the rise throughout Europe and the Middle East.

LeBron wasn't particularly worried about his safety. Nor had he given much thought to American foreign policy and the political implications of the Bush administration's war on terror. At the same time, he hadn't thought a lot about playing in the Olympics. "As an African American kid, your whole mindset growing up is 'I wanna be in the NBA,'" LeBron would later say when reflecting back on his experience. "You don't really understand the importance of playing for your country. It's not preached about. It's not talked about. It's not shown."

But LeBron did understand the importance of loyalty and teamwork. And the notion that he was needed on the American team resonated with him. Tim Duncan and Allen Iverson were the only all-stars from the prior NBA season who were going to Athens. LeBron figured he could play a significant role in helping them bring home a gold medal. Plus, at nineteen, he would be the youngest player to join the USA Men's National Team since NBA players had started competing in the Olympics in 1992. Honored by the distinction and eager to join forces with his fellow Americans to compete against the best basketball players in the world, LeBron headed to training camp in Jacksonville, Florida. He had no idea what he'd gotten himself into.

When LeBron arrived, he was pleasantly surprised to find that he wasn't the only rookie on the team. At the last minute, his friend Carmelo Anthony and Miami Heat point guard Dwyane Wade had been added to the roster. The three of them were the cream of the NBA's rookie crop and they dubbed themselves "the Young Guns." Looking around at the veteran players, LeBron and Carmelo figured they had a good chance of joining Duncan and Iverson in the starting lineup.

"Let's put in the work," LeBron told Carmelo.

Not all the veteran players appreciated the rookies' attitude. New York Knicks point guard Stephon Marbury thought LeBron and Carmelo were a little too cocky and far too chummy. Like LeBron, Marbury had been a high school sensation. In the nineties he'd been a playground legend in Coney Island. But he'd never made the transition to superstar in the NBA. In eight years, Marbury had bounced around to four teams and never gotten close to experiencing the kind of fame and money that had already come LeBron's way. And in New York, even Carmelo was getting more props than Marbury. If it had been up to Knicks fans, they would have swapped Marbury for Melo in a heartbeat.

The resentment between several of the veterans and the rookies was a two-way street. LeBron and Carmelo felt the veterans should have done a better job creating an atmosphere of camaraderie. "They were arrogant," Carmelo said when reflecting on that experience. "They weren't like, 'I got you, young'en. I'll take care of you.' It was not like that. You were out there by yourself."

Head coach Larry Brown was frustrated, too. The players he'd coached in the qualifying tournament a year earlier had been seasoned veterans who had played as a cohesive unit. The current roster had been configured by a committee. Brown had essentially inherited a mishmash of players who had no chemistry. And Team USA had just fifteen practice sessions before heading into competition. True to his coaching style, Brown planned to rely on the veteran players for most of the minutes. During a series of exhibition games in Germany, Serbia, and Turkey, Brown settled on a starting lineup that included:

Allen Iverson, guard
Stephon Marbury, guard
Tim Duncan, center
Richard Jefferson, forward
Shawn Marion, forward

LeBron wasn't happy. Since he had started playing organized basketball as a child, he'd never been on a team where he wasn't a starter. And he hadn't joined the Olympic team just to be a practice player.

Carmelo wasn't pleased, either. He and LeBron were both forwards. And Carmelo believed they were both better forwards than Richard Jefferson and Shawn Marion. "They playin' in front of us?" Carmelo said to LeBron. "What?"

Once LeBron and Carmelo realized they weren't starters, they made a pact before each practice. *If the starters aren't ready to play today, let's smoke these guys.*

On the eve of the final exhibition game before heading to Athens, LeBron and the rest of the team were asleep in a luxury hotel in Istanbul when bombs exploded at two tourist hotels in another part of the city, killing two people and wounding eleven. Kurdish separatists were suspected of being responsible. One day earlier, Lakers forward Lamar Odom had been among a group of players from the American team who had taken a tour in the area where the bombs later went off. Odom had an eerie feeling when he learned about the terrorist attack.

LeBron hadn't taken the tour with Odom. But when US officials briefed the team on the morning after the bombing, LeBron asked more questions than anyone else. He wanted to know what had happened, and he wanted to know what the plan was to ensure the safety of the team. Later that day, a formation of police vehicles escorted the US Olympic team bus from the hotel. And at the arena, LeBron and his teammates walked between two lines of police officers in riot gear when they approached the court. With Tim Duncan leading the way, the US team won the exhibition game. But the Turkish fans were harsh on the American team.

The hostility toward the US team was even more spirited in Athens.

While in Greece, the US team stayed in the Port of Piraeus on the *Queen Mary 2*, the world's largest ocean liner. At that time, first-class accommodations for a transatlantic crossing on the luxury vessel were about $27,000 per person. The team stayed there because the ship provided maximum security for the players. But the luxury ship fed into the pervasive view heading into the Olympics that the US men's basketball team was comprised of arrogant, pampered stars.

In the opening round of competition, Puerto Rico trounced the heavily favored US team, 92–73. The loss marked the first time that the US team had been beaten since NBA players had begun competing in the Olympics in 1992. And Greek spectators roared with approval.

LeBron played just thirteen minutes against Puerto Rico and took only three shots, scoring five points. In the final minutes of the game, the arena was louder than any venue he'd ever played in. Sitting on the far end of the bench, he draped a towel over his head and buried his face in his hands.

Afterward, Coach Brown ripped into his team, questioning their effort and hammering them for failing to appreciate how badly other teams wanted to beat them. Sportswriters back in the States ridiculed the US team, one prominent basketball writer labeling them "a joke." And international fans in Greece reveled at USA basketball's demise. "People no root for U.S.A.," a Lithuanian fan told ESPN. "Because nobody like what U.S.A. is doing rest of world."

LeBron was miserable. Halfway around the world, he spent most of his time stuck on a ship, alone in his room. Come game time, he rode the bench on a team whose coach had decided to rely more and more heavily on players like Stephon Marbury, Richard Jefferson, and Shawn Marion. Meanwhile, the Greek fans were rejoicing at Team USA's loss. LeBron hadn't signed up for any of this. He missed his family. He missed his friends. He missed Ohio.

Despite losing another game—this time to Lithuania—the US team won three games to qualify for the medal round. But it lost to Argentina, 89–81, ensuring that Team USA would not win the gold medal. For LeBron, the loss to Argentina was particularly hard to watch. With his team playing from behind the entire game, LeBron stayed on the bench, logging just three minutes of action. Even Allen Iverson couldn't understand why the most athletically gifted basketball player on the team barely got in the game.

The US ended up winning the bronze.

Dejected and embarrassed, LeBron boarded the team bus for the ride to the airport. Having averaged just eleven minutes and five points per game during the Olympics, he was talking to Carmelo when Stephon Marbury boarded the bus and went after both of them.

"You guys are nothin'!" Marbury shouted. "You didn't help this team."

LeBron and Carmelo went right back at Marbury. The argument quickly escalated.

"Ya'll wanna be buddy-buddy," Marbury said. "Fuck all that buddy-buddy shit."

LeBron and Carmelo had no use for Marbury. And he had no use for them.

"You're never gonna be good," Marbury shouted.

LeBron had heard enough. After thirty-five days overseas, he couldn't wait to get back to the NBA.

In the fall of 2004, *GQ* wanted to profile LeBron. The popular men's fashion and style magazine known for putting Hollywood actors on the cover seldom featured NBA players in its pages. But the magazine's editor was a hoops fan, and he wanted to explore how nineteen-year-old LeBron was handling the pressure of life in the NBA. Aaron Goodwin thought it was a good idea for LeBron to cooperate.

LeBron agreed. And after going to Los Angeles to work on his next Nike commercial, LeBron headed to New York to knock out the *GQ* interview before the Cavaliers started training camp. Maverick Carter, Rich Paul, and Randy Mims accompanied him. They were joined by Mary Ford, the director of public relations at Aaron Goodwin's agency. Chewing Bubblicious gum and wearing baggy shorts, a T-shirt, and a black Nike skullcap, LeBron stood with Ford in the lobby of the W Hotel in Midtown Manhattan, waiting for the writer to arrive.

GQ asked Larry Platt to write the LeBron piece. Platt was the editor of *Philadelphia* magazine and had recently written a biography of 76ers point guard Allen Iverson. An astute observer of the NBA, Platt jumped at the opportunity to write about LeBron for *GQ*. Platt felt the NBA was in real trouble. At the end of the summer, Kobe Bryant had been cleared of the sexual-assault charge when his accuser had ultimately decided not to testify at trial, causing prosecutors to drop the case. But the sordid headlines generated during the yearlong legal wrangling had left a cloud over Kobe and the league. At the same time, friction between Kobe and Shaquille O'Neal resulted in the Lakers trading O'Neal to the Miami Heat, breaking up the league's most dynamic duo. On top of all that, there was the Olympic debacle in Athens. Platt wondered whether LeBron could be the NBA's savior.

When Ford introduced LeBron to Platt, LeBron had no intention of opening up in any sort of substantive way. He'd become guarded about his personal life, especially around journalists.

Looking to establish a quick rapport, Platt tried an old trick—name-dropping. He brought up William Wesley.

LeBron perked up. "You know Wes?" he asked.

"I know Wes from Philly," Platt said.

LeBron smiled and looked across the lobby for his friends. "Yo, yo, yo," he said to them. "This guy knows Wes!"

Maverick and Rich walked over and started telling funny Wes stories.

Platt had made an inroad.

The group headed next door to the Blue Fin, a Times Square restaurant, where Platt intended to interview LeBron over lunch. When they arrived, the restaurant was empty and a hostess informed them that the kitchen was closed for the afternoon.

Blowing a big bubble with his chewing gum, LeBron stepped forward. "Let me see the chef," he said.

Moments later, a manager appeared. Realizing that LeBron James was in the restaurant, the manager arranged for a table to be set. A cook was summoned. Menus were brought out. And although it was midafternoon, LeBron ordered breakfast. Everyone else ordered lunch.

While waiting for the food to arrive, LeBron mercilessly ridiculed Rich.

Rich responded by pulling out an advance copy of a soon-to-be-released comic book featuring LeBron. Pointing at LeBron's depiction, Rich said, "Look at him. He's got this small head and these big-ass ears."

The guys laughed at LeBron.

"This little guy," LeBron told Platt while pointing at Rich, "he's a co-median."

Platt didn't know anything about Maverick, Rich, or Randy. But he was struck by the contrast between them and Allen Iverson's inner circle. While working on Iverson's biography, Platt had concluded that some of the guys around Iverson weren't a good influence. One of them had a long rap sheet. Another one got caught stealing personal property from Iverson and selling it to a pawnshop. Iverson had to fire a third one for being disloyal. But to Platt, LeBron's friends looked like a bunch of kids who were horsing around. Rich seemed like a goofball. It was a welcome change from Iverson's crew, but Platt found it hard to take LeBron's group seriously.

Platt noted one other key difference. Iverson never treated his inner circle like equals. They were on the payroll, and the vibe between them and Iverson reflected that. LeBron's inner circle seemed more like a brotherhood of equals.

A waiter appeared and put a plate full of pancakes and sausages in front of LeBron, along with a heap of sliced bananas. In between bites, LeBron lifted his ass and let loose a thunderous fart. "Damn, Mary," LeBron said, looking at Mary Ford. "Don't be fartin'."

Maverick and Rich cracked up and high-fived each other.

Mary Ford was expressionless. But Platt couldn't help chuckling. The frat house interplay between LeBron and his friends made the experience fun. But Pratt was starting to wonder whether he'd get anything serious out of LeBron. Then Platt asked him a basketball question.

The grin disappearing from his face, LeBron looked Platt in the eye.

"Once I get comfortable with my surroundings out there, it seems like everything just slows down," LeBron said. "I don't want to sound cocky when I say this, but it's like I see things before they happen. I kind of know where the defenders are gonna be. I kind of know where my teammates are gonna be, sometimes before they know."

With his tape recorder running, Platt was struck by the sudden change in LeBron's tone. His voice had gotten deeper. In a matter of seconds, he'd gone from behaving like a playful teen to sounding like a savant.

"My game is really played above time," LeBron continued. "I don't say that like I'm saying I'm ahead of my time. I'm saying, like, if I'm on the court and I throw a pass, the ball that I've thrown will lead my teammate right where he needs to go, before he even knows that that's the right place to go to. I just slow things down to a point where I can control what happens."

Wow, Platt thought. *This guy really is a prodigy.*

By the end of the interview, Platt had concluded that the NBA's future was in good hands with LeBron. Despite the pressures of becoming the league's leading man, at nineteen he appeared remarkably carefree to Platt. When Platt made that observation, he had no idea that LeBron had a high school sweetheart and that the two of them were about to become parents.

When LeBron returned to New York a few weeks later for the *GQ* photo shoot at a loft in Tribeca, Platt was on hand to conduct a follow-up interview. While LeBron posed, Platt noted that the lunch spread included lots of boxes of Fruity Pebbles. When Platt inquired, he was told that the breakfast cereal had been LeBron's only request. Platt made a mental note—if it had been a photo shoot for Allen Iverson, he would have demanded bottles of Cristal champagne.

Cavaliers coach Paul Silas had been impressed with LeBron's ability to make the jump from high school to NBA stardom as a rookie. But Silas was even more amazed when training camp opened in 2004 and he saw how much LeBron had changed during the off-season. He had added a few more pounds of muscle. His outside shot was vastly improved. He'd gotten better at finding the open man when he was double-teamed. And he was much more vocal on the court, taking command and directing his teammates. In all his years as a coach, Silas had never seen a player undergo such a dramatic transformation in such a short period of time. He informed LeBron that he was changing his position from shooting guard to small forward. And he told LeBron that he had the green light to go all out on offense. The team was his.

LeBron liked being back with the Cavaliers, back to what he was used to. And he enjoyed playing for Silas, who appreciated his talents and went out of his way to mentor LeBron on the court. LeBron let Silas know how much he appreciated him, and he assured his coach that he wouldn't let him down.

But toward the end of camp, LeBron stepped away from the team for a few days to be with Savannah. On October 6, 2004, LeBron was present when Savannah gave birth to a boy. For LeBron, it was a life-altering moment that was far more profound than anything he'd experienced as an athlete. For much of his life, LeBron had longed for a father. Suddenly, he was one. Teeming with pride, he wanted his boy to have his name—LeBron Raymone James Jr.

Barely eighteen, Savannah watched her newborn sleeping against LeBron's chest.

Now that he had a baby in his arms, the weight of LeBron's new responsibilities settled on him. He had a family to think about. He had always worked hard to build and maintain an honorable reputation. But now that was even more important. *I can't,* he told himself, *do anything that hurts the reputation of my family.*

LeBron stayed with Savannah and their son for three days before returning to the team. Before he left, they agreed that LeBron would shield her and their son from public scrutiny.

When the press asked about the birth, LeBron declined to say much. He refused to reveal Savannah's name or the name of their child. The *New York Times* referred to Savannah simply as "the mother, who is from Akron." The Associated Press referred to LeBron Jr. as "the baby boy." Without elaborating, LeBron told the *Akron Beacon Journal,* "My main goal [is] to try and be a better father than the one I had. I didn't know him. I didn't know the situation he was in. But I'm going to do my job the best way I can."

In Cleveland's second home game of the season, the Cavaliers trailed the Phoenix Suns, 85–66, at the end of the third quarter. LeBron decided to make good on the promise he'd made to Silas in training camp. In the fourth quarter, LeBron erupted for seventeen points, outscoring the entire Suns team by himself and forcing the game into overtime. The Cavaliers won the game. LeBron finished with thirty-eight points. A few nights later, he put up thirty-three points against the Warriors. Then the Cavaliers traveled to Charlotte to face the Bobcats. Partway through the game, LeBron went airborne to retrieve a pass that had been thrown way too high. At the peak of his leap, his right hand was near the top of the backboard. In one motion, he caught the ball and rammed it through the cylinder on his way down. After the game, a reporter asked him about the dunk.

"I told you I could fly," LeBron said, grinning. "I like it up there. Not too many people up there with me."

The Cavaliers still had a long way to go as a team, but night in and night out, LeBron was dazzling fans in Cleveland and drawing sold-out crowds in other cities throughout the league.

The Detroit Pistons were the reigning NBA champions. The previous year, they had reached the NBA Finals after outlasting the Indiana Pacers in a grueling six-game series in the Eastern Conference Finals. On November 19, 2004, the two teams met at the Palace of Auburn Hills. This time, the Pacers clobbered the Pistons. And with under a minute to play and his team up by fifteen points, Pacers forward Ron Artest slapped the head of Pistons center Ben Wallace while he attempted a layup. Angry, Wallace pushed Artest in the face, triggering whistles and prompting players from both teams to step in to prevent a fight. While the referees huddled to discuss possible ejections, Artest lay down on the scorer's table. A Pistons fan hurled a cup of soda at Artest, who bolted into the stands, sparking a melee that quickly escalated out of control. Pacers players joined Artest in the stands, brawling with fans. Fists flew. A fan threw a metal chair at Pacers center Jermaine O'Neal. The Pacers' radio announcer was trampled, fracturing five of his vertebrae. Fans even streamed onto the court, squaring off with players as police tried to escort them off the floor. With ESPN televising the game, the scene of players' children and other innocent spectators crying in fear was broadcast into viewers' living rooms throughout the country.

Nine players were suspended by the league, several were suspended indefinitely for conduct that the NBA deemed "shocking, repulsive, and inexcusable." Five players were charged with misdemeanor assault and eventually pleaded no contest; they were sentenced to probation and most of them were ordered to undergo anger management counseling. Several fans were also convicted of crimes for their roles in the melee, and some were permanently banned from attending games. The incident—dubbed "the Malice at the Palace"—was the most infamous brawl in NBA history, and it represented the nadir of the league's public image.

The scene in Detroit was anathema to LeBron. Violence between players—never mind violence between players and fans—had no place in the game. Going back to his childhood days in the local rec league in Akron, LeBron had never picked a fight with an opposing player. As he got older and some players targeted him with hard fouls, LeBron played on, choosing to get his revenge with his play instead of his fists. Even when fans shouted disparaging comments at him, including occasional racist epithets during his junior and senior years of high school, LeBron kept his composure. Often the biggest, strongest player on the floor, LeBron never played the bully. From the time he was a little boy, he hated bullies.

But LeBron loved to play mind games with people who underestimated him. Five days after the melee in Detroit, the Cavaliers hosted the Pistons in Cleveland. In a pregame interview with LeBron, a reporter brought up the fact that Pistons head coach Larry Brown had kept him on the bench during the Olympics. The reporter asked if his Olympic experience would be a source of motivation against Brown's team.

"That's over," LeBron said. "I don't need motivation from that to play."

It was true that LeBron didn't need external motivation. But the competitor in him burned hot. And he hadn't forgotten about Athens. "I wish I'd had a better opportunity to showcase my talents," LeBron added in his pregame interview. "That's all it came down to. There ain't no hard feelings."

Before tip-off, LeBron handed Coach Brown a card thanking him for the baby gift that Brown had sent a month earlier. Then LeBron destroyed the Pistons. He started with violent two-handed dunks. Then he dropped jumpers like bombs from all over the perimeter. He banged his way through the paint, spun through double-teams, and flipped the finger roll in a moment of artistry. He even wagged his tongue after sinking a pair of three-pointers to put the game away. By the time LeBron exited the game with two minutes to play, Cleveland fans were on their feet, saluting LeBron with a thunderous ovation. He had poured in a career-high forty-three points.

Coach Silas smiled. *No hard feelings, huh?*

A month after LeBron celebrated his twentieth birthday, *GQ* published its profile of him, calling LeBron "the one man who can lead the troubled league back to the promised land." That same month, *Sports Illustrated* put LeBron on the cover again, this time with a bold question: "Best Ever?" It wasn't hyperbole. Just halfway through his second season, LeBron was already the youngest player in NBA history to score 2,000 points, notch 500 assists, and pull down 500 rebounds.

There were plenty of reasons for rank-and-file players to envy LeBron.

But no one questioned LeBron's bona fides as an elite player. He was chosen to start for the Eastern squad in the NBA All-Star Game in Denver on February 19, 2005. In a corridor beneath the arena before the game, LeBron was surrounded by Shaquille O'Neal, Kobe Bryant, Tim Duncan, Allen Iverson, Yao Ming, Tracy McGrady, and Kevin Garnett.

Iverson looked at LeBron. Then Iverson looked at the other players who were making their first appearance in the All-Star Game—Dwyane Wade, Gilbert Arenas, and Amar'e Stoudemire.

"All these first-timers," Iverson said.

Kevin Garnett laughed as Iverson turned and stared at LeBron, the youngest of the bunch.

LeBron felt everyone's eyes on him.

"He ain't nothin' but sixteen years old," Iverson joked.

The veterans laughed.

When the East and West starters took the floor for the opening tap, they started debating among themselves over which basket belonged to which team. LeBron asserted himself. "We going that way," he said, pointing.

The players kept chirping.

The referee looked at LeBron. "Which basket you want?" he said.

"That basket," LeBron said, pointing. "We going that way."

The referee nodded.

When the action started, LeBron ran the offense for the East. After he knocked down a long jumper, teammate Vince Carter told him, "Way to go, boy. Welcome!"

LeBron smacked Carter's outstretched hand.

On defense, LeBron directed traffic. When his teammate Shaquille O'Neal was about to leave the paint to guard a player coming off a screen, LeBron called him off.

"Switch, Shaq!" LeBron yelled. "Stay there."

Even coming out of time-outs, LeBron acted like a coach on the floor, telling everyone who to guard.

"You got Nash," LeBron told Iverson.

Then he grabbed Dwyane Wade. "You got Ray Allen," LeBron told him.

At twenty, LeBron was the leader among the All-Stars.

Everyone could see that it was only a matter of time before LeBron would lead the Cavaliers to the playoffs.

EIGHTEEN

I'M OLDER NOW

Dan Gilbert was a twenty-two-year-old first-year law student when he started his first company, Rock Financial Corporation, and turned it into one of the most successful independent mortgage banks in the US. Eventually, Gilbert's company was renamed Quicken Loans. By 2004, Quicken Loans was the top-ranked online retail home lender in the industry, closing approximately $12 billion in residential mortgage loans that year. By then, Gilbert had his eye on acquiring the Cleveland Cavaliers. Right before the Cavaliers drafted LeBron, the franchise had been valued at $222 million. After LeBron's rookie year, the team's value had gone up considerably. Gilbert offered to buy the team for $375 million. And in February 2005, the NBA approved the sale of the Cavaliers to Gilbert.

LeBron knew little about Gilbert or how he'd made his fortune. But LeBron had no doubt that Gilbert was going to be much more hands-on than the previous owner. It was also clear that Gilbert saw LeBron as the fulcrum of his $375 million investment. On day one, Gilbert referred to LeBron and said, "It's our job as owners and management to build a team around him that can win championships, and hopefully multiple ones."

A couple of weeks later, LeBron played the best game of his life, scoring fifty-six points against the Raptors in Toronto. It was a spectacular performance, enabling him to eclipse Rick Barry as the youngest player in NBA history to score fifty points in a game. LeBron's scoring outburst also set a franchise record for the Cavaliers. But the Cavs still lost the game, marking their ninth straight defeat on the road.

The next day, the Cavs fired head coach Paul Silas, citing his inability to provide support on the court for LeBron. LeBron liked Silas, but he wasn't surprised that Silas was let go—the players weren't responding to his coaching style. What caught LeBron off guard was the timing of Silas's departure—only eighteen games remained in the regular season and the team was still in the playoff hunt, clinging to the eighth seed. One of the assistant coaches was made interim head coach while Gilbert took it upon himself to search for a permanent replacement.

It was unclear how much Gilbert knew about the intricacies of basketball. But his commitment to winning was unmistakable. He planned to invest millions in upgrading the arena. He was prepared to spend real money on free agents to bolster the roster. He even planned to build a new practice facility for the team.

LeBron had a suggestion. In one of his first conversations with Gilbert, LeBron brought up something he'd raised, to no avail, with the previous ownership group—his displeasure with the team plane. There'd been a few instances when the team's air travel hadn't been the smoothest. LeBron had flown on better planes in high school. In his view, it was time to upgrade. All you had to do was look at the exterior, which still had the old team logo, faded and worn. "If you want to start helping us become a better franchise," he told Gilbert, "we need a new fucking plane."

LeBron had a tone and an expression that made Gilbert smile. He made a mental note about the plane.

The Cavaliers finished the 2004–2005 season 42-40. The winning record demonstrated solid progress for a team that had won only seventeen games the year before LeBron's arrival. But the Cavaliers had collapsed down the stretch and for the second straight season fell one victory shy of qualifying for the playoffs. The day after the season ended, Dan Gilbert fired general manager Jim Paxson. "The new ownership team," Gilbert said, "believes it is time for a new direction in leadership in the basketball operations side of the business."

While Gilbert was busy shaking things up in Cleveland, LeBron was about to rock the NBA. Now that he was a father, he felt an added responsibility to focus on his young family's long-term financial security. *It's time*, LeBron told himself, *to become a man*. Part of that entailed taking personal control of his business affairs. He reached for his phone and punched in Maverick's number.

Maverick had just flown in from Oregon when he picked up the call.

"You in town?" LeBron asked.

"Yeah," Maverick said.

"I wanna come meet you," LeBron told him.

Maverick was on his way to have lunch with his mother. But he could tell from LeBron's tone that something was up. He told LeBron to meet him at his mother's house. Hours later, they were seated opposite each other at the kitchen table.

After catching up, LeBron started talking about what he believed he could become as a player. He'd just finished the season second overall in scoring in the NBA. He was also among the league leaders in assists and steals. Statistically, he had hit milestones that no second-year player had achieved, not even Michael Jordan. Yet LeBron had much higher expectations for himself—he wanted to become the best that had ever played the game. At the same time, he wanted to be just as successful in his off-the-court ventures. And he wasn't satisfied with how things were progressing on that front.

"Mav," LeBron said, "my agent and I are just not seeing eye to eye right now."

Maverick was well aware that Eddie and Gloria had chosen Goodwin to be LeBron's agent.

"I love my mom," LeBron told Maverick. "But I got to make this decision for myself."

Maverick could tell he'd given this a lot of thought.

"It's time, you know?" LeBron said. "I'm older now. I'm twenty years old. I'll be twenty-one in December."

The implications of such a bold move were immediately apparent to Maverick—this was going to be a big fucking deal.

Yet LeBron was calm. He had a plan.

"I want to do things differently than anyone has ever done them before," LeBron said.

Maverick couldn't help wondering what this had to do with him.

For LeBron it was simple. On the court, LeBron was a perfectionist. As such, he needed to remain hyper-focused on his development as a basketball player. No distractions. At the same time, he planned to set up his own company to oversee his marketing and business ventures. But he needed someone to run it. Someone he trusted.

LeBron looked at Maverick and brought up Nike and how much Maverick had learned while working there over the past two years. He felt that

Maverick's experience in Beaverton had groomed him to do something bigger. And although Maverick didn't have a business background per se, he woke up every day convinced that he had to prove himself. He made to-do lists and felt like a failure if he got to the end of the day without checking off every item on his list. LeBron knew that his friend wasn't addicted to money; he was addicted to accomplishing things. Between Maverick's work ethic and his loyalty, LeBron was convinced that he had the right guy.

Maverick took a deep breath. He already had his dream job. There were indoor and outdoor tracks for running. The campus had football fields and baseball diamonds. During lunch, he could play pickup basketball games on state-of-the-art courts. And he got paid to work with talented storytellers whose job was to promote the Nike brand. Best of all, Maverick had fallen in love with the Pacific Northwest. Life was good. He would have been content to spend the rest of his career in Beaverton.

Yet as he sat at his mother's kitchen table, staring at his best friend, Maverick couldn't ignore the sense of intrigue and excitement he felt. LeBron was talking about doing something that had never been done in the NBA—cutting ties with his agent, striking out on his own, and starting a company that would handle his endorsement deals and grow his business ventures. And he was entrusting Maverick to take the helm.

I gotta go for this, Maverick told himself. *I gotta give this a shot.*

It was a huge leap of faith. LeBron was going to leave his agent, and Maverick was going to leave Nike.

LeBron wasn't worried.

Maverick couldn't help being a little anxious, thinking, *If I fuck this up . . .*

Gloria was furious. Convinced that Maverick had pushed LeBron to fire his agent, she telephoned Maverick and cursed him out.

Maverick was caught off guard. But he knew Gloria well. He loved her like family. He even called her Aunt Glo. So he knew full well that when Aunt Glo got hot, it wasn't advisable to try to fight fire with fire.

Gloria made her points—LeBron and Maverick didn't know what in the hell they were doing, and they weren't ready to strike out on their own. After all, they had no experience.

Maverick did not take offense. Instead, he calmly talked her down, explaining that he and LeBron were going to work closely with LeBron's lawyer and that they were going to hire experts. They weren't going to be rash. In other words, they knew what they didn't know. But LeBron had a creative vision for his future, and they were going to work with the right people to execute it.

It would take time for Gloria to come around.

Aaron Goodwin was stunned, too. One moment he was riding a wave as the agent for one of the richest athletes in the world. Then, in early May, he was informed in writing that he was no longer representing Le-Bron. It felt like a wipeout. Dazed, Goodwin wondered what was going on. From his perspective, things could not have been going better for him and LeBron. They had even invested in a restaurant together in Seattle, near Goodwin's office.

But the restaurant in Seattle was symptomatic of the problem—LeBron didn't want to do the traditional things that athletes do with agents, like sink money into a sports bar or simply put his name on this or that. LeBron had much bigger aspirations. He wasn't content to be one of the richest athletes in the world. He wanted to become one of the wealthiest individuals in the world. And he planned to get there with his own guys.

Headlines such as "James Fires Agent" were embarrassing for Goodwin. ESPN reported: "It is expected that Maverick Carter, James's close friend and a former high school teammate, will be part of a team that will take over deal-making responsibilities."

LeBron wasn't talking.

Neither was Maverick.

The NBA players union would only confirm that LeBron no longer had an agent.

Goodwin took the high road. "For nearly three years, I have had the wonderful opportunity to represent LeBron James as his agent," he said in a prepared statement. "I am grateful for the chance to have worked with LeBron and Gloria James. . . . On behalf of Goodwin Sports Management, we wish LeBron and his family the very best."

People in the league office were wondering what the hell was going on. Published reports speculated that LeBron's three friends were taking over. None of them were registered agents. For that matter, none of them had graduated from college, a point that numerous media outlets were highlighting to suggest that LeBron was acting foolishly. There was even speculation that LeBron had axed Goodwin out of envy over the success of Dwyane Wade, who made the playoffs in his second season with the Miami Heat. "Just a guess," wrote *New York Times* columnist Harvey Araton, "but I'd say James, who replaced Goodwin with one of his high school homies, needed a scapegoat and will be lashing out some more until he has what Wade does, the ball and a formidable buffer like Shaq, who has been through the playoff wars."

For LeBron, reading about himself was sometimes a reminder that people talk a lot of shit. *Lashing out?* If anything, LeBron was guilty of saying too little. *Envious of Dwyane Wade?* D-Wade was a friend. Whatever. LeBron at least knew how the old guard in the NBA and in the media looked at Maverick and Rich and Randy—like his high school homies.

LeBron knew he needed expert advice to navigate the finance world. But not the kind of run-of-the-mill input that athletes got from sports agents. Rather, LeBron wanted someone who knew his way around the world of finance the way LeBron knew his way around a basketball court. He wanted a highflier.

In 2005, LeBron met investment banker Paul Wachter. After cutting his teeth at Wall Street firms Kidder, Peabody & Co. and Bear Stearns Companies, Wachter had set out on his own in 1997, founding Main Street Advisors, a boutique financial and asset-management firm for the rich and powerful. His clients included California governor Arnold Schwarzenegger, commodities trader John W. Henry, and network television producer Tom Werner. Wachter had started advising Schwarzenegger when the actor was amassing his estimated $200 million fortune as one of Hollywood's leading men. And Wachter had advised Henry and Werner when their company, New England Sports Ventures, purchased the Boston Red Sox for a record $700 million in 2001.

LeBron couldn't help being impressed with Wachter's clientele. And the fact that Wachter provided investment advice to guys who owned one of the most celebrated professional sports teams in the world was particularly intriguing. The prospect of being the only player in the NBA who was receiving the kind of sophisticated financial guidance that wealthy team owners were able to tap into was very appealing to LeBron.

Wachter wouldn't normally have taken on an athlete as a client. But LeBron wasn't a normal athlete. On top of his NBA salary, he had around $125 million in endorsement deals. There were only three athletes in the world who were earning more money in endorsements than LeBron: Tiger Woods, Germany's Formula One driver Michael Schumacher, and English soccer star David Beckham. Woods and Beckham were in the prime of their careers. Schumacher was at the end of his. LeBron had barely begun.

Yet it wasn't simply LeBron's earning capacity that impressed Wachter. Rather, it was LeBron's entrepreneurial approach and the way his mind worked. To Wachter, LeBron sounded more like a mathematician than a jock. He asked the kind of questions that bankers and investors asked. *He's a numbers guy*, Wachter thought.

Wachter was impressed with Maverick, too. Maverick was a novice when it came to money and investing. But he was malleable. He asked good questions and was eager to learn. In Wachter's view, LeBron had chosen wisely in selecting Maverick as a partner.

In terms of long-term implications, LeBron's decision to go with Wachter as his personal investment banker was probably the most pivotal move he made in his basketball career. Wachter's arrival not only ensured that LeBron had the most sophisticated financial advisor in the NBA, but it also established a conduit for him and his inner circle to meet entertainment moguls, Wall Street titans, and captains of industry. More immediately, however, Wachter helped open LeBron's eyes to new ways of thinking about endorsement deals. Instead of simply lending his name to products, LeBron could take ownership of his image.

Relying on strategic advice from Wachter and legal advice from attorney Fred Nance, LeBron set up LRMR Management Company, LLC. The acronym comprised the first letters of the first names of LeBron, Rich, Maverick, and Randy. The four of them were partners in the company, and Maverick was named CEO. It was a completely unconventional move that positioned LeBron to go beyond simply getting paid for letting companies use his image to sell products. In the future, he would look to form partnerships with companies by seeking an equity stake. No other athlete was doing anything like that.

In the meantime, LeBron had settled on Leon Rose to be his new agent. Rose was a close friend of William Wesley's. And Rose was willing to do things LeBron's way, meaning he'd be the agent of record, but LRMR would be calling the shots.

Rose was also open to mentoring Rich Paul, who was growing interested in becoming a sports agent. With LeBron's backing, Rich was positioned to work under Rose and learn the business much the same way that Maverick had learned when he interned for Lynn Merritt before being hired at Nike.

As far as LeBron was concerned, things were falling into place. Rich was working with Rose. Maverick was CEO of LRMR Management. And thanks to LeBron's influence, the Cavaliers were in the process of putting Randy on the payroll and giving him the job title of player liaison. The Four Horsemen were moving up.

Although NBA league officials had some concerns about LeBron's decision-making, Nike chairman Phil Knight had a different perspective. In July 2005, he and LeBron were at an event when LeBron approached him.

"Phil, can I see you a moment?"

"Of course."

They stepped into a private space.

"When I first signed with you," LeBron said, "I didn't know all that much about the history of Nike. So I've been studying up."

"Oh?" Knight said.

"You're the founder."

"Well. Cofounder. Yes. It surprises a lot of people."

"And Nike was born in 1972," LeBron said.

"Well. Born? Yes. I suppose."

"Right. So I went to my jeweler and had them find a Rolex watch from 1972."

LeBron handed him the watch.

Inspecting it, Knight noticed that LeBron had had it engraved: *With thanks for taking a chance on me.*

Stunned, Knight didn't know what to say. LeBron, in Knight's mind, had been close to a sure thing. But Knight also liked taking chances on people. To him, that was what business was all about. And he liked the way LeBron was taking the same kind of entrepreneurial approach.

LeBron's relationship with Nike was only getting deeper. Shortly after

LeBron met with Knight, Nike sent LeBron to Tokyo, Hong Kong, and Beijing. In each city, he conducted basketball clinics for kids, participated in promotional events, and spoke to the press. It was a slog. But he was determined to become a global brand. And he felt fortunate to have Nike's backing. Everywhere he went in China, he encountered fans who were wearing his shoes, wearing his jersey, and chanting his name.

The sold-out crowd at Continental Airlines Arena in East Rutherford, New Jersey, was on its feet. It was October 27, 2005, and Jay-Z had just finished the set list for his extravagant "I Declare War" concert, which featured a stage set up like the Oval Office. The show had opened dramatically with Jay-Z behind the Resolute desk, flanked by Secret Service agents, while "Public Service Announcement" blasted through the sound system. Then throughout the night, the biggest names in hip-hop made guest appearances onstage. P. Diddy. Kanye West. Nas. For the audience, it was one surprise after another. Now thousands of screaming fans put their hands together in the shape of a diamond, the symbol for Roc-A-Fella Records. They were calling for an encore. They wanted to be surprised one more time.

Backstage, LeBron was hyped up. He was accustomed to performing in his basketball uniform before sold-out crowds. But tonight he was wearing street clothes and boots. Beckoned by Jay-Z, he stepped onto the stage, joining forces with Kanye and P. Diddy and Nas as they performed Jay-Z's hit "Encore."

Can I get an encore, do you want more?
Cookin' raw with the Brooklyn boy
So for one last time I need y'all to roar.

LeBron knew the next line: "Now what the hell are you waitin' for?"
The audience was delirious.

For LeBron the experience was rapturous. His friendship with Jay-Z had become so close that he got invited to do things that no other athlete got invited to do. They communicated almost daily. Jay-Z had gotten to know Maverick and Rich and Randy. He'd also gotten close to Gloria and Savannah, while LeBron had become very friendly with Jay-Z's inner circle and with Beyoncé. LeBron and his friends and family had a standing invitation and backstage passes to any Jay-Z show, and Jay-Z and Beyoncé had a standing invitation and courtside seats to any of LeBron's games.

LeBron and Jay-Z were emerging as two of the most influential African Americans to shape mainstream popular culture. Together, they viewed each other as miracles—one had grown up imitating Michael Jackson and made it out of Bedford-Stuyvesant, and the other had emulated Michael Jordan and made it out of Spring Hill. And they constantly looked out for each other. For instance, around the time that LeBron was being criticized in the media for firing his agent and going into business with his friends, Jay-Z introduced LeBron to Keith Estabrook, the senior VP of corporate communications for Sony Music.

Estabrook oversaw Sony's worldwide media relations. And although PR teams from Nike and the Cavaliers were constantly available to LeBron, Jay-Z figured his friend could use a dedicated expert.

During the summer of 2005, LeBron hired Estabrook to be his personal publicist. In addition to interfacing with Nike and the Cavaliers, Estabrook would work closely with Maverick to manage all of LeBron's national-media interviews and public appearances.

Jay-Z also funneled ideas to LeBron's inner circle. At the "I Declare War" concert in East Rutherford, Jay-Z introduced Maverick to Rachel Johnson, who was P. Diddy's personal stylist. The introduction was both timely and fortuitous.

One week earlier, NBA commissioner David Stern had announced a controversial new dress code requiring all players to wear collared dress shirts or turtlenecks, dress pants, and dress shoes with socks at all team or league functions. Headgear, T-shirts, sneakers, and work boots were prohibited. Chains, pendants, and medallions were also banned. The *New York Times* described the initiative as "the N.B.A.'s latest push to look a little less gangsta and a little more genteel."

Some players had openly pushed back against the new mandate. The mainstream media, for the most part, sided with the commissioner. "Surely leagues have the right to demand a level of presentable appearance from the young personages who represent them," NPR sports commentator Frank Deford said on *Morning Edition*. "And let's be honest, in a very short period of time the snapshot of an NBA player off the court has gone from the impeccable and classy Michael Jordan to what Phil Mushnick of the *New York Post* calls 'players looking like recruitment officers for the Bloods and Crips.'"

Against this backdrop, Maverick got to know Johnson. He was instantly impressed with her background. In many ways, she possessed the same entrepreneurial spirit as he did.

Johnson had been in her junior year of college at Florida A&M University, a historically Black college, when she met Groovey Lew, a hip-hop stylist who worked for Sean Combs (P. Diddy). Johnson had been interested in fashion since she'd been voted best dressed at her high school in Englewood, New Jersey. She experienced an aha moment when Lew complimented her style and told her that Black women were responsible for dressing some very famous men. Inspired, Johnson decided to forgo her plans to become an English teacher. Instead, after college she got a job with *Essence* magazine, where she met a couple of stylists who worked with rappers P. Diddy and the Notorious B.I.G. After learning from them, Johnson got her chance to work as a celebrity-wardrobe stylist for Pharrell Williams and Jamie Foxx. Her career had taken off from there.

Johnson's backstory didn't just resonate with Maverick. LeBron was impressed with her, too. At six feet tall, Johnson looked like she could have played professional basketball. But she was a visionary when it came to fashion and how it could be used to break down racial barriers. She told LeBron that he should be wearing recognizable historic brands. She wanted to bring him to fashion houses where there was very little racial diversity. There was an opportunity to heighten awareness and help fashion designers and brands become more inclusive. And in the process, LeBron, in her mind, could become a trendsetter, someone who could completely change the way NBA players dressed.

"There are men who may have not necessarily felt comfortable wearing what's coming down the runway if they see a waif-y model wearing it," Johnson said. "But a regular 9–5 businessman can look at what LeBron James is wearing and say, 'You know what? Maybe I can do that, too, because he's more like me.'"

Even though she impressed him, when LeBron met Johnson through Jay-Z, he couldn't appreciate what she was contemplating. But the notion of being outfitted by a stylist who dressed some of the biggest names in hip-hop music appealed to him. He hired Rachel Johnson as his personal stylist.

* * *

LeBron couldn't wait to start his third NBA season at home on November 2, 2005. When he pulled up to Gund Arena, it had a new name: Quicken Loans Arena. Fans were dubbing it "the Q." It was a clear sign that Dan Gilbert was putting his stamp on the franchise. Even so, LeBron loomed larger than Gilbert over Cleveland. On the Sherwin-Williams building across the street from the arena, Nike had put up a ten-story mural of LeBron soaring for a dunk with the tagline WE ARE ALL WITNESSES. And when LeBron went inside, it was evident that Gilbert had kept his promise, spending millions in the off-season to upgrade the facilities. There was a brand-new scoreboard overhead. There were new wine-colored seats for the fans to sit in. And the locker room had been fully remodeled to reflect some of LeBron's preferences—every player had a TV, an Xbox, and a stereo installed in his locker.

Gilbert had overhauled the Cavaliers' personnel, too. He'd hired San Antonio Spurs assistant coach Mike Brown to be the new head coach. It was a bold hire. An African American, Brown had no head-coaching experience. And at thirty-five, he was the second-youngest head coach in the league. Gilbert also hired former Cavaliers player Danny Ferry as the new general manager.

With Gilbert giving them the green light to go after free agents, Brown and Ferry signed six new players during the off-season, all of whom were approved by LeBron. They included Larry Hughes and Donyell Marshall, two seasoned veterans who were expected to strengthen the supporting cast around LeBron. And Gilbert personally accompanied Brown and Ferry to an airport, where they literally chased down Cavaliers' seven-foot-three center Zydrunas Ilgauskas, a free agent, who was on his way to meet with another team. The popular Lithuanian player had led the NBA in offensive rebounds, and LeBron had insisted that "Z," as he called him, had to remain in Cleveland. Gilbert convinced Ilgauskas by rewarding him with a five-year deal worth a reported $60 million.

Gilbert had owned the team for only seven months. But he had already learned a vital lesson of the star system in professional sports: whether watching live or on television, fans are attracted to stars. And the brighter the star, the bigger the draw. Recognizing that he had the brightest star in the NBA on his payroll, Gilbert was willing to do whatever was necessary—including setting aside his own ego at times—to keep his organization aligned with his star player. As a result, Gilbert made accommodations for LeBron that weren't available to any other player. For instance, Maverick and Rich were granted full access to all restricted team areas. They were also afforded courtside seats for all home games. And Randy Mims had a seat right behind the Cavaliers bench.

Prior to the game, Savannah approached LeBron near the Cavaliers bench and handed him their one-year-old. LeBron cradled his son, kissed his forehead, and handed him back to Savannah.

Then, with the game about to start, LeBron approached the scorer's table, covered his hands in chalk powder, and clapped them together, creating a cloud of dust and evoking cheers from the sold-out crowd. On one side of the floor, LeBron could see Maverick and Rich. Behind the bench he could see Randy. Along the baseline, LeBron could see Gloria in her front-row seat with Savannah beside her and one-year-old LeBron Jr. on her lap. From now on, the James Gang—LeBron's mom, LeBron's high school sweetheart, and LeBron's son—would be in the front row all the time. There was nothing like going to work and knowing that his family and friends were encircling him. In the background, he had a lawyer, an investment banker, a publicist, and a stylist. He had created the ideal life that he had imagined when he was a boy. Everyone was safe. Everyone was taken care of. Everyone was within sight.

The referee tossed up the opening tip.

NINETEEN

IT'S JUST BASKETBALL

It was after midnight when the Cavaliers landed in Salt Lake City on January 22, 2006. LeBron felt like shit. Hours earlier, he had tweaked his knee in a game against the Warriors. He was battling the flu. The team had lost five straight games on the road. And he'd just gotten word that his mother had been arrested back home and charged with driving under the influence.

After checking in to the team's hotel, LeBron headed to a nearby hospital to have his knee x-rayed. There was swelling, but the X-rays came back negative. An MRI would be scheduled for when LeBron got back to Cleveland. Until then, the best course was to rest the knee by sitting out the final game of the road trip. And a night off would help his body recover faster from the flu. He'd also gotten updates on the situation back home. The lawyers were into it. His mother had posted bond.

Later in the day, LeBron accompanied the team to the Delta Center for the game against the Jazz that evening. A reporter asked him about his mother's arrest. "I don't have all the info on what's going on," LeBron said. "Once I find that out, and once I sit down with my family, you know, I'll be able to comment on it a little bit better."

LeBron knew more than he was letting on. But he was always in protective mode when it came to family. Headlines such as the *Washington Post*'s "James's Mother Is Arrested for DWI" were already appearing online. There was no point in saying anything more. That would only have generated more attention.

Despite being fatigued and sore and having been advised against it, LeBron decided to test his knee. He told head coach Mike Brown he planned to play.

Unaware of LeBron's poor health, Jazz fans were on him from the moment the starting lineups were announced.

LeBron fed off the noise and went into the zone. Layups. Dunks. Spin moves. Fadeaways. Long-range threes. He felt like everything he put up was going in. So he kept shooting. The Jazz looked shell-shocked. The team's head coach, Jerry Sloan, would later admit that his team was "intimidated" by LeBron's dominance. With less than two minutes to play in the game and his team comfortably ahead, LeBron checked out with fifty-one points. He had won over the Utah crowd, which stood and gave him an ovation fit for a king. Barely twenty-one years old, LeBron had surpassed Kobe Bryant, becoming the youngest player in NBA history to reach five thousand career points.

The win in Utah propelled the Cavaliers to a seven-game winning streak. By the All-Star break in February, the Cavaliers were 31-21 and in second place in the Central Division, behind the Detroit Pistons. And LeBron was tearing through opposing defenses. His performance through the first half of the season made him the Eastern Conference's top vote-getter for the 2006 NBA All-Star Game in Houston. No other Cavaliers players were even on the ballot.

Dan Gilbert offered to fly LeBron and his family and friends to Houston for the weekend's All-Star Game festivities. Gilbert also brought along his own family, as well as senior executives in the Cavaliers organization. They took the team plane. The trip was a manifestation of Dan Gilbert's determination to fasten LeBron into the Cavaliers' family for the long haul.

On the flight to Houston, LeBron was playing cards with his friends in the main cabin when the plane suddenly encountered severe turbulence. The lights started flickering. Smoke emanated from the kitchen galley. Various passengers, including Gilbert's wife, who was pregnant at the time, threw up. A flight attendant even broke her ankle.

Oh my God! LeBron thought. *This is it.*

At the peak of the chaos, everyone on board feared for their lives.

But the pilots eventually managed to steady the plane.

LeBron figured he didn't need to say anything more to Gilbert about getting a new team plane. Instead, with everyone still on edge, LeBron attempted to lighten the mood.

"Deal the motherfuckin' cards," he shouted. "I'm here to play cards."

Everyone cracked up.

The plane landed safely in Houston. LeBron led the East team to victory and was named MVP of the game. And Gilbert ordered a new state-of-the-art jet for the team. The media was told that a new team plane would reduce the need for refueling stops and help promote a winning culture that would make Cleveland a more attractive destination for free agents. Both were true. But the real story was that LeBron had entered the exclusive airspace that's typically reserved for owners. There was no other player in the NBA or in any of the other American sports leagues who was flying solo with a team owner the way LeBron was with Gilbert.

Thanks in part to Gilbert's approach, LeBron's transformation within the Cavaliers' organization was happening at warp speed. In LeBron's rookie year, he had gone out of his way not to assert himself too much, trying instead just to fit in with the team. In his third season, the team had been completely remade to fit him.

At the same time, LeBron was reshaping his surroundings in Ohio. Back in 2003, he had paid $2.1 million for a twelve-thousand-square-foot home that sat on nearly six acres of land in Bath Township, north of Akron. A couple of years later, he had demolished the home to make way for his dream house, a thirty-five-thousand-square-foot mansion that he helped design. LeBron's blueprints called for a two-thousand-plus-square-foot master suite, a bowling alley, a barbershop, an in-home movie theater, a three-story aquarium, a sports bar with a wall of television screens, a recording studio, a game room, and a six-car garage. His estate was projected to cost upward of $15 million. He had also purchased a new home for his mother that was located near his property.

After the trip to Houston, while awaiting final approval from the county for his ambitious building design, LeBron took full control of everything that was happening on the court. During a key stretch that started at the beginning of March, the Cavaliers won fifteen out of nineteen games. During that run, LeBron imposed his will on opponents and teammates, demonstrating for the first time in his NBA career his player-coach mentality. When his teammate Donyell Marshall went into a shooting slump, LeBron kept feeding him the ball. In one instance during a game, Marshall had an open look from the top of the key.

"Shoot the ball," LeBron shouted.

Marshall hesitated.

"Shoot the *fucking* ball," LeBron yelled.

Afterward, Marshall thanked LeBron for the confidence boost. Marshall, a thirty-two-year-old veteran, had been brought to Cleveland to help LeBron. But LeBron was helping him.

On the bench, LeBron wasn't shy about telling the head coach what to do, either. But he used humor with Brown so as not to embarrass him. During a time-out during a game in which the Bulls were manhandling LeBron, Coach Brown pulled out his trusty whiteboard and started drawing up plays. Then he erased what he'd drawn and diagrammed a new play. Meanwhile, the time-out was about to expire. Finally, LeBron looked at Brown. "Coach, man, we only got five guys and twenty-four seconds," he said.

The players burst out laughing.

Brown put away his whiteboard.

The exchange between LeBron and Brown was witnessed by *Sports Illustrated* basketball writer Chris Ballard, who was in Cleveland working on yet another profile of LeBron. In addition to getting a front-row seat to LeBron's development on the court, Ballard also experienced the new public relations apparatus that had formed around LeBron. Ballard's interview with him was strictly limited to forty-five minutes. During that time, Ballard was accompanied by three PR reps from the Cavaliers, along with Keith Estabrook, who had flown in from New York. Ballard would later write that Estabrook was "relentless in managing his client's image."

But Ballard was allowed to sit with LeBron while he looked at tape. Perhaps more than any other player in the NBA, he studied video of himself and his opponents. It was a habit he had formed in his rookie season. By his third year, he was like a stick jockey with a remote control—PLAY, PAUSE, REWIND. Alone, he had watched hundreds of hours of game footage to perfect his precision and to gain any advantage he could over his opponents.

Sitting in a windowless room at the Q, LeBron looked at tape from a game against the Celtics a month earlier. Pausing on a play where he was being guarded by Celtics forward Paul Pierce, he recalled for Ballard what he had been seeing in that moment.

"My main focus isn't on the guy that's guarding me, it's on the second level of defense because I feel like I can get past the first guy," LeBron said. "But there comes a time when the weak side can double you, they can load the box on you, and right here"—he pointed to the screen—"I'm not really looking at Paul. I know he's in front of me, but I'm looking at Raef

LaFrentz and [Ryan] Gomes and seeing if they see me or if they prede-termine my move. Right now [the Celtics] don't really know what they're doing back side, so that gave me a good chance to try to drive baseline before they got there."

After the film session, Ballard speculated that LeBron might have been too advanced to be coached. And he reported that Mike Brown had reached out to a former Chicago Bulls coach from the Michael Jordan era for advice on how to sufficiently motivate a player who was so far ahead of everyone else. The former Bulls coach suggested putting LeBron on the second-string team during practice sessions to challenge him. Brown didn't know it, but when LeBron was in high school, he would purposely play on the second string in practices, and he'd tell Coach Dru to spot the first team with a twenty-point lead and set a time limit to simulate the closing min-utes of a game. Then LeBron would work like a dog to lead the reserve team to victory before time ran out. Things turned out similarly in Cleveland once Brown started handicapping LeBron in practice.

Brown had a difficult job. Coaches are programmed to call the shots. But as a rookie head coach, Brown had to learn to be more like a first-time film director working with an Oscar-winning actor. Recognizing that LeBron was a basketball auteur, Brown made sure to give his star player the freedom to create on the fly.

Dan Gilbert was pleased with the way Brown was handling LeBron. The bottom line was that the team was winning. The Cavaliers finished the regular season 50-32. Only two teams in the Eastern Conference—the Pistons and the Heat—had a better record. In Gilbert's first full season as an owner and Brown's first season as a coach, the Cavaliers were headed to the playoffs.

LeBron had butterflies. He hadn't played in a playoff game since his senior year of high school. The stakes were a lot higher now. Cleveland hadn't hosted a playoff game since the nineties. Fans were so ecstatic that they were on their feet during pregame warm-ups, cheering and chanting. The Washington Wizards were in town for Game 1 of the first round of the NBA playoffs. The Q was sold out. And an optimistic fervor permeated the arena.

Wearing a white headband, LeBron stood at the scorer's table, looked into the eyes of the crowd, threw chalk dust into the air, and held up his arms like a savior. He told himself that he had to deliver. Forty-five seconds later, LeBron got the ball at the top of the key, burst past his defender, elevated, and scored, igniting the crowd and banishing the butterflies.

Under the basket and wearing one of LeBron's game jerseys, Gloria jumped to her feet and pointed at LeBron, cheering him on. Next to her, Savannah remained in her seat, clapping and watching LeBron run back on defense. For four years she'd been discreetly cheering him on from the shadows, deftly navigating around the spotlight. Even when the network television cameras focused on Gloria, they managed to miss Savannah, allowing her to remain out of sight.

But Savannah wasn't invisible to LeBron. Her steady courtside presence was like a security blanket. Quiet and reserved, she was the stabilizing influence in his extraordinary life. The more famous LeBron became, the more pretty faces started showing up at his games. But Savannah was the one who was always seated beside Gloria, a testament to her place in LeBron's intimate orbit.

Savannah had always been much more than a pretty face to LeBron. In high school she'd been the girl who captured his heart. Now she was the woman that he went home to every night. His favorite part of the day was seeing their little boy scamper toward him and then lifting him up in the air. That castle LeBron was constructing in the suburbs wasn't for him. It was for them. He and Savannah were building a family together. And over time, as LeBron's celebrity status continued to evolve, the sanctuary of their home would become more and more prized. Until then, he wanted her at every home game right where she belonged, alongside Gloria.

After his first bucket against the Wizards, LeBron was off and running. As if he'd been in this situation a hundred times before, he scored at will in his first NBA playoff game. But the play that brought down the house came at the end of the third quarter when LeBron beat his defender off the dribble, penetrated the lane, elevated, faked out the Wizards' center by looking to his right, and flipped a no-look pass to his left, leading to an easy layup for a teammate.

"Yes!" shouted ABC color analyst Hubie Brown.

"Oh, *beautiful* pass," said play-by-play announcer Mike Breen. "James to Murray."

Chants of "M-V-P, M-V-P," boomed through the arena.

Dan Gilbert was on his feet, fist clenched, yelling along with the fans, swept up in the moment.

Cleveland won by eleven. LeBron finished with 32 points, 11 rebounds, and 11 assists, prompting Mike Breen to declare on the air: "LeBron James's playoff debut is a masterpiece."

Coming off the floor, sweat dripping from his brow, LeBron was stopped by ABC's sideline reporter.

"How did this compare to your wildest dream?" she asked.

"Ah, well," he said, cracking a smile, "I've had some great dreams before."

A few feet away, children in Cavaliers gear stood behind a rope, staring up at him, mouths agape.

"But this is one of the best," LeBron told the reporter.

Then he walked off, passing through a tunnel of fans as he left the court and headed toward the locker room.

Over the next two weeks, he continued to thrill in the series against the Wizards.

In Game 3 at the Verizon Center in Washington, DC, he hit the game-winning shot with 5.7 seconds left on the clock to put the Cavaliers up two games to one.

In Game 5, back in Cleveland, he hit the game-winning shot with ninetenths of a second left in overtime to give his team a 3-2 lead in the series.

Then in Game 6, at the Verizon Center, LeBron got into a shooting match with Wizards all-star point guard Gilbert Arenas. LeBron scored thirty-two points, including a three-point bomb that tied the game and sent it into overtime. Arenas scored thirty-six points. And with fifteen seconds remaining in overtime and his team clinging to a one-point lead, Arenas stepped to the free throw line with a chance to help seal the victory and force a Game 7.

Everyone knew that Arenas was an exceptional free throw shooter. But LeBron knew something about Arenas that no one else on the floor knew. They were friends off the court, and LeBron had invited Arenas to his home more than once to play cards. Whenever Arenas came over, LeBron would also invite Cavaliers' reserve guard Damon Jones to join them. Jones was a terrible cardplayer and ended up owing Arenas a lot of money. Arenas was still waiting for Jones to pay his debt. And LeBron saw this as an opportunity to gain an edge.

After he uncharacteristically missed his first free throw attempt, Arenas stepped back from the foul line to collect himself.

That's when LeBron made his move, walking up from behind and tapping Arenas on the chest. "If you miss these free throws," LeBron told him, "you know who's gonna hit it."

Arenas nodded.

Driving his point home, LeBron tapped Arenas on the chest again and walked away.

It was an unspoken rule in the NBA that you don't approach an opposing player on the free throw line. Arenas's teammates thought that LeBron was being disrespectful and that he had referred to himself when he told Arenas you know who's gonna hit "it," which was a reference to the game-winning shot.

But Arenas knew that LeBron wasn't referring to himself. LeBron was threatening Arenas with the prospect of Damon Jones's hitting the winning shot. And that disrupted Arenas because it got him thinking about the gambling debt. Plus, Damon Jones wasn't in the game and hadn't played all night. *So how was Jones going to hit the game-winning shot?*

Rattled, Arenas clanked the second free throw attempt off the back of the rim.

"Arenas misses both!" ESPN announcer Mike Breen said. "Arenas has had such a huge game and played so well. And two misses right there."

The Wizards players were flummoxed. A sense of unease swept through the arena as the Cavaliers rebounded the ball and called time-out.

On the sideline, Cavs coach Mike Brown made it clear he wanted the ball in LeBron's hands for the final shot. LeBron wanted Damon Jones in the game. LeBron knew that he'd be double-teamed as soon as he got the ball. Jones, however, would be the most unlikely player to take the final shot. He'd likely be left alone.

Jones removed his sweatpants.

LeBron made sure that Jones knew to be ready.

When the two teams returned to the floor, Arenas noticed that Jones had checked into the game. *What the . . . ?* Arenas looked at LeBron.

LeBron smiled at him.

Arenas just turned his head from side to side.

No one else in the building—not the players, not the coaches, not the announcers—knew the mind game that LeBron was playing with Arenas. Even Jones didn't know what LeBron had said to Arenas moments earlier.

After the inbounds pass, LeBron got the ball out beyond the three-point arc and was immediately trapped by two defenders. He split the trap and bounce-passed to a teammate, who quickly kicked the ball to Damon Jones, who was alone in the corner. He launched a three.

"Damon Jones," Breen said as the ball sailed through air. "Puts it in!"

LeBron threw up his fist. The Cavs were up by two with four seconds left.

Frantic, Arenas pushed the ball downcourt and dumped it to a teammate, who threw up a desperate last-second shot that fell short as the buzzer sounded.

LeBron raced to Damon Jones and tackled him. His Cavaliers teammates piled on.

Dumbfounded, ESPN's Mike Breen declared, "Damon Jones, who hasn't played a second the whole game knocks down the winning shot. An incredible finish!"

The Cavaliers had finished off the Wizards. In his first playoff series, LeBron averaged over thirty-five points per game. But it was his poker game that had gotten his team to the next round for a date with the defending Eastern Conference champions.

The Detroit Pistons were an elite team with a starting lineup that was stacked with hard-nosed players who knew what it took to win a championship—Ben Wallace, Richard Hamilton, Rasheed Wallace, Chauncey Billups, and Tayshaun Prince. No one on the Cavaliers roster had ever won an NBA championship. As expected, the Pistons won the first two games at home to take a commanding 2-0 lead in the series. Pistons forward Rasheed Wallace wasted no time bragging publicly that his team was going to win the series. Then the Cavaliers got word that Cavs starting guard Larry Hughes's twenty-year-old brother, who had been born with a heart defect and had undergone a heart transplant during childhood, had died in St. Louis. Hughes and his little brother had been extremely close.

When LeBron found out what had happened, he faced the question that everyone struggles with when someone you care about loses a loved one. *What should I say?* LeBron's message to Hughes was four words: "Family comes before basketball."

Hughes left the team to be with his loved ones in St. Louis. LeBron didn't expect Hughes to return before the series ended, especially with the Cavaliers already down two games.

In Game 3 back in Cleveland, the Cavaliers trailed by three after three quarters. But in the fourth quarter, LeBron scored fifteen points and the Pistons self-destructed down the stretch, enabling the Cavaliers to pull out a victory. Afterward, Rasheed Wallace downplayed the loss. "I know we're going to win it," he told the media. "Tomorrow night is the last game here in this building this year. Y'all can quote me. Put it back page. Front page. Whatever."

Two nights later, with the game tied and the outcome in the balance, LeBron scored the Cavaliers' final four points and Cleveland won, 74–72. The victory knotted the series at 2-2 and assured that the teams would return to Cleveland for Game 6. But with the series headed back to Detroit for Game 5, Wallace continued to run his mouth. "I ain't worried about these cats," he said. "Ain't no way they're going to beat us in no series."

LeBron wasn't one for making predictions. But he wasn't above needling a loudmouth to gain an advantage. "I'm not about going out and talking too much," LeBron said when asked about the Pistons' having to come back to Cleveland for Game 6. "But if the hotels are sold out, yeah, every last one of them can stay at my house. And I'll lock them indoors when it's time to come to the game."

For the third consecutive game, the Cavaliers played Game 5 without starting guard Larry Hughes. LeBron had his best game of the series, slashing and banging his way through the Pistons top-ranked defense to lead all scorers with thirty-two points. The Cavs won, 86–84, silencing the Palace of Auburn Hills.

Pistons fans couldn't believe what they were witnessing. The defending champs were on the ropes and the sports media smelled an upset. *ESPN* declared: "Mighty Pistons Take a Fall."

LeBron put his team's 3-2 lead in perspective. "When you think about it," he said after the game, "it's just basketball. It's not like life or death or anything like that. It's not like they're the big, bad wolf and we're the three little pigs."

* * *

Cleveland fans were ready to celebrate the demise of Detroit. LeBron wasn't. He worried that his team might not be able to maintain the composure that would be necessary to finish the job. No one on the Cavaliers roster had ever been in this situation before. The Pistons, on the other hand, had been in plenty of do-or-die playoff games.

LeBron did his part in Game 6, scoring nearly half of his team's points. But the Pistons did what veteran teams do—played stingy defense and ground out a must-win on the road. Then, back in Detroit for Game 7, he went off in the first half, scoring virtually at will. But in the second half, the Pistons made a defensive adjustment, swarming LeBron, forcing him to give up the ball. The Cavaliers finished the game with an abysmal sixty-one points, and the Pistons escaped with a victory.

As much as he hated losing after being so close to winning, LeBron felt that his team had no reason to hang their heads. In the Cavaliers' first trip to the playoffs with LeBron, they had soundly beaten their first-round opponent and then pushed the defending champs to the limit. LeBron had barely finished showering when he started softening up the Pistons for next time around. "They trapped me," he said in his postgame remarks. "They did a nice job. That's why they keep winning, because defensively they're the best team."

Then he added, "Hopefully, one day, we will be a rival of Detroit."

The Pistons weren't fooled. Not even loudmouth Rasheed Wallace. They knew damn well that the Cavaliers had already arrived as a bona fide rival. The Pistons were lucky to have survived LeBron's offensive onslaught. At twenty-one, he'd led an inexperienced team that had come close to upsetting the defending conference champions. His performance prompted the New York Times to declare: "James's talent gives Cleveland the chance to win anytime, against anyone."

After the scare that LeBron had given the Pistons, the entire NBA could see what was coming.

TWENTY

THE FOUR LeBRONS

The playoffs had been an exhilarating ride for Dan Gilbert. But now that the fun was over, Gilbert had his work cut out for him. LeBron had just one year remaining on his contract with the Cavaliers. If LeBron didn't sign an extension over the summer, he'd become a free agent after the upcoming 2006–2007 season. The prospect of him going elsewhere was something that Gilbert couldn't allow. Yet he was well aware of LeBron's close friendship with Jay-Z, who had recently purchased a small ownership stake in the New Jersey Nets. Recognizing that Jay-Z, like many other NBA owners, would love to lure LeBron away from Cleveland, Gilbert offered LeBron a five-year contract worth $80 million in fully guaranteed money. It would keep LeBron in a Cavs uniform through the 2011–2012 season.

LeBron had no desire to leave Cleveland. He planned to raise his family there. But he'd been studying the NBA's new collective-bargaining agreement, which had a key provision that was particularly relevant to his family's financial future. Under the agreement, players drafted in 2003 were eligible for maximum five-year extensions worth up to $80 million, as Gilbert was offering. But players in LeBron's 2003 draft class also had the option of signing shorter three-year extensions in the $60 million range. Players who chose the three-year extension would forfeit $20 million in guaranteed money, but they'd position themselves to capture even more future revenue by becoming free agents two years earlier.

Normally, agents encourage athletes to seek long-term deals and the maximum amount of guaranteed money. But LeBron's agent, Leon Rose, was advising him to do the opposite—reject Gilbert's five-year offer and sign a three-year extension. It would give LeBron all the leverage at the end of the 2009–2010 season. This approach was also consistent with the overall strategic advice coming from LeBron's investment banker, Paul Wachter, who continued to lean into the idea of LeBron operating as his own corporation. The bottom line was that Dan Gilbert, like every other owner in the NBA, was doing what was in his best financial interests—trying to lock down his biggest asset for as long as possible. LeBron needed to take the same approach with his business decisions, even if that meant that Gilbert wasn't going to like it.

LeBron was averse to conflict. But he wasn't afraid to do what was best for himself and his family. After reading everything that his advisors put in front of him, he knew that he was facing a decision with potentially monumental implications for his and his family's financial future. He knew which way he was leaning, but he wanted time to deliberate on his own before making a final decision.

Time, however, was the one luxury that LeBron didn't have. While Gilbert awaited his answer, LeBron was balancing myriad obligations. He'd made commitments to USA Basketball, which entailed overseas travel to Korea and Japan during the off-season. Nike wanted LeBron to meet with dignitaries and the foreign press while in Asia. Over the summer, LeBron was scheduled to film his most ambitious television commercial to date. His company, LRMR, was launching its website and sponsoring its first big marketing conference in Akron. All the permits had been approved for his estate, and construction was set to begin in August, which meant that he and Savannah had endless details to review with architects and contractors.

On top of everything else, LeBron had taken the lead in his mother's ongoing legal matter in Akron. After Gloria had been humiliated by the publicity around her arrest back in January, LeBron had worked behind the scenes on a variety of fronts to ensure that his mother got all the help she needed and to resolve a difficult situation as quickly and as favorably as possible. In late May, shortly after the Cavaliers were eliminated from the playoffs, the Associated Press reported:

> The mother of the Cleveland Cavaliers' LeBron James was found guilty yesterday of four charges after her SUV nearly hit an unmarked Akron police vehicle and she kicked a window of a patrol car.
>
> Gloria James, 38, pleaded no contest to reckless operation, speeding, disorderly conduct and a reduced count—originally

drunken-driving—of physical control of a motor vehicle under the influence. A fifth count of damaging police property was dismissed.

Judge Lynne Callahan suspended all but three days of a six-month jail term and said James could serve the three remaining days by taking a class on the dangers of drugs and alcohol use. Her license was suspended.

LeBron was his mother's greatest advocate. It was a role that had always come naturally to him. But now that he was a young parent with exceptional means, he was developing a richer appreciation for all that his mother had been through while raising him as a single parent without means. Becoming a father had made him a more empathetic son. Duty bound, he got a great sense of satisfaction and purpose out of being his mother's chief protector.

More and more, LeBron felt like a man who played many different roles, sometimes all in the same day. When life got crazy, he had always found solace on the basketball court. In the summer of 2006, he left the swirl in Ohio for Las Vegas to train with members of the USA Basketball Men's Senior National Team. It had been two years since the bronze medal finish at the Olympics in Athens. And with two years to go until the 2008 Olympic Games in Beijing, LeBron had decided to play on Team USA and start preparing for the next round of international competition. Carmelo Anthony and Dwyane Wade had decided to join him. The three of them were the only holdovers from the team that had played in Athens. They were now joined by a core of other young NBA stars, including Chris Bosh, Dwight Howard, and Chris Paul.

For LeBron, being in the gym with players who were among his best friends in the NBA was a perfect tonic. But a lot had changed since the last time LeBron wore a Team USA uniform. After the debacle in Athens, NBA commissioner David Stern had stepped in, determined to make changes that would entice NBA stars to play in the 2008 Olympic Games in Beijing and restore Team USA's reputation as the world leader in basketball. Stern turned to the former owner of the Phoenix Suns, Jerry Colangelo, and convinced him to become the new director of USA Basketball.

Colangelo's first item of business was to name a new head coach, a process that would require him to navigate the egos of the NBA coaching ranks. Despite the Olympic team's recent troubles, the title of head coach of USA Basketball remained a prestigious honor. To help insulate himself and the selection process from any appearance of favoritism or politics, Colangelo convinced Michael Jordan, Larry Bird, Jerry West, Georgetown basketball coach John Thompson, and North Carolina basketball coach Dean Smith to function as his cabinet. The group ultimately formed a consensus around Duke University's head basketball coach, Mike Krzyzewski. It was unconventional to look to the college ranks for an Olympic coach. But when two of Duke's archrivals—Dean Smith and Michael Jordan—teamed up to lead the charge for Krzyzewski, no one pushed back. Krzyzewski was officially named head coach of Team USA in October 2005.

Krzyzewski was up for the challenge. But he knew going in that he'd have to tone down some aspects of the fiery on-court persona that had made him so successful in Durham, North Carolina. Although Duke routinely attracted the best high school basketball players in the country, Krzyzewski would now be dealing with the most elite players in the world. Coaching blue-chip student-athletes was one thing. Coaching stars was a totally different dynamic. There'd be egos to navigate, relationships to manage, and a talent pool so deep that he'd have to figure out how to get everyone to work together as a single unit.

LeBron didn't know Krzyzewski. But he knew his reputation as Coach K, who was on the same level with UCLA's legendary Wizard of Westwood, John Wooden. Although LeBron had never given serious consideration to playing college basketball, he considered Duke the gold standard among college basketball programs and couldn't help being curious about what it might be like to play under Coach K.

Krzyzewski was even more intrigued by the prospect of coaching LeBron. When LeBron was in high school, Krzyzewski had known he was headed straight for the pros and therefore hadn't bothered recruiting him. And since Krzyzewski rarely attended NBA games, he had never seen LeBron play in person until he met him in the summer of 2006. He was instantly struck by LeBron's physical presence. He had the shoulders of a longshoreman. Yet he could outleap everyone. And as soon as practices started, Krzyzewski could see that he was a virtuoso and far and away the most gifted—and the smartest—player on the floor.

To form a connection with LeBron, Krzyzewski took a cerebral approach. One of the things he wanted LeBron to do was use his voice more effectively as a tool of leadership on the floor. At one point, he stopped practice and approached him.

"When you're standing up, you are only so wide, right?" Coach K said.

LeBron looked at him.

"Your arms are down," Coach K continued. "As soon as you start talking, what happens to your arms?"

LeBron raised his arms.

"Yeah, they go up," Coach K said. "People don't talk with their arms down. Their arms go out."

LeBron wasn't used to being addressed this way by his NBA coaches. This felt like he was in a classroom.

"If you talk on defense," Coach K said, "you will be three times as wide as you are if you don't talk." He demonstrated what he meant. "Your legs will be wider," he explained. "Your arms will be out. You'll have better balance."

All of this was designed to get LeBron to annunciate more authoritatively.

"So your ability to talk and your ability to lead are things I'd like to see you do more of," Coach K said.

The other players were responsive to Coach K's methods, too. It helped that Coach K's assistant coach was Syracuse University head coach Jim Boeheim. Boeheim had recruited Carmelo Anthony and coached him to a national championship. The bond between Carmelo and Boeheim was strong, and it helped establish the coaching staff's credibility with the players and the players' respect for the coaches.

While in Vegas, LeBron settled on what he was going to do about his contract with the Cavaliers. Carmelo, D-Wade, and Chris Bosh were all facing the same question. The only difference was that LeBron had a bigger, more sophisticated team of advisors around him. And after deliberating with them over a period of weeks, LeBron was at peace with his decision. *The Cavs are running a business*, he told himself. *I'm a businessman, too.* He told his agent to tell the Cavaliers that he'd sign a three-year extension.

LeBron's stance put Gilbert in a difficult position. He'd done everything in his power to entice LeBron to commit to Cleveland for the long haul. He'd even agreed to build the team's brand-new practice facility way out near LeBron's new estate, adding another level of convenience to his star player's life. Yet Gilbert now faced a choice—go along with LeBron's preference for a three-year extension or play hardball and insist on five years.

Gilbert couldn't force LeBron's hand. But if push came to shove, Gilbert felt LeBron would cave and sign a five-year extension. He believed that LeBron was too rooted in Ohio to leave—he had never lived outside the state, and he was in the process of constructing his dream home there. Gilbert also believed that LeBron would rather sign for two additional years than risk looking uncommitted to the team and the fans of Cleveland. But drawing a line in the sand would also pose a risk for Gilbert, pitting him against the city's favorite athlete in a contract dispute. Gilbert mapped out in his mind how he'd frame the issue with fans. First, he'd tell Cavaliers fans how much he loved LeBron and how as an owner he'd been doing everything he could to build a team around him that would bring a championship to Cleveland. But Gilbert would also make sure the public understood that LeBron also had to step up by committing to a long-term contract. And if LeBron wasn't willing to sign a long-term deal, Gilbert would have to explore trading him for players who truly wanted to be in Cleveland.

Getting into a protracted contract dispute with LeBron was a risky proposition. After weighing the matter, Gilbert blinked and reluctantly decided against going down the road of tough negotiation tactics. Instead, Gilbert signed off on the three-year extension and trusted that the team would experience enough success over the next three years that LeBron would sign another extension in 2010. It was a decision that required Gilbert to violate one of his cardinal rules of business: *Never give up leverage.*

On July 18, 2006, while in Vegas, LeBron signed a three-year extension, ensuring that he'd be a Cleveland Cavalier for the next four years and then would be a free agent in the summer of 2010.

Dwyane Wade and Chris Bosh made the same choice as LeBron. Both of them signed three-year extensions that would make them free agents in the summer of 2010 as well.

Carmelo Anthony went for the guaranteed $80 million, signing a five-year extension with the Denver Nuggets.

LeBron spent a good chunk of his summer overseas with Wade, Bosh, Anthony, and the rest of Team USA. They dominated an exhibition tournament in Korea. Then they met stiffer competition in the FIBA World Championship in Japan, coming away with the bronze. Despite the third-place finish, LeBron liked the direction in which the team was headed. He and Wade and Bosh, in particular, were developing great chemistry. And under Coach K, a different culture was being created, one that fostered pride in the privilege of playing for the United States of America.

LeBron was also pleased with his burgeoning status in Asia. Thanks in large part to Nike, other than China's Yao Ming, LeBron was the most popular player in Asia. And when he got home, he headed to Hollywood to make a new Nike commercial that would dramatically elevate his popularity at home and abroad. Nike was planning an unprecedented marketing campaign around the rollout of the Nike Zoom LeBron IV sneakers at the start of the 2006–2007 season. The centerpiece of the marketing campaign was a television commercial that featured LeBron playing four versions of himself—LeBron the Kid, LeBron the Athlete, LeBron the Businessman, and LeBron the Wise Man.

When LeBron heard about the concept, he immediately embraced it. "Those are the four guys I act like on an everyday basis," he told Nike.

Once Nike started filming, LeBron started ad-libbing to make the script more authentic. Set to the Kool & the Gang instrumental "Summer Madness," the ad opens with LeBron the Athlete working out in a swimming pool while Wise Man LeBron sits on the pool deck, sipping lemonade. LeBron the Kid is high above the pool on a diving board, next to LeBron the Businessman, who is sweet-talking a woman on his cell phone: "Baby, we can go anytime. You just let me know what's good for you."

LeBron came up with the next line. "You can't get through Detroit trainin' in no pool," Wise Man LeBron tells LeBron the Athlete. "You think Michael train in the pool? No! I don't think so."

The comical exchange reflected what LeBron knew better than anyone else—if the Cavaliers were going to get to the NBA Finals, he had to figure out a way to beat the Detroit Pistons. And no matter how well LeBron played, he was always going to be measured against Michael Jordan.

Nike welcomed LeBron's willingness to poke fun at himself.

To LeBron, filming the Nike commercial was more like play than work. He'd been given the creative license to be himself on-screen. It was a well-kept secret that LeBron was an exceptional swimmer and had an unusual capacity for holding his breath underwater. He also was a pretty good diver. In the commercial, LeBron the Kid leaps off the diving board, landing next to LeBron the Athlete and splashing water on Wise Man LeBron. "Ooh, he got Pops wet," LeBron the Businessman tells the woman on the cell phone.

"Don't make me get out of this seat," Wise Man LeBron says, scolding the Kid.

LeBron the Kid then encourages LeBron the Businessman to dive into the pool, symbolizing LeBron's willingness to try new ventures. When Wise Man LeBron mocks LeBron the Businessman, calling him a "pretty boy," LeBron the Businessman delivers the signature line of the commercial.

"Hold that thought, I'm gonna have to call you back," LeBron the Businessman says. He then flips shut his phone, primps his big Afro, and does a backflip off the diving board as the song reaches a crescendo.

When Nike's Lynn Merritt saw the final cut of the commercial, he was so impressed with LeBron's acting skills that it dawned on him that LeBron might have a legitimate future in Hollywood. Meanwhile, Nike titled the commercial "Swimming Pool" and began purchasing airtime on the networks.

In discussions with Maverick Carter and Paul Wachter, LeBron noted that Berkshire Hathaway chairman Warren Buffett had announced during the summer of 2006 that he was donating 85 percent of his $44 billion personal fortune to five philanthropies. It represented the single largest charitable gift in history. And Buffett said the lion's share of his gift—$31 billion—would go to the Bill & Melinda Gates Foundation. Buffett and Gates were best friends. They were also the two richest men in the world.

LeBron almost never talked about it, but privately he aspired to one day be the richest man in the world. Plenty of people fantasize about that notion. But LeBron made it one of his goals. He'd even given himself a timeline to achieve it—fifteen to twenty years. And unlike others who dreamed of being as rich as Warren Buffett, LeBron could get a private audience with the world's most successful investor and seek his advice.

Wachter knew Buffett and placed a call. And in late September, LeBron and Maverick flew to Nebraska, eager to meet the man that Wall Street admiringly called the Oracle of Omaha.

Looking up at LeBron, Buffett greeted them with a jovial smile and a self-deprecating joke about his basketball skills. He loved the game and had played when he was younger, although "not very well," he liked to quip.

LeBron presented Buffett with a gift—his own official Cavaliers jersey. Buffett loved it.

Standing opposite each other on the marble flooring in the foyer of the Berkshire Hathaway headquarters, LeBron and Buffett were an unlikely pair. LeBron was twenty-one and Buffett was seventy-five. LeBron was a basketball player from inner-city Akron. Buffett was a stockbroker-turned-investor in Omaha. LeBron liked hip-hop and hung out with Jay-Z in loud, crowded arenas. Buffett liked golf and regularly played with Bill Gates in the serenity of Augusta National.

The other big difference was that LeBron's career had just taken off and Buffett's had reached the pinnacle. Yet LeBron and Buffett—the King and the Oracle—were both hubs with lots of powerful connections. And as Buffett gave LeBron a personal tour of the office where he'd spent the past fifty years working his magic, the two men were immediately at ease with each other. And it quickly became apparent that Buffett's success was not produced by magic. It was instead the result of steady effort at becoming exceptional at one thing.

That message was evident as LeBron and Maverick followed Buffett down a narrow hallway lined with framed pictures and mementos. One of those mementos was a balance sheet from his first partnership—Buffett Partnership, Ltd., formed in 1956. The document listed Buffett's six original partners—family members and his college roommate, whom he called "the gang"—and how much equity each one owned at the time. Buffett's share was worth $1,359.16. Eventually, Buffett liquidated his original partnership and reinvested the money in Berkshire Hathaway. Fifty years later, he calculated, an original $10,000 investment in his Buffett Partnership that was reinvested in Berkshire Hathaway was worth about $500 million.

For LeBron and Maverick, walking with Buffett was a transformative experience. He'd been going to work at the same office and making investments from behind the same desk for twice as many years as they'd been alive. It was a sobering testament to the power of consistency and discipline over the long haul.

Above the doorway outside Buffett's office, LeBron recognized a familiar-looking yellow sign with blue lettering that read: INVEST LIKE A

CHAMPION TODAY. It looked just like the famous yellow sign with blue lettering that read PLAY LIKE A CHAMPION TODAY and hung above the stairwell outside the Notre Dame football locker room. It was tradition for every player on the Notre Dame team to touch the sign before entering the field. Buffett had his employees touch his sign at Berkshire Hathaway each morning when they entered the office.

One of the pieces of advice that Buffett gave LeBron was to make monthly investments in low-cost index funds for the rest of his career and beyond. He felt that LeBron should maintain a significant cash reserve, whatever amount made him comfortable. But beyond that, he felt that LeBron should own a piece of America, a diversified piece, acquired over time and held for thirty or forty years. Coca-Cola, which LeBron endorsed and of which Berkshire Hathaway was the third-largest stockholder, was precisely the kind of company Buffett was referring to when he talked about owning a piece of America. The income, he felt, would go up and up over the years.

Buffett also shared a story about him and Bill Gates that had relevance to LeBron. Shortly after Buffett and Gates had met in 1991, they were asked by Bill Gates Sr. to each write down one word that accounted for their success. Buffett and Gates both wrote down the same word: *focus*. Gates believed that the thing you did obsessively between ages thirteen and eighteen was the thing that you had the most chance of being world-class at. As a teenager, Gates had focused on software. Buffett had focused on investments. "It gave me a big advantage to start very young," Buffett explained.

The message was simple, yet profound—like Buffett and Gates, LeBron was world-class at basketball in part because he had been obsessed with it since his youth. In fact, LeBron had established his focus on basketball at an even earlier age than Buffett and Gates had started focusing, respectively, on investing and computer software.

For lunch, Buffett slipped his new Cavs jersey over his white shirt and took LeBron and Maverick to one of his favorite spots in town, the Crescent Moon Ale House. With large wooden ceiling beams, vintage wall hangings, and neon signs that advertised various craft beers, the restaurant had the feel of a Western saloon. Buffett was a regular. Normally, his presence barely raised an eyebrow. But when LeBron walked in with him, everyone noticed.

LeBron and Maverick sat opposite Buffett at a wooden table.

Feeling at home, LeBron chatted with the waitress and ordered a bacon cheeseburger with fries and lemonade mixed with iced tea.

Buffett admired how easily LeBron engaged with people. He had an unusual degree of humility, Buffett felt, for someone of his stature and wealth. Talking with him over lunch, Buffett surmised, *This guy knows more than I did when I was twenty-one.*

Before they finished, Buffett told LeBron that he had to wash down his meal with a milkshake.

LeBron went for the Oreo cookie shake. Then he posed for pictures and signed autographs for people in the restaurant.

Before leaving Omaha, LeBron told Buffett he needed to come to a Cavs game in Cleveland.

Buffett hadn't been to a pro game in years. But he was delighted by the invitation. He said he'd come. And when he did, he'd wear his new Cavs jersey.

LeBron promised him courtside seats.

Buffett had a request of his own. At the Berkshire Hathaway shareholder's meeting held each spring in Omaha, Buffett liked to entertain the thousands of attendees with a funny video presentation to kick things off. He thought it would be hilarious to play LeBron one-on-one in a game of basketball and show that to the shareholders.

LeBron said that could be arranged.

Buffett said there was only one catch—LeBron had to let him win.

LeBron laughed. He was in.

As the plane took off from Omaha, Maverick had reason to smile. His best friend was forging a relationship with *Warren Buffett.* And soon they'd be touching down in New York, where LeBron was scheduled to appear on *Late Show with David Letterman* for the first time. So much was happening so fast.

Not long after he got back home, LeBron had bigger things to think about. He and Savannah learned that she was pregnant with their second child. According to the calendar, the baby would arrive the following June, right when the 2007 NBA Finals were scheduled to take place.

June 2007, LeBron figured, was going to be a busy month.

TWENTY-ONE

THE LONE CAVALIER

Back when LeBron was a high school senior and about to sign with Nike, he had received a letter from consumer-protection advocate Ralph Nader. It read, in part:

> You are on the verge of choosing to immerse yourself in the world of international commerce, which inevitably brings with it a wide array of complicated and difficult challenges and decisions.

Then, after LeBron signed his $90 million Nike deal, Nader issued a more public warning to LeBron. "People say it's unfair to burden an eighteen-year-old with demands of social consciousness," Nader told the *New York Times* in the summer of 2003. "My answer is that he's not getting an eighteen-year-old's salary. This contract proves he has enormous bargaining power, a superstar's physical image."

LeBron hadn't known Nader and had paid no attention to his warnings. At that time, LeBron was preoccupied with more immediate demands, such as graduating from high school and getting ready for the NBA Draft. It hadn't taken long, though, for LeBron to enter the world of international commerce. On Nike's behalf, he had begun making trips to China and other foreign countries right after the conclusion of his rookie season. Business travel abroad in the off-season quickly became the norm. And within the Nike family, it took LeBron just three years to develop an international footprint that was second only to Tiger Woods's. During all that time overseas, LeBron had managed to steer clear of any political trip wires. But superstardom has an inevitable gravitational pull toward complexity and controversy. And by the start of LeBron's fourth season in the NBA, he was unwittingly approaching the first major political dilemma of his professional career.

With the 2008 Summer Olympics in Beijing less than two years away, LeBron's obligations were already mounting by the fall of 2006. USA Basketball and its coach, Mike Krzyzewski, had pegged LeBron to be the leader of the US Olympic team. With hopes of expanding the NBA's reach in China, Commissioner David Stern was looking to LeBron to be the league's ambassador to Beijing. And Nike was already planning to make LeBron the centerpiece of a comprehensive marketing campaign around the Olympics.

Meanwhile, human rights advocates and several celebrities were looking ahead to the 2008 Summer Olympics with a much different agenda—to shine a bright light on China's abysmal human rights record, particularly in the African country of Sudan, where, with Chinese weaponry, government-backed militia groups had slaughtered hundreds of thousands of non-Arab Africans in the country's Darfur region and forced more than 2 million refugees into camps in the neighboring country of Chad. China and Sudan were economic partners. Sudan was China's largest source of offshore oil production; the Sudanese government was using its oil profits from China to purchase arms and munitions that were made by China. And those weapons were being put in the hands of the militia, the Janjaweed, to slaughter villagers in Darfur.

To raise awareness about the crisis, actor George Clooney had visited the Darfur region and then appeared with then-senator Barack Obama at the National Press Club in Washington, DC, earlier in 2006. Senator Obama had described the situation in Darfur as "a slow-rolling genocide." And Clooney had told the press: "What we cannot do is turn our heads and look away and hope that this will somehow disappear. Because if we do, they will. They will disappear."

Activist Eric Reeves, a professor at Smith College in Northampton, Massachusetts, had spent a lot of time in Darfur, and he had dedicated his life to helping the displaced people there. A fiery critic of China, Reeves was in the early stages of mounting a campaign that he was calling the Genocide Olympics. The objective was to apply pressure to China through public embarrassment. Actress Mia Farrow had also visited Darfur and was equally determined to do whatever it took to draw attention to China's role there. Reeves and Farrow felt that those with a high profile—artists, athletes, corporate sponsors—had an obligation to call out China for its role in sustaining the genocide in Darfur. Their goal was to stir the world's consciousness through the 2008 Olympic Games in China. They planned to start by pressuring Oscar-winning director Steven Spielberg, who had been tapped to help choreograph the opening ceremonies in Beijing, to speak out about China's role in Sudan.

LeBron was oblivious to the situation in Darfur. And he had no connection to George Clooney, Mia Farrow, or Steven Spielberg. But in terms of star power, LeBron was in the same small constellation as them. And due to LeBron's profile in China, he was about to encounter what Ralph Nader had referred to years earlier as "complicated and difficult challenges and decisions."

The Cavaliers opened the NBA season at home on November 1, 2006. Nike had purchased all the ad time during ESPN's six o'clock edition of *SportsCenter* that evening. It was the first time in the network's history that an entire episode of *SportsCenter* had been sponsored by a single advertiser. And Nike used all of that airtime to promote LeBron and his new line of sneakers, the Nike Zoom LeBron IV. The centerpiece of the ad campaign was "Swimming Pool," the commercial featuring the four-dimensional personality of LeBron that had been filmed earlier that year. The shoe company had also planned what it called "a digital takeover of home pages on ESPN .com and MTV.com" to promote LeBron and his shoe. And LeBron billboards went up in major cities throughout the country.

Cinematic and hilarious, LeBron's pool ad was like a mini-movie. More than any of his previous commercial spots, this one helped establish him as a pop culture figure who transcended basketball. It was so popular that Nike had plans to air it on all of the major television networks well into the holiday season. When the Cavaliers arrived in New York to play the Knicks in mid-November, Nike had even opened a LeBron pop-up store in Manhattan and had purchased a digital billboard outside Madison Square Garden featuring a nonstop loop of LeBron dunking.

LeBron was flying high and so were the Cavaliers. In early January 2007, the Cavs had the best record in the Eastern Conference.

That same month, a group of human rights organizations, including the NAACP and Amnesty International, gathered in Washington, DC, to discuss how to address human rights violations by China. Eric Reeves spoke at the meeting and forcefully outlined his ideas for a campaign centered around China's role in Darfur. "Darfur advocacy," Reeves said, "needs to link 'Darfur' indissolubly in the world's consciousness with '2008 Olympic Games in China.' China is already rolling out the welcome carpet. These ruthless men must be convinced that their failure to persuade Khartoum to allow UN troops and civilian police into Darfur will make of the Olympics a gigantic protest venue."

Reeves's tactics were dismissed as too aggressive by the groups in attendance. Besides, most activists felt that it would be impossible to make a difference in Darfur by going after the Chinese government.

Frustrated, Reeves walked out.

But an activist named Jill Savitt chased him down outside and introduced herself as a campaign director at Human Rights First, a powerful nonprofit. She'd heard Reeves's speech and wanted to collaborate with him.

Reeves knew he needed help, and he was impressed with Savitt. She was a veteran organizer who had run the campaign that had recruited military leaders to bring US policies on torture and interrogation into compliance with US and international law. Savitt was also media savvy. She had handled the messaging for the Ms. Foundation for Women's Take Our Daughters to Work campaign.

Together, Reeves and Savitt spent the spring securing a $500,000 grant, which they used to found Dream for Darfur, a nonprofit organization with a mission statement to pressure the government of the People's Republic of China to intervene on behalf of civilians in the Darfur conflict. Mia Farrow agreed to join Dream for Darfur and work with Savitt, who set out to develop a national media strategy with a goal of showing China that the Beijing Olympics would be stained if it didn't stop protecting and funding Sudan's regime.

While Reeves and Farrow stepped up their pressure on Steven Spielberg to speak out against China, Savitt attempted to find inroads into the sports world in hopes of identifying some athletes who could help get the International Olympic Committee to hold China accountable.

On a Friday night in Cleveland in late March 2007, the Cavs were way ahead of the Knicks in the fourth quarter when Coach Brown pulled his starters. LeBron took a seat on the bench. Moments later, two-and-a-half-year-old LeBron Jr. slid down from his seat beside Savannah on the baseline and walked toward the Cavs' bench. With the game still in progress, LeBron watched with pride as his boy approached. When he reached the bench, LeBron feigned a serious expression that suggested, *Where do you think you're going, little man?* LeBron Jr. climbed into the empty chair beside his father. Soon, photographers and television cameramen moved in and captured the scene of LeBron relaxing on the bench with his arm around his son.

It was a snapshot of an athlete in his own self-made world. No other Cavaliers player could have an encounter like that because no other player had courtside seats for his family. And LeBron's son was the only child who would be allowed to wander onto the court during a game—all of the courtside security personnel at the Q knew and adored him. And no one in the Cavs organization was going to bother bringing up the fact that league policy prohibited a family member from being on the bench during a game. It was a rule that no one felt like enforcing with LeBron.

In a way, the incident of Savannah's letting LeBron Jr. go sit with his dad during a game was more powerful PR than Nike's commercial featuring the four LeBrons. Although it was spontaneous, the scene couldn't have been better scripted by the NBA in terms of countering the image of players going into the stands and brawling with fans. LeBron's ascension to the top of the NBA was lifting the league's reputation. Nonetheless, the day after the Knicks game, Cavs general manager Danny Ferry got a call from the league office, informing him that it was against league policy for a child to be on the bench during a game.

LeBron knew the call was perfunctory and didn't worry about it. If there had really been a problem, LeBron would have received a call from Commissioner Stern, but Stern was thrilled with all that LeBron had going on in Cleveland—on the day after the Knicks game, LeBron was preparing to host Warren Buffett, who was coming to town for the following day's game.

Since visiting Omaha, LeBron had been emailing back and forth with Buffett. Their communications were both professional and personal in nature. And LeBron was eager to have him at the Q.

It was becoming clear to Buffett that LeBron possessed the same characteristics that Buffett looked for in those who ran the type of companies that Berkshire Hathaway liked to acquire. Early on in his investment career, Buffett had come to appreciate what it takes for someone to build a big, dominant business from nothing—relentless dedication, working weekends, working holidays, giving up vacations, and allowing the business to become part of you. LeBron, in Buffett's view, was like a business. He was turning his love for basketball into an empire the same way that an entrepreneur turns an idea into a big, dominant business—by focusing on it day and night.

Being around Buffett intensified LeBron's commitment to diversifying his investment portfolio and being diligent about planning for his family's long-term financial security. It was a priority that also rubbed off on Maverick, whom LeBron had tasked with looking for investment opportunities that were a good match for him and his personality. Earlier in 2007, Maverick had gotten an idea—that LeBron should invest in a bicycle company. He knew that LeBron biked everywhere, and in the off-season it wasn't unusual for LeBron to ride up to forty miles a day. LeBron even organized an annual King for Kids Bike-A-Thon in Akron. *So why not*, Maverick figured, *invest in something that was so important to LeBron?*

Maverick ran his idea by investment banker Paul Wachter.

A short while later, Wachter came back with a candidate for LeBron to consider: Cannondale.

Cannondale Bicycle Corporation was based in Bethel, Connecticut, and specialized in high-performance bicycles. The company was owned by Pegasus Partners II, a private-equity investment firm in Greenwich, Connecticut. They'd welcome a partner like LeBron. This was a chance for LeBron to acquire a minority-ownership stake in Cannondale.

Maverick wasn't familiar with private equity or how it worked. But he took Wachter's suggestion to LeBron, who liked the prospect of owning a piece of a company rather than simply signing another endorsement deal.

The decision to take an equity stake in Cannondale coincided with a move by LeBron's agent, Leon Rose, to Creative Artists Agency (CAA), one of the largest talent agencies in Hollywood. CAA had tapped Rose to run its new sports practice. LeBron, who was Rose's most important client, opted to continue with Rose as his agent. Rose's move to CAA would give LeBron a more direct link to Hollywood. Moreover, Rich Paul was offered an opportunity to go with Rose to CAA and learn the ropes. Rich took the opportunity.

While Maverick was working on the details of the Cannondale deal with Wachter and Rich set his sights on the transition to CAA with Rose, LeBron welcomed Buffett to Cleveland on March 25, 2007. It was an opportunity for LeBron to introduce Buffett to his family. Wearing a black Nike T-shirt that read WITNESS on the front, Buffett sat courtside next to Maverick and cheered on his friend. The Cavs lost the game. But Buffett's presence overshadowed the scoreboard and signaled to a national television audience that LeBron was aligned with the most powerful investor in the world.

When a reporter asked Buffett why he had traveled to Cleveland to watch LeBron, he quipped, "He wanted a few tips on basketball and I wanted a little advice on money."

The day after Buffett left town, Maverick announced LeBron's new partnership with Cannondale. At twenty-two, LeBron had acquired a piece of a company for the first time.

The same week that Buffett visited Cleveland, the Wall Street Journal published a scathing op-ed titled "The 'Genocide Olympics.'" The controversial headline was the handiwork of activist Eric Reeves. The essay was written by Mia Farrow and her son Ronan Farrow, a nineteen-year-old Yale Law student who had recently traveled to Darfur as a UNICEF spokesperson. The piece, which called China's "One World, One Dream" slogan for the 2008 Olympics a cover for the nightmare in Darfur, purposely targeted Steven Spielberg. They wrote:

> Equally disappointing is the decision of artists like director Steven Spielberg—who quietly visited China this month as he prepares to help stage the Olympic ceremonies—to sanitize Beijing's image. Is Mr. Spielberg, who in 1994 founded the Shoah Foundation to record the testimony of survivors of the Holocaust, aware that China is bankrolling Darfur's genocide?

The op-ed hammered Spielberg and attempted to link him to the term "Genocide Olympics." Mia and Ronan asked a pointed question: "Does Mr. Spielberg really want to go down in history as the Leni Riefenstahl of the Beijing Games?" Leni Riefenstahl was an acclaimed German filmmaker who produced Nazi propaganda movies and later saw her career go down in infamy.

After the piece ran, Spielberg wrote to China's president, Hu Jintao, asking him to intervene in Darfur. His letter prompted China to send an envoy to Khartoum to discuss the prospect of the Sudanese government's allowing UN peacekeeping troops to enter Darfur after passage of a UN Security Council resolution. But Mia Farrow and Eric Reeves were not impressed by the Chinese envoy's visit to Sudan. In their view, Spielberg could do a lot more.

Reeves followed up with an op-ed of his own in the *Boston Globe* titled "Artists Abetting Genocide?" Again, he went hard at Spielberg. "The question for Spielberg is how much China's culpability matters to him," Reeves wrote. "Why would Spielberg or others want to contribute to Beijing's propaganda—especially when it helps Khartoum?"

Up to this point, LeBron had remained out of the field of vision for the activists focused on Darfur. But LeBron's teammate Ira Newble had been reading up on the situation. Newble had been a starter alongside LeBron during the previous two seasons, but now he was thirty-two and in the twilight of his career. He'd been on the bench for most of the current season. Off the court, he was socially conscious, largely due to the influence of his father, who had been a civil rights worker in the sixties. One morning on the way to a shootaround at the Cavs facility, Newble stopped and picked up a copy of *USA Today*, which had a profile of Eric Reeves. It revealed that Reeves had leukemia and had, at times, worked from his hospital bed to help stop the genocide in Darfur.

Inspired, Newble asked the Cavaliers organization to help him track down the activist's contact info.

Reeves was surprised when he received an email from Newble. And then another. And then another. Reeves was a big basketball fan who had played ball in college and knew the game well. But he'd never heard of Ira Newble. Intrigued by his outreach, Reeves telephoned Newble just as the Cavaliers' regular season was winding down.

Newble had a lot of questions about Darfur.

Reeves explained that a genocide was raging there. More than 2.5 million people had been displaced, mainly to eastern Chad. Reeves estimated that there were 350,000 Darfuri non-Arab African refugees in eastern Chad. "It's one of the largest invisible and desperate refugee populations in the world," Reeves explained.

Newble wanted to help.

Reeves told him about Dream for Darfur and its campaign to focus on China and the Olympics in an effort to urge China to act. And he told Newble that he'd put him in contact with his colleague Jill Savitt.

When Savitt reached out to Newble, he said, "What can I do?"

"You can write a letter to the Chinese government," she said. She offered to draft the letter for him.

Newble welcomed the help.

"And maybe you can get your entire team to sign it," Savitt said.

Newble agreed to do his best.

The Cavaliers finished the 2006–2007 regular season with the second-best record in the Eastern Conference. The Detroit Pistons had the best record. With his eye on a rematch with the Pistons in the Eastern Conference Finals, LeBron led the Cavaliers into the first round of the NBA playoffs, and they soundly defeated the Washington Wizards in the first game on April 22, 2007. The next day, Jill Savitt sent Ira Newble a draft letter for him to review and circulate among his teammates. It was addressed to the government of the People's Republic of China. It read, in part:

> China cannot be a legitimate host to the premiere international event in the sporting world—the Summer Olympic Games—while it remains complicit in the terrible suffering and destruction that continues to this day.
>
> As professional athletes and concerned human beings, we call on the People's Republic of China to use all available diplomatic resources and economic pressure to end the agony of Darfur, and to secure access for UN peace support personnel.

Newble shared the letter with his agent, Steve Kauffman, who welcomed his client's activism and likewise got engaged in the issue. Kauffman began networking with Savitt and Reeves and offered to use his contacts and connections to help them with their media campaign. To-

gether, they identified a list of basketball writers and other sports journalists who could write about Newble's letter. Kauffman also strategized
with Newble about the best way to broach the subject of the letter with his
teammates.

With Kauffman's guidance, Newble spoke to Coach Mike Brown and
got permission to talk to his teammates about Darfur.

The Cavaliers swept the Wizards in four games. A day or two later,
Newble addressed the team in the locker room after practice. They listened intently as he told them about the human suffering in Sudan. China,
Newble told them, was buying oil from the Sudanese government, as
well as selling weapons that were being used by the Sudanese military to
slaughter innocent people.

The Cavs' players were shocked. Most of them had never heard of Darfur. And they were unaware that Africans were being slaughtered.

Encouraging them to learn more, Newble handed out a packet to each
player. The packet contained reading materials that Newble had personally
selected and photocopied. There was also a fact sheet. He encouraged his
teammates to read the materials and get back to him with any questions.

Newble made a point of pulling LeBron aside in private. He didn't want
LeBron to feel pressured. "I understand by you being LeBron you have a
lot at stake," Newble told him. "You can't just put your name on *anything*."

LeBron liked Newble. He'd been on the team for four years, and he'd
been a class act on and off the court. But Newble didn't really understand
what *being LeBron* was like. No one did. The weight of the franchise and
the expectations of the city of Cleveland to get the team to the NBA Finals
rested squarely on LeBron's shoulders. The expectations from USA Basketball, the NBA commissioner, and Nike were mounting. And on the personal side, he had things going on that none of his teammates were aware
of. A man had recently surfaced who was claiming to be LeBron's father.
LeBron's lawyer was into it and the story wasn't out there yet. But LeBron
knew that it could become public any time and he'd be facing a new round
of invasive questions about his mother and the identity of his father.

The one person who did understand all that LeBron was balancing was
Savannah. But she was eight months along and about to give birth to their
second child. The reality was that, at twenty-two, LeBron had so much
going on professionally and personally that when Newble approached
him in the middle of the playoffs and told him about the genocide in Dar-

fur, LeBron was already doing all he could to compartmentalize and keep his focus on the task at hand—winning one game at a time.

Nonetheless, LeBron told Newble he'd consider his letter.

Jill Savitt was frustrated. She'd been talking to members of the national media for weeks, trying to get them to write about the connection between Darfur and China. And she was having no luck. But on a brighter note, the Cavaliers organization had been particularly cooperative with Ira Newble's letter-writing campaign. And Steve Kauffman had been invaluable in helping to facilitate press coverage. Savitt had generated a press release to accompany Newble's letter, and she and Kauffman had offered the story as an exclusive to a writer at the *Plain Dealer*. Savitt was just waiting for Newble to get LeBron's signature.

Kauffman, meanwhile, was advising Newble on that front—the strategy was to give LeBron space and time to make his own decision. Until then, Kauffman had to hold off the writer at the *Plain Dealer*, who was itching to go to press. On May 5, Kauffman, Savitt, and Reeves started a text chain.

> **Kauffman:** Have 13 of 15 signatures and writer we promised exclusive wants to run Sunday.
> **Savitt:** Eric and I have had a bit of a rough week working over the Spielberg people. Dealing with Hwood people can be so frustrating. . . . Hope you managed to put off the reporter. . . .
> **Kauffman:** I will send you a list of the players shortly, waiting on LeBron, but will know very shortly.

The Cavs faced the New Jersey Nets in the Eastern Conference Semifinals. As close friends, LeBron and Jay-Z got a kick out of the fact that their teams were going head-to-head. But once the series began, LeBron was all business. The Nets' lineup included veterans Jason Kidd and Vince Carter, two perennial all-stars who had been waiting much longer than LeBron to win an NBA championship. In a nail-biter on May 6, LeBron got past Kidd in the closing seconds at the Q and banked a runner off the glass to give the Cavs an 81–77 victory in Game 1.

A day earlier, more than twenty-seven thousand people had filed into

Berkshire Hathaway's annual shareholders' meeting in Omaha. To kick things off, they watched a video of Buffett going one-on-one with LeBron. The shareholders roared with laughter when Buffett, wearing a headband and white tube socks, dribbled past LeBron. But after all the laughter, Buffett addressed the shareholders and brought up Berkshire's controversial decision to invest in a Chinese oil company called PetroChina. Critics insisted that the company, which was a subsidiary of China National Petroleum, was contributing to the genocide in Darfur. Some of Berkshire's shareholders agreed with the criticism.

Buffett acknowledged the geopolitical implications of Berkshire's investment. And he had previously called the situation in Sudan "deplorable." But he maintained that he could not influence the geopolitical situation in China or Sudan, and he had every intention of continuing his business relationship with PetroChina.

Hours after Buffett finished his remarks, Ira Newble telephoned Jill Savitt with an update on his efforts to get his teammates to sign his letter. "I got everyone to sign except for one person," he told her. Newble still hadn't heard back from LeBron.

Savitt heard the disappointment in Newble's voice.

Suddenly, it dawned on Savitt. *Oh my God*, she thought. *This is gold!*

For weeks, Savitt had been unable to get the national media to connect China to Darfur. If LeBron didn't sign the letter, his Nike shoe contract could end up being the thing that tied China to Darfur.

But Savitt didn't say that to Newble. Instead, she gave him a pep talk and encouraged him to keep working on LeBron. Meantime, she emailed *Sports Illustrated* columnist Rick Reilly, who was working on a column about Mia Farrow and her pressure campaign on Steven Spielberg. "Dunno your deadline," Savitt told Reilly, "but Ira Newble of the Cleveland Cavs has organized 13 of his teammates to sign a letter to the Chinese government about the Olympics/Darfur. . . . If you are interested in including Newble in your piece, let me know."

The next day, the community relations manager for the Cleveland Cavaliers sent Savitt an email. "Per Ira Newble, please find attached scanned copies of the 'Bring the Olympic Dream to Darfur' letter signed by teammates," the Cavs executive wrote. "To decipher the names we have also attached a copy of the players' names in order that they signed the attached letter."

Savitt noticed that LeBron's name still wasn't on the list. Yet the Cavaliers were fully behind Newble's efforts.

That night, LeBron poured in thirty-six points and the Cavs took a 2-0 series lead over the Nets.

With a day off before heading to New Jersey for Games 3 and 4, LeBron was at home on May 10 when the headline "Newble Protesting Genocide in Sudan" ran in the *Plain Dealer*.

"I'm here in the U.S. and I have means to live well and I'm not suffering and then I hear about women and children getting raped and killed and the Sudanese government and the Janjaweed are perpetrating the violence," Newble told the paper. "I had to do something."

The *Plain Dealer* had broken the news that Newble had written a letter to China and the International Olympic Committee and that most of his teammates had signed on to the effort. The paper also raised the big question—would LeBron sign the letter?

LeBron didn't know what to do about Newble's letter. Virtually all of the Cavaliers players had signed it except him. That wasn't what bothered him, though. What troubled him was the realization that he knew that he didn't have a grasp of the situation. When he first heard about Darfur, he didn't know where it was located. He needed a map to find it. Beyond the geography, he was also unfamiliar with the politics and the history of the conflict.

The one thing LeBron did know was that his signature would instantly elevate Newble's letter into an international controversy. The letter clearly pointed the finger at China. It was one thing for Ira Newble and political activists to do that. But was that the right approach for LeBron to take?

Without offering an explanation, LeBron told Newble he had decided not to sign the letter.

Newble didn't need an explanation—he was under contract with Nike, too. Although nowhere close to LeBron's deal, Newble's Nike contract was lucrative to him, and it enabled him to appreciate the difficult spot that LeBron was in. He told LeBron that he respected his decision.

The Cavs headed to New Jersey for Games 3 and 4.

One of LeBron's gifts as a basketball player was his ability to anticipate what was going to happen on the floor, enabling him to orchestrate the action and stay one or two steps ahead of his opponents. But human rights campaigns take place in the political arena, where the stakes are much higher and the players take an all-or-nothing approach. There is no referee. The media tips the scales, weighing in and shaping the narrative. In this environment, there is little room for nuance. Words, especially ones uttered by a political novice, can be akin to matches in the hands of a child. In between Games 3 and 4 in New Jersey, LeBron was asked by a reporter why he hadn't signed Ira Newble's letter. "It was basically not having enough information," LeBron told him. "Any decision I make I have to have extensive knowledge."

Focused on the playoffs, LeBron couldn't see the narrative that was forming around him. Nor did he appreciate how his words would fit into it. He had his own publicist and plenty of savvy advisors. But they were of little help in this situation. Even Steven Spielberg, who had access to the best publicists in Hollywood, was getting pilloried in the press for not speaking out about China's connection to Darfur. On the same day that LeBron talked about not having enough information to get behind a letter to the Chinese government, Spielberg got blasted by Rick Reilly in *Sports Illustrated*. "The King Kong of directors is one of the Beijing Games' 'artistic advisers,' helping to orchestrate the opening and closing ceremonies," Reilly wrote. "But how can a man who decried one holocaust in his finest film—*Schindler's List*—be in bed with a country that is helping to bankroll another?"

The Reilly column showcased how Eric Reeves, Jill Savitt, and Mia Farrow worked. Their strategy from the start had been to get powerful people on their side so they could say to China, "We have all these people with us. Do the right thing." And to win over people like Spielberg, they had started with honey. But when that hadn't worked, they hadn't been afraid to use vinegar. "Once we got mean," Savitt explained, "we got *really mean*."

While Spielberg got the vinegar treatment, LeBron led all scorers in Game 4 and the Cavs took a commanding 3-1 lead as the series shifted back to Cleveland.

On May 16, LeBron woke up in his own bed, refreshed and ready to close out the Nets that night. But before LeBron headed to the Q, the *New York Times* published "Cavalier Seeks Players' Support for Darfur." In a comprehensive and gritty account, senior basketball writer Howard Beck brought the bloodshed in Darfur to LeBron's doorstep. "There's innocent people dying, and it's just a tragedy to stand back and let them do what they're doing," Ira Newble told the *Times*.

Beck's piece included passages from Newble's letter to the Chinese government, along with quotes from Reeves, who praised Newble for being a catalyst for change within the sports world. But the big takeaway from Beck's story was that LeBron hadn't signed the letter. With one sentence, the *Times* focused the Darfur issue on LeBron's shoe contract.

James, one of the NBA's most marketed stars, has a $90 million endorsement contract with Nike, which has extensive dealings in China.

In the story, the mention of LeBron's shoe contract was followed by the answer he'd given a couple of days earlier for not signing the letter: "It's basically not having enough information."

And just like that, the ground shifted beneath LeBron's feet.

As soon as the *Times* piece ran, Jill Savitt's phone started ringing. Every journalist she'd been trying to entice to write about Darfur was suddenly calling and emailing her.

LeBron was out of sync that night. Then, late in the game, he tweaked his knee going for a loose ball and had to leave the game. And the Nets upset the Cavs, forcing the series back to New Jersey.

Meanwhile, Jill Savitt received an email from a writer at Bloomberg who she'd been trying to get to write about Darfur. "Jill," he wrote, "here is the column." The headline read "Lebron James Isn't the Cavalier to Admire Most." The piece, which Bloomberg ran online after Game 5, lambasted LeBron, saying:

Unlike LeBron, Newble can't claim a $90 million endorsement contract with Nike. Ira's mug isn't plastered on downtown Cleveland Landmark Office Towers. Nor does he appear, much less star in, television commercials. This is what Newble does possess: "Courage and conviction," says Mia Farrow the actress and humanitarian.

The campaign had transitioned from honey to vinegar. LeBron was now getting the same treatment as Spielberg. In the Bloomberg piece, Eric

Reeves put pressure on LeBron by praising Newble and his letter. "It's a letter any player of conscience should be able to sign," Reeves said. "Ira is a professional athlete with a connection to the real world. He's not so much in the bubble of NBA stardom that he can't see people are suffering."

Former US senator and basketball Hall of Famer Bill Bradley also sharpened the focus on LeBron without naming him. "You have to decide what it is you want to use your celebrity for," Bradley told Bloomberg. "It's conceivable that some people will choose to never do it, in which case it's unfortunate. There are bigger lives that can be led."

LeBron was blindsided. Over the next few days, one news outlet after another—NPR, Fox, the *Washington Post*, the *Boston Globe*—weighed in. Experts from the Brookings Institution and other foreign-policy analysts were speculating about his motives. For the first time in LeBron's life, people were looking at him through a political lens. And LeBron, for the first time in his professional career, was flat-footed.

Amid the swirl, the Cavs finally finished off the Nets. But as the team headed to Detroit with a trip to the NBA Finals on the line, LeBron was wounded and weary. Basketball had never been this hard.

TWENTY-TWO

ONE FOR THE AGES

Game 1 of the Eastern Conference Finals had gone the way LeBron figured it would go—a tooth-and-nail fight where nothing came easy and neither team could pull away. With fifteen seconds left, the Pistons led by two and the Cavaliers had the ball. During a time-out, LeBron listened as Coach Brown drew up a play that would put the ball in LeBron's hands. Moments later, LeBron caught the ball at the top of the key, drove into the lane, and got a step on defender Tayshaun Prince. With two other defenders closing in, LeBron knew that Donyell Marshall was all alone in the corner. Instinctively, he passed up the shot and whipped the ball to Marshall, who launched a three-pointer for the win.

The ball caromed off the rim and the Pistons secured the long rebound and the victory to take a 1-0 series lead.

LeBron's decision immediately came under scrutiny. In the postgame press conference, he was asked why he hadn't taken the shot to tie the game. "I go for the winning play," LeBron said. "The winning play when two guys come at you and a teammate is open is to give it up. It's as simple as that."

His answer drew instant criticism.

"I've got a problem with the best player on the floor not taking any of these shots down the stretch," TNT analyst Charles Barkley said. "If I'm the best player on the court, I've got to get a shot. That's not a criticism. That's a fact."

Other NBA writers agreed with Barkley's assessment that LeBron shouldn't have passed the ball when the game was on the line. "Kobe Bryant certainly wouldn't have," one writer pointed out. "And Michael Jordan did only when out of options."

LeBron heard the critics. He read the reviews. But he wasn't second-guessing his decision. Way back in grade school, when he had played for Coach Dru, he had learned the importance of passing the ball. By now, giving up the ball to the open man was so ingrained in his game that it was like a muscle reflex—you take what the defense gives you. It was about winning games, not making sure he took the final shot.

After a day off, LeBron and his teammates were getting ready for Game 2 in Detroit when the *Christian Science Monitor* published "On Darfur, LeBron James Drops the Ball," a scathing piece that praised Ira Newble and called LeBron "cowardly."

Newble is hardly the first professional athlete to stick his neck out for a political cause. Tennis great Arthur Ashe denounced apartheid in South Africa; boxer Muhammad Ali resisted the draft during America's war in Vietnam, forsaking his heavyweight crown. But LeBron James, one of the best basketball players in the world, won't lift a finger for Darfur. Here James echoes the dominant hoopster of his youth, Michael Jordan, who has a record of putting profits over principles.

Nike's Lynn Merritt was pissed. The controversy over LeBron's unwillingness to sign Ira Newble's letter had been going full tilt for two weeks. Yet it showed no signs of letting up. On the contrary, with each new article or opinion piece, writers were getting harsher and more personal in their denunciations of LeBron. Merritt blamed Ira Newble for bringing his political agenda into the Cavaliers' locker room. And Merritt also blamed Steve Kauffman for encouraging it.

Fed up, Merritt had a heated call with Kauffman about Newble. "What a pain in the ass he must be to the Cavs bringing this into the workplace," Merritt told Kauffman. "That would be like me coming into your place of employment and asking you to join the Islam Nation."

While Merritt vented, Kauffman, a lawyer, took notes. He also pushed back, unwilling to take any shit from anyone at Nike. As far as Kauffman was concerned, Newble was doing something noble. And Nike ought to be a bit more supportive.

The Pistons won Game 2 to take a 2-0 series lead.

Back in Cleveland, LeBron scored thirty-two points in Game 3 and twenty-five points in Game 4. The Cavs won both games to even the series. But every game was a battle. And every game's outcome hinged on LeBron. When Detroit's hound-him-and-pound-him defensive scheme worked, the Pistons hung on to win. When LeBron outlasted the Pistons' approach, the Cavs won.

As the series shifted back to Detroit for the pivotal fifth game, the Pistons had the edge and were favored to win. That week, *Sports Illustrated* pointed out that it had taken Michael Jordan four straight playoff meetings with the Pistons in the late eighties and early nineties before he figured out how to beat them. It wasn't until the emergence of costar Scottie Pippen and workhorse Horace Grant that Jordan finally got his team to the NBA Finals. "Indeed," *Sports Illustrated* said, "the main lesson from the Jordan era is that one man can't do it alone."

LeBron didn't want to wait four years to beat the Pistons. On May 31, 2007, he entered the Palace of Auburn Hills with a singular focus to win one road game.

Through the first three quarters, LeBron played one of his best games of the playoffs and put his team ahead. But late in the fourth quarter, the Pistons rallied by scoring ten straight points to take the lead, 88–81, with three minutes to play. The momentum had swung, and the Cavs were fading fast. LeBron drove the lane and was raked across the eye by Rasheed Wallace as he attempted a layup. The shot went in, as did the free throw that LeBron was awarded, cutting the lead to 88–84.

Moments later, after a Pistons miss, LeBron stuck a long-range three, drawing his team to within one, 88–87.

On the Cavs next possession, LeBron took another hard shot to the face. Then, after a time-out, he dribbled the ball at the top of the key while being guarded one-on-one. Faking as if he were going left, he crossed over his dribble to his right hand, blew past the defender, and drove into the lane. With a head of steam, he soared above all five Pistons defenders. When forward Tayshaun Prince recognized what was coming, he shielded his head with his arms and ducked out of the way as LeBron rose to the rim and tomahawked a vicious one-handed dunk that shook the backboard. "And stuffed!" announcer Marv Albert yelled.

The Cavs were up, 89–88, with thirty-one seconds to play.

Chauncey Billups answered on the other end with a clutch three-point shot to put Detroit back up by two.

Fifteen seconds remained. LeBron dribbled at the top of the key, looking for an opening. With five Pistons between him and the basket, he blew past Prince.

"James with the *step*," Albert said.

LeBron accelerated and elevated so fast that he hammered home another dunk before Albert could finish his sentence.

The game was tied at ninety-one and headed to overtime.

On the Cavaliers bench, LeBron told his teammates that it was their job to take care of defending the Pistons when Detroit had the ball. "Leave the rest to me," he told them. "I'll take care of the offense."

On the Pistons bench, the coach implored his team to do everything in their power to make it hard on LeBron. "He was going to the floor hard," Chauncey Billups would later say about the Pistons' strategy for stopping LeBron in overtime. "We was putting him on the wood. Hard!"

The first time LeBron touched the ball in overtime, he got whacked. Then he proceeded to score all seven of his team's points in the extra period to give the Cavs the lead, 98–96. Forty seconds remained as LeBron dribbled his way around the three-point arc, looking for a lane to the basket. But none existed. Three players were hounding him and the shot clock was winding down.

"LeBron has to fire," Albert said.

Bouncing off one defender and keeping his dribble, he maneuvered just inside the three-point line and elevated as Billups lunged toward him. While airborne, LeBron adjusted his body, squaring up to face the rim, and let the ball fly.

"And *scores*," Albert said as the shot rattled through the rim.

"Oh *my*!" color commentator Doug Collins said.

"What a shot by LeBron James!" Albert said. "Off balance. Shot clock running down. He had no angle. And he *drilled* it."

LeBron had scored sixteen consecutive points. The Cavs were up, 100–96, with thirty-three seconds left in overtime.

After a time-out, the Pistons rallied and scored four straight points to tie the game and send it into a second overtime.

* * *

This time, when the teams went to the benches, LeBron didn't need to say anything to his teammates. They knew to keep giving him the ball and getting out of the way.

To start the second overtime, LeBron dribbled toward the Pistons bench, then launched a step-back jumper that whipped through the net as he landed out-of-bounds along the Pistons' bench. His team back up by two, LeBron stared down the Pistons bench as he backpedaled away. He had scored twenty-two of his team's last twenty-three points.

The Pistons countered with two baskets to go back up, 104–102.

Guarded one-on-one at the other end, LeBron dribbled the ball at the top of the key, waiting for his teammates to clear out. Seeing the other four Pistons packed around the lane, he juked to his left, getting the defender to lean that way. Then LeBron went the other direction, bounced the ball behind his back from his left hand to his right, creating just enough separation from his defender to elevate and knock down a jumper, tying the game.

Arms folded and mouths open, the Pistons players on the bench stared in disbelief.

Jogging back downcourt, LeBron puffed his cheeks, took a breath, and used his arms to simulate push-ups.

The Pistons went back up, 107–104.

With just over a minute left in the second overtime, LeBron again dribbled at the top of the key, staring down five Pistons defenders, and darted toward Detroit's bench. Being pursued by two defenders, he elevated away from the basket and launched another long-range three, his momentum carrying him out-of-bounds as the ball rattled through the rim.

"*Yes!*" said Albert. "And the game is tied at 107!"

"This is unbelievable," Collins said. "This is Jordanesque."

LeBron had scored twenty-three straight points and twenty-seven of his team's last twenty-eight.

After a Pistons miss, the Cavs got the ball back and called time-out with 11.4 seconds remaining in the second overtime.

Exhausted, LeBron plopped down on the bench beside his teammates, a towel draped over his shoulders, a Gatorade cup in his hand.

Coach Brown pulled out his whiteboard and diagrammed what he wanted to happen on the inbounds play—a screen to free up LeBron so he could get the ball. "Set it here," Brown said, drawing a circle in the lane under the Cavs basket. "Bring LeBron to the top," he continued, drawing a line charting LeBron's path from the screen to the top of the three-point arc.

LeBron's eyes followed Brown's Sharpie.

Brown drew a dotted line from the sideline to LeBron, indicating the path of the inbounds pass. Then he looked up at LeBron. "Make sure you drive it," he shouted, pointing at him. "Take the last shot."

Everyone in the building knew the ball was going to LeBron—no other Cavs player had made a field goal in nearly eighteen minutes of play. The only question was whether LeBron could beat five Pistons off the dribble one more time.

Using the screen to get free, LeBron darted out of the key and caught the inbounds pass at midcourt. His feet just inside the Pistons logo, he cradled the ball in his left hand and surveyed the floor. His teammates cleared out to the far sides of the court. Chauncey Billups crouched in front of him, arms extended. The other four Pistons defenders formed a box in front of the basket. The lane was wide open.

Motionless, LeBron glanced over Billups's head at the clock above the backboard.

"James, working it down," Marv Albert said. "Five seconds . . ."

LeBron sprang to his left, his dribble just inches off the floor, blowing past Billups.

". . . four . . ."

Knifing into the lane with Billups on his right hip and three defenders converging in front of him, LeBron elevated.

". . . three . . ."

In the air, realizing that no one had jumped to contest his shot, he transferred the ball from his left hand to his right.

". . . two . . ."

On the way down, LeBron flipped a scoop shot up off the glass just before his feet touched the floor.

". . . James scores!" Albert shouted.

The Pistons called time-out and Rasheed Wallace threw his hands up in disgust. With 2.2 seconds remaining, the Cavs were up, 109–107.

The crowd was dumbfounded. LeBron hustled to the Cavs bench and chest-bumped one of the assistant coaches so hard that he nearly knocked him to the floor. With Electric Light Orchestra's "Don't Bring Me Down" blaring through the Palace of Auburn Hills, the crowd was stunned.

"Forty-eight points for LeBron James," Marv Albert said. "He has scored the last twenty-five points for Cleveland, twenty-nine of the last thirty. . . . This goes down, no matter what happens here—we still have 2.2 to go—as one of the all-time greatest performances in NBA history."

As the buzzer sounded and a final shot by the Pistons fell short, LeBron felt like he was coming down on the Demon Drop, a roller coaster west of Cleveland that drops ten stories, creating a sensation of free-falling. Drained and barely able to stand, he leaned forward, put his hands on his knees, and stared down at the floor of the Palace of Auburn Hills.

He had played fifty of the game's fifty-eight minutes.

He had scored the Cavs' final 25 points, including all 18 in the two overtime periods, to finish with 48 points, 9 rebounds, and 7 assists.

And he had single-handedly ushered in a changing of the guard in the NBA.

On a Thursday night in the Motor City, LeBron James had broken the Pistons.

Dehydrated and cramping, LeBron needed an IV on the flight back to Cleveland. But he felt better than ever. He knew that the city of Cleveland was about to become the home of the Eastern Conference championship trophy for the first time in history.

Two nights later, tens of thousands of fans packed the streets outside the Q. Inside, the Cavs rolled. Game 6 was the biggest game in franchise history. The Cavs won, 98–82, and the noise in the arena was deafening when the final buzzer sounded. With confetti coming down and fans screaming euphorically, LeBron found Savannah.

Ready to give birth any day, she ran toward LeBron.

He threw his arms around her. Then, like a bodyguard, he led her off the floor and through a gauntlet of cameras. At twenty-two, LeBron had led his team to the NBA Finals in just his fourth season. And he was about to be a father again.

Oh, man, he thought. *It doesn't get any better than this.*

TWENTY-THREE

KINGDOM COME

No one on the Cavaliers' roster had ever played in the NBA Finals. On the other hand, the San Antonio Spurs had practically turned the NBA Finals into an annual destination. Led by two-time NBA Most Valuable Player Tim Duncan, the Spurs had won three championships in the previous seven years. Head coach Gregg Popovich had surrounded Duncan with all-star point guard Tony Parker and a roster stacked with veterans—Manu Ginobili, Bruce Bowen, Robert Horry, and others—whose combined years of championship appearances exceeded those of every other team in the league. From the oddsmakers in Las Vegas to NBA writers around the country, virtually everyone expected the Cavaliers to get routed.

But the outcome of the NBA Finals was almost beside the point. After all, the Cavaliers weren't supposed to be there in the first place. Not so soon, anyway. And not with a starting lineup that included Sasha Pavlovic, Zydrunas Ilgauskas, Daniel Gibson, and Drew Gooden. That LeBron had gotten this squad to the finals in just his fourth pro season was a monumental achievement. Rather than focus on Tim Duncan and the Spurs, the media was still buzzing about LeBron's epic one-man show in Game 5 against Detroit. The *New York Times* called it "hypnotic." *Sports Illustrated* deemed it "immortal." LeBron was getting the kind of superlatives one might expect after a magnum opus performance by a superstar at the pinnacle of his career, not a relative newcomer.

Amid all the hoopla, Darfur became yesterday's news. LeBron's achievement in Game 5 had been so singular and triumphant that it shifted the narrative. LeBron faced no more questions. No more criticism. Now all of the focus was on the start of a new era in basketball—the era of LeBron.

No one was more relieved than Nike's Lynn Merritt. From day one,

Merritt had been LeBron's most passionate advocate within Nike, leading the charge in favor of spending record-setting money to land LeBron and then crafting the deal at the eleventh hour. Not everyone within Nike had been as bullish on LeBron as Merritt had been. There were some within Nike who had felt Merritt had overspent. But no one felt that way after Game 5 in Detroit. Prior to Game 5, Nike had roughly a half dozen people working full-time on LeBron and his brand. After Game 5, that number increased to 150. Even Nike's annual All-American Camp in Indianapolis was renamed the LeBron James Skills Academy and relocated to Akron starting in July 2007. It was further proof that LeBron was making Akron the center of the basketball universe.

Within Nike, the new era was referred to as "AGF," an acronym for After Game Five.

LeBron's first appearance in the NBA Finals was coinciding with James Gandolfini's last performance as Tony Soprano. After eighty-five episodes that had spanned an eight-year period from 1999 to 2007, *The Sopranos*—a series that *New Yorker* editor David Remnick pronounced "the richest achievement in the history of television"—was coming to an end. The final episode was airing on the same night as Game 2 of the NBA Finals. And the complex life of Tony Soprano—a ruthless mob boss who managed to become lovable despite being repulsively brutal—had left such an indelible mark on American culture that pundits from NPR and PBS were debating what the show's popularity said about the country. And everyone from tabloid journalists to television critics were speculating whether Tony Soprano would survive the finale.

The NBA and its broadcast partner, ABC, weren't thrilled about going head-to-head with HBO's juggernaut. From a ratings standpoint, it boiled down to LeBron versus Tony Soprano. To leverage the NBA's leading man, ABC asked LeBron to prerecord an interview, which the network planned to cut into snippets and air in short segments throughout the series.

LeBron was a huge fan of *The Sopranos* and admired Gandolfini's mastery as an actor. Like many Americans, LeBron couldn't help rooting for Tony and got a kick out of his legendary lines, like "I'm the motherfucking fucking one who calls the shots." But LeBron was the antithesis of Tony Soprano, whose family life was tortured—his own mother once put a contract out on him. When asked by ABC to describe his relationship with his mother, LeBron lit up.

"I'm really more proud of her than I am of myself," LeBron said. "Just because of how she helped me grow as a man. And me having a child now, I don't know how she was able to raise me by herself. I give all the praise in the world to single mothers. I don't know how they do it. I couldn't raise my two-year-old by myself."

ABC wasn't used to getting sound bites like that to promote a basketball game.

The Finals opened in San Antonio and to no one's surprise, the Spurs cruised to a 2-0 series lead. Game 1 wasn't close. Game 2, a Sunday night affair, was even more lopsided—the Spurs built a twenty-eight-point lead in the first half and never relented. "For nearly two hours Sunday," the *New York Times* noted, "the Spurs emasculated the Cleveland Cavaliers, further trashed LeBron James' coming-out party and most certainly laid waste to the NBA's U.S. television ratings."

While LeBron and the Cavs were struggling to find their footing on the NBA's biggest stage, over on HBO, Tony Soprano slipped into a booth at Holsten's Ice Cream Parlor, popped a couple of coins in the jukebox, selected Journey's "Don't Stop Believin'," and waited for his wife and kids to join him. The scene looked like a moment of domestic bliss, but it felt like the last supper. By the time the screen went black and the credits rolled, James Gandolfini and costar Edie Falco had performed in the most infamous series finale in television history.

LeBron missed all of that. Flying back to Cleveland, he still believed the Cavs could win.

And for a moment toward the end of Game 3 at the Q, it appeared that LeBron might flip the script. With 5.5 seconds remaining and the Spurs clinging to a three-point lead, Coach Mike Brown drew up a play that called for LeBron to take a game-tying three-point shot. On the Spurs sideline, Coach Popovich told defensive specialist Bruce Bowen to foul LeBron before he could get off a shot.

LeBron knew what was coming. As soon as he sprinted to the top of the key to catch the inbounds pass, he saw Bowen running toward him.

Referee Bob Delaney was just a few feet away as LeBron took one dribble to his left.

Bowen lunged and grabbed LeBron with both hands—Bowen's right hand caught LeBron's right biceps, and his left hand reached around and got hold of the back of LeBron's jersey.

Already starting to elevate, LeBron shook off Bowen and let fly a three-point shot that fell short.

Delaney didn't blow his whistle.

The final buzzer sounded, and the Spurs ran onto the court in jubilation.

LeBron turned to Delaney. "He fouled me!"

Delaney turned his head from side to side, dismissing LeBron's complaint.

"Bob, he *fouled* me," LeBron yelled, pointing at his arm, "right here!"

ABC showed the replay in slow motion. It was clear that LeBron had been fouled.

"LeBron James has a legitimate complaint," color analyst Mike Fratello said on the air.

It didn't matter. The Cavs had lost again, and the Spurs led the series 3-0.

Afterward, LeBron was asked about the missed call at the end.

At that point, LeBron saw no point in calling out the referee. Instead, he took the blame, saying he should have played better.

As soon as he left the arena, LeBron went into family mode. The next day Savannah went to Cuyahoga Falls General Hospital just north of Akron. And a little past midnight on June 14, she gave birth to their second son. They named him Bryce Maximus James. His middle name was based on the character Maximus Decimus Meridius in *Gladiator,* one of LeBron's all-time favorite films.

After a sleepless night, LeBron showed up at the Q for Game 4. Despite being tired, he had an extra bounce in his step, thanks in large part to Bryce's arrival. It also helped that Tom Brady and Gisele Bündchen had flown in and were courtside that night. LeBron and Brady were more acquainted than sports fans realized. A friendly rivalry existed between them, and LeBron got a charge out of playing in front of Brady, who was the only other athlete in American team sports who knew what it was like to be compared to the greatest player of all time. Similar to the way LeBron had grown up idolizing Jordan, Brady had grown up idolizing Joe Montana, who was considered the greatest quarterback of all time. And like LeBron, Brady had set out to reach the heights of his idol. Professionally, LeBron and Brady were still ascending, and they were yoked together in their individual quests to become the greatest of all time.

But in their personal lives, LeBron and Brady were in different places. Brady and Gisele met through a mutual friend on a blind date at a tony restaurant in Greenwich Village. The Brazilian-born supermodel, who had been dubbed by *Rolling Stone* "the Most Beautiful Girl in the World" and who had appeared on more magazine covers than any other model, was worth an estimated $150 million. LeBron and Savannah were teenagers when they had gone on their first date, at an Applebee's in Akron. They'd been together ever since and were building their dream home just a few miles from where they'd grown up. Savannah was fully dedicated to raising their children as a stay-at-home mother. About to turn thirty, Brady had three Super Bowl rings and no children. LeBron, at twenty-two, had two children and was still reaching for his first championship.

After player introductions, a fan held up a sign that read DO IT FOR BRYCE. It was projected on the jumbo screen in the arena, prompting cheers as LeBron approached center court for the opening tip.

Tim Duncan congratulated LeBron on becoming a father for the second time.

Beaming, LeBron threw his arms around Duncan and hugged him.

One by one, the other Spurs players congratulated LeBron.

"James never knew his father," ABC's play-by-play announcer Mike Breen said. "So his mom raised him. And he has such love for what his mother did for him."

ABC cut to the portion of the interview recorded a week earlier where LeBron praised single mothers. "I don't know how they do it," LeBron said, smiling. "I couldn't raise my two-year-old by myself. I couldn't do it."

"Well, now he's got two," Breen said. "He's now a two-time dad. Congratulations to LeBron and his family."

Despite his sleepless night in the hospital, LeBron played all but ninety seconds of Game 4. He finished with 24 points, 10 assists, and 6 rebounds. It was a Maximus-like effort. But the Cavs came up one point short, losing 83–82.

Spurs point guard Tony Parker put the dagger in the Cavs and was named MVP of the finals. As soon as the final buzzer sounded, Parker's fiancée, actress Eva Longoria, ran onto the court, leaped into Parker's arms, wrapped her legs around him, and kissed him. Manu Ginobili smacked the hand of Bruce Bowen. Tim Duncan hugged Gregg Popovich.

LeBron couldn't bear to watch any of it. He turned in silence and headed into the tunnel. He realized he hadn't been mentally prepared to play in the Finals. He'd dreamt about it. He'd wanted it. But there was no substitute for experience. Tim Duncan and Gregg Popovich had just won their fourth title together. Now LeBron had a deeper appreciation for the magnitude of that achievement.

After changing out of his uniform, LeBron congratulated Duncan in a hallway outside the locker rooms.

"Great job, man," Duncan said, hugging him. Duncan encouraged LeBron not to change his approach. "This is going to be your league in a little while," he said.

"I appreciate that," LeBron said.

"But I appreciate you giving us this year," Duncan said with a grin.

LeBron laughed.

Duncan swatted his butt.

LeBron didn't spend much time reflecting on the finals. Days later, he and Maverick hosted a two-day summit in Akron. It was an LRMR event. Maverick was the organizer. LeBron was the draw. Representatives from all of the companies that did business with LeBron—Nike, Coca-Cola, Microsoft, Upper Deck, Bubblicious, and a bunch of other corporate partners—agreed to participate. The purpose of the summit was to expand LeBron's brand globally, particularly in China. Panel sessions included: "China 101: Pop Culture, Media and Sports," "Brand Globalization," and "LeBron Brand in China."

LeBron had asked Mike Krzyzewski to speak at the summit.

Coach K had something weighing heavily on his mind that he wanted to discuss face-to-face with LeBron. The summit provided a perfect opportunity, and Coach K readily accepted the invitation and flew to Akron.

On the night before the summit got underway, LeBron and Maverick invited the corporate sponsors to a private dinner at the Akron Hilton.

Before the main course was served, Coach K delivered a toast. "Over the next two days," he said, looking around the table, "the focus needs to be on LeBron, not your individual companies."

Coach K felt the same way about LeBron with respect to Team USA—LeBron was the most important player on the team. But after Team USA had finished third in Japan the previous summer, Coach K had realized that his mandate—reestablishing the United States atop the world basketball hierarchy—was going to be a steeper climb than he had originally anticipated. In order to get back to the top, Coach K felt that he first needed to create a new culture around the team. And to help him do that, he wanted to add some veteran leadership on Team USA's roster of young stars. The three veterans that Coach K had in mind were Chauncey Billups, Jason Kidd, and Kobe Bryant. But Coach K wasn't going to make any big moves without talking it through with LeBron first.

After the dinner, Coach K and LeBron met alone.

Coach K explained his concerns and how he wanted to address them by recruiting a few veterans. He brought up Jason Kidd first.

"How do you feel about him coming on?" Coach K said.

"Good," LeBron said. "J-Kidd's the best passer in the NBA. I'm really good. But I can learn from him."

LeBron also liked Coach K's suggestion to add Billups, whom LeBron saw as an exceptional defender with a hard-nosed mentality.

When the conversation shifted to Kobe, Coach K took a more diplomatic tack. He viewed Kobe and LeBron as the two alpha males of the NBA. Kobe played with an assassin's mentality and was at the peak of his powers. He was the ultimate competitor. LeBron was the most talented player in the world, a perfect embodiment of muscle, agility, power, and speed. He was the ultimate athlete. Pairing them, Coach K felt, was the surest way to restore Team USA as the world's superpower in basketball at the Beijing Olympics. But there was also the potential for Kobe and LeBron to become Team USA's version of *Top Gun*'s Iceman and Maverick, competing over who was the best. Coach K knew that neither Kobe nor LeBron was cut out to play wingman. He just wanted to ensure that they would embrace each other as teammates.

LeBron was a student of the game. And he appreciated that Coach K was one of the game's great teachers. He also knew that Team USA had gotten their ass kicked in 2004. With him and Kobe joining forces, they'd be doing the ass kicking.

"Nobody prepares like Kobe," LeBron told Coach K.

LeBron didn't say much more.

But Coach K heard what he needed to hear. He was going to get the opportunity to coach the NBA's two top guns.

The next morning, Maverick welcomed everyone to the summit and turned the floor over to LeBron, who addressed sixty-five executives in a large seminar room at the University of Akron. "I'm just very excited about this," he said. "Who would ever have thought we could get you guys to Akron, Ohio? Growing up, we couldn't get anyone to little ol' Akron, Ohio."

Everyone smiled. Especially Coach K.

Even when LeBron had to deal with unpleasant situations, he managed to remain even-keeled. After he got dragged into the lawsuit stemming from the loan that Eddie Jackson and Gloria had taken from Joseph Marsh, LeBron didn't gripe. Without resentment, he looked out for Eddie's and Gloria's interests. Although he had his lawyer, Fred Nance, successfully fend off Marsh's claim for millions of dollars, LeBron ultimately made sure that Marsh was paid in full for the money he had lent Eddie and Gloria. And when Eddie was released from prison, LeBron continued to treat him like a family member.

But questions about the identity of LeBron's biological father persisted. Not long after the NBA Finals ended, LeBron discreetly met with a health-care specialist in Cleveland and submitted a DNA sample. Earlier in 2007, a man had contacted Fred Nance and claimed that he might be LeBron's biological father. Alleging that he'd had a one-time sexual encounter with Gloria back in 1984, he told Nance that he wanted to meet with Gloria to discuss the possibility that his name belonged on the line for the father's name that had been left blank on LeBron's birth certificate. Gloria claimed she'd never met the man, and she wanted nothing to do with him. But after a lot of back-and-forth, Nance arranged a conference call with the man and Gloria. It was contentious. "LeBron's money is for his children," Gloria told the man. After the call, LeBron agreed to take a DNA paternity test. The man agreed to take one, too. Nance made the arrangements.

From the moment his basketball abilities had garnered national exposure, LeBron had been dealing with questions about his father's identity. The most detailed questioning had come in an interview with Bob Costas on HBO when LeBron was eighteen, in 2003.

Costas: Do you know your biological father's whereabouts?

LeBron: No. Not really. I'm not really even concentrating on that. Because I really have my father and my mother all tied up in one. That's Gloria James. At this point, I don't really need nobody else.

Costas: There have been various stories that your biological father may be in prison. He may in fact be dead. He may have been shot some ten years ago.

LeBron: (nodding)

Costas: Do you have a curiosity about that?

LeBron: No. That never really crosses my brain because my friends and family I have now is awesome. I wouldn't trade 'em in for the world.

Costas: So if this guy is still around and if eventually he shows up, have you thought about how that might go?

LeBron: No. I never really thought about it.

LeBron's attitude hadn't changed much since then. Rather than dwelling on questions about his father, he was focused on being an omnipresent father to his sons. Nance had even told the man who was taking a paternity test that LeBron was "indifferent" toward his claim. Nonetheless, LeBron wasn't afraid to take the paternity test.

The samples were sent to a DNA lab in Cincinnati.

By the end of summer, the results came back: the probability of paternity was zero.

Nance advised the man to leave Gloria and LeBron alone.

Days before the Cavaliers were set to open training camp in Cleveland, LeBron and Maverick entered the Time-Life building in New York City. It was a fall day in late September and LeBron had a photo shoot with *Fortune*. The magazine rarely put athletes on the cover—Michael Jordan and Tiger Woods had been exceptions in the nineties. Now it was Le-Bron's turn. But *Fortune* planned to showcase LeBron less as an athlete and more as a bona fide business mogul. The plan was to put LeBron on the cover of a special issue that ranked the twenty-five most powerful people in the business world, starting with Steve Jobs, followed by Rupert Murdoch, Warren Buffett, Bill Gates, the co-CEOs of Google, and so forth. Recognizing that going with LeBron over Jobs would raise questions, *Fortune* planned to feature some clever copy to accompany LeBron's cover image:

Why LeBron James?
Because "if he were an IPO, I'd buy in."

—Warren Buffett

LeBron recognized the significance of the moment. So did stylist Rachel Johnson, who dressed him accordingly in a charcoal-gray suit with a silver pocket square.

Fortune had commissioned portrait photographer Ben Baker to shoot LeBron. Baker lived in the States, but he was from Australia. And that week, Baker's father had come from the land down under to spend time with his son. Accustomed to photographing famous and powerful people, Baker almost never brought anyone along during his shoots. But he and his father were extremely close, and Baker invited him to tag along. While waiting for LeBron to show up, Baker told his father to hang out in the back of the room.

When LeBron walked into the *Fortune* studio, Baker showed him where he wanted him to stand.

While Baker sized up LeBron through his lens, LeBron looked around the room and spotted a man in the back.

"Is that your pops?" LeBron said to Baker.

Baker smiled. "Yeah, that's Dad."

"How you doing, Pops?" LeBron said, nodding at Baker's father.

Baker's father perked up.

LeBron liked the fact that Baker had brought his father to work.

Baker was impressed that LeBron had noticed. He was even more impressed with how easily LeBron loosened up and had fun with the shoot. At one point, Baker had LeBron and Maverick pose together. They seemed, in Baker's eye, to be a refreshing duo—two young guys who were on their way to conquering the world.

After the shoot, LeBron and Maverick went across the street to 30 Rockefeller Plaza, where LeBron was scheduled to rehearse for an upcoming appearance on *Saturday Night Live*.

Baker followed them so he could photograph LeBron in a different setting. Rachel Johnson made sure LeBron had the right look for the *SNL* vibe. This time LeBron put on a sleek black suit with a vest; red, patterned tie; and a matching pocket square.

LeBron had fun rehearsing. After performing live in so many sold-out arenas, he had no trouble standing in front of a small studio audience and reading lines. On the night of the broadcast, LeBron couldn't wait.

"It's great to be here tonight," LeBron said from the edge of the stage. "My name is LeBron James. I play basketball for the Cleveland Cavaliers." He paused for applause.

"For those of you who don't watch basketball," he continued, "this past season we went to the NBA Finals, and we swept the San Antonio Spurs in four games."

The audience laughed.

"And for those of you who do watch basketball, be cool and shut up! There's no reason to ruin it for everybody else."

More than 6 million people tuned in to watch LeBron host *SNL*. His emergence as a pop culture figure was accelerating.

Boston Celtics general manager Danny Ainge didn't catch LeBron on *SNL*. But Ainge had been watching LeBron for a long time. Back in LeBron's junior year, Ainge attended the St. V–Oak Hill game when LeBron had gone head-to-head with Carmelo Anthony. Ainge, at that time, had recently stepped down as head coach of the Phoenix Suns. After watching LeBron, Ainge told *Sports Illustrated* writer Grant Wahl, "If I were a general manager, there are only four or five NBA players that I wouldn't trade to get him right now." When the quote appeared in Wahl's seminal cover story about LeBron—"The Chosen One"—Ainge got flak for having suggested that there were only five NBA players who were better than

LeBron. "He's a high school kid," Ainge heard from more than one of his NBA friends. "What are you talking about?"

A few years later, Ainge ran into Wahl, who told him, "Well, you were right about LeBron." Ainge told Wahl, "No. I was wrong. I should have said I would have traded *anybody* for LeBron." By that time, Ainge was the executive director of basketball operations for the Celtics, a position he'd taken in the summer of 2003, about a month before the NBA Draft. When the Celtics hired him, Ainge told the owners that he'd trade the team's entire roster for LeBron. Ainge wasn't kidding. But he knew that the Cavaliers were never going to trade LeBron.

By the summer of 2007, it had begun to dawn on Ainge, who had spent most of his career as a player trying to beat Michael Jordan, that he was probably going to spend most of his career as an executive trying to beat LeBron. After watching the Cavaliers go from last place to the NBA Finals in just four seasons with LeBron, Ainge concluded that it was going to take a super team to derail him.

In July, while LeBron was gearing up to work out with Kobe for the first time at a Team USA minicamp in Las Vegas, Ainge was wheeling and dealing in Boston to put together a roster capable of competing with LeBron and the Cavaliers in the Eastern Conference. The Celtics had won only twenty-four games the previous year, and all-star forward Paul Pierce was so sick and tired of losing that he wanted to be traded. Instead, Ainge sent three other players to the Seattle SuperSonics for all-star Ray Allen, the best perimeter shooter in the league. Then Ainge enlisted Allen's help to woo his friend, all-star power forward Kevin Garnett, who wanted out of Minnesota. And on July 30, Ainge traded nearly half of the guys left on the Celtics roster—five players, two first-round draft picks, and cash considerations—to the Timberwolves for Garnett.

Suddenly, Paul Pierce didn't want to go anywhere. Pierce, a future Hall of Famer, had never particularly liked LeBron and all the accolades that he garnered. And Ainge's blockbuster moves had given Pierce two more future Hall of Famers to play alongside. No other NBA team boasted that kind of firepower. The Pierce-Garnett-Allen trio was instantly dubbed "the Big Three." And the first time they met with head coach Doc Rivers, he told them: "We're going to win the championship this year!"

NBA experts agreed with Rivers. For its annual NBA preview issue,

Sports Illustrated featured Allen, Garnett, and Pierce, along with the head-line "A Brand-New Green Machine in Boston."

LeBron paid close attention to what was going on in Boston. After spending the previous two years battling the Pistons for supremacy in the Eastern Conference, the Cavaliers had a new foe to contend with. LeBron knew that the green machine was coming for him.

TWENTY-FOUR

FASHION

Jill Demling was the entertainment director at *Vogue* magazine. Among her many duties, she was responsible for booking the magazine's celebrity covers. It was a job that afforded Demling the opportunity to work closely with the fashion industry's top models and Hollywood's A-list actresses. In 2007, Demling had booked Angelina Jolie, Kate Moss, Keira Knightley, Scarlett Johansson, and Charlize Theron. Demling loved her job. But at heart, she was a huge sports fan. Some of her biggest idols were athletes.

Every four years, *Vogue* did a big Olympics portfolio with female athletes from the American team. With the Beijing Games less than a year away, Demling decided to include some male Olympic athletes this time around. The plan was to pair them with female models inside the magazine. On the cover, Demling wanted to feature the ultimate Olympian: LeBron. Toward the end of 2007, Demling reached out to LeBron's representatives.

LeBron didn't read *Vogue*. But to his stylist, Rachel Johnson, *Vogue* was the holy grail. And Johnson explained that being photographed for the cover was a groundbreaking opportunity. In its 116-year history, *Vogue* had never put a Black man on the cover. The only men who had been on the cover were Richard Gere, who had appeared with his then-wife, supermodel Cindy Crawford, in 1992, and George Clooney, who had appeared with Gisele Bündchen back in 2000, when Bündchen was a nineteen-year-old Victoria's Secret angel.

LeBron was willing to pose for the world's most influential fashion magazine, but he wanted to have some fun. So he sent word to Demling that he had one condition: if she wanted to put the best athlete in the world on the cover of *Vogue*, he wanted to be paired with the best model in the world—Gisele.

Demling was well acquainted with Gisele, who at this point had been dating Tom Brady for about a year. Brady and Gisele were very particular about whom Gisele would shoot with, especially if she was shooting with an athlete. Demling understood that Brady would have to sign off on the idea.

LeBron's insistence on working with Gisele seemed like a tall order. But Demling soon discovered that getting Brady to go along with the idea would be a lot easier than expected. It turned out that LeBron had known Brady since the time that Tom and Gisele had first met on their blind date in New York City. Demling was told that Tom did some gambling with Jay-Z and LeBron around that time, and they had remained friends, even though Tom had supposedly lost money to LeBron.

Whatever had gone on between LeBron and Brady wasn't important to Demling. What mattered was that LeBron was "Tom-approved" to shoot with Gisele. And Gisele was willing to travel to Akron to be photographed with LeBron in his hometown. Demling had scored her dream cover. And she brought in the most accomplished portrait photographer in the world to shoot it, Annie Leibovitz.

Leibovitz had first gained prominence when *Rolling Stone* founder Jann Wenner tapped her as the first chief photographer of his fledgling magazine in the early seventies. In addition to covering Vietnam War protests, the launch of Apollo 17, and Richard Nixon's resignation, Leibovitz shot Muhammad Ali, Mick Jagger, Keith Richards, Joan Didion, and Bruce Springsteen. In a photo shoot with John Lennon in 1980, she asked him to take off his clothes. When Yoko Ono offered to remove her top, Leibovitz told her to remain dressed. Leibovitz's Polaroid of Lennon curled up naked beside Ono on the floor of their apartment was taken hours before Lennon was assassinated. It was the most iconic image to ever appear on the cover of *Rolling Stone*. Then, in 1991, when actress Demi Moore was seven months pregnant, Leibovitz photographed her in a tight black dress that showcased her curves. When Leibovitz showed her pictures to *Vanity Fair* editor Tina Brown, she said, "But there is this other picture that I took, but I really did it for just Demi and Bruce Willis." It was a shot of Moore naked. When Brown saw it, she said, "This is the cover." The image was so controversial that Walmart, the nation's largest retailer, deemed it "indecent" and refused to sell the issue. Still, that issue set the record for the most copies sold in *Vanity Fair* history. And Moore loved it. "I understand what impact it had on the world, on women, on our permission to embrace ourselves in a pregnant state," she said.

LeBron had been photographed by the best photographers in sports journalism. But he'd never worked with anyone like Leibovitz. On a cold day in January 2008, LeBron was getting ready to head to the rec center where he had played basketball as a kid. Leibovitz, Gisele, and Demling were already there, getting ready for the shoot. When Rachel Johnson saw that LeBron was dressed in workout clothes, she made him change.

"You're not walking in with these shorts and a T-shirt on," Johnson told him.

LeBron didn't see the big deal. He knew that Nike had provided *Vogue* with apparel for him to put on when he got there. What difference did it make what he wore when he arrived?

To Johnson, it made a big difference. LeBron may have been going to his childhood rec center. But he was entering the upper echelon of the fashion world. Three of the most powerful figures in the industry were inside that old gymnasium. And they would form a first impression the moment that LeBron walked through the door. "You're not going as *the basketball player*," Johnson told LeBron. "You're going as *The Man*. That's who they need to see walking in through the door."

Johnson had LeBron put on a cashmere sweater and a pair of designer pants.

When LeBron walked in, Gisele lit up, Demling was thrilled, and Leibovitz figured this was going to be a fun shoot. LeBron began poking fun at himself and interacting with everyone as if he'd known them for years. He changed into Nike basketball clothes and a pair of his Nike Zoom Soldier II sneakers. Gisele put on a formfitting dress. And Leibovitz directed them on what to do next.

Johnson sensed something memorable was in the works.

Midway through the season, LeBron led the league in scoring. Kobe was second. On January 27, 2008, the Cavaliers played the Lakers in Los Angeles. ABC promoted the game as a duel between the game's two top guns.

LeBron and Kobe didn't disappoint, matching each other bucket for bucket for much of the game. With just over twenty seconds remaining and Cleveland up by one, LeBron dribbled on the perimeter while being guarded by Kobe. The shot clock winding down, LeBron glanced up, took a jab step toward the basket, then stepped back and elevated, releasing a jump shot as Kobe sprang toward him. The perfectly arced ball soared just over Kobe's outstretched hand and whipped through the net, silencing the Staples Center crowd and sealing the victory for the Cavaliers.

LeBron finished with forty-one points and nine rebounds. Kobe had thirty-three points and twelve rebounds.

It was a big win for the Cavaliers. But they remained way behind the Boston Celtics in the quest for the best record in the Eastern Conference. Paul Pierce, Kevin Garnett, and Ray Allen had been dominant. Through the first forty-one games, the Celtics had lost only seven times. The Cavs, on the other hand, had already lost nineteen games.

Feeling a sense of urgency, owner Dan Gilbert authorized a major three-team trade. The Cavaliers shipped seven players—including starters Drew Gooden and Larry Hughes and reserve players Donyell Marshall and Ira Newble—to the Bulls and Sonics. In return, the Cavs received four-time NBA Defensive Player of the Year Ben Wallace, veterans Joe Smith and Wally Szczerbiak, and a young shooting guard named Delonte West. "Our primary goal with this deal is to create a positive impact as we head through the final stretch of the season and into the playoffs," General Manager Danny Ferry said. "This again demonstrates Dan Gilbert's dedication to this organization and city."

When LeBron looked around the NBA, he sensed that many of his peers were afraid to try anything other than playing basketball. Basketball was always going to be LeBron's lodestar. But he embraced the diverse opportunities made possible by his athletic achievements. In early March, the Cavaliers arrived in New York with a retooled lineup to face the Knicks. On the night before the game, after a shootaround with his teammates, LeBron met fifty-eight-year-old Anna Wintour for dinner. The longtime editor in chief of *Vogue* had made reservations at the Waverly Inn in Greenwich Village. Loosely portrayed by Meryl Streep in *The Devil Wears Prada*, Wintour was the most powerful person in the fashion world.

LeBron slid into a corner booth and the two of them discussed everything from Ralph Lauren to the family foundation that LeBron and Savannah had established to help underprivileged children in single-parent households. They also discussed the April issue of *Vogue*, which was going to land on newsstands in the coming days. For the cover, Wintour had approved the most striking image that Leibovitz had shot—LeBron dressed in black athletic wear, his mouth open as if he were roaring, dribbling a ball with his right hand while his left arm is wrapped around Gisele, who wears a strapless dress and looks as though she were about to be carried off. The cover copy read: "Secrets of the Best Bodies: Gisele & LeBron."

LeBron's dinner with Wintour was the start of an unlikely friendship.

The next day, the Cavaliers were getting ready to face the Knicks when Rachel Johnson showed LeBron an advance copy of the April issue of *Vogue*.

While he stared at the cover, Johnson was so proud that her eyes welled up. "Do you understand what this means?" she asked.

LeBron smiled. "Raych, you're making too much of this," he said.

Johnson disagreed. LeBron now occupied the most coveted piece of real estate in the fashion industry. By putting LeBron on the cover of *Vogue* with Gisele, Anna Wintour was essentially telling the fashion world that things were about to change.

Later that night, Wintour sat courtside with Maverick at Madison Square Garden. The court was ringed with stars—Jay-Z, Spike Lee, and an array of other celebrities and Wall Street titans. But Wintour's presence was the biggest sign that LeBron had truly crossed over into a cultural phenomenon. The electric atmosphere in the building was also a tantalizing preview of what the Garden might look like on a nightly basis if LeBron wore a Knicks uniform.

Although LeBron was under contract with the Cavaliers for two more seasons, his upcoming free agency in 2010 already had the city of New York buzzing over the possibility of his joining the Knicks. The tabloids were writing about it. Sports radio hosts couldn't stop talking about it. A group of well-heeled Knicks fans had even created a website called nycforlebron.net that was dedicated to enticing LeBron by offering him his own suite at Yankee Stadium, courtside seats for Gloria James at the Garden, and a Ferrari for LeBron.

While LeBron warmed up, Knicks guard Stephon Marbury spoke to reporters for the first time in forty-nine days. LeBron's former nemesis on the 2004 Olympic team had been feuding with Knicks head coach Isiah Thomas. Peppered with questions about why he hadn't attended any games in a month and a half, Marbury said, "No comment to that." Then, wearing a salmon-colored houndstooth coat, Marbury took a seat on the Knicks bench. His relationship with Thomas had gotten so bad that Marbury's future with the team seemed doomed.

Ignoring the Marbury sideshow, LeBron lit up the Knicks and dazzled the fans with an onslaught of twenty first-half points including a vicious two-handed dunk that elicited gasps, and a thirty-five-foot jump shot that he launched at the buzzer while fading to his left with two defenders on him. The crowd erupted when the ball whipped through the net. In the second half, LeBron poured it on, finishing with 50 points, 10 assists, 8 rebounds, and 4 steals. When he checked out with twenty-three seconds remaining in the game, Knicks fans gave him a standing ovation. Invigorated, LeBron reached the bench just as a fan wearing his jersey ran across the court toward him. With security approaching, the fan told LeBron that he loved the way he played and that he was his favorite player. Flattered, LeBron slapped his hand and thanked him right before security took the fan away and arrested him.

LeBron couldn't ignore how exhilarating it felt to play in New York.

"This ranks really high because of the place where it happened—in the mecca of basketball," LeBron told reporters afterward. "I've dreamed about playing well in this building. To get a standing ovation in the greatest basketball arena in the world is a dream come true for me. It's one of the best things that's ever happened to me."

His words sounded like a nightmare to Cavaliers owner Dan Gilbert.

But Knicks fans were in ecstasy. LeBron's free agency couldn't come fast enough.

LeBron had left town by the time the *Vogue* issue hit newsstands. The cover had the impact of a lightning strike. It was immediately criticized as racist. *Time* magazine's media critic lambasted the "animalistic pose that James struck, which seemed to invoke the savagery of King Kong and perpetuate stereotypes of black male aggression." ESPN's Jemele Hill went further in her critique of LeBron's depiction. "He looks beastly," Hill said. "And if anyone has studied on the history of King Kong or seen any of the imagery that was from the movie, the movie posters—I'm talking about the old ones, you know, from the '30s and stuff—this picture looks exactly like a huge percentage of the pictures they used to put out about King Kong."

Some critics even insisted that Gisele's dress was the same color as the one worn by actress Fay Wray when King Kong carried her to the top of the Empire State Building in the film's climactic scene. Everyone seemed to have an opinion. "I was struck less by the stereotypes at play than by its erotic value," wrote Pulitzer Prize–winning critic Wesley Morris. "It's a hot image, and what's sexy about it is more a matter of celebrity than race. Bündchen doesn't look terrified. She looks exhilarated. And James looks neither mad nor simian: He looks triumphant."

Rachel Johnson thought the King Kong comparisons were misguided. And she felt that the criticism illustrated ignorance on the part of those who were carping the loudest. They had all missed the larger point—LeBron had broken a barrier. By working with Jill Demling and building a relationship with Anna Wintour, LeBron had paved the way for Johnson to start bringing him to fashion houses throughout the world. "There was a huge opportunity there," Johnson explained, "for black men in particular to attend these shows because there was absolutely no diversity present at all."

Thanks to LeBron, other NBA players took an interest in fashion. Soon, LeBron's willingness to wear designer clothes would permeate throughout the league. Johnson started taking other NBA players to fashion houses. Meanwhile, Anna Wintour started courting other NBA players to appear in the pages of *Vogue*. And within three years' time, NBA players would occupy the coveted seat beside Wintour at her annual runway show in New York. The impact of these changes rippled throughout the fashion industry. "All of these stereotypes from a fashion perspective were broken down for men and it just opened things up to make everything about men's fashion become accessible," Johnson said.

The Boston Celtics finished the 2007–2008 regular season with a league-best 66-16 record. It marked the biggest single-season turnaround in NBA history. Kevin Garnett was named NBA Defensive Player of the Year, and Danny Ainge was named NBA Executive of the Year. One thing was clear—if the Cavaliers were going to make a return trip to the NBA Finals, they were going to have to go through Boston.

But the Cavaliers' first-round playoff opponent was the Washington

Wizards. In Game 1, LeBron set the tone for the series when he got up a head of steam and jumped so high to reach an alley-oop pass that his head was above the rim when he reached the ball before jamming it home. "No way!" the announcer yelled. "How on earth does he corral and stuff [that]?"

The Wizards were no match for LeBron. But during the series, he sat down with ESPN's Shelley Smith, who was working on a segment about NBA players and political activism for *Outside the Lines*. It had been a year since LeBron had been blindsided by the refugee crisis in Darfur. And with the Beijing Olympics just months away, the campaign to shame China had resumed. Two months earlier, Steven Spielberg had withdrawn as an artistic advisor to the 2008 Olympic games after trying unsuccessfully for a year to persuade President Hu Jintao of China to intervene to stop Sudan's genocide in Darfur. Spielberg said his conscience would not allow him to continue with business as usual. "Sudan's government bears the bulk of the responsibility for these ongoing crimes but the international community, and particularly China, should be doing more to end the continuing human suffering there," Spielberg said in an official statement. "China's economic, military and diplomatic ties to the government of Sudan continue to provide it with the opportunity and obligation to press for change."

China was furious with Spielberg's stance. But the Hollywood community praised him. "One guy like Steven in a position like that is like one hundred other guys," actor Don Cheadle, who co-wrote the book *Not on Our Watch*, told the *New York Times*.

The question now was whether LeBron would be the one guy in the sports world to follow Spielberg's lead. Shelley Smith asked him about the letter that Ira Newble had asked him to sign a year earlier.

"No one heard my side of the story," LeBron said. "But automatically it's 'LeBron didn't sign the letter. He doesn't care.' But for me to try to create awareness of the situation that's going on in Darfur and other places, for me, in the position I am, I should speak on it and I am gonna speak on it."

LeBron still wasn't settled on what to say, but he had committed to saying something. "At the end of the day," he told Smith, "we're talking about human rights. And people should understand that human rights and people's lives are in jeopardy. We're not talking about contracts here. We're not talking about money. We're talking about people's lives being lost and that means a lot more to me than some money or a contract."

A few nights later, the Cavaliers closed out the Wizards. It was on to Boston.

Twenty-seven-year-old Lisa Taddeo had just gotten her first big break as an aspiring fiction writer. *Esquire*'s editor in chief, David Granger, had commissioned her to write a fictionalized account of Heath Ledger's final days before he was found dead in his SoHo apartment in January 2008. "It becomes theatrically important, after you die, what your last few days are like," Taddeo's provocative account began.

Right after her piece ran, Taddeo got an email from her editor: "Do you want to do LeBron?"

LeBron? Other than knowing that he was a great basketball player, Taddeo was unfamiliar with him. She knew even less about basketball. The proposition sounded intimidating.

She emailed her editor: "Sounds great."

To commemorate the magazine's upcoming seventy-fifth anniversary, *Esquire* was working on a special issue that would profile the seventy-five most influential people of the twenty-first century. The fact that Taddeo had no background in sportswriting was considered a plus. She was a creative writer with a knack for getting people to open up. *Esquire* wanted her to paint an intimate portrait of LeBron.

Taddeo lived alone in New York City. Shortly after getting the assignment, she headed across town to the magazine's headquarters at the Hearst Tower to meet LeBron.

LeBron and Maverick liked the concept of the *Esquire* anniversary issue. The magazine had commissioned sculptor Lincoln Schatz to create something that would unite the seventy-five influencers being profiled. Schatz produced a ten-foot-by-ten-foot translucent box fitted with twenty-four cameras that streamed digital video to twenty-four computers. It was called the Cube. All of the subjects—from Jeff Bezos to Elon Musk to Samantha Power—were encouraged to spend an hour inside the glass structure, doing something that represented their personalities and interests. LeBron chose to crank up Jay-Z and play *NBA 2K8* on Xbox.

Maverick was standing outside the Cube, milling around with staffers from *Esquire* when Taddeo arrived. Astute at reading the room, he pegged her as the journalist well before being introduced.

Intrigued and slightly overwhelmed, Taddeo stood alongside her editor, watching LeBron through the glass. After a while, Maverick perceived that they were waiting on LeBron.

"You need him out?" Maverick said. "I'll get him out."

Maverick rapped on the glass with his knuckles.

LeBron looked up.

"Yo, Bron, let's go," Maverick said. "Time to go."

LeBron stepped out.

"This is Lisa Taddeo," the *Esquire* editor told him. "She's the person that's going to be writing the feature on you."

"Nice to meet you," LeBron said, flashing a smile.

At five one, Taddeo was in awe of LeBron's size. She'd never been so close to someone so big. His height exacerbated her self-consciousness. *He's going to realize that I don't know shit about basketball,* she told herself. *I need to show him that at least I'll be fun to be around.*

The plan was for Taddeo to attend a playoff game so she could see LeBron in action. Then after the season was over, she'd go to Akron and spend a few days with him in his hometown. Her point of contact would be Maverick. Everything ran through Maverick.

Running to his next appointment, LeBron headed for the elevator.

"Oh, I'm going down, too," Taddeo said, squeezing between LeBron and her editor.

A few floors down, the elevator stopped, the doors opened, and a middle-age white man entered.

LeBron didn't make eye contact with him, but he could tell the man was staring at him.

"Are you who I think you are?" the man said.

"Yes," Taddeo blurted out. "And I'm who you think I am."

Confused, the man looked at her blankly.

LeBron laughed and playfully shoved Taddeo.

Taddeo nearly fell over. *God he's strong!* she thought. But she loved it. She'd made LeBron laugh.

Taddeo let Maverick know that she'd see them in Boston.

*   *   *

LeBron knew the series with the Celtics was going to be a battle. The team's captain, Paul Pierce, was one of the fiercest competitors in the NBA, a guy who backed down to no one. Late one night in 2000, Pierce had gotten into a dispute with a gang member at an edgy nightclub in Boston. The gang member stabbed Pierce multiple times. Then nearly a dozen men jumped Pierce, slashing him with knives. One man smashed a bottle across Pierce's temple. Another man used a pair of brass knuckles with a knife attached to it and repeatedly punched Pierce, puncturing a lung and coming within an inch of his heart. Pierce nearly died. But one month after the attack, Pierce left the hospital and played in the Celtics' season opener. He led his team in scoring that night.

Pierce had always resented the fact that so many players had been chosen before him in the NBA Draft. So every time he stepped on the court, he played with a chip on his shoulder. Nicknamed the Truth, he had never cared much for all the accolades that were lavished on LeBron when he entered the league at age eighteen and was nicknamed the King. During a game in LeBron's second season, Pierce was going at it with him. There was some chirping. Things escalated. And Pierce spit toward LeBron and the Cavaliers' bench.

"I'm not sure I hit somebody or not," Pierce later recalled. "But I spit in that direction. And then it just kind of . . . tempers flared up. The next thing you know, we was in the hallway. It was about to go down."

Pierce had been playing on a bad team back then. Now the Celtics were loaded. And the Truth wanted nothing more than to take down the King in a playoff series that would determine supremacy in the Eastern Conference.

LeBron was blanketed by defenders in the first two games in Boston, where the Celtics ground out a 2-0 series lead. Back in Cleveland, the Cavs beat the Celtics in Game 3. Then in Game 4, the series took on the feel of a heavyweight bout. With the Cavs up, 39–33, in the first half, LeBron was streaking toward the basket for what was sure to be a dunk. But Pierce chased him down, fouled him hard from behind, and wrapped his arms around him. With whistles blowing and fans booing, LeBron and Pierce toppled out-of-bounds and into the seats beneath the basket next to Gloria James. As LeBron attempted to shrug himself free and Pierce continued to wrap him up, Gloria sprang from her seat and started screaming at Pierce. With fans shouting obscenities and referees rushing into the melee, Kevin Garnett put his arms around Gloria to keep her away from Pierce. As she pushed him off and continued to shout at Pierce, LeBron yelled at her, "Sit your ass down!"

"There is no love lost between LeBron James and Paul Pierce," TNT's Kevin Harlan said. "None! This rivalry is simmering over."

With the vitriol from the Cleveland fans escalating and security moving in, the players disentangled and walked back onto the floor. LeBron then went up to Pierce, put his arm around him, and tapped him on the chest to say, "It's fine. We're good." Pierce nodded. The crowd roared. And play resumed. After that, LeBron played like a man possessed. Late in the fourth quarter, with his team leading by seven and the crowd on its feet, LeBron accelerated past Pierce and drove right at Garnett, elevated over him, and threw down a violent dunk that went through the rim with such force that the ball ricocheted off Garnett's chest and sent the crowd and the announcers into a frenzy.

"*LeBron James*," Harlan shouted, "with no regard for human life, has given the Cavaliers the biggest lead tonight."

LeBron's monster jam on the NBA's Defensive Player of the Year was a punctuation mark in the hard-fought contest. Scowling, LeBron ran down the court and into the arms of his teammates along the bench. A huge smile then swept across his face as the Q rocked. The series was tied, 2-2.

After the game, LeBron felt bad about what he'd said to his mother in the heat of the moment. When the media asked him about it, he acknowledged his regret. "I told her to sit down in some language I shouldn't have used," he said. "Thank God today wasn't Mother's Day. All I could think about is her. . . . I know my mother. It's fine. We're good."

The Cavs and Celtics split the next two games, setting up Game 7 in Boston on May 18, 2008. "I was like, let us get breaking news that LeBron has torn his ACL or something," Celtics starting center Kendrick Perkins said. "That's how terrified I was of LeBron." A lot of the load was going to rest on Pierce. And with everything on the line, the Celtics organization was looking for a way to give Pierce an edge. And there was no one that inspired Pierce more than hometown hero Tom Brady, who had just led the Patriots to a 16-0 regular season. So one of the team's vice presidents arranged to seat Brady courtside, right alongside the Cavaliers' bench. The intention was to motivate Pierce. And it worked. But Brady's presence also fired up LeBron, resulting in one of the greatest duels in NBA playoff history.

In the first half, LeBron and Pierce accounted for more than half of the total points scored. The Celtics led, 50–40. Pierce had scored twenty-six and LeBron had scored twenty-three. At halftime, Celtics coach Doc Rivers resigned himself to a simple game plan for the second half—put the ball in Pierce's hands and get the hell out of the way. The Cavs always resorted to that plan with LeBron when the chips were down.

At one point in the third quarter, it was as if LeBron and Pierce were playing one-on-one.

7:44   Pierce three-point shot from twenty-five feet—good.

6:33   LeBron jumper from twenty-three feet—good.

6:17   Pierce jumper from seventeen feet—good.

6:01   LeBron three-point shot from twenty-five feet—good.

5:23   Pierce jump shot from twenty-one feet—good.

On and on it went.

Pierce played the game of his life, finishing with forty-one points. LeBron finished with forty-five points. But in the end, it was the superiority of Pierce's supporting cast that tipped the scales. He had stars Garnett and Allen with him down the stretch. LeBron had LeBron. The Celtics prevailed, 97–92, to win the series.

After the game, in the bowels of Boston's TD Garden, Cavaliers coach Mike Brown had trouble controlling his emotions while trying to pay tribute to LeBron's superhuman effort. "LeBron, he's always going to be great in my mind," he said, needing a minute. "He played a hell of a game tonight, trying to get us over the top."

LeBron, meanwhile, paid tribute to his latest rival. "Paul Pierce is one of my favorite players," he said. "I love going against the best, and Paul Pierce is one of those guys."

For LeBron, the loss to the Celtics was an inflection point. After reaching the NBA Finals the year before, the Cavaliers had failed to make it to the Eastern Conference Finals. Following four years of steady progress, the Cavaliers had taken a step backward in LeBron's fifth season. Meanwhile, the Celtics leapfrogged from the worst team in the Eastern Conference to an NBA championship in one season. They beat the Lakers in the NBA Finals.

Paul Pierce had waited nine years for the Celtics to bring in some stars who could help him take his team to the top of the mountain.

LeBron didn't want to wait that long.

TWENTY-FIVE

BEATS

Badass was the word that came to mind when journalist Lisa Taddeo watched LeBron play in the Celtics series. But what was he like off the court? In the off-season she went to Akron in hopes of finding out.

Spending time with LeBron, however, would also mean spending time with Maverick. Early in her reporting for the *Esquire* profile, Taddeo concluded that Maverick was more than LeBron's business partner, that he played a much more vital role—as LeBron's emotional bodyguard. Maverick always had his antenna up. The more famous LeBron became, the higher Maverick's antenna went. No journalist was going to be alone with LeBron.

Maverick had become deft at reading people. He didn't know that much about Taddeo. But it was apparent she was different from the many male sportswriters who had tried to gain access to LeBron over the years: She didn't pretend to care about basketball. She was interested in other things. And he liked her body language. It caused him to drop his guard and allow her to see and hear things that were usually off-limits to sportswriters.

After LeBron led hundreds of children on bikes through the streets of Akron in his annual King for Kids Bike-A-Thon, Maverick invited Taddeo to hang out with him, LeBron, Randy Mims, and Miami Heat guard Dwyane Wade, who was in town to support LeBron's charity. They went to a pub and piled into a corner table in the back.

One of the things Taddeo was interested in was the dynamic between women and powerful men. "Historically," she once observed, "powerful men with slavering appetites have mainly acquired their girlfriends the way a pair of pants gathers lint—rather incidentally. Bill Clinton and his intern. JFK and his secretaries, his stewardess." In terms of power, a basketball player wasn't on the same level as the leader of the free world. But in terms of access to women, an athlete of LeBron's stature existed in a realm of opportunity that even presidents didn't experience. She wondered how LeBron dealt with all of this.

As a journalist, Taddeo had always been good at blending in and being unobtrusive. But it was more challenging than usual with LeBron and his friends. The banter between them—loud and filled with a lot of inside jokes—made Taddeo particularly mindful of the fact that she was the only woman at the table. Yet she wanted them to view her as one of the guys. "You can talk about chicks and tits," she said. "It's cool."

LeBron's friends could be flirtatious at times. Especially Maverick. Taddeo described him as having "Lothario energy." But LeBron was the opposite. Taddeo never saw LeBron flirt with anyone. Moreover, she never even saw LeBron's eyes wander, despite the presence of women almost everywhere he went.

"There was zero sexual anything from LeBron," Taddeo observed. "Not just toward me. But toward any of the young women that were around. And the women around him didn't even appear to be trying to get his attention. It was as if they knew not to."

At the same time, LeBron treated Taddeo like she belonged. When Taddeo was around him, he always made a point of introducing her to people in the community. *He's so nice*, Taddeo thought. *But he isn't being extra nice to me. He's that way to everyone.* He was the kind of person, she concluded, who wouldn't change when he got more and more success. "Everywhere I saw him," Taddeo said, "there was nothing to suggest that he was not totally devoted [to Savannah]. Not even *devoted*—everyone can be devoted. With him it was just this focus, like 'I'm going to be the best player that ever lived. So I'm not going to let anything—drugs, drinking, sex, *anything*—take me down.'"

On the last night that Taddeo was in Akron, Maverick invited her to join him and the guys at a nightclub. She thought about it. But she ultimately passed. She was on her way to writing her memorable opening to her LeBron profile:

Rising from his throne like an urban fairy tale, the great black king stands in his glass house. Looming erect, at six feet eight inches and 250 pounds, he is a pythonic force of length and clout, and all he has to do is crane his neck just so to ever so politely, gingerly, and revolutionarily break the glass ceiling.

Despite not being a sportswriter, Taddeo won an award for exceptional sportswriting for her profile of LeBron.

One night in 2007, LeBron was at home when his high school teammate Romeo Travis showed up. It wasn't unusual for one of LeBron's teammates to drop in unannounced. They had remained tight. But on this occasion, Romeo hadn't come alone. He had brought along Kristopher Belman, an Akron native whom LeBron remembered as "camera man." That's what LeBron and his St. V teammates had started calling Belman back in 2002. That year, Belman had come home to Akron from Los Angeles, where he was studying documentary filmmaking at Loyola Marymount. One of his class assignments was to make a ten-minute short film. Hoping to base his class project on the St. V basketball team, Belman approached Coach Dru and got permission to film a practice during LeBron's junior season. The team was so comfortable with Belman—he was just a college kid with a camera—that Coach Dru allowed him to keep coming around. Belman ended up shooting around four hundred hours of footage during LeBron's junior and senior seasons, including lots of candid interviews with LeBron and his teammates.

LeBron had forgotten how much Belman had been around. And he was surprised to learn that Belman had accumulated so much footage.

Belman explained that after college he had wanted to use the footage to make a feature film about LeBron and his friends and their journey from youth basketball to a national championship at St. V. But all he received was offers from people who wanted to acquire the LeBron footage. Instead, Belman held on to it and teamed up with a former college classmate to produce a documentary titled *More Than a Game*.

Romeo had brought Belman to LeBron's house in hopes that LeBron would look at what Belman had created.

LeBron agreed, and Belman showed him a twelve-minute clip.

Twelve minutes was more than enough time to flood LeBron's mind with memories from a cherished period in his life. "All right," he told Belman. "Whatever you need from me, I'm in."

Belman's biggest need was a distributor. No one was answering his calls. And without a distributor, Belman's film would never appear on television or anywhere else. If LeBron got behind the project, Belman figured, the distributors would come to him.

"I'm down," LeBron told him. "We need to get this done."

Romeo's friendship with LeBron was a game changer for Belman. Overnight, things started to happen. Maverick got involved. So did Paul Wachter. And before long, they came up with an idea: rather than just support the film, LeBron should produce it. Belman's needs presented an opportunity to further expand LeBron's business model.

After a lot of due diligence, in 2007 LeBron and Maverick formed a film and television production company called SpringHill Entertainment. It was named after the Akron apartment complex where LeBron had lived as a teenager. Maverick became the CEO. And *More Than a Game* became SpringHill's first venture. LeBron got Jay-Z to work on the soundtrack, and Maverick worked with some of LeBron's corporate partners, including Coca-Cola and State Farm Insurance, to sponsor the film. With the film scheduled to debut at the Toronto International Film Festival later in the year, the push was on to land a distributor.

It had been three years since Gloria had lit into Maverick after learning that LeBron had decided to fire his agent. But since then, LeBron and Maverick had come a long way. And Gloria was cheering them on. She was particularly impressed with the people they'd chosen to guide them. And Maverick liked to give credit where credit was due. In the summer of 2008, at their annual LRMR marketing summit in Akron, LeBron and Maverick were asked about their business success. "You know," Maverick told the audience, "people tell us, 'You're really smart.' But no. We just have really smart people around us."

LeBron's boldest move as an entrepreneur was empowering Maverick to run LRMR. One of Maverick's more attractive qualities was his willingness to admit what he didn't know. He prided himself on his ability to listen and his willingness to learn. And he never lost sight of the fact that LeBron was the show and Maverick was the man behind the Man. If he accompanied LeBron to a restaurant that was closed, the doors would be opened, and they'd end up being seated and served whatever they wanted. But if Maverick went to the same restaurant by himself, there would be no special treatment. And he was okay with that. After all, Maverick wasn't the one scoring forty-eight points in a playoff game. So he didn't think he deserved the same treatment as LeBron.

LeBron's confidence in Maverick—and their trust and reliance on Paul Wachter—consistently paid off. After taking Wachter's suggestion to invest in a bicycle company in 2007, LeBron received a windfall one year later when Cannondale was acquired by Dorel Industries for approximately $200 million. At the time of the sale, early in 2008, LeBron and LRMR owned 10 percent of the company. As a result, LeBron earned a return that was four times what he had invested. Maverick also profited, earning about $75,000. It was Maverick's first experience with equity income, and he credited Wachter for having recommended Cannondale to them and handling the transactions.

Now that LeBron had tasked him with running SpringHill, Maverick wanted to ensure that their entertainment company got off to a strong start. With that in mind, he suggested that LeBron should write a book. Not an autobiography—it was way too soon for that. And not a memoir. Instead, Maverick felt LeBron could do a limited, coming-of-age memoir that covered his high school years. It could essentially be a companion to the documentary. By publishing the book in tandem with the film, there could be cross-promotion.

But LeBron was going to need a writer. And not just any writer. Maverick wanted to commission someone who had the gravitas and track record to work with LeBron and help elevate the book's profile. An agent LeBron and Maverick trusted recommended Buzz Bissinger, a Pulitzer Prize–winning feature writer for *Vanity Fair*. Bissinger's landmark book, *Friday Night Lights*, had sold over two million copies and been made into a movie starring Billy Bob Thornton. The book had also been the basis of a television drama. Also called *Friday Night Lights*, it aired on NBC and starred Kyle Chandler and Connie Britton.

Bissinger's résumé sparkled with everything that Maverick wanted for LeBron. So Maverick worked with Bissinger's agent, and they secured an advance of approximately $2.5 million for the book, which LeBron and Bissinger shared. The hefty advance was offered with the understanding that LeBron and Bissinger would cowrite the book in LeBron's voice. It was also critical to the book's success that both LeBron and Bissinger do publicity to support the book when it was published.

Although Bissinger had written numerous books, he'd never written one where he didn't have editorial control. But the opportunity to write for LeBron was too lucrative to turn down. Once the terms were finalized, he flew to Ohio in the summer of 2008 to get acquainted with LeBron. They met at his estate, and Maverick joined them.

At fifty-three, Bissinger wasn't easily impressed. But he was in awe when he first laid eyes on LeBron. From an athletic standpoint, he looked like Leonardo da Vinci's Vitruvian Man. *God*, Bissinger thought. *He's perfect.*

But he wondered if LeBron was up for the task at hand—writing a bestseller. "To do a book like this, you have to spend a lot of time," Bissinger told him. "You've got to go deep."

LeBron nodded. But he wasn't familiar with Bissinger's definition of *deep*. Neither was Maverick. That Pulitzer Prize that Bissinger had won was for investigative reporting. His specialty was getting to a person's core and producing immersive, unsparing portraits. In that respect, Bissinger was a curious choice to pair with LeBron. Not that LeBron had anything to hide. But LeBron wasn't interested in letting a journalist drill deep beneath the surface.

Still, Bissinger was skilled. And he got LeBron to talk a little about his mother and his upbringing.

"Sometimes I went to bed not knowing if I was going to see her the next morning," LeBron told him. "I would sometimes go a few nights without seeing her at all. I became afraid that one day I would wake up, and she would be gone forever."

Bissinger's instinct was to ask probing follow-up questions. But he resisted those urges. Instead, he reminded himself why he was there—to make LeBron comfortable and to establish a working rapport. So Bissinger treaded lightly.

One of the things that Bissinger felt was important was to see some of the places that were central to LeBron's story. So Maverick and LeBron took him on a tour of Akron. The three of them hopped in an SUV. Maverick drove. LeBron took the passenger's seat and played tour guide. Bissinger sat in the backseat, taking notes. One of the places they visited was St. V. Although it was summer and school wasn't in session, the gym was full of nine- and ten-year-old kids who were attending a clinic. When LeBron walked in unannounced, the kids screamed with joy and swarmed him.

LeBron's eyes widened, and he opened his arms as the kids wrapped their arms around his waist as if he were Daddy Warbucks.

Bissinger was moved. *Whatever he's not telling me,* Bissinger thought, *one thing is for sure—this is a good man. These kids truly love him.*

At one point while they were driving around Akron, Maverick realized that the SUV was on empty. He pulled into a gas station. But Maverick said he didn't have his wallet. LeBron said he wasn't carrying a wallet, either. They both looked at Bissinger.

Incredulous, Bissinger paid for the gas. *Something's wrong with this,* Bissinger thought. *The hard-up writer must pay for gas for LeBron, who is worth hundreds of millions of dollars?*

Bissinger never got reimbursed.

That night, LeBron and Maverick had dinner with Bissinger. LeBron and Bissinger played video games afterward. Bissinger was no gamer. But he was willing to do whatever it took to establish a connection with LeBron.

By the end of the visit, Bissinger wanted to make sure that he'd have the access he needed to fulfill his mandate. To him, that was going to mean sitting down with Gloria.

"I have to interview your mother," Bissinger told LeBron.

LeBron knew she wouldn't be thrilled.

Not long after Bissinger left Akron, he got word from Maverick that the interview with Gloria was confirmed. As Bissinger composed his questions, he figured there were things in Gloria's past that might be sensitive. So he made a point of focusing on areas that he thought would make her comfortable.

What was LeBron like growing up?

What were his friends like?

In all, he came up with about a dozen questions that he considered softballs. Since this was ultimately LeBron's book, Bissinger figured it made no sense to offend the guy who had commissioned him by asking personal questions that would upset his mother.

But when Bissinger went back to Akron and sat down with Gloria, he realized right away that the interview was going to be contentious. At the outset, Gloria insisted on taping the interview. In addition to being suspicious, she was uncooperative. She declined to answer any of his easy questions. Frustrated, Bissinger abruptly ended the interview. "That's enough," he said.

Gloria seemed surprised when he shut things down.

"It was the most difficult interview I've ever had, really unpleasant," Bissinger recalled. "She agreed to do it because of LeBron. It was just bad. I felt she was an important voice that would lend a lot to the book. But it just wouldn't work."

Bissinger was also discouraged by his inability to get to know LeBron the way he had hoped he would. Despite his best efforts, he had struggled to establish a deeper rapport with LeBron. And he concluded that it hadn't been LeBron's idea to do the book. Rather, it seemed that LeBron was much more interested in supporting the documentary than investing the time it would take to write a book. In all, he spent about ten hours with LeBron.

Frustrated, he knew he'd have to rely heavily on LeBron's high school teammates.

"They'll talk to you," Maverick assured him.

Bissinger liked talking to Maverick. He learned more insightful things about LeBron through him than he did by talking to LeBron. At one point, Maverick told Bissinger: "LeBron hates to be alone."

Bissinger wasn't sure what had made Maverick say that. But that fact struck Bissinger. On one hand, it revealed vulnerability and helped shed light on some of LeBron's actions. On the other hand, it gave Bissinger a deeper respect for Gloria and her decision to place LeBron with a family when he was a young boy. *She realized he had to be with a family*, Bissinger concluded. *That saved LeBron's life. That's when he learned how to live. How to share. How to be in a family. How to have responsibility.*

The more he thought about the situation, the more Bissinger felt that Gloria deserved more credit than she was getting. He just wished that he could delve into that angle of LeBron's story. But it was buried way too deep.

LeBron and Kobe gelled as Olympic teammates. In one of the first Team USA practices before heading overseas, the team members were all lying in a circle at center court, stretching. LeBron started imitating the public address announcer who would be introducing the starting lineups in Beijing.

"Number ten," he said in a deep voice, "from Philadelphia slash Italy."

All the players—Carmelo Anthony, Dwyane Wade, Chris Bosh, Jason Kidd—started laughing. They all knew that Kobe had spent part of his childhood living in Italy.

"The marksman," LeBron continued, his voice deepening, "slash Mamba, Ko-Bee Bryant . . . Bryant . . . Bryant."

The coaches were in stitches, too. Even Kobe couldn't keep a straight face. LeBron made basketball fun. The overall vibe around the US team was totally different than it had been in 2004.

While LeBron was in training camp with his Olympic teammates, Maverick was in Los Angeles meeting with legendary music mogul Jimmy Iovine, the cofounder of Interscope Records. Iovine was in the process of starting a business with Dr. Dre called Beats by Dre. The concept behind the start-up idea was to develop headphones that produced studio-quality sound. Iovine let Maverick try on a pair.

Maverick was a bit of a music connoisseur. But he'd never heard music the way it sounded through the headphones designed by Dr. Dre. It was evident that Iovine wasn't exaggerating when he talked about Beats as a revolutionary product.

At this point, Beats by Dre hadn't gone on the market yet. But Maverick had a thought. He asked Iovine for fifteen pairs. "Watch what I do with them," he told Iovine.

LeBron was just about to fly overseas with his Olympic teammates when Maverick gave him the Beats. LeBron then put a pair in each of his teammates' hands. When Team USA landed in Beijing, every player was wearing Beats by Dre as they walked off the plane. Video of LeBron and Kobe wearing matching headphones was broadcast around the world. It was a fashion statement and masterly stroke of marketing that impressed Iovine and convinced him that he and Dr. Dre should partner with LeBron and Maverick.

LeBron and Kobe had barely gotten settled in Beijing when they were forced to confront political questions about China and Darfur. Earlier in the summer, LeBron had indicated that he'd have more to say about Darfur. But on August 5, 2008, China revoked the visa of former Olympic speed skater Joey Cheek, who had spoken out against the Chinese government. The next day, Kobe and LeBron faced reporters. When Kobe was asked if he had anything to say about Darfur, his answer was curt. "No, not really," he said.

LeBron was asked the same question.

"Basic human rights should always be protected," LeBron said. Then he added, "One thing you can't do is confuse sports and politics."

Kobe had considerably more experience than LeBron when it came to dealing with controversy. And he had no qualms about remaining silent. But the Darfur situation was the first time that LeBron had grappled with a politically charged human rights question. After more than a year, he still hadn't figured out where he stood, and the situation continued to dog him. While inexperienced enough to look up to Kobe's handling of the matter, LeBron was also impressionable enough to take cues from Coach K. When pressed by a reporter, LeBron said, "We are here to concentrate on a gold medal. Sports and politics just don't match."

At the same time, Coach K shot back at a reporter who was working on a piece that questioned whether Kobe and LeBron would speak up on Darfur. "Why would you ask them?" Coach K said to the reporter. "They are not the experts."

When the reporter suggested that Kobe and LeBron were avoiding the issue, Coach K had a different view. "It's not about avoiding an issue; it's about concentrating on one," he said. "I would hope people would be respectful of that."

The issue that Coach K had his team concentrating on was erasing the image of the 2004 American team as a bunch of selfish prima donnas. The way to do that was through camaraderie and a relentless focus on winning the gold. The players had embraced the nickname Redeem Team. And with Kobe as team captain, they weren't just out to win. They were determined to destroy their opponents.

In the first round, Team USA pounded China, winning by thirty-one points. And there was no letting up after that. Through seven games, the American team won each game by an average of thirty points per game. But in the gold medal round, Kobe wasn't taking anything for granted. Team USA faced Spain, a team that featured Kobe's Laker teammate Pau Gasol. Two months earlier, Kobe and Gasol had played together in the NBA Finals against the Celtics. But they were in opposing uniforms now. And Kobe planned to set the tone right away. He gathered his teammates.

"First play of the game, I know what they're gonna run," said Kobe. He had studied his opponent and knew that Spain would set a series of screens to free up the shooter. "Pau's gonna be the last screen. And I'm running through that motherfucker."

"Man, you trippin'," LeBron said. "That's your teammate. You ain't about to do that."

Less than two minutes into the game, Gasol set a screen. Rather than going around Gasol, Kobe ran into him with such force that Gasol went flying and landed on his back. Kobe stared down at him before walking away.

Oh my God! LeBron thought. *Ain't no way we're losing this game. We're about to beat the shit out of Spain.*

For LeBron, that moment was a turning point. He had been prone to attack the rim, not opposing players. But Kobe's aggression altered his approach. LeBron looked at Kobe looking down at Gasol and thought, *This guy's all about winning.*

Team USA had its way with Spain. When Kobe hit a free throw near the end that put a punctuation mark on Team USA's 118–107 victory, LeBron was the first teammate to greet him at the foul line, bump his chest, and roar at him. Chants of "USA, USA" filled the arena.

For the postgame press conference, the entire American team entered the room with their arms locked. "Everybody wants to talk about NBA players being selfish and arrogant and being individuals," Kobe said. "Well, what you saw today was a team bonded together, facing adversity and coming out of here with a big win."

LeBron left China with a completely different outlook from the one he'd had when he'd left Greece four years earlier. Playing for Coach K and being part of such a close-knit group of elite players with a shared commitment to winning had influenced LeBron's outlook. He had already come to grips with the fact that he was going to need a stronger supporting cast to win an NBA championship in Cleveland. He couldn't help feeling that some of his Team USA teammates would make ideal NBA teammates. He was particularly drawn to his friend Dwyane Wade and teammate Chris Bosh. The three of them had developed great court chemistry. They also gelled off the court. And the three of them would be free agents in 2010. LeBron made a mental note.

LeBron seldom cried. But after screening *More Than a Game* with his St. V teammates and coaches at the Toronto International Film Festival in early September, LeBron had tears in his eyes. He hugged his friends, who had tears in their eyes, too. Later that night, LeBron and Maverick had dinner with Jimmy Iovine. They had a lot to celebrate and a lot to discuss. Thanks to Maverick and LeBron, Beats by Dre got tremendous exposure in China. Iovine was so impressed that he offered LeBron and Maverick equity in the start-up. Iovine and Dr. Dre even decided to develop a signature line of the product for LeBron, called Powerbeats. And LeBron planned to give a pair of Beats to all his teammates on the Cavs. Before long, every player in the NBA would want a pair.

There was more. Thanks to SpringHill's involvement in *More Than a Game*, Lionsgate had signed on as the distributor. And Iovine and Interscope Records had agreed to coproduce the film alongside SpringHill.

For LeBron, so much was happening so fast—a gold medal in China, a successful film premiere in Toronto, a partnership that would put Spring-Hill in business with Lionsgate, and a new business opportunity with Jimmy Iovine, one of the most innovative figures in the music industry.

As LeBron ventured further into the worlds of music, film, television, and fashion, his friends in those places began exposing him to politics. After leaving Toronto, LeBron went with Savannah to New York, where David Lauren hosted a cocktail party for the LeBron James Family Foundation at the Ralph Lauren store in New York City. It was a star-studded event that attracted athletes, artists, and television personalities ranging from Jay-Z to Charlie Rose to Serena Williams, who had just won her third US Open days earlier. Even Anna Wintour dropped by to support LeBron and Savannah's efforts to raise awareness for the needs of low-income children. But the name on everyone's lips in New York was Barack Obama, who was running for president. With less than a month to go till Election Day, the forty-seven-year-old senator from Illinois was leading Republican senator John McCain in the polls. The prospect of the country electing its first Black president had people at LeBron and Savannah's party buzzing.

Few people were more energized by Obama's run than Jay-Z. Prior to Obama's candidacy, Jay-Z had never contemplated the possibility of a Black president. "Growing up, if you had ever told a black person from the hood you can be president," Jay-Z reflected, "I'd be like, 'Are you out of your mind? How?'" But Obama had renewed Jay-Z's spirit and given him pride in America. The turning point for Jay-Z had come in April 2008 when Senator Hillary Clinton, who was then challenging Obama for the

Democratic nomination, criticized Obama in a televised debate. The next day, Obama gave a speech and said he wasn't surprised by Clinton's attacks. "When you're running for the presidency," Obama told the crowd, "you've got to expect it. You've just kind of gotta let it . . ." He paused and used his hand to brush the imaginary dirt off his shoulders. It was a reference to Jay-Z's song "Dirt off Your Shoulder." And the crowd went wild when Obama did it. "You know," Obama said, brushing off his other shoulder. "You know."

When Jay-Z saw that, he said to himself, "This is not happening in the world. This is not happening in America." But it was happening. And Jay-Z committed to doing everything possible to get people registered to vote for Obama and to help motivate them to go to the polls on Election Day. Jay-Z also wanted LeBron's help. He told LeBron that he had committed to performing a series of free concerts in Detroit, Miami, and Cleveland. The purpose of those shows was to get people registered to vote for Obama.

LeBron agreed with Jay-Z's long-held view that the only way a Black kid could get out of the projects was by being a rapper or a basketball star. But Obama had inspired Jay-Z, and Jay-Z was spreading that enthusiasm to LeBron.

After the fundraiser in New York, LeBron and Savannah contributed $20,000 to a committee supporting Barack Obama. It marked the first time that they'd donated money to a presidential campaign. Then, on October 23, LeBron walked onto the stage at the jam-packed Q in Cleveland wearing black jeans, a black cap, and a black leather jacket over a black T-shirt that said: VOTE. The Cavaliers' arena was filled with people who had come to hear Jay-Z perform his "Last Chance for Change" concert. They cheered wildly when LeBron welcomed everyone and directed their attention to a giant video screen, which projected a live stream of Barack Obama giving a speech at a rally in Florida.

The crowd at the Q was silent as Obama spoke about his upbringing.

At the conclusion of Obama's speech, LeBron told the crowd, "I want everybody in here, moms, dads, aunts, uncles to get out and vote. November fourth is the most important day of our lives. Everybody in here, get your family out there and vote."

The crowd cheered.

"You know who I'm voting for," LeBron said. "I'm voting for Obama."

The arena went dark. Jay-Z took the stage. A spotlight shone on him.

"Rosa Parks sat so Martin Luther King could walk," Jay-Z told the crowd. "And Martin walked so Obama could run. Obama is running so we can all fly. So let's fly!"

The music started pulsing. LeBron started rapping. And Jay-Z had the building shaking. After his first number, he urged everyone to vote early. "We're here to have fun tonight," Jay-Z said. "But there's an important election coming up. We the youth are going to show them our power." Then he rapped some new lines:

Fuck talkin' 'bout the recession, it's just depressin'
I rock with Obama, but I ain't no politician.

In a matter of months, LeBron had gone from saying that sports and politics don't go together to making campaign donations and using his star power to mobilize voters to get behind Barack Obama.

There was no turning back now.

TWENTY-SIX

MIRACLES AREN'T ENOUGH

Buzz Bissinger had invested a year of his life writing LeBron's memoir. Eager for LeBron's feedback, he sent him and Maverick a draft of the manuscript to read. Then Bissinger returned to Ohio to go over it with them. They gathered at LeBron's kitchen table, where they were joined by Coach Dru Joyce, who had also read the manuscript.

Maverick, who had made notes on his printed copy, led the discussion and offered a series of smart edits, most of which had to do with context. Coach Dru added some important details and flagged a few minor factual inaccuracies.

Bissinger had anticipated that LeBron would want him to cut things from the manuscript—perhaps the mention of his smoking pot or any number of other sensitive topics about his teen years.

But LeBron voiced no concerns with anything Bissinger had written. There was one thing, however, that he wanted Bissinger to add—the fact that the administration at St. V hadn't stood behind him when he'd been accused of accepting vintage jerseys during his senior year. "Jeez," LeBron said. "I've done a lot for this school. The least they can do is support me immediately in a time of tremendous trauma and need."

Recognizing that something that had happened six years earlier still hurt LeBron, Bissinger said he'd be sure to add that episode and LeBron's feelings about it to the narrative.

"I just have one question," LeBron said. "Who is Attila the Hun?"

Hoping for some substantive feedback, Bissinger was deflated. He had included a reference to the infamous ruler of the Hunnic Empire, who had been one of the most feared enemies of the Roman Empire before his death in 453. But by this point, Bissinger didn't feel like explaining.

"It's not important," Bissinger told LeBron. "I'll take him out."

LeBron didn't pick up on Bissinger's frustration. Nor was LeBron trying to be rude. He was just much more invested in the documentary than the book. And he had no understanding of how much work was involved in writing a book. Nor did he appreciate that Bissinger took just as much pride in his craft as LeBron took in his, and writers seek validation much like athletes do.

After going page by page through the manuscript—a process that took about five hours—Bissinger thanked everyone for the input. He was particularly grateful to Maverick. But Bissinger still wasn't sure how LeBron felt.

"So, what do you think of the book?" Bissinger asked.

"The book's good," LeBron said.

Bissinger waited for him to elaborate.

LeBron didn't say more.

He's too young to do a book, Bissinger thought. *He's been in a bubble all his life. How much introspection can he really have—even with all he's gone through—at this age?*

After the trip to Akron, Bissinger made the tweaks suggested by Maverick and Coach Dru. Then he submitted the manuscript to his editor.

"I've been able to go pretty deep with people," Bissinger explained. "But I couldn't get past that initial layer with LeBron. I could not unseal the door."

Ever since LeBron had been in high school, *60 Minutes* had shown interest in doing a segment on him. LeBron wasn't enthused. He didn't watch the news magazine. And as his career progressed, his publicist had reservations about the show's reputation for doing hard-hitting interviews. But at the outset of the 2008–2009 season, LeBron finally agreed to spend some time with correspondent Steve Kroft in what promised to be more of a celebrity profile than a probing interview. When Kroft arrived in Akron, LeBron took him to his high school. Wearing street clothes and holding a basketball, LeBron was showing Kroft the St. V gymnasium when Kroft asked: "Are you any place remotely close to your peak?"

It was hardly a penetrating question. But LeBron wasn't about to elaborate on his ambitions—he was nowhere near the ceiling. Instead, he couched his answer.

"I don't want to say I got a long way to go," he said. "But it's gonna take a little process."

Kroft looked at the ball in LeBron's hand. "Are you going to do anything with this?" he said with a smile.

LeBron looked at the hoop at the other end of the gym. Then he tossed the basketball underhand, as if pitching a softball. It traveled approximately sixty feet through the air and whipped through the net without touching the rim.

Stunned, Kroft cracked up. "How many times can you do that?"

LeBron smiled. "Just one take, baby. Just one take."

To Kroft, it was fun to witness LeBron's magical capabilities and entertain the idea that he was nowhere near his peak, but it was hard to fathom. The 2008–2009 season turned out to be his most dominant to date. He was named MVP of the NBA for the first time, and he led the Cavaliers to sixty-six wins, giving them the best overall record in the league. Over in the Western Conference, Kobe led the Lakers to sixty-five wins. LeBron and Kobe were clearly the two best players in the world, and it seemed they were destined for a head-to-head showdown in the NBA Finals.

The Cavaliers swept the Pistons in the first round of the playoffs and then swept the Atlanta Hawks in the next round. LeBron had expected to face the Celtics in the Eastern Conference Finals. But the Celtics, beset by injuries, were upset by the Orlando Magic, a team led by all-star center Dwight Howard, who had played alongside LeBron in the Olympics.

With Paul Pierce and the Celtics out of the way, LeBron and the Cavaliers appeared to have a clearer path back to the NBA Finals. In Game 1 of the Eastern Conference Finals, in Cleveland, LeBron dominated, converting twenty of his thirty shots and scoring forty-nine points. But the Magic shocked the Cavaliers by pulling out a one-point victory. Then in Game 2, the Cavaliers blew a twenty-three-point lead, allowing the Magic to fight all the way back and take a 95–93 lead with one second remaining on the clock.

With the Cavs on the verge of going down 2-0 in the series, everyone in the lower bowl of the Q stood up. After a time-out, LeBron took his place at the top of the key, waiting for the referee to hand the ball to Cavaliers point guard Mo Williams for the inbounds pass. As a kid, LeBron had rehearsed moments like this, shooting thousands of practice last-second shots in the gym. He even imagined the defender in his face and the sound of the buzzer going off in his head. Now it was time to do it for real. He pointed at Williams, as if to say, *Let's do this.*

The moment the ball was in Williams's hands, LeBron broke for the basket as if he were going to catch a lob pass near the rim for a game-tying dunk attempt. But as soon as his defender started backpedaling, LeBron stopped and popped back out beyond the top of the key. Just as his feet touched down beyond the three-point arc, the pass from Williams arrived in LeBron's hands. With two defenders jumping toward him—one from his left and one from his right—LeBron took six-tenths of a second to catch the ball, elevate, and release a high-arching shot over a pair of outstretched arms. The buzzer sounded as soon as the ball left his hand.

"For three for the win," Marv Albert said as the ball soared through the air.

The shot rattled through the rim.

"Yes!" Albert shouted. "LeBron James at the buzzer!"

It was pandemonium in the Q as the crowd went wild and players mobbed LeBron while confetti rained down. The scoreboard read: Cavaliers 96, Magic 95.

"A miraculous shot by James," Albert continued, hardly able to believe his eyes.

By league rules, the play had to be reviewed to ensure that LeBron had gotten the shot off before time had expired. With the crowd still cheering wildly and confetti stuck to his face, LeBron stepped to the scorer's table and peered over the referees' shoulders as they watched the replay on a monitor. Then LeBron raised his fist. The shot was good. He had finished with thirty-five points, and the Cavs had evened the series, 1-1.

Keeping his index finger raised, LeBron walked triumphantly toward the tunnel, the crowd serenading him with cheers. The last time Cleveland fans had witnessed such a dramatic finish was when Michael Jordan had hit the Shot, which had knocked the Cavaliers out of the playoffs twenty years earlier. In his postgame press conference, LeBron was asked about his shot and Jordan's shot.

"You grew up in this area," a reporter said. "So, you know in the past, the Shot has meant something very different."

LeBron smiled. "Well, that guy's not in the league anymore."

Laughs rippled through the press corps.

Later that night, LeBron got a text from Kobe: "Helluva shot."

* * *

The Cavaliers had the momentum when the series shifted to Orlando for Games 3 and 4. LeBron scored forty-one points in Game 3 and forty-four points in Game 4. He was unstoppable. Yet the Magic won both games to take a commanding 3-1 series lead. Despite LeBron's heroics, the Cavaliers were being outplayed.

Back in Cleveland, LeBron led them to a victory in Game 5, but the Magic easily won Game 6 in Orlando to capture the series. With Orlando fans singing, "Na, na, na, na, hey, hey, goodbye," LeBron didn't bother shaking hands with the Magic. Stunned, he headed for the locker room.

For LeBron, losing the series was hard to take. His team had the best record in the NBA, and he had turned in one of the greatest individual performances in playoff history, averaging 38 points, 8 rebounds, and 8 assists per game in the Eastern Conference Finals. Still, it wasn't enough to get back to the NBA Finals.

Meanwhile, Kobe led his team to the finals, and the Lakers defeated the Magic. It was Kobe's fourth NBA championship.

After six seasons in the NBA, LeBron had established himself as the number one player in the league. But he still didn't have a ring.

Cavaliers' owner Dan Gilbert was feeling the pressure. LeBron had just one year left on his contract. With teams already jockeying for position to lure LeBron out of Cleveland after the 2009–2010 season, Gilbert had to do something to improve the team's chances of winning it all the next year. But what? He'd already spent a fortune to make Cleveland an attractive permanent home for LeBron. The latest project, a state-of-the-art practice facility constructed near LeBron's estate, had been completed. And the Cavs had the third-highest payroll in the NBA. Only the Knicks spent more money on player contracts. Yet the Cavaliers had not managed to deliver a championship to Cleveland. Now that LeBron had just one year remaining on his contract, Gilbert felt compelled to demonstrate to LeBron that his commitment to winning had not waivered.

The one thing Gilbert didn't want to do was fire head coach Mike Brown. After the loss to Orlando, Gilbert had heard the rumblings—that LeBron and his inner circle were exasperated with Brown and wanted him replaced. But LeBron hadn't said that to Gilbert. And the Cavs were coming off a league-best, sixty-six-win regular season, which resulted in Brown's being named NBA Coach of the Year. Gilbert viewed Brown as a man of character and integrity who was a smart and selfless leader. "Mike Brown is a critical element as to why our franchise is growing into the kind of success we all envisioned and hoped to achieve," Gilbert said after Brown received the award. "There is no man more deserving, and it proves to the world that, yes, nice guys *can* indeed finish first."

General Manager Danny Ferry had also made it known that if Brown lost his job, he'd resign in protest. Rather than risk upheaval in the front office, Gilbert stood behind Coach Brown and looked to bring in a big-name player who could bolster the roster. He set his sights on thirty-seven-year-old Shaquille O'Neal. Although O'Neal was the oldest player in the league, he was a future Hall of Fame center who remained one of the NBA's biggest and most accomplished stars. He'd won three NBA titles with Kobe in LA and one title with D-Wade in Miami. Hopeful that pairing Shaq with LeBron would result in a championship for Cleveland, Gilbert traded two starters—Ben Wallace and Sasha Pavlovic—and coughed up $21 million, and O'Neal agreed to join the Cavs.

Gilbert knew that Shaq's age posed some risk. But he looked at the trade as if he were playing poker and this was his all-in moment. He also had a feeling that Kobe's having won another championship would give Shaq—who had a long-standing feud with Kobe—added motivation to win a championship with LeBron.

On June 25, 2009, Danny Ferry stepped to the podium to share the news with the media.

"Did you run this by LeBron?" a reporter asked.

Ferry resented the question. But it cut to the heart of the matter. LeBron had all the power, all the leverage. Every move the Cavaliers made had to be calculated around LeBron. Without him, the Cavaliers would slide back to mediocrity. Or worse.

"We talked to LeBron," Ferry said. "We talked to a few of our players. We have an open level of communication with our team overall."

"How much was this move for LeBron's future beyond next season?" another reporter asked.

"Obviously, LeBron's future is important to our organization," Ferry said. "But this move and our goals are aligned with what our players want, including LeBron."

"Where is Shaq now?" another writer asked.

Dejected, Ferry shrugged. "I'm not sure," he said. "I haven't spoken to him."

Days later, O'Neal rolled into Cleveland in a massive diesel truck with a Superman logo on the front grille. Standing seven one and weighing over 350 pounds, he told the media at his introductory press conference, "I'm still the Dun Dada of all big men." Flanked by Dan Gilbert, Danny Ferry, and Coach Mike Brown, Shaq entertained the reporters. He busted Ferry's chops—"I had to check my computer to see who Danny Ferry was." He laid down the law with Coach Brown—"Other teams are going to have matchup problems against us. But we will not be doubling anybody—ever again." When reporters asked him about playing with LeBron, Shaq made it clear that he knew precisely why he'd been brought in—to keep LeBron from leaving. "My job is to protect the King," he said. "It's LeBron's team. In a perfect world, if we take care of business and win, he has no choice but to stay here. My motto is very simple: 'Win a ring for the King.'"

Dan Gilbert loved the sound of that.

LeBron was vacationing on the French Riviera with Savannah when he got word that Shaq was a Cavalier. LeBron was thrilled. He'd never had a teammate in Cleveland who was a bona fide star. Shaq may have been well past his prime, but he was still a beast on the court. And LeBron thought that he and Shaq were very similar—two big kids who loved to play ball and have fun. LeBron saw the things Shaq had said to the media in Cleveland. "I feel fucking fabulous," Shaq had told one writer. "I feel *good*. I'm the old, old bull that has done it. And I'm now with a new show bull." LeBron loved that Shaq had been where he yearned to go. *I got a teammate that's going to help me get there*, he thought.

After a welcome reprieve in France, LeBron returned to a mounting list of requests. As the reigning MVP of the NBA, the producer of an upcoming documentary, and the founder of two companies, he had a busy summer that was a mix of business and pleasure. He played golf with Warren Buffett and Bill Gates in Sun Valley, Idaho. He was honored as the Best Male Athlete at the BET Awards in Los Angeles. He traveled to Paris to be photographed by fashion photographer Marcel Hartmann. He teamed up with Rihanna to promote the grand opening of a spa in New York City. He hosted Nike's Lynn Merritt at his Nike camp in Akron, and he then returned to China for a Nike-sponsored series of basketball camps. He taped an hour-long interview with Charlie Rose that would air in the fall. And LeBron played himself in an episode of HBO's *Entourage*, appearing as Matt Damon's sidekick.

But the highlight of the off-season was an impromptu visit with President Obama in the Oval Office. LeBron had gone to Washington with Maverick, Rich, and Randy for the premiere of SpringHill's documentary, *More Than a Game*. Although LeBron and his friends didn't have an appointment, President Obama squeezed them into his calendar. LeBron and his friends felt honored to enter the West Wing.

Prior to Obama's run, LeBron had never paid much attention to presidential politics. But since he and Savannah had contributed to Obama's campaign and publicly endorsed his candidacy, LeBron had watched him closely. LeBron knew what it was like to be scrutinized. But President Obama was arguably the most scrutinized person on the planet. Yet he carried himself with a remarkable degree of dignity. LeBron didn't have many role models, but President Obama inspired him. Being in his presence made LeBron want to work even harder to do good in the community and be a good example for young people.

Buzz Bissinger shared an advance copy of the LeBron book, titled *Shooting Stars*, with *Vanity Fair* editor in chief Graydon Carter. After reading it, Carter felt Bissinger had done a masterful job of capturing the inspiring bond between LeBron and his high school teammates. Carter thought that LeBron was wise not to dole out too much personal information about himself. He was also impressed with the prestigious list of LeBron's friends who had provided blurbs for the book: Jay-Z, Warren Buffett, and Mike Krzyzewski. He asked Bissinger what he could do to help launch the book.

"Would you be interested in excerpting it?" Bissinger asked.

"Absolutely," Carter said.

Bissinger was thrilled. An excerpt in *Vanity Fair* would improve the book's chances of becoming a bestseller.

Carter also offered to host a party for the book at the Monkey Bar, the eclectic restaurant he owned in Midtown Manhattan. *Vanity Fair* was known for throwing the go-to party at the Oscars every year. For the book party, Carter put together a guest list of dozens of luminaries from the film, television, and publishing industries.

LeBron had no sense of how unusual it was to get this kind of support for a book launch. But he knew what it was like to be the center of attention. When he walked into the Monkey Bar on September 9, 2009, the day *Shooting Stars* went on sale, he worked the room like a seasoned politician, shaking hands and making small-talk. With everyone approaching him, LeBron made a point of introducing his mother and Savannah, who had accompanied him to the event.

A couple of nights later, LeBron appeared on *The Daily Show with Jon Stewart*. Ostensibly, LeBron was there to plug the book. But LeBron scarcely talked about *Shooting Stars*. Instead, he played along when Stewart toyed with him about joining the Knicks the following year, when he would become a free agent. At one point, Stewart put an I ❤ NEW YORK coffee mug on the table. The audience laughed.

"Are you familiar with our city?" Stewart said. "We have a team. The Knickerbockers. They're a basketball team."

LeBron grinned.

The audience roared with laughter.

"Are you familiar with Shake Shack?" Stewart said. He put a bag of take-out food on the table.

LeBron laughed.

"Have you made up your mind yet?" Stewart asked. "Are you gonna stay in Cleveland? Have you thought about another city to play in?"

"Well, I'm in New York now, with you," LeBron said. "So, I'm here now."

The audience loved it.

LeBron grinned. "We'll see," he said.

Bissinger wasn't thrilled with LeBron's failure to promote the book on the show. Both of their names appeared on the cover, and they were supposed to be a team when it came to doing publicity. But while Bissinger was doing every talk show and television interview that the book publicist lined up, LeBron showed little interest in doing book publicity. The book reviews weren't glowing, either. *New York Times* book critic Dwight Garner called *Shooting Stars* "a modest book . . . that reads like a better-than-average young adult novel." Not exactly high praise. Although the review praised LeBron as "smart" for collaborating with Bissinger, it went on to suggest that Bissinger had forced words—"brooding," "spark and bite," "the taunting cruelty that is basketball," "a prickly bunch"—into LeBron's mouth. "That's the language of a professional writer, and it doesn't feel like James's language," Garner wrote. "It breaks the spell this narrative tries to cast."

Bissinger was frustrated. Despite LeBron's star power, Bissinger's decorated record, the *Vanity Fair* excerpt, blurbs by celebrities, and plenty of media hits, the book did not sell well. It didn't make the *New York Times* bestseller list. The experience left a bad taste in Bissinger's mouth.

Dan Gilbert wasn't pleased with LeBron, either. He found nothing funny about LeBron's interview with Jon Stewart, which felt like an opportunity for LeBron to flirt with the Knicks. Gilbert also didn't appreciate what LeBron was saying about his future plans. While interviewing LeBron, Charlie Rose revealed a private conversation they'd had earlier in the summer.

> **Rose:** You and I were on the golf course, and you said to me, "I'm going to play this year and then I'm going to look at all the options. I owe that to myself and my mother and people who are a part of LeBron's team."
>
> **LeBron:** Right.
>
> **Rose:** How will you decide? That's the question.
>
> **LeBron:** Well, I want to win. . . . Without question I think Danny [Ferry] and the GMs and the ownership has been great. But at the same time, you know, as an athlete and competitor, you want to continue to be successful at the highest level.

For Gilbert, LeBron's words weren't reassuring. He wasn't encouraged by LeBron's body language, either. When LeBron arrived at training camp, Gilbert felt he looked bored and disengaged. Especially at Media Day. Leaning against a wall behind a semicircle of Cavaliers beat writers, LeBron delivered rote answers and a forced smile.

Nearby, head coach Mike Brown was asked about his relationship with LeBron. "LeBron allows me to coach him," Brown said.

Brown's answer made Gilbert cringe. Brown was in his fifth season as head coach. He was the NBA Coach of the Year. And LeBron *allowed* Brown to coach him? *What the . . . ?*

While the media flocked around LeBron, Gilbert was approached by journalist Scott Raab, a Cleveland native who wrote for *Esquire*. An avid fan of Cleveland sports, Raab felt that the Cavaliers were on the cusp of finally winning an NBA title. He told Gilbert that he planned to write a book about the 2009–2010 season. Then he asked Gilbert if he thought LeBron would stay past the season.

Gilbert shrugged. "Nobody knows," he told Raab. "I think he will."

Raab opined that there was no way LeBron would leave Cleveland. No way!

Gilbert wanted to believe that. But privately, he had his doubts, although he wasn't going to admit that to a journalist.

The Cavaliers were off to a 3-2 start. On November 4, 2009, LeBron was at home, watching Game 6 of the World Series, when the Yankees players raced out of the dugout and mobbed pitcher Mariano Rivera after he got Phillies outfielder Shane Victorino to ground out to end the game. The Yankees had won their twenty-seventh championship. A huge Yankees fan, LeBron texted Derek Jeter to congratulate him. Then he texted Alex Rodriguez. Then pitcher CC Sabathia.

The following night, after losing a close game at home, LeBron flew with his team to New York and checked into a hotel in Midtown. The city was preparing for a ticker-tape parade for the Yankees. But New Yorkers awoke to a full-page letter from LeBron on the back cover of the New York *Daily News*. It began:

> Thank you for welcoming me back to New York City, one of my favorite places to play in the world. The Big Apple has always been good to me, so I wanted to do something special to show my appreciation.

In the letter, LeBron announced that he had arranged for seven gyms around the city to host high school players for free open runs. LeBron's idea was to give kids a warm, safe place to play now that the weather had turned cold.

New Yorkers were thrilled. The Yankees were champs again, and LeBron was talking about the Big Apple like it was his future home.

LeBron slept through the parade. But when he stepped onto the floor at Madison Square Garden that evening, members of the Yankees were sitting courtside with Jay-Z. The atmosphere felt like a playoff game. Knicks fans wore LeBron jerseys and held up pictures of LeBron superimposed in a Knicks uniform. A Knicks fan wearing a LeBron Knicks jersey and a Yankees cap held up a sign with one such picture and the words *236 Days*.

Before the opening tip, the Yankees players were announced and received a standing ovation. LeBron rose to his feet and clapped as Frank Sinatra's "New York, New York" played through the sound system.

LeBron scored nineteen points in the first quarter. After dropping a fadeaway three-pointer, LeBron slapped Jay-Z's hand. He closed the quarter with another three at the buzzer. Then he looked at the Yankees players and flashed three fingers. Knicks fans were going crazy. The Cavaliers were up, 40–21.

LeBron lived for moments like that. The bigger the stage, the better he performed. The crowd's reaction felt fulfilling.

The Knicks fought back in the second half. But LeBron was in control the entire night. He finished with 33 points, 9 assists, and 8 rebounds, leading his team to a 100–91 victory. Before he could get off the court, he was cornered by ESPN's Doris Burke.

"Madison Square Garden," Burke said. "This stage. Describe what it's like for a guy of your stature."

"This is the mecca of basketball," LeBron said. "There's so many memories that's happened in this building. It's a legendary ball court. As a competitor and a guy that knows history, you would *love* to play here."

At around two o'clock in the morning on November 27, 2009, Tiger Woods's wife chased him out of their home and pursued him down the driveway, golf club in hand, as he fled in his SUV, careened into a fire hydrant, and crashed into a tree in a neighbor's front yard. After his wife took the golf club to the SUV windows, Tiger ended up on the ground. His mother, who had been staying in Tiger's house, came running outside, yelling, "What happened?" It was the beginning of the biggest fall from grace in the history of sport.

LeBron didn't have a relationship with Tiger Woods, but they had some things in common. They were both dubbed "The Chosen One" by

Sports Illustrated. They both lived up to the hype and were considered the best in the world in their respective sports. And they were both among the wealthiest athletes. Tiger was the first athlete to earn $1 billion, and according to *Forbes*, he was the richest athlete in the world. LeBron was in the top five. The biggest source of their wealth came from Nike, where they were the company's two most important athletes. In the Nike pecking order, Tiger was first, and LeBron was second. But that was about to change.

On November 27, LeBron awoke in Charlotte, where the Cavaliers were set to play the Bobcats later that night. When he first saw the news, he wondered the same thing that Tiger's mother had wondered. But within a matter of days, Tiger was engulfed in an epic infidelity scandal. One woman after another came forward to reveal sexual relations with Tiger, shattering his carefully cultivated image.

At first, LeBron did not anticipate how Tiger's situation would impact him. Nor could he relate to the complicated set of circumstances that had led to Tiger's dilemma. But by the time the Cavaliers arrived in Los Angeles for a Christmas Day matinee against the Lakers, Tiger had stepped away from golf to save his marriage, and virtually all his corporate sponsors other than Nike had dropped him. His career was on hold, and his personal life was in shambles. At Nike, the torch quietly passed to LeBron, whose reputation positioned him to become the company's new leading man.

LeBron was far more focused on Kobe and the Lakers than on Tiger. For the second year in a row, the Cavaliers and Lakers appeared destined to meet in the NBA Finals. The Lakers were 23-4 and the Cavaliers were 22-8. In a nationally televised game that the NBA hyped as a duel between the league's two biggest stars, LeBron and Kobe put on a show, combining for sixty-one points and seventeen assists. In the end, LeBron got the upper hand, and the Cavaliers won going away, 102–87.

When the Lakers came to Cleveland a month later, LeBron and Kobe went toe-to-toe again. In the fourth quarter, LeBron scored twelve straight points to put his team up. Kobe poured in thirty-one points. But LeBron scored thirty-seven. During a time-out with twenty-three seconds left, Cleveland fans gave LeBron a standing ovation as he pranced along the sideline, mouthing the words of "Forever" from the *More Than a Game* soundtrack that blared through the arena:

The passion in the flame is ignited
You can't put it out once we light it.

The Cavaliers were rolling.

Shaquille O'Neal had come to Cleveland determined to win another title. He knew when he arrived that LeBron was the toast of the town. LeBron's stature in Cleveland reminded Shaq of how big he had been in Los Angeles back in the early 2000s when the Lakers were dominating the league. But early on, Shaq also saw something he didn't recognize—an organization that was totally beholden to one player. LeBron's influence was so pervasive that the head coach was powerless. "Our coach, Mike Brown, was a nice guy," Shaq observed. "But he had to live on the edge because nobody was supposed to be confrontational with LeBron. Nobody wanted him to leave Cleveland, so he was allowed to do whatever he wanted to do."

Shaq liked playing with LeBron. He especially appreciated the way LeBron had created such an inclusive culture among the players. "This is the funnest, funniest team I've ever been on in my life," Shaq said. "LeBron, everyplace we go, he'll send a text—'Hey, meet us at the steakhouse, eight o'clock, meet us at the movies, we got a party tonight.' This is a very, very close-knit group." Yet Shaq sensed the potential for trouble ahead. At one point during the season, Coach Brown was leading the team through a film session. Everyone watched a play where LeBron didn't hustle back on defense after a missed shot. Rather than saying anything, Coach Brown went to the next play, where Mo Williams basically did the same thing. "Yo, Mo, we can't have that," Coach Brown told him. "You've got to hustle a little more." At that point, teammate Delonte West stood up. "Hold up, now," West said. "You can't be pussyfooting around like that. Everyone has to be accountable for what they do, not just some of us."

"I know, Delonte," Coach Brown said. "I know."

Shaq observed that LeBron frequently ignored Brown during the 2009–2010 season. And Brown went out of his way to avoid confrontation. It was awkward. Nonetheless, for the second year in a row, the Cavaliers finished the regular season with the best overall record in the NBA at 61-21. And after easily dispatching the Chicago Bulls in the first round of the playoffs, the Cavaliers looked poised to manhandle the Boston Celtics in the Eastern Conference Semifinals.

Celtics general manager Danny Ainge was not optimistic. The Celtics hadn't had a great season. They'd won fifty games. But they'd struggled down the stretch and were playing uninspiring basketball. The way LeBron was playing, Ainge figured the Celtics had little chance of standing up to the Cavaliers.

Prior to Game 1 in Cleveland, Celtics head coach Doc Rivers tried to inspire his players to fight tooth and nail against LeBron and his teammates. "They want to have fun," Rivers barked. "Our job is to make this no fun. To make this fucking war. To make this brutal. To make this shit hard. To make it so hard that they give in."

The Celtics came out swinging in Game 1 in Cleveland. LeBron scored thirty-five points and led his team to victory. But it was clear that the Celtics weren't going to go down without a fight. Prior to the start of Game 2, LeBron was awarded the MVP trophy for the 2009–2010 season. It was the second straight year that he'd taken home the honor. But the pregame ceremony seemed to ignite the Celtics, who pounded the Cavaliers that night to even the series at 1-1.

When the series shifted to Boston, LeBron attempted to snuff out the Celtics' hopes. He came out firing and scored twenty-one points in the first quarter. The romp was on. LeBron finished with thirty-seven points and the Cavs won, 124–95, handing the Celtics their worst home-court playoff loss in team history. Boston fans booed the Celtics off the floor.

None of this surprised Ainge. LeBron was playing like the best player in the league, and Celtics captain Paul Pierce was playing like a shadow of the player who had stood up to LeBron back in 2008. The Cavs were up, 2-1. The Celtics badly needed to win Game 4.

With a chance to seize control of the series, LeBron appeared distracted in Game 4. His passes were off the mark and repeatedly ended up in the hands of the Celtics. His point production was down, too. At the same time, Celtics point guard Rajon Rondo had the game of his life, scoring 29 points, snaring 18 rebounds, and handing out 13 assists. One of those assists proved to be a turning point in the game. Late in the third quarter, Rondo was streaking toward the Celtics basket for a breakaway layup. LeBron, whose signature defensive play was chasing down play-ers from behind and swiping away layups with perfectly timed leaps, was closing in. Sensing LeBron's presence, Rondo elevated. Just as LeBron went airborne to block his shot, Rondo whipped a behind-the-back pass to a trailing teammate. Fooled, LeBron found himself up in the air and out of position as Rondo's teammate dunked the ball, igniting the Celtics crowd.

While the Celtics went on a run, the Cavaliers imploded. Trying to compensate for the drop-off in LeBron's scoring, Coach Brown substituted players in and out, hoping to find a lineup that could muster some points. It looked chaotic, and at one point, Shaq fumed at Brown on the sideline. Meantime, Celtics fans reveled in LeBron's lackluster performance, chant-ing "M-V-P" when Rondo touched the ball. The Celtics cruised to a 97–87 win to even the series at 2-2.

LeBron seldom had an off game. In those rare instances, he always bounced back with a strong performance in the next game. But at the start of Game 5 in Cleveland, he did something he'd never done in his seven-year career—he attempted only one shot and failed to score a single point in the first quarter. The second quarter was even worse—LeBron took three shots and missed all of them. At halftime, he had registered a mere eight points, all from the foul line. The Celtics, meanwhile, were running away with the game.

LeBron's teammates were befuddled. Especially Shaq. "There's no question in Game 5 LeBron was kind of out of it," O'Neal would later say. "I always believed he could turn it on at any moment, but for some reason he didn't. . . . It was weird."

By the fourth quarter, the unthinkable happened—Cleveland fans were booing LeBron. And with just over eight minutes remaining in the game, the Cavaliers trailed, 92–68, and fans were flocking to the exits. Sitting stone-faced in his courtside seat, Cavs owner Dan Gilbert undid his top button, loosened his tie, and folded his arms across his chest. It looked to him like LeBron had quit. In the most important game of the season, LeBron shot three for fourteen and the Celtics won, 120–88. It was the worst home defeat in the Cavaliers' playoff history. Gilbert was beside himself.

LeBron's postgame statements added to the perception that he was disconnected from the team. "I put a lot of pressure on myself to be the best player on the court," he said. "When I'm not, I feel bad for myself because I'm not going out there and doing the things I know I can do."

He knew he'd played poorly. But he had no patience for people questioning his commitment by pointing to one bad game. "I spoil a lot of people with my play," he said. "When you have three bad games in a seven-year career, it's easy to point that out."

With the Celtics up, 3-2, and the series headed back to Boston, the criticism of LeBron escalated. On Twitter, Bill Simmons, who had recently been deemed "America's most famous sports columnist," encouraged fans to chant "New York Knicks" when LeBron shot free throws. And when LeBron stepped to the free throw line for the first time in Game 6 in Boston, the crowd greeted him with the chant: "New York Knicks. New York Knicks." The taunts dogged LeBron through the game.

LeBron played better than he had in Games 4 and 5. But the final minutes were stunning. Trailing by ten points, the Cavaliers appeared to give up. Boston fans started singing, "LeBron is leaving." And as the final second ticked off the clock and Boston fans were on their feet, LeBron hugged the Celtics players one by one, congratulating them and wishing them well. He had tallied 27 points, 19 rebounds, and 10 assists. Those were great numbers for any other player. But more was expected from the greatest player in the game, especially in such a big moment.

Sitting in TD Garden, Celtics GM Danny Ainge tried to process what he had witnessed. "I don't know what was going on," Ainge said. "But he was not the LeBron James I had seen in 2008." In all his years playing against Michael Jordan, Ainge had never seen him disappear in a playoff series. "That never happened to Michael, where he wasn't, for sure, the best player in a series, even if his team lost," Ainge said.

Ainge wasn't the only one who was studying LeBron's performance in Boston. As LeBron walked off the court, removed his jersey, and disappeared into the tunnel, Miami Heat general manager Pat Riley was watching him on television. *Beaten again*, Riley thought. *Seven years of banging his head against the wall.*

Determined to see LeBron in a Heat uniform, Riley was already plotting how to lure him away from Cleveland.

After taking a shower and getting dressed, LeBron stepped to the podium in the press room beneath TD Garden. Peppered by questions about his future, LeBron parried. "You can never predict the future," he said. "But at the same time, you hope for things that's much brighter than what's going on right now."

Donning a pair of sunglasses and a backpack, he left the room.

Although LeBron wouldn't officially become a free agent until July 1, the most highly anticipated off-season in NBA history was officially underway.

TWENTY-SEVEN

THE SUMMER OF LeBRON

The morning after the Cavaliers were eliminated by the Celtics, a sports gossip website published a story alleging that LeBron's teammate Delonte West had been having an affair with Gloria James. Citing an unnamed source, the website claimed that LeBron had learned about the sordid situation right before Game 4 in Boston. It was a vile, unsubstantiated rumor. But in the vacuum created by LeBron's inexplicable lack of engagement in Games 4 and 5, the tale gained traction on the internet. Within hours, *Barstool Sports* picked up the story. Then *Deadspin* weighed in. Soon, the rumor was trending on Twitter. Delonte West was taking heat. One respected NBA player tweeted: "Just heard a rumor, say it ain't so Delonte."

LeBron wasn't on social media—up to this point, he'd resisted joining Twitter. But he saw the way the internet and Twitter could weaponize a nasty rumor. With each tweet, Gloria was being humiliated over and over. It was sport for the gossipmongers. Determined to put a stop to it, LeBron engaged his attorney.

Fred Nance thought the story was morally despicable. He also determined it met the legal definition of defamation. But at first blush, Nance felt the rumor was so off the wall and idiotic that it didn't warrant a denial. Yet rather than dying down, the uncontested rumor continued to gain traction over the weekend. After further consideration, Nance sent a cease-and-desist letter to the proprietor of the gossip website on May 17. "I am the attorney for Gloria and LeBron James," Nance's letter began. "I am writing to demand that you Cease and Desist in repeating the lies you have been instrumental in spreading regarding Gloria James. They are categorically false and per se defamatory."

While Nance was dealing with the gossip site, Maverick Carter had a different problem on his hands—Buzz Bissinger had weighed in on Le-Bron's free agency. In an op-ed in the *New York Times*, Bissinger suggested that LeBron was "terrified to leave home" and that he needed to get out of Cleveland "for his own emotional and professional growth."

In hindsight, Bissinger felt like a sellout for having written LeBron's book. The money was good. But Bissinger was ashamed. Unabashedly honest, he eventually told a group of students at Harvard's Nieman Foundation for Journalism that the book was "a piece of shit . . . but the money was really good, so . . ."

In his *Times* piece, Bissinger called LeBron's performance in Game 5 in Boston "astounding" and "inexcusable." And he made the case that Le-Bron was not the greatest player in the history of the game. "He has never shown anything close to the killer mentality and step-it-up of the players he is most compared to, Michael Jordan and Magic Johnson," Bissinger wrote. "He is not in the same category as Kareem Abdul-Jabbar. Or Kobe Bryant." Bissinger closed his essay by speaking directly to LeBron. "It is time to leave home," Bissinger said.

Maverick wasn't happy. He had brought Bissinger in. And thanks to Maverick, Bissinger had sat at LeBron's kitchen table. The piece in the *Times* felt like an act of betrayal. Maverick's job was to protect LeBron. It distressed him to think that a writer he had backed would do this to his friend.

Suddenly, Maverick was no longer on speaking terms with Bissinger.

Meanwhile, LeBron was getting hammered by the pundits. "LeBron James was made for the regular season," Skip Bayless said on ESPN2's *1st and 10*. "He's a regular-season dynamo. He's made for our *SportsCenter* plays of the night because he's always number one in the regular season. Postseason time . . . he's the most overrated, overhyped superstar in my history in this business."

Under the NBA rules, Dan Gilbert had the upper hand in terms of how much money he could spend to keep LeBron in Cleveland. The Cavaliers were allowed to offer LeBron up to $126 million over six years. The other teams hoping to sign LeBron were restricted to offering him a five-year contract worth up to $96 million. The system was intended to discourage star players from changing teams. But Gilbert knew it would take more than money to keep LeBron in Cleveland. He also knew that the relationship between LeBron and Coach Mike Brown was dysfunctional. Although Brown was the most successful coach in the team's history, Gilbert decided to make a change. In late May, he fired Brown.

"The expectations of this organization are very high," Gilbert said in an official statement. "And, although change always carries an element of risk, there are times when that risk must be taken to break through to new, higher levels of accomplishment. This is one of those times."

LeBron said nothing about Brown's termination. But his teammates were upset. "If you're going to lay all the blame on Coach Brown and think that's going to solve everything, you've got another thing coming," said Zydrunas Ilgauskas.

"Do I think he deserved it? No," Mo Williams weighed in. "I'm hurt because I like him a lot."

But an influential writer who had Gilbert's ear agreed with the decision.

"Had to happen," wrote *Esquire*'s Scott Raab. "I've never seen a team so openly quit on a coach as the Cavs in Game 6 against the Celtics. . . . It was sad, it was ugly, and it was clearly a fuck-you to Brown from the team—and especially from its leader, LeBron James."

After Gilbert fired Brown, General Manager Danny Ferry resigned.

Meantime, Gilbert was getting antsy. Since the season ended, he hadn't heard boo from LeBron.

The Celtics made it back to the NBA Finals, where they faced the Lakers. During Game 2, Maverick sat courtside next to the Lakers bench, alongside Ari Emanuel and Mark Dowley. Emanuel, the CEO of William Morris Endeavor, was Hollywood's most powerful agent. His clients included Oprah Winfrey, Martin Scorsese, Dwayne Johnson, and Donald Trump. Widely considered the best agent of his generation, Emanuel also had influential political connections. His brother, Rahm Emanuel, was President Obama's chief of staff.

At WME, Emanuel relied on Mark Dowley for strategic input. Dowley was a marketing guru and a senior partner at the agency. Early on, he had attended one of the first marketing summits hosted by LRMR in Akron. Impressed by what Maverick was doing for LeBron, Dowley had

struck up a friendship that eventually turned into a business relationship. While Leon Rose handled LeBron's NBA contracts, WME handled
LeBron's television commercial contracts and other entertainment opportunities.

The fact that Maverick was seated between Emanuel and Dowley at a
Lakers game was a testament to just how far he had come since his days
as an intern at Nike. Now he rubbed shoulders with Hollywood titans.
During halftime of Game 2, Maverick spotted broadcaster Jim Gray approaching. Gray greeted everyone. Then he asked about LeBron.

"Maverick, how's this free agency process going?" Gray asked.

"Good," Maverick said. "There'll be a lot going on, a lot of interest."

After some more chitchat, Gray cut to the chase. "I'd like to do the first
interview with LeBron after he decides where he's going," he said.

"I'll let him know," Maverick replied.

"I did one with him in high school, one when he got drafted, his first
game in Sacramento," Gray said. "I have interviewed him so many times."

"You don't have to explain all that," Maverick told him.

After the game, Maverick and Emanuel had dinner together. And they
ran into Gray again. Still angling to be part of LeBron's announcement,
Gray proposed another idea. "What we should do is a live show," he said.
"Announce his decision right there, on the air."

Intrigued, Maverick had questions.

Gray expounded on his idea. "You produce the show," Gray said. "You
own the show."

"That's a brilliant idea," Emanuel interjected.

"I get to do the interview," Gray continued. "And you have LeBron
make the announcement where he's going to go."

"Maverick," Emanuel said, "you ought to do that."

"Okay," Carter said, looking at Emanuel. "You want to handle it?"

"Yeah. Let's do this."

Gray was giddy.

After talking to Gray, Emanuel and Maverick telephoned Dowley and
shared Gray's pitch. Emanuel wanted Dowley's opinion on how receptive
the networks might be.

"Could we sell this to somebody?" Emanuel asked.

"Yeah, we could," Dowley said, hesitating. "But I think there's a higher-
order thing to do."

"What do you mean?" Maverick asked.

"Look, I think we could sell it to a number of partners," Dowley said. "However, I think we should give all the money away."

"Why?" Emanuel asked.

"Yeah, why?" Carter echoed.

"Because I think we're gonna piss a lot of people off," Dowley said.

Emanuel welcomed Dowley's perspective and wanted him to elaborate.

Conceptually, Dowley loved the idea of giving LeBron his own platform. After all, he was successful enough that he no longer needed to rely on the sports media to make or frame the news. He could make and frame the news himself. He could go to a network like ESPN and set the terms for a one-hour show. But this would be a first. And the traditional media outlets might misinterpret it and even feel threatened by it.

Emanuel was well versed in what Dowley was getting at—anytime you do something revolutionary, and people don't understand it, the easiest thing to do is to criticize it. That had been the story of Emanuel's career.

Dowley just didn't want to see LeBron get criticized.

Neither did Emanuel or Maverick.

The three of them brainstormed ways to blunt the criticism. The best idea they came up with was to add another dimension to the opportunity by donating the sponsorship money to kids who play sports.

Maverick brought up the Boys & Girls Clubs. LeBron was a big supporter. He and Jay-Z did a lot of work for the clubs behind the scenes.

Dowley felt that if they found corporate sponsors, they could easily cover the cost of producing the show and also pass along millions of dollars to the Boys & Girls Clubs.

"That's a good idea," Emanuel said.

Maverick agreed, and he was confident that LeBron would love the concept.

Dowley and Maverick agreed to work out all the details. But it was going to require Emanuel's influence to get ESPN on board. An hour of prime-time programming was a big ask, one that would require sign-off from the network's top executive, John Skipper.

"I'll call Skipper to get the time," Emanuel said.

*   *   *

James Gandolfini and Edie Falco hadn't worked together since they'd filmed the final episode of *The Sopranos* in 2007. But in June 2010, they were reunited to help the New York Knicks land LeBron. Knicks owner James Dolan coveted LeBron. And he'd approved an unorthodox gimmick to recruit him. The idea was to make a short film they were calling *City of Winners* that would feature a cavalcade of New York celebrities pitching LeBron on the virtues of the city.

The Knicks commissioned Rocco Caruso, a little-known independent filmmaker who specialized in eccentric films seen by very few people. Caruso had no interest in celebrity, and he barely knew the difference between a basketball and a baseball. But he did know Edie Falco. They had gone to school together. Although Falco didn't follow LeBron, she agreed to participate, especially when she learned that Gandolfini, a big Knicks fan, had agreed to be in the film.

With Falco and Gandolfini on board, Caruso reached out to Jonathan Hock, an experienced sports documentary filmmaker who had gotten his start with NFL Films. Caruso asked Hock to direct the film. A New York native and lifetime Knicks fan, Hock had watched his team languish into futility under Dolan's leadership. The opportunity to work for the team to create a pitch for LeBron was invigorating. *How often*, Hock thought, *do you get a chance to really do something for your team for real?*

Over a one-week period in June, Hock frantically conducted a slew of documentary-style interviews. Alec Baldwin helicoptered in from the Hamptons to be interviewed at the Garden. Rudy Giuliani and retired Yankees slugger Reggie Jackson did back-to-back interviews one day. Another day, Harvey Weinstein and Robert De Niro were filmed at Miramax's Tribeca offices. Comedian Chris Rock, New York Rangers star Mark Messier, and Knicks legend Walt Frazier all went on camera. Hock even interviewed Donald Trump in his office at Trump Tower. It was the most stressful shoot of the project. After Hock's crew set up the lights and cameras, Trump walked in and impatiently asked, "What are we doing?"

"We're convincing LeBron to come to the Knicks," Hock told him.

"My friend, LeBron," Trump said, taking a seat.

Trump's staff had sent special instructions on how to light him for the interview. The orange gel that was applied to his hair was a certain thickness to ensure that the color accentuated his hair in the proper manner. Otherwise, you'd see through his hair to his head.

While the crew hustled to set things just right, Trump kept looking at his watch. "This is taking too much time," he groused.

When Hock was finally ready, Trump looked into the camera and spoke to LeBron as if they were old buddies. Then, after answering a few questions, he looked at Hock. "This is taking too much time," he said. "I gotta go."

For Hock, the highlight of the project was going to Gandolfini's apartment to shoot a scene with him and Falco. Unlike the other participants, Gandolfini and Falco were going to be in character as Tony and Carmela Soprano. There were three cameras on tripods and a lot more lights. When Gandolfini walked in, he was sporting a big thick beard.

"Whatta you wanna do?" Gandolfini said.

Hock had written a short script. The premise was that Carmela was a New York City real estate agent and Tony wanted her to find a place suitable for his friend LeBron, who was moving to the city.

Gandolfini ran his fingers through his beard while he thought about it for a minute. "Well," he said, "let's do it like I'm in the witness-protection program."

Hock loved the concept—Tony and Carmela would pick up where the last episode of *The Sopranos* ended. They were now living in witness protection in New York City.

Gandolfini and Falco got into character and set the scene—Carmela seated at the kitchen table, looking at real estate listings on her iPad, Tony getting up from the couch and approaching her to look at options.

Carmela: Mansion on Fifth Avenue.
Tony: Not elegant enough.
Carmela (clicks to the next option): Gracie Mansion.
Tony: Not historic enough.

After Tony rejects a couple more options, Carmela swipes to a web page featuring Madison Square Garden.

Tony: That's the place. That's the only place in New York great
    enough for LeBron.

Behind the camera, Hock was mesmerized. "Just to watch them feed off each other," Hock recalled. "Then after Edie called up MSG on the iPad, Gandolfini looked over at the camera and gave this look like 'I know this is a big joke, LeBron. But if you do want to come to New York, it would be pretty cool.' I happened to be behind the camera that he looked into at that moment. I got chills."

Days later, Hock delivered a DVD of the finished film to the Knicks executives at the Garden.

LeBron was incredulous when Maverick pitched the idea of producing a one-hour television program to announce his decision. "We can get five million dollars just for me saying where I'm going to go play?" LeBron asked.

It sounded absurd. But Maverick wasn't exaggerating. He and Mark Dowley had been talking to LeBron's corporate partners and they were all lining up. Maverick pointed out to LeBron that he wouldn't profit from the show. All the proceeds would go to the Boys & Girls Clubs.

LeBron was wrestling with his decision to leave Cleveland. The last thing he wanted to do was get in the weeds about the details of how he was going to announce his plans. He left that to Maverick. But the selling point for him was the idea of donating money from the ESPN show to the Boys & Girls Clubs. Months earlier, LeBron had spent a day with Jay-Z, mentoring children at a Boys & Girls Club in Dallas. It was one of the most enjoyable days he'd had all season. He gave Maverick the green light to go forward.

Meanwhile, Fred Nance informed LeBron that there were more legal problems. Leicester Bryce Stovell, the man who had surfaced in 2008 and claimed he'd had sex with Gloria when she was a teenager, had decided to file a lawsuit. He was claiming that the paternity test he'd taken two years earlier had been tampered with. Stovell was also alleging that various public statements LeBron and Gloria had made about LeBron's absentee father were defamatory to him. Stovell was seeking $4 million.

Nance was confident that Stovell's suit would ultimately be dismissed. But the litigation wouldn't be resolved overnight. And in the meantime, there would be more misinformation about LeBron's family that would make its way into the public square. It was one more thing that LeBron was going to have to deal with.

LeBron was also getting pushback over his decision to announce his plans on ESPN. Although the rest of the media had not yet learned of the idea, NBA commissioner David Stern had caught wind of it and was indignant. Stern wasn't privy to the corporate-sponsorship aspect and the fact that money generated by the show would flow to the Boys & Girls Clubs. He was focused on the league's image, and he was convinced that LeBron's plan was a bad look for the NBA. Stern tried to dissuade LeBron, but that didn't work. So Stern reached out directly to ESPN president John Skipper, urging not to go through with the idea. That didn't work, either. Even though ESPN was the NBA's most important business partner—the network was paying the league $485 million for the rights to broadcast games in the upcoming season—Skipper wouldn't back away from his decision to give LeBron the airtime. Weighing both sides, Skipper thought it was worth doing the show for relationship purposes with Ari, Maverick, and LeBron. The commissioner's inability to stop the show solidified his concern that LeBron had too much power. And that didn't sit well with him.

Unfazed by all that was swirling around him, LeBron stood in a room in a warehouse on the Hudson River in Manhattan, surrounded by a couple dozen people who were applying powder to his skin, touching up his hair, and making sure that his clothes fit just right. It was June 25, and LeBron was doing a photo shoot with *GQ*. Posing for the camera, he paid little attention when the door on the opposite end of the room opened and an inconspicuous man walked in.

Writer J. R. Moehringer hadn't expected to find himself in a warehouse. Nor had he ever been around LeBron. But Moehringer was a master at profiling superstar athletes. A Pulitzer Prize–winning writer who had penned a bestselling memoir titled *The Tender Bar*, Moehringer had been handpicked a few years earlier by Andre Agassi to write the tennis star's autobiography. Titled *Open*, Agassi's collaboration with Moehringer came out on the heels of LeBron's book with Bissinger. But the reception to Agassi's book was vastly different from LeBron's. The *New York Times* called *Open* "one of the most passionately anti-sports books ever written by a superstar athlete—bracingly devoid of triumphalist homily and star-spangled gratitude." Calling Agassi's selection of Moehringer as his collaborator "inspired," the *Times* raved, "The result is not just a first-rate

sports memoir but a genuine bildungsroman, darkly funny yet also an-
guished and soulful."

Open was a number one bestseller, and Moehringer was in demand
to profile other sports stars. *GQ* asked him to profile Kobe Bryant, which
required Moehringer to spend a lot of time with the notoriously private
Lakers star during the 2009–2010 season. Moehringer got Kobe to open
up about his longtime feud with Shaq, his attitude toward pain, and the
geniuses he looked to for inspiration—Leonardo da Vinci and Daniel Day-
Lewis. The piece was so insightful that shortly after it was published, *GQ*
asked Moehringer to shadow LeBron during his decision-making process.

Standing just inside the door and staring at all the stylists and photo
assistants fawning over LeBron, Moehringer thought of a line from
nineteenth-century journalist Margaret Fuller: "For precocity some great
price is always demanded sooner or later in life." Suddenly, Moehringer's
train of thought was interrupted by a man coming toward him.

LeBron's publicist, Keith Estabrook, told him that the shoot was running late and encouraged him to come back in a little while.

Moehringer stepped out and got a cup of coffee. While waiting, he
pulled out *Shooting Stars*, which he'd been reading in preparation for the
interview. He'd quickly noticed that the book sidestepped what Moehringer figured were the more traumatic parts of LeBron's childhood. Methodical in his preparation, Moehringer had reached out to Bissinger and
asked him about LeBron's relationship with his mother. "He's utterly, totally devoted to her," Bissinger told Moehringer.

LeBron didn't know Moehringer. But after his experience with
Bissinger, LeBron wasn't eager to talk to another writer. He was tired of
having other people trying to tell his story. It didn't occur to LeBron that
writers, especially the uber-talented ones—Wahl, Taddeo, Bissinger, and
now Moehringer—were part of his story. Nor did he fully appreciate that
they were gifted creators and that with a little recognition on his part, he
could have inspired them to portray him in a more textured and thoughtful
way. But LeBron's attitude toward writers had been colored by bad experiences with *ESPN The Magazine* and other publications earlier in his life.
As a result, he didn't seem to value writers, never mind see them as allies.

Wearing a sleeveless shirt and a pair of sunglasses, LeBron entered the
room where Moehringer was waiting and took a seat. When Moehringer
asked if he was stressed about his upcoming decision, LeBron insisted

that his mindset was quite the opposite. "It's a very exciting time for me," he said.

The reality was that LeBron was under enormous pressure. Ohio was his home. He'd never lived elsewhere. His family was settled there. His inner circle was there. Yet LeBron desperately wanted to win championships, and he'd concluded that he needed to go elsewhere and play with other stars for that to happen. "My emotions won't be involved and will not affect what my decision will ultimately be," LeBron told Moehringer.

Moehringer wondered if any of his heavyweight friends, such as Warren Buffett, had weighed in with advice on which team to choose.

LeBron said that none of his friends were weighing in.

Moehringer was skeptical but moved on. He brought up the comment LeBron had made during the Celtics series: "I spoil a lot of people with my play." It was an opportunity for LeBron to provide context for what was interpreted as a self-absorbed remark.

But LeBron doubled down. "I love our fans," he said. "Cleveland fans are awesome. But I mean, even my family gets spoiled at times watching me doing things that I do, on and off the court."

Insisting that he didn't understand spoiled people, LeBron added that his upbringing had conditioned him to keep quiet about disappointment. "That's what keeps me humble, because I know my background, know what my mother went through," he said. "I never get too high on my stardom or what I can do. My mom always says, and my friends say, 'You're just a very low-maintenance guy.'"

Intrigued by the phrase *low-maintenance*, Moehringer brought up Kobe, who traveled to and from home games via private helicopter.

At the mention of Kobe, LeBron lowered his sunglasses and flashed an expression that Moehringer interpreted as: *No one is less low maintenance than Kobe.* Without saying a word, LeBron raised his glasses back over his eyes.

Moehringer had observed that the greatest athletes were fueled by anger. Jordan was notorious for playing with fury. Tom Brady played with an enormous chip on his shoulder after he was skipped over in the NFL Draft. Kobe, Moehringer pointed out, resented Shaq and then resented everyone else after his situation in Colorado. Perhaps LeBron wasn't angry enough.

"Are you a sports psychologist?" LeBron said.

Moehringer reminded LeBron that he had previously acknowledged that he might not possess Kobe's killer instinct. "That still true?" Moehringer asked.

"I hope not," LeBron said. "I don't think so. I think I've gotten to a point now in my career where I do feel like I have a killer instinct."

Moehringer shared his theory: in sports, anger equals success.

"That's an awesome theory," LeBron said.

Sizing up LeBron, Moehringer thought: *He sounds like a big kid.*

Eventually, they got around to talking about Gloria.

"She doesn't hold her tongue," LeBron told him. "If she sees something that she believes isn't right or is right, she's going to speak about it." LeBron said he had recently begged her not to get a tattoo. She'd done it anyway.

"What does it say?" Moehringer asked.

"Queen James," he said.

Keith Estabrook stepped in—time was up.

They agreed to a second interview in Akron during the first week of July.

Besides the Cavaliers, five teams were competing for LeBron's services—the Brooklyn Nets, New York Knicks, Miami Heat, Chicago Bulls, and Los Angeles Clippers. Representatives from each team were scheduled to make pitches to LeBron as soon as the free agency period started on July 1. That day, executives from the Nets and Knicks traveled to Cleveland. At 11:00 a.m., Jay-Z led a contingency of Nets executives into a downtown office building. In an eighth-floor conference room, he introduced them to LeBron.

LeBron knew Nets head coach Avery Johnson and Nets president Rod Thorn, considered one of the smartest executives in the league. But LeBron was intrigued to meet the Nets' owner, Mikhail Prokhorov, a Russian billionaire who stood at six eight. Flanked by his agent, Leon Rose, and Maverick, LeBron listened with interest as Prokhorov outlined his vision of the team's bright future, highlighted by the new arena being built in Brooklyn. Prokhorov also appealed to LeBron's vanity, making it clear that he wanted to help him become a billionaire athlete with broader global appeal.

Jay-Z pitched LeBron, too. But he didn't push. They were close friends. And the friendship wasn't going to rise or fall based on LeBron's decision.

LeBron knew how Jay-Z felt. And as much as he considered Jay-Z a brother, he'd already resolved that he wasn't going to let that influence his decision-making process.

After two hours, the Nets executives exited, and the Knicks delegation entered. Owner James Dolan had brought along team president Donnie Walsh; head coach Mike D'Antoni; the president of Madison Square Garden Sports, Scott O'Neil; and former-Knicks-star-turned-executive Allan Houston.

The Knicks also tried to sell LeBron on the idea that he could earn $1 billion in combined salary and endorsements if he joined the team. The organization had gone as far as to commission a study by a consulting firm to demonstrate that LeBron's earning power would be greatest in New York.

LeBron loved playing in the Garden. He loved New York City. But he wasn't impressed with James Dolan. Ever since Dolan had taken over the Knicks, the team had been a virtual disaster. His presence was a deterrent in LeBron's mind.

But LeBron didn't let on that he was leery. Neither did Rose nor Maverick.

At one point, the Knicks delegation showed LeBron the video.

LeBron was amused. He wasn't interested in guys like Trump—*a phony*—and Weinstein—*bad vibes*. He loved seeing De Niro—*Vito Corleone!* But LeBron got the biggest kick out of Gandolfini—*Tony fucking Soprano was making him an offer he couldn't refuse.*

When the video ended and the smiles receded, LeBron hit the Knicks with a question: How were they going to fit him and two other stars under the salary cap?

The Knicks did not have a satisfactory answer.

While LeBron was in a room with the Knicks brass, Dwyane Wade and Chris Bosh were in Chicago, meeting separately with prospective teams. But Wade's and Bosh's free agency meetings weren't drawing the attention of the basketball world. LeBron was what the *New York Times* described as "a 25-year-old prince of the planet," and all eyes were on him. When he emerged from the office building with Maverick and Leon Rose late that afternoon, a gauntlet of cameramen and reporters were on the street. And Cavaliers fans lined the sidewalk, holding signs that pleaded with him to stay in Cleveland. His eyes hidden behind dark shades, LeBron stared straight ahead, showing no emotion.

That night, LeBron sat alone in his home, watching a password-protected video presentation on his iPad. Sent to him by the Miami Heat, it was a prelude to the next day's meeting. And it was very different from the celebrity sales pitch from the Knicks. The Heat video was more like something put together by a Wall Street firm. It had numbers, statistics, charts, and graphs. As if prepping for an exam, LeBron watched it enough times to memorize it.

While LeBron studied, Leon Rose met privately with Miami Heat president Pat Riley. Rose knew that LeBron, Dwyane Wade, and Chris Bosh had been talking for months about playing together. It was an idea that had really taken hold during the Beijing Olympics. And it picked up steam during the 2009–2010 season. Riley felt this gave him an advantage. The Heat was one of the only teams in the running for LeBron that had ample cap space to sign him and Wade and Bosh. The key was convincing LeBron, which was why Riley wanted to grease the wheels with Rose before making his pitch.

Riley knew he was coming behind the Knicks. But he was the antithesis of James Dolan. For starters, Riley knew basketball and he knew what the great players wanted more than anything—championships. Riley had been plotting to get LeBron in a Heat uniform for years. And he was confident that money wasn't going to be the deciding factor. Nor would location matter. LeBron, Riley figured, would move to the Black Hills of South Dakota if that was what it took to win an NBA championship. But Riley did have the benefit of offering South Beach.

It was 11:00 a.m. on July 2 when LeBron returned to the eighth-floor conference room in the IGM building and took a seat on one side of a large conference table. He faced Heat owner Micky Arison, Head Coach Erik Spoelstra, General Manager Andy Elisburg, vice president of Basketball Operations Nick Arison, and former Heat star Alonzo Mourning. They all sat. But Riley stood and rested his hands on the back of his chair and looked at LeBron. "We want you to understand that we are going to make sure the main thing remains the main thing," he said.

LeBron stared at him. "The main thing is to make sure the main thing remains the main thing?"

Maverick smiled. He recognized the reference from Stephen R. Covey's bestselling book *First Things First*.

"It's the beginning of the book," Riley told LeBron.

LeBron nodded.

"Now, the main thing with us," Riley said, looking to the men flanking him, "is winning championships."

LeBron locked onto Riley's eyes as if they were the only two people in the room.

"We think you and Chris and Dwyane can do something really special," he said.

Then Arison and Spoelstra talked about long-term goals for the team, and they made a brief video presentation. When it concluded, Riley reached into his briefcase, removed a small mesh bag, and placed it on the table.

"What's in there?" LeBron said.

Riley pushed the bag across the table.

LeBron opened it and rings spilled out. He picked one up. "What are these rings?" he asked.

Riley explained they were a collection of his all-star rings, championship rings, and Hall of Fame ring. Over his career as a player and a coach, he had amassed six titles with the Lakers and one with the Heat. Every championship team he'd been a part of, he explained, included one star and two superstars.

LeBron understood what Riley was implying—he and D-Wade were superstars, Bosh was a star, and in Miami the three of them could play for an organization that was helmed by someone who had won seven championships.

"It's essential," Riley said. "You're not going to win a championship just bringing in guys. Cleveland has tried to do everything for you. But they just could not break loose with the players they needed to win a championship."

To LeBron, Riley stood out from everyone else he had met with. He knew what it took to win championships. He had the jewelry to prove it. And he'd done his homework in terms of how to make room for the salaries to accommodate LeBron, Bosh, and Wade. Without a doubt, Miami was the clearest path to a championship.

The meeting went on for three hours. By the end, Riley was confident that he had landed LeBron. But he was also fully aware that if LeBron left Cleveland for Miami, the news was going to hit the NBA like a bomb. He hoped LeBron and his team were ready for the fallout, and he wondered if they had any fear.

"Afraid?" Maverick said. "Us?"

"Shit's going to hit the fan, man," Riley said.

The only thing Mark Dowley hadn't figured out was where to stage Le-Bron's ESPN show. With less than a week to go before decision day, Dowley finally proposed his hometown—Greenwich, Connecticut. It was near a regional airport. His home could serve as a staging area. And there was a Boys & Girls Club in town.

Maverick went along with the idea.

So, on July 4, Dowley telephoned the president of the Boys & Girls Club and started making the arrangements. Time and secrecy were of the essence. They had four days to set everything up. In the meantime, Dowley didn't want the press to catch wind of the plan.

While Dowley was on the phone with local officials in Greenwich, LeBron mulled over his options. After the final round of meetings with the Bulls and Cavaliers, he knew what he wanted to do. That afternoon, he texted Wade: *Hey, can you get on a call in the next hour?*

Cool, Wade replied.

Wade reached out to Bosh.

Now that the three of them had met with their potential suitors, the dream of playing together seemed to finally be within reach.

Wade looped in LeBron and Bosh for a three-way call. LeBron led the conversation.

"Miami's got the cap space if all three of us are willing to go," LeBron said.

Wade loved what he was hearing. Miami had been his home for his entire career. The prospect of his two friends' joining him there was the ideal scenario in his mind.

"You in?" Wade said.

"I'm in," LeBron said.

"I'm in," Wade said.

"I'm in," Bosh said.

It was decided.

LeBron didn't mention his plans to announce his decision on ESPN.

* * *

On July 6, J. R. Moehringer entered the basketball arena at the University of Akron. Keith Estabrook intercepted him in the lobby and informed him that his interview with LeBron would occur in the gym while LeBron watched a scrimmage between NBA players and blue-chip high school recruits.

Interviewing LeBron in a loud gym while he watches a game? Moehringer couldn't think of a worse location. No wonder LeBron had little appreciation for writers. His publicist didn't seem to understand a writer's vocation, either.

Moehringer and Estabrook spent the next few minutes walking around the arena, looking for a more suitable space. When they ducked into a quiet room with air-conditioning, Moehringer said it was perfect. Estabrook said it wouldn't work for LeBron, who he said wouldn't like being in a strange room with a stranger. Instead, Estabrook led Moehringer to the locker room. It smelled like a giant sweaty jockstrap. But Estabrook said LeBron would be comfortable there. Plus, the room had a television, which would enable LeBron to watch the World Cup during the interview. Moehringer couldn't help thinking of Napoleon, who had agreed to a portrait but refused to sit still for the painter.

Before leaving the locker room, Estabrook lowered his voice and told Moehringer to ask LeBron about Chicago. And New York. And Miami.

Confused, Moehringer turned the tables and said he had a feeling that LeBron was heading to the Knicks.

Estabrook's eyes widened. Offering no clarity on which team LeBron was joining, he nonetheless assured Moehringer of one thing—the Dwyane Wade–Chris Bosh thing that was being talked about in the media wasn't going to happen.

Moehringer didn't know what to believe. The *New York Times* was reporting that Michael Jordan's former consigliere, William "Worldwide Wes" Wesley, was trying to broker a deal that would pair LeBron with New Orleans Hornets all-star point guard Chris Paul. It was well known that LeBron and Paul were tight. It was also rumored that Wesley, who had some history with LeBron, would play a significant role in his decision-making process. Irritated, Maverick called the *Times* and told a reporter: "All the Wes rumors are untrue and he will not be at the meetings. Wes has nothing to do with where he goes."

While Moehringer waited, LeBron was in the gym, playing a pickup game with Chris Paul. Dwyane Wade, meanwhile, was down in Miami, texting LeBron. But LeBron wasn't responding. Anxious about LeBron's radio silence, Wade texted Bosh: *CB, you talk to Bron?*

Nah, I ain't talked to him, Bosh responded.

It had been two days since the three of them had agreed to join forces in Miami. Wade and Bosh were starting to wonder if LeBron was having second thoughts.

When LeBron finally entered the locker room, he sank into a leather couch and started looking at his BlackBerry. He had lots of texts, including some from Wade.

Moehringer thanked him for making time for the interview.

LeBron said nothing.

Moehringer asked him how the free agency process was going.

"Tiring," LeBron said, his attention shifting to the TV and a World Cup soccer match.

After some more questions and answers that yielded little insight, Moehringer was about to ask the most sensitive one on his list—*Do you ever think about your father?* But right before he posed it, LeBron's sons, three and five, charged into the room and piled onto the couch with him.

Happy to see them, LeBron encouraged them to be quiet during the interview. The boys weren't having it. "Stay and be quiet," he told them. "Or go outside and be loud. Which is it?"

"Loud," Bronny said.

"All right, go," LeBron said.

As they dashed out, Moehringer saw an opening. He asked if being a father made LeBron think about his father.

"No," LeBron said flatly, his eyes back on the soccer game.

Moehringer was pretty good at detecting bullshit. And he was pretty sure that LeBron was bullshitting him. Bissinger had told Moehringer that when LeBron was asked a sensitive question—especially ones about his mother or anything to do with his father—his voice changed to a hollow sound. Bissinger had referred to it as "a flat affect," which was exactly what Moehringer was hearing.

But Moehringer didn't know that LeBron and his mother had just been sued by a man who was claiming to be LeBron's father and who was insisting that LeBron and Gloria had defamed him by saying derogatory things about LeBron's absentee father to the media over the years. So far, the lawsuit was under wraps. And LeBron wasn't about to bring it up.

"I'm not downgrading my father or blasting him," he told Moehringer. "Because I don't know what he may have been going through at the time. I'm not one of those to judge without knowing. I was too young to understand."

LeBron kept his focus on the television. But he kept talking about his father. "Without him, first of all, I wouldn't be here in this world," he said. "And then, secondly, I may have got a lot of genes from him, and that's part of the reason why I am who I am today. . . . I mean, it's not all anger. It's not all anger at all."

On the brink of the most monumental decision of his career, LeBron was thinking a lot about a man he'd never met. Over the years, LeBron had worked hard to present a strong public persona about growing up fatherless. But just beneath the surface there was a lot of vulnerability. Moehringer had gotten to the place that Bissinger hadn't been able to access.

"Would you like to meet your father?" Moehringer asked.

"No," LeBron said.

"Really?"

"Right now?" LeBron asked. "At twenty-five? No."

"Maybe later?"

LeBron was ready to end the questions. "Maybe," he said. "Yeah."

A few minutes later, Estabrook came back to say time was up.

Relieved, LeBron headed back to the gym.

While Moehringer was interviewing LeBron, the news broke that LeBron would announce his decision on July 8 on ESPN. Suddenly, Dwyane Wade and Chris Bosh were on the phone with each other. "What the fuck is going on?" Wade asked. Bosh was wondering the same thing. Maybe, they feared, LeBron had changed his mind.

Moehringer was unaware that the news of the ESPN show had already leaked when Estabrook approached him a little while after the interview and discreetly told him that LeBron was going to make an announcement in two days. When Moehringer said he'd like to be there when it happened, Estabrook looked around the gym to make sure no one was close enough to hear him. Then he whispered, "Fly to New York." Moehringer pressed for details. Estabrook told him to call when he landed. He'd get more instructions at that point.

That afternoon, after Moehringer took off, LeBron activated his Twitter account and tweeted for the first time: "Hello World, the Real King James is in the building 'Finally.' My Brother @oneandonlycrp3 [Chris Paul] gas'd me up to jump on board so I'm here. Haaaa."

By that evening, LeBron had ninety thousand followers.

On the morning of July 7, LeBron attended his basketball camp at the University of Akron. One of the attendees was a high school student who had taken a bus all the way from Chicago. LeBron shook his hand, and the high schooler introduced himself: Anthony Davis.

While LeBron played a pickup game with Davis, the share price of the New York Knicks' parent company fell amid published reports suggesting that LeBron was likely spurning the Knicks for the Heat. Then, during the noon hour, Dwyane Wade and Chris Bosh appeared on ESPN's *SportsCenter*. In a live interview with Michael Wilbon, Wade confirmed that he was re-signing with the Heat, and Bosh confirmed that he was joining Wade in Miami.

"Dwyane," Wilbon said, "reports about you guys talking with LeBron already, saying, 'C'mon down here and join us.' Where do those discussions stand now? And do you think you're going to have him?"

No longer certain, Wade smiled. "It's no secret that myself and Chris and LeBron are all good friends," he began. "Of course we would love for LeBron to join Miami. . . . But LeBron's going to make his own decision. And that's a decision we will all be in front of the TV tomorrow to wait for."

Wade and Bosh had barely finished announcing their intentions when President Obama's press secretary, Robert Gibbs, stepped to the lectern to deliver the White House daily briefing. The main topic was the BP oil spill in the Gulf of Mexico. At one point, a reporter raised his hand.

Reporter: I have an issue of transcendent importance. Where does the president think LeBron James should play basketball?

Gibbs: We were talking about this earlier today. After the apparent news of Miami acquiring Chris Bosh, I think the president still believes he would look quite good in a Bulls uniform. I hope that does not lead to NBA tampering charges.

Another reporter: In all seriousness, are you concerned that that might annoy people in Cleveland?

Gibbs: I'm sure it will.

Laughter filled the room.

Gibbs: I think the people in Cleveland . . . We all have seen . . .

While Gibbs tried to remind everyone that the president was a Bulls fan, the press persisted.

Reporter: A somewhat serious follow-up. People in Cleveland did take it sort . . . They are very sensitive when it comes to these things—the president rooting against them. And they never catch a break. Sure, he roots for the Bulls. But this might actually really bother people.

Gibbs: Again, I'm sure it will.

The fact that the White House had weighed in on LeBron's decision showed just how out of hand the situation had gotten. Meanwhile, the backlash to ESPN's plan to give LeBron an hour in prime time was mounting online and on social media. "An hour show?" one prominent sports commentator blogged. "WTF?"

ESPN was taking hits, too. "ESPN insists it hasn't handed over the network keys to LeBron," tweeted *New York Times* writer Don Van Natta Jr. "He just picks the time slot, the interviewer and gets all the ad $ for his charity."

LeBron went to the gym on the morning of July 8. Then he met up with Maverick and Rich Paul. It was decision day. The three of them were about to uproot themselves and leave Ohio. Maverick had worked with Ari Emanuel, Mark Dowley, and ESPN on every detail of LeBron's announcement. Rich had worked with Leon Rose on LeBron's meetings with the various suitors and the negotiations with Pat Riley and the Heat. And LeBron had positioned himself to be the most sought-after player in the history of the NBA.

Riding high, the three of them were joined by Savannah and boarded a private jet that was headed for Greenwich. It was time to shock the world.

TWENTY-EIGHT

"HESTER PRYNNE IN A HEADBAND"

Fans in NBA cities across America huddled around television screens in homes and in sports bars. As eager as everyone else to find out where LeBron was going, Dwyane Wade hosted a watch party down in Miami. "I don't know what the hell is about to go on," Wade told a friend. "I wasn't this nervous at the draft." But Wade told himself that no matter what LeBron decided, he and Bosh were going to be strong in Miami.

Suddenly, Wade saw LeBron appear on-screen, sitting opposite Jim Gray on a stage that had been erected in the center of the gymnasium at the Boys & Girls Club. LeBron looked out of sorts. And it felt like forever before Gray finally asked, "LeBron, what's your decision?"

Wade was on edge as LeBron hemmed and hawed.

"Um, this fall I'm going to take my talents to South Beach and join the Miami Heat," he finally said.

Cheers erupted at Wade's party in Miami. "Oh, man!" Wade told his guests. "It's showtime."

The kids in the gymnasium groaned.

The crowd outside the Boys & Girls Club started booing.

In Cleveland, scorned fans took to the streets.

On social media, LeBron was getting lampooned.

Pat Riley's warning—*Shit's gonna hit the fan*—was already happening.

J. R. Moehringer, who had come to Greenwich to chronicle the evening, couldn't believe what he was witnessing. *There were so many other, better ways to do this*, he thought. Blaming the people closest to LeBron, Moehringer hustled out of the gym, tracked down publicist Keith Estabrook, and asked him why they had staged *The Decision* in Greenwich.

"Neutral location," he said.

Moehringer pointed out that they were in deep Knicks country. Most of the kids in the gym and practically everyone outside wanted him to play for the Knicks. Greenwich was hardly a neutral site.

Estabrook shrugged.

Afterward, LeBron and his team hung out in Greenwich with Kanye West, listening to tracks from his forthcoming album, *My Beautiful Dark Twisted Fantasy*. Meanwhile, the situation in Cleveland escalated. Fans set fire to LeBron's jersey. The police made arrests. And Dan Gilbert fanned the flames by posting a caustic letter to Cleveland sports fans on the Cavaliers' website. Ripping LeBron for being "cowardly" and "narcissistic," Gilbert personally guaranteed that the Cavaliers would win an NBA championship before LeBron won one. "The good news is that this heartless and callous action can only serve as the antidote to the so-called 'curse' on Cleveland, Ohio," Gilbert wrote. "The self-declared former 'King' will be taking the 'curse' with him down south. And until he does 'right' by Cleveland and Ohio, James (and the town where he plays) will unfortunately own this dreaded spell and bad karma."

Gilbert didn't stop there. Later that night, he talked to an Associated Press reporter and got even more personal in his criticism of LeBron. "He has gotten a free pass," Gilbert told the AP. "People have covered up for him for way too long. Tonight, we saw who he really is."

Gilbert owned the Cavaliers. But he was acting as if he owned LeBron. And now that LeBron had chosen to walk away from the Cavaliers, Gilbert had no reservations about saying the one thing that would cut LeBron to the bone. "He quit," Gilbert told the AP. "Not just in Game 5, but in Game 2, 4, and 6. Watch the tape. The Boston series was unlike anything in the history of sports for a superstar."

Gilbert's attack on LeBron was so pointed and so public that even the rival Celtics were shocked. "When Dan Gilbert did that," said Danny Ainge, "I'll never forget thinking, 'Why would you do that?'" In professional sports, players come and go. Coaches come and go. It's the nature of the business. When a player moves on via free agency, the prudent course is for his previous team to be gracious and thank him for giving his all to a franchise. "It's not about who's better, or who's right, or who's wrong," Ainge said. "It's about staying positive. Because you just never know what could possibly happen down the road."

In the heat of the moment, Gilbert wasn't looking down the road. He was busy burning down every bridge that connected LeBron to Cleveland. "It's not about him leaving," Gilbert told the AP. "It's the disrespect. It's time for people to hold these athletes accountable for their actions. Is this the way you raise your children? I've been holding this all in for a long time."

LeBron was conditioned to project a tough exterior. But beneath the surface, he was sensitive. Especially when it came to how he was perceived. Gilbert had attacked LeBron where he was emotionally vulnerable.

As far as Gloria was concerned, Gilbert had drawn blood with his cutting remarks, and she was ready to go to war with anyone who attacked her son's work ethic and integrity.

Savannah was upset, too. Everyone in LeBron's camp was. But on the flight to Florida later that night, they were too shell-shocked by the overall scope of the animosity toward LeBron from fans and the media to say anything.

After landing in Miami in the predawn hours and being greeted by Pat Riley on the tarmac, LeBron and Savannah got a few hours' sleep at the W Hotel. By the time LeBron woke up later that morning, his reputation was in meltdown. Sportswriters, pundits, bloggers, and news anchors were hammering him. Fans from every city other than Miami were tearing into him on Twitter. It was hard to find anyone other than Heat fans who had anything good to say about him. Just about everyone with a platform was following the herd mentality in the media. And ESPN's Bill Simmons was among those leading the charge. Years earlier, after pitcher Roger Clemens had left the Boston Red Sox to sign with the Toronto Blue Jays, Simmons, a die-hard Red Sox fan, had written a column titled "Is Clemens the Antichrist?" The morning after LeBron announced he was going to Miami, Simmons referred to his column about Clemens. "I hated that guy as much as you could hate a professional athlete without things getting creepy," Simmons said. "And you know what? What LeBron did to Cleveland last night was worse. Much worse."

It would have been easy to dismiss Simmons's Antichrist reference as hyperbole. But Simmons had a huge following. And like Dan Gilbert, he made his criticism of LeBron personal. "I blame the people around him," Simmons said. "I blame the lack of a father figure in his life."

Rich Paul had never cared for Simmons, and he wasn't surprised by the tone of Simmons's criticism of LeBron. Simmons had a history with

LeBron. It had started all the way back at the 2003 NBA Draft, when sportscaster Mike Tirico had said on the air, "There [LeBron] is with his mom, Gloria. Gloria sacrificed a lot. Gave birth to LeBron when she was sixteen. . . . On their own at nineteen, living on assistance, food stamps, and now here they are. . . . It's a great American story." In response, Simmons wrote: "What about parents who stayed together, worked hard, provided for their children and put them through school? Since when did not practicing birth control and lucking out because of DNA become a 'sacrifice'?"

As far as Rich was concerned, Simmons was showing his true colors. "A lot of that has to do with race," Paul said about Simmons. "He wouldn't have said that about Larry Bird."

While the rest of the basketball world was criticizing him, LeBron headed to his new place of employment—the American Airlines Arena, home of the Miami Heat—to sign his contract. When he arrived, LeBron was told that the team was throwing a big party that night for the fans. And LeBron, Wade, and Bosh were headlining it. *What?* LeBron had had no idea anything was planned. He was exhausted. It had been less than twenty-four hours since he'd sat with Jim Gray in the Boys & Girls Club in Greenwich. And he was getting pilloried.

Nonetheless, he agreed to participate.

Outside, thousands of fans were chanting: "Let's go Heat! Let's go Heat!" Inside, every seat in the arena was occupied. The floor was packed with fans, too. Pat Riley, in a black suit, black tie, and white shirt, sat with owner Micky Arison in seats not far from the stage that had been erected at one end of the arena. Television stations in Miami were covering the event live, as was ESPN. "Miami's new dream team—LeBron, Dwyane, and Chris—hitting the stage in a *big* way tonight, and fans are going crazy," one of the network affiliates reported from outside the arena.

Wearing a white headband and a fresh new Heat uniform with the number 6, LeBron stood next to Wade and Bosh, listening as one of the rally coordinators gave them instructions. "I'm gonna bring you into the back of the stage," the man told them. "I'm gonna load the three of you on the lift." Moments later, LeBron, Wade, and Bosh rose through an opening in the stage. Laser lights flashed. Flames shot into the air and smoke enveloped the stage. Like rock stars, LeBron, Wade, and Bosh turned, faced the crowd, and strutted off the platform while music fit for a Marvel movie blared and thousands of fans screamed deliriously.

Introduced as "the three kings," they took a seat on high-backed chairs and addressed the crowd. "This surpasses a dream come true," Wade began. "To have an opportunity to team up with arguably the best trio to ever play the game of basketball is amazing."

It was a big statement considering that LeBron and Bosh had never won a championship and Wade had won one. But LeBron got even more carried away than Wade when he started predicting how many championships they were going to win together. "Not two, not three, not four, not five," LeBron told the crowd. Wade and Bosh laughed hysterically, and the crowd roared. LeBron kept going. "Not six, not seven."

The more LeBron boasted, the more he revved up the fans. And the harder Wade and Bosh laughed. "And when I say that," LeBron continued, "I really believe it. I'm not just up here blowing smoke at none of these fans, because that's not what I'm about. I'm about business. And we believe we can win multiple championships if we take care of business and do it the right way."

Riley was the one person who wasn't smiling when LeBron was making predictions. This was the risk of putting players onstage without a script and without time to rehearse. Staring sternly at the stage, his hands clasped beneath his chin, Riley had been around long enough to know that the Heat still had a long, hard road in front of them. Every team in the league would be gunning for them. And LeBron's words were giving opponents even more motivation to beat the Heat.

The rally in Miami further amped up the criticism on LeBron, which quickly spread well beyond the sports pages. Every news outlet, from CNN to the nightly news broadcasts on the major networks, was weighing in on LeBron's decision. Even *New York Times* political columnist Maureen Dowd criticized LeBron. In a column titled "Miami's Hoops Cartel," Dowd ripped LeBron's "narcissistic announcement." Quoting LeBron's own words—"'I wanted to do what was best, you know, for LeBron James'"—Dowd wrote, "It's always a bad sign when people begin talking about themselves in the third person. He seems to have no idea of the public relations damage he has inflicted on himself."

LeBron didn't care that much about what the pundits said. But he cared deeply about how he was viewed by NBA legends. And in the immediate aftermath of his decision, sportswriters had latched on to some off-the-cuff remarks by Michael Jordan. After playing in a celebrity golf tournament in Nevada, Jordan was asked about LeBron's joining forces with Wade and Bosh. "There's no way, with hindsight, I would've ever called up Larry [Bird], called up Magic Johnson and said, 'Hey, look, let's get together and play on one team,'" Jordan said. "In all honesty, I was trying to beat those guys." The fact was that Jordan did have a future Hall of Fame teammate in Scottie Pippen, not to mention several other bona fide stars on the Bulls roster, to help him beat his rivals. Moreover, LeBron's chief rivals were Paul Pierce and Kobe Bryant, and he wasn't calling them up to say, "Let's get together." Rather, he had called two of his close friends and Olympic teammates to assemble a team that could compete with the Celtics' star-laden team that Danny Ainge had assembled and the Kobe Bryant–Coach Phil Jackson juggernaut that had won five championships in Los Angeles.

Nonetheless, TNT's Charles Barkley, a friend of Jordan's, took a public swipe at LeBron. "He'll never be Jordan," Barkley said days after LeBron made his decision. "This clearly takes him out of the conversation. . . . There would have been something honorable about staying in Cleveland and trying to win it as 'The Man.'"

LeBron noted Barkley's comments. He also noted that Barkley had spent his entire career being the Man on teams—in Philadelphia, Phoenix, and Houston—that never won a championship.

Commissioner David Stern didn't mind debates between NBA legends. But he hated PR gaffes that hurt the league's brand. And as far as Stern was concerned, *The Decision* was a royal blunder born of hubris. He placed most of the blame on LeBron's team. "It was terrible," Stern said. "It is fair to say that we knew it was going to be terrible, and we tried very hard for it not to happen." Stern added, "The advice that he received on this was poor." From Stern's perspective, the over-the-top televised announcement had brought out the worst in some fans and triggered some unseemly behavior from individuals who should have known better. Stern couldn't do much about fans who set fire to jerseys. But he publicly reprimanded Dan Gilbert and fined the Cavaliers organization for Gilbert's letter and his remarks to the AP. Stern also took issue with the Reverend Jesse Jackson, who had held a press conference to publicly condemn Gilbert. "His feelings of betrayal personify a slave master mentality," Jackson had said. "He sees LeBron as a runaway slave."

Stern felt the slave reference was over the top.

* * *

Five days after predicting he and his new teammates would win seven championships in Miami, LeBron rolled out of bed at his mansion outside Akron and went to St. V to work out at the gym. Feeling as though the whole world was against him, he was glad to be back in familiar territory with friends and family. Deep down, he was already wondering, *What would it be like to come back and play for the Cavaliers again?*

After finishing his workout, LeBron talked to J. R. Moehringer on the phone. In their last conversation before he would file his story, Moehringer brought up Gilbert's letter. LeBron acknowledged that he'd read it. "Me and my family have seen the character of that man," LeBron told him. "[The letter] made me feel more comfortable that I made the right decision."

Moehringer knew that LeBron had built his dream home in Ohio. He wondered aloud whether LeBron could continue to live there now that he was a member of the Heat.

"I'm in Akron as we speak," LeBron said. "I'm at home. I'm going to spend a lot of the summer here."

Moehringer was surprised.

"This is my home," LeBron continued. "Akron, Ohio, is my home. I will always be here. I'm still working out at my old high school."

Listening to LeBron, Moehringer thought of an observation that Bissinger had shared shortly after watching LeBron onstage with Wade and Bosh during the rally in Miami. "When I saw the look on his face sitting there with Wade and Bosh, for all the anger everyone else has, it was clear LeBron had died and gone to heaven," Bissinger said. "Pop psychology is always dangerous, but he really is replicating his high school experience."

Bissinger's conclusion was consistent with something Moehringer had felt—that high school might have been the only time in LeBron's life when he'd felt completely safe, and that maybe his desire to rekindle that time period had factored into his decision to go play with Wade and Bosh.

With any star of LeBron's magnitude, it was difficult to distinguish the truth from the rumors and the mythology. But in LeBron's case, he was forthcoming about the fact that he didn't like to be alone. Yet he was very particular about who he surrounded himself with. As far back as middle school, he had curated the group around him, choosing his friends carefully and recruiting specific players, such as Romeo Travis, to transfer to St. V. He had done the same thing when he'd formed his inner circle, recruiting Rich and Randy to work with him and Maverick.

Despite the need for companionship, LeBron wasn't an anybody-will-do kind of guy. People had to pass his test. And now, after several years of playing together on Team USA and getting to know each other, LeBron had chosen Wade and Bosh as the players he wanted to win championships with.

After getting to know Kobe—a loner who kept his teammates at a distance—Moehringer admired the loyalty that LeBron showed his friends. Moehringer also felt that LeBron's team had done him no favors. In his *GQ* piece, "Three Weeks in Crazyville," which ran in August, Moehringer referred to the PR aspect of LeBron's announcement as a foreseeable "train wreck." "You could actually see the cow wander onto the tracks, hear the brakes screeching, feel the cars decoupling and the caboose go flying," he wrote. "His handlers were said to be trying to build his brand. He's branded all right. He's Hester Prynne in a headband."

Seeing his best friend compared to the fictional character in Nathaniel Hawthorne's *The Scarlet Letter* stung Maverick. As the one who had championed the idea to announce LeBron's decision on ESPN, Maverick felt responsible for the hit to LeBron's reputation. *I have really ruined something for my best friend and my business partner*, he told himself.

Maverick viewed criticism as a sign of failure. And in the aftermath of *The Decision*, his confidence was shaken. Normally, he was a goal-oriented overachiever. He was addicted to the sense of accomplishing things and moving up the ladder. Now it dawned on him, *Holy shit! This is really going to derail me and prevent me from checking a lot of the boxes I want to check off in my life.* Suddenly, he felt his goals were in jeopardy.

No NBA player wanted to knock LeBron's headband off more than Paul Pierce. When Pierce found out that LeBron had joined Wade and Bosh in

Miami, he told a few close friends, "Ain't nobody gonna beat them." But Pierce would never admit that publicly. And he sure as hell wasn't going to give an inch when the Celtics hosted the Heat in the first game of the new NBA season on October 26, 2010. Longtime *Boston Globe* basketball writer Bob Ryan called the contest between Miami and Boston "the most hyped opening game in the history of the league."

Boston fans relished the fact that LeBron's first game in a Heat uniform was taking place on the same court where his career with the Cavaliers had come to an ignominious end five months earlier. Adding to the drama, Shaq had joined the Celtics during the off-season.

Wade and Bosh didn't fully appreciate the animosity that Boston fans felt toward LeBron. When LeBron stepped onto the floor at TD Garden, the chorus of boos filled the arena. And they continued to boo him when the starting lineups were announced and when he touched the ball. LeBron led all scorers with thirty-one points. But in the fourth quarter, when the Celtics pulled away from the Heat, chants of "O-ver-ra-ted" echoed through the Garden. The Celtics won, 88–80.

"This is a work in progress," LeBron said afterward. "We all know Rome wasn't built in one day."

"This is one of eighty-two," Wade said. "I'm sorry if everyone thought we was gonna go 82-0. It just ain't happenin'."

Just over two weeks later, the Heat hosted the Celtics in Miami. Again, the game was hard fought. And again, the Celtics won. Afterward, Pierce tweeted: "It's been a pleasure to bring my talents to South Beach."

LeBron was used to Pierce's tactics. LeBron's teammates were not. The day after Pierce's tweet, Heat enforcer Udonis Haslem was asked about it. "Paul who?" Haslem said to the press. Then Haslem gave the reporters some advice on how to learn more about Pierce. "Look up the definition of studio gangster," Haslem said. More than one journalist had to look online to learn that in hip-hop parlance, a "studio gangster" was a wannabe gangster who rapped about the gangster lifestyle.

The Cavs-Celtics rivalry was over. The Heat-Celtics rivalry was on.

On a Sunday afternoon in November, LeBron was at home in Miami, watching the Cleveland Browns play the New York Jets on television. He was also tweeting about the game. *Esquire* writer Scott Raab was also watching the game and tweeting. But Raab was tweeting about LeBron, calling him a "loser" and a "gutless punk."

The Heat saw Raab's tweets. The team also noticed the next day when Raab referred to him as "the Whore of Akron" in his *Esquire* blog.

Later that day, Raab got an email from Tim Donovan, the Miami Heat's head of media relations. "Scott," Donovan wrote, "you are no longer welcome at our building and will not be credentialed moving forward."

The next day, Raab published Donovan's email. "I suspect that Tim objected to something I wrote yesterday," he said. "I referred to LeBron James as the Whore of Akron—maybe that was it."

LeBron was still getting used to Twitter. But he was now up to nearly one million followers. He didn't like the way he and his fellow athletes were targeted on the social media platform. So he decided to retweet some of the racist, hateful tweets about him. One of the tweets referred to him as "a big nosed big lipped bug eyed nigger. Ur greedy, u try to hide ur ghettoness." Other tweets referred to him as a "bitch" and suggested to LeBron: "why don't u speak by laying ur head under a moving car."

The tweets only scratched the surface of what LeBron had experienced since *The Decision*. The public reaction to him was notably different than what Tiger Woods experienced in the aftermath of his adultery scandal. For nineteen consecutive days—a record that surpassed the terrorist attacks on 9/11—Tiger was on the cover of the *New York Post* with headlines such as "I'm a Cheetah" and "Tiger's Wife Turns Tail." In the media, Tiger was ridiculed and mocked. But Tiger's situation was personal, and he owned up to his mistakes and apologized to his family and the golf community in a televised speech. When Tiger returned to the golf course after taking a brief hiatus from the sport, he was greeted by huge crowds and rousing ovations.

LeBron, on the other hand, had become the most hated man in all of sports. He was relentlessly booed and heckled in arenas throughout the country. It seemed that even people who didn't follow basketball were rooting against him and the Heat.

More than 250 media credentials were issued for LeBron's first game back in Cleveland. When the Heat arrived at the Q on December 2, 2010, extra security measures had been implemented. Fourteen security guards were stationed around the Heat's bench. And police officers lined the corridor that led from the locker room to the court. In single file with his team-mates, LeBron jogged out of the tunnel and toward the floor. Fans close enough to touch LeBron screamed at him.

"Liar!" one fan yelled.

"Punk!" said another.

"Akron hates you, too!" said another.

A man with a phone in one hand and a beer in the other leaned within inches of LeBron and spewed obscenities at him while a burly cop looked on in silence.

LeBron knew the Q was going to be a hostile environment. But this was different. One fan held up a sign depicting a crudely drawn stick fig-ure of LeBron on his knees next to the words WHAT SHOULD YOU DO? BEG FOR MERCY.

Another sign read: LIKE FATHER, LIKE SON.

LeBron stared straight ahead, saying nothing.

"This is the most hate I've seen, ever!" recalled the Heat's head of secu-rity. "The signs and the looks on the fans' faces. We got there three hours before the game and it was packed. It was loaded. There was just so much anger in the air.

"I just tried to keep my eye on LeBron more than I normally do and just stay close, even as he's going to the table to do the powder, or when he goes in the game, just constantly watching for avenues of entrances for the fans," he continued. "When I think back on it, just the pure hate that I saw . . . I'd never seen it in that fashion in an enclosed arena."

The booing was so loud that it drowned out the TNT announcers. "I have been around basketball for twenty-five to thirty years and have never seen [such] an electricity in a building and the intensity in a building for a regular-season game," one of the announcers said. "This feels like a Game 7 of an NBA Finals right now."

To the Heat players it felt a lot more ominous than a championship game. For one night, the Q felt more like the Roman Colosseum. "That was one of those games I was most afraid of to play in," Chris Bosh re-called. And Zydrunas Ilgauskas, who had followed LeBron from Cleve-land to Miami, was unnerved by the fans of his former team. "It was the most hostile arena I'd ever been in," Ilgauskas said. "It felt like if they would've [had the chance], they'd have torn us to pieces."

LeBron had an eerie feeling. But once he and his teammates started doing their pregame layup drill, he felt safer. The crowd was serenading him with "ass-hole, ass-hole," but LeBron was itching to play. The first time he touched the ball, a fan yelled, "Take his head off." But LeBron knocked down the shot. And then another. And another.

During time-outs, fans threw things at the Heat bench. One fan even hurled a battery. But by halftime, the Heat were up by twenty and LeBron was having a monster game. Dan Gilbert was so angry that he left his seat and didn't return for the second half.

In the third quarter, LeBron poured it on, erupting for twenty-one points. With his team up by thirty, he drained a fallaway three-point shot from the corner, right in front of the Cavs bench. Then he turned and glared at his former team as he jogged past them. Someone shouted at him to "shut the fuck up."

With his team so far ahead, Coach Spoelstra sat LeBron for the entire fourth quarter. He still ended up with 38 points, 8 assists, and 5 rebounds. And the Heat won, 118–90. After the game, Dan Gilbert talked to *Esquire's* Scott Raab and explained why he hadn't come back to his seat for the second half. "I was literally afraid of going out on that court," Gilbert told Raab. "I knew what the asshole was doing, and I didn't want to . . . Sometimes I lose my . . . He was taunting. He was loving every second of it. I wouldn't have physically gone after him, but I would have probably said and done some things that I would have regretted. So I didn't come out."

LeBron's return to Cleveland was a turning point in the season for both teams. After that game, the Cavaliers went on a record losing streak. And the Heat won eighteen of their next nineteen games. But the animosity toward LeBron didn't subside. When the Heat were in New York to play the Knicks on December 17, the front page of the New York *Daily News* featured a photo of LeBron and the headline "LeBum's the Word." The *New York Post* reminded readers that LeBron could have been the King of New York. "But he took the safe path to Miami; now he'll always be . . . LeCHICKEN."

The Heat were on a ten-game winning streak and LeBron's return to Madison Square Garden was the hottest ticket in town. Celebrities packed the seats in the lower bowl. Drake. Maxwell. Liam Neeson. Paul Simon. Bill O'Reilly. Fabolous. Jessica White. Craig Robinson. DJ Clue. Joe Jonas.

Tracy Morgan. Matthew Modine. Spike Lee. Woody Allen. This was theater at its finest. And Knicks fans came ready to unload on LeBron.

"Fuck you, LeBron!" a fan shouted as the national anthem concluded.

On the Heat's first possession, LeBron drained a three, silencing a deafening chorus of boos. The Heat built a lead. But the Knicks stormed back in the second quarter. LeBron single-handedly fended off the run. Slashing. Dunking. Knocking down jump shot after jump shot. For Knicks fans, it was a painful reminder of what might have been. He finished with 32 points, 11 rebounds, and 10 assists. The Heat throttled the Knicks by twenty-two.

As the Heat were hitting their stride and starting to dominate other teams, more NBA pundits took shots at LeBron for having joined forces with Wade and Bosh. One of the most common digs was that Celtics legend Larry Bird and Lakers legend Magic Johnson—longtime archrivals—never would have joined forces. It was a silly comparison, given that Bird and Johnson had played on teams that were loaded with future Hall of Fame players. But eventually, Bird spoke out in defense of LeBron. "I didn't get mad at him for going down there," he said. "It hurt a lot of people's feelings. But shit, it's his life. It's his game." And when a reporter tried to bait Bird into criticizing LeBron for the way that he handled his decision announcement, Bird said, "He's just a kid, you know? I mean, come on. We all make stupid mistakes. I made a million of them. So what the hell?"

LeBron had just turned twenty-six. It was January 11, 2011, and he was in his hotel room in Los Angeles, watching the Cavs-Lakers game on television. The next night, the Heat would play the Clippers. But LeBron was keeping tabs on his old team. The Lakers destroyed them, 112–57, handing Cleveland the worst loss in team history. LeBron tweeted: "Karma is a bitch."

Without LeBron, Gilbert's franchise collapsed. The Cavaliers finished the 2010–2011 season 19-63. It was the second-worst record in the NBA. The Heat, on the other hand, finished the regular season with the second-best record in the Eastern Conference at 58-24. And after breezing through the first round of the playoffs, Miami faced Boston in the Eastern Conference Semifinals. It was the showdown that basketball fans wanted to see.

The Celtics had essentially had their way with the Heat during the regular season. In Game 1, Pierce and his teammates resorted to a familiar approach—bully ball. When Heat bench player James Jones hit a string of three-point shots, Pierce went chest-to-chest with him and bumped his head into Jones's face. Then Pierce got into a shoving match with Wade. While Pierce ran his mouth, the referee hit him with a technical foul and ejected him. But the Heat were clearly rattled.

On the sideline, LeBron took over the huddle, imploring his teammates to ignore the antics. "They gonna try to do everything besides basketball to get us out of our heads," LeBron shouted. "Let's just beat 'em in basketball!"

The Heat rallied and took Game 1, 99–90.

In Game 2, LeBron punished the Celtics. With thirty-five points, he led all scorers, and the Heat won again.

But in Boston, the Celtics prevailed in Game 3. And Game 4 turned into a shoot-out between LeBron and Pierce. With the Celtics on the verge of evening up the series at 2-2, LeBron led the Heat into overtime, where they went on to win, 98–90, and take a commanding 3-1 series lead.

Back in Miami, Dwyane Wade played his best game of the series in Game 5, leading all scorers. But the score was tied with 2:10 remaining in the game when LeBron pulled up with Pierce in his face and nailed a three. Then he hit another three in Pierce's face to put Miami up by six. Heat fans roared as LeBron mimicked a locomotive, huffing and puffing next to Pierce. The Celtics called time-out. On the inbounds pass, LeBron stole the ball from Pierce, who stood flat-footed as LeBron streaked downcourt and tomahawked it through the rim with two hands, sending the crowd into a frenzy and putting the Heat up by eight. After another time-out, the Celtics turned it over again and the ball ended up in LeBron's hands. Holding it for the last shot, LeBron looked at Pierce, and then blew by him for a layup. He had scored the team's final ten points, all at Pierce's expense. LeBron had finally beaten Boston's Big Three, and the Heat were moving on in the playoffs.

After making quick work of the Chicago Bulls in the Eastern Conference Finals, LeBron and the Heat advanced to the NBA Finals, where they faced the Dallas Mavericks.

Behind strong performances by Wade and Bosh, the Heat won Game 1 in Miami. Wade led the way in Game 2, and the Heat were having their way again. With just over seven minutes remaining in the fourth quarter, Wade hit a three-point shot to cap off a 13–0 run that put the Heat up, 88–73. "The Heat have blown this game open," the announcer said on ABC as LeBron and Wade celebrated in front of the Dallas bench.

After a time-out, a minute passed before either team scored. Then the Mavericks hit a jumper. Then a layup. Then a couple of free throws. Then another layup. With four and a half minutes left, the Heat's lead had been cut to seven.

LeBron hit two free throws to put his team back up by nine.

Then Jason Kidd hit a three to cut the lead to six. Jason Terry followed with a bucket to pull the Mavericks within four with three minutes to play.

The entire Heat team had suddenly gone cold. But LeBron's absence during the Mavericks' run was more conspicuous. He had gone to Miami to win championships. This was the moment to assert himself and seize the moment.

Mavericks star Dirk Nowitzki, a seven-footer with a trademark fall-away jump shot that was essentially indefensible due to his height, was trying to win his first championship, too. A thirty-two-year-old native of Germany, Nowitzki had spent his entire thirteen-year NBA career in Dallas. Like LeBron, he'd been a free agent in 2010. But Nowitzki had quietly re-signed with Dallas, saying, "Ultimately, that was where my heart was at." He also felt he had "unfinished business" in Dallas—in all those years as the team's best player, Nowitzki had only been to the NBA Finals once, in 2006, when they'd lost to Dwyane Wade and the Miami Heat. Nowitzki was determined to win a championship for Dallas.

With 2:43 remaining in Game 2, Nowitzki scored to pull his team within two.

On the other end of the floor, LeBron missed two three-point-shot attempts.

Then Nowitzki tied the game with a layup.

After Wade missed a three, Nowitzki nailed a three, capping an astonishing 20–2 run by the Mavericks and putting his team ahead 93–90 with twenty seconds remaining.

After a time-out, Miami's Mario Chalmers hit a quick three to tie the game.

With twenty-four seconds left, Nowitzki called for the ball again. Out on the perimeter, the seven-footer took his time, allowing the game clock to run down before making his move to the basket and scoring with just three seconds left on the clock to put Dallas up, 95–93. The Miami crowd was silent.

On the other end, LeBron passed the ball to Wade for a desperation heave that wasn't close. After being down by fifteen with six minutes to play, the Mavericks had come all the way back, and Nowitzki had scored his team's final nine points. The Mavericks were the first team since Michael Jordan's Chicago Bulls in 1992 to overcome a fifteen-point deficit in the fourth quarter and win an NBA Finals game.

There was still a long way to go in the series, but Pat Riley was concerned. He'd played and coached in enough championships to know that a little thing can give an underdog hope and change the outcome of a series.

The Heat held on to win Game 3 in Dallas by two points and take a 2-1 series lead. But for the third straight game, LeBron had gone quiet in the fourth quarter. When asked about that after the game, he got defensive. Then in Game 4, Dallas once again mounted a fourth-quarter comeback and won the game, 86–83, knotting the series at 2-2. Wade and Bosh played well. But LeBron had one of the worst games of his postseason career, scoring just eight points. "I didn't play well, especially offensively," he admitted afterward. "I know that. I've got to do a better job of helping this team win basketball games, especially late, no matter what it is."

After Game 4, LeBron's disappearance in fourth quarters became the main story line of the finals. After being so dominant against the Celtics and the Bulls, LeBron was fading against the Mavericks. Labeling him "the league's most confounding superstar," the New York Times noted: "Most alarming of all, James has been silent when the Heat has needed him most, in a series of breathtakingly tense fourth quarters. James is averaging a feeble 2.3 points in fourth quarters, going 3 for 12 from the field." ESPN pointed out that LeBron hadn't scored a basket in the final ten minutes of Games 2, 3, or 4.

LeBron looked at the Heat as Wade's team. LeBron was the bigger star, but Wade had spent his career in Miami. LeBron felt obligated to help his friend win a championship.

"Obviously, he feels like he let me down," Wade said after Game 4. "Obviously, I understand he's going to respond."

But the Mavericks won Game 5 decisively at home, and Wade bruised his hip in the game. With the Heat trailing, 3-2, the series shifted back to Miami. On the night before Game 6, LeBron and Wade worked out at the arena, trying to get in sync.

That night, ESPN published a graphic that showed nearly every state in the country was rooting for Dallas to win Game 6. LeBron wouldn't admit it. But the constant reminder that everyone was rooting against him had become a drag.

Nowitzki shot miserably in the first half of Game 6, missing all but one of his eleven shots. Still, Dallas clung to a two-point lead at halftime. With Wade struggling to score, LeBron and Bosh shouldered the load. But neither of them took over the game. Meanwhile, Nowitzki saved his best performance for the end, scoring ten points in the fourth quarter and pushing the Mavericks to a twelve-point lead with eight minutes to play. Mavericks' fans scattered throughout the arena started chanting, "Let's go, Mavs!" And Heat fans began heading for the exits.

LeBron looked dazed when the final horn sounded and the Mavericks began celebrating on the Heat's home court. In the tunnel leading to Miami's locker room, Bosh crumpled to the floor. On his hands and knees, his face buried in his hands, he wept. Staff walked past him as if he were a homeless man on a crowded city street. Finally, Wade helped Bosh to his feet and helped get him to the locker room. "It just wasn't how I thought it was going to be," Bosh later said. "I thought we were going to win."

The Heat locker room felt like a trauma unit. Coach Spoelstra tried to steady his players. "You're an extremely hardworking group that did sacrifice and do all the right things," Spoelstra told them. "You put yourself in a position to win the whole thing. You just didn't."

LeBron wasn't in the mood to hear anything. On social media, he was already getting trashed. "Hey LeBron, ya choked bitch," one fan tweeted. Even Dan Gilbert took to Twitter to gloat over LeBron's demise. "Mavs NEVER stopped & now entire franchise gets rings," Gilbert tweeted. "Old Lesson for all: There are NO SHORTCUTS. NONE."

Dressed in a blue suit and tie with a handkerchief in his jacket pocket, LeBron entered the media room to face the press. Taking a seat beside Wade, he rested his elbows on the table and clasped his hands.

"Does it bother you that so many people are happy to see you fail?" a reporter asked.

"Absolutely not," LeBron said, fighting back emotion. "At the end of the day, all the people that are rooting on me to fail, they got to wake up tomorrow and have the same life that they had before they woke up today. They got the same personal problems that they had today. I'm going to continue to live the way that I want to live. Continue to do the things that I want to do with my family and be happy with that."

TWENTY-NINE

A REAL DARK PLACE

The morning after losing the NBA Finals, Dwyane Wade didn't get out of bed. He stayed in his room all day. Had his meals brought in. Refused to see or talk to anyone. When his kids knocked on the door early in the afternoon, trying to get him to come out and play ball, he hollered, "Not right now." When they returned a few hours later with the same request, he told them the same thing. Instead, Wade watched his favorite movie, *Coming to America*. It reminded him that despite the crushing loss to the Mavericks, he still had to be a father. When his children returned around dinnertime and one of them said, "Dad, let's go play before it gets dark," Wade finally emerged from his bedroom and joined them outside. The next morning, Wade woke up and came to grips with the fact that the outcome of the NBA Finals was not a bad dream. It was reality. *Okay, bro,* he told himself. *You still got responsibilities. Time to get back to life.*

LeBron couldn't rebound that fast. He was in a much darker place. Losing the finals had mortified him, especially after all the "three kings" hype and his "not six, not seven" preseason boasting about championships. But humiliation wasn't the only thing LeBron was feeling. For the first time in his career, he'd lost his grip on the court and had become insecure about his identity as a basketball player. The blowback from his "taking my talents to South Beach" had transformed him into the most polarizing figure in professional sports. The hatred, night in and night out, had made the 2010–2011 season a miserable, exhausting experience. And the situation had forced him into a role he wasn't cut out to play—the villain. All the pretending—the glaring, the scowling—was a disguise that had ultimately worn him down. By the time the Heat reached the finals, LeBron was overthinking things so much that he disappeared in critical stretches when the games were on the line. Now that the season was finally over, he was so mentally and emotionally drained that he didn't want to see anyone.

But Pat Riley had lined up exit interviews with each Heat player before everyone scattered for the summer. LeBron's interview was set for 3:00 p.m.

Begrudgingly, LeBron arrived at Riley's office right on time. Riley was still meeting with Bosh. Offered a seat while he waited, LeBron declined. He wasn't about to wait around. Instead, he entered Riley's office.

"You're late," he told Riley, walking toward the window and staring blankly outside.

Bosh stood. "We can finish this later," he told Riley.

LeBron kept looking out the window.

Bosh ducked out, and LeBron started pacing back and forth in front of Riley's desk.

"You can go if you want," Riley said. "We don't have to have this meeting."

LeBron shook his head and kept pacing.

"Look, you had a great year," Riley said.

LeBron didn't want to hear it. They were supposed to win the championship. But he didn't say that. He didn't say *anything*.

Riley ended the meeting.

LeBron had hit rock bottom. Savannah tried to talk to him. So did Maverick. And Gloria. And Wade. LeBron ignored all of them. Suddenly, the man who couldn't stand to be alone had turned off his phone and sequestered himself inside his place in Coconut Grove. Alone in his thoughts and wallowing in misery, he realized that basketball wasn't fun anymore. "I had built my whole life on being happy about the game of basketball . . . and going out and playing with joy," LeBron said. "Then in one year, because of everything that had happened, I was playing to prove people wrong."

There was no one LeBron wanted to prove wrong more than Dan Gilbert, who had gone for LeBron's jugular by accusing him of being selfish. From a basketball standpoint, nothing hurt LeBron more than the perception of being self-centered. As far back as high school he had prided himself on being a team player. He'd taken that approach in the NBA, establishing a reputation as an unselfish player with the Cavaliers. Yet Gilbert had branded him as a narcissist.

In LeBron's mind, his actions were the opposite of narcissism—he had left Cleveland, where he was the face of the franchise, to go to Miami, where someone else was the face of the franchise. LeBron was so determined to win a championship that he'd been willing to play second fiddle on Wade's team. And to counter the perception that he was selfish, he had forced himself into a supporting role in Miami, sometimes going out of his way to make sure he didn't come off like a player who was upstaging the team's leading man.

Yet when the team lost, it was LeBron's fault. At least that's how it felt. Every publication from *Sports Illustrated* to the *New York Times* to *Slam* magazine was dissecting LeBron's performance. He was trending on Twitter. He was all over ESPN and CNN. The public scrutiny had become too much. There was only so much one man could take. So he turned off his phone. Shut down his social media. Avoided his television. And spent a lot of time listening to Barry White and Curtis Mayfield.

"I went to a real dark place for about two weeks," LeBron recalled. "I wasn't talking to nobody. I was just in my room. I was looking like Tom Hanks in *Cast Away*. My beard had grown all the way out."

During this period, LeBron didn't have anyone in the NBA he could turn to for guidance. Michael Jordan or Kobe Bryant would have been ideal candidates. But LeBron wasn't close to either of them. And there wasn't anyone else in the league who was at LeBron's level in terms of talent and celebrity status. Instead, LeBron turned to Jay-Z, the only friend he had who could relate to him and his situation.

Jay-Z empathized with LeBron. One of the things that he had long admired most about LeBron was that he worked just as hard on his reputation as he did on his game. As a young man who had grown up in a single-parent home, LeBron recognized the role that men like Frankie Walker and Coach Dru had played in his life. He considered those men saviors. And from the moment he joined the NBA, LeBron had embraced the responsibility of being a role model to other young men, especially to kids who were growing up in circumstances like his. By making a conscious effort, he had avoided many of the pitfalls of celebrity and wealth that had tripped up his contemporaries. Free of scandal, he had developed a golden image. Then one false step had changed everything. The reputation he'd worked so hard to build had vaporized.

From Jay-Z's vantage point, LeBron had lived his life very carefully, never daring to stray from the straight-and-narrow path to basketball stardom that he'd been on since his freshman year at St. V. He'd spent his entire life in and around Akron, where everything was familiar. Going to Miami had been a big change. He'd been naive to think that it would be fun and that championships would come easily. Now he knew better. The decision to go to Miami had broken the blissful cocoon that LeBron had created for himself in Ohio.

Jay-Z's own life experience had positioned him to help LeBron. Back when they were becoming friends, in 2003, Jay-Z had been at a similar crossroads in his career, where he was questioning a lot of things about himself and his future. He'd had to remind himself, "I love music. Music saves me every day." During the summer of 2011, Jay-Z reminded LeBron how much he loved basketball, and that basketball saved him every day. The key word that Jay-Z emphasized to his friend was *remember*.

Remember where you came from.

Remember what got you to this point in your life.

Remember why you love the game.

It was simple yet profound advice from one world-class entertainer to another.

Even while off the grid, LeBron made the news. For weeks, the media in Miami had speculated on his whereabouts and his well-being. Then, on June 29, LeBron resurfaced. That night, he took Savannah to see U2 at Sun Life Stadium. Afterward, they hung out with Bono, who had many more years of experience living in the spotlight and dealing with the extreme highs and lows that it breeds. The next day, LeBron posted a picture of him and Savannah with Bono and captioned it "Yesterday was a good day." It was the first time he'd been seen in public or on social media since the NBA Finals. One of the Miami papers ran a headline: "LeBron James Alive, at U2 Concert."

After the show, LeBron and Savannah headed home to Ohio, where LeBron reached back to his roots and redoubled his commitment to get better. He stepped up his training regimen, biking close to one hundred miles some days on trails on the outskirts of Akron. He also reached out to his first high school coach, Keith Dambrot, and started working out with him. He hadn't spent much time with Dambrot since high school. But LeBron wanted to return to the basketball player he had been before his life had gotten away from him. He figured Dambrot's no-nonsense approach was just what he needed.

"You have to do more things you don't want to do," Dambrot told him that summer. "You have to do more offensive and defensive rebounding, moving without the ball, all the basics that made you great going back to the beginning."

Eventually, LeBron watched film of his performance in the finals against Dallas. He didn't like what he saw of himself in the fourth quarter of Games 4 and 5, when he essentially stopped scoring. He spent the rest of his summer focusing on areas he wanted to strengthen—his footwork, his ballhandling, and developing a low-post game.

During the off-season, LeBron got a call from Wade, who had gone away on vacation. He invited LeBron to join him so they could train together and talk about making some changes.

When he got there, Wade told him he'd been doing a lot of thinking. It was time for LeBron to cut loose. To take over. To not feel constrained by the idea that the Heat was Wade's team.

The conversation with Wade was a breakthrough that deepened their friendship and altered the dynamic between them as teammates. The Heat was going to be a very different team going forward.

Although he didn't talk about it, LeBron regretted doing the interview with Jim Gray on ESPN. It was a mistake that he was determined not to repeat. The aftermath of that decision convinced LeBron that he'd reached a point where he needed more than a publicist. He needed a communications guru who was more of a strategic thinker, someone who could better help him repair his image and navigate the perils of his celebrity status. He didn't have to go far to find the right person for the job.

Earlier in 2011, LeBron and Maverick had formed a strategic business partnership with Fenway Sports Group, one of the largest sports, media, and entertainment companies in the world. All the drama in Miami had overshadowed the significance of LeBron's new alliance. Fenway's portfolio of companies included the Boston Red Sox; Liverpool FC, an English Premier League soccer club; Roush Fenway Racing, a NASCAR racing team; the New England Sports Network; and two of the most renowned venues in sports—Fenway Park in Boston and Anfield stadium in Liverpool. The partnership between FSM and LRMR meant that all of LeBron's future business, marketing, endorsement, and philanthropic endeavors around the globe would be handled by some of the most strategic thinkers in the entertainment industry, including Fenway group's founder, Tom Werner. As part of the agreement, LeBron and Maverick acquired an interest in Liverpool FC, which *Forbes* ranked as the sixth-most valuable sports team in the world. It was an opportunity that enabled LeBron to become the first active player to own a piece of a professional sports team.

One of the unforeseen opportunities arising from the Fenway group collaboration was LeBron's introduction to Adam Mendelsohn, a world-class public relations strategist who had done work for Werner's group. Mendelsohn had been deputy chief of staff to Governor Arnold Schwarzenegger before starting his own communications firm, Mercury Public Affairs. Mercury specialized in crisis management for politicians and celebrities. In 2011, there was no athlete in American team sports who had a dedicated communications operative as sophisticated and experienced as Adam Mendelsohn.

Right after LeBron started training for the next season, the NBA locked out the players. At the time, the collective-bargaining agreement afforded 57 percent of basketball income to players. The owners wanted to reduce the percentage. Dan Gilbert was among those pushing hardest for the reduction. Part of Gilbert's frustration with the players was rooted in the fact that his franchise had drafted LeBron and then watched him depart for another team when he was at the pinnacle of his career.

It had taken LeBron seven years to become an unrestricted free agent. Gilbert didn't appreciate that LeBron had had the audacity to exercise the leverage that he had accumulated under the system that the owners had put in place. In many ways, LeBron's move to Miami had been a seismic shift that was rippling across the league. On the court, he was public enemy number one. But off the court, every player in the NBA—particularly the stars—stood to benefit from LeBron's decision to take less money in favor of joining forces with other players in hopes of winning championships.

During the lockout, HarperCollins published Scott Raab's book *The Whore of Akron: One Man's Search for the Soul of LeBron James*. The book opened with an encounter between Raab and LeBron in the locker room at the Q in April 2010. At the time, Raab had been convinced that LeBron was going to re-sign with the Cavaliers. He had approached LeBron and said, "I saw Oscar in his prime. Michael. Magic. All of them. And you're the best basketball player I've ever seen. Thank you." LeBron replied, "That means a lot to me. Thanks."

Then Raab wrote: "I feel remorse unto grief about that night in the locker room with LeBron. I'm sorry, truly sorry, that I didn't haul off and kick him square in the nuts. . . . King James. The Chosen One. The Whore of Akron. I dropped that last one on him myself, after he left to join the Miami Heat."

The book was wildly popular and critically acclaimed. The Associated Press called it "laugh-out-loud [funny]." *Sports Illustrated* deemed it "rollicking and profane." Even Buzz Bissinger weighed in, calling the book "hilarious, heartfelt, and wincingly honest." Raab's critique of LeBron was blistering. But his unflinching account of his own life was far more powerful. And it was Raab's self-inspection that distinguished the book from other sports memoirs and prompted *Slate* magazine to name it Best Book of the Year. "The guy doesn't like LeBron James," wrote Stefan Fatsis. "Not the point. *The Whore of Akron* is about a basketball player the way *Moby-Dick* is about a whale."

While working on his book, Raab had multiple conversations with Gilbert. Although Raab was judicious about what he shared from those conversations, his revelations about Gilbert's thoughts on LeBron's departure were blunt and harsh. "It's still a shock," Gilbert told Raab. "I can't believe he actually did this. It's just unreal. He fucks the entire city and then on top of it dances on your grave—it's unbelievable. There's no words for it—the amount of rage."

LeBron was learning to pay less attention to what people said and wrote about him, but it was hard to ignore a book that picked the scabs off of some fresh wounds. But he drew strength from his family and trudged on. When the lockout finally ended and the shortened 2011–2012 season began on December 25, LeBron was in Dallas, where the Heat were set to open the season against the Mavericks. LeBron looked on as Nowitzki and his teammates received their championship rings. Then the game started. And LeBron played like a one-man wrecking crew.

During the off-season, Erik Spoelstra had met with his staff and told them that they had to stop trying to force a system of basketball on Le-

Bron. LeBron, he said, was an unconventional player, and they'd been trying to make him play in a conventional system. Going forward, Spoelstra wanted to give LeBron the freedom to be more creative and allow the system to run through him. "We have to open our minds and develop a system where LeBron James is the best player in the world every night," Spoelstra told his assistants.

In the season opener against Dallas, LeBron looked like a liberated player. Free to play any position he chose—sometimes he brought the ball up like a point guard, sometimes he posted up like a big man, and at times he just improvised on the fly—LeBron led all scorers with thirty-seven points. He was dominant in every phase of the game. And the reigning NBA champions were no match for the Heat.

On December 30, days after thrashing the Mavericks, LeBron turned twenty-seven. The following night, he invited fifty of his closest friends and family to a private New Year's Eve dinner at an exclusive hotel in South Beach. During the lockout, LeBron had decided that it was time to finally tie the knot with Savannah. She'd been his soulmate since they were teenagers in high school. And they functioned like a married couple—raising their two children and building a home together. But LeBron had never popped the question. And Savannah had no intention of rushing him. "I've definitely not put a fire under his ass," she told *Harper's* right after LeBron had signed with Miami. "We're really comfortable with the way things are now. And it's not up to me. When it happens, it happens."

For LeBron, the time had come. "Just like how I needed to take that next step as a player," he said, "I also needed to take that next step as a man."

Around midnight, he went to Wade, who was holding the engagement ring. Nervous, LeBron asked him for the ring.

"You ready?" Wade asked.

"If you don't give me the ring right now," LeBron told him, "I ain't gonna do it."

Moments later, with his friends and family looking on, LeBron dropped to one knee and looked up at Savannah.

The Heat were rolling. And LeBron was having the most dominant season of his career. He was still getting booed in every arena outside Miami. But over the course of the 2011–2012 season, LeBron was quietly shedding his villain image.

While the team was on a layover at the airport in Oklahoma City, LeBron noticed some helicopter pilots in military uniforms had approached the Heat's security in hopes of taking a picture with the players. But most of the Heat players were napping, and security turned down the request. "Hey, hey," LeBron said, "any of these military guys can take a picture with us." Then he roused his teammates. "Hey, everybody, get up," he said. "Get in a circle here."

He later explained why he did that. "These are guys who put their life in danger every day," he said. "If it wasn't for them, we wouldn't be free. . . . They do so many great things for America, for all of us. The least we could do was take a picture with them."

Even away from the court, LeBron had stepped up as the team's leader. At the NBA All-Star Game in Orlando on February 26, 2012, LeBron got into a shootout with Kevin Durant. They both finished with thirty-six points. But LeBron's teammates were more impressed with what LeBron did in the weeks that followed, after learning that a seventeen-year-old Black youth named Trayvon Martin had been shot and killed during the All-Star Game. Martin lived with his mother in Miami, but he had gone to stay with his father in Sanford, a town outside Orlando. Wearing a gray hooded sweatshirt, he stepped out during halftime to get some candy at a nearby 7-Eleven. He never came back. With his hood up and rain coming down, Martin crossed paths with a neighborhood crime watch volunteer named George Zimmerman, who called 911. "Hey, we've had some break-ins in my neighborhood," he told the dispatcher. "And there's a real suspicious guy." After providing a few descriptors—gray hoodie, appears like he's up to no good—Zimmerman was asked to describe him further. "He looks Black," he told the dispatcher. The police responded. But by the time they arrived, Zimmerman had shot Martin, who was found facedown in the grass, a bag of Skittles in his pocket.

Protesters called for the arrest of Zimmerman, who claimed self-defense under Florida's Stand Your Ground law. LeBron first heard about Trayvon Martin's death from Dwyane Wade's girlfriend. It turned out that the Heat were Martin's favorite team and LeBron was his favorite player. LeBron and Wade spent several days discussing how to use their influence to bring attention to the injustice of Martin's death. In the meantime, civil rights leaders held rallies, millions of people marched in cities across the country, and the Justice Department opened a federal investigation into the killing.

On March 23, the Heat were in Detroit to face the Pistons. That morning, President Obama appeared in the Rose Garden to introduce the next head of the World Bank. A reporter asked the president about Trayvon Martin. Unprepared to make a formal statement, the president spoke from the heart. "I think all of us have to do some soul-searching to figure out how does something like this happen," Obama said. "And that means we examine the laws and the context for what happened, as well as the specifics of the incident." He added: "If I had a son, he'd look like Trayvon."

The president's sentiments resonated with LeBron. He had *two* sons. And they certainly looked like Trayvon Martin. That notion that any young Black man in a gray hoodie could be Trayvon Martin was chilling. And right after President Obama's Rose Garden remarks, LeBron and Wade asked all of their teammates to gather at the team hotel for a team photo. They all wore gray hoodies. It was a provocative image. That afternoon, LeBron shared the picture on Twitter, along with the caption: "#WeAreTrayvonMartin #Hoodies #Stereotyped #WeWantJustice."

For LeBron, this was a turning point in his evolution as an activist. No athlete in the world had more Twitter followers than LeBron. By choosing to use his social media platform to bring attention to the unjust killing of an unarmed Black teenager, LeBron was venturing into an area that no other contemporary American athlete of his stature—Jordan, Kobe, Tiger, Tom Brady—had dared to go. And there was a realization on his part that there was no turning back.

Around the time that LeBron joined the Heat, journalist Lee Jenkins took over the NBA beat at *Sports Illustrated*. Shortly after LeBron hired Adam Mendelsohn, Jenkins approached him. LeBron was putting up MVP numbers, and Jenkins wanted to profile him. The piece, he intimated, would be strictly a basketball story.

After a fair amount of pestering by Jenkins, Mendelsohn trusted him enough that he lined up a one-hour interview for him with LeBron. It was set to take place when the Heat were in the New York area to play the Knicks and Nets on back-to-back days.

Tired, LeBron stepped off the team bus on April 14, 2012, and entered the Westin in Jersey City. While his teammates checked into their rooms, LeBron sank into a booth opposite Jenkins in the hotel's restaurant. Wearing a stocking cap, LeBron ordered a cup of chamomile tea with honey.

"Where you from?" LeBron asked.

"San Diego," Jenkins said.

"That's my second-favorite city in the world," LeBron said.

Jenkins was surprised. "What's your favorite city?" he asked.

LeBron flashed a quizzical expression. "Well, Akron," he said.

Jenkins was different from the feature writers who had previously sat down with LeBron over the years. Sensitive and soft-spoken, he was a student of the game of basketball. But his real strength was that he had empathy as a writer. It was a quality that couldn't be taught in journalism school.

At the same time, LeBron had evolved from the teenager who got in Grant Wahl's rental car, or the young man who stepped in the elevator with Lisa Taddeo at the Hearst Tower in 2007, or the guy who Buzz Bissinger had bought gas for in 2008, or the one who J. R. Moehringer had followed around in 2010. He'd matured in many ways. And now that he worked with Mendelsohn, LeBron was more open to the idea of talking to a writer who was looking to chronicle his transformation. Within an hour of meeting Jenkins, LeBron became introspective about his first season in Miami.

"I lost touch with who I was as a basketball player and a person," LeBron told him. "I got caught up in everything that was going on around me, and I felt like I had to prove something to people, and I don't know why. Everything was tight, stressed."

He also opened up about his evolving view toward his father. "My father wasn't around when I was a kid," he told Jenkins. "And I used to always say, 'Why me? Why don't I have a father? Why isn't he around? Why did he leave my mother?' But as I got older, I looked deeper and thought, 'I don't know what my father was going through, but if he was around all the time, would I be who I am today?' It made me grow up fast. It helped me be more responsible. Maybe I wouldn't be sitting here right now."

Jenkins was impressed. He reassured LeBron that the more he was willing to reveal, the better he could do as a writer.

Sipping his tea, LeBron made a mental note.

At the end of the interview, Jenkins thanked LeBron for the time.

"When you win your first title in a couple months," Jenkins told him, "I want to do this again."

LeBron liked the sound of that.

Two nights later at the Prudential Center in Newark, Nets fans passionately booed LeBron. But with Wade sitting out with an injury and his team down in the fourth quarter, LeBron took over the game, scoring seventeen consecutive points in the final four minutes to lead the Heat to victory. It was a display of utter dominance. Sitting courtside, Jay-Z marveled as the crowd started chanting, "M-V-P! M-V-P!" The Heat won the game, and LeBron had won over the Nets' fans.

The applause lifted LeBron. As soon as the game ended, he removed his headband and his sneakers and handed them to Jay-Z's nephew, bringing a smile to the boy's face. Then he hugged Jay-Z.

Lee Jenkins was there to witness it all. When LeBron spotted him, he walked over. Thinking about the conversation they'd had two days earlier and the importance of allowing Jenkins to see him more intimately, LeBron said, "Does this work?"

Jenkins assured him that it did.

Happy, LeBron walked off in his socks.

Jenkins's story—"After Tumultuous First Year in Miami, LeBron Returns a New Man"—cast LeBron in a new light, and made the case that he had completed "one of the finest all-around seasons in the NBA's modern era." The sportswriters and broadcasters agreed, overwhelmingly choosing him as the NBA's MVP. And the Heat finished the regular season with the best record in the Eastern Conference and the odds-on favorites to win the NBA Finals. But in the Eastern Conference Semifinals, the Heat fell behind two games to one to the Pacers. LeBron knew that if the Heat lost Game 4 in Indiana and fell behind, 3-1, they would almost surely lose the series. This was not the time to be a team player. It was time to carry the team.

In Game 4, LeBron never let up. And in the second half, when Pacers players were tired and wheezing, he played as if he had an extra gear. "You're a marathon runner!" Coach Erik Spoelstra shouted at him. "You're not supposed to get tired."

Pat Riley studied LeBron that night and knew he was witnessing his moment of truth. "It was the first time I've ever seen him absolutely exhausted," Riley said. "He doesn't get exhausted. He took a breath and then went back in, and he closed them out."

LeBron finished the game with forty points. Miami won the game. More important, LeBron had broken the Pacers' will. The Heat won the next two games to close out the Pacers and advanced to face the Celtics in the Eastern Conference Finals.

The Heat were heavily favored. Pierce and Garnett were getting on in years. And the Celtics were dealing with a slew of injuries. "We're tired and old and banged up," Celtics coach Doc Rivers admitted.

In the first two games, the Heat took a 2-0 series lead. But when the series shifted to Boston, the Celtics ground out two wins to even the series. Then, in the pivotal Game 5 in Miami, the Celtics led, 87–86, with a minute remaining. LeBron guarded Pierce, who had the ball out beyond the three-point arc. Pierce had shot poorly all night. Nonetheless, he stepped back and let fly a long three-point shot that banked off the backboard and through the goal, putting his team up by four and sealing the game. The Celtics had won three straight.

Down 3-2 and heading back to Boston for Game 6, LeBron and the Heat looked finished. Controversy swirled around the team. It was being blasted by the pundits. LeBron was being mocked. Spoelstra's job security was being questioned. There was even talk of breaking up the Big Three. "Not only is this series over," said ESPN's Stephen A. Smith. "Everything's over in Miami."

But when LeBron took the floor in Boston on June 7, 2012, he was a very different player from the one who had faced the Mavericks a year earlier in the NBA Finals. Standing on the parquet floor, he had the eyes of a killer. He never smiled. He didn't say a word to anyone. He just glared. Looking at him, Pat Riley thought, *LeBron looks primal.*

And that was the LeBron that Riley wanted to see.

Moments into the game, LeBron blew past Pierce and hammered down a violent dunk that rattled TD Garden. Next time down the floor, he pulled up on Pierce and nailed a jumper. Then LeBron dunked again. Then a spin move. Then a jab step. Then a layup. He hit nine of his first ten shots. But he still never smiled. He never spoke. He just kept glaring. And scoring. On one offensive rebound, he leaped so high that he nearly hit his head on the rim before tomahawking the ball through the goal. Even his teammates were collectively saying, "Holy shit!" LeBron scored thirty points *in the first half.*

The Celtics were on the ropes. And LeBron kept attacking. With 7:15 remaining in the game, Pierce and Garnett slumped on the Celtics bench, wiping away sweat, when LeBron sliced through the lane and scored his forty-fifth point, putting the Heat up by twenty-five and silencing the Garden. Pierce hung a towel over his head.

Looking on, Riley reveled. "He was a cobra," Riley said of LeBron afterward. "A leopard. A tiger hunched over his prey."

LeBron finished with 45 points, 15 rebounds, and 5 assists. It was the first time since 1964 that an NBA player had put up such numbers in a playoff game. The last player to do so had been Wilt Chamberlain with 50 points, 15 rebounds, and 6 assists. When LeBron finally left the court, the tunnel leading to the locker room was lined with Boston police officers. With fans screaming obscenities at him, LeBron passed between the cops. Suddenly he felt liquid landing on his head. A fan had thrown an open container of beer on him. Saying nothing, LeBron licked his lips and ducked into the tunnel in silence. He later told *Sports Illustrated*, "If I was a fan, and someone came into our building and did to us what I did to them, I'd probably have thrown a beer on him too."

LeBron's performance in Game 6 was the most clutch performance of his career. Displaying unparalleled physical conditioning and technical precision, he single-handedly altered the destiny of two franchises in one night. The Eastern Conference Finals marked the last time that the Celtics Big Three would ever play together. And the Heat's Big Three were ascending to a run of NBA dominance. But on a personal level, LeBron had silenced his critics. The *New York Times* declared his play in Game 6 as "one of the most brilliant performances of his brilliant career." ESPN's Stephen A. Smith said, "This is arguably one of the greatest performances we've ever seen. It's the first time that I can recall seeing one man beating an entire team." But it was Paul Pierce's eyes that said it best—in the waning minutes of Game 6, Pierce sat on the bench, looking at LeBron, knowing his team had been pummeled by the best player on the planet.

*   *   *

The following night in Miami, the Celtics fought valiantly. At the end of the third quarter, the score was 73–73. But Pierce, Garnett, and Allen were exhausted and broken down. LeBron, Wade, and Bosh took over down the stretch. Dunking. Sprinting. Dishing out assists. Miami's Big Three scored all twenty-eight of the Heat's points in the final quarter, while limiting the Celtics to just six points in the last nine minutes. With the Celtics succumbing, LeBron pulled up from long range and launched a three-point shot from well beyond the arc. As the shot clock expired, the ball dropped through the net, sending the crowd into a frenzy and putting the dagger in the Celtics. With the building shaking, LeBron stood as if frozen, his shooting arm extended, his wrist limp. It was a great feeling, a moment that he wanted to savor.

The Heat were headed back to the NBA Finals. But this time around, LeBron's head was clear. He knew that he was on the cusp of winning his first NBA title.

THIRTY

THE TAKEOVER

ABC hyped the 2012 NBA Finals matchup between the Miami Heat and the Oklahoma City Thunder as a showdown between "arguably the two best players on the planet"—LeBron and twenty-three-year-old Kevin Durant, who was appearing in the finals for the first time. The two superstars shined brightly. Durant put on a scintillating offensive exhibition. And with twenty-three-year-old Russell Westbrook relentlessly attacking the rim and the sharpshooting of twenty-two-year-old James Harden, the young Thunder team took Game 1 and demonstrated that they were not intimidated by the Heat.

But LeBron was in a much different headspace than he'd been in during the 2011 finals against the Mavericks. Despite losing the first game, LeBron had never been more confident. He opened Game 2 in Oklahoma City by soaring through the air on a fast-break dunk that ignited an 18–2 run, and the Heat never looked back. They won Game 2. Then, when the series shifted to Miami, the Heat won Game 3 to take a 2-1 series lead.

Game 4, in LeBron's mind, would dictate the outcome of the series. If the Thunder won, they'd reclaim the momentum and anything could happen. If the Heat won, it was over. No team had ever come back from a 3-1 deficit to win the NBA Finals. So when the Thunder raced out to a seventeen-point lead in the first quarter, LeBron asserted himself, carrying the Heat all the way back to tie the game. With just under six minutes left in the fourth quarter and the teams deadlocked at ninety, LeBron stumbled and fell while driving on Durant, turning the ball over. As the Thunder took off downcourt, LeBron was slow to get up. After a scrum at the other end, Wade got the ball back and threw it ahead to LeBron, who put up an awkward shot. But it went in and put the Heat up by two.

Signaling to the bench that he needed to come out, LeBron collapsed on the court.

The sight of LeBron on his knees silenced the arena.

LeBron knew he wasn't injured. Yet he was in trouble. The muscles in his legs had locked up, and the cramps were so severe that he couldn't walk. A teammate and the trainer carried him off the court and had him lie down in front of the bench. "Ah, shit!" LeBron screamed, writhing in pain as the trainer straddled him and deep-massaged his quads.

With LeBron receiving treatment and fluids on the sideline, the Heat failed to score on four consecutive possessions. Meanwhile, Durant scored four straight points, and the Thunder reclaimed the lead, 94–92.

Stoic, Pat Riley surveyed the situation from his seat. This, he figured, was LeBron's moment of truth. The Thunder had seized the momentum, and time was running out. If LeBron didn't dig deep, the game—and perhaps the series—would be lost.

With determination, LeBron got up and limped to the scorer's table, bringing the crowd to its feet. As soon as LeBron checked back in, Bosh scored to tie the game at ninety-four. Then, after a Thunder turnover, Wade passed the ball to LeBron at the top of the key, well beyond the three-point line. With the shot clock winding down and the fans chanting, "Let's go Heat!" LeBron knew his legs wouldn't allow him to drive. Instead, he elevated and fired.

"Bang!" yelled ABC's Mike Breen. "*LeBron James* from downtown!"

The arena erupted in pandemonium. LeBron's three-pointer had put the Heat up by three.

Grimacing, LeBron turned and limped back on defense. He'd just hit one of the most clutch shots of his career, but he was in too much pain to celebrate. He was afraid he might not be able to remain on the floor.

"This place is exploding right now," Breen shouted over the noise.

After another defensive stop, Wade scored to put Miami up by five.

Miami's 7–0 run was just enough cushion. With a minute to play, LeBron's quads seized up so badly that he pulled himself out of the game. And the Heat held on to win by six and take a 3-1 series lead.

Two nights later, LeBron sat in front of his meticulously neat locker, slowly putting on his uniform. Savoring the moment, he knew the Heat were going to close out the Thunder. After four hard-fought games, Miami had broken Oklahoma City's will. The drama was over. The championship was within his grasp.

Game 5 was anticlimactic. LeBron led the Heat with twenty-six. Bosh added twenty-four. Wade contributed twenty. It was a businesslike performance, a balanced team effort. The Heat romped over the Thunder, building a twenty-five-point fourth-quarter lead and clinching the series in a dominant show of force.

LeBron was the unanimous choice for NBA Finals MVP. But when the final horn sounded, LeBron found Durant, wrapped his arms around him, and held him close. There was no gloating, no showboating, just deep respect for Durant's talent, and empathy for what Durant was feeling.

The mood in the Heat locker room after the game was euphoric. By the time LeBron reached the media room for his postgame press conference, his voice was hoarse, his mood subdued. "I dreamed about this moment for a long time," he said, his mind wandering back to the dark place he had found himself in a year earlier. "I'm thankful for the fact that I have a family—a fiancée and two kids. . . . It took me to hit rock bottom to realize what I needed to do as a professional athlete and as a person."

Instead of talking about winning the Finals, LeBron was reflecting on his growth. "The best thing that happened to me last year was us losing the Finals," he said, clearing his throat. "It humbled me. . . . I knew I was going to have to change as a basketball player and I was going to have to change as a person."

Suddenly, LeBron looked older and sounded wiser. He was taking stock of the path he'd been on since he'd picked up a basketball while living with the Walker family during grade school. "No one had gone through that journey," he said. "So I had to learn on my own. All the ups and downs—everything that came along with it—I basically had to figure it out on my own."

Overcome with gratitude, LeBron nonetheless hadn't forgotten any of the painful words that Dan Gilbert had said about him along the way. Even Gilbert's tweet from a year earlier when the Heat had lost to the Mavericks in the finals—"There are NO SHORTCUTS"—was still fresh in LeBron's mind. Sitting between the gold NBA championship trophy and his gold finals MVP trophy, LeBron straightened the brim of his new championship cap and looked into the cameras. "I did it the right way," he said. "I didn't shortcut anything. I put a lot of hard work and dedication in. And hard work pays off."

A couple of nights later, LeBron was sitting on the terrace of the Ritz Carlton in Coconut Grove with his sons. He reached for his phone and texted Maverick: *It just finally hit me. I'm a champion.*

The plane ride from Miami to New York felt like the start of a new phase. Two years earlier, David Letterman had ripped him for going to Miami. And Letterman's barbs had hurt. Nonetheless, LeBron said yes when Letterman invited him back on his show after the Finals.

Wearing a sport coat, jeans, and sneakers, LeBron stood backstage in the Ed Sullivan Theater, waiting for his cue. He wondered how the audience would react. He knew there would be a couple of stagehands with signs that would instruct the studio audience to CLAP. But still. How enthusiastic would they be?

"Ladies and gentlemen," Letterman said, "on Thursday night our first guest led his team to victory against the Oklahoma City Thunder. Won his first NBA championship. Ladies and gentlemen, from your Miami Heat, here's Finals MVP LeBron James."

The audience erupted as the house band broke into Power Station's "Some Like It Hot" and LeBron emerged from the shadows and stepped into the spotlight. After the stagehands dropped their signs, the crowd kept standing and cheering. Smiling at the crowd and waving, LeBron thought: *Wow!* Even after the band stopped playing, the audience kept going.

LeBron finally took a seat.

"This championship changes many things in your life, doesn't it?" Letterman asked.

"Absolutely," LeBron said, beaming. "I went from being ringless on Wednesday night to having a ring on Thursday night."

But the transformation went way beyond winning a ring. Two years earlier, he'd been the villain of professional sports, the target of derision and hatred. He'd gone through something that transcended sports. His goal had always been to win an NBA championship. But now that he'd finally reached the summit of his profession, the bigger achievement was the resurrection of his reputation. He'd won the respect of his peers, his opponents, and even his critics.

* * *

When Team USA assembled to get ready for the 2012 Summer Olympics in London, a few weeks after the NBA Finals concluded, Coach Mike Krzyzewski viewed LeBron in a new light. He now saw him as unique among all players who had ever played the game. "The evolution I saw in LeBron was a big-time change," Krzyzewski said. "By 2012, even Kobe understood that it was LeBron's team."

LeBron led a roster that included Durant, Westbrook, and Harden—the three stars he had just been beaten in the finals. But they were champing at the bit to play alongside LeBron, as were newcomers Kevin Love and nineteen-year-old Anthony Davis. And the veterans who had been on the team in 2008—Kobe, Chris Paul, and Carmelo Anthony—all looked at LeBron differently now.

That summer, Coach K treated LeBron differently, too. Each day, Coach K would create a practice plan. But before implementing it, he'd show it to LeBron and ask, "What do you think?" And LeBron would make suggestions. In some instances, LeBron's input would result in dramatic changes to Coach K's approach. But Coach K was not coddling LeBron; rather, he was collaborating with him. And LeBron was reciprocating. Each day, he'd ask Coach K, "What do you need from me today?"

It was also apparent to Coach K that LeBron's profile on the global stage had changed. By 2012, he was arguably the most famous athlete in the world. On July 16, when Team USA played an exhibition game against Brazil at the Verizon Center in Washington, DC, President Barack Obama and First Lady Michelle Obama attended. Vice President Joe Biden joined them. Prior to the game, Obama wanted to speak to the team in the locker room.

LeBron and each of the players stood in front of their lockers as the Secret Service took their places. When the president entered, he approached LeBron, smiled, and took his hand. "What's up, champ?" he said.

LeBron could feel the eyes of his teammates upon him. Kevin Durant and Russell Westbrook and Anthony Davis were the up-and-coming superstars of the league. But in this moment, they were in awe of LeBron's stature and the way he handled himself. The leader of the free world was in their locker room, and he was addressing LeBron like a friend.

When the game began, the president, First Lady, and vice president were seated in the front row near Team USA's basket. LeBron had never performed in front of such a distinguished group. Recognizing the enormity of the moment, he drove the lane in traffic. Feeling like he could fly, he muscled his way above the defenders and went airborne. His eyes nearly even with the front of the rim, he threw down a one-handed dunk that electrified the arena and brought a "Did you see that?" smile to the face of the First Lady. As LeBron landed and turned to run back downcourt, President Obama looked at Biden, raised his eyebrows, and grinned. The American team was in good hands.

In London, with a starting lineup that featured LeBron, Kobe, and Durant, Team USA dominated. Spain, which had numerous NBA players on its roster, was the only team capable of putting up a fight. But when the two teams met in the gold medal game, it was apparent that Team USA was simply too deep and too talented to be denied. Plus, the camaraderie between the American players was stronger than on any team LeBron had ever played on. They defeated Spain, 107–100.

Overcome with joy, LeBron found Coach K on the court. The two of them threw their arms around each other, and Coach K spoke to him as if he were addressing his own son. No player, Coach K intimated, had done more to help him rehabilitate Team USA's reputation after the team hit its nadir in Greece back in 2004. Over the course of eight years, Coach K and LeBron had transformed the culture around Olympic basketball, making it a source of patriotic pride for NBA stars to wear the red, white, and blue uniform. And in the London Olympics, especially, LeBron had been so invested, as one basketball writer pointed out, that he "did everything except carve the gold medals by hand."

Coach K's praise filled LeBron with pride. A little while later, he stood between Durant and Westbrook on an elevated platform. When an Olympics official approached, LeBron bowed his head, enabling the official to slip the gold medal over his head and around his neck. He was the only player other than Michael Jordan to win a gold medal, an NBA championship, and an NBA MVP Award in the same year.

Examining the medal, LeBron felt on top of the world.

When LeBron got back home, he met with his inner circle—Randy Mims, Rich Paul, and Maverick Carter. They'd been through a lot together and had come a long way.

Randy had been at LeBron's side as his personal assistant from day one, and the complexity of that job had increased dramatically over the past nine years. Randy was the ultimate confidant, working closely with the NBA, the Heat, Team USA, LeBron's various film and television projects, his business partners, his advertising partners, his lawyers and agents, and his friends. LeBron had elevated Mims to chief of staff. No other NBA player had someone with such a title. But no other NBA player had demands on him the way LeBron did. Randy's responsibilities grew as LeBron's profile grew. It was a role that Randy had embraced and perfected.

But Rich and Maverick were looking to branch out. Rich had been itching for a while to start his own sports agency. He felt overlooked and underutilized at Creative Arts Agency. And he was eager to show the world what he could do. "I learned nothing at C.A.A.," he would later tell the *New Yorker*. "Because there was no investment in me for me to learn anything. There was no plan. I used my personal skill set that I grew up with for these opportunities." By the summer of 2012, Rich was finally ready to make the leap. He had decided to leave the big Hollywood agency and form Klutch Sports Group.

LeBron could relate to the way Rich felt. He also believed that Rich's upbringing and unique life experiences had prepared him to become an exceptional agent for young Black players. "A lot of these kids that are being brought into these situations and being drafted, they are first-generation moneymakers, they are from the inner city," LeBron said. "They are from what we call the hood. And Rich and I are from that as well, so he can relate to these kids. There is nothing they've seen that he hasn't seen."

Rich had something much bigger in mind than simply building an agency. He wanted to change the way business was done in the NBA. But he knew that it was going to be an uphill battle, especially in the beginning, just to convince players to sign with him. Historically, there had been very few Black sports agents. There was a well-entrenched mentality within the Black community, Rich felt, that conditioned young players to expect to see white head coaches and white agents in the rooms where the decisions were being made about their futures. "We have to change that," Rich said.

LeBron agreed. And he was prepared to do something that would accelerate Rich's career aspirations and lend instant credibility to his friend as an agent. LeBron told Rich that if he was ready to leave CAA, LeBron was ready to leave with him.

* * *

On September 12, 2012, shock waves rippled across the NBA when the news broke that LeBron had split with his agent, Leon Rose, and left CAA to join Klutch Sports Group. The implications weren't lost on the NBA commissioner or on other established agents. With only one client, Rich's upstart Cleveland-based agency would have been easy to dismiss. But the fact that Rich Paul's sole client was the most powerful player in the NBA meant that Klutch was a force to be reckoned with. And other NBA agents couldn't help wondering how long it would be before other players started signing with Klutch.

The news also raised some eyebrows in Hollywood, where LeBron had been instrumental in building CAA's sports division. Not long after LeBron had gone with Leon Rose to CAA, other superstar athletes had followed, including Peyton Manning, Derek Jeter, and Real Madrid's Cristiano Ronaldo. Would LeBron's latest move start a new trend?

Initially, LeBron and Rich remained quiet about their intentions. But twenty-four hours after their new venture became public, LeBron sent a powerful message to his millions of followers on Twitter: "#THETAKEOVER."

Right away, players around the NBA took notice. And some of the players who had worked with Rich at CAA started signing on with Klutch.

While Rich was getting his business going in Cleveland, Maverick was planting SpringHill Entertainment's flag in Hollywood. A year earlier, SpringHill had successfully launched its second project, an animated series about a family of four called *The LeBrons*. Based loosely on the popular Nike commercial called "The 4 LeBrons," the new animated series explored the four facets of LeBron's personality—"kid," "athlete," "business," and "wise." It debuted on YouTube in April 2011 and ended up running for three seasons.

Then, while LeBron was busy winning an NBA title with the Heat, Maverick got a call from Fenway group chairman Tom Werner, who proposed an idea. Through a series of discussions, the idea evolved into a sitcom about a basketball player who relocates his family after signing with a new team. They called it *Survivor's Remorse* and pitched it to the premium cable network Starz, which ordered a first season and targeted 2014 for the show's premiere.

For Maverick, Hollywood was a foreign world with its own language. But one of the many benefits of merging with the Fenway group was that Maverick got to work closely with Werner, who had a stellar history of producing television programs. Plus, Maverick continued to work closely with Ari Emanuel and Mark Dowley at WME. Much as he had learned under Lynn Merritt at Nike, Maverick was now learning how to navigate Hollywood by riding along with the most experienced pros in the business. His vision was to grow SpringHill into a creative company that produced movies, television shows, and content for digital platforms.

Together, LeBron, Maverick, Rich, and Randy were doing a very American thing—inventing opportunities. LeBron was a new kind of superstar athlete, one who had both the desire and the economic might to change the business model of the NBA and to be a power player in Hollywood while he was in the heyday of his basketball career. No athlete had ever been able to realize such grand ambitions while maintaining mastery of his sport.

Danny Ainge knew the Celtics had a problem. There was a crack in the team's facade. Shooting guard Ray Allen felt underappreciated. For years, he'd been the quiet costar to Paul Pierce and Kevin Garnett. But now Rajon Rondo had developed an even louder voice in the locker room, and Allen had had enough. Besides, he was nearing the end of his career and he wanted to win another championship before retiring. And that wasn't going to happen with the Celtics.

Pat Riley sensed that Allen wasn't happy in Boston. And he seized the opportunity to lure the best three-point shooter in the NBA to Miami. He knew just how to do it—by convincing Allen that he was wanted. Riley made it clear to Allen that LeBron wanted him in Miami. D-Wade wanted him. Bosh wanted him. They were built to win more championships, and Allen's sharpshooting could be critical to winning back-to-back championships.

Ainge loved Allen as a player. They were also close friends. To keep Allen in Boston, Ainge offered him nearly twice as much money as he stood to earn in Miami. But Allen chose the Heat. In the end, Ainge wasn't surprised that Allen went to play with LeBron. He wished him the best and they remained friends.

But Allen's teammates felt jilted. Especially Pierce and Garnett. For five years they'd been in the trenches together. They'd won a title together.

They'd confided in each other. They'd spent time in each other's homes. "I thought we formed a brotherhood here in Boston," Pierce said.

The way Allen left—without giving Pierce and Garnett a heads-up—stung. They thought he at least would have called. The fact that he had walked away from them to play with LeBron in Miami felt like an act of betrayal. They hated Miami. LeBron was their archrival. They'd just lost to those guys in an epic, seven-game Eastern Conference Finals series.

The emotions evoked by Allen's bolting to Miami were still raw when the Heat hosted the Celtics in the season opener on October 30, 2012. Prior to the game, the Celtics had to sit through a ceremony in which Commissioner David Stern awarded the Heat players their championship rings. When Allen checked into the game late in the first quarter, he walked over to the Celtics bench to greet his former team. When Allen extended his hand, Garnett ignored him. Pierce avoided him, too.

Moments later, Allen caught a pass deep in the corner and nailed a three. With LeBron and Wade leading the way, and Allen chipping in nineteen points off the bench, the Heat rolled over the Celtics. The Heat looked poised to be even better than they'd been in the previous season.

On January 21, 2013, President Obama got big cheers from the servicemen and -women at the commander in chief's inaugural ball when he said, "I've got a date with me. . . . She makes me a better man and a better president. . . . Some may dispute the quality of our president, but nobody disputes the quality of our First Lady." Michelle Obama stepped onstage wearing a ruby-red dress. And the two of them slow-danced while Jennifer Hudson sang Al Green's "Let's Stay Together."

LeBron had very few men that he considered role models. President Obama was at the top of the list. LeBron and Savannah had contributed to his reelection campaign. And they were thrilled that Obama would be in office for four more years.

Days after the inauguration festivities, the Heat visited the White House to be honored for winning the NBA Finals the previous year. Wearing a navy-blue suit, a blue checkered shirt, a tie, and a pair of fashionable black glasses, LeBron stood with his teammates in a semicircle behind the president, who praised the team's achievements and cracked a few jokes. But he had something more serious he wanted to bring up.

"Let me just say one thing about these guys," Obama said. "There's a lot of focus on what happens on the court. But what's also important is what happens off the court. And I don't know all these guys. But I do know LeBron and Dwyane and Chris."

LeBron felt chills as the president spoke.

"One of the things I'm proudest of is that they take their roles as fathers seriously," Obama continued. "And for all the young men out there who are looking up to them all the time, for them to see somebody who cares about their kids and is there for them day in and day out, that's a good message to send. It's a positive message to send, and we're very proud of them for that."

The audience applauded.

Nothing made LeBron prouder than being singled out for being a good father. And to hear something like that from the president of the United States had him thinking about how far he'd come.

Suddenly, the president turned, looked at LeBron, and motioned for him to step forward. "C'mon, LeBron," he said.

LeBron approached the dais with a basketball for the president. It had been signed by all the players. "Am I supposed to say something?" LeBron asked.

"You can if you want," Obama said, taking the ball from him. "It's your world, man."

Everyone cracked up.

LeBron stepped to the microphone and faced the president. "On behalf of myself and my teammates, we just want to thank you for the hospitality, for allowing us to be in the White House," he said.

LeBron paused and looked back at his teammates. "I mean, we're in the White House!"

They laughed.

LeBron and Obama looked each other in the eye and smiled.

Then LeBron turned back toward his teammates again.

"I mean, we're kids from Chicago. And Dallas, Texas. And Michigan and Ohio and *South Dakota*," LeBron said. The room erupted. "And we're in the White House right now! This is like . . ." He paused, barely containing his emotions. "Mama, I made it!"

President Obama applauded and everyone else did, too.

*   *   *

For LeBron, *The Decision* seemed like a lifetime ago. The 2012–2013 season was his most enjoyable one yet. At one point, he and his teammates went fifty-three days without losing a game. During that period, the Heat won twenty-seven straight games, marking the second-longest winning streak in NBA history. The more they won, the harder teams tried to take them down. In a game in Chicago, LeBron was driving when Bulls guard Kirk Hinrich wrapped him up and took him down to the floor. LeBron expected the officials to call a flagrant foul. But they didn't. Then, in the fourth quarter, LeBron was collared around the shoulders and taken down again. This time the refs called a flagrant foul. But after reviewing the play on a video monitor, the officials downgraded the call to a routine foul.

LeBron protested. In his mind, neither of those fouls had been basketball plays. They'd been more like wrestling moves. Minutes later, LeBron was guarding Hinrich when he spotted Bulls forward Carlos Boozer heading in his direction to set a screen. Bracing himself, LeBron lowered his shoulder into Boozer's chest. The refs blew the whistle and called a flagrant foul on LeBron.

LeBron and the Heat were furious at what they perceived as a double standard. A couple of days later, Celtics president Danny Ainge weighed in. Asked about the questionable calls during a radio show, Ainge said: "I don't think either one of those were flagrant, and I think the one—LeBron against Boozer—was flagrant. I think that it's almost embarrassing that LeBron would complain about officiating."

Pat Riley was fed up with Ainge. Two days later, a bunch of beat writers were talking to Coach Erik Spoelstra when the Heat's head of PR emerged from the locker room with an official statement from Riley. It read: "Danny Ainge needs to shut the fuck up and manage his own team. He was the biggest whiner going when he was playing, and I know that because I coached against him."

Ainge fired back with his own official statement: "I stand by what I said. . . . I don't care about Pat Riley. He can say whatever he wants. I don't want to mess up his Armani suits and all that hair goop. It would be way too expensive for me."

With Ainge and Riley sparring in the press and Ray Allen thriving in Miami, the Celtics-Heat rivalry was winding down. At the end of the 2012–2013 season, Ainge traded Pierce and Garnett to the Brooklyn Nets, and the Celtics began to rebuild. Meanwhile, the Heat finished the season with the best record in the NBA. And for the second straight year, LeBron was named the league's MVP, joining Michael Jordan, Bill Russell, Wilt Chamberlain, and Kareem Abdul-Jabbar as the only players to win four or more NBA MVP Awards.

To no one's surprise, the Heat reached the NBA Finals for the third consecutive year. This time they faced the San Antonio Spurs. For LeBron, it was a rematch against an old foe, Tim Duncan, who had led San Antonio in the sweep of the Cavaliers back in the 2007 Finals. The Spurs still had their other two core players from back then, namely Tony Parker and Manu Ginobili. But they had added a budding star, twenty-one-year-old Kawhi Leonard. The Spurs were trying to win their fifth championship with Duncan. The Heat were seeking back-to-back titles.

The two teams were so evenly matched that they alternated victories through the first five games, with the Spurs up, 3-2, when the series shifted back to Miami for Game 6. But by the end of the fourth quarter, the Spurs had seized control. With twenty-eight seconds remaining, Manu Ginobili hit two free throws to put his team up, 94–89. Chewing his gum like a machine, Pat Riley stood with his arms folded across his chest as Miami fans streamed for the exits and the arena's security staff started putting up yellow tape along the outskirts of the court to keep people from interfering with the upcoming Spurs celebration. "Gonna be hard for Miami to live with this finish," the Heat's play-by-play announcer said on the radio.

Seconds later, LeBron hit a three to cut the Spurs lead to two.

Then Duncan inbounded the ball to Leonard, who was one of the team's best free throw shooters. Immediately fouled, Leonard went to the line with a chance to seal the victory. But he missed his first attempt. He made the second, putting the Spurs back up by three. The Heat had life.

With nine seconds on the clock, LeBron launched another three to tie. It rimmed out. But Chris Bosh outhustled three Spurs and grabbed the rebound. Surrounded, he kicked it to Ray Allen in the corner. With a man in his face, Allen launched a three-pointer that touched nothing but net as it went through the cylinder with five seconds left on the clock. The sharpshooter from the Celtics had saved the Heat from defeat and sent the game into overtime, where Miami prevailed, 103–100.

* * *

Game 7 was a classic. The score was tied after one quarter. It was tied at halftime. It was tied in the fourth quarter. And in the end, it came down to LeBron and Duncan. With his team down by two, Duncan missed a shot at the rim with forty seconds left. Then he missed a tap-in rebound attempt. Either shot would have tied the game. Angry at himself, Duncan smacked the floor with both hands.

On the other end, with Leonard lunging at him, LeBron never considered passing. He stepped up and nailed a jumper to put Miami up by four. Then, after a Spurs time-out, LeBron intercepted a pass intended for Duncan, sealing the victory. LeBron had finished with a herculean thirty-seven points—tying an NBA record set in the 1950s for points scored in a Game 7 Finals win—and twelve rebounds, and the Heat were crowned champions for the second year in a row. LeBron was named MVP of the Finals again.

While the Heat fans celebrated, LeBron and Duncan embraced at mid-court. Seven years earlier, Duncan had told LeBron, "This is going to be your league in a little while." Duncan was amazed at how much LeBron had reinvented his game since then. He had developed into one of the most reliable outside shooters in the league. And his physical conditioning remained unparalleled.

After the game, LeBron joined Magic Johnson, Jalen Rose, and Bill Simmons for a courtside interview. The irony of sharing this triumphant moment with Simmons, a guy who had crossed the line with his barbs at LeBron and LeBron's mother over the years, wasn't lost on him. But LeBron kept it cordial. When Magic and Rose talked about LeBron's performance and pointed out that he had won two straight Finals MVPs, LeBron deflected the praise.

"I'm just a kid from Akron, Ohio," he said. "Statistically, I'm not even supposed to be here."

Magic and Rose nodded.

"You know," LeBron said, pointing at Rose. "You know," he continued, pointing at Magic. "So the fact that I can walk into an NBA locker room and see James on the back of an NBA jersey . . ."

When the interview was winding down, Magic turned to LeBron.

"LeBron," he said, "and I'm serious, too. I've seen *everybody* play. You are the *only* guy, I think, who can become the greatest who has ever played this game."

Biting his lip, LeBron looked down.

"What are you gonna do now?" Magic asked.

Magic was referring to what it was going to take for LeBron and the Heat to win a third-straight championship.

But LeBron was contemplating something bigger.

THIRTY-ONE

GETTING A GRIP

LeBron was a dreamer. And by age twenty-eight, many of his basketball dreams had come true. Yet his dedication to his career had delayed the completion of another dream that he'd had since he was a little boy—to be part of a family consisting of a husband and a wife with children, living in a big, warm home that was filled with love. Early on, LeBron's idealized vision of family life was influenced by television shows like *The Fresh Prince of Bel-Air* and *The Cosby Show*. In one respect, the grand estate LeBron had built outside Akron and his luxury home in Miami were reflections of the fictional houses occupied by Will Smith and the Huxtables. But in a more authentic sense, LeBron and Savannah had nurtured a relationship that had withstood the traps and temptations of celebrity and fame. They'd been together for twelve years. And LeBron wanted their wedding to resemble the fairy-tale life that he felt they were creating together.

On September 14, 2013, LeBron and Savannah invited their closest friends to witness their nuptials in LeBron's favorite city outside of Akron—San Diego. News helicopters hovered above the Grand Del Mar hotel. But LeBron and Savannah had gone to great lengths to keep every aspect of the ceremony private. They had no interest in an exclusive arrangement with a photographer from a celebrity magazine. They thwarted the paparazzi by erecting huge tents to shield the guests upon arrival. Even the chapel and the reception area were shrouded by tents. And everyone on the guest list was instructed to turn off their phones and avoid posting pictures on social media.

For LeBron and Savannah it was an ideal wedding, topped off by their good friends Jay-Z and Beyoncé serenading them with "Crazy in Love." It was hard to believe that their first date at the Outback Steakhouse in Akron had led to this moment. But by now, they were used to the uniqueness of their life together. And they knew the words to the song that captured the new phase they were entering:

History in the making
Part two, it's so crazy right now.

After the reception, LeBron and Savannah jetted off to Italy for their honeymoon.

LeBron and Savannah had fully adapted to life in Miami. They had a beautiful home there. The boys had adjusted. Savannah had gotten involved in the community, helping underprivileged children. And the tropical climate beat Cleveland's, especially in the winter.

The basketball was good, too. LeBron had won back-to-back championships, and the Heat were on a quest to win three straight titles. In the history of the NBA, only three teams—the Bill Russell Celtics in the sixties, Michael Jordan's Bulls in the nineties, and Kobe and Shaq's Lakers in the early 2000s—had managed to achieve the feat. LeBron hoped he and his teammates would join that exclusive club.

Heading into the 2013–2014 season, Pat Riley likened the Heat to a Broadway show that was in its fourth year of an amazing run. The team had the greatest leading man in the game, along with big-name costars. The Heat drew the biggest crowds in every city they visited. They were the talk of the league. And the organization had developed a national profile that transcended basketball.

Midway through the season, when the Heat returned to the White House on January 14, 2014, to be honored for their second championship, the players looked as though they were right at home. Beforehand, head coach Erik Spoelstra, Dwyane Wade, and Ray Allen agreed to record a public service announcement in support of Michelle Obama's "Let's Move!" anti-obesity initiative. With the camera rolling, Spoelstra played the role of television correspondent. Holding a microphone, he asked Wade and Allen about the importance of healthy eating.

"You can take it from me, eating the right foods can make you a better athlete," Wade said.

Suddenly, LeBron and the First Lady sneaked in behind Wade, Allen, and Spoelstra. LeBron held up a miniature backboard. Michelle Obama dunked a miniature basketball. "Oooh!" she shouted, disrupting the interview and prompting Wade and Allen to turn around.

"In your *face!*" LeBron said.

Everyone cracked up.

LeBron and the First Lady had turned the White House into a fun house. That afternoon, after President Obama recognized the team for winning back-to-back championships, Ray Allen presented Obama with an official Heat jersey with the name *POTUS* and the number *44* sewn on the back. And Coach Spoelstra gave Obama a championship trophy replica that had been signed by all the players. It included Obama's name.

An avid Bulls fan, Obama joked: "You guys are winning me over."

LeBron's connection with the Obamas was deepening. Shortly after the White House visit, President Obama asked for LeBron's help with his signature legislative achievement—the Affordable Care Act.

Also known as Obamacare, the universal-healthcare initiative included the establishment of a government website, HealthCare.gov. And in December 2013, applicants had started signing up for health insurance through the website. Under the law, the deadline for open enrollment was set to end on March 31, 2014. Millions of eligible applicants—many of whom were minorities—had yet to enroll. Obama appealed to LeBron for help with encouraging people to register.

With Adam Mendelsohn now a member of his inner circle, entrusted with protecting and enhancing LeBron's public image, LeBron was kept up to speed on political affairs that related to him. He was aware that the Republican Party had opposed Obama's healthcare legislation. He also understood that by getting involved, he'd likely face some political backlash. Indeed, when Senate Minority Leader Mitch McConnell learned that the Obama administration was enlisting a few prominent athletes to help register people for health insurance, he contacted the NBA and the NFL to discourage it. And Steve Scalise, a high-ranking Republican in the House of Representatives, wrote the leagues about the Obama administration's efforts, saying, "I would caution you against being coerced into doing their dirty work for them."

LeBron didn't consider it dirty work. At a point in his career when he was earning tens of millions of dollars per year to endorse consumer products, he wanted to volunteer his time and use his visibility to help the president. LeBron knew that a lot of African Americans needed health insurance, and he hoped his voice would encourage them to sign up. He recorded a public service announcement that aired on ESPN, ABC, TNT, and NBA TV in March 2014.

Obama praised LeBron for his willingness to get involved. "When you think about some of our greatest sports heroes—Muhammad Ali, Bill Russell, Arthur Ashe—they spoke out on issues that mattered at pretty critical times," Obama told the press.

As the 2013–2014 regular season wound down, speculation was mounting about LeBron's future in Miami. When LeBron had signed with Miami in 2010, his contract had included a provision that enabled him to opt out after the 2014 season and become an unrestricted free agent. Wade and Bosh had the same provisions in their contracts. But as a practical matter, LeBron was the only one of Miami's Big Three whose plans were the subject of intense scrutiny. Wade had spent his entire career in Miami and had no intention of playing elsewhere. And Bosh wanted to stay put in Miami and continue to play with LeBron and Wade. LeBron, on the other hand, was once again in a position to become the most coveted free agent in the NBA.

With Rich Paul poised to handle LeBron's upcoming contract negotiations, Mendelsohn managed the messaging to the press. His approach was simple: say nothing.

But off the record, Mendelsohn was back-channeling with Lee Jenkins at *Sports Illustrated*. By this point, Jenkins had gone through Mendelsohn for access to LeBron on several big pieces he'd written for *Sports Illustrated* over the previous few years. He'd earned Mendelsohn's trust and LeBron's respect.

Jenkins knew that LeBron's decision whether to remain in Miami in 2014 had the potential to be just as explosive as his decision to leave Cleveland in 2010. With that in mind, Jenkins was looking for an exclusive. And he came up with an idea.

In mid-April 2014, *Sports Illustrated* had published an essay written by Duke freshman basketball player Jabari Parker, who, instead of calling a press conference as was customary, announced on SI.com that he was leaving college to enter the NBA Draft. The response to Parker's essay had been overwhelmingly positive. Jenkins emailed a link to Parker's essay to

Mendelsohn, suggesting it might be a blueprint for what LeBron could do to announce his plans at the end of the season.

Mendelsohn filed the idea away.

The Heat finished the season with the second-best record in the Eastern Conference. Poised to defend their championship title, Miami won the first two games of the first round of the playoffs against the Charlotte Bobcats.

The team was in Charlotte preparing for Game 3 when a scandal broke. TMZ published audio recordings of Donald Sterling, the eighty-year-old married owner of the Los Angeles Clippers, talking to his thirty-one-year-old mistress, V. Stiviano, who had posted a photo of herself with former Lakers star Magic Johnson on her Instagram page.

> **Sterling:** In your lousy fucking Instagrams, you don't have to have yourself walking with black people. It bothers me a lot that you want to promote, broadcast that you're associating with black people.
>
> **Stiviano:** Do you know that you have a whole team that's black that plays for you?
>
> **Sterling:** Do I know? I support them and give them food and clothes and cars and houses. Who gives it to them? Does someone else give it to them? Who makes the game? Do I make the game, or do they make the game?

Stiviano had recorded the conversation, along with many other ones, on her cell phone.

When they were released by TMZ, the NBA playoffs were suddenly in doubt. The Clippers' players were contemplating a walkout. Their playoff opponent—the Warriors—were poised to join them. It was a crisis for Adam Silver, who had just succeeded David Stern as NBA commissioner a couple of months earlier. Calling the comments "disturbing and offensive," the league announced it was investigating whether the voice on the recordings was Sterling's.

When LeBron arrived at the arena in Charlotte hours after the tapes had become public, the Heat beat writers asked his opinion on the situation. Without consulting Adam Mendelsohn or anyone else, LeBron didn't hesitate. "If the reports are true," he began, "it's unacceptable. It's unacceptable in our league. It doesn't matter if you're black, white, Hispanic, or whatever the case may be. . . . And as the commissioner of our league, they have to make a stand. And they have to be very aggressive with it. . . . We just can't have that in our league."

LeBron mentioned that one of his best friends, Chris Paul, played for the Clippers. "I can only imagine what's going through his head," LeBron said before pointing out that the NBA was too high-profile to let this slide. "There is no room for Donald Sterling in our league," he said.

The reporters in the room immediately sensed the magnitude of the moment. LeBron played for the Heat. But he was the ambassador for the sport. And he had the self-awareness to recognize that his words mattered.

A reporter asked a follow-up question.

"There are only thirty owners and four hundred–plus of us," LeBron said. "I can only imagine if a player came out and said something of that stature what would happen to us as players. So I believe in [Commissioner] Adam [Silver]. I believe in the NBA and they have to do something, and do something very fast and quickly before this really gets out of hand. Like I said, there is no room for Donald Sterling in our league. There it is."

Minutes later, *Sun Sentinel* sports columnist Ira Winderman tweeted: "LeBron James, 'There is no room for Donald Sterling in our league.'" Other journalists tweeted it. Headlines appeared. LeBron's opinion went viral.

The Heat won that night. But that was beside the point. Standing in a cramped locker room in North Carolina, a Black athlete had called for the governing body of a sports league to strip a white billionaire of his ownership of a team. It was an inflection point in American sports that marked the beginning of a change in the power dynamic between athletes and owners.

Sterling had a checkered past when it came to racism. "Donald Sterling's racial history is on the record," sportscaster Bryant Gumbel said on NBC's *Meet the Press* the next day. "David Stern and the NBA owners knew the kind of a man Donald Sterling was long before this."

The difference this time was that the game's greatest player had called out the league. And players were talking seriously about sitting out the playoffs.

Three days after LeBron spoke out, the NBA banned Sterling for life, and Adam Silver said the league would try to force him to sell the team, an unprecedented step that would require the approval of three-fourths of the league's owners. "It would be a rare," the *New York Times* reported, "if not unprecedented, move for a North American professional sports league—made even more unusual by the fact that the NBA is punishing Mr. Sterling for comments he made in a private conversation."

But Silver was determined. "We stand together in condemning Mr. Sterling's views," he said. "They simply have no place in the NBA."

Before the owners voted, Sterling sold the team to Microsoft CEO Steve Ballmer.

The Heat steamrolled through the playoffs. With LeBron leading the way, they reached the NBA Finals, where the Spurs awaited.

All season long, San Antonio had played with one goal in mind—to avenge the loss to the Heat in the previous NBA Finals. No one was more motivated than Tim Duncan, who had not stopped thinking about the two shots he had missed at the rim near the end of Game 6 that could have enabled them to win. At thirty-seven, Duncan knew this might be his last shot at redemption.

For LeBron, it was his third time going head-to-head with Duncan in the Finals. When the two of them shook hands before the start of Game 1 in San Antonio on June 5, 2014, LeBron said to Duncan: "Me and you again."

Duncan smiled. But he was dead set in his resolve to win this time.

The Spurs won the first game by fifteen.

LeBron put the Heat on his back and led all scorers with thirty-five points in Game 2. And the Heat won by two points to even the series.

With the next two games set to be played in Miami, Pat Riley was confident that the Heat were on their way to a third straight title. But the Spurs dominated Games 3 and 4, winning by nineteen and twenty-one points, respectively, to take a commanding 3-1 lead. Then, after Miami jumped out to a big lead in Game 5, the Spurs stormed back and finished off the Heat to win the Finals. It was Duncan's fifth championship in fifteen seasons.

While the confetti fell in San Antonio, you could hear a pin drop in the Heat locker room.

And questions about LeBron's future instantly took center stage. As soon as LeBron sat down beside Wade for their joint postgame press conference, a reporter said, "Obviously, you have a very big decision coming up. What do you think your timetable will be on your decision?"

"I haven't really thought about that just yet," LeBron said.

Moments later, another reporter said, "LeBron, you said in February you couldn't picture yourself leaving Miami. Do you still feel that way?"

LeBron hesitated. "I mean, I'll deal with my summer when I get to that point." He paused again. "You guys are trying to find answers," he said. "I'm just not going to give you one."

Pat Riley had been around the NBA for more than forty-five years. During that time, he'd developed a philosophy for what it took to establish a basketball dynasty—keep the star players together, *especially* when you lose. Sports dynasties were generally defined as teams that won three or more championships with the same core personnel. In the eighties, the Lakers had won five championships with Magic Johnson and Kareem Abdul-Jabbar. Riley had coached them for four of those championships, and he liked to point out that during that great Lakers run, Magic and Kareem had failed to win the championship five times. But when they fell short, they always regrouped and came back strong the following season.

Similarly, the Celtics were considered one of the greatest teams in the eighties, with Larry Bird, Robert Parish, and Kevin McHale. They had won three championships, which meant that they hadn't won nine times. But the core players had stayed together.

Michael Jordan and Scottie Pippen had stayed together for eleven years and won six titles together.

Then there were the San Antonio Spurs. In seventeen years, they'd won the championship five times. During that period, they'd come up short twelve times. But they had kept Tim Duncan and the core players together. And after a seven-year drought since their last championship, they had won another one. It was the ultimate testament to the importance of staying together.

When Riley sized up the Heat's situation after the 2014 Finals, he felt they were on the cusp of becoming a dynasty—in four years, they'd been to the championship four times and won twice. If LeBron, Wade, and Bosh stayed together for as long as Jordan and Pippen had played together or as long as Magic and Kareem had, there was no reason why the Heat couldn't win five or six championships.

With that in mind, a few days after the loss to the Spurs, Riley scheduled exit interviews with the Heat players. The mood in these meetings was subdued. That didn't surprise Riley. He hated losing as much as the players did. But there was one encouraging aspect of these one-on-one sessions—Wade and Bosh signaled a desire to stay together and compete for more titles. They just needed some time off to recuperate.

Riley's meeting with LeBron, however, was different.

Like everyone else on the team, LeBron was frustrated over the loss to the Spurs. But he wasn't despondent the way he had been in 2011 after losing to the Mavericks. This time, LeBron had adopted Riley's view that championships were extremely hard to come by in the NBA, and the fact that the Heat had been to four straight finals and won two was impressive.

But LeBron wasn't prepared to commit to staying in Miami. He told Riley that he needed some time to think about what he was going to do. He wanted to meet with his team. He made no promises and offered no timetable.

Riley didn't press, figuring it wouldn't do any good. He didn't have the kind of close personal relationship with LeBron that would have enabled him to appeal to his sense of loyalty. As the team's chief executive, Riley had chosen to maintain an arm's-length relationship with LeBron. They typically communicated via text or in brief encounters after practice or in the hallway. For Riley, this was a strategic decision. He had decided at the outset of LeBron's tenure in Miami that he wasn't going to pander to the team's biggest star the way the Cavaliers had.

When the meeting ended, there was no warm embrace. Riley got hugs and kisses after winning championships the previous two years. Now there was just a handshake.

That night, Riley went home to his wife of forty-plus years, Chris Rodstrom, and poured himself a scotch. And he reached for one of his favorite LPs, removed it from the sleeve, placed it on the record player, and dropped the needle. Then they downed Johnnie Walker Blue while listening to James Ingram's "Just Once" and reminiscing about when they'd been young and ambitious and achievement-oriented.

We're back to bein' strangers
Wonderin' if we ought to stay
Or head on out the door.

Riley couldn't help fearing that LeBron was heading out the door.

The next morning, Riley was scheduled to address the media. Struggling to conceal his frustration over the prospect of LeBron's leaving, he sat down in the pressroom at the Heat's headquarters, took a deep breath, and exhaled. "Good morning, everybody," he said, looking at the press corps. Then he chuckled under his breath. "You wanna trend something?" he said, smacking the table with both hands. "I'm pissed! Okay? So go ahead. Get it out there."

Riley balled up his tongue in his cheek and waited for the first question.

A reporter asked him to address the level of concern within the organization about the Big Three and keeping them together.

Riley had anticipated that. But he had no intention of letting the press steer the conversation. He planned to use the press conference to send a message to LeBron.

"Bear with me for a minute," Riley said. "I think we need to have a perspective about things. I think everybody needs to get a grip. Media. Heat players. The organization. All of our fans. You gotta get a grip on greatness and on teams."

Riley rattled off the previous NBA dynasties and pointed out that the greatest teams in the history of the league had lost more championships than they had won.

"This stuff is hard," Riley told the media. "You gotta stay together. If you got the guts. You don't find the first door and run out of it."

Riley uncharacteristically sounded like the one who was losing his grip.

"What happened last year with San Antonio?" he said. "Did they run? They faced it. And they came back. And we saw the result. We will find out what we're made of here. It's not about options. It's not about free agency. We have a chance to do something significant. We have a tremendous opportunity here for long-term success. But don't think we're not gonna get beat again. So just get a grip. Everybody. That's my message to the players also."

"Have you shared that with them?" a reporter asked.

"They're hearing it right now," Riley said.

LeBron heard Riley loud and clear. But he didn't appreciate being lectured. It bothered LeBron that when a player had an opportunity to decide his own fate, he faced questions and criticism. But when a team executive traded or cut players, it was considered business.

LeBron shared Riley's view about dynasties. LeBron was a basketball historian. He knew all about the Lakers and the Celtics and the Bulls. And after four years in Miami, LeBron had personally experienced what it took to win championships.

LeBron also knew that the Heat were primed to win more titles and that if he stayed with Wade and Bosh in Miami, he stood the best chance of winning as many titles as Magic or Jordan.

But LeBron was different than Magic and Jordan. As much as he wanted to accumulate more rings and trophies, the one thing LeBron wanted most was to deliver a title to Cleveland. Growing up, he'd fantasized about being a superhero. He had imagined what it would be like to look over a city and take down bad guys. As an adult, his definition of "bad guys" included poverty, abandonment, and hopelessness. He was uniquely positioned, he felt, to fight those things.

But in order to do that, he had to go home.

THIRTY-TWO

WHO AM I TO HOLD A GRUDGE?

On June 24, LeBron opted out of his contract with the Heat, officially becoming a free agent.

Riley was beside himself. And the silence from LeBron was maddening. Back in 2010, Riley had dealt with Leon Rose, a familiar foe who had worked with him to land the Big Three in Miami. But now Rich Paul was in charge. He didn't operate the way Rose did. And although Rich was young and still learning the business, he was an experienced poker player. When it came to LeBron's intentions, Rich never tipped his hand. He provided no information to the Heat and made no promises.

Rich knew where LeBron wanted to end up. And he understood why. But there were a lot of hurdles to clear for LeBron to get back to Cleveland.

For starters, LeBron had to convince his family. Savannah had gotten used to Miami, and she still hadn't forgotten that fans back in Cleveland had burned LeBron's jerseys. Then there was Gloria. She was vehemently opposed to LeBron's playing for Dan Gilbert again. In Gloria's mind, Gilbert had crossed the line with his personal attacks on her son's reputation. Now LeBron wanted to go play for that man again?

"Fuck that," Gloria said. "We ain't going back."

LeBron had no illusions about Gilbert. Deep down, he saw racism in Gilbert's words and deeds back in 2010. But LeBron's motivation for going back to Cleveland was bigger than his tiff with Gilbert. "You know what, Mom," LeBron told her, "it ain't really about that."

Gloria struggled to understand why LeBron would play for the Cavs again.

"It's more of a bigger picture," LeBron said. "It's more all of these kids and all of these people need inspiration and a way to get out. And I believe I'm that way out."

"You go back," she told him. "I ain't going back with you."

LeBron also had significant pushback from Maverick, who had uprooted four years earlier to follow LeBron to Miami. One of the reasons that LeBron and Maverick's relationship had endured was that Maverick had never been a yes-man. He was never afraid to speak his mind. They went back and forth over LeBron's desire to return to Cleveland. Maverick thought it was a mistake. LeBron said it was progress over pride. Ultimately, they agreed to disagree. But Maverick had no intention of following his best friend back home.

"I ain't going back to Cleveland this time," Maverick told LeBron. After all, LeBron wasn't the only one with personal aspirations.

As a kid, Maverick hadn't dreamt about making movies. Nor had he set out to become a television and film producer. But since they'd formed SpringHill and he'd started spending so much time going back and forth to Hollywood, Maverick had figured out that what he really wanted to do was tell stories. And he wanted to build a platform for athletes to tell their own stories. A platform that bypassed journalists. But in order to do that, he couldn't be in Cleveland.

"I'm going to LA," Maverick told LeBron.

The longer they'd been together, the more LeBron had valued Maverick's instincts. It was Maverick who had struck up the relationship with Jimmy Iovine, which had led LeBron to go into business with Iovine and Beats back in 2008. And in the spring of 2014, while the Heat had been in the playoffs, Apple had acquired Beats for $3 billion. At the time of the Apple acquisition, LeBron's equity stake in the audio products company was valued at $30 million. In LeBron's mind, going into business with Beats had been the best financial decision he'd made since signing with Nike at the end of his senior year of high school.

He supported Maverick's relocation to Hollywood.

When LeBron declared his free agency, Dan Gilbert started maneuvering. He figured it was a long shot to get LeBron back. But he was determined to do everything possible to make the Cavaliers look attractive. It was no small chore. The Cavs were a fledgling team that had finished 33-49 in 2013–2014. But they'd been lucky in the draft lottery, where they inexplicably landed the number one overall pick, which they used to select Andrew Wiggins, a promising young star.

The team had also fired its coach and hired David Blatt, one of the most successful coaches in European basketball history.

Gilbert's most important task, however, was convincing the team's star point guard, Kyrie Irving, to re-sign with the team. Irving was a twenty-two-year-old phenom whom the Cavaliers had selected with the number one overall pick in 2011. He'd been the NBA Rookie of the Year and a two-time all-star. But Irving was entering the final year of his rookie contract. If the Cavaliers had any chance of landing LeBron, they were first going to have to secure Irving.

When the free agency period officially began on July 1, 2014, Gilbert entered Irving's home one minute after midnight and met with him and his agent. Less than two hours later, Gilbert tweeted: "Looking forward to the next 6 years of @KyrieIrving in CLE. Just shook hands & intend to sign on the 10th."

Then Irving sent out his own tweet: "I'm here for the long haul Cleveland!!!"

Gilbert had offered Irving a five-year, $90 million contract extension.

Speculation about LeBron and his future was garnering as much attention as speculation about Hillary Clinton, who was figuring out whether to run for president in 2016. The *New Yorker* dubbed LeBron and Hillary "the Deciders." "As they pondered—James, where to play; Clinton, whether to run—the country looked on, rapt, while the press scurried to break news on an announcement that both figures would make only in their own good time," the magazine's Ian Crouch wrote in the summer of 2014.

Lee Jenkins wasn't scurrying. He'd spent four years establishing the inside track. After the NBA Finals, Jenkins had reached out to Mendelsohn again about his suggestion that LeBron consider revealing his decision through a first-person essay that Jenkins would help him write. On the Fourth of July, Jenkins was with his family at a parade in San Diego when he got a call from Mendelsohn.

"We like the idea," Mendelsohn told him. "I think that could work."

Thrilled, Jenkins wondered about the next steps.

"Be ready early in the week to go to Miami, Rio, or Vegas," Mendelsohn told Jenkins.

Miami and Vegas made sense. But Rio?

LeBron, Jenkins was told, might be down there for the World Cup.

Mendelsohn gave Jenkins no hints about which team LeBron was leaning toward. But they agreed that LeBron would break the news on the *Sports Illustrated* website. Before hanging up, Mendelsohn told Jenkins to stand by for instructions on where to meet LeBron to work on the essay. And he gave Jenkins some parting instructions.

"You can't tell anybody why," Mendelsohn said. "You can't tell anybody anything."

Pat Riley was frustrated over the lack of communication from LeBron. But Rich Paul was focused on Dan Gilbert. As far as Rich was concerned, Gilbert had talked a lot of shit about his client. And before Rich could explore the prospect of LeBron's returning to Cleveland, Gilbert needed to clear the air with LeBron. And that was only going to happen in a face-to-face conversation.

Gilbert welcomed the opportunity. And on July 6, he flew to Miami to meet with LeBron, Rich, and Maverick.

For Gilbert, it was a surreal situation. He was flying beneath the radar into Pat Riley's backyard in hopes of saying the right things to get LeBron to return to the city that had burned his jerseys. He wished he could take back all those things he'd said and done. But at least he'd finally removed his scathing letter from the team's website. Now he planned to seek forgiveness.

They convened at a house in Miami. It was the first time the two men had been in a room together since before *The Decision*. At the outset, Gilbert told LeBron how sorry he was. They'd had seven great years together and one terrible night, Gilbert suggested. "I let all the emotion and passion for the situation carry me away," Gilbert said. "I wish I had never done it. . . . I wish I could take it back."

LeBron acknowledged that he had made some mistakes, too. If he'd had it to do over again, there were plenty of things he'd have done differently. But LeBron preferred to look forward at this point, not backward.

Without indicating which direction he was leaning, LeBron inquired about Gilbert's plans to do what it would take to win a championship.

Gilbert was surprised and relieved that LeBron was willing to talk about the future. And he launched into all the things the team had already done over the summer—signing number one draft pick Andrew Wiggins, hiring head coach David Blatt and assistant coach Tyronn Lue, and coming to terms with Kyrie Irving on a long-term deal. He told LeBron that everything was coming together.

LeBron made no commitments. Nor did Rich.

Afterward, Gilbert flew to Sun Valley, Idaho, for the annual Allen & Company retreat. And LeBron flew to Las Vegas to host his Nike basketball camp.

On July 8, the Republican National Committee announced that Cleveland had been chosen to host the 2016 convention. Florida senator Marco Rubio promptly tweeted: "Congrats to Cleveland on being awarded the #GOP2016 convention. But you still aren't getting @KingJames back!" That afternoon, Lee Jenkins got word to fly to Las Vegas and check into the Wynn hotel and await further instructions.

The next day, Dan Gilbert was summoned to meet with LeBron and his camp in Las Vegas. Unsure what to expect, Gilbert boarded his plane in Sun Valley and headed for the desert. Then he spent three hours in a room with LeBron and Rich, who made it clear that this wasn't a negotiation. Rich outlined LeBron's terms. He wanted a two-year deal with an opt-out clause after the first season. If the Cavaliers weren't doing what LeBron wanted after one year, he'd be free to walk and go elsewhere. This gave LeBron all the flexibility and the upper hand.

After LeBron had left Cleveland in 2010, Gilbert vowed to never let a player obtain so much leverage over him again. But Gilbert knew that the only way he was going to get LeBron back was to acquiesce. Privately, Gilbert couldn't help admiring the fact that LeBron had the balls to make take-it-or-leave-it demands, and the smarts to insist on renewable contracts after each year. LeBron's team had mastered the ins and outs of the salary cap, and they had the foresight to realize that the numbers were going to go up exponentially in 2017 when the league entered a new TV deal with the networks. By not locking into a long-term contract the way Kyrie Irving had, LeBron stood to make a lot more money through one-year contracts.

After the meeting, Gilbert let Rich know that he would accept LeBron's terms. And he immediately set in motion a three-team trade that would off-load a few players from the Cavs' payroll, freeing up cap space to sign LeBron.

On the same day that LeBron and Rich met with Gilbert, they had also scheduled a meeting with Riley and the Heat's general manager, Andy Elisburg. Before leaving Miami, Riley told Elisburg to pack the two championship trophies that the team had won with LeBron. With Riley planning to use them as motivation, Elisburg put them in protective cases. Riley also packed a bottle of wine from a vineyard in Napa Valley whose motto was "A Promise Made and a Promise Kept." Back when LeBron had signed with the Heat, Maverick had given Riley a bottle of wine from the same winery.

But when Riley and Elisburg arrived at LeBron's suite, Riley was disappointed to discover that Maverick, whom he respected, wasn't there. It was just LeBron, Rich, and Randy Mims, and they were watching the World Cup. They didn't bother to turn the game off when the meeting started. Riley discreetly told Elisburg not to bother unpacking the trophies.

The meeting lasted about an hour. Riley reiterated that Miami was the best path to more championships. And the Heat had the money and the willingness to bring in another player or two to complement LeBron, Wade, and Bosh. Irritated, at one point Riley asked the guys to mute the television. When the meeting ended, Riley didn't have a great feeling.

That night, Mendelsohn called Lee Jenkins and told him to come to LeBron's room the following morning.

Wearing a black stocking cap, shorts, and a tank top, LeBron sat on a sofa, eating scrambled eggs and picking at fruit. The television was tuned to ESPN. From his fifty-eighth-story suite atop the Wynn, he had an expansive view of the Strip. But the distant haze made it hard to see the mountains on the horizon.

In his mind, however, LeBron had a very clear picture of the future. In October, Savannah was expecting their third child, a little girl. And she would be born in Ohio, where LeBron intended to resettle his family and bring a championship to Cleveland. He was clearly choosing the harder path. The Cavs were at best a mediocre team with a head coach who had never coached in the NBA and a roster that was nowhere near as talented or experienced as the one he was leaving behind. He could already feel the weight of his decision.

Lee Jenkins entered the suite, greeted Mendelsohn and Maverick, and sat down, noting that LeBron looked a lot more at ease than he had four years earlier when he'd announced his decision to join the Miami Heat.

"Way more at ease," LeBron said, sipping carrot juice.

Jenkins was not at ease. He was sitting on one of the biggest scoops in sports history. It was imperative that he focus. He had to ask LeBron the questions that would elicit answers he could then craft into an essay.

"What does your home mean to you?" Jenkins asked.

LeBron started talking. An hour later, he stopped.

Jenkins felt LeBron had given him plenty to work with.

"I don't know if it's a fairy tale," LeBron told Jenkins. "But I hope it ends the way most of them end."

Jenkins went back to his room and started writing. The clock was ticking.

On July 11, LeBron was up before the sun. He was about to shock the NBA world for the second time in four years. And he planned to get an early start.

Jenkins had barely slept. But he was running on adrenaline. And after getting LeBron's sign-off, he sent the essay to his editor at *Sports Illustrated* in New York around 10:30 Eastern time.

While a small team back at the magazine's headquarters in New York prepared to launch LeBron's piece on SI.com, LeBron and his team boarded a private plane headed for Miami. Dwyane Wade accompanied them. They'd been together for four glorious years. During that time, they'd gotten so close that they would say "I love you" to each other in the same manner that brothers express affection. Wade wanted nothing more than for them to stay together. But he had never once appealed to LeBron to come back. And now he knew that LeBron had made up his mind.

"It was fun, wasn't it?" he said to LeBron.

LeBron was somber. It had indeed been fun in Miami. But it was time to do something hard in Cleveland.

Before his plans became public, LeBron wanted to tell Riley himself. Rich punched in the number. When Riley answered, Rich handed LeBron the phone.

"I want to thank you for four years," LeBron began.

Riley didn't need to hear the next sentence. It was over. And he was too pissed to speak. He had thought he'd have LeBron for eight more years. He figured they'd end up building a dynasty that would top the Lakers dynasty in the eighties. But LeBron had walked out the door. Hell, the Heat weren't even going to win a third title. *Goddamn it!*

Meanwhile, Rich called Gilbert.

"Dan, congratulations," he said. "LeBron is coming home."

Shortly after noon Eastern time on July 11, 2014, LeBron's 952-word essay appeared on SI.com. It began:

> Before anyone ever cared where I would play basketball, I was a kid from Northeast Ohio. It's where I walked. It's where I ran. It's where I cried. It's where I bled. It holds a special place in my heart. People there have seen me grow up. I sometimes feel like I'm their son.

You didn't have to read any further to know that LeBron James was doing the unthinkable. He was going back to Cleveland.

LeBron's decision to enlist Lee Jenkins to help craft his announcement was a masterstroke that created a sharp contrast to his choice four years earlier to participate in a live spectacle with Jim Gray. The method of communicating the two most important decisions of his basketball career had both been proposed by members of the media. But the approaches of the two journalists had been quite different. Gray's job was to land big interviews, and he got a charge out of being on television with LeBron. For Jenkins, the reward was being chosen to write for the greatest athlete of his generation. Jenkins knew that no one would remember his role in the process. But he knew that he had proposed the idea and that LeBron had trusted him to help him change his narrative. And no paragraph did that more than the one that dealt with LeBron's willingness to forgive Dan Gilbert. In his essay, LeBron said:

> I've met with Dan, face-to-face, man-to-man. We've talked it out. Everybody makes mistakes. I've made mistakes as well. Who am I to hold a grudge?

Who am I to hold a grudge? With seven words, LeBron had flipped the script and done something more impressive than scoring fifty points in a game. On ESPN, Shannon Sharpe acknowledged that he could not have forgiven Gilbert, especially not after he called LeBron a quitter. "LeBron James is a bigger man than I can ever be," Sharpe said on *First Take*.

"I would not have forgiven Dan Gilbert, either," Stephen A. Smith said. "What he said about LeBron was clearly beyond the pale."

Even frequent LeBron critic Skip Bayless admitted being "dumbfounded" by LeBron's willingness to return to the Cavs. "I thought that bridge had been burned *to the ground*," Bayless said on the air.

LeBron knew that his stance toward Gilbert would raise a lot of eyebrows. But he had enough self-awareness to realize he had mishandled his departure from Cleveland. And in order to achieve the one objective that he and Gilbert shared—bringing a championship to Cleveland—the two of them were going to have to compromise. Shortly after his essay landed on SI.com, LeBron shared it with his 75 million followers on Instagram and Twitter, along with a photo of himself in a Cavs uniform and the words "I'm coming home."

In Miami, Pat Riley was scrambling. Dwyane Wade was a wingman without a leader. Chris Bosh was seriously considering an offer to sign with the Houston Rockets. Ray Allen, who was also a free agent, was thinking about following LeBron to Cleveland. Riley's lieutenant, Andy Elisburg, felt like he was living the scene in *Jerry Maguire* when all the clients head for the exits.

Riley wanted to lash out at LeBron. "It was personal for me," Riley later explained. "It just was. I had a very good friend who talked me off the ledge and kept me from going out there and saying something like Dan Gilbert."

Instead, before the end of the day, Riley issued a formal statement:

While I'm disappointed by LeBron's decision to leave Miami, no one can fault another person for wanting to return home. The last four years have been an incredible run for South Florida, HEAT fans, our organization and for all of the players who were part of it. LeBron is a fantastic leader, athlete, teammate and person, and we are all sorry to see him go.

Privately, Riley seethed. And Elisburg was so overcome with anger and emotion that he started having chest pains and feared he was having a heart attack. Desperate for some peace of mind, he got in his car and started driving north. It felt like the Heat were suddenly on a road to nowhere.

But in Cleveland, the reaction to LeBron's announcement was immediate and every bit as emotional as when LeBron had said he was leaving town for South Beach. Only this time the city streets were filled with the sound of cheers and car horns. Radio stations started playing Diddy's "Coming Home," Kanye West's "Homecoming," and Bon Jovi's "Who Says You Can't Go Home." Fans calling the Cavaliers' ticket line encountered an automated message: "All circuits are busy now." Within eight hours, the Cavaliers had sold out of season tickets. *Forbes* predicted that the value of the Cavaliers franchise had jumped $100 million in one day. And oddsmakers in Las Vegas had the Cavaliers as a 4–1 bet to win the NBA championship in 2015.

"Stuff like this doesn't happen to Cleveland," one fan on the street outside Quicken Loans Arena told a television reporter.

Even President Obama weighed in. "The president is a big fan of LeBron's," press secretary Josh Earnest said from the White House briefing room. "I think it's a pretty powerful statement about the value of a place you consider home."

On ABC's *World News Tonight*, Diane Sawyer declared, "The king is coming home."

In Dan Gilbert's home, his eight-year-old boy approached him and said, "Daddy, does this mean I can finally wear my LeBron jersey again?"

"Yes, it does, son," Gilbert said. "Yes, it does!"

THIRTY-THREE

POWER BROKER

LeBron had learned a lot in Miami. Especially in terms of understanding what it took to reach the summit of the NBA and capture a title. He wouldn't repeat the mistake he'd made of brashly predicting that the Heat would win at least seven championships when he'd joined the team. This time he wanted to manage expectations.

"I'm not promising a championship," he said in his SI.com essay. "I know how hard that is to deliver. We're not ready right now."

Even for the Heat team with superstars and a roster of veteran role players, the mountain had been a steep climb. Now, other than LeBron, the Cavs didn't have anyone who had breathed that rare air. Assembling a championship-caliber team and getting it in shape to go the distance was going to be a process. Step one was forming a nucleus of stars.

LeBron had no doubt that twenty-two-year-old Kyrie Irving was going to be an excellent wingman. Although Irving lacked D-Wade's experience, he possessed rare talent. A magician with the basketball, he had the best handle in the NBA. And for a six-foot-two point guard, Irving had an uncanny ability to get to the rim and score. LeBron saw an opportunity to mentor Irving and help him become a bona fide superstar.

But the Cavs needed a third star, and LeBron knew whom he wanted. Hours after announcing his decision to return to Cleveland, he reached out to Minnesota Timberwolves power forward Kevin Love. They had played together on the US Olympic team that had won the gold medal in London. Although Love wasn't a free agent, LeBron knew he was frustrated in Minnesota, where he'd been a three-time all-star. In 2013–2014, Love had been one of the top scorers in the league, averaging more than twenty-six points per game. He had also averaged twelve rebounds per game. Despite Love's impressive numbers, LeBron was more interested in his exceptional basketball IQ. He'd fit well with LeBron and Irving. *He's a great piece*, LeBron thought.

LeBron had been recruiting good players to his teams since his freshman year at St. V. But his ability to look at players as pieces of a championship puzzle was a new dimension in his approach to the game. After being around Riley for four years, he had developed a general manager's mindset. He knew how to identify holes in a roster, spot players who could fill them, and figure out ways to lure them to his team while navigating the league's salary cap. Cleveland would have to offer Minnesota a lot in order to pry Love away. But first he had to get Love's buy-in. He did it by offering Love the one thing he craved—the opportunity to win a ring.

Love was invigorated by the call. The fact that the greatest player in the world was making a personal appeal was beyond flattering.

"I'm in," Love told LeBron.

LeBron's life had hit warp speed. In between team building, relocating his family back to Ohio, preparing for the arrival of his third child, and jetting off to China for his annual summer Nike clinics, he was also scrambling to memorize lines. Well before deciding to return to Cleveland, he had been chosen by actress Amy Schumer to appear with her in the movie *Trainwreck*. His scenes were set to be shot in New York City in July 2014.

The timing wasn't ideal. But LeBron had to focus. This was his first acting role in a major motion picture. A lot was riding on his performance. Thanks in part to all the groundwork Maverick had been doing at Spring-Hill, he was already under consideration for various acting roles in other films. *Trainwreck*, in many respects, was going to be his screen test.

LeBron seldom got nervous. But the thought of being on set with Schumer, Matthew Broderick, Bill Hader, and others made him anxious. They were accomplished actors and comedians. He wasn't used to following a script. But from the first time that director Judd Apatow said, "Action," LeBron embraced the moment. Even when he forgot his lines, he made everyone laugh by poking fun at himself. It was clear to Schumer that he was a natural in front of the camera. And LeBron's ability to ad-lib convinced Apatow that they'd made the right choice in casting him.

But LeBron hadn't forgotten what Pat Riley had told him back in 2010:

"*The main thing is to keep the main thing the main thing.*" The main thing for LeBron was to deliver a championship to Cleveland. So, behind the scenes, he continued to orchestrate personnel moves for the Cavs. Step two in his process was recruiting some veteran role players with championship experience who could complement him, Irving, and Love.

LeBron considered Mike Miller and James Jones to have been key components of the Heat's championship teams in 2012 and 2013. They weren't marquee players. But they had come off the bench and delivered big buckets during crunch time. They also epitomized the concept of *team* basketball. Miller and Jones, LeBron felt, were just the kind of poised players that the Cavs needed. And they were both free agents.

Once Miller and Jones learned that LeBron was headed for Cleveland, they both indicated a willingness to follow him.

LeBron also liked the idea of adding free agent Shawn Marion, a fifteen-year veteran who had won a championship with Dallas in 2011. He went way back with Marion, who had played with him on the US Olympic team in 2004.

At thirty-six, Marion was a consummate pro who yearned for one more title run before calling it quits. And playing with LeBron in Cleveland offered him his best chance to go out on top.

Dan Gilbert did his part by closing the deals. Four years earlier, Gilbert had felt Pat Riley had stolen LeBron and sent the Cavaliers into a tailspin. Now Miami was reeling, and Gilbert was the beneficiary of LeBron's willingness to leverage his influence and attract talent to Cleveland.

Over the summer, the Cavs signed Miller, Jones, and Marion to contracts. Then Gilbert authorized a blockbuster trade to get Kevin Love, sending Anthony Bennett, the number one overall pick in the 2013 NBA Draft, and Andrew Wiggins, the number one overall pick in the 2014 draft, to Minnesota.

The team hated to part with Wiggins, who looked like a future star. But the Timberwolves had been adamant in their demands, and the Cavs knew how LeBron felt about Love. Right after the Cavs announced the Love trade, LeBron tweeted at him: "Welcome to the Land."

For the second time in four years, LeBron's decision to leave one team for another had reconfigured the balance of power in the NBA. When *Sports Illustrated* published its annual NBA preview issue in the fall, it featured LeBron, Kyrie Irving, and Kevin Love on the cover, along with the headline "All the King's Men."

On October 30, the night the Cavaliers opened the 2014–2015 season at home against the Knicks in a nationally televised game, Nike unveiled its most ambitious LeBron commercial since signing him to his $90 million shoe deal back in 2003. By this point, Nike had sold more than $340 million in shoes from the LeBron line of sneakers. But the sneaker sales figures were hardly an adequate measure of the symbiotic relationship between Nike and LeBron. For more than a decade, Nike had been framing his career through sophisticated advertising campaigns in the United States. And in China, he had spent ten consecutive summers as Nike's chief ambassador, a situation that enriched Nike and him in the two biggest economies in the world.

Nike viewed LeBron's decision to return home as an epic chapter in his personal narrative. In this instance, LeBron was framing his own story. Capitalizing on the moment, Nike turned to a duo of Hollywood filmmakers to help create a commercial that resembled a mini-documentary. Titled "Together," the two-minute biopic had an inspirational theme: one city and one goal, a championship.

The filmmakers shot in Cleveland and used over five hundred local people as extras. LeBron's mother and Coach Dru were featured, leading fans out of the stands and onto the court to join LeBron in a team huddle. "We gonna grind for this city," he exhorted his teammates in the commercial. "The whole city of Cleveland. That's what it's all about. It's time to bring them something special."

Nike aired the ad on TNT and ESPN during the pregame programming of the season opener, and the Cavaliers showed it on the Q's giant video board prior to the opening tip. LeBron's homage to Cleveland was so stirring that fans in the arena dabbed their eyes and roared with pride when the commercial ended with him leading an arena full of fans in a chant:

LeBron: Cleveland on three. One. Two. Three.
Fans: Cleveland!

* * *

For Dan Gilbert, the situation was exhilarating. His roster was star-studded. His arena was once again sold out. His team was back on national television. The Cavaliers had the top selling merchandise in the NBA. Cleveland had been restored to the center of the basketball universe. And the city's fans were enraptured.

Gilbert was as thrilled as anyone. Yet it was clear that he wasn't in control. Gilbert owned the team. But it was more like he was along for the ride and LeBron was doing the steering. After his four-year stint in Miami, LeBron had accrued enough power to dictate terms wherever he chose to go to pursue another championship. He and Maverick and Rich had figured out something that team owners had long understood but most players did not: in the NBA, the talent has the leverage. No one was purchasing season tickets or turning on the television to see whether Dan Gilbert or any other owner won or lost. They tuned in to see stars perform. And LeBron was the biggest draw in the game. Any number of franchises and cities would have rolled out the red carpet for him. But he had chosen Cleveland. He was the only player who could single-handedly turn the Cavaliers into an instant title contender. In that respect, Gilbert needed him a lot more than he needed Gilbert.

LeBron knew that he was in a position of strength. And he saw it as an opportunity. At the start of the season, when the NBA announced $24 billion in new television deals with ESPN and TNT, he spoke up. He wanted every owner in the league to know that the next round of collective-bargaining negotiations between the owners and the players was going to be different. Last time around, the owners had extracted concessions from the players union by insisting that the league couldn't afford some of the players union's demands. "The owners were telling us that they were losing money," he told the *New York Times* in October 2014. "There is no way they can sit in front of us and tell us that right now."

LeBron and his team had studied the numbers. He knew that the league's television revenues had just tripled. Meantime, the value of NBA franchises was skyrocketing. The Los Angeles Clippers had recently sold for an unprecedented sum of $2 billion. By publicly putting the owners on notice, he was altering the economic relationship between owners and players.

Journalist Scott Raab, author of *The Whore of Akron*, had been deeply critical of LeBron when he'd left Cleveland for Miami. But Raab had come to admire him, as well as Maverick Carter and Rich Paul. "I don't think they were ever taken seriously by Dan Gilbert or Pat Riley," Raab said. "I don't think they ever saw or understood how savvy and determined LeBron and Maverick and Rich were to build their own empire. By the time Gilbert and Riley realized they'd been outsmarted, it was out of their hands."

Raab now rooted for LeBron to succeed. "When LeBron came back, he talked about a calling beyond basketball," Raab told NPR. "So, when he came back, I really felt hope had returned. I unfairly slagged him for not being Moses. And guess what? He comes back as sort of a Moses figure."

One month into the season, the Cavs arrived in New York to face the Knicks on the same day that a grand jury on Staten Island decided not to indict a white New York City police officer whose choke hold had led to the death of Eric Garner, an unarmed Black man. LeBron faced questions about the grand jury's decision and its broader implications.

"This is our country, the land of the free, and we keep having these incidents happen," LeBron told reporters at the team's shootaround. "Innocent victims or whatever the case may be. Our families are losing loved ones."

As LeBron spoke to reporters, protesters took to the streets of New York.

"It's a sensitive subject right now," he continued. "Violence is not the answer. And retaliation isn't the solution."

Two nights later, LeBron noted that Chicago Bulls guard Derrick Rose wore a black T-shirt with the words I CAN'T BREATHE on it during warm-ups before a game against the Golden State Warriors. The NBA had a strong stance against players wearing anything other than league-issued apparel during warm-ups. Rose's shirt had raised a few eyebrows, especially at the league office. LeBron, however, liked the shirt and respected Rose for wearing it.

Then LeBron got a call from Jay-Z. The Cavs would be playing the Nets in Brooklyn on December 8. A group of social justice advocates were planning to protest outside the Barclays Center that evening. The organizers of the protest were in the process of printing I CAN'T BREATHE T-shirts. With Jay-Z's help, they hoped to get one into LeBron's hands.

LeBron recognized the enormity of the moment. The Cavs-Nets game was already primed to be a high-profile event. Prince William and his wife, the former Kate Middleton, now the Duchess of Cambridge, were on a three-day visit to the United States and were scheduled to attend. They were going out of their way to watch LeBron play, and he was scheduled to meet privately with them after the game.

With so many members of the foreign press on hand to cover the royals' visit, LeBron weighed whether to wear a politically charged T-shirt. He was frequently solicited to get behind social causes. Most of the time, he declined. His threshold for engaging was whether the issue hit home for him. When it didn't, he'd move on and not look back. When something resonated with him, he'd act. And he'd come to terms with the fact that no matter what he decided, he was going to face criticism. So he had resolved to do what felt right in his gut and live with the fallout. He'd make a game-time decision on what to do here.

With Jay-Z's help, T-shirts were smuggled into the arena. Then one of the Nets players delivered a couple of T-shirts to the Cavs' locker room. Outside, protesters from an emerging movement called Black Lives Matter chanted, "Hands up, don't shoot." Others staged a "die in," lying down on the street. A wall of New York City police officers stood between the protesters and the entrance to the Barclays Center. For security reasons, the royal couple delayed their arrival.

About thirty minutes before the opening tip, LeBron emerged from the locker room in a yellow Cavs warm-up jacket. All eyes were on him as he reached the floor, removed his jacket, and revealed his black T-shirt with white lettering. Kyrie Irving had also decided to wear the shirt. The two of them had not discussed the matter. But during warm-ups, LeBron made eye contact with Irving and nodded.

Irving nodded back at LeBron.

Several Nets players also wore the T-shirts, including LeBron's old rival Kevin Garnett. In this moment, they were unified by something bigger and more important than wins and losses.

Suddenly, the game was an afterthought as cable news channels cut to the Barclays Center.

"A remarkable scene just unfolded moments ago here in New York,"

MSNBC's Chris Hayes said as live footage of LeBron warming up aired on television screens across the country. "Cavs star LeBron James took the court for warm-ups in this T-shirt, bearing the words 'I Can't Breathe,' the last words uttered by Eric Garner, repeated eleven times as he was subjected to the police choke hold."

The game was in its second half when Prince William and Kate entered the arena and took their courtside seats. Minutes later, during a time-out, Jay-Z and Beyoncé walked across the floor and greeted them while the crowd cheered. It was one spectacle after another. LeBron and Kyrie put on a show and led the Cavs to victory.

After the game, the press surrounded LeBron's locker and tried to bait him into saying more about the police brutality that had led to Eric Garner's death.

"LeBron, what was the message you were sending by wearing the T-shirt?" a reporter asked.

"It was a message to the family that I'm sorry for their loss, sorry to his wife," he said. "That's what it's about. Everybody else gets caught up in everything besides who is *really* feeling it. And that's the family."

"There's no larger message—" the reporter began.

"How larger can it be?" LeBron interrupted.

"I'm just saying—" the reporter began.

"How larger can it be than to pay respect to the family?" LeBron said, cutting him off again. "Obviously, we know our society needs to do better. But like I said before, violence is not the answer, and retaliation is not the solution."

The royal couple was waiting for LeBron in a private room. When he entered, he presented them with gifts on behalf of the NBA. As the three of them posed for pictures, he treated them like family, putting his arm around the duchess. The image of LeBron with his hand on Kate's shoulder was an instant sensation on social media, touching off an international controversy. The British tabloids lambasted LeBron for breaking royal protocol. In America, CNN's Piers Morgan, a Brit, criticized him. "You do not put your sweaty arm around the future queen of England," Morgan said. "LeBron James, you may call yourself King James. You are not a real king. . . . Hands off the duchess."

To quell the uproar, Buckingham Palace took the unusual step of issuing a formal statement:

The Duke and Duchess of Cambridge very much enjoyed their time in the US, including attending the NBA game and meeting LeBron.

When members of the Royal Family meet people they want them to feel as comfortable as possible. There is no such thing as Royal protocol.

LeBron ignored the royal dustup. He cared a lot more about the league's response to his decision to wear a T-shirt with a message on it.

"I respect Derrick Rose and all of our players for voicing their personal views on important issues," Commissioner Adam Silver told the press. "But my preference would be for our players to abide by our on-court attire rules." Silver was walking a political tightrope.

But the next day, Kobe Bryant arranged for the entire Lakers team to wear the I CAN'T BREATHE shirts during warm-ups before a game in Los Angeles. After LeBron, Kobe was the most influential player in the league. He rarely spoke out. But in this instance he went out of his way to dismiss the notion that his decision to wear the shirt was a comment on race relations in America. "I think it would be a serious disservice to limit this to a race issue; it's a justice issue," Bryant told the press. "You are kind of seeing a tipping point right now, in terms of social issues."

In America, Tom Brady and Tiger Woods were the only male athletes with a celebrity profile and level of achievement on par with LeBron's. But neither of them had ever spoken out on social issues or matters of political concern. Because of his stature, LeBron's speaking out drew a lot of notice.

Days after the game between the Cavs and the Nets, President Obama addressed the situation. "We went through a long stretch there where [with] well-paid athletes the notion was 'Just be quiet and get your endorsements and don't make waves,'" Obama said. "LeBron is an example of a young man who has, in his own way and in a respectful way, tried to say, 'I'm part of this society, too,' and focus attention."

Obama added, "I'd like to see more athletes do that. Not just around this issue, but around a range of issues."

Adam Silver recognized that it was futile to try to hold back the tide. The NBA was emerging as a platform for social change.

* * *

There was more than a foot of snow on the ground when LeBron trudged into his family foundation's office in Akron wearing Nike shower shoes with socks, sweatpants, a T-shirt, and a coat on a cold, gray morning in February 2015. The night before, the Cavs had beaten the 76ers to improve to 30-20. Tired and grumpy, he would rather have been home, resting. But Adam Mendelsohn had arranged for him to meet with a feature writer from the *Hollywood Reporter*.

Marisa Guthrie had been pursuing LeBron for a cover story for nearly two years. Guthrie was one of the most respected writers in Hollywood, and she'd been impressed by the production company that he and Maverick were building. Mendelsohn knew that Guthrie had profiled many luminaries in the entertainment industry. The fact that she wanted to profile LeBron was an exceptional opportunity. But Mendelsohn hadn't wanted LeBron on the cover of Hollywood's most influential publication when he was navigating the transition from Miami to Cleveland. The optics would have sent the wrong message. So, Mendelsohn had put Guthrie off then. But now that LeBron was deep into the basketball season and *Trainwreck* was soon to be in theaters, Mendelsohn felt that the timing was right.

LeBron brought Savannah and their eleven-week-old daughter, Zhuri, along for the interview.

Aware that Savannah didn't do interviews and generally kept a very low profile, Guthrie was surprised to see her and the baby.

Savannah greeted Guthrie like an old friend, giving her a hug and a peck on the cheek.

Guthrie felt an instant connection. She, too, had recently given birth to a little girl, who was born one day after Zhuri. Guthrie also related to the fact that Savannah wasn't wearing any makeup and was carrying a diaper bag.

To break the ice with LeBron, Guthrie asked if he missed anonymity.

"It's been so long, I don't remember," LeBron said.

Guthrie sensed that LeBron wasn't in the mood to say much. He looked like he was weighted down by the burden of trying to deliver a title to Cleveland.

With Mendelsohn looking on, Guthrie worked through her list of questions, and LeBron went through the motions. Eventually, Guthrie brought up the recent death of twelve-year-old Tamir Rice, a Black youth who had been shot by Cleveland police while waving a toy gun in a park.

LeBron's demeanor instantly changed.

"I have those conversations with my boys," LeBron said. "They have tons of play guns. None of them look real. We have Nerf guns that are lime green and purple and yellow. But I don't even let them take them out of the house."

Guthrie asked LeBron and Savannah if they had talked to their sons about what to do if they were ever stopped by the police.

"Absolutely," LeBron said. "And the talk is, 'You be respectful. You do what's asked. And you let them do their job. And we'll take care of the rest after. You don't have to boast and brag and automatically think it's us against the police.'"

Guthrie had hit on something that mattered deeply to LeBron.

"I've had one or two encounters with the police in my life that were nothing," he continued. "But sometimes you just got to shut up. It's that simple. Just be quiet and let them do their job and go on about your life and hopefully things go well."

"For everybody," Savannah chimed in.

Guthrie had covered Hollywood for a long time. She found it refreshing to hear someone of LeBron's stature talk so freely and honestly about issues that had become so polarizing. "LeBron feels those things in a way that a middle-class white woman can't," Guthrie said. "I never had to confront that the way he did. And he *wanted* to talk about it because he knew that what he said might make a difference."

At the end of February, LeBron appeared on the cover of the *Hollywood Reporter* for the first time. Titled "LeBron James Reveals Ambitious Plan to Build Hollywood Empire," Guthrie's 3,400-word profile highlighted an array of projects that LeBron and Maverick had in the works through their SpringHill production company. Their comedy *Survivor's Remorse* had been picked up by the premium cable network Starz. LeBron had signed on to costar alongside comedian Kevin Hart in a movie called *Ballers* for Universal Pictures. And Maverick was in discussions with Warner Bros. about the prospect of LeBron starring in a sequel to *Space Jam*. Guthrie's story positioned LeBron, Maverick, and SpringHill as an up-and-coming force in the film and television industry. But Guthrie also made one subtle point that was important to LeBron—that his immediate priority was winning a championship for Cleveland.

* * *

At 51-29, the Cavaliers finished the regular season with the second-best record in the Eastern Conference. Down the stretch, LeBron, Irving, and Love had hit their stride. And to strengthen the roster, the team made some late-season acquisitions, adding veterans J. R. Smith, Iman Shumpert, and Kendrick Perkins.

The Cavs swept the Celtics in the opening round of the playoffs. But in Game 4, Kevin Love got tangled up with a Celtics player who clamped down on Love's arm and yanked it so hard that it popped out of the shoulder joint. Love ran off the court in agony. The injury required season-ending surgery.

The loss of Love was significant. Without him, the Cavs struggled in the beginning of the next round against the Bulls. Trailing 2-1, the Cavs faced a must-win situation in Game 4 in Chicago. With 1.5 seconds remaining and the score tied, 84–84, Cavaliers head coach David Blatt drew up a play that called for LeBron to inbound the ball under the Cavs' basket. But LeBron ignored Blatt and told his teammates, "Just get me the ball."

Reserve guard Matthew Dellavedova did exactly what LeBron said. When the ref handed him the ball, Dellavedova zipped it to LeBron, who had faked like he was going to go to the hoop and instead cut toward the Bulls' bench. In one motion, he caught the pass, elevated, and launched a fallaway shot.

"LeBron fires," said ESPN's Mike Breen.

The horn sounded while the ball was in the air and LeBron was landing out-of-bounds.

"It's good!" Breen yelled. "LeBron James at the buzzer!"

The United Center crowd was stunned as LeBron's teammates mobbed him at the scorer's table. The series was tied, 2-2, and heading back to Cleveland.

The Bulls never recovered, and the Cavs won the next two games to close out the series and advance to the Eastern Conference Finals, where the top-seeded Atlanta Hawks awaited.

In Game 1 in Atlanta, Kyrie Irving had to scale back his minutes due to tendinitis in his left knee. J. R. Smith picked up the slack, scoring twenty-eight points to go along with LeBron's thirty-one. The Cavs won the opener. Then Irving's tendinitis forced him to miss Games 2 and 3. Matthew Dellavedova started in his place. Other role players stepped up. And LeBron took care of the offense, averaging over thirty points per game. The Cavs were up, 3-0, when Irving returned for Game 4, which Cleveland won by thirty to sweep Atlanta.

For the fifth year in a row, LeBron was headed to the NBA Finals, a feat that no player other than Bill Russell and his Celtics teammates in the sixties had achieved. But the Cavaliers were a long shot to win.

The Golden State Warriors were by far the best team in the NBA in 2014–2015. Led by first-year head coach Steve Kerr and a young trio of stars—twenty-four-year-old Klay Thompson, twenty-four-year-old Draymond Green, and twenty-six-year-old NBA MVP Stephen Curry—the Warriors had gone 67-15 during the regular season. Only five teams in NBA history had finished with a better record.

Curry and Thompson, who were nicknamed "the Splash Brothers" for the way their prolific three-point shooting splashed the net, came out firing in Game 1 at Oracle Arena in Oakland. Between them, they scored forty-seven points. But LeBron was unstoppable. He scored forty-four, and Irving added twenty-three. The two teams battled to a tie after four quarters.

But in overtime, Irving's knee buckled while he was driving against Klay Thompson. Irving had played forty-four minutes. Now he had to be helped off the floor. X-rays revealed he had fractured his kneecap.

The Warriors prevailed in overtime to take a 1-0 series lead.

With Love already out, LeBron looked at the loss of Irving as a huge blow to the team, especially at this stage. The challenge of beating the Warriors had suddenly become even more herculean. But LeBron was undaunted. Obsessed with delivering a championship to Cleveland, he looked around the locker room and embraced a "next man up" approach. Matthew Dellavedova would have to start at point guard and go head-to-head with Curry. J. R. Smith and Iman Shumpert were going to have to score more points. Tristan Thompson needed to grab more rebounds. And on defense, everyone was going to have to dig deep and help on the perimeter.

The Warriors, meanwhile, smelled blood heading into Game 2. But with Dellavedova harassing Curry all night, the Warriors' best player struggled to make shots. On the other end, LeBron relentlessly attacked the rim with drives and dunks. In a play that summed up the game, he drove to the basket and was fouled by Draymond Green, who collided with him in the air and hammered him in the face with a forearm. Yet it was Green who went sprawling and ended up on the floor. LeBron was a one-man wrecking crew. He finished with 39 points, 16 rebounds, and 11 assists. And the Cavs won by two points in overtime, shocking the crowd at Oracle. When the final buzzer sounded, LeBron slammed the ball onto the hardwood, clenched his fists, and let out a guttural roar.

Exhausted, LeBron was leaving the court and heading toward the tunnel when a white woman in Warriors garb screamed at him: "LeBron, how does it feel to be a pussy ass bitch?"

He stopped and glared at her.

"Hey!" an arena security guard shouted. "Watch your mouth, woman."

It galled LeBron that a random stranger would say something so vile to a married father with three young children and get away with it. But he held his tongue and continued toward the locker room. With the series tied at 1-1, he was eager to get home.

In Game 3 at the Q, LeBron got into a shootout with Curry and Thompson. LeBron scored forty. Curry and Thompson combined for forty-one. And Dellavedova played the game of his life, chipping in twenty. The Cavs won again, 96–91, to take an improbable 2-1 series lead.

The New York Times opined that LeBron had turned the series into his "personal playground." Through the first three games, he'd taken 107 shots and scored 123 points, effectively putting his teammates on his back and the city of Cleveland on edge. "I know our team is fighting for our lives," LeBron said before Game 4. "We're undermanned. We're undermatched. And we're fighting."

And that was all Cleveland fans could ask. LeBron and a bunch of role players with a blue-collar approach were pushing a heavily favored super-team to the brink. The Warriors responded by winning Game 4 to even the series. Then in Game 5, back in Oakland, Curry put up thirty-seven, including seventeen in the fourth quarter. Four other Warriors players scored in double figures. LeBron was unstoppable—he scored 40 points, grabbed 14 rebounds, and dished out 11 assists. But the Warriors won by thirteen and took a 3-2 series lead.

Afterward, the press pointed out that LeBron appeared to be playing. with a lot of confidence, even though Irving and Love were out of action. "Do you feel a lot less pressure this Finals run just because you are under-manned?" a reporter asked.

"I feel confident because I'm the best player in the world," LeBron said, pausing while the cameras clicked. "It's that simple."

The rivalry between LeBron and Curry had taken center stage. And it had produced the most entertaining NBA Finals since the days of Michael Jordan. LeBron was outperforming Curry. But in the end, Curry had a superior team around him. In Game 6 in Cleveland, LeBron played forty-seven of forty-eight minutes, scoring thirty-two points to go along with nineteen rebounds and nine assists. Curry scored twenty-five, while four of his teammates scored in double figures, and Golden State outlasted the Cavaliers to win the game and capture the championship.

Although Andre Iguodala was named Finals MVP, plenty of sports-writers noted that this was a rare instance when a member of the los-ing team deserved the honor. LeBron was the first player in NBA Finals history to lead both teams in points, assists, and rebounds for the entire series. He had scored 40 points or more three times and *averaged* over 35 points, 13 rebounds, and 9 assists per game. It was one of the most dom-inant Finals performances in history and by far the greatest Finals effort of his career.

But none of that eased the pain of seeing the Warriors celebrating on the court at Quicken Loans Arena. Long after all his teammates had left the building, LeBron sat at his locker, a towel over his shoulders. Drained and alone, he pondered. Winning a title in Cleveland was a lot harder than he'd thought it would be. At age thirty, he wasn't getting any younger. And the Warriors were just getting started.

THIRTY-FOUR

DELIVERANCE

In the summer of 2015, LeBron reflected on his decision to move back home. For the most part, it was turning out the way he had hoped. Savannah and the kids were comfortable in the familiar protective shell of northeast Ohio. His oldest son was thriving on an AAU basketball team. His family foundation was making a profound impact on the community—he had partnered with Chase Bank and the University of Akron to guarantee four-year scholarships for high school students in Akron who graduated with a 3.0 grade point average. Over one thousand students earned full-ride scholarships in the first year of the program.

Going home hadn't hurt LeBron's business pursuits, either. In 2015 he and Maverick signed a development deal with Warner Bros. that enabled SpringHill to develop films and television shows in partnership with a major Hollywood studio. And Warner Bros. and Turner Sports invested more than $15 million in Uninterrupted, a digital media platform that he and Maverick designed for athletes to speak their mind, much the way he had in his *Sports Illustrated* essay. At the same time, he was negotiating a first-of-its-kind lifetime endorsement deal with Nike worth a reported $1billion. And with all that LeBron had going on in Hollywood, he and Savannah had purchased a 9,400-square-foot home in Brentwood for $21 million.

But his main objective in returning to Cleveland—to deliver a championship—remained unfulfilled. The Golden State Warriors stood in the way of the fairy-tale ending LeBron had imagined when he left Miami. He figured the Warriors were only going to get better and become even more of an obstacle. Yet, night after night, he had a recurring dream of what it would feel like to win one for Cleveland.

After some time off, he readied himself for another run at the title. First, he made sure the Cavs would re-sign Kevin Love, Tristan Thompson, and Iman Shumpert. Then he agreed to another one-year contract. He also intensified his workouts, refined his already-stringent diet, and talked one-on-one with key teammates to get them mentally prepared for the season ahead. While Love was rehabbing from shoulder surgery, he gave him a pep talk, telling him how much the team needed him to come back at full strength.

From the start of the 2015–2016 season, LeBron kept a close eye on the Warriors, recording their games and watching them in the middle of the night. He got accustomed to hearing the play-by-play announcer say the same three words: "Curry. Three. Good." With Curry knocking down three-point shots at a record clip, the Warriors looked like a team that might never lose. The NBA record for consecutive wins to open a season was fifteen. It had stood since 1949. But the Warriors shattered the mark. By mid-December, Golden State was 24-0. "They have by far the best player in basketball right now in Steph Curry," NBA analyst David Aldridge told NPR. "And I say that knowing that LeBron James is incredibly talented and gifted and is a great player, but what Curry's doing is remarkable."

The Cavaliers, meanwhile, struggled to play up to LeBron's standards. They were the top team in the Eastern Conference. Nonetheless, midway through the season, the team fired head coach David Blatt and replaced him with Tyronn Lue, who was more popular among the players. In the second half of the season, the team lost more games under Lue than it had under Blatt. LeBron was at wit's end.

Although he was living in Los Angeles and had his hands full running SpringHill, Maverick Carter kept close tabs on the situation in Cleveland. He recognized what was happening. Some of the Cavs players weren't as committed as LeBron felt they should be. But Maverick also knew that LeBron was a perfectionist. Toward the end of the regular season, Maverick called him. "You get paid a lot of money to do something you're better at than anybody else in the world," Maverick told him. "So just do that. Don't worry about this guy or that guy, or what anybody else is. Just play."

The Cavs finished the regular season with the best record in the Eastern Conference at 57-25. The Warriors, meanwhile, finished with the best record in NBA history at 73-9. Curry led the league in scoring, set the NBA record for three-pointers made in a season, and was voted MVP for the second straight year. The Warriors were the only team with three players—Curry, Thompson, and Green—named to the all-star team in 2016. And Steve Kerr was named Coach of the Year. The Warriors were so dominant and so popular that some writers started referring to them as America's team.

LeBron had heard enough about how great the Warriors were. And it irked him when Curry was characterized as the best player in the world. Curry was a newly minted star who was known for freakishly accurate long-range shooting, handling the ball as if it were a yo-yo, and steals. He was a master showman who'd had two phenomenally entertaining seasons, and he was deserving of the MVP honors. But LeBron had been the most talented basketball player on the planet for thirteen years. For most of that time, he had to carry his team. His ability to play all five positions made him difficult to categorize. And his overall body of work from the NBA to the Olympics was on a different plane from Curry's. In LeBron's view, the words *most valuable* were open to interpretation, and there was a difference between being the most valuable player and being the best player in a particular season.

Colin Cowherd of Fox Sports agreed. He suggested that Curry wasn't as important to his team's success as LeBron had been in Miami or Cleveland. "I'm not sure this league has ever had a single player as valuable as LeBron James," Cowherd said. He added: "Steph Curry should win 'Best Player of the Year,' while LeBron is the real MVP."

The Cavs gelled at the right time and breezed through the playoffs, sweeping two teams and never being challenged. The Warriors, on the other hand, were nearly knocked off by Kevin Durant and the Oklahoma City Thunder in the Western Conference Finals. After being down, 3-1, the Warriors came back and won the series.

A rematch between the Cavaliers and the Warriors was a gold mine for the NBA and its network partners. The 2016 NBA Finals pitted one of the best teams in NBA history against one of the best players in NBA history. The Warriors were trying to repeat as champions. LeBron was on a quest to win a championship for Cleveland. And the debate over who was the superior player—Curry or LeBron—would be settled on the floor. From a ratings standpoint, ABC had the best drama on television.

The Warriors trounced the Cavs in Games 1 and 2 in Oakland, winning both games by a combined forty-eight points. In Game 3 in Cleveland, the Cavs responded, pounding the Warriors by thirty. But in the pivotal Game 4 on June 10, Curry erupted, nailing seven three-pointers and scoring thirty-eight points. Thompson added twenty-five, silencing the crowd and giving the Warriors a commanding 3-1 series lead. The Splash Brothers were all smiles when they left the Q.

The Cavs looked doomed. No team had ever come back from a 3-1 deficit to win the NBA Finals. And the Warriors hadn't lost three games in a row all season. But an altercation between LeBron and Draymond Green near the end of Game 4 proved to be a turning point in the series. Green had been verbally and physically harassing LeBron throughout the game. With less than three minutes to play and the Warriors up by ten, LeBron had had enough. When Green set a screen, LeBron pushed his way through it. Green went down, and LeBron stepped over him in his pursuit of the play. Attempting to stand up while LeBron was straddling him, Green swiped at LeBron's groin. LeBron took exception. They went chest-to-chest, exchanged words, and started shoving. Both players were whistled for fouls that had no impact on the game's outcome.

The altercation between LeBron and Green escalated in the postgame press conferences. When asked about LeBron's reaction to Draymond Green, Klay Thompson mocked LeBron by saying that the NBA was "a man's league," and that trash talk was part of the game. "I don't know how the man feels," Thompson said. "But obviously, people have feelings. People's feelings get hurt. I guess his feelings just got hurt."

While Thompson was talking to the press, LeBron was in the locker room, assuring his teammates that they had the Warriors right where they wanted them. He told his teammates that they were not going to lose another game.

Then, when LeBron entered the media room, a reporter referenced Thompson's words and asked him if he cared to comment.

"What did you say Klay said?" LeBron asked.

"Klay said, 'I guess he just got his feelings hurt,'" the reporter repeated.

Holding a microphone, LeBron dropped his chin to his chest and laughed.

The press chuckled.

"My goodness," he said, grinning. "I'm not gonna comment on what

Klay said." He paused and laughed again. Then he looked the reporters in the eye. "It's so hard to take the high road," LeBron said with a smile. "I've been doing it for thirteen years. It's so hard to continue to do it. And I'm gonna do it again."

LeBron didn't need additional motivation. But Thompson had manufactured some.

Later that night, LeBron wound down with Savannah. Around two thirty in the morning they watched *Eddie Murphy Raw*. After laughing hysterically for about ninety minutes, he sent a predawn group text to his teammates. They were due to board a plane for Oakland later that day. But LeBron had a message for them first. "I know we're down 3-1," he said. "But if you don't think we can win this series, then don't get on the fucking plane."

LeBron was playing a game within the game. He'd been to the NBA Finals seven times, and he knew how hard it was to win back-to-back titles. He also understood that a seven-game series is a battle of attrition, and mental discipline plays a big part in who prevails. The Warriors were acting like a team that was entitled to the trophy. LeBron thought that was a big mistake.

After the Cavaliers arrived in Oakland, the NBA announced that Draymond Green was suspended for Game 5. He'd been retroactively assessed a flagrant foul for a "retaliatory swipe of his hand to the groin" of LeBron. As a stand-alone incident, Green's flagrant foul didn't warrant a suspension. But Green was a provocateur, and earlier in the postseason he'd twice been assessed flagrant fouls, once for throwing a Houston Rockets player to the floor, and once for kicking an Oklahoma City player between the legs. Under the NBA's rules, Green's third flagrant foul during the playoffs automatically triggered a one-game suspension.

LeBron knew the rules when he had stepped over Green. Longtime *New York Times* sports columnist Harvey Araton suggested that LeBron was essentially saying to Green: "Care to check out my groin?" By goading Green, LeBron had beaten him at his own game. Basketball writers dubbed Green the "Nutcracker." But Green's disqualification was no laughing matter to the Warriors. A tenacious rebounder and shot blocker, Green was the anchor of the defense. He was also the team's emotional leader who set the tone by doing the dirty work that enabled Curry and Thompson to flourish.

Prior to Game 5, LeBron got himself in the right frame of mind by watching *The Godfather Part II*. One scene—when crime boss Michael Corleone, bent on revenge, pays a surprise visit to Frankie Pentangeli—captured the way he felt toward Green and the Warriors.

Frankie: I wish you woulda let me know you were coming. I
   coulda prepared something for you.
Corleone: I didn't want you to know I was coming.

In Green's absence, the Cavs manhandled the Warriors. The big men controlled the paint, and LeBron and Kyrie each scored forty-one points. It was the first time in league history that teammates scored forty-plus points in a Finals game. The Cavs won by fifteen. As the final buzzer sounded, Curry attempted a meaningless layup. Even though the game was over, LeBron blocked Curry's shot, sending a not-so-subtle message to the league's MVP. Afterward, the *New York Times* declared that LeBron "remains the best hoop-playing specimen on the planet."

The Warriors were still up, 3-2. But now they had to go back to Cleveland, where Warriors coach Steve Kerr was worried that LeBron would take control of the series. As a player, Kerr had won five NBA championships, including three straight with the Chicago Bulls in the Michael Jordan era. Kerr knew the amount of mental toughness that was required to win back-to-back titles. "It just doesn't *happen*," he told his players after Game 5. "It's harder than that."

For the Cavaliers, Game 6 was the biggest game in franchise history. Feeding off the crowd's energy, they stormed to a 31–9 lead. Draymond Green was back in the lineup, but he played tentatively. The Cavs were much more physical, and the Warriors never matched their energy level. During one stretch in the second half, LeBron scored eighteen straight points. He wasn't just dominating the Warriors. He was bullying them. In the fourth quarter, when LeBron should have needed a breather, he told Coach Lue, "I'm not coming out." Then, with four minutes remaining and his team up by thirteen, Curry drove to the basket and head-faked, hoping to get LeBron up in the air. But LeBron didn't bite. Instead, he waited for Curry to attempt a layup and swatted his shot out-of-bounds. He glared at Curry and barked a message: *Get that weak shit out of my house!* The Q erupted. It had never felt so good to be a Cavs fan.

Moments later, on the other end of the court, Curry tried to poke the ball out of LeBron's hands and got whistled for his sixth foul. Angry over the call, Curry lit into the referee and flung his mouthpiece, hitting a fan who was seated courtside. The referee assessed Curry a technical foul and ejected him. It was the first time in Curry's career that he'd been thrown out of a game. He got jeered leaving the court.

In contrast, LeBron played forty-three minutes and scored forty-one points for the second consecutive game. The Cavs won by fourteen and evened the series at 3-3. Afterward, Steve Kerr unloaded on the officials for the way they had treated Curry. "He's the MVP of the league," Kerr said. "He gets six fouls called on him. Three of them were absolutely ridiculous. LeBron flops on the last one. Jason Phillips falls for that flop. This is the MVP of the league, and we're talking about these touch fouls in the NBA Finals." Meanwhile, Curry's wife tweeted that the game was rigged. "I won't be silent," she said.

The NBA fined Kerr for singling out a referee by name. Curry was fined for hurling his mouthpiece and hitting a fan. And his wife took down her tweet.

The Warriors were unraveling.

In the Cavs' locker room, LeBron smiled. "They fucked up, *mentally* and *physically*," he told his team. "I'm telling you. They. Fucked. Up."

Game 7, back in Oakland, was the closest contest of the series. There were twenty lead changes and eighteen ties. And with under two minutes remaining, the score was knotted at eighty-nine when Kyrie Irving drove the lane and tossed up a floater. The play that would define LeBron's legacy and reverse Cleveland's sports history had begun.

Irving missed his floater. Warriors forward Andre Iguodala grabbed the rebound and took off downcourt, passing the ball ahead to Curry. With a defender in front of him and Iguodala streaking to the basket, Curry bounce-passed the ball back to him. Iguodala was fourteen feet from the hoop when he caught Curry's pass in stride, took two steps, and elevated for a layup.

Trailing the play, LeBron was on the opposite side of the court and twenty-one feet from the basket when Iguodala caught Curry's pass. *I can get it*, he told himself. With a head of steam and a three-foot vertical leap, LeBron took flight. In the air, he had to navigate three obstacles—to stay clear of the rim, avoid fouling Iguodala, and reach the ball before it reached the glass. His chest was level with Iguodala's head when LeBron pinned the ball against the backboard, next to the square above the rim. The ball then ricocheted into J. R. Smith's hands. Golden State's go-ahead layup had been diverted midflight.

The play happened so fast—an analysis would later reveal that LeBron had raced sixty feet in 2.67 seconds, topping out at an estimated twenty miles per hour—that the announcers didn't grasp the significance of the feat until they watched it on slow-motion replay. "Oh . . . my . . . goodness," ABC's Jeff Van Gundy said. "Great pass by Curry. Running hard by Iguodala. And superhuman defensive recovery by LeBron James."

On the other end, with the shot clock winding down and Curry guarding him out beyond the three-point line, Kyrie stepped back and launched, burying a clutch shot and putting his team up, 92–89. Then Curry, unable to shake Kevin Love, forced up a three that caromed off the back of the rim and into the hands of LeBron, who was fouled. LeBron made a free throw to put Cleveland up by four with ten seconds to play, sealing the victory. Moments later the Warriors missed a desperation heave as the buzzer sounded.

"It's over! It's over!" shouted ABC's Mike Breen as Kevin Love hoisted LeBron off his feet. "Cleveland is a city of champions once again. The Cavaliers are NBA champions."

The Cavs mobbed LeBron. In the chaos, Maverick Carter raced onto the court and hugged his friend.

Overcome, LeBron crumpled to his knees.

When he'd played on the Heat and finally won his first championship, he had not lost his composure. Nor had he cried after winning the second title in Miami. But this was different, more epic than he had dreamed. Digging out of a 3-1 hole to beat a team that had seemed invincible, against the odds he had delivered for the people of northeast Ohio. Cleveland's fifty-two-year championship drought was over. This was what he'd come home for.

LeBron put his face to the floor and wept.

THIRTY-FIVE

BELIEVELAND

The 2016 NBA Finals were LeBron's magnum opus, and Game 7 drew ABC's largest audience ever for an NBA game. A record 45 million viewers were tuned in when LeBron's chase-down block of Andre Iguodala helped end fifty-two years of heartache. For so long, Cleveland had been defined by infamous moments—the Drive, the Fumble, the Shot, and the Decision. Now it had a legendary moment—the Block. It would rank as the most iconic shot block of all time and become the signature play of LeBron's career, an outcome that he relished due to the magnitude of the game and the fact that his legacy was defined by a defensive play that helped his team win a championship.

LeBron was still pinching himself when more than 1.3 million people poured into downtown Cleveland for a victory parade on June 22. News helicopters hovered overhead, horns blared, sirens whistled, and people scaled buildings, trees, street signs, and lampposts to get a glimpse of the team. Joined by Savannah and his children, LeBron sat atop the backseat of a convertible as it eased to a stop and the throng pressed around him, their arms extended above their heads. With a cigar in his mouth, he stood, spread his arms, and looked over the sea of cell phone cameras aimed up at him. It was a rapturous moment. "We did it," he told Savannah.

After the parade, with his teammates seated behind him on a stage in front of the convention center and chants of "M-V-P" echoing in the air, LeBron addressed the fans. "What's going on right now is still so surreal to me that it still hasn't hit me," he said. "For some crazy-ass reason, I believe I'm gonna wake up and it's gonna be Game 4 all over again. And I'll be like, 'Shit, we're down 2-1 still.'"

Browns legend Jim Brown stood on the stage, smiling and nodding his approval.

Then LeBron spent fifteen minutes talking about his teammates, singling out each one, thanking them for their contributions, and praising their talents. He never talked about himself.

"I'm nothing without this group behind me," LeBron said. "Shit. Let's get ready for next year."

He put the mic down and the crowd roared.

LeBron's transformation from the most reviled athlete in America in 2010 to the most admired player in the NBA was complete. You didn't have to have a connection to Cleveland to be inspired by LeBron's achievement. By going home and keeping his word, he'd cemented his legacy as a sports hero. "James's career," the *New York Times* declared, "was now the stuff of bildungsroman." In terms of basketball, it almost didn't matter what happened next. At thirty-one, a defining stage of his life was behind him.

The sphere of his influence had never been wider. And that summer, he was emboldened to focus on another aspect of his legacy. During the finals, Muhammad Ali had died. The older LeBron got, the more he appreciated Ali's courage and marveled at what he'd endured. When LeBron got invited to present at the ESPYs, he wanted to do something to honor Ali.

More Black men had died at the hands of police that summer, including Philando Castile, a thirty-two-year-old cafeteria worker who had been pulled over by police in St. Paul, Minnesota, for driving with a broken taillight. When Castile reached for his license and registration, the police shot him multiple times. Castile's girlfriend and her four-year-old daughter were in the vehicle. The incident was captured on video. Castile died in the hospital.

LeBron was already an active member of a partnership that had been formed between the NBA and the Obama administration to bridge divides and defuse tensions in communities. He planned to use the ESPYs platform to speak out on this issue. Dwyane Wade, Carmelo Anthony, and Chris Paul agreed to join him. The four of them joined hands onstage at the Microsoft Theater in Los Angeles and called on their fellow athletes in all sports to take action against racism, gun violence, and social injustice in communities of color. LeBron told the audience:

We all feel helpless and frustrated by the violence. We do. But that's not acceptable. It's time to look in the mirror and ask ourselves what we are doing to create change. . . .

I know tonight we're honoring Muhammad Ali. The GOAT. But to do his legacy any justice, let's use this moment as a call to action for all professional athletes to educate ourselves. It's for these issues. Speak up. Use our influence. And renounce all violence.

And most importantly, go back to our communities, invest our time, our resources, help rebuild them, help strengthen them, help change them. We all have to do better.

As LeBron leaned into the idea of using the NBA as a force for social change, the landscape of the league underwent a seismic shift. After seeing LeBron and the Cavaliers overcome a 3-1 deficit and LeBron win his third title, free agent Kevin Durant decided to leave the Oklahoma City Thunder and sign with the Warriors. Back in 2010, when LeBron had announced he was leaving Cleveland for Miami, Durant had been praised as "the anti–LeBron James" for re-signing with Oklahoma City. But after nine seasons in the NBA and no championships, the twenty-seven-year-old superstar had a different outlook. Having been unable to beat Curry and the Warriors in the Western Conference Finals, Durant was now ready to join them. Taking a cue from LeBron, he announced his plans in an essay on the Players' Tribune website in early July.

With Durant and Curry joining forces, the Warriors became a virtual all-star team that was headlined by two of the three best players in the game. Writing in the *New York Times Magazine*, Sam Anderson likened the situation to if Jimi Hendrix had joined the Rolling Stones after losing to them in a battle of the bands. ESPN's Stephen A. Smith called Durant's decision "the weakest move I've ever seen from a superstar." Yet it was also a testament to the profound impact LeBron had had on the NBA. His move to Miami had ushered in a new era where the power to assemble superteams had transferred from owners and executives to players. And while Durant took some criticism, it was minimal and short-lived. In the economics of professional sports, the NBA was at the forefront of player empowerment.

Similarly, LeBron's willingness to use his resources and his platform to effect social change had established him as a leader whose voice carried great weight well beyond the NBA. A few weeks after his remarks at the ESPYs, San Francisco 49ers quarterback Colin Kaepernick took a knee during the playing of the national anthem prior to a preseason game. "I am not going to stand up to show pride in a flag for a country that oppresses black people and people of color," he told NFL media. "To me, this is bigger than football and it would be selfish on my part to look the other way. These are bodies in the street and people getting paid leave and getting away with murder."

Several professional athletes, including members of the Women's National Basketball Association, started kneeling during the anthem to show solidarity with Kaepernick. But LeBron took a different tack and chose to stand for the anthem. Unlike the NFL, the NBA had a rule requiring its players to stand during the anthem. But that wasn't why LeBron chose to stand. "That's who I am, that's what I believe," he said. "But that doesn't mean I don't respect and don't agree with what Colin Kaepernick is doing. You have the right to voice your opinion, stand for your opinion, and he's doing it in the most peaceful way I've ever seen someone do something."

Steph Curry also chose to stand for the anthem. And like LeBron, he said he respected Kaepernick's decision, calling it "a bold step."

The controversy around athletes' protesting during the national anthem coincided with the final months before a presidential election. Republican nominee Donald Trump employed divisive campaign tactics. He had accused the Mexican government of sending rapists and drug dealers to the US southern border. At rallies, he'd pledged to build a wall to keep immigrants out, encouraged his supporters to "knock the crap out of" hecklers, and led "Lock her up" chants referring to his opponent, Democratic nominee Hillary Clinton.

With Trump gaining on Clinton in the polls, LeBron thought it was critical to do his part to help her win. He was getting ready to endorse her, when the *Washington Post* published a video recording of Trump making vulgar comments about women. The recording was from September 2005. Trump's wife, Melania, was pregnant at the time, and Trump was making a cameo appearance on the television show *Days of Our Lives*. On the set he started bragging about his efforts to seduce a married woman. "I did try and fuck her," Trump said. "I moved on her like a bitch." Then Trump bragged to *Access Hollywood*'s Billy Bush, "When you're a star, they let you do it. You can do anything. Grab 'em by the pussy."

The comments sparked outrage and numerous Republican senators and governors called for Trump to withdraw from the race. But Trump refused. And a few nights later, during a debate with Clinton, he characterized his comments as "locker room talk."

Professional athletes across the political spectrum took exception to Trump's claim that bragging about sexual assault was locker room banter. They felt Trump had insulted athletes by roping them into his situation. But LeBron was one of the few athletes who publicly challenged Trump's statement. "We don't disrespect women in no shape or fashion in our locker rooms," he told reporters. "I have a mother-in-law, a wife, a mom, and a daughter, and those conversations just don't go on in our locker room."

LeBron took it a step further, publishing an op-ed for *Business Insider* in support of Clinton. Although he didn't know Clinton personally, he felt it was critical that she prevail against Trump. And from his association with Obama, he was confident that Clinton would further Obama's domestic agenda. Plus, LeBron felt it would be good for the country to elect a female president. He wrote:

> We must address the violence, of every kind, the African American
> community is experiencing in our streets and seeing on our TVs. I
> believe rebuilding our communities by focusing on at-risk children
> is a significant part of the solution. However, I am not a politician. I
> don't know everything it will take finally to end the violence. But I
> do know we need a president who brings us together and keeps us
> unified. Policies and ideas that divide us more are not the solution.

It bothered LeBron that Clinton was trailing Trump in Ohio. Hoping to give her a lift, he campaigned with her. Two days before the election, they met backstage at Cleveland's Public Auditorium. "As big as you are, as busy as you are," Clinton told him, "it humbles me that you'd take the time to do this."

"Of course," LeBron said.

Moments later, he stepped onstage with Clinton and was greeted by raucous applause. "I want people to understand how I grew up in the inner city," LeBron said. "I was one of those kids and was around a community that was like, 'Our vote doesn't matter.' But it really does. It really, really does."

LeBron had energized the hometown crowd. And he made it clear why he thought it was imperative to vote for Clinton. Referring to his charitable foundation and its mission to help children advance through education, he said, "President Hillary Clinton can make their dreams become a reality, which is very important to me. And I believe that this woman right here can continue that."

On Election Night, the Cavs lost to the Hawks at home. After the game, LeBron and Savannah stayed up most of the night, monitoring the election returns. It was difficult to watch Trump win one key battleground state after another. It was especially painful to see him carry Ohio. The next morning, Clinton conceded to Trump. "We owe him an open mind and a chance to lead," she said. "Our constitutional democracy enshrines the peaceful transition of power. We don't just respect that; we cherish it."

LeBron was disheartened. Obama had been a powerful example for his sons and so many other young people. Similarly, LeBron felt Clinton would have been a great role model for his daughter and countless other young girls. But Trump had been so divisive that LeBron had trouble visualizing him as a role model for young people. Over breakfast, he told Savannah that they were going to have to step up their efforts and use their influence to be a bigger catalyst for positive change.

LeBron knew that players and coaches throughout the NBA feared the worst with Trump. "You walk in and see the faces of your players, most of them who have been insulted directly as minorities," said Warriors coach Steve Kerr. "It's very shocking. All of a sudden, you're faced with the reality that the man who's going to lead you has routinely used racist, misogynist, insulting words." Spurs coach Gregg Popovich and Clippers coach Doc Rivers voiced similar sentiments. But LeBron had over 200 million followers on social media, many of whom were young people. He felt a responsibility to strike a more encouraging tone.

"Minorities and Women in all please know that this isn't the end, it's just a very challenging obstacle that we will overcome!!" he said on Instagram. "To all the youth out there I PROMISE I'll continue to lead u guys every single day without no hesitation!! Time to educate and even more mold my children into being the greatest model citizens they can become in life!"

Donald and Melania Trump visited the White House to meet with the Obamas and start the transition process on November 10, 2016. Coincidentally, it was the same day that the Cavaliers went to the White House to be honored by President Obama. Before the ceremony, LeBron and his teammates met with members of the Obama administration in the Roosevelt Room to discuss ways to improve relations between law enforcement and members of the community in Cleveland. LeBron also spent time with the First Lady. No one spoke Trump's name. But he was in the back of everyone's mind.

Obama was upbeat when he and Vice President Joe Biden gathered the team before an enthusiastic audience on the South Lawn.

"Welcome to the White House and give it up for the *world champion* Cleveland Cavaliers," he said with a smile. "That's right. I said *world champion* and *Cleveland* in the same sentence."

Everyone laughed.

"That's what we're talking about when we're talking about hope and change," he said.

Everyone laughed again.

Obama poked fun at the players. He poked fun at himself. Then he got serious. "You can learn a lot about somebody's character by the way they play basketball," he said.

The players straightened up.

"When you see LeBron James, it is not just his power and his speed and his vertical," Obama continued. "It is his unselfishness. It is his work ethic. It is his determination."

Pensive, LeBron lowered his chin to his chest.

"You saw it when this kid from Akron broke down and fell to his knees," Obama said, "when he realized that he'd finally fulfilled a promise that he'd made all these years ago and delivered that championship back to northeast Ohio. Through it all, Cleveland was always Believeland."

LeBron cherished these White House visits. It was richly gratifying to stand shoulder to shoulder with his teammates and be praised by a leader he revered. No American president had done more to bring Black athletes into the nation's political process, involving them in his campaigns and seeking their assistance in accomplishing his domestic agenda. In his book *The Audacity of Hoop: Basketball and the Age of Obama*, Alexander Wolff argued that Obama leveraged basketball "more often and more effectively than any previous president had used any sport." For the league, the Obama years corresponded with an unprecedented rise in the economic power and cultural influence of NBA players. For LeBron, Obama's presidency had been a golden opportunity to learn from a master statesman and to become his friend and ally.

Obama had treated basketball as a tool to inspire and unify people. He made sure to get the message across one last time. "These Cavs exemplify a growing generation of athletes that are using their platforms to speak out," Obama said. "Kevin [Love] combatting campus sexual assault. LeBron on issues like gun violence and working with Michelle to help more kids go to college."

LeBron wished time could stand still. He knew this was the last time he'd ever be at the White House with the president and First Lady who had played a transformative role in his life.

THIRTY-SIX

U BUM

In his third season back in Cleveland, LeBron improved in each of the major statistical categories. He scored more points, grabbed more rebounds, and dished out more assists per game than he had in the previous two seasons. And at thirty-two, he averaged nearly thirty-eight minutes per game. But his actions away from the court were what distinguished his fourteenth season in the NBA.

On the team's first trip to New York to face the Knicks, in November 2016, LeBron chose not to stay at Trump SoHo, a hotel that the team had booked long before the presidential election. He got his own hotel, and a group of teammates joined him. The move made national headlines, with the *New York Times* declaring, "LeBron James Boycotts Donald Trump's Hotel." LeBron told reporters he wasn't trying to make a statement about Trump. "At the end of the day, I hope he's one of the best presidents ever for all of our sakes—for my family, for all of us," he said. "But just my personal preference. It would be the same if I went to a restaurant and decided to eat chicken and not steak."

Self-assured, LeBron understood that athletes had various economic levers to pull, and he was willing to use them. Trump SoHo was a popular hotel among professional sports teams visiting New York. After LeBron publicly opted to stay elsewhere, roughly twenty sports teams and several other corporate clients stopped staying there. Within a year, the Trump Organization reached an agreement with the hotel to remove the Trump name from the property. Meanwhile, several NBA teams had independently stopped staying at Trump-branded properties in other cities.

LeBron made a point not to publicly criticize President Trump. He went to great lengths to avoid even mentioning his name. But he took a different approach when Knicks president Phil Jackson disparaged his friends with a racially charged word. In an interview that ESPN ran in November 2016, Jackson called LeBron's decision to leave Miami "a slap in the face" to Pat Riley and the Heat organization. Then Jackson opined that LeBron expected special treatment. "When LeBron was playing with the Heat, they went to Cleveland and he wanted to spend the night," Jackson told ESPN. "They don't do overnights. Teams just don't. . . . You can't hold up the whole team because you and your mom and your posse want to spend an extra night in Cleveland."

Maverick Carter was offended. On Twitter, he tagged Jackson and posted a screenshot of the dictionary's definition of *posse*: "a body of men, typically armed, summoned by a sheriff to enforce the law." It would have been one thing, Maverick felt, if Jackson had said LeBron's *agent* or *business partners*. "Yet because you're young and black," he said, "he can use the word." *Every step we take*, Maverick thought, *they remind us*, *"You ghetto."*

LeBron agreed with Maverick, and while contemplating how to respond, he learned that Jackson had previously used the word *posse* in his 2004 book, *The Last Season*, in which he had written:

> As talented as [LeBron James] definitely appears to be, I don't believe any nineteen-year-old should be playing in the NBA. These young men grow so dependent on their posses, who fetch their cars and their girls, that they can't possibly develop into mature, self-sufficient human beings. One day, I'm convinced, we'll find out the true extent of the psychological damage that's been caused.

LeBron had long respected Jackson as a coach who had won six championships with the Bulls and five championships with the Lakers. But it hurt to hear Jackson speak so disrespectfully about his friends, not to mention LeBron himself. When LeBron turned pro, he had put Maverick, Rich, and Randy in position to succeed. There had been no handouts. Just a lot of hard work and persistence. It had taken fourteen years to get where they were. Now Maverick was the founder and CEO of a successful entertainment company in Hollywood. Rich was the founder and CEO of Klutch Sports Group, which had a burgeoning number of NBA players as clients. And Randy was the executive administrator of player programs and logistics for the Cavaliers organization.

"It just sucks that now at this point," LeBron told reporters, "the title for young African Americans is the word *posse*. If you go and read the definition of what that word *posse* is, it's not what I've built over my career. It's not what I stand for. It's not what my family stands for. I believe the only reason he used that word is because he sees young African Americans trying to make a difference."

Jackson had coached legendary players from Michael Jordan to Kobe Bryant. Neither of them came to his defense. But Knicks star Carmelo Anthony wasn't afraid to put Jackson's comments in context. "To some people, the word 'posse' might not mean anything," Anthony said. "To some other people it could be a derogatory statement. It all depends on who you mention it to, and who you're talking about. In this case, [Jackson] was talking about five black men." Although Anthony was diplomatic, he made it clear that he thought the president of his team had used poor judgment.

By this point, Maverick and Rich were highly regarded for their business acumen by players throughout the NBA, and many of them rallied behind LeBron. And with the Knicks floundering, the media blasted Jackson for his arrogance.

LeBron made it clear that he had lost all respect for Jackson, but he said he wasn't looking for an apology and moved on. He was less forgiving when it came to TNT's Charles Barkley, who'd criticized him for being "inappropriate" and "whiny." On the heels of Jackson's comments, Barkley insinuated during an NBA broadcast that LeBron was holding something over Dan Gilbert's head by publicly advocating for the team to add another playmaker to the roster. "He's got Kyrie Irving and Kevin Love," Barkley said. "He wants everybody. He doesn't want to compete. He wanna be the favorite all the time. It just pissed me off that a guy that great doesn't want to compete."

Barkley was notorious for criticizing NBA stars. Years earlier, his negative comments about his close friend Michael Jordan had ended their relationship and Jordan famously ghosted him. Barkley had also sparred with other players. Although LeBron had been a frequent target of Barkley's barbs—he had called LeBron's decision to sign with Miami a "punk move," and he'd liked to remind the TNT audience that LeBron would never be considered a top five player in NBA history—LeBron had ignored him. But after years of holding his tongue, he decided to put Barkley in his place.

"I'm not the one who threw somebody through a window," LeBron told ESPN. "I never spit on a kid. I never had unpaid debt in Las Vegas. I never said, 'I'm not a role model.' I never showed up to All-Star Weekend on Sunday because I was in Vegas all weekend partying. All I've done for my entire career is represent the NBA the right way. Fourteen years. Never got in trouble. Respected the game. Print that."

It was jarring to hear a player speak so candidly about another member of the NBA family, and the media anticipated retaliation. A couple of nights later, Barkley responded on TNT's *Inside the NBA*: "I have no problem with what LeBron said. . . . I did some stupid things in my life. That being said, I have never said anything personal about a guy. And I'm never going to. Ever!"

Shaquille O'Neal, who was Barkley's broadcast partner on TNT, reminded him on the air that he had made it personal when he had said that LeBron didn't like to compete. "You took it personal with that man," O'Neal said. "And that man took it personal with you."

The Cavs finished the 2016–2017 season with the second-best record in the Eastern Conference. After sweeping both opponents in the opening rounds of the playoffs, they faced the Celtics in the Eastern Conference Finals. Celtics president Danny Ainge had retooled the team by drafting budding stars like twenty-year-old Jaylen Brown and twenty-two-year-old Marcus Smart, and Boston was the top seed in the conference. But Cleveland dominated and advanced to the finals to face Golden State for the third straight year.

Once again, the NBA and ABC had a showcase championship series featuring the game's biggest stars. But while LeBron was in Oakland preparing for Game 1 of the Finals, he got word that the authorities in Los Angeles were investigating a hate crime that had occurred at his Brentwood property, where the N-word had been painted on the front gates of the house. Fortunately, Savannah and the children were back in Ohio. After checking on them, LeBron thought about Mamie Till, who insisted on an open coffin after her fourteen-year-old son, Emmett, was brutally beaten and murdered by two white men in Mississippi in the fifties.

LeBron was on edge when he arrived at the arena and addressed the media. "This is kind of killing me inside right now," he said. "No matter how much money you have, no matter how famous you are, no matter how many people admire you, being black in America is . . . it's tough."

Then he brought up Emmett Till's mother. "She wanted to show the world what her son went through as far as a hate crime and being black in America," he said.

For basketball writers, this was unlike any NBA Finals press conference they'd attended.

"Obviously," LeBron said, "you see I'm not my normal energetic self. It will pass. That's fine. I'm figuring it out."

LeBron's words resonated with baseball slugger Hank Aaron. "I can understand what LeBron is saying, because I felt the same way that he does," Aaron told the *Atlanta Journal-Constitution* prior to Game 1. In the early seventies, when Aaron was closing in on Babe Ruth's home run record, he was inundated with death threats and hate mail from those who didn't want to see a Black man reach baseball's holy grail. "As I got older, I was able to deal with it a little better," he said. "But I would go home at night and say, 'What did I do wrong?' Even now, I am eighty-two and I think about some of the things that happened. I just wanted to play baseball."

LeBron used to want to just play basketball. But those days were long gone. The mantle of being the most famous black athlete in America had unrelenting weight.

LeBron shined in Game 1 and throughout the Finals. So did Kyrie Irving. As a duo, they were at their zenith. Irving averaged over twenty-nine points per game in the finals. And LeBron became the first player in NBA history to average a triple-double in the finals with 33.6 points, 12 rebounds, and 10 assists per game. But the Cavs were no match for the Warriors. Kevin Durant, Steph Curry, Klay Thompson, Draymond Green, and the rest overwhelmed Cleveland and won the series in five games. Durant was named Finals MVP.

LeBron embraced Durant after the final buzzer sounded. NBA pundits had widely criticized Durant for taking an easier route to the championship by joining the Warriors. LeBron didn't see it that way. He loved competing against Durant and the Warriors. And in LeBron's view, the Warriors were built to last. Their four all-stars were in their twenties. LeBron, on the other hand, had just completed his fourteenth season. If Cleveland was going to keep pace with Golden State, the Cavaliers were going to have to get some help for LeBron and Irving.

But over the summer, LeBron was blindsided when he found out that the Cavaliers were trading Irving to the Celtics. After the 2017 Finals, Irving had gone to Dan Gilbert and demanded a trade. Gilbert hadn't alerted LeBron. Nor had Irving.

Celtics president Danny Ainge was intrigued when he found out through Irving's agent that Irving wanted out of Cleveland. The Celtics had just drafted Jayson Tatum to bolster a championship-caliber roster. The Cavaliers were the only team standing in the way of Boston regaining supremacy in the Eastern Conference. And the opportunity to subtract Irving from Cleveland's roster and add him to Boston's represented a coup. At twenty-five, Irving was a four-time all-star and had developed into one of the most elite talents in the NBA. From Ainge's perspective, Irving's best years were ahead of him.

The fact that Irving wanted to leave LeBron and a team that had been to three straight NBA Finals didn't surprise Ainge. "It's not always about just winning," Ainge said. "On the surface it didn't make sense that Kyrie should want to leave LeBron and the Cleveland Cavaliers. But it doesn't make sense that people get divorced over silly things. Emotions are real. We're talking about kids in their twenties. The emotional part is a very real element."

A year earlier, when the Cavs had won the title, Irving had compared LeBron to Beethoven composing a symphony. But after three years with LeBron, Irving wanted out from playing in his shadow. Boston seemed like a place where he would be the brightest star and lead a team to a title.

LeBron didn't want the Cavs to go through with the deal. Irving still had three years remaining on his contract, so he lacked the leverage to force a trade. But by the time LeBron stepped in, all that remained was for Irving to pass a physical and the league to sign off. The player LeBron had taken under his wing and tried to mentor was gone. And he hadn't bothered to say goodbye.

Privately, LeBron was hurt. Publicly, he wished Irving well on Twitter: "That's the only way to be kid! Special talent/guy! Nothing but respect and what a ride our 3 years together. . . ."

While LeBron was coming to terms with the loss of his wingman, President Trump held a political rally in Huntsville, Alabama. In front of a predominantly white audience, Trump talked about athletes who knelt during the national anthem to protest police brutality and racial injustice. "Wouldn't you love to see one of these NFL owners, when somebody disrespects our flag, to say, 'Get that son of a bitch off the field right now. Out. He's fired.'" The crowd cheered. "He's fired!" Trump repeated, energizing the crowd.

By this point, Kaepernick was out of the NFL, and the controversy over kneeling during the anthem had died down. But Trump's broadside rekindled the issue. Many of his supporters voiced their support on social media. At the same time, plenty of NFL players felt that the president's rhetoric was racially divisive and dangerous. Attempting to defuse the situation, NFL commissioner Roger Goodell issued a diplomatically worded statement in support of the players. But Trump lashed out at Goodell on Twitter: "Tell them to stand!"

LeBron couldn't believe it. A month earlier a "Unite the Right" rally of white nationalists had turned deadly in Charlottesville when a neo-Nazi purposely plowed his car into a crowd of counter protesters, killing a woman and injuring dozens. Trump insisted there were "very fine people on both sides." And now Trump was more animated about a Black athlete who chose to peacefully protest racism by kneeling than he'd ever been about white supremacists marching through Charlottesville. LeBron was already stewing over the situation when he woke up on September 23, 2017, and saw that Trump had also turned his ire on Steph Curry.

After Trump's speech in Alabama, Curry told reporters on September 22 that if it were up to him, the Warriors wouldn't go to the White House. "I don't know why he feels the need to target certain individuals rather than others," Curry said at a press conference after the team's first practice of the season. "I have an idea of why, but it's kind of beneath the leader of a country to go that route. It's not what leaders do."

The next morning, at 8:45 Eastern time, Trump tweeted: "Going to the White House is considered a great honor for a championship team. Stephen Curry is hesitating, therefore invitation is withdrawn!"

Curry was LeBron's rival. But LeBron had seen enough. The president was using sports as a wedge. That morning, at 11:17 Eastern time, LeBron tweeted at Trump: "U bum @StephenCurry30 said he ain't going! So therefore ain't no invite. Going to White House was a great honor until you showed up!"

Other athletes and coaches had previously taken issue with Trump's words and actions. But LeBron was the first to confront Trump so forcefully and so directly. The reaction was immediate and profound. That afternoon, Draymond Green was asked by reporters what he thought of LeBron's tweet. "He called him a bum," Green said, smiling. "I respect it." Kobe Bryant tweeted that a president "whose words inspire dissension and hatred can't possibly 'Make America Great Again.'" The University of North Carolina's national championship basketball team announced that it would not be going to the White House. And the next day, players throughout the NFL knelt in solidarity during the national anthem. Within twenty-four hours, LeBron's tweet had been liked by 1.5 million people and retweeted more than 620,000 times, far surpassing Trump's most popular post—his all-caps victory tweet on Election Day—which was retweeted 335,000 times. LeBron's tweet ended up being the most retweeted tweet in the world by an athlete in 2017. "Turns out, the basketball superstar is better at uniting Americans than the commander in chief," quipped *Slate* magazine.

With four characters and one space, LeBron's "U bum" tweet had redefined the way athletes engaged in political speech. And although it hadn't been his intention, he was now front and center in a battle between athletes and the president over race and social justice. The *New York Times* ran the headline "Trump Attacks Warriors' Curry. LeBron James's Retort: 'U Bum.'" The *New Yorker*'s David Remnick wrote: "How is it possible to argue with the sentiment behind LeBron James's concise tweet at Trump: 'U Bum'? It isn't."

And LeBron didn't back away from what he had said. When the Cavaliers had their Media Day during training camp, the press asked whether he regretted calling the president a bum. LeBron said he didn't.

"He doesn't understand the power that he has for being the leader of this beautiful country," LeBron said. "He doesn't understand how many kids, no matter the race, look up to the president of the United States for guidance. For leadership. For words of encouragement."

LeBron paused. "That's what makes me more sick than anything—that we have someone, this is the number one position in the world. You guys agree?" LeBron looked around the room at the reporters. "Being the president of the United States is the most powerful position in the world," he continued. "And we're at a time when the most powerful position in the world has an opportunity to bring us closer together as a people and inspire the youth and put the youth at ease, saying that it's okay for me to walk down the street and not be judged because of the color of my skin or because of my race. He has no recognition of that, and he doesn't even care!"

LeBron brought it back to the original question about whether he regretted calling the president a bum. "No," he said. "Because if I did, I would have deleted my tweet."

His choice of words had provided cover for other athletes to speak out. His statement also had laid bare an unspoken disconnect between many Black players and white owners. Plenty of NFL and NBA owners had given financial support to Trump, including Dan Gilbert, whose Quicken Loans mortgage lending company had contributed $750,000 to Trump's inauguration.

LeBron didn't hear from Gilbert after his "U bum" tweet. But Gilbert got an earful from people who were enraged by LeBron's comment. The messages left on Gilbert's voicemail were some of the most vile and racist things he'd ever heard. For Gilbert, it was eye-opening.

"There's an element of racism that I didn't even realize existed in this country," Gilbert said on CNBC's *Squawk Box.* "It was some of the most disgusting things I've ever heard people say. And you could hear it in their voice. It wasn't even about the issue. They went to who they really are."

Gilbert wasn't the only owner whose eyes were opened in the aftermath of LeBron's tweet and the protests that spread throughout professional sports. Numerous team owners in the NBA and the NFL openly backed the players, even after the president called on fans to boycott NFL games if players continued to kneel during the anthem. And players across the NBA and the NFL were galvanized in their protests throughout the 2017–2018 season. After the Philadelphia Eagles defeated the New England Patriots in the 2018 Super Bowl, numerous Eagles players made it clear that they would not visit the White House. Trump, in turn, canceled the team's visit.

Snow was falling in Akron, Ohio, on January 14, 2018. It was the night before the Cavaliers hosted the Warriors, and LeBron was giving Kevin Durant a guided tour of his hometown. They were in the backseat of an

SUV being driven by ESPN broadcaster Cari Champion. With a camera mounted to the dashboard, Champion facilitated a conversation between LeBron and Durant that began with them talking about what it was like to compete against each other. But it quickly took a turn when LeBron brought up Muhammad Ali and how he was stripped of his heavyweight title and jailed for refusing to fight in Vietnam. Durant admired LeBron's willingness to go there. Glancing in the rearview mirror, Champion said, "We are at a watershed moment in this country. LeBron, you called the president a bum."

"Straight up," he said.

Durant smiled. "Straight up."

"How do you describe the climate for an athlete with a platform who wants to talk about what's happening in the world?" Champion said.

"The number one job in America," LeBron said, "is [held by] someone who doesn't understand the people, and really don't give a fuck about the people. . . . While we can't change what comes out of that man's mouth, we can continue to alert the people that watch us—that listen to us—that this is not the way."

"We're talking about leadership and what's going on in our country," Durant said. "I feel like our team, as a country, is not run by a great coach."

Champion suggested that some people think that being wealthy Black men would insulate LeBron and Durant from racism.

"I'm a Black man with a bunch of money and having a crib in Brentwood and having the word 'nigger' spraypainted over my gate," LeBron said.

"That's crazy," Durant said.

"No matter how far money or access or how high you become in life as an African American man or female, they will always try to figure out a way to let you know that you are still beneath them," LeBron said. "You either cave into that notion or you just chalk it up and say, 'You know what? I'm gonna paint over this goddamn gate and I'm gonna make it taller.'"

As a young teen, Durant had idolized LeBron. Now he looked up to him for other reasons. "You had your first son," Durant said. "Then you had another son. Then you had a daughter. For me, I'm not even at that point in my life. How do you become a better father and husband every day?"

"What really helped me out becoming a parent was what I went through as a kid—not having a dad," he said, explaining his approach to parenting. "I have three kids and I'm still learning how to be a better husband and how to be a better father."

"So it's an ongoing process," Durant said.

"It's never-ending, bro," LeBron said. "All you can hope at the end of the road is that you've given your kids enough life lessons to where when it's time for them to live their lives, they can flourish on their own."

Durant nodded. So did Champion.

"It's the same with being a husband," LeBron said. "When you know you're committed, then everything else takes care of itself."

"Man," Durant said, "that's good."

It was an extraordinary conversation between the two greatest basketball players in the world. When it aired a month later, Fox News host Laura Ingraham seized on what LeBron said about Trump. Mocking LeBron and Durant as "barely intelligible" and "ungrammatical," she mocked them on her program *The Ingraham Angle*. "Must they run their mouths like that?" she said. "Unfortunately, a lot of kids—and some adults—take these ignorant comments seriously. . . . And it's always unwise to seek political advice from someone who gets paid a hundred million dollars a year to bounce a ball."

In many ways, Ingraham was doing exactly what LeBron had described—figuring out a way to let them know that they were still beneath her. But in doing so, she had purposely ignored one of the most poignant and honest conversations with the country's two most prominent Black athletes discussing marriage, parenting, and the struggle to be true to your beliefs. Instead, Ingraham went out of her way to take them down.

"Oh, and LeBron and Kevin," she said, "You're great players. But no one voted for you. Millions elected Trump to be their coach. . . . So keep the political commentary to yourself or, as someone once said, shut up and dribble."

Ingraham's broadside aired days before the NBA All-Star game in Los Angeles. The backlash was swift. *New York Times* opinion columnist Maureen Dowd wrote: " 'Shut up and dribble.' Those four words sum up the attitude of Donald Trump and his acolytes toward athletes who speak out when the president uses sports to foment racial animosity and rile up his base." Athletes and coaches across the country lamented Ingraham's comments. Durant called them "racist." But LeBron saw Ingraham's ignorance as an opportunity. The day after her show aired, he held a press conference in the lead-up to the All-Star game. "The best thing she did is help me create more awareness," he said. "I get to sit up here and talk about social injustice and equality. So thank you, whatever her name is. I don't even know her name."

The basketball writers loved that LeBron didn't know her name. Maverick Carter didn't know what's-her-name either. But he had an idea—they should take the phrase "shut up and dribble" and use it as the basis of a television show. LeBron agreed. They started brainstorming and ultimately came up with an eight-part documentary series called "More Than an Athlete." ESPN+ agreed to air it. LeBron and Maverick produced it.

Despite being at the forefront of player activism, LeBron's on-court performance in his fifteenth season didn't taper off. By the time LeBron turned thirty-three near the midpoint of the season, he led the league in field goals and he was second in points scored and minutes played. Warriors coach Steve Kerr argued that LeBron might be better at thirty-three than he was at twenty-eight. "How many players are better in Year 15 than in Year 10?" Kerr said. "Go down the list: Michael, Bird, Magic, Wilt, Kareem, Bill Russell. A lot of them didn't even get to 15 years. Were any of them better in Year 15 than in Year 10? I can't imagine."

But the Cavs had a tumultuous year. They struggled to win consistently. Coach Tyronn Lue had to take a leave of absence due to job-related anxiety. And the Cavaliers made so many trades during the season that many of the players from the championship roster were shipped elsewhere. With so much chaos, the Cavs limped into the playoffs as the fourth seed in the Eastern Conference, and the primary question looming over the franchise was whether LeBron's time in Cleveland was up.

It was a question LeBron had been contemplating for a while. His relationship with Gilbert was purely transactional. The franchise was in turmoil. And LeBron had his children to consider. His oldest son Bronny was in middle school, and LeBron and Savannah were considering where to live during their sons' high school years. One option was Los Angeles, where he had purchased another home in Brentwood during the season. But in the meantime, LeBron geared up for one final playoff run in Cleveland.

With a depleted roster and several players nursing injuries, the Cavs survived a bruising seven-game series in the opening round against Indiana when LeBron scored forty-five points and led them to victory in Game 7. LeBron single-handedly beat the top-seeded Toronto Raptors with one dramatic shot after another, including a buzzer-beater he banked off the backboard to win Game 3, and a backbreaking fallaway near the end of Game 4 where he shot over the backboard as he was landing out-of-bounds. On ESPN, Stephen A. Smith called LeBron's performance "superhuman" and added, "You're just running out of superlatives to describe what this man is doing."

After sweeping Toronto, Cleveland faced Boston in the Eastern Conference Finals. With Kyrie Irving sitting out the series with an injury, Boston built a 3-2 series lead. But LeBron scored forty-six points to win Game 6. Then with Kevin Love out with a concussion, LeBron played all forty-eight minutes in Game 7 in Boston and notched 35 points, 15 rebounds, and 9 assists to lead Cleveland to an improbable victory. It was the first time in NBA history that the Boston Celtics had lost a Game 7 at home. "No one person has ever shouldered more and gotten his team to the Finals," analyst Jeff Van Gundy said. "He'll never have a greater achievement than getting *this* team to the Finals."

For LeBron it was his eighth straight trip to the NBA Finals. And for an unprecedented fourth straight year, the Cavaliers faced the Warriors. Although the series was a colossal mismatch, LeBron hoped his team could flip a switch one last time and find a way to beat Golden State. In Game 1, LeBron scored 51 points, but his team lost in overtime. In awe, Steve Kerr said, "They have a guy who is playing basketball at a level that I'm not sure anybody's ever seen before."

The Warriors swept the Cavs. But LeBron turned in one of his grittiest performances as a Cavalier, playing virtually every minute of all four games, averaging 34 points, 8.5 rebounds, and 10 assists per game.

Nonetheless, the final showdown between the Cavaliers and Warriors was marked by a spirit of political solidarity by the two teams, particularly LeBron and Curry. A headline in the *New York Times* during the finals—"LeBron James and Stephen Curry Unite Against White House Visits"—signified how much the political climate in the NBA had changed in four years. "I know whoever wins this series, no one wants an invite," LeBron said.

Near the end of Game 4 in Cleveland, the Warriors were up by twenty-five points with 4:03 remaining when the ball went out-of-bounds. Seeing

Cavs bench players waiting at the scorer's table, LeBron knew his time was up. As the crowd rose to its feet and started to cheer, LeBron fist-bumped Draymond Green, Kevin Durant, Andre Iguodala, and Klay Thompson. The applause escalating and chants of "M-V-P" booming through the Q, LeBron approached Curry, who patted him on the behind and joined the Cleveland fans in applause. After LeBron took a seat on the bench and the game resumed, the "MVP" chants got louder. Another chapter in LeBron's life was ending. The fans felt it. And so did LeBron. The 2017–2018 season had been one of the hardest in his career. More than ever, he was glad he had come home. Now he could chase other dreams.

THIRTY-SEVEN

A MAN IN FULL

On July 1, 2018, Rich Paul's agency released a one-sentence press release on Twitter: "LeBron James, four time NBA MVP, three time NBA finals MVP, fourteen time NBA All-Star, and two time Olympic gold medalist has agreed to a four year, $154 million contract with the Los Angeles Lakers."

The matter-of-fact announcement was in stark contrast to the way LeBron had previously left Cleveland. And Dan Gilbert's reaction was profoundly different as well. Within hours, he released his own statement. "LeBron, you came home and delivered the ultimate goal," Gilbert wrote, "a championship that united generations of Clevelanders, both living and past. . . . Nothing but appreciation and gratitude for everything you put into every moment you spent in a Cavaliers uniform. We look forward to the retirement of the famous #23 Cavs jersey one day down the line."

It was a classy ending to a comeback story for the ages.

Although he was heading to LA, LeBron made it clear that northeast Ohio would always be home. On July 30, 2018, he was back in Akron with his family and friends to announce something that would change more lives than the championship banner hanging in the Q—the opening of his I Promise School, which he and Savannah had constructed for underprivileged children. Wearing a suit and tie, LeBron stood on a stage in front of the new institution and looked out at the members of the community and the educators who supported the venture. Then he looked down and saw Maverick Carter, Rich Paul, and Randy Mims seated together in the front row. Their presence took him back. "When you were a kid growing up in Akron, Ohio, and so many things were happening," he said, "gun violence and drugs and things were going on, what stopped you from going the other way? Looking out I see my friends right now that I've been with since I was six, seven years old."

Maverick, Rich, and Randy locked eyes on him.

"They're the reason that kinda stopped me from going the other way."

The school opened with 240 students. Each of them would receive free tuition, uniforms, transportation within two miles, breakfast and lunch and snacks, bicycles and bike helmets. There was also a food pantry for families, GEDs and job placement services for parents, and guaranteed tuition to the University of Akron for all graduates.

After the opening ceremonies, LeBron sat down for an interview with CNN's Don Lemon to discuss the school and his efforts to help educate children. During the interview, Lemon shifted the conversation to President Trump.

"What would you say to the president if he was sitting right here?" Lemon asked.

"I would never sit across from him," LeBron said.

"You don't want to talk to him?" Lemon asked.

"No," LeBron said. "I'd sit across from Barack, though."

It was a historic moment. The most famous athlete in America said he would not talk to the president of the United States.

LeBron elaborated. "Our president is kind of trying to divide us."

"Kind of?" Lemon said.

"Yeah, he is. I don't want to say kind of. He is dividing us. And what I noticed over the last few months is that he's used sports to divide us. That's something I can't relate to because I know that [playing] sports was the first time I was ever around someone white."

LeBron used the opportunity to suggest that sports had a way of breaking down racial barriers, as it did for him as a teen with white students. "I got an opportunity to see them and learn about them," he said. "And they got an opportunity to learn about me, and we became very good friends."

Hours after the interview aired, President Trump tweeted: "LeBron James was just interviewed by the dumbest man on television, Don Lemon. He made LeBron look smart, which isn't easy to do. I like Mike!"

In one swipe, the president demeaned the intelligence of two Black men, dragged Michael Jordan—"Mike"—into the fray, and once again put LeBron at the focal point of a national discussion on race. The next day, *CBS Saturday Morning* opened the show with: "Our top story this morning, President Trump taking to Twitter overnight to bash NBA superstar LeBron James. . . ." It was the top story across the country. LeBron took the high ground, putting out a tweet of his own: "Let's get it kids! Love you guys." The tweet included a link to his I Promise School.

Los Angeles Lakers owner Jeanie Buss put out a statement: "We could not be more proud to have LeBron James as part of our Lakers family. He is an incredibly thoughtful and intelligent leader and clearly appreciates the power that sports has to unite communities and inspire the world to be a better place."

Rival Steph Curry weighed in: "Keep doing you @kingjames!"

Even the First Lady came to LeBron's defense. Reporting from CNN's *The Situation Room* on August 16, 2018, Wolf Blitzer said, "The First Lady, Melania Trump, contradicts her husband once again, praising LeBron James for his charitable work, after her husband attacks him." The First Lady put out a formal statement indicating she'd like to visit the I Promise School.

But the biggest surprise came when Michael Jordan entered the fray. The debate over whether Jordan or LeBron was the greatest player of all time would go on for years to come. But there would never be a question about which one of them had done more to influence social change. LeBron had used his position and his resources to lean into a range of political issues, from gun violence to racism to voting rights. Jordan had famously avoided anything political during and after his career. But Trump had invoked Jordan's name in his tweet, and Jordan paid LeBron a high compliment: "I support LJ," Jordan said. "He's doing an amazing job for his community."

While the fallout over Trump's attack on LeBron continued to swirl in the US, LeBron traveled to China, where he wore a T-shirt that said I AM MORE THAN AN ATHLETE while addressing a large audience at the Shanghai Theatre Academy. He then took his message of athlete activism to Paris and Germany, where he visited the site of the Berlin Wall and told the press, "People just need some hope."

When he returned to the States, he stopped in New York, where he received a Harlem's Fashion Row award for his philanthropic work. LeBron used the opportunity to unveil his latest Nike shoe, which was a women's sneaker inspired by strong African American women. With his mother, his wife, and his daughter on hand, he took the podium and paid tribute to them. Thanking his mother for raising him by herself, he pointed out that the insoles of his new Nike shoes were covered with the words that described his mom—*strength*, *loyalty*, *dignity*, and *courage*. "Every time someone puts their foot in the shoe, that's what they're standing on," he said. "Because of you, Gloria James, I'm able to be in a position today where I can give back and showcase why I believe African American women are the most powerful women in the world."

LeBron looked around at the room full of women. "This pretty girl right here," he said, nodding at his daughter, "this is my rock. People always told me, 'If you ever have a girl, she'll change you.' I was like, 'Nah. Impossible. Ain't nobody changing me.' Then three years ago this bright spot happened in our family. And not only did she change me, but she made me a better person—a more dedicated person, a stronger person. I guess a more sensitive person that realized that I have so much more of a responsibility to women in general. So, thank you, Zhuri. I love you, baby girl."

Savannah beamed.

LeBron looked at her and paused. With a room full of women looking at him, LeBron revealed a lot about his personality and why the bond between them was so strong. "Savannah was with me, shooting in the gym, when I had absolutely nothing," he said.

It was easy to get emotional when he thought about how far they'd come and how much they'd been through together.

But the time for reflection was over. The Lakers were about to open training camp. He had to get to LA for the next chapter in his life.

EPILOGUE

On a warm, sunny afternoon in mid-September 2018, LeBron entered a popular sushi restaurant near his new home in Brentwood. Wearing shorts and a T-shirt and carrying a lumbar-support pillow, he sat down with Adam Mendelsohn and Marisa Guthrie from the *Hollywood Reporter*. Mendelsohn handed him a bottle of wine. It was a gift for LeBron's wedding anniversary, the following day. Mendelsohn asked whether LeBron would take a day off from his workout regimen.

LeBron gave him a funny look. "That's like asking, 'Am I going to breathe tomorrow?'" he said. "Of course I'm gonna work out."

LeBron was heading into his sixteenth season, but he was training more relentlessly than he had trained when he entered the league as a rookie. Guthrie admired LeBron's work ethic. She'd spent part of the previous day with him on the Warner Bros. lot in Burbank, where LeBron and Maverick kept an office in a blue Cape Cod–style house that had been used as a set for *Gilmore Girls*. It had been four years since Guthrie first profiled LeBron. Now she was doing a cover story on him and the growth of SpringHill Entertainment and his athlete-empowerment brand Uninterrupted, which produced *The Shop* on HBO. While still playing at an elite level in the NBA, LeBron was building an empire in Los Angeles.

"Go ahead," LeBron said, positioning the lumbar support behind his lower back. "You can ask me questions."

Guthrie took out her recording device. But as soon as people spotted LeBron, they approached and wanted to take selfies with him.

"Not right now," LeBron said politely. "We're gonna do an interview."

Guthrie asked LeBron if he ever longed for anonymity.

"I'm not an anonymous guy," LeBron told her. "You gotta understand, I'm an only child. I *like* people."

Guthrie asked about the new slate of projects that LeBron and Maverick had lined up. That week, NBC and the CW Network had both announced new shows with SpringHill. Maverick had also signed deals for new projects with HBO, including a documentary on Muhammad Ali. LeBron and Maverick had a crime drama in the works with Netflix, along with a limited series starring Octavia Spencer. But Maverick had provided Guthrie with a scoop for her story—he had just convinced *Black Panther* director Ryan Coogler to produce the new *Space Jam* movie for Warner Bros. LeBron, who was starring in the film, couldn't wait to start shooting.

"Coogler gave this generation's kids something I didn't have when I was a kid," LeBron said. "And that's a superhero movie with an African-American cast."

For LeBron, the chance to work with Coogler on *Space Jam* represented the fulfillment of a childhood dream. "I always wanted to be a superhero," he said. "Batman was my favorite. But I knew I could never be Bruce Wayne. I never felt like I could be the president of a multibillion-dollar company."

Now LeBron was worth an estimated $1 billion, and Warner Bros. had cast LeBron to play himself in a live-action/animated film alongside Bugs Bunny, Daffy Duck, and other cartoon characters from the Looney Tunes gang. In many ways, LeBron's move to Los Angeles had the makings of a real-life Hollywood ending to his storied basketball career.

While LeBron and Guthrie talked, Rich Paul showed up and sat down at the table next to them. Rich had been busy, too. In addition to negotiating LeBron's four-year, $154 million deal with the Lakers, he had recruited a slew of new clients to join his Klutch Sports Group. And as he took a call on his cell phone, he was closing in on one of the league's biggest superstars, New Orleans Pelicans center Anthony Davis, who had just fired his agent a few days earlier. Guthrie couldn't help overhearing the conversation. When Rich hung up, he turned to her and said, "Don't say anything."

Guthrie assured him that he didn't need to worry. That wasn't the story she was there to write.

A week later, LeBron and twenty-eight employees from his teams at SpringHill and Uninterrupted appeared on the cover of *Hollywood Reporter* with the headline "LeBron Takes L.A." The magazine called LeBron "one of the town's hottest producers."

* * *

Similarly, Rich was one of the NBA's hottest agents. That same week, Klutch Sports Group announced that Anthony Davis had signed with Rich. And soon Rich would begin talking to Davis about joining the Lakers and teaming up with LeBron.

But as LeBron prepared to play his first game in a Laker uniform, he was dreaming about a different future teammate—his eldest son, Bronny, who was already attracting interest from college basketball recruiters. For some time, LeBron had wondered what it would be like to play in the NBA with Bronny. LeBron wasn't ready to share his dream with the public. But at the start of the 2018 season, he let the world know how he felt about Bronny. On Instagram he wrote:

> Happy 14th Bday to my first born Bronny! U make me proud every single day to say you're my son. Continue to set a great example to your lil brother, sister, and being the man of the house when your pops is on the road for work. I love the young man you've grown into and this is just the beginning! Looking forward to continuing seeing your growth in everything you do! Love you Bronny! #ProudDad.

The 2018–2019 season was a frustrating one. The Lakers failed to reach the playoffs. But in the summer of 2019, Rich orchestrated a trade that brought Anthony Davis to Los Angeles. That same year, Rich left Cleveland and moved to Beverly Hills, where he bought a multimillion-dollar home. Later that year, he met singer-songwriter Adele when she approached him at a party and said, "Do you want to sign me?" They became friends and eventually started seeing each other.

LeBron and Anthony Davis led the Lakers to the NBA championship in 2020. It was LeBron's fourth title, and he became the first player to be named NBA Finals MVP with three different teams.

Shortly after the finals, LeBron and Savannah purchased the Beverly Hills estate that previously belonged to Katharine Hepburn. Meanwhile, back in Akron, LeBron opened House Three Thirty, a sixty-thousand-square-foot facility staffed with bankers and financial advisors, who were on hand to assist low-income families with financial planning. The venture was financed through a partnership between the LeBron James Family Foundation and JPMorgan Chase.

LeBron was also heavily involved in the 2020 election. He formed a political organization called More Than a Vote to combat voter suppression by helping minorities register and get them to the polls. It was a direct response to Republican-led efforts in states like Georgia to make it harder for people of color to vote.

On January 6, 2021, LeBron watched on television as a mob of Trump supporters stormed and ransacked the US Capitol. LeBron couldn't help noticing that the mob was predominantly white and that there were no troops or reinforcements to help the overwhelmed Capitol police force. The next day, LeBron appeared at a postgame press conference wearing a T-shirt that said DO YOU UNDERSTAND NOW? "We live in two Americas," he told the media. "And if you don't understand that or don't see that after seeing what you saw yesterday, then you really need to take a step back." He reflected on the violent images from the previous day. "If those were my kind storming the Capitol," he added, "what would have been the outcome? And I think we all know. There's no ifs, ands, or buts—we already know what would've happened to my kind if anyone would have even got close to the Capitol, let alone storm inside the offices."

In 2021, the production company that LeBron and Maverick formed in 2007 had a valuation of nearly $1 billion. And through their partnership with Fenway Sports Group, LeBron and Maverick became part owners of the Boston Red Sox and the Liverpool Football Club in 2021. "For me and my partner Maverick to be the first two black men to be a part of that ownership group . . . is pretty damn cool," LeBron said. "It gives me and people that look like me hope and inspiration that they can be in a position like that as well, that it can be done. It gives my kids at my I Promise School more and more inspiration as well."

The year 2021 was a big one for Rich, too. His Klutch Sports Group had negotiated $1.8 billion in NBA and NFL contracts. And Rich and Adele decided to go public with their dating relationship by attending an NBA playoff game together. "What are people going to say?" Rich asked her. "That you signed me," Adele said.

Rich and Adele had courtside seats. A few seats down from them, LeBron sat next to Randy Mims. The Lakers weren't in the playoffs. But LeBron took stock of his situation. All of the Four Horsemen were still together, living in LA, and experiencing wild success. And Savannah and the children were thriving on the West Coast. Life had turned out just the way he'd hoped it would. Basketball had been immeasurably good to him. And even though he would soon be forty, he felt as though he could play for many years to come.

During the 2022-2023 season, his fifth with the Lakers and his twentieth season overall, LeBron turned thirty-eight. Less than two months later, on February 7, 2023, he reached the milestone of 38,388 points, surpassing Kareem Abdul-Jabbar as the NBA's all-time leading scorer.

Only one basketball dream remained—playing in an NBA game with his eighteen-year-old son, Bronny, who was set to graduate from high school in 2023.

ACKNOWLEDGMENTS

I'll start with the writers.

LeBron's high school years were covered extensively by a slew of first-rate scribes from the *Akron Beacon Journal* and *Plain Dealer*, led by David Lee Morgan, Jr., Terry Pluto, Tim Rogers, and Brian Windhorst. I don't know what's going on in Utah. But when I wanted to know what was going on in Akron from 1999 to 2003, I looked to the reporting of Morgan, Pluto, Rogers, and Windhorst.

Some of the best basketball writers in the business covered LeBron's pro career and his stints on the US Olympic team. But for me, a handful stood out. The day-to-day reporting by *New York Times* writers Liz Robbins, Howard Beck, and Scott Cacciola was insightful, smart, and pleasurably entertaining. Columnist Ira Berkow, a magician with words, wrote the first national profile of LeBron, and it's a beauty. Michael Holley, a consummate pro, wrote the second profile on LeBron, and it's largely overlooked. I relied on it for an important scene in the biography. Mike Wise and Tom Friend both penned penetrating pieces that informed this biography. Larry Platt wrote a marvelous feature for *GQ* that was full of windows into LeBron and his inner circle in the early days. Then there's Chris Ballard and Jack McCallum—two veteran *Sports Illustrated* writers who penned exceptional features on LeBron over the years.

Other sports writers whose work influenced and informed mine include Jonathan Abrams, Harvey Araton, Frank Litsky, Jere Longman, Jackie MacMullan, Chris Mannix, Dave McMenamin, Michael Powell, William C. Rhoden, S.L. Price, Billy Witz, and Adrian Wojnarowski.

Similarly, a group of feature writers from the worlds of fashion, business, music, politics, and entertainment produced illuminating pieces that were a great resource. They include Tim Arango, Isaac Chotiner, Joe

Drape, Sean Gregory, Boaz Herzog, Charles McGrath, Jason Quick, Lisa Robinson, Eli Saslow, Robert Sullivan, Touré, and Patrick Varone.

I am most indebted to a decorated group of journalists who produced seminal works on LeBron over the years. This list includes some of my generation's finest storytellers in print journalism: Grant Wahl, Lisa Taddeo, Buzz Bissinger, J. R. Moehringer, Lee Jenkins, Marisa Guthrie, and Wright Thompson. One of the highlights of working on this biography was getting to know Grant, whose reporting style reflected his endearing personality traits—kindness, humility, and empathy. It's no wonder he wrote the *Sports Illustrated* cover story that introduced LeBron to the world. Lisa is a wildly entertaining writer . . . and one helluva an interview. Buzz—the best name in journalism, and from my perspective, the book you wrote with LeBron was a masterpiece! J. R.—if you ever decide to teach journalism, I'll go back to school. There's a reason LeBron trusted Lee to write the essay announcing his return to Cleveland. Hats off to the writer who is confident enough to stay out of sight. Marisa is a paragon of professionalism and a navigator. She's a writer I will encourage my young daughter to emulate. Wright is a terrible dresser, but he's an intrepid reporter and lyrical writer.

I'd be remiss if I didn't thank the dozens of senior executives, editors, and staff at *Sports Illustrated*, ESPN, *Vanity Fair*, and *The Hollywood Reporter* for helping to facilitate interviews, provide context, search files, track down data and information, and answer my various written queries. I'm also grateful to the librarians, archivists, and editors at the *Akron Beacon Journal*, *Plain Dealer*, and *Miami Herald* for assisting me with the retrieval of enough stories to fill binders.

Tim Bella and John Gaughan did yeoman work on the research front.

Next there's my colleagues.

It takes a lot of hands and bright minds to produce a biography of this magnitude. While writing is a long and often lonely marathon, I am fortunate to run with a true and trusted team. There's the Brain Trust—Richard Pine, Jofie Ferrari-Adler, and Jon Karp. The Secret Weapon—Dorothea H. The Confidants—Justin L, Jeff K, Andy D, Steve Y, Bill M, Eric Z, and the Wisest One. The Reliables—John from Southport, AEK, Justin from Chester, and Jeanne and Steve, who keep me around and give me a place to write at The Garde. And The Pros who make the book sing and soar—Jonathan Evans, David Kass, Carolyn Kelly, Meredith Vilarello, Paul O'Halloran, Eliza Rothstein, Gideon Pine, Jeff Miller, and Kelvin·Bias.

Then there's the family. Lydia is my ultimate brain trust, secret weapon, and confidant. She's also my lover. I was smitten the first time I took her on a date to Ivar's in Seattle in 1988. I'm still smitten. And Tennyson Ford, Clancy Nolan, Maggie May, and Clara Belle lived this biography with me. But no book—no professional achievement—matches the pride and joy I feel from being their father.

SOURCE NOTES

When reporting what LeBron said, I relied on statements he's made—in interviews, in speeches, in press conferences, in appearances on his various digital platforms, in documentary films, and during competition or other events that were videotaped—and on his writings, primarily those in his book, *Shooting Stars* (cowritten with Buzz Bissinger), in his diary entries in *SLAM* magazine in 2001–2002, in his essays, and on his social media platforms. I also relied on interviews with individuals who recounted direct conversations with him. Similarly, when reporting LeBron's *thoughts*, I relied on satatements and writings in which he discussed his thinking. I also relied on statements from individuals with whom LeBron shared his thinking.

In most instances where I've described scenes, I interviewed at least one source who was present or had firsthand knowledge of what took place. I also relied on video footage, photographs, and previously published accounts. Where I've reconstructed dialogue, I attempted to interview at least one person who was a party in the conversation or was a witness to the conversation. Additionally, I pulled quotations and dialogue from video footage, press conference transcripts, podcast transcripts, interviews, emails, text messages, court records, and previously published works.

Unless otherwise indicated in these notes, direct quotations derive from the roughly 250 interviews conducted for this book, from written responses to inquiries I sent to sources, from hundreds of pages of court records, or from hundreds of hours of video footage. Some of those whom I interviewed asked not to be identified. While I did not quote anonymous sources, I found their input valuable.

Chapter 1: What Just Happened?

2   *"the Four Horsemen"*: Noam Bernstein, "The 4 Horsemen of the NBA: LeBron James, Maverick Carter, Rich Paul and Randy Mims," ClutchPoints, May 28, 2020.

2   *John Skipper, to green-light an hour*: James Andrew Miller and Tom Shales, *Those Guys Have All the Fun: Inside the World of ESPN* (New York: Little, Brown, 2011).

2   *his own show*: Sean Gregory, "The LeBron James Hour: Is This Prime-Time Overkill?," *Time*, July 8, 2010.

2   *uneasy over the way*: Joe Drape, "An Agent of Change," *New York Times*, August 17, 2014.

2   *acquired by Apple*: Billy Steele, "Apple's $3 Billion Purchase of Beats Has Already Paid Off," *Engadget*, May 28, 2019.

2   *"If he were an IPO"*: Tim Arango, "LeBron Inc.," *Fortune*, December 10, 2007.

3   *on track to crest $1 billion*: "Forbes: Tiger Woods Becomes Billionaire, Joining LeBron James and Michael Jordan," Athletic, June 10, 2022.

3   *James was determined to be the first*: Associated Press, "LeBron James—Beyond His Years, beyond the Hype," ESPN.com, December 10, 2005

3   *Woods had crashed his SUV*: Jeff Benedict and Armen Keteyian, *Tiger Woods* (New York: Simon & Schuster, 2018).

3   *surpassed Jay-Z in popularity*: Chris Yuscavage, "LeBron James Is More Powerful Than Dr. Dre, Oprah, and Jay Z, According to Forbes," Complex, July 3, 2014.

3   *"C'mon LeBron" campaign*: "Mayor Bloomberg and NYC & Company Launch 'C'mon LeBron' Campaign," press release, June 3, 2010; see also Alan Feuer, "Luring a Star: Big City Beckons; Cleveland Begs," *New York Times*, June 4, 2010; and *Shattered: Hope, Heartbreak, and the New York Knicks*, podcast, Athletic, March 29, 2021.

3   *A Russian billionaire*: Adrian Wojnarowski, "Nets' LeBron Pursuit: From Russia, with Love," Yahoo! Sports, September 24, 2009.

3   *President Obama weighed in*: Associated Press, "President Obama Lobbies for LeBron James to Make Move to Chicago Bulls," New York *Daily News*, May 23, 2010.

4   *wanted to be wanted*: LeBron James, "More Than an Athlete," ESPN+, November 27, 2018. In this interview, LeBron said, "I was 25 years old and I wanted to be liked by everybody."

4   *the way people perceived him*: Ibid.

4   *"I'm just not the guy"*: Darnell Mayberry, "Low-Key Kevin Durant Announces Contract Extension via Twitter," *Oklahoma City News*, July 8, 2010.

4   *"Jordan and Kobe would never do this"*: Sean Gregory, "The LeBron James Hour: Is This Prime Time Overkill?" *Time*, July 8, 2010.

4   *James read what was written*: James, "More Than an Athlete."

4   *Riley showed up with his championship rings*: Ian Thomsen, *The Soul of Basketball* (Boston: Houghton Mifflin Harcourt, 2018).

5   *at the Greenwich Boys & Girls Club*: Michael Lee, "Remembering 'The Decision': The Day a Boys & Girls Club Was The Coolest Place on Earth," Athletic, July 8, 2020.

5   *donated to Boys & Girls Clubs*: Martenzie Johnson, "How LeBron James used 'The Decision' to Raise More Than $2 Million for the Boys & Girls Club," Andscape, July 8, 2020.

5   *tweeting for the first time*: LeBron James, tweet from @KingJames, July 6, 2010.

5 *off the grid in Hawaii*: Logan Hill, "Demented Genius," *New York*, November 19, 2010.

6 *"Let them know"*: Jim Gray, *Talking to Goats* (New York: William Morrow, 2020).

7 *called the Cavaliers*: Joe Drape, "An Agent of Change," *New York Times*, August 17, 2014.

7 *"When he said, 'I'm signing for three years,' "*: Scott Raab, *The Whore of Akron* (New York: Harper Perennial, 2011).

7 *"Wish me luck"*: J. R. Moehringer, "Three Weeks in Crazyville," *GQ*, August 16, 2010.

9 *"a narcissistic fool"*: Dan Ohlmeyer, "The 'Decision' Dilemma," ESPN, July 21, 2010.

9 *"shameless"*: Ibid.

9 *"an egotistical self-promoter"*: Ibid.

9 *"our society hit rock bottom"*: Richard Deitsch, "ESPN's LeBron Circus Good for TV Ratings, Bad for Sports Media," *Sports Illustrated*, July 9, 2010.

9 *"Foreplay from Jim Gray"*: Ibid.

9 *"milking best done on a farm"*: Ibid.

9 *"the new Evil Empire"*: Harvey Araton, "Miami in Pinstripes," *New York Times*, July 8, 2010.

9 *"Dear Cleveland"*: Dan Gilbert, "Letter from Cavs Owner Dan Gilbert," posted on July 8, 2010.

10 *"shameful display"*: Ibid.

10 *leader and architect*: Maverick Carter, "More Than an Athlete," ESPN+, November 27, 2018.

10 *disappear in a hole*: Ibid.

10 *"What the hell just happened?"*: James, "More Than an Athlete."

10 *so awkwardly quiet*: Rich Paul, "More Than an Athlete," ESPN+, November 27, 2018.

10 *"We fucked up"*: Carter, "More Than an Athlete."

10 *"You got no fucking idea"*: Tony Soprano quote comes from the IMDb page for the character "Tony Soprano."

10 *James loved* The Sopranos: Pablo S. Torre, "LeBron: The Sequel," *ESPN The Magazine*, February 27, 2017.

11 *I don't think he ever cared*: Moehringer, "Three Weeks in Crazyville."

11 *Riley was waiting for James*: Thomsen, *The Soul of Basketball*.

Chapter 2: Glo and Bron

12 *he'd seen things no child should see*: Grant Wahl, "Ahead of His Class," *Sports Illustrated*, February 18, 2002. Also see Associated Press, "LeBron James—Beyond His Years, Beyond the Hype," ESPN, December 10, 2005, where LeBron said, "I've seen a lot of stuff that kids my age just don't see. I don't want to go back to what I've seen when I was 7, 8, 9 years old." Also see the interview LeBron did with Stuart Scott on ESPN during his senior year of high school. "When I was living in Elizabeth Park, where you was talking about, in the projects. Those were hard times. You see everything, crackheads to drug dealers to gunshots every night, to police sirens. It just made me strong."

12 *finding his mother alive*: LeBron James and Buzz Bissinger, *Shooting Stars* (New York: Penguin Press, 2009). Also see *More Than a Game*, directed by Kristopher Belman (Lionsgate, October 2009). The quotes differ slightly in the book and the documentary.

12 *"Like it or not . . . that's how my mom treated me"*: Ibid.

12 *"those police sirens are for her"*: "LeBron James Talks to Larry King," transcript, CNN, June 2, 2010. LeBron told King: "I grew up on the north side of Akron, lived in the projects. So those scared and lonely nights—that's every night. You hear a lot of police sirens, you hear a lot of gunfire. Things that you don't want your kids to hear growing up. When you're there and you know your mother's not home, you never know if those police sirens are for her. Or if those gunshots were intended towards her. So those are the nights, almost every night, that would stand [out] hearing those sounds and hoping and wishing that it wasn't your parent on the other end."

13 *If I'm ever lucky enough*: See James and Bissinger, *Shooting Stars*.

14 *"The moment I wake up"*: For the lyrics to Dionne Warwick's "I Say a Little Prayer," see https://genius.com/Dionne-warwick-i-say-a-little-prayer-lyrics.

14 *Western Reserve Psychiatric Habilitation Center*: Information about the statutory rescission of the citizens advisory board can be found at Casetext.com.

14 *439 Hickory Street*: Martin Rodgers, "How Akron Differs from Cleveland on LeBron James," *USA Today*, October 27, 2014. See also Brandon Castel, "A Cavalier Who's Anything But: How LeBron James Lifts Akron's Kids," *Forbes*, September 4, 2014; Ben Golliver, "Video: LeBron James Returns to Cleveland in New Beats by Dre Ad," *Sports Illustrated*, October 19, 2014.

14 *"She shut that shit down early"*: LeBron James, *The Shop*, season 1, episode 2, HBO, 2018.

14 *"It's me and you"*: Ibid.

14 *"I grew up resenting my father"*: Ibid.

14 *" 'Fuck Pops' "*: Ibid.

15 *Gloria started seeing Eddie Jackson*: David Lee Morgan Jr. *LeBron James: The Rise of a Star* (Cleveland: Gray & Company, 2003).

15 *"To meet Gloria's mother"*: Ibid.

15 *a Little Tikes basketball hoop*: Transcript from *More Than a Game*.

15 *Freda had suffered a heart attack*: Freda M. James obituary, *Akron Beacon Journal*, December 28, 1987.

16 *How would she manage without her mother?*: Tim Rogers, "LeBron Closely Guards His Inner Circle," *Plain Dealer*, February 11, 2002.

16 *"Christmas is not a happy time for me"*: Ibid.

17 *"It's not safe here"*: Eli Saslow, "Lost Stories of LeBron, Part 1," *ESPN The Magazine*, October 17, 2013.

17 *"when my son and I ran out of food and went hungry"*: Gloria James in a Walmart commercial released in April 2021.

17 *"I was a scared, lonely young boy"*: See James and Bissinger, *Shooting Stars*.

17 *"Being uprooted as a very young child"*: Ibid.

17 *"I didn't like looking for trouble"*: Ibid.

17 *"You guys like football?"*: Saslow, "Lost Stories of LeBron, Part 1." See also Eddie Kim, "How to Build a School with LeBron James," MEL, September 24, 2018; Bob Gurnett, *LeBron James, GOAT: Making the Case for Greatest of All Time* (New York: Sterling Children's Books, 2019); Pablo S. Torre, "Lost Stories of LeBron, Part 2," *ESPN The Magazine*, October 18, 2013; Hunter Atkins, "Lost Stories of LeBron, Part 3," *ESPN The Magazine*, October 19, 2013.

18 *LeBron liked to draw*: Saslow, "Lost Stories of LeBron, Part 1."

18 *"How much football have you played?"*: Ibid.

18 *he raced eighty yards for a touchdown*: Ibid. For more information on LeBron's peewee football exploits, see the *Akron Beacon Journal* archive.

19 *"I was tired of picking him up"*: Ibid.

19 *sapped some of the joy*: See James and Bissinger, *Shooting Stars*. For information on Frankie and Pam Walker, see Saslow, "Lost Stories of LeBron, Part 1."

19 *"He didn't have a normal childhood"*: Transcript from *More Than a Game*.

19 *"I hated raising him that way"*: Tim Rogers, "LeBron Closely Guards His Inner Circle," *Plain Dealer*, February 11, 2002.

Chapter 3: If You Pass the Ball

21 *she try to visit*: See James and Bissinger, *Shooting Stars*.

22 *His teacher, Karen Grindall*: Eli Saslow, "Lost Stories of LeBron, Part 1," *ESPN The Magazine*, October 17, 2013.

22 *"I got the stability I craved"*: See James and Bissinger, *Shooting Stars*.

22 *Walker introduced him to basketball*: Tim Rogers, "The LeBron Phenomenon," *Plain Dealer*, February 10, 2002.

23 *LeBron had never played one-on-one*: Ibid.

23 *couldn't believe it when Scar killed Mufasa*: LeBron James, *Road Trippin* podcast, Uninterrupted, March 6, 2017.

23 *a sentimental side to LeBron*: Ibid.

24 *When Smith started crying, James started crying*: Ibid.

24 The Fresh Prince of Bel-Air: Information about *The Fresh Prince of Bel-Air* is from the IMDb page "*The Fresh Prince of Bel-Air*" and the page "Papa's Got a Brand New Excuse."

24 *"This young man right here"*: Tania Ganguli, "LeBron James Left Akron, but with an Imprint That Keeps Getting Bigger," *Atlanta Journal-Constitution*, August 15, 2018.

25 *"he was the first one to give me a basketball"*: Rogers, "The LeBron Phenomenon."

25 *Joyce had aspired to coach football*: *More Than a Game*. See also James and Bissinger, *Shooting Stars*.

26 *she treated LeBron like a fourth child*: Rogers, "LeBron Closely Guards His Inner Circle."

26 *wiping away his tears*: Ibid.

26 *"What we did for you . . . we did because we love you"*: Ibid.

26 *"Without that time spent at the Walkers"*: See James and Bissinger, *Shooting Stars*.

26 *"I know she hated to do it"*: Ibid.

27 *"There are times when I want to take him"*: Rogers, "LeBron Closely Guards His Inner Circle."

29 *"Bron, if you pass the ball"*: Terry Pluto, "Lessons Learned as Young Player Stick with James in NBA," *Akron Beacon Journal*, April 20, 2004.

30 *"The word 'ball hog' was something"*: Dan Woike, "LeBron James Isn't a Pure Scorer?" *Los Angeles Times*, March 6, 2022.

30 *LeBron filed into Coach Dru's minivan*: For accounts of LeBron's early years with Coach Dru, see James and Bissinger, *Shooting Stars* and *More Than a Game*.

30 *"You guys are going to do something special"*: Ibid.

31   *"I cried like there was no tomorrow"*: Ibid.

31   *"He loved his mother to death"*: Brad Townsend, "Flashback: Thirteen Years Ago, We Visited LeBron James' High School and Saw the Future," *Dallas Morning News*, June 21, 2016.

32   *"The great force of history"*: Eddie S. Glaude Jr., "The History That James Baldwin Wanted America to See," *The New Yorker*, June 19, 2020.

32   *write down three things they wanted to be*: See James and Bissinger, *Shooting Stars*. LeBron has told various versions of this story over the years. See *Nike Battlegrounds*, episode 1. See also Brandon Lilly, "It's Decisions, Decisions for LeBron James," *New York Times*, July 12, 2002.

33   *a kid named Willie McGee*: For Willie McGee's background, see James and Bissinger, *Shooting Stars* and *More Than a Game*.

34   *"One thing about Bron"*: See transcript from *More Than a Game*.

34   *"You and I are good friends"*: Ibid.

35   *"They were more giving"*: Ibid.

36   *"Y'all from Akron?"*: Ibid.

Chapter 4: We All We Got

38   *Little Dru kept a pull-up bar*: See *More Than a Game*.

38   *the only Black kids at the Jewish Community Center*: See James and Bissinger, *Shooting Stars*.

39   *"I wish we had more niggers on this team"*: See *Dambrot v. Central Michigan University*, 839 F. Supp. 477 (E.D. Mich. 1993). Also see *Dambrot v Central Michigan University*, United States Court of Appeals, Sixth Circuit, June 5, 1995.

39   *"It was not used in any racially offensive manner"*: Ibid.

39   *"All the people who said he should be fired"*: Ibid.

39   *"Obviously, I made mistakes"*: Tom Gaffney, "Dambrot Back on the Bench," *Akron Beacon Journal*, July 21, 1998.

40   *"We checked and we liked"*: Ibid.

40   *"I was already having fantasies"*: See James and Bissinger, *Shooting Stars*.

41   *"Man, I don't think this is gonna work"*: Ibid.

41   *"Dad, they're not gonna give me"*: Ibid.

41   *" 'I'm not fucking with white people' "*: Rachel Herron, "People Get Slammed for Calling LeBron Racist for Saying He Had to Adjust to His White High School," BET, August 30, 2018.

42   *"We all we got"*: See James and Bissinger, *Shooting Stars*.

43   *Maverick had been named*: "How Maverick Carter Went from Intern to CEO," interview with Andrew Hawkins 2020, *Kneading Dough*, Uninterrupted, 2020.

43   *play poker and shoot craps*: Ibid.

43   *Maverick's father had done prison time*: Ibid.

44   *LeBron looked up to Maverick*: Ben Cohen, "LeBron James's Business Partner Maverick Carter Talks Talent in the NBA, Hollywood and Beyond," *Wall Street Journal*, May 11, 2022.

45   *"Maverick . . . was the main reason"*: Mark Anthony Green, "Meet Maverick Carter, the Man behind LeBron's Billion Dollar Nike Deal," *GQ*, May 17, 2016.

45   *Dambrot used the word "nigger"*: See *Dambrot v. Central Michigan University*, 839 F.

Supp. 477 (E.D. Mich. 1993). See also *Dambrot v. Central Michigan University*, United States Court of Appeals, Sixth Circuit, June 5, 1995; "Judge Dismisses Lawsuit against Central Michigan U," *Chronicle of Higher Education*, January 5, 1994.

46 *"I understand you're pimping"*: See *More Than a Game*.

46 *"White people aren't going to take care of you"*: See James and Bissinger, *Shooting Stars*.

46 *"You're all fucking traitors"*: Ibid.

Chapter 5: The Freshman

49 *"Jay, just don't let my baby get hurt"*: Christopher Kamrani and Bill Oram, "LeBron James as Randy Moss? NFL Teams Were Interested." Athletic, February 15, 2021.

49 *being around so many white people*: See James and Bissinger, *Shooting Stars*. See also Charles McGrath, "N.B.A. Star, Now Memoirist, on Hometown Court," *New York Times*, September 4, 2009.

50 *Patrick Vassel*: Kerry Clawson, "Theater Career Goes in Surprise Direction," *Akron Beacon Journal*, October 17, 2019.

51 *Brophy and Coach Murphy stepped away*: Jonathan Abrams, "LeBron James: Two Sports, One Superstar," *New York Times*, May 2, 2009. For more information, see *Mark Murphy and LeBron*: Tim Graham, "LBJ and NFL: A Fantasy Based in Reality," ESPN, July 7, 2010. Also *Jay Brophy (Dolphins) and LeBron*: Joe Rose, "Ex-Dolphin Jay Brophy Talks about Coaching LeBron in High School Football," *Sun-Sentinel*, February 9, 2011.

52 *"All you had to do was look at him"*: Kamrani and Oram, "LeBron James as Randy Moss?"

52 *"There's no sense in leaving him"*: Ibid.

53 *"That was fucking terrible"*: See James and Bissinger, *Shooting Stars*.

53 *"What the fuck is that?"*: Ibid.

54 *the death stare*: Ibid.

54 *Maverick felt it was his duty*: Brian Windhorst, "Carter Keeps Irish Riding High," *Akron Beacon Journal*, December 19, 1999.

55 *Barbara Wood, the school's librarian*: See https://stvm.com/staff/barbara-wood-v65.

56 *"no such thing as fiddy cent"*: Terry Pluto, "They Knew Him Then, They Know Now," *Plain Dealer*, May 5, 2009.

56 *search engine called Google*: Ibid.

57 *"I don't care if I score two points"*: David Lee Morgan Jr., "St. V-M Star Carter Is Maverick in Name Only," *Akron Beacon Journal*, March 21, 2000.

58 *"I will always love you"*: Dick Zunt, "Champion Irish Were Young, but Never Frazzled," *Plain Dealer*, March 26, 2000.

Chapter 6: The Most Crooked Street in America

59 *Chris Dennis arrived*: Zach Helfand, "LeBron James Never Forgot Where He Came From and They Didn't Forget Him," *Los Angeles Times*, October 27, 2014.

59 *"I saw a kid that will be better"*: Marc J. Spears, "The Weekend Bay Area Trip That Helped Make LeBron James a Star," Yahoo! Sports, June 1, 2015. See also Ron Kroichick, "An NBA Hopeful at 16 on Display in Berkeley," SFGate, July 31, 2001; and Ron Kroichick, "LeBron Made Impression with Oakland AAU Team as Teen," SFGate, June 3, 2015.

59 *Vaccaro preferred to be called Sonny*: Ric Bucher, "The Last Don," *ESPN The Magazine*, October 28, 2002.

60 *Jordan to the richest athlete-endorsement deal*: Megan Armstrong, "David Falk: Michael Jordan's Nike Contract the Best, Worst Deal I've Ever Made," Bleacher Report, May 11, 2020.

60 *Nike sold over $126 million*: Information on the number of shoes sold during Michael Jordan's first year with Nike was taken from David Falk's comment in the Netflix documentary series *The Last Dance*.

60 *ABCD Basketball Camp*: Robyn Norwood, "Tale of Two Camps," *Los Angeles Times*, July 5, 1992.

61 *Andrews agreed to offer him a roster spot*: Spears, "The Weekend Bay Area Trip That Helped Make LeBron James a Star."

62 *"Have you guys ever heard of"*: Ibid.

63 *"What's up, big fella?"*: Ibid. See also Associated Press, "Leon Powe Happy to Remain in the East," August 13, 2009.

63 *Powe was raised by a single mother*: Jay King, "Leon Powe: Down, but Not Out for the Count," Bleacher Report, May 24, 2009. See also Mark Fainaru-Wada, "Oakland Tech Star's Mother Dies," SFGate, March 22, 2002; Jesse Dorsey, "The 50 Most Inspirational Figures in NBA History," Bleacher Report, November 1, 2012.

63 *family moved twenty times*: Rusty Simmons, "Leon Powe Tries to Prove Knee Is Healthy," SFGate, July 20, 2012.

63 *ended up in foster care*: Jonathan Okanes, "Celtics' Powe Returns Fostering Care and Hope," *East Bay Times*, December 25, 2008; see also Scott Ostler, "A Grown Man Taking Care of Business," SFGate, August 17, 2006.

63 *LeBron related to that*: For information on the relationship between LeBron James and Leon Powe, see Jeff Faraudo, "Cleveland Cavaliers' Leon Powe Not Surprised to See LeBron James Go," *East Bay Times*, July 13, 2010; Jeff Faraudo, "LeBron James' Basketball Rise Came Through Bay Area," *Mercury News*, June 1, 2015.

64 *"You grew two inches last night!"*: Tom Friend, "Next: LeBron James," *ESPN The Magazine*, December 10, 2002.

64 *introduced him to Urban Meyer*: Melissa Rohlin, "LeBron James Was Recruited by Football Coach Urban Meyer," *Los Angeles Times*, August 2, 2012; "The Football History of LeBron James," NFL News, May 21, 2018. See also Joon Lee, " 'He Was a Man amongst Boys': Catching Up with LeBron James' High School QBs," Bleacher Report, February 13, 2007.

64 *"Why don't you come up to Notre Dame?"*: Ibid.

65 *LeBron knew Romeo*: See James and Bissinger, *Shooting Stars*. See also Ryan Jones, "Real Friends," *SLAM*, March 24, 2016.

65 *an "arrogant dickhead"*: See James and Bissinger, *Shooting Stars*.

66 *"Too many whites at this school"*: Ibid.

67 *a virtual basketball factory*: Brian Windhorst, "Oak Hill: Simply the Best," *Akron Beacon Journal*, January 13, 2001.

67 *a standing ovation*: Terry Pluto, "Loss Hurts, but Irish Stand Tall," *Akron Beacon Journal*, January 15, 2001.

67 *LeBron began to cry*: David Lee Morgan Jr., *LeBron James: The Rise of a Star* (Cleveland: Gray & Company, 2003).

67 *Romeo let go of his emotions*: Pluto, "Loss Hurts, but Irish Stand Tall."

68 *"It's supposed to hurt"*: Ibid.

68 *Dajuan Wagner of Camden High*: Associated Press, "Trial Next Month for Dajuan Wagner," *New York Times*, April 10, 2001.

68 *guilty of simple assault and threatening*: Associated Press, "Dajuan Wagner Given Probation," *New York Times*, July 3, 2001.

69 *"I didn't go looking for trouble"*: See James and Bissinger, *Shooting Stars*.

70 *outfitting LeBron's team with sneakers*: Terry Pluto, "Shoe Companies Pull Off Feat at High School Level," *Akron Beacon Journal*, February 4, 2001.

70 *"Best sophomore in the country, my ass"*: See James and Bissinger, *Shooting Stars*.

70 *first national AAU tournament*: Brian Windhorst, "As a Sophomore in 2001, James Caught the Eye of Many Agent Hopefuls," *Akron Beacon Journal*, February 16, 2004.

70 *LeBron held an ice cream cone*: Spears, "The Weekend Bay Area Trip That Helped Make LeBron James a Star."

72 *"Now let me welcome everybody"*: For lyrics to Tupac's "California Love," see https://genius.com/2pac-california-love-lyrics.

72 *"Now on the sidewalk"*: For lyrics to "Mack the Knife" as sung by Bobby Darin, see https://genius.com/Bobby-darin-mack-the-knife-lyrics.

73 *"I'm with the family"*: Spears, "The Weekend Bay Area Trip That Helped Make LeBron James a Star."

74 *"LeBron, look, I'm not gonna tell you"*: Ibid.

74 *"Coach, my shorts are bothering me"*: Ibid.

Chapter 7: The Lad

76 *Maverick Carter came to grips*: William C. Rhoden, "For Maverick Carter, Running King James' Empire Was Always the Game Plan," Andscape, May 25, 2018. See also Kevin Moore, "Who Is LeBron James' Best Friend, Maverick Carter?" Sportscasting, November 1, 2020.

76 *Carter wanted to be around to help him navigate*: Tim Rogers, "LeBron Closely Guards His Inner Circle," *Plain Dealer*, February 11, 2002.

77 *"He used us"*: See James and Bissinger, *Shooting Stars*.

77 *LeBron felt scorned*: Ibid.

77 *"I want you to take over"*: See *More Than a Game*.

78 *"They'll play hard for you"*: See James and Bissinger, *Shooting Stars*.

78 *"Dru, how can you say no?"*: See *More Than a Game*.

78 *"Once Coach Dru had been selected"*: See James and Bissinger, *Shooting Stars*.

79 *introduced himself as Greg Ryan*: Maverick Carter interview with Chris Broussard, *In the Zone with Chris Broussard* podcast, episode FS1, 2017.

79 *they'd entered basketball heaven*: Ibid.

79 *Ryan invited LeBron and Maverick to come back*: Ibid.

79 *LeBron had to travel to Colorado*: Tim Rogers, "SVSM's James Grows in Stature, Respect," *Plain Dealer*, June 20, 2001.

80 *"the best mother . . . hands down"*: Carmelo Anthony, *Where Tomorrows Aren't Promised* (New York: Gallery Books, 2021).

80 *a gold chain with a Jesus emblem*: Ibid.

80 *the city had 256 murders that year*: Ibid.

80 *"I felt like I had known LeBron my whole life"*: Ibid.

81 *the best basketball player he'd seen at the festival*: See James and Bissinger, *Shooting Stars*.

81 *A playground legend, Cooke was projected*: Harvey Araton, "Star-to-Be Who Never Was," *New York Times*, March 3, 2012.

81 *"I'm going in trying to be MVP"*: LeBron James, "Basketball Diary with LeBron James," *SLAM*, 2001.

81 *"The main thing I want to tell you guys"*: *Lenny Cooke*, documentary, directed by Benny Safdie and Josh Safdie (Under the Milky Way, December 6, 2013).

82 *"When are you gonna play me one-on-one?"*: Ibid.

82 *"What I want for LeBron is happiness"*: Ira Berkow, "Hitting the Lottery as a Junior?" *New York Times*, July 9, 2001.

83 *"That's a lot of money"*: Ibid.

83 *"a 16-year-old from St. Vincent–St. Mary"*: Ibid.

85 *"How'd he make that?"*: See footage from Safdie and Safdie, *Lenny Cooke*.

85 *"That kid over there"*: Ibid.

Chapter 8: A Different Floor

87 *LeBron saw him as a father figure*: Tim Rogers, "LeBron Closely Guards His Inner Circle," *Plain Dealer*, February 11, 2002. See also Grant Wahl, "Ahead of His Class," *Sports Illustrated*, February 18, 2002.

87 *Jackson wanted to play an active role*: Ibid.

87 *Jackson went to see an old friend*: See *Magic Arts & Entertainment, et al. v. Eddie Jackson, Jr., et al.*

87 *a dancer with Chippendales*: Ibid.

87 *an initial advance to Jackson*: See *Magic Arts & Entertainment, Inc. and Joseph B. Marsh v. Eddie G. Jackson, Jr. and Gloria James*.

88 *Jackson signed a promissory note*: Ibid.

88 *charged with disorderly conduct*: Tim Elfrink, "LeBron James' Troubled Ex-Stepfather Eddie Jackson Arrested for DUI in Miami Beach," *Miami New Times*, February 12, 2014.

88 *Maverick met Merritt*: Maverick Carter interview with Jay Williams, "Maverick Carter on Building the LeBron James Empire," NPR, January 4, 2022. See also the Carter interview with Andrew Hawkins, "How Maverick Carter Went from Intern to CEO," *Kneading Dough*, Uninterrupted, 2020.

88 *"How does Nike decide"*: Ibid.

89 *Merritt was impressed with Maverick's*: Lisa Taddeo, "LeBron James: The Rise of the Superathlete," *Esquire*, October 2008.

89 *in Jordan's inner sanctum*: Maverick Carter interview with Chris Broussard, *In the Zone with Chris Broussard* podcast. See also Erik García Gundersen, "Maverick Carter Recalls First Time He and LeBron Met Michael Jordan: 'Black Jesus in the Flesh,' " *LeBron Wire (USA Today)*, April 30, 2020; Arjun Athreya, " 'Black Jesus in the Flesh': LeBron James' Crazy Fanboy Moment When He Met Michael Jordan for the First Time," *Essentially Sports*, April 29, 2020.

90 *LeBron ended up guarding Jerry Stackhouse*: Ibid.

90 *they spotted a red Ferrari*: Ibid.

90 *"Ho-lee shit"*: Ibid.

91 *"It was like listening to God speak"*: Ibid.

91 *"I didn't get to play with Mike"*: LeBron James, "Basketball Diary with LeBron James," *SLAM*, 2001.

92 *"I see folk with long cars and fine clothes"*: For lyrics to Ray Charles's "Them That Got," see https://genius.com/Ray-charles-them-that-got-lyrics.

92 *He hated being a spectator*: Tim Rogers, "James Will Play Football," *Plain Dealer*, August 28, 2001.

93 *Eddie and Gloria flew to Oregon*: Wahl, "Ahead of His Class." See also Tom Friend, "Lining Up for LeBron," *ESPN The Magazine*, December 19, 2002.

93 *R&B singer Aaliyah had died*: Ibid.

93 *"Tomorrow is not promised to anyone"*: Rogers, "James Will Play Football."

93 *Eddie found a broker in North Carolina*: Friend, "Lining Up for LeBron."

93 *"Jay, take care of my baby"*: Christopher Kamrani and Bill Oram, "LeBron James as Randy Moss? *The Athletic*, February 15, 2021.

94 *"do you mind signing some autographs"*: Ibid.

94 *"They showed us love"*: Ibid.

95 *"Coach, I've got ESPN Classics"*: Jonathan Abrams, "LeBron James: Two Sports, One Superstar," *New York Times*, May 2, 2009.

96 *"I broke my left index finger"*: James, "Basketball Diary with LeBron James."

97 *LeBron could look out the window and see*: See LeBron James and Buzz Bissinger, *Shooting Stars* (New York: Penguin Press, 2009).

97 *LeBron burst through the gym doors*: Michael Holley, "Akron Prep Star a Jump Ahead of Pack," *Chicago Tribune*, November 24, 2001.

98 *he expected to control the rights to the film*: See *Magic Arts & Entertainment v. Eddie Jackson*.

98 *meet with Lionel Martin*: Ibid. Information also obtained from the IMDb page titled "Lionel Martin."

99 *borrowed from Marsh to purchase a used Ford*: See *Magic Arts & Entertainment v. Eddie Jackson*. See also Tom Friend, "Next: LeBron James," *ESPN The Magazine*, December 10, 2002.

99 *"There's LeBron James"*: Holley, "Akron Prep Star a Jump Ahead of Pack."

99 *He would never play organized football again*: Bill Bender, "The Hit, the Photo, and a Lasting Legend: The Untold Story of LeBron James' Last HS Football Game," *Sporting News*, November 22, 2021.

99 *"You almost expect to wake up"*: Tom Reed, "LeBron's Legacy Larger Than Life," *Akron Beacon Journal*, November 29, 2001.

99 If people want to turn us into arrogant victors: See James and Bissinger, *Shooting Stars*.

99 *"We bring knife to fistfight, kill your drama"*: For lyrics to Jay-Z's "Takeover," see https://genius.com/Jay-z-takeover-lyrics.

100 *"None of those poses mattered"*: See James and Bissinger, *Shooting Stars*.

100 *"We only got one"*: James, "Basketball Diary with LeBron James," *Slam*, 2001.

101 *Romeo used a series of obscenities*: See James and Bissinger, *Shooting Stars*.

101 *"bitches" and "hos"*: Ibid.

101 *a holiday tournament in Delaware*: Brandon Lilly, "Talent Show Thrives for Delaware Resort," *New York Times*, December 30, 2001.

101 *LeBron's seventeenth birthday*: See James and Bissinger, *Shooting Stars*.

Chapter 9: Get in the Car

104 *William Wesley, considered by many*: Alex French, "Is This the Most Powerful Man in Sports?" *GQ*, June 20, 2007.

104 *"I thought he worked for the Secret Service"*: Ibid.

104 *introduced LeBron to Jay-Z*: Ibid.

105 *"Where's Mama?"*: Wahl, "Ahead of His Class."

105 *Bill Clinton meeting his idol*: Bethania Palma, "Yes, This Photograph Shows Bill Clinton Meeting JFK," Snopes, March 18, 2022.

105 *"That's my guy"*: Wahl, "Ahead of His Class."

106 *Michael LeBrecht, a fledgling photographer*: "Grant Wahl on LeBron James and 'The Chose One Cover,'" *SI Vault Podcast, Sports Illustrated*, February 20, 2017.

108 *to put a high school athlete on the cover*: Hank Hersch, "Hey World, Look What I Can Do," *Sports Illustrated*, September 1, 1986.

108 *For the editors, it was a big decision*: "Grant Wahl on LeBron James and 'The Chose One Cover.'"

109 *Fans showed up at the school*: Tom Reed, "Hype Taking Toll on James, Irish?" *Akron Beacon Journal*, February 18, 2002.

109 *"Maybe naively, I didn't really understand"*: See LeBron James and Buzz Bissinger, *Shooting Stars* (New York: Penguin Press, 2009).

109 *6,700 fans packed the arena*: David Lee Morgan Jr., "By George, Irish on a New Streak," *Akron Beacon Journal*, February 18, 2002.

110 *fans were lined up twelve-deep*: See footage in *More Than a Game*.

110 *"We love you, LeBron!"*: See *More Than a Game*.

110 *girls, screaming*: Ibid.

110 *"Girls at our hotels"*: Ibid.

111 *"made us all into rock stars"*: See James and Bissinger, *Shooting Stars*.

112 *He even tried marijuana*: Tom Friend, "Next: LeBron James," *ESPN The Magazine*, December 10, 2002.

112 *LeBron went to see the school's production of* Annie: David Morgan, "James Is Handling Flood Well," *Akron Beacon Journal*, March 23, 2002.

113 *largest crowd ever for a high school game in Ohio*: Chris Tomasson, "LeBron Scores with Fans," *Akron Beacon Journal*, March 14, 2002.

113 *$200 a ticket*: Ibid.

113 Nobody can mess with us: See James and Bissinger, *Shooting Stars*.

113 *sneaking girls into their rooms*: Ibid.

114 *"What are you doing?"*: Ibid. See also a video that can be found on YouTube, "Roger Bacon v. Akron (with LeBron James)—3/23/2002," posted October 15, 2014; John Stegeman, "Book Remembers the Day Roger Bacon Beat LeBron," *Catholic Telegraph*, Jan-

uary 31, 2013; Mike Dyer, "Roger Bacon's 2002 State Championship Win over LeBron James' Team Gets Sweeter Each Year," WCPO—ABC Cincinnati, February 24, 2020.

Chapter 10: Hustle

115 *when LeBron needed to get away, he'd call Maverick*: Tim Rogers, "LeBron Closely Guards His Inner Circle," *Plain Dealer*, February 11, 2002.

115 *started using the term* inner circle: Ibid.

115 *LeBron was like gold*: Mike Wise, "Manchild Approaches the Promised Land," *New York Times*, December 5, 2002.

115 If you haven't been in the circle: Ibid.

115 *standing in the Akron-Canton Airport*: Joe Drape, "An Agent of Change," *New York Times*, August 17, 2014.

115 *Houston Oilers football jersey*: Isaac Chotiner, "LeBron James's Agent Is Transforming the Business of Basketball," *The New Yorker*, May 31, 2010.

116 *the owner telephoned Paul*: S. L. Price, "The King Maker," *Sports Illustrated*, June 12, 2009.

117 *"The biggest difference between this year's St. V team"*: See LeBron James and Buzz Bissinger, *Shooting Stars* (New York: Penguin Press, 2009).

117 *"Dad, don't worry about it"*: Ibid.

118 *To them, Paul was an outsider*: Price, "The King Maker."

118 *Paul—a self-made man*: Drape, "An Agent of Change."

118 *"I'll be right there"*: Ibid.

119 *LeBron landed hard on his wrist*: Chris Tomasson, "LeBron Breaks His Left Wrist in Game," *Akron Beacon Journal*, June 9, 2002.

119 *"Why me?"*: Tom Friend, "Next: LeBron James," *ESPN The Magazine*, December 10, 2002.

120 *lifestyle magazine* Robb Report: Price, "The King Maker."

120 *how Marvin Gaye had died*: Ibid.

120 *"Get your shit together"*: Ibid.

121 *"The conversations that we were having"*: Ibid.

124 *authorities accused Jackson of mortgage fraud*: Bill Livingston, "A Summer of Upheaval for LeBron," *Plain Dealer*, June 23, 2002. See also "Police Raid House Owned by LeBron's Mentor," Associated Press, July 23, 2002.

124 *LeBron had known Mims since LeBron was four*: Marc Spears, "LeBron and His Friends Are Telling Their Story for the First Time," ESPN, November 19, 2018.

Chapter 11: Prime Time

129 *the way girls were looking at LeBron*: Mike Wise, "Manchild Approaches the Promised Land," *New York Times*, December 5, 2002.

129 *"There are a lot of females"*: Ibid.

129 *Even LeBron's teammates were basking*: See *More Than a Game*, directed by Kristopher Belman (Lionsgate, October 2009).

129 *"Just protect yourself"*: Wise, "Manchild Approaches the Promised Land."

130 *a cheerleader and a softball player*: Patrick Varone, "LeBron James's Lady," *Harper's Bazaar*, August 9, 2010.

130 *"I'll take his number"*: Alex Butler, "LeBron James Took Wife Savannah to AppleBee's, Outback Steakhouse on First Dates," UPI, December 22, 2017.

130 *Brinson didn't call*: Ibid.

130 *profit-sharing arrangement with Time Warner Cable*: "Cable Guy: LeBron James Heads for Pay-Per-View," Associated Press, November 8, 2002.

130 *games on pay-per-view*: Tom Friend, "Next: LeBron James," *ESPN The Magazine*, December 10, 2002.

130 *ESPN and St. V came to terms on an arrangement*: Jere Longman with John Fountain, "Phenom's School Tried to Avoid Getting Caught Up in the Game," *New York Times*, February 8, 2003.

130 *The school did not charge a rights fee*: Ibid.

132 *Brand-new gold carpet*: See LeBron James and Buzz Bissinger, *Shooting Stars* (New York: Penguin Press, 2009).

132 *bringing in girls and drinking alcohol*: See James and Bissinger, *Shooting Stars*.

132 *"Can you imagine the headlines"*: Ibid.

133 *Corey Jones was the only junior*: Ibid.

133 *"Are you all right?"*: Ibid.

134 *Willie ended up winning*: Ibid.

134 *"This is our last year together"*: See *More Than a Game*.

134 *"could have cried and bitched about it"*: Ibid.

135 *he admitted to mortgage fraud*: Friend, "Next: LeBron James."

135 *studying* Macbeth: Terry Pluto, "They Knew Him Then, They Know Him Now," *Plain Dealer*, May 5, 2009.

135 *"Till he unseam'd"*: *The Tragedy of MacBeth*, http://shakespeare.mit.edu/macbeth/full .html.

135 *teacher Shawn-Paul Allison*: Pluto, "They Knew Him Then, They Know Him Now."

136 *"If I wasn't in the rap game"*: For lyrics to "Things Done Changed" by Christopher Wallace (Biggie Smalls), see https://genius.com/The-notorious-big-things-done -changed-lyrics.

136 *his 3.2 GPA*: Ernesto Soliven, "NBA Stars' GPAs Revealed: Are You Smarter Than a High School LeBron James or Steph Curry?," Basketball Network, August 19, 2022. See also Brad Townsend, "Flashback: Thirteen Years Ago, We Visited LeBron James' High School and Saw the Future," *Dallas Morning News*, June 21, 2016.

136 *sketching a picture of Macbeth*: Pluto, "They Knew Him Then, They Know Him Now."

136 *placed it in a bank vault*: Ibid.

138 *most-watched event on ESPN2 in two years*: Darren Rovell, "Time Warner Expects to Lose $30,000 on Deal," ESPN, February 20, 2003.

138 *ESPN faced renewed criticism*: Jay Bilas, "Did 'LeBron Mania' Go Too Far?" ESPN, December 17, 2002.

138 *Billy Packer said that Vitale and Walton*: "James' National TV Debut Draws Crowd, Media, Sponsors," *Sports Business Journal*, December 13, 2002.

138 *"They're not giving the kid any money"*: Ibid.

139 *referred to as a "narcissist"*: Friend, "Next: LeBron James."

139 *"a testy, diminutive woman"*: Ibid.

140 *LeBron played it cool and invited her*: Nasha Smith, "LeBron and Savannah James

Have Been Together for Almost 2 Decades. Here's a Timeline of Their Love Story," *Business Insider*, July 19, 2019.

140 *Brinson had never seen LeBron play basketball*: Patrick Varone, "LeBron James's Lady," *Harper's Bazaar*, August 9, 2010.

140 Wow, *she thought. This guy is pretty popular*: Ibid.

140 *Born August 27, 1986, Savannah Brinson*: Rajani Gurung, "Savannah Brinson Bio: Career, Net Worth & Love Life," Players Bio, August 31, 2022. See also Corinne Sullivan, "Who Is Savannah James? LeBron James's Wife Is Truly His Perfect Match," *Cosmopolitan*, May 10, 2022.

140 *a black and pink two-piece outfit*: Robert Sullivan, "How Savannah and LeBron James Are Changing Lives in Their Hometown," *Vogue*, August 15, 2017.

140 *seared into his memory*: Ibid.

140 *home on time*: Ibid.

140 *respected their rules*: Ibid.

141 *left behind her take-home container*: Varone, "LeBron James's Lady."

Chapter 12: Trading Places

142 *"Dear Mr. Morgan"*: Larry Platt, "The Education of LeBron James," *GQ*, February 15, 2005.

142 *It can't hurt to have a writer*: Ibid.

143 *dealership in Los Angeles whose clients included*: David Lee Morgan Jr., "Hummer Bears Tag of Dealer in Calif.," *Akron Beacon Journal*, January 14, 2003.

143 *Gloria approached U.S. Bank in Columbus, Ohio*: David Lee Morgan Jr. and Terry Pluto, "James' Mother Secured Car Loan," *Akron Beacon Journal*, January 17, 2003.

144 *Frederick R. Nance was arguably the most revered*: Ashby Jones, "The Man Who Carried LeBron's Legal Bags," *Wall Street Journal*, July 2, 2010.

144 *helped revitalize Cleveland's economy*: H. K. Wilson, "Frederick R. Nance: The Legal Futurist Who Helped Remake a Great City," *Attorney at Law Magazine*, May 14, 2015.

144 *candidate to become the next commissioner*: Ibid.

144 *Nance received an unusual request—to meet a kid*: Jordan Poll, "National Sports and Entertainment Lawyer Enjoys Career Beyond His Wildest Expectations," *Oakland County Legal News*, January 23, 2018.

145 *A thirty-foot-long white Cadillac Escalade*: Grant Wahl, "The Continuing Education of LeBron James," *Sports Illustrated*, January 13, 2003.

145 *LeBron popped his head through the sunroof*: Ibid.

146 *brand-new white uniforms*: See LeBron James and Buzz Bissinger, *Shooting Stars* (New York: Penguin Press, 2009).

Chapter 13: Higher Education

150 *inmate number 38980-060*: See letter from Joseph B. Marsh to Eddie G. Jackson Jr. at the Federal Correctional Institution in Loretto, Pennsylvania, dated September 23, 2003.

150 *Eddie promised to write*: See correspondence from Eddie Jackson in the court file for *Magic Arts & Entertainment and Joseph B. Marsh v. Eddie G. Jackson, Jr. and Gloria James*, Case No. 2003-10-5848.

151 *St. V had vaulted to the number one spot*: Brian Windhorst, "Irish's Eyes on Top Spot," *Akron Beacon Journal*, January 6, 2003.

151 *the victory over Mater Dei*: Ben Bolch, "He Shoots Below Par at Pauley," *Los Angeles Times*, January 5, 2003.

151 *one of the best days of their lives*: See *More Than a Game*.

152 *inquired about LeBron's Hummer*: Frank Litsky, "Basketball; LeBron James's S.U.V. Prompts an Investigation," *New York Times*, January 14, 2003.

153 *"Asked how she could secure such a loan"*: Ibid.

153 *LeBron went out and dropped fifty points*: Tim Rogers, "LeBron's 50 Points Drive Irish," *Plain Dealer*, January 15, 2003.

153 *"I really think this is a class issue"*: David Lee Morgan Jr. and Terry Pluto, "James' Mother Secured Car Loan," *Akron Beacon Journal*, January 17, 2003.

154 *"As the national media jumped"*: See James and Bissinger, *Shooting Stars*.

154 *"Like a good son, LeBron James sees his mom"*: Scott Fagerstrom, "James' Problems Began with Misguided Mother," *Akron Beacon Journal*, February 2, 2003.

155 *"There's something in there for you"*: Phil Trexler, "James Takes a Shot at Return to Team," *Akron Beacon Journal*, February 5, 2003.

155 *Muscaro finally cleared LeBron*: Tom Withers, "LeBron James Cleared in Hummer Inquiry," Associated Press, January 28, 2003.

156 *LeBron would not be talking to Muscaro*: Trexler, "James Takes a Shot at Return to Team."

156 *driving back to Akron when he got a call*: Ibid.

156 *banned for the remainder of the season*: Mike Wise, "Basketball; LeBron James Is Ruled Ineligible after Taking Gifts," *New York Times*, February 1, 2003.

156 *"In talking with the store's personnel"*: David Lee Morgan Jr., "St. V-M Star Loses Eligibility over Jerseys," *Akron Beacon Journal*, February 1, 2003.

157 OHSAA SUCKS: Carol Biliczky and David Lee Morgan Jr., "St. V-M Faithful Show Support," *Akron Beacon Journal*, February 1, 2003.

157 *LeBron buried his face in his hands*: See James and Bissinger, *Shooting Stars*.

158 *"I want to start by apologizing"*: Ibid.

159 *"People couldn't wait for him to fail"*: Biliczky and Morgan Jr., "St. V-M Faithful Show Support," *Akron Beacon Journal*, February 1, 2003.

160 *Vassel even ended up getting interviewed*: Mike Wise, "Manchild Approaches the Promised Land," *New York Times*, December 5, 2002.

161 *winning by one point*: Ben Bolch, "James Tries to Make Case in Pleas Court," *Los Angeles Times*, February 5, 2003.

161 *LeBron's sit-down with Sanders aired on CBS*: Tatiana Morales, "LeBron James: Nothing I Regret More," CBS News, February 3, 2003.

161 *"Don't tell me he hasn't had his hand out"*: Tom Friend, "Please Don't Cry for LeBron James," *ESPN The Magazine*, February 3, 2003.

162 *James R. Williams*: "U.S. Attorney's Office Remembers Former U.S. Attorney, Honorable Judge James R. Williams," press release, United States Attorney's Office for the Northern District of Ohio, November 9, 2020.

162 *Muscaro failed to notify LeBron*: Trexler, "James Takes a Shot at Return to Team."

163 *Camera shutters clicked when LeBron skipped*: Terry Pluto, "LeBron Back in Style," *Akron Beacon Journal*, February 9, 2003.

163 *Busloads of fans from Akron*: "Show Goes On: LeBron James to Visit Trenton," *New York Times*, February 7, 2003.

163 *scalpers were getting $2,500 per ticket*: Pluto, "LeBron Back in Style."

163 *"This world is mine for the taking"*: For lyrics to Eminem's "Lose Yourself," see https://genius.com/Eminem-lose-yourself-lyrics.

164 *LeBron went off for fifty-two points*: Ben Bolch, "LeBron Is Too Much for Westchester," *Los Angeles Times*, February 9, 2003.

164 *"That's how you play basketball!"*: Susan Vinella, "James Back with Force," *Plain Dealer*, February 9, 2003.

165 *the leading man passed the trophy to a role player*: David Lee Morgan Jr., "James Scores 22, but Hands MVP Trophy to Junior Guard," *Akron Beacon Journal*, February 17, 2003.

Chapter 14: In the Room

166 *McDonald's All-American high school basketball game*: Bill Finley, "The LeBron James Show Is Coming to the End of Act I," *New York Times*, March 27, 2003.

166 *Scouts from all twenty-nine NBA teams*: Tom Reed, "Pro Scouts Drool over McDonald's," *Akron Beacon Journal*, March 25, 2003.

167 *stayed in touch through phone calls*: Sam Fulwood III, "Imprisoned Advisor Still Has LeBron's Ear," *Plain Dealer*, March 13, 2003.

167 *Eddie wrote letters to LeBron*: Ibid.

168 *the prospect of Goodwin's representing LeBron*: Tom Reed, "As Expected, Goodwin to Represent St. V-M Star," *Akron Beacon Journal*, May 15, 2003.

168 *"I recruited LeBron James for more than a year"*: Steve Kelley, "Agent Tried to Avoid Bright Light of Publicity," *Seattle Times*, May 16, 2003.

168 *"I thank Gloria and Eddie all the time"*: Reed, "As Expected, Goodwin to Represent St. V-M Star."

168 *attorney Fred Schreyer*: Terry Pluto, "The Franchise: LeBron James and the Remaking of the Cleveland Cavaliers—Chapter 8," Cleveland.com, December 12, 2007.

169 *Marsh had started dealing more exclusively with Gloria*: See *Magic Arts & Entertainment and Joseph Marsh v. Eddie G. Jackson, Jr. and Gloria James*, Case No. 2003-10-5848.

169 *"Gloria James, LeBron's mother, has expressed"*: Letter from Joe Marsh to Spike Lee, March 26, 2003.

169 *"If Spike Lee is unavailable"*: Letter from Joe Marsh to Gloria James, April 29, 2003.

169 *Marsh made two payments to Gloria*: See copies of the checks in the court file.

169 *LeBron knew that Eddie had dealings with Marsh*: See "Answer of Defendant LeBron James" in *Joseph B. Marsh v. LeBron James*, Case No. 2003-12-7432.

171 *entering the NBA Draft*: "James Officially Declares for Draft," *Washington Post*, April 26, 2003.

171 *"It's been a longtime goal"*: Tom Reed, "Star Says He Could Help Cavs," *Akron Beacon Journal*, April 26, 2003.

171 *his own signature sneaker, the S. Carter*: Matt Walty, "Jay Z's Reebok Deal Changed the Sneaker Industry Forever," Complex, December 4, 2016.

172 *Paul Fireman pulled out a pen*: Boaz Herzog and Jason Quick, "Just Shoe It," *Seattle Times*, June 23, 2003.

172 *LeBron had no idea what Fireman was doing*: Maverick Carter and LeBron James,

"LeBron James Talks First Generation Wealth and Betting on Himself," *Kneading Dough*, Uninterrupted, January 12, 2018.

172   *Goodwin picked it up*: Aaron Dodson, "Fifteen Years Ago, Reebok and Adidas Wanted Him Badly—So How Exactly Did LeBron James End Up with Nike?" The Undefeated, May 23, 2018.

172   *Gloria cried*: Ibid.

172   *Maverick stood and undid the top buttons*: Ibid.

172   Holy shit, *he thought*: Carter and James, "LeBron James Talks First Generation Wealth and Betting on Himself."

172   *LeBron was at a loss for words*: Ibid.

172   *rent was around $22 a month*: Chris Ballard, "Their Decision," *Sports Illustrated*, October 2022.

172   *Gloria was ready to walk out*: Dodson, "Fifteen Years Ago, Reebok and Adidas Wanted Him Badly."

172   *Schreyer agreed*: Herzog and Quick, "Just Shoe It."

173   *Stoic, LeBron pushed the check*: Tyler Rucker, "Reebok CEO Reveals LeBron James Was Unfazed by $10 Million Signing Offer: 'I See LeBron Stoic. He Wasn't Impressed,'" Sportskeeda, November 28, 2002. See also Complex Sneakers tweet from @complexsneakers, November 26, 2002.

173   *He's a man already*: Dodson, "Fifteen Years Ago, Reebok and Adidas Wanted Him Badly."

173   I can't believe I left that on the table: Carter and James, "LeBron James Talks First Generation Wealth and Betting on Himself."

173   Anger Management, *atop the box office charts*: ABC News, "Actor Jack Nicholson Gets Angry over Shaq's Foul Call," ABC News, May 10, 2003.

174   *"This is the NBA!"*: "Nicholson Gets Court Rage," BBC News, May 11, 2003.

178   *Nike had also stocked the room*: Dodson, "Fifteen Years Ago, Reebok and Adidas Wanted Him Badly."

178   *Lynn Merritt had thought of everything*: Ibid.

178   *LeBron insisted on being in the room*: Brian Windhorst, "When LeBron Learned the Power of Saying No," ESPN, March 20, 2019.

178   *Phil Knight realized that LeBron wanted*: Ibid.

179   *dinner at Lynn Merritt's home*: Ibid.

179   *"I can't say I would have turned it down"*: Carter and James, "LeBron James Talks First Generation Wealth and Betting on Himself."

180   *"I want to go with Nike"*: Herzog and Quick, "Just Shoe It."

Chapter 15: Crazy Right Now

181   *had won a title since 1964*: Mike Axisa, "LeBron James Calls Out Jose Mesa for Blown Save in Game 7 of 1997 World Series," CBS Sports, June 20, 2016.

182   *Sian had accepted a football scholarship*: See *More Than a Game*, directed by Kristopher Belman (Lionsgate, October 2009); LeBron James and Buzz Bissinger, *Shooting Stars* (New York: Penguin Press, 2009).

182   *Romeo and Little Dru were heading*: Ibid.

182   *Standing beside St. V librarian Barb Wood*: Brian Windhorst, "Fate? Karma? Who Cares?" *Akron Beacon Journal*, May 23, 2003.

183 *phone lines at the Cavaliers' front office were jammed*: Tom Reed, "Just Another Day for LeBron," *Akron Beacon Journal*, May 24, 2003.

183 *favorite action figure was Batman*: Marisa Guthrie, "LeBron James Is Already Winning Hollywood," *Hollywood Reporter*, September 20, 2018.

184 *rap artists and basketball players*: Lisa Robinson, "Jay-Z Has the Room," *Vanity Fair*, October 1, 2013.

184 *Jay-Z had grown up in a public housing*: Ibid.

184 *Jay-Z was close to his mother*: Dean Baquet, "Jay-Z Discusses Rap, Marriage and Being a Black Man in Trump's America," *New York Times*, November 29, 2017.

185 *"Hard enough to match the pain of my pop"*: For lyrics to Jay-Z's "December 4th," see https://genius.com/Jay-z-december-4th-lyrics.

185 *Jay-Z had loved to read and write down rhymes*: Baquet, "Jay-Z Discusses Rap, Marriage and Being a Black Man in Trump's America."

185 *turned to drug dealing*: Lisa Robinson, "Jay-Z Has The Room," *Vanity Fair*, October 1, 2013.

185 *"You enter the room, your résumé enters"*: Ibid.

185 *LeBron's and Jay-Z's lives intersected at a time*: Touré, "Superstardom Is Boring: Jay-Z Quits (Again)," *New York Times*, November 16, 2003.

186 *grand opening of his 40/40 Club*: Ibid.

186 *a private conversation with Timothy Zachery Mosley*: Ibid.

186 *"It's not like it was with Big and Pac"*: Ibid.

187 *"Yes, whoo, ow, it's so crazy right now"*: For lyrics to Beyoncé's "Crazy Right Now," see https://genius.com/Beyonce-crazy-in-love-lyrics.

187 *"Hip-hop's corny now"*: Touré, "Superstardom Is Boring: Jay-Z Quits (Again)."

187 *"A house with some grass"*: LeBron James interview, *On the Record with Bob Costas*, HBO, Summer 2003.

188 *"I want you to go work there"*: Andrew Hawkins, "How Maverick Carter Went from Intern to CEO," *Kneading Dough*, Uninterrupted, 2020.

188 *"I've already worked it out for them to hire you"*: Ibid.

188 *"If you got a hunch, bet a bunch"*: Ibid.

188 *LeBron's conversation with Randy Mims*: Marc Spears, "LeBron and His Friends Are Telling Their Story for the First Time," ESPN, November 19, 2018.

188 *LeBron offered Rich an annual salary of $50,000*: Joe Drape, "An Agent of Change," *New York Times*, August 17, 2014. (Note: Elsewhere, the salary figure has been reported to be $48,000; see Isaac Chotiner, "LeBron James's Agent Is Transforming the Business of Basketball, *The New Yorker*, May 31, 2021.)

189 *started calling themselves the Four Horsemen*: Spears, "LeBron and His Friends Are Telling Their Story for the First Time."

189 *a $13 million, three-year contract*: Associated Press, "Deal Worth Almost $13 Million in First Three Years," July 3, 2003. See also Brian Windhorst, "James, Cavs Make It Official," *Akron Beacon Journal*, July 4, 2003.

189 *"Listen, man, I just want to tell you"*: Aaron Dodson, "Fifteen Years Ago, Reebok and Adidas Wanted Him Badly—So How Exactly Did LeBron James End Up with Nike?" The Undefeated, May 23, 2018.

190 *"It's nothing personal"*: Ibid.

190 Shit, he didn't need to do that: Ibid.

190 *Nike had signed an endorsement deal with Kobe Bryant*: Dow Jones Newswire, "Nike Signs Kobe Bryant to $40 Million Contract," *Wall Street Journal*, June 25, 2003.

191 *"Bryant's track record as a sneaker pitchman is spotty"*: Ibid.

191 *Jay-Z's "Roc the Mic" tour passed through Cleveland*: Video can be found on YouTube, "Jay-Z and LeBron James—Rocking The Bus (Roc The Mic Tour)—2003," posted August 15, 2018. See also "Jay-Z, 50 Cent Ready to 'Roc The Mic'," *Billboard*, May 1, 2003.

Chapter 16: Pressure

193 *Colorado charged Kobe Bryant with sexually assaulting*: Mike Wise and Alex Markels, "Kobe Bryant Charged with Felony Sexual Assault," *New York Times*, July 18, 2003.

193 *"I'm innocent"*: Ibid.

193 Sports Illustrated *even put Kobe's mug shot on the cover*: *Sports Illustrated*, July 28, 2003.

193 *"As with all allegations"*: Wise and Markels, "Kobe Bryant Charged with Felony Sexual Assault."

193 *Coca-Cola signed LeBron to a six-year endorsement deal*: Tracie Rozhon, "Coke Signs Deal with N.B.A. Rookie," *New York Times*, August 22, 2003.

194 *"Beyond immeasurable damage to Mr. Bryant's once-flawless"*: Ibid.

195 *"I think the NBA has done him a disservice"*: March Schmitt Boyer, "A Changing of the Guard," *Plain Dealer*, October 29, 2003.

195 *Charles Barkley ironically declares, "I am not a role model"*: Associated Press, "LeBron James—Beyond His Years, Beyond the Hype," ESPN, December 10, 2005.

195 *"That's ridiculous"*: Ibid.

195 *"I have no problem being a role model"*: Ibid.

196 *"This can't be messed up"*: Jack McCallum, "You Gotta Carry That Weight: LeBron James Enters the NBA," *Sports Illustrated*, October 27, 2003.

197 *"However, I did write her"*: Letter from Eddie Jackson to Joseph Marsh, July 21, 2003.

197 *"As I stated over the phone"*: Letter from Eddie Jackson to Joseph Marsh, September 30, 2003.

197 *Marsh sued Jackson and Gloria*: See *Magic Arts & Entertainment and Joseph B. Marsh v. Eddie G. Jackson, Jr. and Gloria James*, Case No. 2003-10-5848.

197 *Marsh also sued LeBron*: See *Joseph B. Marsh and Magic Arts & Entertainment, Inc. v. LeBron James*, Case No. 2003-12-7432.

197 *LeBron denied that Eddie Jackson had acted with his authority*: Ibid.

198 *"LeBron is going to help me"*: McCallum, "You Gotta Carry That Weight: LeBron James Enters the NBA."

199 *Kings issued 340 credentials*: Chris Broussard, "James Answers Hype with Standout Debut," *New York Times*, October 30, 2003.

200 *LeBron hadn't learned how to play basketball on playgrounds*: Terry Pluto, "Lessons Learned as Young Players Stick with James in NBA," *Akron Beacon Journal*, April 20, 2004.

200 *"He used to hit that shot on Willie"*: David Lee Morgan Jr., "Ex-Teammates Are Thrilled for LeBron," *Akron Beacon Journal*, October 31, 2003.

201 *LeBron led all scorers*: Broussard, "James Answers Hype with Standout Debut."

201 *Dressed in a stylish black suit, Gloria waited*: Brian Windhorst, "James Debut Muted by Loss," *Akron Beacon Journal*, October 31, 2003.

201 *threw her arms around him*: Ibid.

201 *first NBA game were off the charts*: Brian Windhorst, "Ratings for Cavs Opener Skyrocket," *Akron Beacon Journal*, October 31, 2003.

202 *Cavaliers traded Ricky Davis*: "Cavs Part with Davis," ESPN, December 15, 2003.

202 *"Turns out Nike's gone clean-cut"*: Seth Stevenson, "The Second Coming," *Slate*, January 12, 2004.

203 *sold out everywhere before Christmas*: Bloomberg News, "Nike Says LeBron James Sneaker Had Strong Debut," *New York Times*, December 24, 2003.

203 *Savannah Brinson learned that she was pregnant*: Patrick Varone, "LeBron James's Lady," *Harper's Bazaar*, August 9, 2010.

203 What am I going to tell my parents?: Ibid.

203 What's going to happen to LeBron's career?: Ibid.

203 *Bawling, Savannah informed LeBron*: Ibid.

203 *"It's not going to slow me down"*: Ibid.

Chapter 17: No Hard Feelings

204 *an unexpected invitation*: Clen Adams, "Cavaliers' LeBron James Added to 2004 USA Basketball Men's Senior National Team," NBA, May 14, 2004.

204 *NBA players had security concerns*: Liz Robbins, "After Anxious Morning, Basketball Team Plays On," *New York Times*, August 11, 2004. See also Liz Robbins, "Olympics; Security at Summer Games in Athens Is Topic A, B and C for U.S. Basketball," *New York Times*, April 29, 2004.

204 *"As an African American kid"*: " 'What Did We Just Watch?': An Oral History," ESPN, August 30, 2019.

205 *the youngest player to join the USA*: Clen Adams, "Cavaliers' LeBron James Added to 2004 USA Basketball Men's Senior National Team," NBA, May 14, 2004.

205 *He had no idea what he'd gotten himself into*: Nate Penn, "Dunk'd: An Oral History of the 2004 Dream Team," *GQ*, July 27, 2012.

205 *"the Young Guns"*: Scott Polacek, "Carmelo Anthony Details 2004 Olympics Pact with LeBron," Bleacher Report, May 4, 2020.

205 *"Let's put in the work"*: Ibid.

205 *"They were arrogant"*: Ibid.

205 *Larry Brown was frustrated*: Eddie Maisonet, "The Miseducation of the 2004 U.S. Men's Olympic Basketball Team," Bleacher Report, September 5, 2017.

206 *just to be a practice player*: Liz Robbins, "James Is Earning His Wings," *New York Times*, November 21, 2004.

206 *they made a pact*: Polacek, "Carmelo Anthony Details 2004 Olympics Pact with LeBron."

206 *bombs exploded*: Robbins, "After Anxious Morning, Basketball Team Plays On."

206 *Kurdish separatists were suspected*: Jared Malsin, "Turkey Blames Kurdish Militants for the Bombing," *Wall Street Journal*, November 15, 2022. See also George Packer, "The Playing Field," *The New Yorker*, August 22, 2004.

206 *LeBron asked more questions than anyone*: Ibid.

206 *police officers in riot gear*: Ibid.

207 *the* Queen Mary 2: Diane Pucin, "Ship of Dream Teams," *Los Angeles Times*, August 26, 2004.

207 *the US team had been beaten*: Damon Hack, "Puerto Rico Upsets United States Men," *New York Times*, August 15, 2004. See also *Puerto Rico beats the U.S.*: Video can be found on YouTube, "Puerto Rico End USA Basketball's Sixteen Year Unbeaten Streak—Athens 2004 Replay," posted on June 26, 2020.

207 *Coach Brown ripped into his team*: Liz Robbins, "Brown Blasts U.S. Team after Loss to Puerto Rico," *New York Times*, August 16, 2004.

207 *labeling them a "joke"*: Nate Penn, "Dunk'd: An Oral History of the 2004 Dream Team," *GQ*, July 27, 2012.

207 *"nobody like what U.S.A. is doing rest of world"*: Ibid.

207 *LeBron was miserable*: Ibid.

208 *"You guys are nothin'!"*: Scott Polacek, "Carmelo Anthony Details 2004 Olympics Pact with LeBron," Bleacher Report, May 4, 2020.

208 *couldn't wait to get back to the NBA*: Robbins, "James Is Earning His Wings."

210 *"Don't be fartin'"*: Platt, "The Education of LeBron James."

210 *"Once I get comfortable with my surroundings"*: Ibid.

210 *"My game is really played above time"*: Ibid.

211 *Paul Silas had been impressed*: Ibid.

211 *Silas was even more amazed*: Robbins, "James Is Earning His Wings."

211 *Savannah gave birth to a boy*: "NBA Star Says Baby's at Home," Associated Press, October 6, 2004.

212 I can't, *he told himself,* do anything that hurts the reputation: Robbins, "James Is Earning His Wings."

212 *refused to reveal Savannah's name*: "NBA Star Says Baby's at Home."

212 *"the mother, who is from Akron"*: Robbins, "James Is Earning His Wings."

212 *"My main goal"*: "NBA Star Says Baby's at Home."

212 *"I told you I could fly"*: Robbins, "James Is Earning His Wings."

213 *Fists flew*: Associated Press, "Brawl Between Pistons and Pacers Spills into Crowd," *New York Times*, November 19, 2004. See also video on YouTube, "The Infamous 'Malice at the Palace' Fight Needs a Deep Rewind—2004 Pacers-Pistons," posted December 11, 2018.

213 *Nine players were suspended*: Kevin Omuya, "Who Threw the Beer at Malice at the Palace: The Untold Story of Malice at the Palace," Sports Brief, October 26, 2022.

214 *"That's over"*: Robbins, "James Is Earning His Wings."

214 *youngest player in NBA history to score 2,000 points*: Platt, "The Education of LeBron James."

Chapter 18: I'm Older Now

216 *Dan Gilbert was a twenty-two-year-old*: For biographical information on Dan Gilbert, see "Bloomberg Billionaire Index" page for Dan Gilbert; see also *Forbes* profile on Daniel Gilbert.

216 *valued at $222 million*: Christina Gough, "Cleveland Cavaliers Franchise Value from 2003 to 2022," Statista, December 7, 2022.

216 *Gilbert offered to buy the team for $375 million*: Associated Press, "Gund Gets $375 Million in Sale of Cavaliers," *Los Angeles Times*, January 4, 2005.

216 *NBA approved the sale*: Associated Press, "Cavaliers Sale Approved," *Los Angeles Times*, March 1, 2005.

216 *the best game of his life, scoring fifty-six points*: Liz Robbins, "Cavaliers Join Trend and Fire Silas," *New York Times*, March 22, 2005.

216 *the Cavs fired head coach Paul Silas*: Ibid.

217 *"we need a new fucking plane"*: LeBron James, *Road Trippin'* podcast, episode 61, Uninterrupted, December 11, 2017. See also, Chris Yuscavage, "That Time LeBron James Was 100 Percent Sure He Was Going to Die in a Plane Crash," Complex, December 11, 2017.

217 *Dan Gilbert fired general manager*: "Cavaliers GM Paxson Fired after Chaotic Season," *Seattle Times*, April 22, 2005.

217 *It's time . . . to become a man*: Associated Press, "LeBron James—Beyond His Years, Beyond the Hype," ESPN, December 10, 2005.

217 *"You in town?"*: Maverick Carter interview, *The Colin Cowherd Podcast*, April 11, 2021.

218 *opposite each other at the kitchen table*: Ibid.

218 *"not seeing eye to eye right now"*: Tim Arango, "Lebron Inc.," *Fortune*, December 10, 2007.

218 *Gloria had chosen Goodwin*: Maverick Carter interview with Jay Williams, "Maverick Carter on Building the LeBron James Empire," NPR, January 4, 2022. See also Carter interview with Andrew Hawkins, "How Maverick Carter Went from Intern to CEO," *Kneading Dough*, Uninterrupted, 2020.

218 *"I love my mom"*: Ibid.

218 *"I'm older now"*: Arango, "Lebron Inc."

218 *"I want to do things differently"*: Ibid.

219 *Maverick had fallen in love*: Carter interview, *The Colin Cowherd Podcast*.

219 I gotta go for this: Ibid.

219 If I fuck this up: Ibid.

219 *Gloria was furious*: Carter interview with Jay Williams. See also Carter interview with Andrew Hawkins.

219 *called her Aunt Glo*: Ibid.

219 *what did they know?*: Ibid.

220 *Maverick did not take offense*: Ibid.

220 *Aaron Goodwin was stunned*: Bob Finnan, "James Fires Agent," *News Herald*, May 11, 2005.

220 *invested in a restaurant together*: Howard Beck, "Knicks Visit West Coast with Hope for Playoffs," *New York Times*, March 25, 2005.

220 *"It is expected that Maverick Carter"*: Darren Rovell, "LeBron Fires Agents, Possibly in Favor of Friend," ESPN, May 10, 2005.

220 *Goodwin took the high road*: Finnan, "James Fires Agent."

221 *"one of his high school homies"*: Harvey Araton, "For Miami, the Real Diesel Is Wade," *New York Times*, May 13, 2005.

221 *LeBron met investment banker Paul Wachter*: Stephanie Mehta, "Meet the L.A. Investor Advising LeBron James, Bono, and Billie Eilish," *Fast Company*, March 9, 2021.

221 *impressed with Wachter's clientele*: Laura M. Holson with Geraldine Fabrikant, "Schwarzenegger the Investor Relies on Expert Advice," *New York Times*, August 24, 2003.

222 He's a numbers guy: Elena Bergeron, "Very Smart Player," ESPN, October 18, 2013.

222 *LeBron had chosen wisely*: Ibid.

222 *set up LRMR Management Company*: Ibid.

222 *Rose was a close friend of William Wesley's*: Yaron Weitzman, "Inside Look at How Leon Rose Rebuilt the Knicks: 'We Need Quickley,' " *New York Post*, March 9, 2021.

223 *"Phil, can I see you a moment?"*: Phil Knight, *Shoe Dog* (New York: Scribner, 2016).

223 *"So I went to my jeweler"*: Ibid.

224 *LeBron to Tokyo, Hong Kong, and Beijing*: Steve Gleydura, "The World According to LeBron," *Cleveland Magazine*, December 18, 2006.

224 *"I Declare War" concert*: Kelefa Sanneh, "A Show of Solidarity, with a Few Surprises," *New York Times*, October 29, 2005.

224 *he stepped onto the stage*: Tom Breihan, "Jay-Z Brings Nas Onstage, Disses No One," *Village Voice*, October 28, 2005.

224 *"Can I get an encore"*: For lyrics to Jay-Z's "Encore," see https://genius.com/Jay-z-encore-lyrics.

224 *friendship with Jay-Z had become so close*: Larry Platt, "The Education of LeBron James," *GQ*, February 15, 2005.

225 *imitating Michael Jackson*: Lisa Robinson, "Jay-Z Has the Room," *Vanity Fair*, October 1, 2013.

225 *Jay-Z introduced LeBron to Keith Estabrook*: Chris Ballard, "LeBron Act II," *Sports Illustrated*, April 24, 2006.

225 *Jay-Z introduced Maverick to Rachel Johnson*: Adena Andrews, "Rachel Johnson Embraces Role as NBA Stylist," ESPNW, February 7, 2012.

225 *P. Diddy's personal stylist*: Tim Murphy, "Put Me in That Suit, Coach," *New York Times*, April 27, 2011.

225 *a controversial new dress code*: John Eligon, "N.B.A. Dress Code Decrees: Clothes Make the Image," *New York Times*, October 19, 2005.

225 *"Surely leagues have the right"*: Frank Deford, "NBA's New Dress Code Policy Sparks Furor," NPR, October 26, 2005.

226 " *'recruitment officers for the Bloods and Crips' "*: Ibid.

226 *She told LeBron that he should be wearing*: Andrews, "Rachel Johnson Embraces Role as NBA Stylist."

227 *a ten-story mural of LeBron*: Associated Press, "LeBron James—Beyond His Years, Beyond the Hype."

227 *Gilbert had kept his promise*: Ballard, "LeBron Act II."

227 *wine-colored seats*: Liz Robbins, "In Cleveland, It's Good to Be the King," *New York Times*, April 30, 2006.

228 *LeBron cradled his son*: Associated Press, "LeBron James—Beyond His Years, Beyond the Hype."

Chapter 19: It's Just Basketball

229 *his mother had been arrested*: Associated Press, "LeBron James' Mom Charged with Drunken Driving," ESPN, January 21, 2006.

229 *"I don't have all the info"*: "James's Mother Is Arrested for DWI," *Washington Post*, January 20, 2006.

230 Oh my God! *LeBron thought.* This is it: LeBron James, *Road Trippin'* podcast, episode 61, Uninterrupted, December 11, 2017.

230 *"Deal the motherfuckin' cards"*: Ibid.

231 *Gilbert ordered a new state-of-the-art jet*: Liz Robbins, "In Cleveland, It's Good to Be the King," *New York Times*, April 30, 2006.

231 *paid $2.1 million for a twelve-thousand-square-foot home*: Jim Carney, "LeBron Will Soon Call Bath Mansion Home," *Akron Beacon Journal*, December 5, 2000. See also "Real Estate Transfers for January 31, 2004," *Akron Beacon Journal*.

231 *thirty-five-thousand-square-foot mansion*: Bob Dyer, "King James Builds a Castle of a Home," Real CavsFans, March 27, 2007. See also "LeBron James Building Mega-Mansion," UPI, March 27, 2007.

231 *LeBron's blueprints*: "LeBron James Will Build again on his Bath Township Property," *Akron Beacon Journal*, May 3, 2013.

231 *"Shoot the ball"*: Chris Ballard, "LeBron Act II," *Sports Illustrated*, April 24, 2006.

232 *"Coach, man, we only got five guys"*: Ibid.

232 *"relentless in managing his client's image"*: Ibid.

232 *"My main focus isn't on the guy"*: Ibid.

234 *His favorite part of the day*: See home video posted on Instagram.

234 *lifting him up in the air*: See home video posted on Instagram.

236 *"If you miss these free throws"*: Video can be found on YouTube, "Gilbert Arenas on What LeBron Told Him before Missing 2 Clutch FTs in 2006 Playoffs—Episode 12," posted on December 11, 2020. See also "The Game That LeBron James Disrespected Gilbert Arenas, Insane Game 6 Duel Highlights 2006 Playoffs," YouTube video, posted on August 24, 2018.

237 *Rasheed Wallace wasted no time bragging*: Howard Beck, "Rasheed Wallace Guarantees Victory, Again," *New York Times*, May 15, 2006.

237 *Larry Hughes's twenty-year-old brother*: Jeff Douglas, "Cavaliers Mourn Loss of Hughes' Brother," Associated Press, May 16, 2006.

238 *"Family comes before basketball"*: Howard Beck, "Promises. Promises. Game 6 Is Needed After All," *New York Times*, May 16, 2006.

238 *"I ain't worried about these cats"*: Ibid.

238 *"it's just basketball"*: Howard Beck, "Cool Cavaliers Win in Detroit," *New York Times*, May 18, 2006.

239 *"James's talent gives Cleveland the chance"*: Clifton Brown, "Pistons' Kryptonite Dazes James and Cavaliers," *New York Times*, May 22, 2006.

Chapter 20: The Four LeBrons

240 *a small ownership stake in the New Jersey Nets*: Dean Baquet, "Jay-Z Discusses Rap, Marriage and Being a Black Man in Trump's America," *New York Times*, November 29, 2017.

240 *Gilbert offered LeBron a five-year contract*: Liz Robbins, "With Eyes on Bigger Money, James Signs," *New York Times*, July 13, 2006.

241 *"Gloria James, 38, pleaded no contest"*: Associated Press, "James' Mother Is Sentenced," *New York Times*, May 27, 2006.

242 *Developing a richer appreciation for all that his mother*: Associated Press, "LeBron James—Beyond His Years, Beyond the Hype," ESPN, December 10, 2005.

244 *The Cavs are running a business*: Associated Press, "LeBron James—Beyond His Years, Beyond the Hype."

245   *LeBron signed a three-year extension*: Liz Robbins, "In Deal Fit for a King, James Stays a Cavalier," *New York Times*, July 9, 2006. See also Associated Press, "LeBron Officially Signs Contract Extension with Cavs," ESPN, July 18, 2006.

245   *Anthony went for the guaranteed $80 million*: Associated Press, "Anthony Signs Five-Year, $80M Contract," Associated Press, July 12, 2006.

249   *the most popular player in Asia*: Chris Ballard, "LeBron Act II," *Sports Illustrated*, April 24, 2006.

246   *Nike was planning an unprecedented marketing campaign*: Stuart Elliott, "With LeBron James, Nike Ads Hit the Streets Where You Live," *New York Times*, October 31, 2006.

246   *LeBron playing four versions of himself*: Adam Fusfeld, "Four LeBrons Will Try to Appeal to Your Social Sensibilities in Ways That One Couldn't," *Business Insider*, January 18, 2011.

246   *"Those are the four guys I act like"*: Lynn Zinser, "James Cool and Mature, Just as He Wants to Be," *New York Times*, November 14, 2006.

247   *When Nike's Lynn Merritt saw the final cut*: Steve Gleydura, "The World According to LeBron," *Cleveland Magazine*, December 18, 2006.

247   *donating 85 percent of his $44 billion personal fortune*: Timothy O'Brien and Stephanie Saul, "Buffett to Give Bulk of His Fortune to Gates Charity," *New York Times*, June 26, 2006.

247   *he aspired to one day be the richest man in the world*: Associated Press, "LeBron James—Beyond His Years, Beyond the Hype." In this interview, LeBron said, "In the next 15 to 20 years, I hope I'll be the richest man in the world. That's one of my goals. I want to be a billionaire."

247   *Wachter knew Buffett and placed a call*: Pablo S. Torre, "LeBron: The Sequel," *ESPN The Magazine*, February 27, 2017.

247   *LeBron and Maverick flew to Nebraska*: "LeBron Hobnobs with Rich (Buffett), Famous (Letterman)," Associated Press, September 21, 2006.

248   *a transformative experience*: Zameena Mejia, "Warren Buffett Said LeBron James Has a 'Money Mind'—Here's Why," CNBC, October 22, 2018.

250   This guy knows more than I did: Sarah Berger, "What Impressed Warren Buffett When He First Met LeBron James—And It Wasn't His Basketball Skills," CNBC, April 17, 2019.

250   *the Oreo cookie shake*: "LeBron Hobnobs with Rich (Buffett), Famous (Letterman)."

250   *a funny video presentation*: Matt Koppenheffer, "Quick Take: The Annual Berkshire Videos," Motley Fool, May 5, 2007.

Chapter 21: The Lone Cavalier

251   *"You are on the verge of choosing to immerse yourself"*: Harvey Araton, "As the 'Next Jordan,' Should James Try to Be Unlike Mike?" *New York Times*, May 24, 2003.

251   *"People say it's unfair"*: Ibid.

252   *George Clooney had visited the Darfur region*: "Clooney, Senators Urge Action on Darfur," CNN, April 28, 2006.

252   *Barack Obama at the National Press Club*: Holli Chmela, "Thousands Rally in Support of American Aid to Darfur," *New York Times*, May 1, 2006.

252 *"What we cannot do is turn our heads"*: "Clooney, Senators Urge Action on Darfur."

252 *Activist Eric Reeves*: Nicholas Kristof, "Heroes of Darfur," *New York Times*, May 7, 2006.

252 *Actress Mia Farrow had also visited*: Ian Greenberg, "Changing the Rules of the Games," *New York Times Magazine*, March 30, 2008.

253 *pressuring Oscar-winning director Steven Spielberg*: Ibid.

253 *Nike had purchased all the ad time*: "LeBron James Returns in Second Season of 'The LeBrons' to Debut Zoom LeBron IV Shoe," Nike press release, October 26, 2006.

253 *"a digital takeover"*: Stuart Elliott, "With LeBron James, Nike Ads Hit the Streets Where You Live," *New York Times*, October 31, 2006.

253 *pop-up store in Manhattan*: Ibid.

253 *a group of human rights organizations*: Greenberg, "Changing the Rules of the Games."

254 *Jill Savitt chased him down*: Ibid.

256 *King for Kids Bike-A-Thon*: Mary Schmitt Boyer, "Cycling's Slam Dunk," *Bicycling*, April 30, 2010.

256 *Wachter came back with a candidate*: Pablo S. Torre, "LeBron: The Sequel," *ESPN The Magazine*, February 27, 2017.

256 *he took Wachter's suggestion to LeBron*: Ibid.

256 *an equity stake in Cannondale*: Thomas J. Ryan, "LeBron James Buys Stake in Cannondale," SGB Media, March 26, 2007.

256 *Rich Paul was offered an opportunity to go*: Joe Drape, "An Agent of Change," *New York Times*, August 17, 2014.

257 *LeBron welcomed Buffett to Cleveland*: Associated Press, "Odd Couple: Billionaire Buffett Sees Buddy LeBron James Play," *Denver Post*, March 25, 2007.

257 *"The 'Genocide Olympics' "*: Ronan Farrow and Mia Farrow, "The Genocide Olympics," *Wall Street Journal*, March 28, 2007.

257 *"the Leni Riefenstahl of the Beijing Games?"*: Ibid.

258 *"The question for Spielberg"*: Eric Reeves, "Artists Abetting Genocide," *Boston Globe*, April 16, 2007.

258 *Newble stopped and picked up a copy of USA Today*: Steve Springer, "Opening Eyes to Darfur," *Los Angeles Times*, May 19, 2008.

259 *"China cannot be a legitimate host"*: Letter provided to the author.

260 *Newble addressed the team*: Springer, "Opening Eyes to Darfur."

260 *Newble handed out a packet to each player*: Ibid.

262 *a video of Buffett going one-on-one with LeBron*: Karen Richardson, "Buffett Plays Basketball," *Wall Street Journal*, May 5, 2007.

262 *Berkshire's controversial decision to invest in a Chinese oil company*: Richard Dooling, "The Wizard Drops the Curtain," *New York Times*, May 9, 2007.

262 *Buffett acknowledged the geopolitical implications*: Susan Lisovicz, "Being Buffett . . . and Blunt," CNN Money, May 7, 2007.

262 *But he maintained that he could not influence*: Ibid.

263 *"I'm here in the U.S. and I have means"*: Branson Wright, "Newble Protesting Genocide in Sudan," *Plain Dealer*, May 10, 2007.

264 *"It was basically not having enough information"*: Howard Beck, "Cavalier Seeks Players' Support for Darfur," *New York Times*, May 16, 2007.

264 *"The King Kong of directors is one of"*: Rick Reilly, "Mia's Olympic Mettle," *Sports Illustrated*, May 14, 2007.

265 *"Unlike LeBron, Newble can't claim a $90 million endorsement"*: Scott Soshnick, "LeBron James Isn't the Cavalier to Admire Most," Bloomberg, May 17, 2007.

266 *"It's a letter any player of conscience"*: Ibid.

266 *Hall of Famer Bill Bradley also sharpened the focus*: Ibid.

Chapter 22: One for the Ages

267 *"I go for the winning play"*: Associated Press, "The Pistons Slow James and Escape with a Win," *New York Times*, May 22, 2007.

267 *"I've got a problem with the best player"*: Associated Press, "LeBron Criticized for Passing Ball," *Deseret News*, May 23, 2007.

267 *"Kobe Bryant certainly wouldn't have"*: Ibid.

268 *"LeBron James . . . won't lift a finger for Darfur"*: Jonathan Zimmerman, "On Darfur, LeBron James Drops the Ball," *Christian Science Monitor*, May 24, 2007.

269 *"the main lesson from the Jordan era"*: Ian Thomsen, "Not Quite Ready Yet," *Sports Illustrated*, May 28, 2007.

273 *coming down on the Demon Drop*: Liz Robbins, "Dazzling Display Takes Everything Out of James," *New York Times*, June 2, 2007.

Chapter 23: Kingdom Come

274 *"hypnotic"*: Liz Robbins, "James Puts on Scoring Clinic in Overtime," *New York Times*, June 1, 2007.

274 *"immortal"*: Jack McCallum, "His Kingdom Come," *Sports Illustrated*, June 11, 2007.

275 *James Gandolfini's last performance*: Joan Acocella, "Gandolfini: Rest in Peace," *The New Yorker*, June 22, 2013.

275 *"the richest achievement in the history of television"*: David Remnick, "Postscript: James Gandolfini, 1961–2013," *The New Yorker*, June 19, 2013.

275 *the complex life of Tony Soprano*: Dave Itzkoff, "James Gandolfini Is Dead at 51; a Complex Mob Boss in 'The Sopranos,' " *New York Times*, June 19, 2013.

275 *speculating whether Tony Soprano would survive the finale*: Willy Staley, "Why Is Every Young Person in America Watching 'The Sopranos'?" *New York Times Magazine*, October 3, 2021.

276 *"I'm really more proud of her"*: See LeBron James interview with ABC.

276 *"For nearly two hours Sunday"*: Howard Beck, "Spurs Overpower Cavaliers in Game 2," *New York Times*, June 11, 2007.

277 *gave birth to their second son*: Liz Robbins, "With Sweep of Cavs, Spurs Are Champions Again," *New York Times*, June 15, 2007.

277 *named him Bryce Maximus James*: Ibid.

277 *Maximus Decimus Meridius in* Gladiator: Adam Duerson, "The Beat," *Sports Illustrated*, June 25, 2007.

277 *After a sleepless night*: Robbins, "With Sweep of Cavs, Spurs Are Champions Again."

278 *like LeBron, Brady had set out to reach the heights*: Jeff Benedict, *The Dynasty* (New York: Avid Reader Press, 2020).

278 *Brady and Gisele met through a mutual friend*: Ibid.

278 *"the Most Beautiful Girl in the World"*: Ibid.

279 *LeBron couldn't bear to watch*: Robbins, "With Sweep of Cavs, Spurs Are Champions Again."

279 *Maverick hosted a two-day summit in Akron*: Tim Arango, "Lebron Inc.," *Fortune*, December 10, 2007.

279 *"China 101: Pop Culture"*: Ibid.

279 *a private dinner*: Ibid.

280 *"the focus needs to be on LeBron"*: Ibid.

281 *LeBron ultimately made sure that Marsh was paid in full*: "Defendant LeBron James' 'Motion to Make Deposit in Court,' " April 5, 2005. It reads, in part: "Defendant LeBron James hereby moves the Court . . . to deposit with the Court the sum of $138,334.00 on the ground that defendant does not contest that plaintiffs are owed this amount as repayment on a $100,000 loan (plus interest) that plaintiffs made to defendant Eddie G. Jackson, Jr. on or about July 2001." Case No. 2003-10-5848. Subsequently, the court ordered a summary judgment in favor of Gloria James on May 3, 2015.

281 *LeBron discreetly met with a healthcare specialist in Cleveland*: See *Stovell v. James*, United States District Court for the District of Columbia, Civil Action No. 10-1059.

281 *claimed that he might be LeBron's biological father*: Ibid.

281 *Gloria claimed she'd never met the man*: Ibid.

281 *"LeBron's money is for his children"*: Ibid.

281 *a DNA paternity test*: Ibid.

282 *"Do you know your biological father's whereabouts?"*: LeBron James interview, *On the Record with Bob Costas*, HBO, Summer 2003.

282 *"I never really thought about it"*: Ibid.

282 *LeBron wasn't afraid to take the paternity test*: See Memorandum Opinion in *Stovell v. James*, United States District Court for the District of Columbia, Civil Action No. 10-1059.

283 *"if he were an IPO, I'd buy in"*: Arango, "Lebron Inc."

284 *"If I were a general manager"*: Grant Wahl, "Ahead of His Class," *Sports Illustrated*, February 18, 2002.

285 *Ainge was wheeling and dealing*: Michael Holley, *The Big Three* (New York: Hachette, 2020).

285 *Paul Pierce was so sick and tired*: Chris Mannix, "Moments of Truth," *Sports Illustrated*, October 2021.

285 *Ainge's blockbuster moves had given Pierce*: Ibid.

285 *The Pierce-Garnett-Allen trio*: Holley, *The Big Three*.

Chapter 24: Fashion

287 *the entertainment director at* Vogue: Jill Demling interview, *Future of Fashion Business* podcast, October 19, 2021.

287 *booking the magazine's celebrity covers*: Stephanie Saltzman, "Jill Demling Is Exiting Her Role as 'Vogue' Entertainment Director," Fashionista, October 17, 2018.

287 *Demling wanted to feature the ultimate Olympian*: Jill Demling interview, *Collectible Daily* podcast, May 11, 2021.

287 Vogue *was the holy grail*: Adena Andrews, "Rachel Johnson Embraces Role as NBA Stylist," ESPNW, February 7, 2012.

287 *never put a Black man on the cover*: Ibid.

287 *Richard Gere . . . and George Clooney*: "LeBron James to Appear on Vogue's Cover," Associated Press, March 15, 2008.

287 *he wanted to be paired with the best model*: Jill Demling interview, *Collectible Daily* podcast.

287 *Demling was well acquainted with Gisele*: Ibid.

288 *Brady and Gisele were very particular*: Ibid.

288 *Demling understood that Brady would have to sign off*: Ibid.

288 *Tom did some gambling with Jay-Z and LeBron*: Ibid.

288 *Leibovitz had first gained prominence*: Robin Pogrebin, "Annie Leibovitz Revisits Her Early Years," *New York Times*, February 13, 2019.

288 *a photo shoot with John Lennon*: Alina Cohen, "How Annie Leibovitz Perfectly Captured Yoko and John's Relationship," Artsy, December 6, 2019.

288 *Leibovitz told her to remain dressed*: Interview with Annie Leibovitz, https://www .youtube.com/watch?v=FJdc3MyLWs8&ab_channel=Witnify.

288 *Demi Moore was eight months pregnant*: Lucy Handley, "The Vanity Fair Photo of a Pregnant, Naked Demi Moore Was Never Meant to Appear in Public," CNBC, May 9, 2018.

288 *"But there is this other picture"*: Ibid.

288 *a shot of Moore naked*: Ibid.

288 *image was so controversial*: George Lois, "Flashback: Demi Moore," *Vanity Fair*, June 22, 2011.

288 *"I understand what impact it had"*: Handley, "The Vanity Fair Photo of a Pregnant, Naked Demi Moore Was Never Meant to Appear in Public."

289 *"You're not walking in with these shorts"*: Rachel Johnson interview with Eric Rutherford, uploaded to YouTube on February 11, 2020.

289 *"You're going as The Man"*: Ibid.

290 *LeBron met . . . Anna Wintour for dinner*: Page Six, "Cover Boy Chic," *New York Post*, March 6, 2008.

291 *"Do you understand what this means?"*: Andrews, "Rachel Johnson Embraces Role as NBA Stylist."

291 *"Raych, you're making too much of this"*: Johnson interview with Eric Rutherford.

292 *LeBron lit up the Knicks*: Howard Beck, "With Marbury Watching, James Scores 50 Points at Garden," *New York Times*, March 6, 2008.

292 *"This ranks really high"*: Ibid.

292 Vogue *issue hit newsstands*: "Vogue Cover with LeBron Stirs Up Controversy," Associated Press, March 25, 2008.

292 *"He looks beastly"*: Jemele Hill, "LeBron Should Be More Careful with His Image," ESPN, March 21, 2018. See also "Some Call LeBron James Cover Offensive," NPR, March 27, 2008.

293 *"its erotic value"*: Wesley Morris, "Monkey Business," *Slate*, March 31, 2008.

294 *Steven Spielberg had withdrawn as an artistic advisor*: Helene Cooper, "Spielberg Drops Out as Advisor to Beijing Olympics in Dispute over Darfur Conflict," *New York Times*, February 13, 2008.

294 *"Sudan's government bears the bulk"*: Ibid.

294 *"No one heard my side of the story"*: Shelley Smith via ESPN, "LeBron James Breaks Silence on Darfur," ABC News, May 19, 2008.

294 *"At the end of the day"*: Ibid.

295 *"It becomes theatrically important, after you die"*: Lisa Taddeo, "The Last Days of Heath Ledger," *Esquire*, April 2008.

295 *commissioned sculptor Lincoln Schatz*: "Esquire's Portrait of the 21st Century, 2008, Cube," www.lincolnschatz.com.

296 *"You need him out?"*: Lisa Taddeo, "LeBron James: The Rise of the Superathlete," *Esquire*, October 2008.

296 *"Yo, Bron, let's go"*: Ibid.

297 *The gang member stabbed Pierce*: The account of Paul Pierce's attack come from over two thousand pages of documents from the Boston Police Department, Boston Police Homicide Unit, crime scene photographs, Suffolk County grand jury transcripts, and transcripts of tape-recorded interviews with police.

297 *nearly a dozen men jumped Pierce*: Ibid.

297 *brass knuckles with a knife*: Ibid.

297 *puncturing a lung*: Ibid.

297 *Pierce spit toward LeBron*: Brian Windhorst, "History of the James-Pierce Feud," *True Hoop* blog, ESPN, May 28, 2012.

298 *"Let us get breaking news that LeBron has torn"*: Eve Peyser, "Winning Friends, Influencing People," *Vanity Fair*, December/January 2023.

299 *"He played a hell of a game tonight"*: Howard Beck, "Pierce Wins Duel: Celtics Take Series," *New York Times*, May 19, 2008.

299 *"Paul Pierce is one of my favorite players"*: Ibid.

Chapter 25: Beats

301 Badass *was the word*: Lisa Taddeo, "LeBron James: The Rise of the Superathlete," *Esquire*, October 2008.

301 *"powerful men with slavering appetites"*: Lisa Taddeo, "Rachel Uchitel Is Not a Madam," *New York*, April 12, 2010.

302 *"Rising from his throne like an urban fairy tale"*: Taddeo, "LeBron James: The Rise of the Superathlete."

303 *Romeo Travis showed up*: Transcript of Kristopher Belman interview with Debbie Lynn Elias, October 2009.

303 *remembered as "camera man"*: Ibid.

303 *Belman approached Coach Dru*: Ibid.

303 *Brought Belman to LeBron's house*: John Jurgensen, "Long Shot," *Wall Street Journal*, October 9, 2009.

303 *a twelve-minute clip*: Ibid.

303 *"Whatever you need from me"*: Transcript of Belman interview with Debbie Lynn Elias.

304 *"I'm down"*: John Jurgensen, "Long Shot," *Wall Street Journal*, October 9, 2009.

304 *film and television production company called SpringHill*: Marisa Guthrie, "LeBron James Is Already Winning Hollywood," *Hollywood Reporter*, September 10, 2018.

304 *SpringHill's first venture*: Anita Elberse, "LeBron James: Building a Hollywood Empire," *Harvard Business School*, October 24, 2017.

304 *Jay-Z to work on the soundtrack*: Jurgensen, "Long Shot."

304 *Coca-Cola and State Farm Insurance*: Ibid.

304 *"people tell us, 'You're really smart'"*: Taddeo, "LeBron James: The Rise of the Super-athlete."

304 *empowering Maverick*: Maverick Carter interview with Jay Williams, "Maverick Carter on Building the LeBron James Empire," NPR, January 4, 2022. See also Carter interview with Andrew Hawkins, "How Maverick Carter Went from Intern to CEO," *Kneading Dough*, Uninterrupted, 2020. In this interview, Maverick said, "I wouldn't . . . be in the position I am if I wasn't empowered by LeBron."

304 *ability to listen*: Ibid.

304 *willingness to learn*: Ibid.

305 *Cannondale was acquired by Dorel Industries*: "Dorel Buys Cannondale," Bicycle Retailer, February 4, 2008.

305 *LeBron earned a return*: Carter interview with Andrew Hawkins.

305 *Maverick also profited*: Ibid.

305 *An agent LeBron and Maverick trusted*: Charles McGrath, "N.B.A. Star, Now Memoirist, on Hometown Court," *New York Times*, September 4, 2009.

305 *sold over two million copies*: "The Exchange: Buzz Bissinger," *The New Yorker*, November 5, 2009.

305 *Maverick worked with Bissinger's agent*: Ibid.

305 *too lucrative to turn down*: Buzz Bissinger, "Twidiot," *New Republic*, June 21, 2010.

309 *cofounder of Interscope Records*: Ben Sisario, "Jimmy Iovine Knows Music and Tech," *New York Times*, December 30, 2019.

309 *Beats by Dre*: Ben Sisario, "Jimmy Iovine, a Master of Beats, Lends Apple a Skilled Ear," *New York Times*, May 28, 2014.

309 *hadn't gone on the market yet*: Carter interview with Jay Williams.

309 *"Watch what I do with them"*: Jason Whitlock, "Maverick Carter Out to Silence Critics," Fox Sports, April 7, 2011.

309 *every player was wearing Beats*: Ibid.

309 *marketing that impressed Iovine*: J. Freedom Du Lac, "Speakerheads," ESPN, February 5, 2013.

309 *Dr. Dre should partner with LeBron*: Jimmy Iovine interview with Jason Kelly, "How Rich Paul, Fueled byLeBron, Built a Billion-Dollar Empire," Bloomberg, February 4, 2021.

309 *China revoked the visa*: "Darfur Work May Have Led to Revoked Visa," NPR, August 6, 2008.

309 *Joey Cheek, who had spoken out*: Juliet Macur, "Lost Boy of Sudan Is Chosen to Carry U.S. Flag," *New York Times*, August 6, 2008.

309 *"No, not really"*: "Will Kobe, LeBron Pass on Darfur?" Yahoo! News, August 7, 2008.

310 *"Basic human rights"*: Ibid.

310 *"We are here to concentrate on a gold medal"*: Ibid.

311 *"Everybody wants to talk about"*: Pete Thamel, "USA Basketball Returns to the Top," *New York Times*, August 24, 2008.

311 *LeBron had tears in his eyes*: Associated Press, "LeBron James Goes Hollywood," *Los Angeles Times*, September 7, 2008.

312 *dinner with Jimmy Iovine*: Ibid.

312 *Powerbeats*: Ibid.

312 *Interscope Records had agreed to coproduce*: Du Lac, "Speakerheads."

315 *David Lauren hosted*: Carol Hastings, "Ralph Lauren and LeBron James Team Up for Charity," Cleveland.com, September 12, 2008.

312 *energized by Obama's run*: Lisa Robinson, "Jay-Z Has the Room," *Vanity Fair*, October 1, 2013.

312 " *'Are you out of your mind?' "*: Ibid.

313 *"When you're running for the presidency"*: Ibid.

313 *brush the imaginary dirt off*: Ibid.

313 *"This is not happening in the world"*: Ibid.

313 *Jay-Z wanted LeBron's help*: Associated Press, "Jay-Z, LeBron James Hosting Obama Rally," *Hollywood Reporter*, October 23, 2008.

313 *a series of free concerts*: Randy Lewis, "Jay-Z Shows Will Support Obama," *Los Angeles Times*, October 2, 2008.

313 *LeBron and Savannah contributed $20,000*: Dan Labbe, "James, Jay-Z Energize Rally at the Q for Obama," Cleveland.com, October 30, 2008.

313 *T-shirt that said*: "LeBron James Hosts Concert for Obama," Buchtelite, October 30, 2008.

313 *"You know who I'm voting for"*: Ibid.

314 *"Rosa Parks"*: Ibid.

314 *"Fuck talkin' 'bout the recession"*: Ibid.

Chapter 26: Miracles Aren't Enough

315 *"I've done a lot for this school"*: "The Exchange: Buzz Bissinger," *The New Yorker*, November 5, 2009.

316 *"Are you any place remotely close to your peak?"*: Steve Kroft, "The Incredible Drive of LeBron James," CBS News, March 26, 2009.

317 *Magic shocked the Cavaliers*: William C. Rhoden, "Magic Has Superman, but LeBron James Comet to the Rescue," *New York Times*, May 29, 2009.

318 *"that guy's not in the league anymore"*: Howard Beck, "James's Last Shot Saves Cavaliers," *New York Times*, May 23, 2009.

319 *state-of-the-art practice facility*: Howard Beck, "As James Plot Swirls, the Cavaliers Dig In," *New York Times*, November 25, 2008.

320 *"Mike Brown is a critical element"*: "Mike Brown Wins NBA's 2008-2009 Coach of the Year Award," press release, Cleveland Cavaliers, April 20, 2009.

320 *oldest player in the league*: Scott Raab, "Shaq: 'My Job Is to Protect the King,' " *Esquire*, June 2010.

320 *titles with Kobe in LA*: Howard Beck, "Shaquille O'Neal Traded to Cleveland Cavaliers," *New York Times*, June 25, 2009.

320 *O'Neal agreed to join the Cavs*: Ibid.

320 *if he were playing poker*: Howard Beck, "Cavaliers' Sense of Urgency Spurs James, O'Neal and Owner," *New York Times*, October 10, 2009.

320 *"Did you run this by LeBron?"*: Scott Raab, *The Whore of Akron* (New York: Harper Perennial, 2011).

320 *"Where is Shaq now?"*: Ibid.

321 *Superman logo on the front grille*: Raab, "Shaq: 'My Job Is to Protect the King.' "

321 *"I'm still the Dun Dada"*: Ibid.

321 *"I had to check my computer"*: Ibid.

321 *"It's LeBron's team"*: Ibid.

321 *"I feel fucking fabulous"*: Ibid.

321 a teammate that's going to help: Transcript of LeBron James interview with Charlie Rose, September 25, 2009.

321 *golf with Warren Buffett*: Joe Flint, "LeBron Plays Sun Valley," *Los Angeles Times*, July 7, 2009.

321 *teamed up with Rihanna*: "Rihanna Joins Up with LeBron," NikeLeBron.net, June 18, 2009.

322 *visit with President Obama*: Associated Press, "LeBron visits White House," ESPN, June 16, 2009.

322 *a party for the book*: Leon Neyfakh, "Graydon Carter Throws Big Bash-ket for LeBron at Monkey Bar," *The Observer*, September 10, 2009.

322 *the Monkey Bar*: Leslie Kaufman, "An Insiders' Clubhouse (Apply at the Door)," *New York Times*, August 12, 2008.

323 *"Are you familiar with our city?"*: Transcript of LeBron James interview with Jon Stewart on *The Daily Show*.

323 *"a modest book"*: Dwight Garner, "An N.B.A. Giant and How He Grew," *New York Times*, September 8, 2009.

324 *"the language of a professional writer"*: Ibid.

324 *Bissinger was frustrated*: Karen Long, "Buzz Bissinger Calls His Book with LeBron James 'An Epic Failure,' " *Plain Dealer*, June 26, 2012.

324 *"You and I were on the golf course"*: Transcript of James interview with Charlie Rose.

324 *"LeBron allows me to coach him"*: Raab, *The Whore of Akron*.

324 *Brown's answer made Gilbert cringe*: Ibid.

325 *"Nobody knows"*: Ibid.

325 *LeBron texted Derek Jeter*: Brian Lewis, "Knicks Hope to Become 'Apple' of LeBron's Eye," *New York Post*, November 6, 2009.

325 *"Thank you for welcoming me back"*: Open letter from LeBron James, New York *Daily News*, November 6, 2009.

326 *LeBron slept through the parade*: Jonathan Abrams, "James Brings Buzz to Garden, but Keeps Plans to a Murmur," *New York Times*, November 6, 2009.

326 *LeBron was in control*: Howard Beck, "Fans at Garden Were Thrilled, but Not by Knicks," *New York Times*, November 6, 2009.

326 *Tiger Woods's wife chased him out*: Jeff Benedict and Armen Keteyian, *Tiger Woods* (New York: Simon & Schuster, 2018).

326 *"What happened?"*: Ibid.

326 *biggest fall from grace*: Jonathan Mahler, "The Tiger Bubble," *New York Times Magazine*, March 24, 2010.

327 *first athlete to earn $1 billion*: Benedict and Keteyian, *Tiger Woods*.

327 *sponsors other than Nike had dropped him*: Larry Dorman, "Tiger Woods as Pitchman Slips from View," *New York Times*, December 8, 2009.

328 *"The passion and the flame"*: For the lyrics to "Forever," written by Drake, Kanye West, Lil Wayne, and Eminem, see https://genius.com/Drake-kanye-west-lil-wayne-and-eminem-forever-lyrics.

328 *"nobody was supposed to be confrontational with LeBron"*: Shaquille O'Neal with Jackie MacMullan, *Shaq Uncut: My Story* (New York: Grand Central, 2011).

328 *"every place we go, he'll send a text"*: Raab, "Shaq: 'My Job Is to Protect the King.' "

328 *"Yo, Mo, we can't have that"*: O'Neal with MacMullan, *Shaq Uncut.*

328 *Shaq observed that LeBron frequently ignored Brown*: Ibid.

329 *"They want to have fun"*: Ian Thomsen, *The Soul of Basketball* (Boston: Houghton Mifflin Harcourt, 2018).

330 *"There's no question in Game 5 LeBron was kind of out of it"*: O'Neal with MacMullan, *Shaq Uncut.*

331 *"I put a lot of pressure on myself to be the best player"*: Howard Beck, "Cleveland Boos James as Celtics Dominate," *New York Times*, May 11, 2010.

331 *"I spoil a lot of people"*: Ibid.

331 *"America's most famous sports columnist"*: Noam Cohen, "Writing a Sports Column Far from Print, and the Game," *New York Times*, November 15, 2009.

331 *encouraged fans to chant*: Erik Gallant, "Did Bill Simmons' 'Celtics Chants' Twitter Account Work in Game 6?" MassLive, May 14, 2010.

331 *LeBron stepped to the free throw line*: Howard Beck, "Cavs' Run Ends; Uncertainty Starts," *New York Times*, May 13, 2010.

331 *Beaten again, Riley thought*: Thomsen, *The Soul of Basketball.*

Chapter 27: The Summer of LeBron

333 *a sports gossip website published*: Barry Petchesky, "Anatomy of a Rumor: How the Gloria James/Delonte West Sex Story Went Viral," Deadspin, May 21, 2010.

333 *"I am the attorney for Gloria and LeBron James"*: Email from Frederick R. Nance, May 17, 2010.

334 *"terrified to leave home"*: Buzz Bissinger, "LeBron's Next Leap," *New York Times*, May 19, 2010.

334 *"a piece of shit"*: Paige Williams, "Buzz Bissinger on Heart, Luck, Honesty, Critics and the Importance of Switching Things Up," Nieman Reports, May 25, 2012.

334 *"never shown anything close to the killer mentality"*: Bissinger, "LeBron's Next Leap."

334 *Gilbert had the upper hand*: Howard Beck, "Does LeBron James Need New York and the Knicks?" *New York Times*, November 5, 2009.

335 *"The expectations of this organization"*: "Cavs Fire Brown before $4.5M Deadline," ESPN, May 24, 2010.

335 *"If you're going to lay all the blame"*: Ibid.

335 *"Do I think he deserved it?"*: Ibid.

335 *"Had to happen"*: Scott Raab, "Did LeBron James Get His Head Coach Fired?" *Esquire*, May 24, 2010.

336 *"Maverick, how's this free agency"*: James Andrew Miller and Tom Shales, *Those Guys Have All the Fun: Inside the World of ESPN* (New York: Little, Brown, 2011).

336 *"There'll be a lot going on"*: Ibid.

336 *more chitchat*: Ibid.

336 *"I'd like to do the first"*: Jim Gray, *Talking to Goats* (New York: William Morrow, 2020).

336 *"I'll let him know"*: Ibid.

336 *"I did one with him"*: Ibid.

336 *"You don't have to explain"*: Ibid.

336 *"What we should do is a live show"*: Ibid.

336 *"That's a brilliant idea"*: Miller and Shales, *Those Guys Have All the Fun.*

336 *"I get to do the interview"*: Ibid.

336 *"you ought to do that"*: Ibid.

336 *"You want to handle it?"*: Ibid.

336 *"Let's do this"*: Ibid.

337 *the story of Emanuel's career*: Connie Bruck, "Ari Emanuel Takes on the World," *The New Yorker*, April 19, 2021.

338 *Gandolfini and Edie Falco hadn't worked together*: *Shattered: Hope, Heartbreak, and the New York Knicks* podcast, *The Athletic*, March 29, 2021.

338 *Knicks commissioned filmmaker*: Ibid.

338 *he did know Edie Falco*: "Production Update," *Filmmaker*, Winter 1998.

338 *reached out to Jonathan Hock*: *Shattered: Hope, Heartbreak, and the New York Knicks*.

340 *a day with Jay-Z*: Theo Bark, "Jay-Z & LeBron James to Mentor Students in Dallas," Boombox, February 12, 2010.

340 *decided to file a lawsuit*: *Stovell v. James*, Civil Action No. 10-1059.

341 *weighing both sides, Skipper thought*: Miller and Shales, *Those Guys Have All the Fun*.

341 *LeBron stood in a room in a warehouse*: J. R. Moehringer, "Three Weeks in Crazyville," *GQ*, August 16, 2010.

341 *a bestselling memoir*: J. R. Moehringer, *The Tender Bar* (New York: Hyperion, 2005).

341 *handpicked a few years earlier*: Andre Agassi, *Open* (New York: Knopf, 2009).

341 *"one of the most passionately"*: Sam Tanenhaus, "Andre Agassi's Hate of the Game," *New York Times*, November 20, 2009.

341 *"a first-rate sports memoir"*: Ibid.

342 *notoriously private Lakers star*: J. R. Moehringer, "Kobe Bryant Is in It to Win It," *GQ*, March 1, 2010.

342 *Leonardo da Vinci and Daniel Day-Lewis*: Ibid.

342 *"For precocity some great price"*: Moehringer, "Three Weeks in Crazyville."

343 *"My emotions won't be involved"*: Ibid.

343 *"That's what keeps me humble"*: Ibid.

343 *No one is less low-maintenance*: Ibid.

343 *"Are you a sports psychologist?"*: Ibid.

344 *"She doesn't hold her tongue"*: Ibid.

344 *Nets and Knicks traveled to Cleveland*: *Shattered: Hope, Heartbreak, and the New York Knicks*.

344 *become a billionaire athlete*: Ibid.

344 *friendship wasn't going to rise or fall*: Lisa Robinson, "Jay-Z Has the Room," *Vanity Fair*, October 1, 2013.

345 *commission a study*: Jonathan Abrams and Howard Beck, "James Hears Nets' and Knicks' Pitches," *New York Times*, July 1, 2010.

345 *delegation showed LeBron the video*: *Shattered: Hope, Heartbreak, and the New York Knicks*.

345 *Bosh were in Chicago*: Abrams and Beck, "James Hears Nets' and Knicks' Pitches."

345 *"prince of the planet"*: Harvey Araton, "Knicks Have Little to Offer LeBron James," *New York Times*, July 1, 2010.

346 *grease the wheels with Rose*: Jonathan Abrams, "Knicks Quietly Make Another Run at James," *New York Times*, July 4, 2010.

346 *Riley had been plotting*: Ian Thomsen, *The Soul of Basketball* (Boston: Houghton Mifflin Harcourt, 2018).

346 *"We want you to understand"*: Ibid.

346 *Stephen Covey's bestselling book*: Stephen R. Covey, A. Roger Merrill, and Rebecca R. Merrill, *First Things First* (New York: Simon & Schuster, 1994).

347 *"It's the beginning of the book"*: Thomsen, *The Soul of Basketball*.

347 *"the main thing with us . . . is winning championships"*: Ibid.

347 *"What's in there?"*: Ibid.

347 *"What are these rings?"*: Ibid.

348 *"Shit's going to hit the fan"*: Ibid.

348 Hey, can you get on a call?: *D. Wade: Life Unexpected*, directed by Bob Metelus (Imagine Documentaries), Disney+, 2020.

348 *"Miami's got the cap space"*: Ibid.

348 *"You in?"*: Ibid.

349 Interviewing LeBron in a loud gym: Moehringer, "Three Weeks in Crazyville."

349 *Wesley, was trying to broker*: Adrian Wojnarowski, "Inside Look at LeBron's Free-Agent Coup," Yahoo! News, July 16, 2010.

349 *Irritated, Maverick called the* Times: Ibid.

349 *"Wes has nothing to do"*: Jonathan Abrams, "Advisor to James Will Not Meet with N.B.A. Suitors," *New York Times*, June 29, 2010.

350 Nah, I ain't talked to him: *D. Wade: Life Unexpected*.

350 *"Stay and be quiet"*: Moehringer, "Three Weeks in Crazyville."

351 *"I'm not downgrading my father"*: Ibid.

351 *"What the fuck is going on?"*: *D. Wade: Life Unexpected*.

353 *Maverick had worked with Ari Emanuel*: Miller and Shales, *Those Guys Have All the Fun*.

Chapter 28: "Hester Prynne in a Headband"

355 *"I don't know what the hell"*: *D. Wade: Life Unexpected*, directed by Bob Metelus (Imagine Documentaries), Disney+, 2020.

355 *"Neutral location"*: J. R. Moehringer, "Three Weeks in Crazyville," *GQ*, August 16, 2010.

356 *Fans set fire*: "Cleveland Fans 'Stunned' by LeBron's Decision to Play for Miami," Associated Press, July 8, 2010.

356 *"cowardly" and "narcissistic"*: Dan Gilbert, letter posted on July 8, 2010.

356 *"He has gotten a free pass"*: "Dan Gilbert Says LeBron James 'Quit' During the Playoffs," Associated Press, July 9, 2010.

357 *"Is Clemens the Antichrist?"*: Bill Simmons, "Is Clemens the Antichrist?" *Grantland*, October 26, 2005.

357 *"I blame the people around him"*: William J. Simmons, "Welcome to the All-LeBron Sound-Off," ESPN, July 9, 2010.

358 *"What about parents who stayed together"*: Bill Simmons, "Sports Guy's Vault: Draft Diary 2003," *Grantland*, June 27, 2003.

358 *"A lot of that has to do with race"*: Isaac Chotiner, "LeBron James's Agent Is Transforming the Business of Basketball," *The New Yorker*, May 31, 2021.

359 *"narcissistic announcement"*: Maureen Dowd, "Miami's Hoops Cartel," *New York Times*, July 10, 2010.

360 *"There's no way"*: "Jordan Wouldn't Have Called Magic, Bird," ESPN, July 10, 2010.

360 *"It was terrible"*: Ian Thomsen, *The Soul of Basketball* (Boston: Houghton Mifflin Harcourt, 2018).

360 *"a slave master mentality"*: Jeanne Marie Laskas, "LeBron James," *GQ*, February 18, 2014.

631 *"Me and my family have seen"*: Moehringer, "Three Weeks in Crazyville."

362 *Kobe—a loner*: J. R. Moehringer, "Kobe Bryant Is in It to Win It," *GQ*, March 1, 2010.

362 *This is really going to derail me*: Maverick Carter interview, *The Colin Cowherd Podcast*, April 11, 2021.

364 *"you are no longer welcome"*: Scott Raab, "The Miami Heat Don't Want My Talents in South Beach," *Esquire*, November 16, 2010.

364 *"a big nose big lipped"*: Brian Windhorst, "LeBron James Shares Hateful Tweets," ESPN, October 20, 2010.

364 *LeBron's first game back in Cleveland*: Dave McMenamin and Brian Windhorst, "A Moment LeBron James and Cleveland Will Never Forget," ESPN, November 20, 2018.

365 *"This is the most hate I've seen, ever!"*: Ibid.

366 *"I knew what the asshole was doing"*: Scott Raab, *The Whore of Akron* (New York: Harper Perennial, 2011).

366 *"LeCHICKEN"*: Howard Beck, "Vilified by Fans, but Exiting Victorious," *New York Times*, December 17, 2010.

367 *"I didn't get mad at him"*: Thomsen, *The Soul of Basketball*.

Chapter 29: A Real Dark Place

373 *"Not right now"*: *D. Wade: Life Unexpected*, directed by Bob Metelus (Imagine Documentaries), Disney+, 2020.

374 *"We can finish this later"*: Ian Thomsen, *The Soul of Basketball* (Boston: Houghton Mifflin Harcourt, 2018).

374 *"You can go if you want"*: Ibid.

374 *LeBron had hit rock bottom*: Lee Jenkins, "After Tumultuous First Year in Miami, LeBron Returns a New Man," *Sports Illustrated*, April 24, 2012.

374 *sequestered himself*: Ibid.

375 *Tom Hanks in Cast Away*: Ibid.

376 *"I love music"*: Lisa Robinson, "Jay-Z Has the Room," *Vanity Fair*, October 1, 2013.

376 *Remember where you came from*: Jenkins, "After Tumultuous First Year in Miami, LeBron Returns a New Man."

378 *LeBron's introduction to Adam Mendelsohn*: Maurice Peebles, "LeBron James, Adam Mendelsohn, and the Politicization of Sports Superstardom," Complex, July 2014.

379 *"I saw Oscar in his prime"*: Scott Raab, *The Whore of Akron* (New York: Harper Perennial, 2011).

379 *"laugh-out-loud fun"*: Ibid.

380 *"We have to open our minds"*: Lee Jenkins, "Miami Heat's LeBron James Named SI's 2012 Sportsman of the Year," *Sports Illustrated*, December 3, 2012.

380 *"a fire under his ass"*: Patrick Varone, "LeBron James's Lady," *Harper's Bazaar*, August 9, 2010.

380 *"I also needed to take that next step as a man"*: Jenkins, "After Tumultuous First Year in Miami, LeBron Returns a New Man."

381 *"any of these military guys"*: "LeBron James Overruled Team Security," *SLAM*, March 26, 2012.

381 *"If it wasn't for them"*: Ibid.

381 *Trayvon Martin had been shot*: Greg Botelho, "What Happened the Night Trayvon Martin Died," CNN, May 23, 2012.

381 *Zimmerman, who called 911*: Cara Buckley, "Zimmerman Judge Bars Testimony on 911 Call," *New York Times*, June 22, 2013.

381 *LeBron first heard about Trayvon*: "Hoodies Up," *30 for 30 Podcasts*, season 2, episode 1, November 14, 2017.

382 *"I think all of us have to do some soul-searching"*: "Remarks by the President on Trayvon Martin," Office of the Press Secretary, White House, July 19, 2013.

382 *LeBron and Wade asked all of their teammates*: "Heat Don Hoodies after Teen's Death," ESPN, March 23, 2012.

382 *They all wore gray hoodies*: Ibid.

382 *picture on Twitter*: Ibid.

383 *sank into a booth*: Jenkins, "After Tumultuous First Year in Miami, LeBron Returns a New Man."

383 *"I lost touch with who I was"*: Ibid.

384 *Jenkins was there to witness*: Ibid.

384 *"You're a marathon runner!"*: Jenkins, "Miami Heat's LeBron James Named SI's 2012 Sportsman of the Year."

384 *"He doesn't get exhausted"*: Ibid.

384 *LeBron looks primal*: Ibid.

386 *"He was a cobra"*: Ibid.

386 *"If I was a fan"*: Ibid.

386 *"one of the most brilliant performances"*: Howard Beck, "James Takes Game 6 Personally," *New York Times*, June 7, 2012.

Chapter 30: The Takeover

391 It just finally hit me: Lee Jenkins, "Promise Keeper," *Sports Illustrated*, July 2, 2012.

392 *exhibition game against Brazil*: Matt Compton, "Taking in Team USA," Obama White House Archives, July 17, 2012.

394 *start his own sports agency*: Joe Drape, "An Agent of Change," *New York Times*, August 17, 2014.

394 *"I learned nothing at C.A.A."*: Isaac Chotiner, "LeBron James's Agent Is Transforming the Business of Basketball," *The New Yorker*, May 31, 2010.

394 *"A lot of these kids"*: Ibid.

395 *LeBron had split with his agent*: Brian Windhorst, "LeBron Chooses Rich Paul as Agent," ESPN, September 13, 2012.

395 *Maverick was planting*: Joe Rhodes, "Sprinting Downcourt to the High Life," *New York Times*, September 16, 2014.

395 *called it* Survivor's Remorse: Ibid.

396 *a very American thing*: Michael Eric Dyson, *Jay-Z: Made in America* (New York: St. Martin's Press, 2019).

397   *"I've got a date with me"*: "The Inauguration Party," *Time*, January 22, 2013.

397   *Heat visited the White House*: "2012 NBA Champions the Miami Heat Visit the White House (2013)," YouTube video, posted on January 28, 2013.

398   *"It's your world, man"*: Ian Crouch, "LeBron James: You Are Loved," *The New Yorker*, March 1, 2013.

399   *"I don't think either one of those were flagrant"*: Kevin Arnovitz, "Pat Riley to Danny Ainge: Shut Up," ESPN, March 29, 2013.

399   *"Ainge needs to shut the fuck up"*: Ibid.

399   *"I don't care about Pat Riley"*: Ibid.

Chapter 31: Getting a Grip

403   *LeBron's idealized vision*: LeBron James, *Road Trippin'* podcast, Uninterrupted, March 6, 2017.

403   *Jay-Z and Beyoncé serenading them*: Kurt Helin, "Jay-Z, Beyoncé Performed at LeBron's Wedding," NBC Sports, September 16, 2013.

404   *"History in the making"*: For lyrics to Beyoncé's "Crazy Right Now," see https://genius .com/Beyonce-crazy-in-love-lyrics.

405   *"You guys are winning me over"*: Ethan Skolnick, "At White House, Obama Takes Friendly Jabs at Miami Heat," Bleacher Report, January 14, 2014.

405   *Obama appealed to LeBron for help*: Alexander Wolff, *The Audacity of Hoop* (Philadelphia: Temple University Press, 2016).

405   *Leader Mitch McConnell*: Ibid.

405   *"I would caution you"*: Ibid.

406   *"some of our greatest sports heroes"*: Ibid.

406   *written by Duke freshman*: Jabari Parker, *Sports Illustrated*, April 17, 2014.

407   *audio recordings of Donald Sterling*: "Don't Bring Black People to My Games," TMZ, April 25, 2014.

407   *"disturbing and offensive"*: Richard Sandomir, "Commissioner Sees Basis for Ousting Clippers' Owner," *New York Times*, April 29, 2014.

408   *"no room for Donald Sterling in our league"*: Billy Witz, "LeBron James Shows a Growing Willingness to Take the Lead on Social Issues," *New York Times*, June 7, 2014.

408   *"Donald Sterling's racial history"*: *Meet the Press* transcript, April 27, 2014.

409   *"It would be a rare"*: Richard Sandomir, "Commissioner Sees Basis for Ousting Clippers' Owner," *New York Times*, April 29, 2014.

412   *"We're back to bein' strangers"*: For lyrics to James Ingram's "Just Once," see https:// www.lyrics.com/lyric/498316/James+Ingram/Just+Once.

Chapter 32: Who Am I to Hold a Grudge?

414   *Rich knew where LeBron wanted to end up*: Joe Drape, "An Agent of Change," *New York Times*, August 17, 2014.

414   *"Fuck that"*: Des Bieler, "LeBron James Says He Returned to Cavaliers Despite Family's Anger at Owner's Letter," *Washington Post*, June 9, 2017.

414   *"it ain't really about that"*: Ibid.

415   *had significant pushback from Maverick*: Maverick Carter interview with Jay Williams, "Maverick Carter on Building the LeBron James Empire," NPR, January 4, 2022.

415   *progress over pride*: Ibid.

415   *"I ain't going back to Cleveland"*: Maverick Carter interview, *The Colin Cowherd Podcast*, April 11, 2021.

415   *Apple had acquired Beats*: "Apple to Acquire Beats Music & Beats Electronics," press release, Apple News Room, May 28, 2014.

415   *LeBron's equity stake*: Polly Mosendz, "LeBron James Just Made $30 Million from His Headphones Deal," *The Atlantic*, June 12, 2014.

416   *Irving a five-year, $90 million*: "Irving, Cavs Agree to Extension," ESPN, July 1, 2014.

416   *"As they pondered"*: Ian Crouch, "LeBron James and Hillary Clinton: The Deciders," *The New Yorker*, July 11, 2014.

417   *a face-to-face conversation*: Drape, "An Agent of Change."

417   *on July 6, he flew to Miami*: Ibid.

417   *He wished he could take back*: Haley O'Shaughnessy, "A Brief History of the Complicated Relationship between LeBron James and Dan Gilbert," The Ringer, June 5, 2018.

417   *Gilbert told LeBron how sorry he was*: Drape, "An Agent of Change."

417   *"I let all the emotion and passion"*: Adrian Wojnarowski, "How LeBron James Forgave Cavs Owner Dan Gilbert," Yahoo! Sports, July 11, 2014.

417   *LeBron preferred to look forward*: Drape, "An Agent of Change."

419   *a three-team trade*: Paul Palladino, "Cavaliers Trade Jack to Nets, Zeller to Celtics in Three-Team Deal," *Sports Illustrated*, July 9, 2014.

419   *a meeting with Riley*: Scott Cacciola, "The Decision Is Reversed, and Cleveland Is in a Forgiving Mood," *New York Times*, July 11, 2014.

419   *pack the two championship trophies*: Wright Thompson, "Pat Riley's Final Test," *ESPN The Magazine*, April 25, 2017.

419   *not to bother unpacking the trophies*: Ibid.

419   *fifty-eighth-story suite atop the Wynn*: Lee Jenkins, "Closer Look at LeBron James's Return to Cleveland," *Sports Illustrated*, July 15, 2014.

420   *"I don't know if it's a fairy tale"*: Ibid.

421   *"I want to thank you for four years"*: Thompson, "Pat Riley's Final Test."

421   *too pissed to speak*: Ibid.

421   *"Dan, congratulations"*: Drape, "An Agent of Change."

421   *"Before anyone ever cared"*: LeBron James, essay in *Sports Illustrated*, July 11, 2014.

421   *"I've met with Dan"*: Ibid.

422   *"It was personal for me"*: Thompson, "Pat Riley's Final Test."

423   *Privately, Riley seethed*: Ibid.

423   *Diddy's "Coming Home"*: Jenkins, "Closer Look at LeBron James's Return to Cleveland."

423   *franchise had jumped $100 million*: Mike Ozanian, "$100 Million from Cleveland to Miami," *Forbes*, July 11, 2014.

423   *"Yes, it does, son"*: "Reaction to LeBron's Decision to Rejoin Cavs," Reuters, July 11, 2014.

Chapter 33: Power Broker

424 *"I'm not promising a championship"*: LeBron James, essay in *Sports Illustrated*, July 11, 2014.

424 *"going to be a process"*: Harvey Araton, "For LeBron James, It's Home, and It's a Job Again," *New York Times*, October 5, 2014.

424 *he reached out*: Chris Fedor, "A Phone Call from LeBron James," Cleveland.com, August 26, 2014.

425 *"I'm in"*: Ibid.

425 *in the movie* Trainwreck: Marisa Guthrie, "LeBron James Pulls Back on Hollywood Projects," *Hollywood Reporter*, August 28, 2014.

427 *"All the King's Men"*: *Sports Illustrated*, October 27, 2014.

427 *Nike unveiled its most ambitious*: "LeBron James' New Nike 'Together' Commercial Was a 'Very Hush-Hush' Cleveland Project," Associated Press, October 31, 2014.

427 *$340 million in shoes*: Matt Fitzgerald, "LeBron James Tops Nike Shoe Sales," Bleacher Report, March 18, 2014.

427 *ten consecutive summers*: Darren Griffin, "LeBron James Visits China for 12th Straight Nike Summer Tour," Nice Kicks, September 13, 2016.

428 *"The owners were telling us"*: Harvey Araton, "Owners Can't Line Their Pockets Now and Cry Poverty Later, LeBron James Says," *New York Times*, October 6, 2014.

429 *"I unfairly slagged him for not being Moses"*: Bill Littlefield, "A Sportswriter's Love-Hate-Love Relationship with LeBron James," NPR, March 31, 2017.

429 *decided not to indict*: J. David Goldman and Al Baker, "Waves of Protests after Grand Jury Doesn't Indict Officer in Eric Garner Chokehold Case," *New York Times*, December 3, 2014.

429 *"This is our country"*: Marissa Payne, "LeBron James Talks Eric Garner," *Washington Post*, December 5, 2014.

429 *protesters took to the streets*: Goldman and Baker, "Waves of Protests after Grand Jury Doesn't Indict Officer in Eric Garner Chokehold Case."

429 *"Violence is not the answer"*: Zach Schonbrum, "For LeBron James and Other Stars, the Political Is Personal," *New York Times*, December 8, 2014.

429 *Derrick Rose wore a black T-shirt*: Scott Cacciola, "At Nets' Game, a Plan for a Simple Statement Is Carried Out to a T," *New York Times*, December 9, 2014.

429 *a call from Jay-Z*: Ibid.

430 *When something resonated with him*: Schonbrum, "For LeBron James and Other Stars, the Political Is Personal."

430 *he was going to face criticism*: Ibid.

430 *T-shirts smuggled into the arena*: Cacciola, "At Nets' Game, a Plan for a Simple Statement Is Carried Out to a T."

430 *protesters from an emerging movement*: Scott Cacciola, "A Long, Complex Day on the Hardcourt," *New York Times*, December 8, 2014.

431 *William and Kate entered*: Matt Flegenheimer, "With Prince William Away in Washington, Catherine Charms Harlem Crowds," *New York Times*, December 8, 2014.

431 *Jay-Z and Beyoncé walked across*: Ibid.

431 *"How larger can it be?"*: William C. Rhoden, "Social Convictions: Don't Tuck Neatly into N.B.A.'s Interests," *New York Times*, December 9, 2014.

431 *presented them with gifts*: Cacciola, "A Long, Complex Day on the Hardcourt."

431 *"your arm around the future queen"*: Sierra Marquina, "Piers Morgan on LeBron James Breaking Protocol," *US Weekly*, December 9, 2014.

432 *"The Duke and Duchess of Cambridge"*: Joe Vardon, "Buckingham Palace: No Foul on LeBron James," Cleveland.com, December 12, 2014.

432 *"I respect Derrick Rose"*: Cacciola, "At Nets' Game, a Plan for a Simple Statement Is Carried Out to a T."

432 *Kobe Bryant arranged for*: Chris Greenberg, "Kobe Bryant, Lakers Teammates Wear 'I Can't Breathe' T-Shirts," *Huffington Post*, December 10, 2014.

432 *"We went through a long stretch"*: Alexander Wolff, *The Audacity of Hoop* (Philadelphia: Temple University Press, 2016).

434 *"I have those conversations with my boys"*: Marisa Guthrie, "LeBron James Reveals Ambitious Plans to Build Hollywood Empire," *Hollywood Reporter*, February 11, 2015.

434 *"The talk is, 'You be respectful' "*: Ibid.

436 *fractured his kneecap*: Harvey Araton, "Kyrie Irving out of N.B.A. Finals with Broken Kneecap," *New York Times*, June 5, 2015.

436 *"next man up"*: Ibid.

437 *"personal playground"*: Scott Cacciola, "LeBron James and Cavaliers Hold Off Warriors," *New York Times*, June 20, 2015.

Chapter 34: Deliverance

439 *four-year scholarships*: Karen Farkas, "University of Akron's Pledge to Offer Free Ride," Cleveland.com, August 14, 2015.

439 *a development deal with Warner Bros.*: Marisa Guthrie, "LeBron James Is Already Winning Hollywood," *Hollywood Reporter*, September 20, 2018.

439 *lifetime endorsement deal with Nike*: Emmett Knowlton, "LeBron James' Business Partner Confirms Lifetime Deal with Nike Is Worth over $1 Billion," *Business Insider*, May 17, 2016.

440 *"They have by far the best player"*: "Golden State Warriors Lead NBA with Record 19-0 Start," *All Things Considered*, NPR, December 1, 2015.

440 *"You get paid a lot of money"*: Lee Jenkins, "The Promise Keeper," *Sports Illustrated*, June 20, 2016.

441 *the words* most valuable: Des Bieler, "LeBron James: Steph Curry Deserves MVP Award, but 'Valuable' Is Open to Debate," *Washington Post*, May 11, 2016.

441 *"I'm not sure this league has ever"*: Ibid.

443 *Draymond Green was suspended*: Scott Cacciola, "Warriors' Draymond Green Suspended for Game 5 after LeBron James Episode," *New York Times*, June 12, 2016.

443 *a "retaliatory swipe"*: "Suspended Draymond Green Watches Game 5 Next Door," ESPN, June 12, 2016.

443 *"Care to check out my groin?"*: Harvey Araton, "With a Swat of Stephen Curry, LeBron James Jolted a Debate," *New York Times*, June 18, 2016.

443 *"then don't get on the fucking plane"*: Tristan Thompson interview on *The Herd with Colin Cowherd*, October 13, 2020.

444 *watching* The Godfather Part II: Troy L. Smith, "Watching 'The Godfather Part 2' Scenes That May Have Inspired LeBron James' Game 5," Cleveland.com, June 14, 2016.

444 *"the best hoop-playing specimen"*: Michael Powell, "Warriors Wobble in an Altered Continuum," *New York Times*, June 14, 2016.

445 *a technical foul and ejected*: Billy Witz, "For Stephen Curry, an Unfamiliar Walk to the Locker Room," *New York Times*, June 17, 2016.

445 *"I won't be silent"*: Ibid.

446 *sixty feet in 2.67 seconds*: Shea Serrano, "Which Are Better, LeBron's Dunks or LeBron's Blocks," The Ringer, December 6, 2017.

Chapter 35: Believeland

447 *ABC's largest audience ever*: Ben Cafardo, "Most Watched NBA Game in ABC History," ESPN Press Room, June 20, 2016.

447 *45 million viewers*: John Koblin, "Game 7 of NBA Finals Draws Close to 31 Million Viewers," *New York Times*, June 20, 2016.

448 *"the stuff of bildungsroman"*: Marc Tracy, "The Arc of the LeBron James Story Reaches Its Climax," *New York Times*, June 21, 2016.

448 *didn't matter what happened*: Ibid.

448 *Muhammad Ali had died*: Robert Lipsyte, "Muhammad Ali Dies at 74," *New York Times*, June 4, 2016.

448 *Philando Castile*: Mitch Smith, "Minnesota Officer Acquitted in Killing of Philando Castile," *New York Times*, June 16, 2017.

449 *"We all feel helpless"*: Transcript of 2016 ESPY Awards, July 13, 2016.

449 *"We all have to do better"*: Ibid.

449 *free agent Kevin Durant*: Benjamin Hoffman, "Kevin Durant to Join the Golden State Warriors," *New York Times*, July 4, 2016.

449 *Jimi Hendrix had joined the Rolling Stones*: Sam Anderson, "The Moody Monkish Genius of Kevin Durant," *New York Times Magazine*, June 6, 2021.

450 *"These are bodies in the street"*: Cindy Boren, "A Timeline of Colin Kaepernick's Protests against Police Brutality," *Washington Post*, August 26, 2020.

450 *"That's who I am"*: Des Bieler, "LeBron James, Steph Curry Say They Will Stand for the National Anthem," *Washington Post*, September 26, 2016.

450 *"a bold step"*: Ibid.

450 *"I did try and fuck her"*: "Transcript: Donald Trump's Taped Comments about Women," *New York Times*, October 8, 2016.

451 *"Grab 'em by the pussy"*: Ibid.

451 *"locker room talk"*: Shelby Miller, "LeBron James on Donald Trump: 'That's Trash Talk, We Don't Disrespect Women," Cleveland 19 News, October 12, 2016.

451 *"I got a mother-in-law, a wife"*: Ibid.

451 *in support of Clinton*: Des Bieler, "LeBron James Officially Endorses Hillary Clinton for President," *Washington Post*, October 2, 2016.

451 *"We must address the violence"*: LeBron James, "Why I'm Endorsing Hillary Clinton," *Business Insider*, October 2, 2016.

451 *"As big as you are"*: Lee Jenkins, "Crowning the King," *Sports Illustrated*, December 1, 2016.

451 *"I want people to understand"*: Ibid.

452 *difficult to watch*: Adam Kilgore, "LeBron James on Future White House Visit," *Washington Post*, November 11, 2016.

452 *"You walk in and see the faces"*: "Steve Kerr Discusses Election," *Sports Illustrated*, November 9, 2016.

453 *Cavaliers went to the White House*: Jessica Contrera, "In an Unusual Show of Politics, LeBron James Campaigned for Hillary Clinton," *Washington Post*, November 10, 2016.

453 *time with the First Lady*: Ibid.

453 *"Cleveland was always Believeland"*: Cindy Boren and Marissa Payne, "President Obama as Cavaliers Visit the White House," *Washington Post*, November 10, 2016.

454 *No American president had done more*: Alexander Wolff, *The Audacity of Hoop*, (Philadelphia: Temple University Press, 2016).

Chapter 36: U Bum

455 *"At the end of the day"*: Scott Cacciola, "LeBron James Boycotts Donald Trump's Hotel, Then Beats Up Knicks," *New York Times*, December 7, 2016.

455 *clients stopped staying there*: Sarah Maslin Nir, "Final Nights at the Trump SoHo before Trump Checks Out," *New York Times*, November 23, 2017.

455 *remove the Trump name*: Jonathan O'Connell and David A. Fahrenthold, "Trump's Name Is Coming off His SoHo Hotel," *Washington Post*, November 22, 2017.

456 *"a slap in the face"*: Jackie MacMullan, "Phil Jackson," ESPN, November 14, 2016.

456 *"your mom and your posse"*: Ibid.

456 *"because you're young and black"*: Matt Moore, "Maverick Carter Takes Issue with Phil Jackson's Comments," CBS Sports, November 14, 2016.

456 "You ghetto": Ibid.

456 *"As talented as [LeBron James] definitely appears"*: Joe Vardon, "LeBron James Doesn't Want Apology from Phil Jackson," Cleveland.com, January 11, 2019.

457 *"To some people"*: Kelly Dwyer, "Carmelo Anthony, Like His Friend LeBron James, Isn't a Fan of Phil Jackson's Comments," Yahoo! Sports, November 15, 2016.

458 *"I'm not the one who threw somebody"*: Victor Mather, "Fed Up, LeBron James Fires Back at Charles Barkley," *New York Times*, January 31, 2017.

458 *where the N-word had been painted*: Scott Cacciola and Jonah Engel Bromwich, "LeBron James Responds to Racial Vandalism," *New York Times*, May 31, 2017.

459 *"being black in America is . . . tough"*: Ibid.

459 *first player in NBA history*: Billy Witz, "After Loss, LeBron James Faces the Future," *New York Times*, June 13, 2017.

460 *demanded a trade*: Scott Cacciola, "Seismic N.B.A. Trade Sends Kyrie Irving to Celtics for Isaiah Thomas," *New York Times*, August 22, 2017.

460 *Irving had compared LeBron to Beethoven*: Marcy Tracy, "The Arc of the LeBron James Story Reaches Its Climax," *New York Times*, June 21, 2016.

460 *LeBron didn't want the Cavs*: James Lloyd, "As Tensions Mount, the Distance between LeBron James and the Cavaliers Is Growing," The Athletic, February 6, 2018.

460 *"That's the only way to be kid!"*: Kyle Boone, "LeBron Bid Kyrie Irving Goodbye on Twitter," CBS Sports, August 23, 2017.

461 *"Get that son of a bitch off the field"*: Alexander Burns, "Defying Trump, Athletes Intensify Debate on Race and Protest," *New York Times*, September 24, 2017.

461 *a neo-Nazi purposely plowed his car*: Paul Duggan and Justin Jouvenal, "Neo-Nazi Sympathizer Pleads Guilty to Federal Hate Crimes for Plowing Car into Protestors," *Washington Post*, April 1, 2019.

461   *"very fine people on both sides"*: Glenn Kessler, "The 'Very Fine People' at Charlottes-ville: Who Were They?" *Washington Post*, May 8, 2020.

461   *"I don't know why he feels the need"*: Scott Cacciola, "Stephen Curry, on a 'Surreal Day,' Confronts a Presidential Snub," *New York Times*, September 28, 2017.

461   *LeBron tweeted at Trump: "U bum"*: Ken Belson and Julie Hirschfeld Davis, "Trump Attacks Warriors' Curry. LeBron James's Retort: 'U Bum,' " *New York Times*, September 23, 2017.

462   *North Carolina's national championship*: Ibid.

462   *the most retweeted tweet*: Daniel Politi, "James' 'U Bum' Tweet Is Way More Popular Than Any of the President's Messages," *Slate*, September 24, 2017.

462   *"Turns out, the basketball superstar"*: Ibid.

462   *"How is it possible"*: David Remnick, "The Racial Demagoguery of Trump's Assaults on Colin Kaepernick and Steph Curry," *The New Yorker*, September 23, 2017.

463   *$750,000 to Trump's inauguration*: "Cavs Owner Dan Gilbert Reveals He Received Racist Voicemails," *Akron Beacon Journal*, September 30, 2017.

465   *"Shut up and dribble"*: Emily Sullivan, "Laura Ingraham Told LeBron James to Shut Up and Dribble," NPR, February 19, 2018.

465   *backlash was swift*: Maureen Dowd, "An Anti-Trump Slam Dunk," *New York Times*, June 13, 2020. See also Jonah E. Bromwich, "N.B.A. Players Respond to Laura Ingra-ham's Comments on LeBron James," *New York Times*, February 16, 2018.

466   *the basis of a television show*: Des Bieler, "LeBron James Turns 'Shut up and Dribble' into Title of Showtime Series," *Washington Post*, August 7, 2018.

467   *"They have a guy who is playing basketball"*: Kevin O'Connor, "The Cavaliers Wasted LeBron's Finals Masterpiece," *The Ringer*, June 1, 2018.

467   *"I know whoever wins this series"*: Benjamin Hoffman, "LeBron James and Stephen Curry Unite against White House Visits," *New York Times*, June 5, 2018.

Chapter 37: A Man in Full

469   *a one-sentence press release*: Jeff Zillgitt, "Why LeBron James Chose the Los Angeles Lakers," *USA Today*, July 1, 2018.

469   *Dan Gilbert's reaction*: Joseph Zucker, "Cavaliers' Dan Gilbert Thanks LeBron James," Bleacher Report, July 2, 2018.

469   *opening of his I Promise School*: James Dator, "LeBron James Opened a Public School In Akron for At-Risk Kids," SB Nation, July 30, 2018.

470   *an interview with CNN's Don Lemon*: Christine Caron, "Trump Mocks LeBron James's Intelligence and Calls Don Lemon 'Dumbest Man' on TV," *New York Times*, August 4, 2018.

470   *demeaned the intelligence of two Black men*: Michael Powell, "Donald Trump and the Black Athlete," *New York Times*, August 5, 2018.

471   *"We could not be more proud"*: Katherine Rosman, "Lady of the Lakers," *New York Times*, January 2, 2021.

471   *First Lady put out a formal statement*: Adam Wells, "Melania Trump Issues LeBron James Statement," Bleacher Report, August 4, 2018.

471   *"I support LJ"*: Charlotte Carroll, "Michael Jordan Responds to Donald Trump's Le-Bron James Tweet," *Sports Illustrated*, August 4, 2018.

471 *Harlem's Fashion Row award*: Marisa Guthrie, "LeBron James Is Already Winning Hollywood," *Hollywood Reporter*, September 20, 2018.

471 *strong African American women*: Dominique Fluker, "Meet the Four Black Women Who Created LeBron James's Newest Shoe," *Forbes*, September 10, 2018.

Epilogue

473 *a set for* Gilmore Girls: Marisa Guthrie, "LeBron James Is Already Winning Hollywood," *Hollywood Reporter*, September 20, 2018.

473 *"I'm not an anonymous guy"*: Ibid.

474 *"Coogler gave this generation's kids"*: Ibid.

475 *Davis had signed with Rich*: Isaac Chotiner, "LeBron James's Agent Is Transforming the Business of Basketball," *The New Yorker*, May 31, 2021.

475 *Paul orchestrated a trade*: Ibid.

475 *met singer-songwriter Adele*: Nardine Saad, "Adele Calls It the 'Easiest' Relationship She's Ever Had," *Los Angeles Times*, November 15, 2021.

475 *"Do you want to sign me?"*: Abby Aguirre, "Adele on the Other Side," *Vogue*, October 7, 2021.

476 *More Than a Vote*: Jonathan Martin, "LeBron James and Other Stars Form a Voting Rights Group," *New York Times*, June 10, 2020.

476 *"We live in two Americas"*: Dave McMenamin, "Los Angeles Lakers' LeBron James: U.S. Capitol Siege Shows 'We Live in Two Americas,' " *ESPN*, January 8, 2021.

476 *"What are people going to say?"*: Saad, "Adele Calls It the 'Easiest' Relationship She's Ever Had."

477 *Only one basketball dream remained*: Chris Ballard, "The Decision," *Sports Illustrated*, October 2022.

INDEX

ABOUT THE AUTHOR

JEFF BENEDICT is the #1 *New York Times* bestselling author of seventeen nonfiction books, including *Tiger Woods* (with Armen Keteyian) and *The Dynasty*. He is also a television and film producer and has been a special-features writer for *Sports Illustrated* and the *Los Angeles Times*. He lives with his wife and children in Connecticut.